OUR AMERICAN SISTERS

OUR AMERICAN SISTERS

WOMEN IN AMERICAN LIFE AND THOUGHT

FOURTH EDITION

JEAN E. FRIEDMAN
UNIVERSITY OF GEORGIA

WILLIAM G. SHADE
LEHIGH UNIVERSITY

MARY JANE CAPOZZOLI
ADELPHI UNIVERSITY

D. C. HEATH AND COMPANY
LEXINGTON, MASSACHUSETTS   TORONTO

Copyright © 1987 by D.C. Heath and Company.
Previous editions copyright © 1982 by D.C. Heath and Company; and 1976, 1973 by Allyn and Bacon, Inc.

Published simultaneously in Canada.

Printed in the United States of America.

International Standard Book Number: 0-669-11020-5

Library of Congress Catalog Card Number: 86-81268

PREFACE

In 1981, Gloria Steinem appeared at Lehigh University to commemorate that formerly all-male institution's first decade of coeducation. Thirteen hundred people attended and responded enthusiastically to her message. She recalled an earlier appearance in 1970, when one-third that number turned out to jeer. That visit, along with the developments of the late 1960s, led in part to the publication of the first edition of *Our American Sisters*. Putting together a decent anthology at that time meant searching for a few obscure articles or excerpting segments from books dedicated to other subjects. In the 1970s, however, women's history in the United States came of age. The problem today is choosing from the wide range of excellent articles and books that have appeared since 1970.

This new edition is a major revision of the extremely successful third edition, published in 1982. In this edition we have attempted to respond to suggestions from friends and colleagues who have used the previous editions in their classes. Accordingly, the basic structure of the book has been retained, and the essays continue to reflect our conception of women's history as expressed in the introduction. *Our American Sisters* is a comprehensive anthology of writings on the history of American women that includes extensive material on the colonial era and the nineteenth century. We have tried to choose essays that combine readability with a high scholarly standard.

The content, however, has broadened to include six new essays that incorporate the most recent scholarship in the field. These essays reflect a greater regional, ethnic, and social diversity among women, as well as the growing sophistication of women's history. They introduce new quantitative data and ideological perspectives that should challenge the students and make this edition more interesting to teach. Only five essays remain from the original edition in 1973. New scholarship has altered some of their findings, but we have retained them because they pose questions of continuing relevance.

Limitations of space have made it impossible to include every fine essay that has appeared since the last edition, or to touch upon every important subject that now troubles students of women's history. We therefore refer students to reading materials that analyze the ethnic, religious, and sexual values of American women and that explore significant debates, such as the existence of a distinctive female culture. As women's history has matured and feminism has expanded its perspectives, the territory has grown and the problems are compounded. The introductions to each section have been revised, and up-to-date bibliographies have been added to guide interested students. Finally, we are pleased that our author team has expanded to three: we welcome Mary Jane Capozzoli as an associate in this new edition.

J.E.F.
W.G.S.
M.J.C.

CONTENTS

⪽ 3 ⪼
The Progressive Impulse
Page 263

⪽ 4 ⪼
The Illusion of Equality
Page 415

INTRODUCTION

Two decades ago one of the leading historians in the United States warned his colleagues that their traditional approaches to American history seriously perverted the subject. At the time, David Potter was referring to the way in which historians have ignored women and have belittled their role in American history. Major generalizations about the American character have totally ignored women, and when historians have commented upon women, their views have been wildly inconsistent. In part this situation was a product of ignorance. Only a handful of relevant monographs existed in the 1960s, and the treatment of women in general studies was woefully inadequate. Few aspects of the history of women in America had drawn serious attention. As late as 1969 Gerda Lerner could write, "The striking fact about the historiography of women is the general neglect of the subject by historians."

By the mid-1970s the situation changed dramatically. The emergence of the movement for women's liberation heightened women's consciousness of their position in American society and led to demands for college courses that would enable women to regain their history. By 1975 approximately ninety colleges offered interdisciplinary majors in Women's Studies; of the over 4,000 courses on women, there were approximately 300 on the history of American women. At the same time, historians—many of whom were feminists—revealed a new concern for the subject. The number of texts and monographs has grown geometrically. Scholarly journals are increasingly open to studies concerning women. Rarely does an issue of the *American Quarterly*, *Journal of Social History*, *Journal of Interdisciplinary History* or even the conservative *Journal of American History*, fail to include at least one relevant article, and new journals such as *Feminist Studies*,

Women's Studies, and *Signs* are devoted entirely to the subject.* Conferences on the history of women have been sponsored across the country. The programs of the annual meetings of major historical organizations feature growing numbers of sessions on women. By almost any measure, the history of women is now attracting unparalleled interest.

The origins of this dramatic change in the historical treatment of women can be found in the shift in attitudes toward women in American society, in the rise of women's professional aspirations and their place in the history profession, and in a renewed interest in social history and historical sociology. Although all historians of women are not feminists—feminist history is not simply propaganda for the movement—the revival of interest in the history of women is intimately linked to the revival of feminism in the past decade.

Earlier in this century, the passage of the Nineteenth Amendment sparked a good deal of professional interest in the history of American women, and a number of major books on the subject appeared during the interwar period. Feminism was probably in better repute in the 1920s than at any time in American history before the 1960s. During that decade the birthrate fell precipitously, and increasing numbers of women entered graduate schools. The proportion of women earning M.A.'s and Ph.D.'s rose dramatically to a high point in 1930 and then declined slightly during the Great Depression. The number of women college professors grew, although most taught in women's colleges. At the time that this generation of women was entering the history profession, several influential historians, as part of their rebellion against the legalistic and narrowly political focus of their predecessors, showed heightened interest in the role of women in history.

The fascination of Progressive historians with social and economic aspects of history and their tendency to view American history in terms of the conflict between conservatives and reformers led at least two of the most important and widely read male historians of this era to study the role of women in American history. In 1922, Arthur Schlesinger, in *New Viewpoints in American History,* included an essay on women that protested "the pall of silence" cast over the subject. Later in the

---

*In the past two decades fourteen historical journals have devoted entire issues to aspects of women's history: *American Jewish History* 70 (September 1980); *American Quarterly* 22 (Winter 1978); *Baptist History and Heritage* 12 (January 1977); *Current History* 70 (May 1976); *History of Education Quarterly* 15 (Spring 1974); *Journal of Presbyterian History* 52 (Summer 1974); *Journal of Urban History* 4 (May 1978); *Labor History* 17 (Winter 1976); *Teacher's College Record* 76 (February 1974); *Pacific Historical Review* 49 (May 1980); *Utah Historical Quarterly* 46 (Spring 1978); *Journal of Popular Culture* 15 (Winter 1981); *Pennsylvania Magazine of History and Biography* 107 (January 1983); and *American Historical Review* 80 (June 1984).

decade Charles and Mary Beard co-authored the extremely influential book *The Rise of American Civilization*, which strongly emphasized the economic importance of women. During the interwar years men and women influenced by the Progressive school of history integrated discussions of women's roles into studies of social history and produced a number of classic monographs on women in America.

Although historians trained in the 1920s and 1930s maintained their concern for the history of women, by 1940 a reversal of earlier trends became apparent. The feminists, whose story Schlesinger thought "one of the noblest chapters in the history of American democracy," fell into increasing public disrepute. The birthrate rose dramatically as the post-World War II generation of women appeared dominated by what sociologist Jesse Bernard has called the "Motherhood Mania." The percentage of women completing M.A. and Ph.D. degrees declined as the birthrate climbed. At the same time, the attitudes of academic men toward women changed for the worse. Men were condescending toward their female colleagues and resisted hiring new women. During this strange interlude, attention to the history of women faded; even areas of American life in which women had traditionally played important roles went unstudied. When families in America were once again growing and the role of the homemaker was exalted in the media, the historical study of the family languished. The study of political, diplomatic, and economic elites characterized the historiography of these years.

In the early 1960s, attitudes towards the study of the history of women began to change as each of the trends that characterized the preceding decades was reversed. Feminism and feminist issues gained renewed popularity. In the late 1950s, the birthrate once again began to fall. Each year the number of young women choosing to continue their education increased: The proportion of women holding Ph.D.'s in history has risen dramatically since the nadir of the 1950s. At the same time, the attitudes towards women of male colleagues born since the late 1930s are a distinct improvement over those of the previous generation. Finally, the 1960s witnessed a revival of interest in social history and the processes of social change that has broadened the concept of legitimate subjects of history. The "new" social history, which studies sexual behavior and sex roles, the effects of demographic change, religious and ethnic conflict, and marriage and the family, has suddenly "rediscovered" women everywhere in the American past.

Before the present revival of women's history, most historians writing about women focused narrowly on the history of the feminist movement and on what Schlesinger called women's "contributions to American national progress." Since this approach characterized the writings of the feminist chroniclers, it was only natural that the

Progressive historians, who were sympathetic to the feminist cause and concerned with reform, carried these views over into professional history. But a more comprehensive approach to the history of women is necessary if we are to recapture the wealth and texture of women's lives in the American past.

Taking into consideration the trends of current scholarship, we have divided American history into four chronological periods of rather unequal length, but which nonetheless seem to present a sense of surface continuity in relation to the history of American women. Each section is preceded by an introduction that outlines the major unifying themes of the period and relates the essays to these themes. Within each period we have included material bearing on the three most distinctive aspects of the history of American women: society's definition of the nature of women and women's roles; the actual working conditions of women and the social and economic functions that women perform; and women's response to their special intellectual, socioeconomic, and political problems. Finally, several essays have been included to show the differential effects of changes in these areas on subgroups of women, taking into account the influences of region, class, race, religion, and ethnicity. It is our hope that this relatively simple organizational structure will highlight the importance of the essays and facilitate the integration of this excellent recent scholarship into a more comprehensive framework for the study of the American past.

Suggested Readings

General Histories and Collections of Essays

Banner, Lois. *Women in Modern America.* Englewood Cliffs, NJ: Prentice-Hall, 1975.

Banner, Lois. *American Beauty.* Chicago: University of Chicago Press, 1983.

Berkin, Ruth Carol, and Norton, Mary Beth, eds. *Women of America: A History.* Boston: Houghton Mifflin Co., 1979.

Cantor, Milton and Laurie, Bruce, eds. *Sex, Class and the Woman Worker.* Westport: Greenwood Press, 1977.

Cott, Nancy F. and Pleck, Elizabeth H., eds. *A Heritage of Her Own.* New York: Simon & Schuster, 1979.

Cowan, Ruth Schwartz. *More Work for Mother: The Ironies of Household Technology from the Open Hearth to the Microwave.* New York: Basic Books, 1983.

Degler, Carl. *At Odds: Women and the Family in America from the Revolution to the Present.* New York: Oxford University Press, 1980.

Demos, John, and Boocock, Sarane Spence, eds. *Turning Points: Historical and Sociological Essays on the Family.* Chicago: University of Chicago Press, 1978.

Ehrenreich, Barbara, and English, Dierdre. *For Their Own Good: 150 Years of the Experts' Advice to Women.* Garden City, NY: Doubleday, 1978.

Flexner, Eleanor. *Century of Struggle: The Women's Rights Movement in the United States.* Cambridge: Harvard University Press, 1975.

Foner, Philip S. *Women in the American Labor Movement From the First Trade Unions to the Present.* New York: The Free Press, 1982.

George, Carol V.R., ed. *"Remember the Ladies": New Perspectives On Women in American History.* Syracuse: Syracuse University Press, 1975.

Giddings, Paula. *When and Where I Enter: The Impact of Black Women on Race and Sex in America.* New York: William Morrow and Company, 1984.

Goodfriend, Joyce, and Christie, Claudia. *Lives of American Women: A Survey with Documents.* Boston: Little, Brown & Co., 1981.

Gordon, Michael, ed. *The American Family in Social-Historical Perspective.* New York: St. Martin's Press, 1983.

Hareven, Tamara K., ed. *Family and Kin in Urban Communities, 1700-1930.* New York: New Viewpoint, 1977.

———, ed. *Transitions: The Family and Life Course in Historical Perspective.* New York: Academic Press, 1978.

———, and Vinovskis, Maris A., eds. *Family and Population in Nineteenth Century America.* Princeton: Princeton University Press, 1979.

Harley, Sharon, and Tenborg-Penn, Rosalyn, eds. *The Afro-American Woman: Struggles and Images.* Port Washington, NY: Kenniket Press, 1978.

Harris, Barbara J. *Beyond Her Sphere: Women and the Professions in American History.* Westport, CT: Greenwood Press, 1978.

Hartman, Mary, and Banner, Lois W., eds. *Clio's Consciousness Raised: New Perspectives on the History of Women.* New York: Harper & Row, 1974.

Hymowitz, Carol, and Weissman, Michale. *A History of Women in America.* New York: Bantam Books, 1978.

James, Edward T., and James, Janet W., eds. *Notable American Women, 1607-1950: A Biographical Dictionary.* 3 vols. Cambridge: Harvard University Press, 1971.

James, Janet Wilson, ed. *Women and American Religion.* Philadelphia: University of Pennsylvania Press, 1980.

Jones, Jacqueline. *Labor of Love, Labor of Sorrow: Black Women, Work, and the Family from Slavery to the Present.* New York: Basic Books, 1985.

Kerber, Linda K., and Mathews, Jane De Hart. *Women's America.* New York: Oxford University Press, 1982.

Kessler-Harris, Alice. *Out to Work: A History of Wage-Earning Women in the United States.* New York: Oxford University Press, 1982.

Leavitt, Judith W. " 'Science' Enters the Birthing Room: Obstetrics in America Since the Eighteenth Century." *Journal of American History* 70 (September 1983): 281-304.

_____, ed. *Women and Health in America: Historical Readings.* Madison: University of Wisconsin Press, 1984.

Lerner, Gerda. *The Woman in American History.* Reading, MA: Addison-Wesley, 1971.

_____. *The Majority Finds Its Past.* New York: Oxford University Press, 1979.

Margolis, Maxine L. *Mothers and Such: Views of American Women and Why They Changed.* Berkeley: University of California Press, 1984.

Matthaei, Julie. *An Economic History of Women in America: Women's Work, the Sexual Division of Labor and the Development of Capitalism.* New York: Schocken Books, 1982.

Newton, Judith L., Ryan, Mary P., and Walkowitz, Judith R., eds. *Sex and Class in Women's History.* London: Routledge & Kegan Paul, 1983.

Oakley, Ann. *Women's Work: The Housewife Past and Present.* New York: Vintage Books, 1974.

Riegel, Robert E. *American Women: A Story of Social Change.* Teaneck, NJ: Fairleigh-Dickinson Press, 1970.

Rosaldo, Michelle Zimbalist, and Lamphere, Louise, eds. *Women, Culture and Society.* Stanford: Stanford University Press, 1974.

Rosenberg, Charles, ed. *The Family in History.* Philadelphia: University of Pennsylvania Press, 1975.

Rothman, Sheila. *Woman's Proper Place: A History of Changing Ideas and Practices, 1870 to the Present.* New York: Basic Books, 1978.

Ryan, Mary P. *Womanhood in America From Colonial Times to the Present.* New York: New Viewpoints, 1975.

Scholten, Catherine M. ed. *Childbearing in American Society, 1650-1850.* New York: New York University Press, 1985.

Scott, Anne. *Making Invisible Women Visible.* Urbana: University of Illinois Press, 1984.

Sinclair, Andrew. *The Better Half.* New York: Harper & Row, 1965.

Smith, Page. *Daughters of the Promised Land.* Boston: Little, Brown & Co., 1970.

Snitow, Ann, *et. al. Powers of Desire.* New York: Monthly Review Press, 1983.

Sochen, June. *Herstory: A Woman's View of American History.* New York: Alfred Publishing Co., 1974.

_____. *Movers and Shakers: American Women Thinkers and Activists, 1900-1970.* New York: Quadrangle Books, 1973.

Steady, F.S. ed. *Black Women Cross Culturally.* Cambridge, MA: Schenkman Press, 1981.

Sterling, Dorothy. *Black Foremothers: Three Lives.* Old Westbury, NY: The Feminist Press, 1979.

Weiner, Lynn Y. *From Working Girl to Working Mother: The Female Labor Force in the United States, 1820-1980.* Chapel Hill: University of North Carolina Press, 1985.

Wells, Robert V. *Revolutions in Americans' Lives: A Demographic Perspective on the History of Americans, Their Families and Their Society.* Westport, CT: Greenwood Press, 1982.

Werbel, Kathryn. *Mirror, Mirror: Images of Women Reflected in Popular Culture.* Garden City, NY: Anchor Books, 1977.

Wolock, Nancy. *Women and the American Experience.* New York: Oxford University Press, 1983.

Historiography

Brumberg, Joan J., and Tomes, Nancy. "Women in the Professions: A Research Agenda for American History." *Reviews in American History* 10 (June 1982): 275-96.

Carroll, Bernice A., ed. *Liberating Women's History: Theoretical and Critical Essays.* Urbana: University of Illinois Press, 1976.

Freedman, Estelle B. "The New Woman: Changing Views of Women in the 1920s." *Journal of American History* 61 (1974): 372-93.

_____. "Sexuality in Nineteenth Century America: Behavior, Ideology and Politics." *Reviews in American History* 10 (1982): 196-215.

Faragher, John Mack. "History from the Inside-Out: Writing the History of Women in Rural America." *American Quarterly* 33 (1981): 537-57.

Ferher, Marianne A. "Women and Work: Issues of the 1980s." *Signs* 8 (1982): 273-95.

Gordon, Ann D., Buhle, Mari Jo, and Schrom, Nancy E. "Women in American Society: An Historical Contribution." *Radical America* 5 (1971): 3-66.

Green, Rayna. "Review Essay: Native American Women." *Signs* 6 (1980): 248-67.

Jensen, Joan M., and Miller, Darlis. "The Gentle Tamers Revisited: New Approaches to the History of Women in the American West." *Pacific Historical Review* 49 (1980): 173-213.

May, Elaine Tyler. "Expanding the Past: Recent Scholarship on Women in Politics and Work." *Reviews in American History* 10 (December 1982): 216-33.

Norton, Mary Beth. "Review Essay: American History." *Signs* 5 (1979): 324-37.

Ryan, Mary P. "The Explosion of Family History." *Reviews in American History* 10 (December 1982): 181-95.

Sickerman, Barbara, Monter, E. William, Scott, Joan Wallach, Sklar, Kathryn Kish. *Recent United States Scholarship on the History of Women.* Washington: American Historical Association, 1980.

Sickerman, Barbara. "A Review Essay: American History," *Signs* 1 (1975): 461-85.

Sklar, Kathryn Kish. "American Female Historians in Context, 1770-1930," *Feminist Studies* 3 (1975): 171-84.

Smith-Rosenberg, Carroll. "The New Woman and the New History," *Feminist Studies* 3 (1975): 185-98.

Zangrando, Joanna Schneider. "Women's Studies in the United States: Approaching Reality." *American Studies International* 14 (Autumn 1975): 15-36.

Anthologies of Primary Sources

Baxandall, Rosalyn, Gordon, Linda, and Reverby, Susan, eds. *America's Working Women: A Documentary History, 1600-Present.* New York: Vintage Books, 1976.

Brownlee, W. Elliot, and Brownlee, Mary H., eds. *Women in the American Economy: A Documentary History, 1675-1927.* New Haven: Yale University Press, 1976.

Buhle, Mary Jo, and Buhle, Paul, eds. *The Concise History of Woman Suffrage.* Urbana: University of Illinois Press, 1978.

Cott, Nancy F., ed. *Root of Bitterness: Documents of the Social History of American Women.* New York: E.P. Dutton & Co., 1972.

Dublin, Thomas. ed. *Farm to Factory: Women's Letters, 1830-1860.* New York: Columbia University Press, 1981.

Foner, Philip S., ed. *Mother Jones Speaks: Collected Writings and Speeches.* NY: Monad, 1983.

Holmes, Kenneth L., ed. *Covered Wagon Women: Diaries and Letters From the Western Trails, 1840-1890.* Vol 1: 1840-1849. Glendale, CA: Clark, 1983.

Kraditor, Aileen, ed. *Up From the Pedestal: Selected Writings in the History of American Feminism.* Chicago: Quadrangle Books, 1968.

Lerner, Gerda, ed. *Black Women in White America.* New York: Pantheon Books, 1972.

———. *The Female Experience.* Indianapolis: Bobbs-Merrill, 1977.

Martin, Wendy, ed. *The American Sisterhood.* New York: Harper & Row, 1972.

Rossi, Alice S., ed. *The Feminist Papers: From Adams to de Beauvoir.* New York: Columbia University Press, 1973.

Seller, Maxine, ed. *Immigrant Women.* Philadelphia: Temple University Press, 1981.

Sochen, June, ed. *The New Feminism in Twentieth Century America.* Lexington, MA: D.C. Heath and Co., 1971.

Sterling, Dorothy, ed. *We Are Your Sisters: Black Women in the Nineteenth Century.* NY: Norton, 1984.

Stoehr, Taylor, ed. *Free Love in America: A Documentary History.* New York: AMS Press, 1979.

OUR AMERICAN SISTERS

~1~

COLONIAL WOMEN

From the settlement of Jamestown until the outbreak of the American Revolution, the colonists struggled to establish a stable society based upon the English model. In each new settlement they recreated familiar social, political and economic institutions in an attempt to reaffirm the ideals and values of English civilization. The new environment and the absence of central authority, however, altered institutions and attitudes sometimes immediately, but more often gradually. Colonial society slowly evolved into one quite different from that of the mother country; by the mid-eighteenth century, the transplanted Englishman had become a "new man," an American. The effects of this process upon the status of women highlight their anomalous position in American history.

The first mainland colonies were founded as business ventures, and it was not until the decision was made to establish societies in the New World that any significant number of women were transported across the Atlantic. The fact that men outnumbered women throughout the colonial period accounted for the earlier age at which colonial women married and the greater liberties and privileges they enjoyed in relation to European women. Colonial women existed as essential subordinates, however, in a largely patriarchial culture where they were subject to paternal decisions. A father's control of the land gave him the power to determine his daughter's marriage partners and settlements, and to delay property inheritance. Nonetheless, several meliorating circumstances—the scarcity of women, isolation of settlements and a limited labor supply—increased the woman's value to the family and the community. Carl Degler has emphasized that "the wife and mother in the rude settlement on or near the frontier was more than a housekeeper; she was an indispensable part of the apparatus of survival." In an economy dominated by farms and small shops, women worked side by side with men and often ran large plantations or carried on the family business following the death of a husband or father. Of necessity, few jobs were deemed inappropriate for colonial women, and they worked outside the home as blacksmiths and barbers, tanners and tavern keepers. Their contributions, however, were still considered marginal to the market economy.

The lives of most women were generally circumscribed within the family, where wives were expected to be subservient to their husbands. Political rights were almost completely restricted to men as heads of families, and access to the professions was closed to women on the grounds that they should, in the words of Puritan leader John Winthrop, "refrain from such things as proper for men whose minds are stronger." Although colonial Americans considered piety a major feminine grace, only a few denominations allowed women to preach. In general they followed the admonition of St. Paul that "women keep silent in the churches." In her challenge to Puritan orthodoxy in the mid-1630s, Anne Hutchinson, the most famous woman preacher of the colonial era, expressed women's frustration with the limitations imposed upon them by traditional roles and by the magistrates' fears of the socially destructive consequences of women's departure from their proper sphere. Consideration of the prevailing sex/gender system as well as the complexities of Puritan theology highlights the nature of the Antinomian controversy of the 1630s in Massachusetts Bay. As Mary Ryan has reminded us, colonial Americans "viewed the whole of society as an intricate series of ranks, a profusion of finely graded positions of authority and subordination, which neither male nor female could circumvent." Violation of gender norms, therefore, seemed to invite moral and civil anarchy, threatening the entire social order and undermining the very basis of civilization as they knew it.

The family was an essential element of the community and a sphere in which women shared joint responsibility for a variety of religious, social and economic functions. The roles of husband and wife were less neatly compartmentalized than they would become in the nineteenth century. This cooperation and intimacy between husbands and wives sometimes led colonial women into business and political affairs, where they shared their husbands' lives, mending political fences or fomenting revolution.

The Puritan community placed strong emphasis on the social role of the family and on close surveillance of moral life. Yet, the New England colonists were neither so unrealistic about human nature nor so sexually repressive as has often been charged. They were well aware that sexual intercourse was a human necessity and believed that marriage was the proper place for it. Although they were unable to contain all sexual impulses wholly within the bounds of marriage— illicit sexual intercourse was common—the Puritan magistrates encouraged early marriage and took every means to insure peaceful cohabitation. Adultery was severely punished, but divorces and annulments were relatively easy to obtain.

Perhaps the most interesting aspect of the Puritan attitude toward sexual intercourse was the degree to which the magistrates acknowledged and respected the sexual needs of women as well as men. John Demos's analysis of the court records of Plymouth in "Husbands and Wives" reveals only minor traces of a double standard. Patterns of decision making within the family show that in their day-to-day lives these women stood more nearly equal to their husbands than has generally been supposed. This may explain why foreign observers believed these women occupied a higher status than their European counterparts. Sexual roles were not rigidly defined, and mutuality of obligation and affection often characterized Puritan marriages.

Outside colonial New England, beyond the reaches of the Puritan social order, women retained even more bargaining power regarding their economic status. As Lois Green Carr and Lorena S. Walsh show in "The Planter's Wife," most women who emigrated into seventeenth-century Maryland were indentured servants who married after their term of service. Because they were outnumbered by men, they had a relatively free choice of partners. Once married, women labored to increase their husbands' property and status. Recognition of the contribution made by women to the marital partnership led husbands to bequeath more than the customary one-third of their property to wives and, in addition, to name the wives executors of their estates. One such woman was the remarkable Margaret Brent, executrix of the estate of Governor Leonard Calvert. She has been described by Julia Cherry Spruill as one of the "most prominent personages" in Maryland, "whose business and public activities fill many pages of court records."

By the eighteenth century, common social practice, specific legislation, and the development of equity law freed married women from complete domination by their husbands and gave them a certain amount of legal autonomy unknown under the Common Law. In contrast to the English double standard, the New England colonies maintained a single standard of sexual fidelity. The Whiggish trends at the time of the War for Independence resulted in the revival of the Puritan morality that distinguished Republican "virtue" from English "corruption." As a result, divorces, which had been rare, were granted to increasing numbers of women on the grounds of adultery. It should not be forgotten, however, that colonial society was basically masculine in orientation. Attitudes toward women during the period remained traditional, differing little from those of contemporary Europeans. The belief in the inferiority of women was universal. While American women were far better off then their English sisters and while in some areas their legal position improved during this period, women—particularly those who were married—suffered numerous legal and social restrictions imposed by the widespread acceptance of the idea of coverture (women's inferior status under the law).

Little is known about the lives of the many Afro-American women who suffered as slaves in the colonies, but certain things may be inferred from the work of recent historians. Although their status, along with that of Afro-American men, undoubtedly evolved from servant to slave for life, one of the first references to slavery in colonial records concerns a woman: in 1639 a Massachusetts woman refused to allow her master to mate her with a black man on the grounds that such was "beyond her slavery." Early in the eighteenth century the status of slavery was codified and conditions became increasingly severe. Nearly everywhere miscegenation, which had been widespread during the previous century, was outlawed, and acts of manumission (voluntary emancipation of a slave by the owner) declined. Due to the nature of the tasks to which they were assigned, slave women may have adjusted more easily to their new lives and to the rigors of slavery than did African men. Yet there are numerous instances of resistance to their masters from these women, whose unhappy lives were made harsher by physical and sexual abuse, and the double bind of working for their masters while running their own families in the quarters.

While the slave population was heavily concentrated in the southern colonies, surprising numbers could be found in northern urban areas. Blacks made up fifteen percent of Philadelphia's population by mid-century and had spilled over into the surrounding counties of southeastern Pennsylvania. As Jean Soderlund makes clear in "Black Women in Colonial Pennsylvania," the fortunes of slavery were closely tied to the available labor supply. Black women in the North often did agricultural work as in the South, but in Philadelphia they were usually domestics. Among these urban slaves there were also a large number of female-headed households, although husbands may have resided nearby. When given the chance, most black women opted for freedom and for a time "Philadelphia was the center of both the white and black abolitionist movements in America."

The Revolution led to the abolition of slavery in the northern states, but had little positive effect on the status of the vast majority of blacks enslaved below the Mason-Dixon line. Emancipation did bring certain benefits to the free blacks of the North. The black family was strengthened and Afro-American women were able to exercise some leadership in churches and mutual aid societies. There were even modest increases in educational opportunity for free black women. Nonetheless, economic advancement was limited; most black women continued to be employed as domestics. Even freedom itself proved hazardous for black women, who were liable to be kidnapped and resold into slavery.

During the Revolution, American women aided the patriot cause in a variety of ways. They voiced opposition to the Stamp Act, the hated tea tax and the Coercive Acts; they formed the Daughters of Liberty as a counterpart to the Sons of Liberty. Two famous women, Ester De Berdt Reed and Sara Bache, Benjamin Franklin's daughter, headed an effort to supply troops with badly needed clothing, and many lesser-known women moved into the growing, war-related textile industry. Although the American Revolution produced no great heroine, Molly Pitcher and Margaret Corbin were noted for their courage in battle, and Deborah Sampson Gannett later claimed to have served in the Continental Army disguised as Robert Shurtleff. One Philadelphia woman wrote her husband detailing her support for the Revolution, "I know this—that as free I can die but once; but as a slave I shall not be worthy of life. I have the pleasure to assure you that these are the sentiments of all my sister Americans." Yet the Revolution brought only modest change in women's status or men's attitudes toward them. The brilliant and witty Abigail Adams chided her husband, "I cannot say, that I think you are very generous to the ladies; for whilst you are proclaiming peace and goodwill to men, emancipating all nations, you insist upon retaining an absolute power over all wives."

Joan Hoff Wilson's essay, "The Illusion of Change: Women and the American Revolution," argues that colonial women's gains during these years were due to the sexual imbalance and the labor shortage, and thus reflected necessity rather than "any fundamental change in sexist values transplanted from Europe." In tracing economic and demographic changes in the Revolutionary period, Wilson reveals that new technological demands created by the war encouraged a specialization that changed women's economic function. Women's status in the household was reduced, and new social institutions, such as schools, increasingly discharged traditional parental responsibilities. The decline of parental authority, the glorification of motherhood, women's circumscribed sphere of influence and growing sexual repression characterized the "family in transition."

The education of women mirrored the society's attitudes. Illiteracy among women was rampant, with perhaps as many as two-thirds of the women in sixteenth-century New England unable to sign their names. In the following century, women's literacy improved, but at the end of the colonial period Kenneth A. Lockridge has shown that "female illiteracy remained quite common and women were always at a distinct disadvantage in obtaining basic education." Even those in school found opportunities limited. In the lower grades, boys and girls attended school together, but beyond that point the colleges, which trained men for the professions, and the grammar schools, which prepared men for the colleges, were closed to women as a matter of course. When coeducation became more popular at the end of the eighteenth century, advocates like Benjamin Rush emphasized the republic's need for educated mothers rather than the intellectual equality of women. Linda K. Kerber's essay "Daughters of Columbia" traces the post-Revolutionary debate over the proposals of Rush, Charles Brockden Brown, and Judith Sargent Murray—the author of the "Constantia" letters—for the education of women.

Kerber shows that, even among citizens of the new republic, traditional views of woman's role persisted, and the seemingly radical proposals for their education were limited. Americans of the revolutionary generation were forced to reconcile the role of women with the new political autonomy implicit in Enlightenment thought. "The model republican woman was to be self-reliant," Kerber has written elsewhere, "but her competence did not extend to the making of political decisions. Her political task was accomplished within the confines of her family. The model republican woman was a mother." In this fashion, women were assigned a definite political role in the new republic, but one that integrated traditional female domesticity with the quest for a virtuous citizenry. Women were to take part in the civic culture vicariously, through their influence on their sons and husbands.

By the end of the eighteenth century, the lives of American women were undergoing noticeable changes. The ambivalent relationship between motherhood and citizenship was reflected in other areas of life. Improved educational opportunity increasingly narrowed the gap between male and female literacy. The birth rate was declining, and women were gaining control over their own marital and sexual lives. But the close relationship between husband and wife that had characterized the seventeenth century continued to exist only on the frontier and in rural areas, where men and women, of necessity, shared the harsh responsibilities of home and family. In the urban areas and among the upper classes, the roles of men and women were becoming more clearly differentiated and the first signs of the so-called Victorian morality appeared. This increasing differentiation of sex roles and the acceptance of English ideals concerning the relations of the sexes was related to the appearance of sharper class distinctions and growing economic specialization, which separated the functions of men and women both physically and psychologically. Page Smith has argued that "in the creation of a middle-class, essentially urban style of life, women who early had shared in the direction of farms and the rigors of pioneer existence, were expected to preside gracefully over drawing rooms." Such changes affected women's self-perceptions and the attitudes of others toward them. Julia Cherry Spruill has noted that "the eighteenth century saw a decline in the vigor and self-reliance of women in wealthier families and a lessening of their influence in public matters."

In the South the idealization of white womanhood was intertwined with the growth of slavery and anxieties concerning miscegenation. Racial attitudes and sexual myths were closely related in early America, and the degradation of blacks had deep effects upon white women. In the early eighteenth century the discussion of sex was fairly open, and sexual activity was an accepted part of life. With the development of slavery, sexual relations in the southern colonies became warped, and a distinctive double standard emerged that irreparably scarred southern women of both races.

It is difficult to generalize about the condition of women in colonial America. After the early years, the risk of disease decreased, and both life expectancy and fertility were greater than in England. But the lot of colonial women was neither a uniform nor an easy one. Society in the eighteenth century differed from that in the seventeenth century, and the situations of women differed accordingly. The imbalance between the sexes disappeared. Sexual discipline became looser and premarital pregnancy far more common. Class, region, race and status also determined that colonial women led varied lives. While the sexual boundaries were not so clearly drawn as they would become in the nineteenth century, life was difficult for colonial women. Their work was hard; continuous pregnancy and child care jeopardized their health. Death in childbirth was a horror that, in one way or another, touched the life of every women. The idea that these years represented a "golden age" for women is clearly a myth.

∽ 1 ∽
HUSBANDS AND WIVES
JOHN DEMOS

No aspect of the Puritan household was more vital than the relationship of husband and wife. But the study of this relationship raises at once certain larger questions of sex differentiation: What were the relative positions of men and women in Plymouth Colony? What attributes, and what overall valuation, were thought appropriate to each sex?

We know in a general way that male dominance was an accepted principle all over the Western World in the seventeenth century. The fundamental Puritan sentiment on this matter was expressed by Milton in a famous line in *Paradise Lost:* "he for God only, she for God in him " and there is no reason to suspect that the people of Plymouth would have put it any differently. The world of public affairs was nowhere open to women—in Plymouth only males were eligible to become "freemen." Within the family the husband was always regarded as the "head"—and the Old Colony provided no exceptions to this pattern. Moreover, the culture at large maintained a deep and primitive kind of suspicion of women, solely on account of their sex. Some basic taint of corruption was thought to be inherent in the feminine constitution—a belief rationalized, of course, by the story of Eve's initial treachery in the Garden of Eden. It was no coincidence that in both the Old and the New World witches were mostly women. Only two allegations of witchcraft turn up in the official records of Plymouth,[1] but other bits of evidence point in the same general direction. There are, for example, the quoted words of a mother beginning an emotional plea to her son: "if you would beleive a woman beleive mee. . . ."[2] And why *not* believe a woman?

The views of the Pilgrim pastor John Robinson are also interesting in this connection. He opposed, in the first place, any tendency to regard women as "necessary evils" and greatly regretted the currency of such opinions among "not only heathen poets . . . but also wanton Christians." The Lord had created both man and woman of an equal perfection, and "neither is she, since the creation more degenerated than he from the primitive goodness."[3] Still, in marriage some principles of authority were essential, since "differences will arise and be seen, and so the one must give way, and apply unto the other; this, God and nature layeth upon the woman, rather than upon the man." Hence the proper attitude of a wife towards her husband was "a reverend subjection."[4]

However, in a later discussion of the same matter Robinson developed a more complex line of argument which stressed certain attributes of inferiority assumed to be inherently feminine. Women, he wrote, were under two different kinds of subjection. The first was framed "in innocency" and implied no "grief" or "wrong" whatsoever. It reflected simply the woman's character as "the weaker vessel"—weaker, most obviously, with respect to intelligence or "understanding." For this was a gift "which God hath . . . afforded [the man], and means of obtaining it, above the woman, that he might guide and go before her."[5] Robinson also recognized that some men abused their position of authority and oppressed their wives most unfairly. But *even so*—and this was his central point—resistance was not admissible. Here he affirmed the second kind of subjection laid upon woman, a subjection undeniably "grievous" but justified by her "being first in transgression." In this way—by invoking the specter of Eve corrupting Adam in paradise—Robinson arrived in the end at a position which closely approximated the popular assumption of woman's basic moral weakness.

Yet within this general framework of masculine superiority there were a number of rather contrary indications. They seem especially evident in certain areas of the law. Richard B. Morris has written a most interesting essay on this matter, arguing the improved legal status of colonial women by comparison to what still obtained in the mother country.[6] Many of his conclusions seem to make a good fit with conditions in Plymouth Colony. The baseline here is the common law tradition of England, which at this time accorded to women only the most marginal sort of recognition. The married woman, indeed, was largely subsumed under the legal personality of her husband; she was virtually without rights to own property, make contracts, or sue for damages on her own account. But in the New World this situation was perceptibly altered.

Consider, for example, the evidence bearing on the property rights of Plymouth Colony wives. The law explicitly recognized their part in the accumulation of a family's estate, by the procedures it established for the treatment of widows. It was a basic principle of inheritance in this period—on both sides of the Atlantic—that a widow should have the use or profits of one-third of the land owned by her husband at the time of his death and full title to one-third of his movable property. But at least in Plymouth, and perhaps in other colonies as well, this expressed more than the widow's need for an adequate living allowance. For the laws also prescribed that "if any man do make an irrational and unrighteous Will, whereby he deprives his Wife of her reasonable allowance for her subsistencey," the Court may "relieve her out of the estate, notwithstanding by Will it were otherwise disposed; especially in such case where the Wife brought with her good part of the Estate in Marriage, or hath by her diligence and industry done her part in the getting of the Estate, and was otherwise well deserving."[7] Occasionally the Court saw fit to alter the terms of a will on this account. In 1663, for example, it awarded to widow Naomi Silvester a larger share of her late husband's estate than the "inconsiderable pte" he had left her, since she had been "a frugall and laborious woman in the procuring of the said estate."[8] In short, the widow's customary "thirds" was not a mere dole; it was her *due.*

But there is more still. In seventeenth-century England women were denied the right to make contracts, save in certain very exceptional instances. In Plymouth Colony, by contrast, one finds the Court sustaining certain kinds of contracts involving women on a fairly regular basis. The most common case of this type was the agreement of a widow and a new husband, made *before* marriage, about the future disposition of their respective properties. The contract drawn up by John Phillips of Marshfield and widow Faith Doty of Plymouth in 1667 was fairly standard. It stipulated that "the said Faith Dotey is to enjoy all her house and land, goods and cattles, that shee is now possessed of, to her owne proper use, to dispose of them att her owne free will from time to time, and att any time, as shee shall see cause." Moreover this principle of separate control extended beyond the realm of personal property. Phillips and widow Doty each had young children by their previous marriages, and their agreement was "that the children of both the said pties shall remaine att the free and proper and onely dispose of theire owne naturall parents, as they shall see good to dispose of them."[9] Any woman entering marriage on terms such as these would seem virtually an equal partner, at least from a legal standpoint. Much rarer, but no less significant, were contracts made by women *after* marriage. When Dorothy Clarke wished to be free of her husband Nathaniel in 1686, the Court refused a divorce but allowed a separation. Their estate was then carefully divided up by contract to which the wife was formally a party.[10] Once again, no clear precedents for this procedure can be found in contemporary English law.

The specific terms of some wills also help to confirm the rights of women to a limited kind of ownership even within marriage. No husband ever included his wife's clothing, for example, among the property to be disposed of after his death. And consider, on the other side, a will like that of Mistress Sarah Jenny, drawn up at Plymouth in 1655. Her husband had died just a few months earlier, and she wished simply to "Despose of som smale thinges that is my owne proper goods leaveing my husbands will to take place according to the true Intent and meaning thereof."[11] The "smale thinges" included not only her wardrobe, but also a bed, some books, a mare, some cattle and sheep. Unfortunately, married women did not usually leave wills of their own (unless they had been previously widowed); and it is necessary to infer that in most cases there was some sort of informal arrangement for the transfer of their personal possessions. One final indication of these same patterns comes from wills which made bequests to a husband and wife separately. Thus, for example, Richard Scalis of Scituate conferred most of his personal possessions on the families of two married daughters, carefully specifying which items should go to the daughters themselves and which to their husbands.[12] Thomas Rickard, also of Scituate, had no family of his own and chose therefore to distribute his property among a variety of friends. Once again spouses were treated separately: "I give unto Thomas Pincin my bedd and Rugg one paire of sheets and pilloty . . . I give and bequeath unto Joane the wife of the aforsaid Thomas Pincin my bason and fouer sheets . . . I give and bequeath unto Joane Stanlacke my Chest . . . unto Richard Stanlacke my Chest . . . unto Richard Stanlacke my best briches and Dublit and ould Coate."[13]

The questions of property rights and of the overall distribution of authority within a marriage do not necessarily coincide; and modern sociologists interested in the latter subject usually emphasize the process of decision-making.[14] Of course, their use of live samples gives them a very great advantage; they can ask their informants, through questionnaires or interviews, which spouse decides where to go on vacation, what kind of car to buy, how to discipline the children, when to have company in, and so forth. The historian simply cannot draw out this kind of detail, nor can he contrive any substantial equivalent. But he is able sometimes to make a beginning in this direction; for example, the records of Plymouth do throw light on two sorts of family decisions of the very greatest importance. One of these involves the transfer of land, and illustrates further the whole trend toward an expansion of the rights of married women to hold property. The point finds tangible expression in a law passed by the General Court in 1646: "It is enacted &c. That the Assistants or any of them shall have full power to take the acknowledgment of a bargaine and sale of houses and lands . . . And that the wyfe hereafter come in & consent and acknowledg the sale also; but that all bargaines and sales of houses and lands made before this day to remayne firm to the buyer notwithstanding the wife did not acknowledge the same."[15] The words "come in" merit special attention: the authorities wished to confront the wife personally (and even, perhaps, privately?) in order to minimize the possibility that her husband might exert undue pressure in securing her agreement to a sale.

The second area of decision-making in which both spouses shared an important *joint* responsibility was the "putting out" of children into foster families. For this there was no statute prescribing a set line of procedure, but the various written documents from specific cases make the point clearly enough. Thus in 1660 "An Agreement appointed to bee Recorded" affirmed that "Richard Berry of Yarmouth with his wifes Concent and other frinds; hath given unto Gorge Crispe of Eastham and his wife theire son Samuell Berry; to bee att the ordering and Disposing of the said Gorge and his wife as if hee were theire owne Child."[16] The practice of formally declaring the wife's consent is evident in all such instances, when both parents were living. Another piece of legal evidence describes an actual deathbed scene in which the same issue had to be faced. It is the testimony of a mother confirming the adoption of her son, and it is worth quoting in some detail. "These prsents Witnesse that the 20th of march 1657–8 Judith the wife of William Peaks acknowlidged that her former husband Lawrance Lichfeild lying on his Death bedd sent for John Allin and Ann his wife and Desired to give and bequeath unto them his youngest son Josias Lichfeild if they would accept of him and take him as theire Child; then they Desired to know how long they should have him and the said Lawrance said for ever; but the mother of the child was not willing then; but in a short time after willingly Concented to her husbands will in the thinge."[17] That the wife finally agreed is less important here than the way in which her initial reluctance sufficed to block the child's adoption, in spite of the clear wishes of her husband.

Another reflection of this pattern of mutual responsibility appears in certain types of business activity—for instance, the management of inns and taverns ("ordinaries" in the language of the day). All such establishments were licensed by the General Court; hence their history can be followed, to a limited degree, in the official Colony Records. It is interesting to learn that one man's license was revoked because he had recently "buryed his wife, and in that respect not being soe capeable of keeping a publicke house."[18] In other cases the evidence is less explicit but still revealing. For many years James Cole ran the principal ordinary in the town of Plymouth, and from time to time the Court found it necessary to censure and punish certain violations of proper decorum that occurred there. In some of these cases Cole's wife Mary was directly implicated. In March 1669 a substantial fine was imposed "for that the said Mary Cole suffered divers psons after named to stay drinking on the Lords day . . . in the time of publicke worshipp."[19] Indeed the role of women in all aspects of this episode is striking, since two of the four drinking customers, the "divers psons after named," turned out to be female. Perhaps, then, women had considerable freedom to move on roughly the same terms with men even into some of the darker byways of Old Colony life.

The Court occasionally granted liquor licenses directly to women. Husbands were not mentioned, though it is of course possible that all of the women involved were widows. In some cases the terms of these permits suggest retail houses rather than regular inns or taverns. Thus in 1663 "Mistris Lydia Garrett" of Scituate was licensed to "sell liquors, alwaies provided . . . that shee sell none but to house keepers, and not lesse than a gallon att a time;"[20] and the agreement with another Scituate lady, Margaret Muffee, twenty years later, was quite similar.[21] But meanwhile in Middlebury one "Mistress Mary Combe" seems to have operated an ordinary of the standard type.[22] Can we proceed from these specific data on liquor licensing to some more general conclusion about the participation of women in the whole field of economic production and exchange? Unfortunately there is little additional hard evidence on one side or the other. The Court Records do not often mention other types of business activity, with the single exception of milling; and no woman was ever named in connection with this particular enterprise. A few more wills could be cited—for instance, the one made by Elizabeth Poole, a wealthy spinster in Taunton, leaving "my pte in the Iron workes" to a favorite nephew.[23] But this does not add up to very much. The economy of Plymouth was, after all, essentially simple—indeed "underdeveloped"—in most important respects. Farming claimed the energies of all but a tiny portion of the populace; there was relatively little opportunity for anyone, man *or* woman, to develop a more commercial orientation. It is known that in the next century women played quite a significant role in the business life of many parts of New England,[24] and one can view this pattern as simply the full development of possibilities that were latent even among the first generations of settlers. But there is no way to fashion an extended chain of proof.

Much of what has been said so far belongs to the general category of the rights and privileges of the respective partners to a marriage. But what of their duties, their basic responsibilities to one another? Here, surely, is another area of major importance in any assessment of the character of married life. The writings of John Robinson help us to make a start with these questions, and especially to recover the framework of ideals within which most couples of Plymouth Colony must have tried to hammer out a meaningful day-to-day relationship. We have noted already that Robinson prescribed "subjection" as the basic duty of a wife to her husband. No woman deserved praise, "how well endowed soever otherwise, except she frame, and compose herself, what may be, unto her husband, in conformity of manners."[25] From the man, by contrast, two things were particularly required: "love . . . and wisdom." His love for his wife must be "like Christ's to his church: holy for quality, and great for quantity," and it must stand firm even where "her failings and faults be great." His wisdom was essential to the role of family "head"; without it neither spouse was likely to find the way to true piety, and eventually to salvation.

It is a long descent from the spiritual counsel of John Robinson to the details of domestic conflict as noted in the Colony Records. But the Records are really the only available source of information about the workings of actual marriages in this period. They are, to be sure, a negative type of source; that is, they reveal only those cases which seemed sufficiently deviant and sufficiently important to warrant the attention of the authorities. But it is possible by a kind of reverse inference to use them to reconstruct the norms which the community at large particularly wished to protect. This effort serves to isolate three basic obligations in which both husband and wife were thought to share.

There was, first and most simply, the obligation of regular and exclusive cohabitation. No married person was permitted to live apart from his spouse except in very unusual and temporary circumstances (as when a sailor was gone to sea). The Court stood ready as a last resort to force separated couples to come together again, though it was not often necessary to deal with the problem in such an official way. One of the few recorded cases of this type occurred in 1659. The defendant was a certain Goodwife Spring, married to a resident of Watertown in the Bay Colony and formerly the wife and widow of

Thomas Hatch of Scituate. She had, it seems, returned to Scituate some three or four years earlier, and had been living "from her husband" ever since. The Court ordered that "shee either repaire to her husband with all convenient speed, . . . or . . . give a reason why shee doth not." [26] Exactly how this matter turned out cannot be determined, but it seems likely that the ultimate sanction was banishment from the Colony. The government of Massachusetts Bay is known to have imposed this penalty in a number of similar cases. None of the extant records describe such action being taken at Plymouth, but presumably the possibility was always there.

Moreover, the willful desertion of one spouse by the other over a period of several years was one of the few legitimate grounds for divorce. In 1670, for example, the Court granted the divorce plea of James Skiffe "haveing received sufficient testimony that the late wife of James Skiffe hath unlawfully forsaken her lawfull husband . . . and is gone to Roanoke, in or att Verginnia, and there hath taken another man for to be her husband." [27] Of course, bigamy was always sufficient reason in itself for terminating a marriage. Thus in 1680 Elizabeth Stevens obtained a divorce from her husband when it was proved that he had three other wives already, one each in Boston, Barbadoes, and a town in England not specified. [28]

But it was not enough that married persons should simply live together on a regular basis; their relationship must be relatively peaceful and harmonious. Once again the Court reserved the right to interfere in cases where the situation had become especially difficult. Occasionally both husband and wife were judged to be at fault, as when George and Anna Barlow were "severly reproved for theire most ungodly liveing in contension one with the other, and admonished to live otherwise." [29] But much more often one or the other was singled out for the Court's particular attention. One man was punished for "abusing his wife by kiking her of from a stoole into the fier," [30] and another for "drawing his wife in an uncivell manor on the snow." [31] A more serious case was that of John Dunham, convicted of "abusive carriage towards his wife in continuall tiranising over her, and in pticulare for his late abusive and uncivill carryage in endeavoring to beate her in a deboist manor." [32] The Court ordered a whipping as just punishment for these cruelties, but the sentence was then suspended at the request of Dunham's wife. Sometimes the situation was reversed and the woman was the guilty party. In 1655, for example, Joan Miller of Taunton was charged with "beating and reviling her husband, and egging her children to healp her, bidding them knock him in the head, and wishing his victuals might coak him." [33] A few years later the wife of Samuel Halloway (also of

Taunton) was admonished for "carryage towards her husband . . . soe turbulend and wild, both in words and actions, as hee could not live with her but in danger of his life or limbs."[34]

It would serve no real purpose to cite more of these unhappy episodes—and it might indeed create an erroneous impression that marital conflict was particularly endemic among the people of the Old Colony. But two general observations are in order. First, the Court's chief aim in this type of case was to restore the couple in question to something approaching tranquility. The assumption was that a little force applied from the outside might be useful, whether it came in the form of an "admonition" or in some kind of actual punishment. Only once did the Court have to recognize that the situation might be so bad as to make a final reconciliation impossible. This happened in 1665 when John Williams, Jr., of Scituate, was charged with a long series of "abusive and harsh carriages" toward his wife Elizabeth, "in speciall his sequestration of himselfe from the marriage bed, and his accusation of her to bee a whore, and that especially in reference unto a child lately borne of his said wife by him denied to bee legittimate."[35] The case was frequently before the Court during the next two years, and eventually all hope of a settlement was abandoned. When Williams persisted in his "abuses," and when too he had "himself . . . [declared] his insufficency for converse with weomen,"[36] a formal separation was allowed—though not a full divorce. In fact, it may be that his impotence, not his habitual cruelty, was the decisive factor in finally persuading the Court to go this far. For in another case, some years later, a separation was granted on the former grounds alone.[37]

The second noteworthy aspect of all these situations is the equality they seem to imply between the sexes. In some societies and indeed in many parts of Europe at this time, a wife was quite literally at the mercy of her husband—his prerogatives extended even to the random use of physical violence. But clearly this was not the situation at Plymouth. It is, for example, instructive to break down these charges of "abusive carriage" according to sex: one finds that wives were accused just about as often as husbands. Consider, too, those cases of conflict in which the chief parties were of opposite sex but not married to one another. Once again the women seem to have held their own. Thus we have, on the one side, Samuel Norman punished for "strikeing Lydia, the wife of Henery Taylor,"[38] and John Dunham for "abusive speeches and carriages"[39] toward Sarah, wife of Benjamin Eaton; and, on the other side, the complaint of Abraham Jackson against "Rose, the wife of Thomas Morton, . . . that the said Rose, as hee came from worke, did abuse him by calling of him lying rascall and rogue."[40] In short, this does *not* seem to have been a society characterized by a really pervasive, and operational, norm of male dominance. There is no evidence at all of habitual patterns of deference in the relations between the sexes. John Robinson, and many others, too, may have assumed that woman was "the weaker vessel" and that "subjection" was her natural role. But as so often happens with respect to such matters, actual behavior was another story altogether.

The third of the major obligations incumbent on the married pair was a normal and exclusive sexual union. As previously indicated, impotence in the husband was one of the few circumstances that might warrant a divorce. The reasoning behind this is nowhere made explicit, but most likely it reflected the felt necessity that a marriage produce children. It is worth noting in this connection some of the words used in a divorce hearing of 1686 which centered on the issue of a man's impotence. He was, according to his wife, "always unable to perform the act of generation."[41] The latter phrase implies a particular view of the nature and significance of the sexual act, one which must have been widely held in this culture. Of course, there were other infertile marriages in the same period which held together. But perhaps the cause of the problem had to be obvious—as with impotence—for the people involved to consider divorce. Where the sexual function appeared normal in both spouses, there was always the hope that the Lord might one day grant the blessing of children. Doubtless for some couples this way of thinking meant year after year of deep personal disappointment.

The problem of adultery was more common—and, in a general sense, more troublesome. For adultery loomed as the most serious possible distortion of the whole sexual and reproductive side of marriage. John Robinson called it "that most foul and filthy sin, . . . the disease of marriage," and concluded that divorce was its necessary "medicine."[42] In fact, most of the divorces granted in the Old Colony stemmed from this one cause alone. But adultery was not only a strong *prima facie* reason for divorce; it was also an act that would bring heavy punishment to the guilty parties. The law decreed that "whosoever shall Commit Adultery with a Married Woman or one Betrothed to another Man, both of them shall be severely punished, by whipping two several times . . . and likewise to wear two Capital Letters A.D. cut out in cloth and sewed on their uppermost Garments . . . and if at any time they shall be found without the said Letters so worne . . . to be forthwith taken and publickly whipt, and so from time to time as often as they are found not to wear them."[43]

But quite apart from the severity of the prescribed punishments, this statute is interesting for its definition of adultery by reference to a married (or bethrothed) *woman*. Here, for the first time, we find some indication of difference in the conduct expected of men and women. The picture can be filled out somewhat by examining the specific cases of adultery prosecuted before the General Court down through the years. To be sure, the man involved in any given instance was judged together with the woman, and when convicted their punishments were the same. But there is another point to consider as well. All of the adulterous couples mentioned in the records can be classified in one of two categories: a married woman and a married man, or a married woman and a single man. There was, on the other hand, no case involving a married man and a single woman. This pattern seems to imply that the chief concern, the essential element of sin, was the woman's infidelity to her husband. A married man would be punished for his part in this aspect of the affair—rather than for any wrong done to his own wife.

However, this does not mean that a man's infidelities were wholly beyond reproach. The records, for example, include one divorce plea in which the wife adduced as her chief complaint "an act of uncleanes" by her husband with another woman.[44] There was no move to prosecute and punish the husband—apparently since the other woman was unmarried. But the divorce was granted, and the wife received a most favorable settlement. We can, then, conclude the following. The adultery of a wife was treated as both a violation of her marriage (hence grounds for divorce) *and* an offense against the community (hence cause for legal prosecution). But for comparable behavior by husbands only the former consideration applied. In this somewhat limited sense the people of Plymouth Colony do seem to have maintained a "double standard" of sexual morality.

Before concluding this discussion of married life in the Old Colony and moving on to other matters, one important area of omission should at least be noted. Very little as been said here of love, affection, understanding—a whole range of positive feelings and impulses— between husbands and wives. Indeed the need to rely so heavily on Court Records has tended to weight the balance quite conspicuously on the side of conflict and failure. The fact is that the sum total of actions of divorce, prosecutions for adultery, "admonitions" against habitual quarreling, does not seem terribly large. In order to make a proper assessment of their meaning several contingent factors must be recognized; the long span of time they cover, the steady growth of the Colony's population (to something like 10,000 by the end of the century),[45] the extensive jurisdiction of the Court over many areas of domestic life. Given this overall context, it is clear that the vast majority of Plymouth Colony families never once required the attention of the authorities. Elements of disharmony were, at the least, controlled and confined within certain limits.

But again, can the issue be approached in a more directly affirmative way? Just how and how much, did feelings of warmth and love fit into the marriages of the Old Colony? Unfortunately our source materials have almost nothing to say in response to such questions. But this is only to be expected in the case of legal documents, physical remains, and so forth. The wills often refer to "my loveing wife"—but it would be foolish to read anything into such obvious set phrases. The records of Court cases are completely mute on this score. Other studies of "Puritan" ideals about marriage and the family have drawn heavily on literary materials—and this, of course, is the biggest gap in the sources that have come down from Plymouth Colony. Perhaps, though, a certain degree of extrapolation is permissible here; and if so, we must imagine that love was quite central to these marriages. If, as Morgan has shown, this was the case in Massachusetts Bay, surely it was also true for the people of Plymouth.[46]

There are, finally, just a few scraps of concrete evidence on this point. As previously noted, John Robinson wrote lavishly about the importance of love to a marriage—though he associated it chiefly with the role of the husband. And the wills should be drawn in once again, especially those clauses in which a man left specific instructions regarding the care of his widow. Sometimes the curtain of legal terms and style seems to rise for a moment and behind it one glimpses a deep tenderness and concern. There is, for example, the will written by Walter Briggs in 1676. Briggs's instructions in this regard embraced all of the usual matters—rooms, bedding, cooking utensils, "lyberty to make use of ye two gardens." And he ended with a particular request that his executors "allow my said wife a gentle horse or mare to ride to meeting or any other occasion she may have, & that Jemy, ye neger, catch it for her."[47] Surely this kind of thoughtfulness reflected a larger instinct of love—one which, nourished in life, would not cease to be effective even in the fact of death itself.

NOTES

1. The first occurred in 1661, in Marshfield. A girl named Dinah Silvester accused the wife of William Holmes of being a witch, and of going about in the shape of a bear in order to do mischief. The upshot, however, was a suit for defamation

against Dinah. The Court convicted her and obliged her to make a public apology to Goodwife Holmes. *Plymouth Colony Records*, III, 205, 207, 211. The second case (at Scituate, in 1677) resulted in the formal indictment of one Mary Ingham—who, it was said, had bewitched a girl named Mehitable Woodworth. But after suitable deliberations, the jury decided on an acquittal. *Plymouth Colony Records*, V, 223–24.

2. From a series of depositions bearing on the estate of Samuel Ryder, published in *Mayflower Descendant*, XI, 52. The case is discussed in greater detail below, pp. 165–66.

3. *The Works of John Robinson*, ed. Robert Ashton (Boston, 1851), I, 236.

4. *Ibid.*, 239–40.

5. *Ibid.*, 240.

6. Richard B. Morris, *Studies in the History of American Law* (New York, 1930), Chapter III, "Women's Rights in Early American Law."

7. Brigham *The Compact with the Charter and Laws of the Colony of New Plymouth*, 281.

8. *Plymouth Colony Records*, IV, 46.

9. *Ibid.*, 1643–64. For another agreement of this type, see *Mayflower Descendant*, XVII, 49 (the marriage contract of Ephraim Morton and Mistress Mary Harlow). The same procedures can be viewed, retrospectively, in the wills of men who had been married to women previously widowed. Thus when Thomas Boardman of Yarmouth died in 1689 the following notation was placed near the end of his will: "the estate of my wife brought me upon marriage be at her dispose and not to be Invintoried with my estate." *Mayflower Descendant*, X, 102. See also the will of Dolar Davis, *Mayflower Descendant*, XXIV, 73.

10. *Mayflower Descendant*, VI, 191–92.

11. *Mayflower Descendant*, VIII, 171.

12. *Mayflower Descendant*, XIII, 94–96.

13. *Mayflower Descendant*, IX, 155.

14. See, for example, Robert O. Blood, Jr., and Donald M. Wolfe, *Husbands and Wives* (Glencoe, Ill., 1960), esp. ch. 2.

15. Brigham, *The Compact with the Charter and Laws of the Colony of New Plymouth*, 86.

16. *Mayflower Descendant*, XV, 34.

17. *Mayflower Descendant*, XII, 134.

18. *Plymouth Colony Records*, IV, 54.

19. *Plymouth Colony Records*, V, 15.

20. *Plymouth Colony Records*, IV, 44.

21. *Plymouth Colony Records*, VI, 187.

22. *Ibid.*, 141.

23. *Mayflower Descendant*, XIV, 26.

24. Elizabeth Anthony Dexter, *Colonial Women of Affairs* (Boston, 1911).

25. *The Works of John Robinson*, I, 20.

26. *Plymouth Colony Records*, III, 174.

27. *Plymouth Colony Records*, V, 33.

28. *Plymouth Colony Records*, VI, 44–45.

29. *Plymouth Colony Records,* IV, 10.

30. *Plymouth Colony Records,* V, 61.

31. *Plymouth Colony Records,* IV, 47.

32. *Ibid.,* 103–4.

33. *Plymouth Colony Records,* III, 75.

34. *Plymouth Colony Records,* V, 29.

35. *Plymouth Colony Records,* IV, 93.

36. *Ibid.,* 125.

37. *Plymouth Colony Records,* VI, 191.

38. *Plymouth Colony Records,* V, 39.

39. *Ibid.,* 40.

40. *Plymouth Colony Records,* IV, 11.

41. *Plymouth Colony Records,* VI, 191.

42. *The Works of John Robinson,* I, 241.

43. Brigham, *The Compact with the Charter and Laws of the Colony of New Plymouth,* 245–46.

44. *Plymouth Colony Records,* III, 221.

45. There are three separate investigations dealing with this question: Bowen, *Early Rehoboth,* I, 15–24; Joseph B. Felt, "Population of Plymouth Colony," in American Statistical Association *Collections,* I, Pt. ii (Boston, 1845), 143–44; and Bradford, *Of Plymouth Plantation,* xi.

46. See Edmund Morgan, *The Puritan Family* (New York, 1966), esp. 46 ff.

47. *Plymouth Colony Records,* VI, 134–35.

~ 2 ~
THE PLANTER'S WIFE: THE EXPERIENCE OF WHITE WOMEN IN SEVENTEENTH-CENTURY MARYLAND

LOIS GREEN CARR AND LORENA S. WALSH

Four facts were basic to all human experience in seventeenth-century Maryland. First, for most of the period the great majority of inhabitants had been born in what we now call Britain. Population increase in Maryland did not result primarily from births in the colony before the late 1680s and did not produce a predominantly native population of adults before the first decade of the eighteenth century. Second, immigrant men could not expect to live beyond age forty-three, and 70 percent would die before age fifty. Women may have had even shorter lives. Third, perhaps 85 percent of the immigrants, and practically all the unmarried immigrant women, arrived as indentured servants and consequently married late. Family groups were never predominant in the immigration to Maryland and were a significant part for only a brief time at mid-century. Fourth, many more men than women immigrated during the whole period.[1] These facts—immigrant predominance, early death, late marriage, and sexual imbalance—created circumstances of social and demographic disruption that deeply affected family and community life.

We need to assess the effects of this disruption on the experience of women in seventeenth-century Maryland. Were women degraded by the hazards of servitude in a society in which everyone had left community and kin behind and in which women were in short supply? Were traditional restraints on social conduct weakened? If so, were women more exploited or more independent and powerful than women who remained in England? Did any differences from English experience which we can observe in the experience of Maryland women survive the

From *William and Mary Quarterly* 34 (October, 1977), pp. 542–571. Reprinted by permission.

transformation from an immigrant to a predominantly native-born society with its own kinship networks and community traditions? The tentative argument put forward here is that the answer to all these questions is Yes. There were degrading aspects of servitude, although these probably did not characterize the lot of most women; there were fewer restraints on social conduct, especially in courtship, than in England; women were less protected but also more powerful than those who remained at home; and at least some of these changes survived the appearance in Maryland of New World creole communities. However, these issues are far from settled, and we shall offer some suggestions as to how they might be further pursued.

Maryland was settled in 1634, but in 1650 there were probably no more than six hundred persons and fewer than two hundred adult women in the province. After that time population growth was steady; in 1704 a census listed 30,437 white persons, of whom 7,163 were adult women.[2] Thus in discussing the experience of white women in seventeenth-century Maryland we are dealing basically with the second half of the century.

Marylanders of that period did not leave letters and diaries to record their New World experience or their relationships to one another. Nevertheless, they left trails in the public records that give us clues. Immigrant lists kept in England and documents of the Maryland courts offer quantifiable evidence about the kinds of people who came and some of the problems they faced in making a new life. Especially valuable are the probate court records. Estate inventories reveal the kinds of activities carried on in the house and on the farm, and wills, which are usually the only personal statements that remain for any man or woman, show something of personal attitudes. This essay relies on the most useful of the immigrant lists and all surviving Maryland court records, but concentrates especially on the surviving records of the lower Western Shore, an early-settled area highly suitable for tobacco. Most of this region comprised four counties: St. Mary's, Calvert, Charles, and Prince George's (formed in 1696 from Calvert and Charles). Inventories from all four counties, wills from St. Mary's and Charles, and court proceedings from Charles and Prince George's provide the major data.[3]

Because immigrants predominated, who they were determined much about the character of Maryland society. The best information so far available comes from lists of indentured servants who left the ports of London, Bristol, and Liverpool. These lists vary in quality, but at the very least they distinguish immigrants by sex and general destination. A place of residence in England is usually given, although it may not represent the emigrant's place of origin; and age and occupation are often noted. These lists reveal several characteristics of immigrants to the Chesapeake and, by inference, to Maryland.[4]

Servants who arrived under indenture included yeomen, husbandmen, farm laborers, artisans, and small tradesmen, as well as many untrained to any special skill. They were young: over half of the men on the London lists of 1683–1684 were aged eighteen to twenty-two. They were seldom under seventeen or over twenty-eight. The women were a little older; the great majority were between eighteen and twenty-five, and half were aged twenty to twenty-two. Most servants contracted for four or five years service, although those under fifteen were to serve at least seven years.[5] These youthful immigrants represented a wide range of English society. All were seeking opportunities they had not found at home.

However, many immigrants—perhaps about half[6]—did not leave England with indentures but paid for their passage by serving according to the custom of the country. Less is known about their social characteristics, but some inferences are possible. From 1661, customary service was set by Maryland laws that required four-year (later five-year) terms for men and women who were twenty-two years or over at arrival and longer terms for those who were younger. A requirement of these laws enables us to determine something about age at arrival of servants who came without indentures. A planter who wished to obtain more than four or five years of service had to take his servant before the county court to have his or her age judged and a written record made. Servants aged over twenty-one were not often registered, there being no incentive for a master to pay court fees for those who would serve the minimum term. Nevertheless, a comparison of the ages of servants under twenty-two recorded in Charles County, 1658–1689, with those under twenty-two on the London list is revealing. Of Charles County male servants (N = 363), 77.1 percent were aged seventeen or under, whereas on the London list (N = 196), 77.6 percent were eighteen or over. Women registered in Charles County court were somewhat older than the men, but among those under twenty-two (N = 107), 5.5 percent were aged twenty-one, whereas on the London list (N = 69), 46.4 percent had reached this age. Evidently, some immigrants who served by custom were younger than those who came indentured, and this age difference probably characterized the two groups as a whole. Servants who were not only very young but had arrived without the protection of a written contract were possibly of lower social origins than were servants who came under indenture. The absence of skills among Charles County servants who served by custom supports this supposition.[7]

Whatever their status, one fact about immigrant women is certain: many fewer came than men. Immigrant lists, headright lists, and itemizations of servants in inventories show severe imbalance. On a London immigrant list of 1634–1635 men outnumbered women six to one. From the 1650s at least until the 1680s most sources show a ratio of three to one. From then on, all sources show some, but not great, improvement. Among immigrants from Liverpool over the years 1697–1707 the ratio was just under two and one half to one.[8]

Why did not more women come? Presumably, fewer wished to leave family and community to venture into a wilderness. But perhaps more important, women were not as desirable as men to merchants and planters who were making fortunes raising and marketing tobacco, a crop that requires large amounts of labor. The gradual improvement in the sex ratio among servants toward the end of the century may have been the result of a change in recruiting the needed labor. In the late 1660s the supply of young men willing to emigrate stopped increasing sufficiently to meet the labor demands of a growing Chesapeake population. Merchants who recruited servants for planters turned to other sources, and among these sources were women. They did not crowd the ships arriving in the Chesapeake, but their numbers did increase.[8]

To ask the question another way, why did women come? Doubtless, most came to get a husband, an objective virtually certain of success in a land where women were so far outnumbered. The promotional literature, furthermore, painted bright pictures of the life that awaited men and women once out of their time; and various studies suggest that for a while, at least, the promoters were not being entirely fanciful. Until the 1660s, and to a less degree the 1680s, the expanding economy of Maryland and Virginia offered opportunities well beyond those available in England to men without capital and to the women who became their wives.[10]

Nevertheless, the hazards were also great, and the greatest was untimely death. Newcomers promptly became ill, probably with malaria, and many died. What proportion survived is unclear; so far no one has devised a way of measuring it. Recurrent malaria made the woman who survived seasoning less able to withstand other diseases, especially dysentery and influenza. She was especially vulnerable when pregnant. Expectation of life for everyone was low in the Chesapeake, but especially so for women.[11] A woman who had immigrated to Maryland took an extra risk, though perhaps a risk not greater than she might have suffered by moving from her village to London instead.[12]

The majority of women who survived seasoning paid their transportation costs by working for a four- or five-year term of service. The kind of work depended on the status of the family they served. A female servant of a small planter—who through about the 1670s might have had a servant[13]—probably worked at the hoe. Such a man could not afford to buy labor that would not help with the cash crop. In wealthy families women probably were household servants, although some are occasionally listed in inventories of well-to-do planters as living on the quarters—that is, on plantations other than the dwelling plantation. Such women saved men the jobs of preparing food and washing linen but doubtless also worked in the fields.[14] In middling households experience must have varied. Where the number of people to feed and wash for was large, female servants would have had little time to tend the crops.

Tracts that promoted immigration to the Chesapeake region asserted that female servants did not labor in the fields, except "nasty" wenches not fit for other tasks. This implies that most immigrant women expected, or at least hoped, to avoid heavy field work, which English women—at least those above the cottager's status—did not do.[15] What proportion of female servants in Maryland found themselves demeaned by this unaccustomed labor is impossible to say, but this must have been the fate of some. A study of the distribution of female servants among wealth groups in Maryland might shed some light on this question. Nevertheless, we still would not know whether those purchased by the poor or sent to work on a quarter were women whose previous experience suited them for field labor.

An additional risk for the woman who came as a servant was the possibility of bearing a bastard. At least 20 percent of the female servants who came to Charles County between 1658 and 1705 were presented to the county court for this cause.[16] A servant woman could not marry unless someone was willing to pay her master for the term she had left to serve.[17] If a man made her pregnant, she could not marry him unless he could buy her time. Once a woman became free, however, marriage was clearly the usual solution. Only a handful of free women were presented in Charles County for bastardy between 1658 and 1705. Since few free women remained either single or widowed for long, not many were subject to the risk. The hazard of bearing a bastard was a hazard of being a servant.[18]

This high rate of illegitimate pregnancies among servants raises lurid questions. Did men import women for sexual exploitation? Does John Barth's Whore of Dorset have a basis outside his fertile imagination?[19] In our opinion, the answers are clearly No. Servants were economic investments on the part of planters who needed labor. A female servant in a household where there were unmarried men must have both provided and faced temptation, for the pressures were great in a society in which men outnumbered women by three to one.

Nevertheless, the servant woman was in the household to work—to help feed and clothe the family and make tobacco. She was not primarily a concubine.

This point could be established more firmly if we knew more about the fathers of the bastards. Often the culprits were fellow servants or men recently freed but too poor to purchase the woman's remaining time. Sometimes the master was clearly at fault. But often the father is not identified. Some masters surely did exploit their female servants sexually. Nevertheless, masters were infrequently accused of fathering their servants' bastards, and those found guilty were punished as severely as were other men. Community mores did not sanction their misconduct.[20]

A female servant paid dearly for the fault of unmarried pregnancy. She was heavily fined, and if no one would pay her fine, she was whipped. Furthermore, she served an extra twelve to twenty-four months to repay her master for the "trouble of his house" and labor lost, and the fathers often did not share in this payment of damages. On top of all, she might lose the child after weaning unless by then she had become free, for the courts bound out bastard children at very early ages.[21]

English life probably did not offer a comparable hazard to young unmarried female servants. No figures are available to show rates of illegitimacy among those who were subject to the risk,[22] but the female servant was less restricted in England than in the Chesapeake. She did not owe anyone for passage across the Atlantic; hence it was easier for her to marry, supposing she happened to become pregnant while in service. Perhaps, furthermore, her temptations were fewer. She was not 3,000 miles from home and friends, and she lived in a society in which there was no shortage of women. Bastards were born in England in the seventeenth century, but surely not to as many as one-fifth of the female servants.

Some women escaped all or part of their servitude because prospective husbands purchased the remainder of their time. At least one promotional pamphlet published in the 1660s described such purchases as likely, but how often they actually occurred is difficult to determine.[23] Suggestive is a 20 percent difference between the sex ratios found in a Maryland headright sample, 1658–1681, and among servants listed in lower Western Shore inventories for 1658–1679.[24] Some of the discrepancy must reflect the fact that male servants were younger than female servants and therefore served longer terms; hence they had a greater chance of appearing in an inventory. But part of the discrepancy doubtless follows from the purchase of women for wives. Before 1660, when sex ratios were even more unbalanced and the expanding economy enabled men to establish themselves more quickly, even more women may have married before their terms were finished.[25]

Were women sold for wives against their wills? No record says so, but nothing restricted a man from selling his servant to whomever he wished. Perhaps some women were forced into such marriages or accepted them as the least evil. But the man who could afford to purchase a wife—especially a new arrival—was usually already an established landowner.[26] Probably most servant women saw an opportunity in such a marriage. In addition, the shortage of labor gave women some bargaining power. Many masters must have been ready to refuse to sell a woman who was unwilling to marry a would-be purchaser.

If a woman's time was not purchased by a prospective husband, she was virtually certain to find a husband once she was free. Those famous spinsters, Margaret and Mary Brent, were probably almost unique in seventeenth-century Maryland. In the four counties of the lower Western Shore only two of the women who left a probate inventory before the eighteenth century are known to have died single.[27] Comely or homely, strong or weak, any young woman was too valuable to be overlooked, and most could find a man with prospects.

The woman who immigrated to Maryland, survived seasoning and service, and gained her freedom became a planter's wife. She had considerable liberty in making her choice. There were men aplenty, and no fathers or brothers were hovering to monitor her behavior or disapprove her preference. This is the modern way of looking at her situation, of course. Perhaps she missed the protection of a father, a guardian, or kinfolk, and the participation in her decision of a community to which she felt ties. There is some evidence that the absence of kin and the pressures of the sex ratio created conditions of sexual freedom in courtship that were not customary in England. A register of marriages and births for seventeenth-century Somerset County shows that about one-third of the immigrant women whose marriages are recorded were pregnant at the time of the ceremony—nearly twice the rate in English parishes.[28] There is no indication of community objection to this freedom so long as marriage took place. No presentments for bridal pregnancy were made in any of the Maryland courts.[29]

The planter's wife was likely to be in her mid-twenties at marriage. An estimate of minimum age at marriage for servant women can be made from lists of indentured servants who left London over the years 1683–1684 and from age judgments in Maryland county court records. If we assume that the 112 female indentured servants going to Maryland and Virginia whose ages are given in the London lists served full four-year terms, then only 1.8 percent married before age twenty, but 68 percent after age twenty-four.[30] Similarly, if the 141 women whose ages were judged in Charles County between 1666 and 1705 served out their terms according to the custom of the country, none married before age twenty-two, and half were twenty-five or over.[31] When adjustments are made for the ages at which wives may have been purchased, the figures drop, but even so the majority of women waited until at least age twenty-four to marry.[32] Actual age at marriage in Maryland can be found for few seventeenth-century female immigrants, but observations for Charles and Somerset counties place the mean age at about twenty-five.[33]

Because of the age at which an immigrant woman married, the number of children she would bear her husband was small. She had lost up to ten years of her childbearing life[34] —the possibility of perhaps four or five children, given the usual rhythm of childbearing.[35] At the same time, high mortality would reduce both the number of children she would bear over the rest of her life and the number who would live. One partner to a marriage was likely to die within seven years, and the chances were only one in three that a marriage would last ten years.[36] In these circumstances, most women would not bear more than three or four children—not counting those stillborn—to any one husband, plus a posthumous child were she the survivor. The best estimates suggest that nearly a quarter, perhaps more, of the children born alive died during their first year and that 40 to 55 percent would not live to see age twenty.[37] Consequently, one of her children would probably die in infancy, and another one or two would fail to reach adulthood. Wills left in St. Mary's County during the seventeenth century show the results. In 105 families over the years 1660 to 1680 only twelve parents left more than three children behind them, including those conceived but not yet born. The average number was 2.3, nearly always minors, some of whom might die before reaching adulthood.[38]

For the immigrant woman, then, one of the major facts of life was that although she might bear a child about every two years, nearly half would not reach maturity. The social implications of this fact are far-reaching. Because she married late in her childbearing years and because so many of her children would die young, the number who would reach marriageable age might not replace, or might only barely replace, her and her husband or husbands as child-producing members of the society. Consequently, so long as immigrants were heavily predominant in the adult female population, Maryland could not grow much by natural increase.[39] It remained a land of newcomers.

This fact was fundamental to the character of seventeenth-century Maryland society, although its implications have yet to be fully explored. Settlers came from all parts of England and hence from differing traditions—in types of agriculture, forms of landholding and estate management, kinds of building construction, customary contributions to community needs, and family arrangements, including the role of women. The necessities of life in the Chesapeake required all immigrants to make adaptations. But until the native-born became predominant, a securely established Maryland tradition would not guide or restrict the newcomers.

If the immigrant woman had remained in England, she would probably have married at about the same age or perhaps a little later.[40] But the social consequences of marriage at these ages in most parts of England were probably different. More children may have lived to maturity, and even where mortality was as high newcomers are not likely to have been the main source of population growth.[41] The locally born would still dominate the community, its social organization, and its traditions. However, where there were exceptions, as perhaps in London, late age at marriage, combined with high mortality and heavy immigration, may have had consequences in some ways similar to those we have found in Maryland.

A hazard of marriage for seventeenth-century women everywhere was death in childbirth, but this hazard may have been greater than usual in the Chesapeake. Whereas in most societies women tend to outlive men, in this malaria-ridden area it is probable that men outlived women. Hazards of childbirth provide the likely reason that Chesapeake women died so young. Once a woman in the Chesapeake reached forty-five, she tended to outlive men who reached the same age. Darrett and Anita Rutman have found malaria a probable cause of an exceptionally high death rate among pregnant women, who are, it appears, peculiarly vulnerable to that disease.[42]

This argument, however, suggests that immigrant women may have lived longer than their native-born daughters, although among men the opposite was true. Life tables created for men in Maryland show that those native-born who survived to age twenty could expect a life span three to ten years longer than that of immigrants, depending upon the region where they lived. The reason for the improvement was doubtless immunities to local diseases developed in childhood.[43] A native woman developed these immunities, but, as we shall see, she also married earlier than immigrant women usually could and hence had more children.[44] Thus she was more exposed to the hazards of childbirth and may have died a little sooner. Unfortunately, the life

TABLE 1 Bequests of Husbands to Wives, St. Mary's and Charles Counties, Maryland, 1640 to 1710

		Dower or Less	
	N	N	%
1640s	6	2	34
1650s	24	7	29
1660s	65	18	28
1670s	86	21	24
1680s	64	17	27
1690s	83	23	28
1700s	74	25	34
Totals	402	113	28

Source: Wills, I-XIV, Hall of Records, Annapolis, Md.

tables for immigrant women that would settle this question have so far proved impossible to construct.

However long they lived, immigrant women in Maryland tended to outlive their husbands—in Charles County, for example, by a ratio of two to one. This was possible, despite the fact that women were younger than men at death, because women were also younger than men at marriage. Some women were widowed with no living children, but most were left responsible for two or three. These were often tiny, and nearly always not yet sixteen.[45]

This fact had drastic consequences, given the physical circumstances of life. People lived at a distance from one another, not even in villages, much less towns. The widow had left her kin 3,000 miles across an ocean, and her husband's family was also there. She would have to feed her children and make her own tobacco crop. Though neighbors might help, heavy labor would be required of her if she had no servants, until— what admittedly was usually not difficult—she acquired a new husband.

In this situation dying husbands were understandably anxious about the welfare of their families. Their wills reflected their feelings and tell something of how they regarded their wives. In St. Mary's and Charles counties during the seventeenth century, little more than one-quarter of the men left their widows with no more than the dower the law required—one-third of his land for her life, plus outright ownership of one-third of his personal property. (See Table 1.) If there were no children, a man almost always left his widow his whole estate. Otherwise there were a variety of arrangements. (See Table 2.)

TABLE 2 Bequests of Husbands to Wives with Children, St. Mary's and Charles Counties, Maryland, 1640 to 1710

	N	All Estate		All or Dwelling Plantation for Life		All or Dwelling Plantation for Widowhood		All or Dwelling Plantation for Minority of Child		More than Dower in Other Form		Dower or Less or Unknown	
		N	%	N	%	N	%	N	%	N	%	N	%
1640s	3	1	33	33								2	67
1650s	16	1	6	2	13	1	6	1	6	4	25	7	44
1660s	45	8	18	8	18	2	4	3	7	9	20	15	33
1670s	61	4	7	21	34	2	3	3	5	13	21	18	30
1680s	52	5	10	19	37	2	4	2	4	11	21	13	25
1690s	69	1	1	31	45	7	10	2	3	10	14	18	26
1700s	62			20	32	6	10	2	3	14	23	20	32
Totals	308	20	6	101	33	20	6	13	4	61	20	93	30

Source: Wills, I-XIV.

During the 1660s, when testators begin to appear in quantity, nearly a fifth of the men who had children left all to their wives, trusting them to see that the children received fair portions. Thus in 1663 John Shircliffe willed his whole estate to his wife "towards the maintenance of herself and my children into whose tender care I do Commend them Desireing to see them brought up in the fear of God and the Catholick Religion and Chargeing them to be Dutiful and obedient to her."[46] As the century progressed, husbands tended instead to give the wife all or a major part of the estate for her life, and to designate how it should be distributed after her death. Either way, the husband put great trust in his widow, considering that he knew she was bound to remarry. Only a handful of men left estates to their wives only for their term of widowhood or until the children came of age. When a man did not leave his wife a life estate, he often gave her land outright or more than her dower third of his movable property. Such bequests were at the expense of his children and showed his concern that his widow should have a maintenance which young children could not supply.

A husband usually made his wife his executor and thus responsible for paying his debts and preserving the estate. Only 11 percent deprived their wives of such powers.[47] In many instances, however, men also appointed overseers to assist their wives and to see that their children were not abused or their property embezzled. Danger lay in the fact that a second husband acquired control of all his wife's property, including her life estate in the property of his predecessor. Over half of the husbands who died in the 1650s and 1660s appointed overseers to ensure that their wills were followed. Some trusted to the overseers' "Care and good Conscience for the good of my widow and fatherless children." Others more explicitly made overseers responsible for seeing that "my said child . . . and the other [expected child] (when pleases God to send it) may have their right Proportion of my Said Estate and that the said Children may be bred up Chiefly in the fear of God."[48] A few men—but remarkably few—authorized overseers to remove children from households of stepfathers who abused them or wasted their property.[49] On the whole, the absence of such provisions for the protection of the children points to the husband's overriding concern for the welfare of his widow and to his confidence in her management, regardless of the certainty of her remarriage. Evidently, in the politics of family life women enjoyed great respect.[50]

We have implied that this respect was a product of the experience of immigrants in the Chesapeake. Might it have been instead a reflection of English culture? Little work is yet in print that allows comparison of the provisions for Maryland widows with those made for the widows of English farmers. Possibly, Maryland husbands were making traditional wills which could have been written in the communities they left behind. However, Margaret Spufford's recent study of three Cambridgeshire villages in the late sixteenth century and early seventeenth century suggests a different pattern. In one of these villages, Chippenham, women usually did receive a life interest in the property, but in the other two they did not. If the children were all minors, the widow controlled the property until the oldest son came of age, and then only if she did not remarry. In the majority of cases adult sons were given control of the property with instructions for the support of their mothers. Spufford suggests that the pattern found in Chippenham must have been very exceptional. On the basis of village censuses in six other counties, dating from 1624 to 1724, which show only 3 percent of widowed people heading households that included a married child, she argues that if widows commonly controlled the farm, a higher proportion should have headed such households. However, she also argues that widows with an interest in land would not long remain unmarried.[51] If so, the low percentage may be deceptive. More direct work with wills needs to be done before we can be sure that Maryland husbands and fathers gave their widows greater control of property and family than did their English counterparts.

Maryland men trusted their widows, but this is not to say that many did not express great anxiety about the future of their children. They asked both wives and overseers to see that the children received "some learning." Robert Sly made his wife sole guardian of his children but admonished her "to take due Care that they be brought up in the true fear of God and instructed in such Literature as may tend to their improvement." Widowers, whose children would be left without any parent, were often the most explicit in prescribing their upbringing. Robert Cole, a middling planter, directed that his children "have such Education in Learning as [to] write and read and Cast accompt I mean my three Sonnes my two daughters to learn to read and sew with their needle and all of them to be keept from Idleness but not to be keept as Comon Servants." John Lawson required his executors to see that his two daughters be reared together, receive learning and sewing instruction, and be "brought up to huswifery."[52] Often present was the fear that orphaned children would be treated as servants and trained only to work in the fields.[53] With stepfathers in mind, many fathers provided that their sons should be independent before the usual age of majority, which for girls was sixteen but for men twenty-one. Sometimes fathers willed that their sons should inherit when they were as young as sixteen, though more often eighteen. The sons could then escape an incompatible stepfather, who could no longer exploit their labor or property. If a son was already close to age sixteen, the father might bind him to his mother until he reached majority or his mother died, whichever came first. If she lived, she could watch out for his welfare, and his labor could contribute to her support. If she died, he and his property would be free from a stepfather's control.[54]

What happened to widows and children if a man died without leaving a will? There was great need for some community institution that could protect children left fatherless or parentless in a society where they usually had no other kind. By the 1660s the probate court and county orphans' courts were supplying this need.[55] If a man left a widow, the probate court—in Maryland a central government agency—usually appointed her or her new husband administrator of the estate with power to pay its creditors under court supervision. Probate procedures provided a large measure of protection. These required an inventory of the movable property and careful accounting of all disbursements, whether or not a man had left a will. William Hollis of Baltimore County, for example, had three stepfathers in seven years, and only the care of the judge of probate prevented the third stepfather from paying the debts of the second with goods that had belonged to William's father. As the judge remarked, William had "an uncareful mother."[56]

Once the property of an intestate had been fully accounted and creditors paid, the county courts appointed a guardian who took charge of the property and gave bond to the children with sureties that he or she would not waste it. If the mother were living, she could be the guardian, or if she had remarried, her new husband would act. Through most of the century bond was waived in these circumstances, but from the 1690s security was required of all guardians, even of mothers. Therefore the courts might actually take away an orphan's property from a widow or stepfather if she or he could not find sureties—that is, neighbors who judged the parent responsible and hence were willing to risk their own property as security. Children without any parents were assigned new families, who at all times found surety if there were property to manage. If the orphans inherited land, English common law allowed them to choose guardians for themselves at age fourteen—another escape hatch for children in conflict with stepparents. Orphans who had no property, or whose property was insufficient to provide an income that could maintain them, were expected to work for their guardians in return for their maintenance. Every year the county courts were expected to check on the welfare of orphans of intestate parents and remove them or their property from guardians who abused them or misused their estates. From 1681, Maryland law required that a special jury be impaneled once a year to report neighborhood knowledge of mistreatment of orphans and hear complaints.

This form of community surveillance of widows and orphans proved quite effective. In 1696 the assembly declared that orphans of intestates were often better cared for than orphans of testators. From that time forward, orphans' courts were charged with supervision of all orphans and were soon given powers to remove any guardians who were shown false to their trusts, regardless of the arrangements laid down in a will. The assumption was that the deceased parent's main concern was the welfare of the child, and that the orphans' court, as "father to us poor orphans," should implement the parent's intent. In actual fact, the courts never removed children—as opposed to their property—from a household in which the mother was living, except to apprentice them at the mother's request. These powers were mainly exercised over guardians of orphans both of whose parents were dead. The community as well as the husband believed the mother most capable of nurturing his children.

Remarriage was the usual and often the immediate solution for a woman who had lost her husband.[57] The shortage of women made any woman eligible to marry again, and the difficulties of raising a family while running a plantation must have made remarriage necessary for widows who had no son old enough to make tobacco. One indication of the high incidence of remarriage is the fact that there were only sixty women, almost all of them widows, among the 1,735 people who left probate inventories in four southern Maryland counties over the second half of the century.[58] Most other women must have died while married and therefore legally without property to put through probate.

One result of remarriage was the development of complex family structures. Men found themselves responsible for stepchildren as well as their own offspring, and children acquired half-sisters and half-brothers. Sometimes a woman married a second husband who himself had been previously married, and both brought children of former spouses to the new marriage. They then produced children of their own. The possibilities for conflict over the upbringing of children are evident, and crowded living conditions, found even in the households of the wealthy, must have added to family tensions. Luckily, the children of the family very often had the same mother. In Charles County, at least, widows took new husbands three times more often than widowers took new wives.[59] The role of the mother in managing the relationships of half-brothers and half-sisters or stepfathers and stepchildren must have been critical to family harmony.

Early death in this immigrant population thus had broad effects on Maryland society in the seventeenth century. It produced what we might call a pattern of serial polyandry, which enabled more men to marry and to father families than the sex ratios otherwise would have permitted. It produced thousands of orphaned children who had no kin to maintain them or preserve their property, and thus gave rise to an institution almost unknown in England, the orphans' court, which was charged with their protection. And early death, by creating families in which the mother was the unifying element, may have increased her authority within the household.

When the immigrant woman married her first husband, there was usually no property settlement involved, since she was unlikely to have any dowry. But her remarriage was another matter. At the very least, she owned or had a life interest in a third of her former husband's estate. She needed also to think of her children's interests. If she remarried, she would lose control of the property. Consequently, property settlements occasionally appear in the seventeenth-century court records between widows and their future husbands. Sometimes she and her intended signed an agreement whereby he relinquished his rights to the use of her children's portions. Sometimes he deeded to her property which she could dispose of at her pleasure.[60] Whether any of these agreements or gifts would have survived a test in court is unknown. We have not yet found any challenged. Generally speaking, the formal marriage settlements of English law, which bypassed the legal difficulties of the married woman's inability to make a contract with her husband, were not adopted by immigrants, most of whom probably came from levels of English society that did not use these legal formalities.

The wife's dower rights in her husband's estate were a recognition of her role in contributing to his prosperity, whether by the property she had brought to the marriage or by the labor she performed in his household. A woman newly freed from servitude would not bring property, but the benefits of her labor would be great. A man not yet prosperous enough to own a servant might need his wife's help in the fields as well as in the house, especially if he were paying rent or still paying for land. Moreover, food preparation was so time-consuming that even if she worked only at household duties, she saved him time he needed for making tobacco and corn. The corn, for example, had to be pounded in the mortar or ground in a handmill before it could be used to make bread, for there were very few water mills in seventeenth-century Maryland. The wife probably raised vegetables in a kitchen garden; she also milked the cows and made butter and cheese, which might produce a salable surplus. She washed the clothes, and made them if she had the skill. When there were servants to do field work, the wife undoubtedly spent her time entirely in such household tasks. A contract of 1681 expressed such a division of labor. Nicholas Maniere agreed to live on a plantation with his wife and child and a servant. Nicholas and the servant were to work the land; his wife was to "Dresse the Victualls milk the Cowes wash for the servants and Doe allthings necessary for a woman to doe upon the s[ai]d plantation."[61]

We have suggested that wives did field work; the suggestion is supported by occasional direct references in the court records. Mary Castleton, for example, told the judge of probate that "her husband late Deceased in his Life time had Little to sustaine himselfe and Children but what was produced out of ye ground by ye hard Labour of her the said Mary."[62] Household inventories provide indirect evidence. Before about 1680 those of poor men and even middling planters on Maryland's lower Western Shore—the bottom two-thirds of the married decendents—[63] show few signs of household industry, such as appear in equivalent English estates.[64] Sheep and woolcards, flax and hackles, and spinning wheels all were a rarity, and such things as candle molds were nonexistent. Women in these households must have been busy at other work. In households with bound labor the wife doubtless was fully occupied preparing food and washing clothes for family and hands. But the wife in a household too poor to afford bound labor—the bottom fifth of the married decedent group—might well tend tobacco when she could.[65] Eventually, the profits of her labor might enable the family to buy a servant, making greater profits possible. From such beginnings many families climbed the economic ladder in seventeenth-century Maryland.[66]

The proportion of servantless households must have been larger than is suggested by the inventories of the dead, since young men were less likely to die than old men and had had less time to accumulate property. Well over a fifth of the households of married men on the lower Western Shore may have had no bound labor. Not every wife in such households would necessarily work at the hoe—saved from it by upbringing, ill-health, or the presence of small children who needed her care—but many women performed such work. A lease of 1691, for example, specified that the lessee could farm the amount of land which "he his wife and children can tend."[67]

Stagnation of the tobacco economy, beginning about 1680, produced changes that had some effect on women's economic role.[68] As shown by inventories of the lower Western Shore, home industry increased, especially at the upper ranges of the economic spectrum. In these households women were spinning yarn and knitting it into clothing.[69] The increase in such activity was far less in the households of the bottom fifth, where changes of a different kind may have increased the pressures to grow tobacco. Fewer men at this level could now purchase land, and a portion of their crop went for rent.[70] At this level, more wives than before may have been helping to produce tobacco when they could. And by this time they were often helping as a matter of survival, not as a means of improving the family position.

So far we have considered primarily the experience of immigrant women. What of their daughters? How were their lives affected by the demographic stresses of Chesapeake society?

On of the most important points in which the experience of daughters differed from that of their mothers was the age at which they married. In this woman-short world, the mothers had married as soon as they were eligible, but they had not usually become eligible until they were mature women in their middle twenties. Their daughters were much younger at marriage. A vital register kept in Somerset County shows that some girls married at age twelve and that the mean age at marriage for those born before 1670 was sixteen and a half years.

Were some of these girls actually child brides? It seems unlikely that girls were married before they had become capable of bearing children. Culturally, such a practice would fly in the face of English, indeed Western European, precedent, nobility excepted. Nevertheless, the number of girls who married before age sixteen, the legal age of inheritance for girls, is astonishing. Their English counterparts ordinarily did not marry until their mid- to late twenties or early thirties. In other parts of the Chesapeake, historians have found somewhat higher ages at marriage than appear in Somerset, but everywhere in seventeenth-century Maryland and Virginia most native-born women married before they reached age twenty-one.[71] Were such early marriages a result of the absence of fathers? Evidently not. In Somerset County, the fathers of very young brides—those under sixteen—were usually living.[72]

Evidently, guardians were unlikely to allow such marriages, and this fact suggests that they were not entirely approved. But the shortage of women imposed strong pressures to marry as early as possible.

Not only did native girls marry early, but many of them were pregnant before the ceremony. Bridal pregnancy among native-born women was not as common as among immigrants. Nevertheless, in seventeenth-century Somerset County 20 percent of native brides bore children within eight and one half months of marriage. This was a somewhat higher percentage than has been reported from seventeenth-century English parishes.[73]

These facts suggest considerable freedom for girls in selecting a husband. Almost any girl must have had more than one suitor, and evidently many had freedom to spend time with a suitor in a fashion that allowed her to become pregnant. We might suppose that such pregnancies were not incurred until after the couple had become bethrothed, and that they were consequently an allowable part of courtship, were it not that girls whose fathers were living were usually not the culprits. In Somerset, at least, only 10 percent of the brides with fathers living were pregnant, in contrast to 30 percent of those who were orphans.[74] Since there was only about one year's difference between the mean ages at which orphan and non-orphan girls married, parental supervision rather than age seems to have been the main factor in the differing bridal pregnancy rates.[75]

Native girls married young and bore children young; hence they had more children than immigrant women. This fact ultimately changed the composition of the Maryland population. Native-born females began to have enough children to enable couples to replace themselves. These children, furthermore, were divided about evenly between males and females. By the mid-1680s, in all probability, the population thus began to grow through reproductive increase, and sexual imbalance began to decline. In 1704 the native-born preponderated in the Maryland assembly for the first time and by then were becoming predominant in the adult population as a whole.[76]

This appearance of a native population was bringing alterations in family life, especially for widows and orphaned minors. They were acquiring kin. St. Mary's and Charles counties wills demonstrate the change.[77] (See Table 3.) Before 1680, when nearly all those who died and left families had been immigrants, three-quarters of the men and women who left widows and/or minor children made no mention in their wills of any other kin in Maryland. In the first decade of the eighteenth century, among native-born testators, nearly three-fifths mention other kin, and if we add information from sources other than wills—other probate records, land records, vital registers, and so

TABLE 3 Resident Kin of Testate Men and Women Who Left Minor Children, St. Mary's and Charles Counties 1640 to 1710

	Families N	No Kin % Families	Only Wife % Families	Grown Child % Families	Other Kin % Families
			A.		
1640-1669	95	23	43	11	23
1670-1679	76	17	50	7	26
1700-1710	71	6	35[a]	25	34[b]
			B.		
1700-1710					
Immigrant	41	10	37	37	17
Native	30		33[c]	10	57[d]

Notes: [a]If information found in other records is included, the percentage is 30.

[b]If information found in other records is included, the percentage is 39.

[c]If information found in other records is included, the percentage is 20.

[d]If information found in other records is included, the percentage is 70.

For a discussion of wills as a reliable source for discovery of kin see n. 78. Only 8 testators were natives of Maryland before 1680s; hence no effort has been made to distinguish them from immigrants.

Source: Wills, I-XIV.

on—at least 70 percent are found to have had such local connections. This development of local family ties must have been one of the most important events of early Maryland history.[78]

Historians have only recently begun to explore the consequences of the shift from an immigrant to a predominantly native population.[79] We would like to suggest some changes in the position of women that may have resulted from this transition. It is already known that as sexual imbalance disappeared, age at first marriage rose, but it remained lower than it had been for immigrants over the second half of the seventeenth century. At the same time, life expectancy improved, at least for men. The results were longer marriages and more children who reached maturity.[80] In St. Mary's County after 1700, dying men far more often than earlier left children of age to maintain their widows, and widows may have felt less inclination and had less opportunity to remarry.[81]

We may speculate on the social consequences of such changes. More fathers were still alive when their daughters married, and hence would have been able to exercise control over the selection of their sons-in-law. What in the seventeenth century may have been a period of comparative independence for women, both immigrant and native, may have given way to a return to more traditional European social controls over the creation of new families. If so, we might see the results in a decline in bridal pregnancy and perhaps a decline in bastardy.[82]

We may also find the wife losing ground in the household polity, although her economic importance probably remained unimpaired. Indeed, she must have been far more likely than a seventeenth-century immigrant woman to bring property to her marriage. But several changes may have caused women to play a smaller role than before in household decision-making.[83] Women became proportionately more numerous and may have lost bargaining power.[84] Furthermore, as marriages lasted longer, the proportion of households full of step-children and half-brothers and half-sisters united primarily by the mother must have diminished. Finally, when husbands died, more widows would have had children old enough to maintain them and any minor brothers and sisters. There would be less need for women to play a controlling role, as well as less incentive for their husbands to grant it. The provincial marriage of the eighteenth century may have more closely resembled that of England than did the immigrant marriage of the seventeenth century.

If this change occurred, we should find symptoms to measure. There should be fewer gifts from husbands to wives of property put at the wife's disposal. Husbands should less frequently make bequests to wives that provided them with property beyond their dower. A wife might even be restricted to less than her dower, although the law allowed her to choose her dower instead of a bequest.[85] At the same time, children should be commanded to maintain their mothers.

St. Mary's County wills show most of the symptoms, although exhortations of fathers to children to help their mothers are not included. (See Table 4.) But bequests of dower more or less increased by a fifth, and widowhood restrictions began to appear. Evidently, as demographic conditions became more normal, St. Mary's County widows began to lose ground to their children, a phenomenon that deserves further study.

It is time to issue a warning. Whether or not Maryland women in a creole society lost ground, the argument hinges on an interpretation of English behavior that also requires testing. Either position supposes that women in seventeenth-century Maryland obtained power in the household which wives of English farmers did not enjoy. Much of the evidence for Maryland is drawn from the disposition of property in wills. If English wills show a similar pattern, similar inferences might be drawn about English women. We have already discussed evidence from English wills that supports the view that women in

TABLE 4 Bequests of Husbands to Wives with Children, St. Marys County, Maryland, 1710-1777

Date	N	All Estate		All or Dwelling Plantation for Life		All or Dwelling Plantation for Widowhood[a]		More than Dower in Other Form		Dower or Less or Unknown[b]	
		n	%	n	%	n	%	n	%	n	%
1710-19	38	1	3	12	32	2	5	10	26	14	37
1720-29	65	4	6	23	35	0	0	15	23	23	35
1730-39	58	2	3	17	29	5	9	9	16	25	43
1740-49	73	1	1	20	27	6	8	10	14	36	49
1750-59	79	2	3	26	33	11	14	8	10	31	39
1760-69	92	2	2	35	38	10	11	5	5	40	43
1770-77	66	1	3	17	26	10	15	12	18	26	39
Totals	471	13	3	150	32	44	9	69	15	195	41

a. Includes instances of all or dwelling plantation for minority of child (N=11)
b. Includes instances of provisions for maintenance or houseroom (N=5)
Sources: Wills XIII-XLI
Note: This table is a revision of the Table IV printed in the original article.

Maryland were favored; but the position of seventeenth-century English women—especially those not of gentle status—has been little explored.[86] A finding of little difference between bequests to women in England and in Maryland would greatly weaken the argument that demographic stress created peculiar conditions especially favorable to Maryland women.

If the demography of Maryland produced the effects here described, such effects should also be evident elsewhere in the Chesapeake. The four characteristics of the seventeenth-century Maryland population—immigrant predominance, early death, late marriage, and sexual imbalance—are to be found everywhere in the region, at least at first. The timing of the disappearance of these peculiarities may have varied from place to place, depending on date of settlement or rapidity of development, but the effect of their existence upon the experience of women should be clear. Should research in other areas of the Chesapeake fail to find women enjoying the status they achieved on the lower Western Shore of Maryland, then our arguments would have to be revised.[87]

Work is also needed that will enable historians to compare conditions in Maryland with those in other colonies. Richard S. Dunn's study of the British West Indies also shows demographic disruption.[88] When the status of wives is studied, it should prove similar to that of Maryland women. In contrast were demographic conditions in New England, where immigrants came in family groups, major immigration had ceased by the mid-seventeenth century, sex ratios balanced early, and mortality was low.[89] Under these conditions, demographic disruption must have been both less severe and less prolonged. If New England women achieved status similar to that suggested for women in the Chesapeake, that fact will have to be explained. The dynamics might prove to have been different;[90] or a dynamic we have not identified, common to both areas, might turn out to have been the primary engine of change. And, if women in England shared the status—which we doubt—conditions in the New World may have had secondary importance. The Maryland data establish persuasive grounds for a hypothesis, but the evidence is not all in.

NOTES

1. Russell R. Menard, "Economy and Society in Early Colonial Maryland" (Ph.D. diss., University of Iowa, 1975), 153–212, and "Immigrants and Their Increase: The Process of Population Growth in Early Colonial Maryland," in Aubrey C. Land, Lois Green Carr, and Edward C. Papenfuse, eds., *Law, Society, and Politics in Early Maryland* (Baltimore, 1977), 88–110, hereafter cited as Menard, "Immigrants and Their Increase"; Lorena S. Walsh and Russell R. Menard, "Death in the Chesapeake: Two Life Tables for Men in Early Colonial Maryland," *Maryland Historical Magazine,* LXIX (1974), 211–227. In a sample of 806 headrights Menard found only two unmarried women who paid their own passage ("Economy and Society," 187).

2. Menard, "Immigrants and Their Increase," Fig. 1: William Hand Browne *et al.,* eds., *Archives of Maryland* (Baltimore, 1883–   ). XXV, 256, hereafter cited as *Maryland Archives.*

3. Court proceedings for St. Mary's and Calvert counties have not survived.

4. The lists of immigrants are found in John Camden Hotten, ed., *The Original Lists of Persons of Quality; Emigrants; Religious Exiles; Political Rebels; . . . and Others Who Went from Great Britain to the American Plantations, 1600–1700* (London, 1874); William Dodgson Bowman, ed., *Bristol and America: A Record of the First Settlers in the Colonies of North America, 1654–1685* (Baltimore, 1967 [orig. publ. London, 1929]); C. D. P. Nicholson, comp., *Some Early Emigrants to America* (Baltimore, 1965); Michael Ghirelli, ed., *A List of Emigrants to America, 1682–1692* (Baltimore, 1968); and Elizabeth French, ed., *List of Emigrants to America from Liverpool, 1697–1707* (Baltimore, 1962 [orig. publ. Boston, 1913]). Folger Shakespeare Library, MS. V.B. 16 (Washington, D.C.), consists of 66 additional indentures that were originally part of the London records. For studies of these lists see Mildred Campbell, "Social Origins of Some Early Americans," in James Morton Smith, ed., *Seventeenth-Century America: Essays in Colonial History* (Chapel Hill, N.C., 1959), 63–89; David W. Galenson, " 'Middling People' or 'Common Sort'?: The Social Origins of Some Early Americans Reexamined," *William and Mary Quarterly* (forthcoming). See also Menard, "Immigrants and Their Increase," Table 4.1, and "Economy and Society," Table VIII-6; and Lorena S. Walsh, "Servitude and Opportunity in Charles County," in Land, Carr, and Papenfuse, eds., *Law, Society, and Politics in Early Maryland,* 112–114, hereafter cited as Walsh, "Servitude and Opportunity."

5. Campbell, "Social Origins of Some Early Americans," in Smith, ed., *Seventeenth-Century America,* 74–77; Galenson, " 'Middling People' or 'Common Sort'?" *WMQ* (forthcoming). When the ages recorded in the London list (Nicholson, comp., *Some Early Emigrants)* and on the Folger Library indentures for servants bound for Maryland and Virginia are combined, 84.5% of the men (N = 354) are found to have been aged 17 to 30, and 54.9% were 18 through 22. Of the women (N = 119), 81.4% were 18 through 25; 10% were older, 8.3% younger, and half (51.2%) immigrated between ages 20 and 22. Russell Menard has generously lent us his abstracts of the London list.

6. This assumption is defended in Walsh, "Servitude and Opportunity," 129.

7. *Ibid.,* 112–114, describes the legislation and the Charles County data base. There is some reason to believe that by 1700, young servants had contracts more often than earlier. Figures from the London list include the Folger Library indentures.

8. Menard, "Immigrants and Their Increase," Table I.

9. Menard, "Economy and Society," 336–356; Lois Green Carr and Russell R. Menard, "Servants and Freedmen in Early Colonial Maryland," in Thad W. Tate and David A. Ammerman, eds., *Essays on the Chesapeake in the Seventeenth Century* (Chapel Hill, N.C., 1979); E. A. Wrigley, "Family Limitation in Pre-Industrial England," *Economic History Review*, 2d Ser., XIX (1966), 82–109; Michael Drake, "An Elementary Exercise in Parish Register Demography," *ibid.*, XIV (1962), 427–445; J. D. Chambers, *Population, Economy, and Society in Pre-Industrial England* (London, 1972).

10. John Hammond, *Leah and Rachel, or, the Two Fruitfull Sisters Virginia and Mary-land . . .*, and George Alsop, *A Character of the Province of Mary-land . . .*, in Clayton Colman Hall, ed., *Narratives of Early Maryland, 1633–1684*, Original Narratives of Early American History (New York, 1910), 281–308, 340–387; Russell R. Menard, P. M. G. Harris, and Lois Green Carr, "Opportunity and Inequality: The Distribution of Wealth on the Lower Western Shore of Maryland, 1638–1705," *Md. Hist. Mag.*, LXIX (1974), 169–184; Russell R. Menard, "From Servant to Freeholder: Status Mobility and Property Accumulation in Seventeenth-Century Maryland," *WMQ*, 3d Ser., XXX (1973), 37–64; Carr and Menard, "Servants and Freedman," in Tate and Ammerman, eds., *Essays on the Chesapeake*; Walsh, "Servitude and Opportunity," 111–133.

11. Walsh and Menard, "Death in the Chesapeake," *Md. Hist. Mag.*, LXIX (1974), 211–227; Darrett B. and Anita H. Rutman, "Of Agues and Fevers: Malaria in the Early Chesapeake," *WMQ*, 3d Ser., XXXIII (1976), 31–60.

12. E. A. Wrigley, *Population and History* (New York, 1969), 96–100.

13. Menard, "Economy and Society," Table VII-5.

14. Lorena S. Walsh, "Charles County, Maryland, 1658–1705: A Study in Chesapeake Political and Social Structure" (Ph.D. diss., Michigan State University, 1977), chap. 4.

15. Hammond, *Leah and Rachel*, and Alsop, *Character of the Province*, in Hall, ed., *Narratives of Maryland*, 281–308, 340–387; Mildred Campbell, *The English Yeoman Under Elizabeth and the Early Stuarts*, Yale Historical Publications (New Haven, Conn., 1942), 255–261; Alan Everitt, "Farm Labourers," in Joan Thirsk, ed., *The Agrarian History of England and Wales, 1540–1640* (Cambridge, 1967), 432.

16. Lorena S. Walsh and Russell R. Menard are preparing an article on the history of illegitimacy in Charles and Somerset counties, 1658–1776.

17. Abbot Emerson Smith, *Colonists in Bondage: White Servitude and Convict Labor in America, 1607–1776* (Chapel Hill, N.C., 1947), 271–273. Marriage was in effect a breach of contract.

18. Lois Green Carr, "County Government in Maryland, 1689–1709" (Ph.D. diss., Harvard University, 1968), text, 267–269, 363. The courts pursued bastardy offenses regardless of the social status of the culprits in order to ensure that the children would not become public charges. Free single women were not being overlooked.

19. John Barth, *The Sot-Weed Factor* (New York, 1960), 429.

20. This impression is based on Walsh's close reading of Charles County records. Carr's close reading of Prince George's County records, and less detailed examination by both of all other 17th-century Maryland court records.

21. Walsh, "Charles County, Maryland," chap. 4; Carr, "County Government in Maryland," chap. 4, n. 269. Carr summarizes the evidence from Charles, Prince George's, Baltimore, Talbot, and Somerset counties, 1689-1709, for comparing punishment of fathers and mothers of bastards. Leniency toward fathers varied from county to county and time to time. The length of time served for restitution also varied over place and time, increasing as the century progressed. See Charles County Court and Land Records, MS, L #1, ff. 276-277, Hall of Records, Annapolis, Md. Unless otherwise indicated, all manuscripts cited are at the Hall of Records.

22. Peter Laslett and Karla Osterveen have calculated illegitimacy ratios—the percentage of bastard births among all births registered—in 24 English parishes, 1581-1810. The highest ratio over the period 1630-1710 was 2.4. Laslett and Osterveen, "Long Term Trends in Bastardy in England: A Study of the Illegitimacy Figures in the Parish Registers and in the Reports of the Registrar General, 1561-1960," *Population Studies*, XXVII (1973), 267. In Somerset County, Maryland, 1666-1694, the illegitimacy ratio ranged from 6.3 to 11.8. Russell R. Menard, "The Demography of Somerset County, Maryland: A Preliminary Report" (paper presented to the Stony Brook Conference on Social History, State University of New York at Stony Brook, June 1975), Table XVI. The absence of figures for the number of women in these places of childbearing age but with no living husband prevents construction of illegitimacy rates.

23. Alsop, *Character of the Province*, in Hall, ed., *Narratives of Maryland*, 358.

24. Maryland Headright Sample, 1658-1681 (N = 625); 257.1 men per 100 women; Maryland Inventories, 1658-1679 (N = 584); 320.1 men per 100 women. Menard, "Immigrants and Their Increase," Table I.

25. A comparison of a Virginia Headright Sample, 1648-1666 (N = 4,272) with inventories from York and Lower Norfolk counties, 1637-1675 (N = 168) shows less, rather than more, imbalance in inventories as compared to headrights. This indicates fewer purchases of wives than we have suggested for the period after 1660. However, the inventory sample is small.

26. Only 8% of tenant farmers who left inventories in four Maryland counties of the lower Western Shore owned labor, 1658-1705. St. Mary's City Commission Inventory Project, "Social Stratification in Maryland, 1658-1705" (National Science Foundation Grant GS-32272), hereafter cited as "Social Stratification." This is an analysis of 1,735 inventories recorded from 1658 to 1705 in St. Mary's, Calvert, Charles, and Prince George's counties, which together constitute most of the lower Western Shore of Maryland.

27. Sixty women left inventories. The status of five is unknown. The two who died single died in 1698. Menard, "Immigrants and Their Increase," Table I.

28. Menard, "Demography of Somerset County," Table XVII; Daniel Scott Smith and Michael S. Hindus, "Premarital Pregnancy in America, 1640-1971: An Overview," *Journal of Interdisciplinary History*, V (1975), 541. It was also two to three times the rate found in New England in the late 17th century.

29. In Maryland any proceedings against pregnant brides could have been brought only in the civil courts. No vestries were established until 1693, and their jurisdiction was confined to the admonishment of men and women suspected of fornication unproved by the conception of a child. Churchwardens were to inform the county court of bastardies. Carr, "County Government in Maryland," text, 148-149, 221-223.

30 The data are from Nicholson, comp., *Some Early Emigrants.*

31. Charles County Court and Land Records, MSS, C #1 through B #2.

32. Available ages at arrival are as follows:

Age under	12	13	14	15	16	17	18	19	20	21	22	23	24	25	26	27	28	29	30
Indentured (1682–1687)			1		1	6	2	9	9	8	29	19	6	5	6	2	3	1	2	3
Unindentured (1666–1705)	8	5	12	4	7	18	16	13	34	9	11	2	1	1					

Terms of service for women without indentures from 1666 on were 5 years if they were aged 22 at arrival; 6 years if 18–21; 7 years if 15–17; and until 22 if under 15. From 1661 to 1665 these terms were shorter by a year, and women under 15 served until age 21. If we assume that (1) indentured women served 4 years; (2) they constituted half the servant women; (3) women under age 12 were not purchased as wives; (4) 20% of women aged 12 or older were purchased; and (5) purchases were spread evenly over the possible years of service, then from 1666, 73.9% were 23 or older at marriage, and 66.0% were 24 or older; 70.8% were 23 or older from 1661 to 1665, and 55.5% were 24 or older. Mean ages at eligibility for marriage, as calculated by dividing person-years by the number of women, were 24.37 from 1666 on and 23.42 from 1661 to 1665. All assumptions except (3) and (5) are discussed above. The third is made on the basis that native girls married as young as age 12.

33. Walsh, "Charles County, Maryland," chap. 2; Menard, "Demography of Somerset County," Tables XI, XII.

34. The impact of later marriages is best demonstrated with age-specific marital fertility statistics. Susan L. Norton reports that women in colonial Ipswich, Massachusetts, bore an average of 7.5 children if they married between ages 15 and 19; 7.1 if they married between 20 and 24; and 4.5 if they married after 24. Norton, "Population Growth in Colonial America: A Study of Ipswich, Massachusetts," *Pop. Studies,* XXV (1971), 444. Cf. Wrigley, "Family Limitation in Pre-Industrial England," *Econ. Hist. Rev.,* 2d Ser., XIX (1966), 82–109.

35. In Charles County the mean interval between first and second and subsequent births was 30.8, and the median was 27.3 months. Walsh, "Charles County, Maryland," chap. 2. Menard has found that in Somerset County, Maryland, the median birth intervals for immigrant women between child 1 and child 2, child 2 and child 3, child 3 and child 4, and child 4 and child 5 were 26, 26, 30, 27 months, respectively ("Demography of Somerset County," Table XX).

36. Walsh, "Charles County, Maryland," chap. 2.

37. Walsh and Menard, "Death in the Chesapeake," *Md. Hist. Mag.,* LXIX (1974), 222.

38. Menard, using all Maryland wills, found a considerably lower number of children per family in a similar period: 1.83 in wills probated 1660–1665; 2.20 in wills probated 1680–1684 ("Economy and Society," 198). Family reconstitution not surprisingly produces slightly higher figures, since daughters are often underrecorded in wills but are recorded as frequently as sons in birth registers. In 17th-century Charles County the mean size of all reconstituted families was 2.75. For marriages contracted in the years 1658–1669 (N = 118), 1670–1679 (N = 79), and 1680–1689 (N = 95), family size was 3.15, 2.58, and 2.86, respectively. In

Somerset County, family size for immigrant marriages formed between 1665 and 1695 (N = 41) was 3.9. Walsh, "Charles County, Maryland," chap. 2; Menard, "Demography of Somerset County," Table XXI.

39. For fuller exposition of the process see Menard, "Immigrants and Their Increase."

40. P. E. Razell, "Population Change in Eighteenth-Century England. A Reinterpretation," *Econ. Hist. Rev.*, 2d Ser., XVIII (1965), 315, cites mean age at marriage as 23.76 years for 7,242 women in Yorkshire, 1662–1714, and 24.6 years for 280 women of Wiltshire, Berkshire, Hampshire, and Dorset, 1615–1621. Peter Laslett, *The World We Have Lost: England before the Industrial Age*, 2d ed. (London, 1971), 86, shows a mean age of 23.58 for 1,007 women in the Diocese of Canterbury, 1619–1690. Wrigley, "Family Limitation in Pre-Industrial England," *Econ. Hist. Rev.*, 2d Ser., XIX (1966), 87, shows mean ages at marriage for 259 women in Colyton, Devon, ranging from 26.15 to 30.0 years, 1600–1699.

41. For a brief discussion of Chesapeake and English mortality see Walsh and Menard, "Death in the Chesapeake," *Md. Hist. Mag.*, LXIX (1974), 224–225.

42. George W. Barclay, *Techniques of Population Analysis* (New York, 1958), 136n; Darrett B. and Anita H. Rutman, " 'Now-Wives and Sons-in-Law': Parental Death in a Seventeenth-Century Virginia County," in Tate and Ammerman, eds., *Essays on the Chesapeake*; Rutman and Rutman, "Of Agues and Fevers," *WMQ*, 3d Ser., XXXIII (1976), 31–60. Cf. Peter H. Wood, *Black Majority: Negroes in Colonial South Carolina from 1670 through the Stono Rebellion* (New York, 1974), chap. 3.

43. Walsh and Menard, "Death in the Chesapeake," *Md. Hist Mag.*, LXIX (1974), 211–227; Menard, "Demography of Somerset County."

44. In Charles County immigrant women who ended childbearing years or died before 1705 bore a mean of 3.5 children (N = 59); the mean for natives was 5.1 (N = 42). Mean completed family size in Somerset County for marriages contracted between 1665 and 1695 was higher, but the immigrant-native differential remains. Immigrant women (N = 17) bore 6.1 children, while native women (N = 16) bore 9.4. Walsh, "Charles County, Maryland," chap. 2; Menard, "Demography of Somerset County," Table XXI.

45. Among 1735 decedents who left inventories on Maryland's lower Western Shore, 1658–1705, 72% died without children or with children not yet of age. Only 16% could be proved to have a child of age. "Social Stratification."

46. Wills, I, 172.

47. From 1640 to 1710, 17% of the married men named no executor. In such cases, the probate court automatically gave executorship to the wife unless she requested someone else to act.

48. Wills, I, 96, 69.

49. *Ibid.*, 193–194, 167, V, 82. The practice of appointing overseers ceased around the end of the century. From 1690 to 1710, only 13% of testators who made their wives executors appointed overseers.

50. We divided wills according to whether decedents were immigrant, native born, or of unknown origins, and found no differences in patterns of bequests, choice of executors, or tendency to appoint overseers. No change occurred in 17th-century Maryland in these respects as a native-born population began to appear.

51. Margaret Spufford, *Contrasting Communities: English Villagers in the Sixteenth and Seventeenth Centuries* (Cambridge, 1974), 85-90, 111-118, 161-164.

52. Wills, I, 422, 182, 321.

53. For example, *ibid.*, 172, 182.

54. Lorena S. Walsh, " 'Till Death Do Us Part': Marriage and Family in Charles County, Maryland, 1658-1705," in Tate and Ammerman, eds., *Essays on the Chesapeake.*

55. The following discussion of the orphans' court is based on Lois Green Carr, "The Development of the Maryland Orphans' Court, 1654-1715," in Land, Carr, and Papenfuse, eds., *Law, Society, and Politics in Early Maryland*, 41-61.

56. Baltimore County Court Proceedings, D, ff. 385-386.

57. In 17th-century Charles County two-thirds of surviving partners remarried within a year of their spouse's death. Walsh, "Charles County, Maryland," chap. 2.

58. See n. 26.

59. Walsh, " 'Till Death Do Use Part,' " in Tate and Ammerman, eds., *Essays on the Chesapeake.*

60. *Ibid.*

61. *Maryland Archives*, LXX, 87. See also *ibid.*, XLI, 210, 474, 598, for examples of allusions to washing clothes and dairying activities. Water mills were so scarce that in 1669 the Maryland assembly passed an act permitting land to be condemned for the use of anyone willing to build and operate a water mill. *Ibid.*, II, 211-214. In the whole colony only four condemnations were carried out over the next 10 years. *Ibid.*, LI, 25, 57, 86, 381. Probate inventories show that most households had a mortar and pestle or a hand mill.

62. Testamentary Proceedings, X, 184-185. Cf. Charles County Court and Land Records, MS, I #1, ff. 9-10, 259.

63. Among married decedents before 1680 (N = 308), the bottom two-thirds (N = 212) were those worth less than £150. Among all decedents worth less than £150 (N = 451), only 12 (about 3%) had sheep or yarn-making equipment, "Social Stratification."

64. See Everitt, "Farm Labourers," in Thirsk, ed., *Agrarian History of England and Wales*, 422-426, and W. G. Hoskins, *Essays in Leicestershire History* (Liverpool, 1950), 134.

65. Among married decedents, the bottom fifth were approximately those worth less than £30. Before 1680 these were 17% of the married decedents. By the end of the period, from 1700 to 1705, they were 22%. Before 1680, 92% had no bound labor. From 1700 to 1705, 95% had none. Less than 1% of all estates in this wealth group had sheep or yarn-making equipment before 1681. "Social Stratification."

66. On opportunity to rise from the bottom to the middle see Menard, "From Servant to Freeholder," *WMQ*, 3d Ser., XXX (1973), 37-64; Walsh, "Servitude and Opportunity," 111-133, and Menard, Harris, and Carr, "Opportunity and Inequality," *Md. Hist. Mag.*, LXIX (1974), 169-184.

67. Charles County Court and Land Records, MS, R #1, f. 193.

68. For 17th-century economic development see Menard, Harris, an Carr, "Opportunity and Inequality," *Md. Hist. Mag.*, LXIX (1974), 169-184.

69. Among estates worth £150 or more, signs of diversification in this form appeared in 22% before 1681 and in 67% after 1680. Over the years 1700-1705,

the figure was 62%. Only 6% of estates worth less than £40 had such signs of diversification after 1680 or over the period 1700–1705. Knitting rather than weaving is assumed because looms were very rare. These figures are for all estates. "Social Stratification."

70. After the mid-1670s information about landholdings of decedents becomes decreasingly available, making firm estimates of the increase in tenancy difficult. However, for householders in life cycle 2 (married or widowed decedents who died without children of age) the following table is suggestive. Householding decedents in life cycle 2 worth less than £40 (N = 255) were 21% of all decedents in this category (N = 1,218).

	£0–19				£20–39		
	Deced-ents N	Land Unkn. N	With Land N	With Land %	Deced-ents N	Land Unkn. N	With Land N	With Land %
To 1675	10	0	7	70	34	2	29	91
1675 on	98	22	40	53	113	16	64	66

In computing percentages, unknowns have been distributed according to knowns.

A man who died with a child of age was almost always a landowner, but these were a small proportion of all decedents (see n. 45).

Several studies provide indisputable evidence of an increase in tenancy on the lower Western Shore over the period 1660–1706. These compare heads of households with lists of landowners compiled from rent rolls made in 1659 and 1704–1706. Tenancy in St. Mary's and Charles counties in 1660 was about 10%. In St. Mary's, Charles, and Prince George's counties, 1704–1706, 30–35% of householders were tenants. Russell R. Menard, "Population Growth and Land Distribution in St. Mary's County, 1634–1710" (ms report, St. Mary's City Commission, 1971, copy on file at the Hall of Records); Menard, "Economy and Society," 423; Carr, "County Government in Maryland," text, 605.

71. Menard, "Immigrants and Their Increase," Table III; n. 40 above.

72. Menard, "Demography of Somerset County," Table XIII.

73. Ibid., Table XVII; P. E. H. Hair, "Bridal Pregnancy in Rural England in Earlier Centuries," Pop. Studies, XX (1966), 237; Chambers, Population, Economy, and Society in England, 75; Smith and Hindus, "Premarital Pregnancy in America," Jour. Interdisciplinary Hist., V (1975), 537–570.

74. Menard, "Demography of Somerset County," Table XVIII.

75. Adolescent subfecundity might also partly explain lower bridal pregnancy rates among very young brides.

76. Menard develops this argument in detail in "Immigrants and Their Increase." For the assembly see David W. Jordan, "Political Stability and the Emergence of a Native Elite in Maryland, 1660–1715," in Tate and Ammerman, eds., Essays on the Chesapeake. In Charles County, Maryland, by 1705 at least half of all resident landowners were native born. Walsh, "Charles County, Maryland," chaps. 1, 7.

77. The proportion of wills mentioning non-nuclear kin can, of course, prove only a proxy of the actual existence of these kin in Maryland. The reliability of such a measure may vary greatly from area to area and over time, depending on the character of the population and on local inheritance customs. To test the reliability of the will data, we compared them with data from reconstituted families

in 17th-century Charles County. These reconstitution data draw on a much broader variety of sources and include many men who did not leave wills. Because of insufficient information for female lines, we could trace only the male lines. The procedure compared the names of all married men against a file of all known county residents, asking how many kin in the male line might have been present in the county at the time of the married man's death. The proportions for immigrants were in most cases not markedly different from those found in wills. For native men, however, wills were somewhat less reliable indicators of the presence of such kin; when non-nuclear kin mentioned by testate natives were compared with kin found by reconstitution, 29% of the native testators had non-nuclear kin present in the county who were not mentioned in their wills.

78. Not surprisingly, wills of immigrants show no increase in family ties, but these wills mention adult children far more often than earlier. Before 1680, only 11% of immigrant testators in St. Mary's and Charles counties mention adult children in their wills; from 1700 to 1710, 37% left adult children to help the family. Two facts help account for this change. First, survivors of early immigration were dying in old age. Second, proportionately fewer young immigrants with families were dying, not because life expectancy had improved, but because there were proportionately fewer of them than earlier. A long stagnation in the tobacco economy that began about 1680 had diminished opportunities for freed servants to form households and families. Hence, among immigrants the proportion of young fathers at risk to die was smaller than in earlier years.

In the larger population of men who left inventories, 18.2% had adult children before 1681, but in the years 1700–1709, 50% had adult children. "Social Stratification."

79. Examples of some recent studies are Carole Shammas, "English-Born and Creole Elites in Turn-of-the-Century Virginia," in Tate and Ammerman, eds., *Essays on the Chesapeake*; Jordan, "Political Stability and the Emergence of a Native Elite in Maryland," *ibid.*; Lois Green Carr, "The Foundations of Social Order: Local Government in Colonial Maryland," in Bruce C. Daniels, ed., *Town and Country: Essays on the Structure of Local Government in the American Colonies* (Middletown, Conn., 1978); Menard, "Economy and Society," 396–440.

80. Allan Kulikoff has found that in Prince George's County the white adult sex ratio dropped significantly before the age of marriage rose. Women born in the 1720s were the first to marry at a mean age above 20, while those born in the 1740s and marrying in the 1760s, after the sex ratio neared equality, married at a mean age of 22. Marriages lasted longer because the rise in the mean age at which men married—from 23 to 27 between 1700 and 1740—was more than offset by gains in life expectancy. Kulikoff, "Tobacco and Slaves: Population, Economy, and Society in Eighteenth-Century Prince George's County, Maryland" (Ph.D. diss., Brandeis University, 1976), chap. 3; Menard, "Immigrants and Their Increase."

81. Inventories and related biographical data have been analyzed by the St. Mary's City Commission under a grant from the National Endowment for the Humanities, "The Making of a Plantation Society in Maryland" (R 010585-74-267). From 1700 through 1776 the percentage of men known to have had children, and who had no adult child at death, ranged from a low of 32.8% in the years 1736–1738 to a high of 61.3% in the years 1707–1709. The figure was over 50% for 13 out of 23 year-groups of three to four years each. For the high in 1707–1709 see comments in n. 78.

82. On the other hand, these rates may show little change. The restraining effect of increased parental control may have been offset by a trend toward increased sexual activity that appears to have become general throughout Western Europe and the United States by the mid-19th century. Smith and Hindus, "Premarital Pregnancy in America," *Jour. Interdisciplinary Hist.*, V (1975), 537-570; Edward Shorter, "Female Emancipation, Birth Control, and Fertility in European History," *American Historical Review*, LXXVIII (1973), 605-640.

83. Page Smith has suggested that such a decline in the wife's household authority had occurred in the American family by—at the latest—the beginning of the 19th century (*Daughters of the Promised Land: Women in American History* [Boston, 1970], chaps. 3, 4).

84. There is little doubt that extreme scarcity in the early years of Chesapeake history enhanced the worth of women in the eyes of men. However, as Smith has observed, "the functioning of the law of supply and demand could not in itself have guaranteed status for colonial women. Without an ideological basis, their privileges could not have been initially established or subsequently maintained" (*ibid.*, 38-39). In a culture where women were seriously undervalued, a shortage of women would not necessarily improve their status.

85. Acts 1699, chap. 41, *Maryland Archives*, XXII, 542.

86. Essays by Cicely Howell and Barbara Todd, printed or made available to the authors since this article was written, point out that customary as opposed to freehold tenures in England usually gave the widow the use of the land for life, but that remarriage often cost the widow this right. The degree to which this was true requires investigation. Howell, "Peasant Inheritance in the Midlands, 1280-1700," in Jack Goody, Joan Thirsk, and E. P. Thompson, eds., *Family and Inheritance: Rural Society in Western Europe, 1200-1800* (Cambridge, 1976), 112-155; Todd, " 'In Her Free Widowhood'; Succession to Property and Remarriage in Rural England, 1540-1800" (paper delivered to the Third Berkshire Conference of Women Historians, June 1976).

87. James W. Deen, Jr., "Patterns of Testation: Four Tidewater Counties in Colonial Virginia," *American Journal of Legal History*, XVI (1972), 154-176, finds a life interest in property for the wife the predominant pattern before 1720. However, he includes an interest for widowhood in life interest and does not distinguish a dower interest from more than dower.

88. Richard S. Dunn, *Sugar and Slaves: The Rise of the Planter Class in the English West Indies, 1624-1713* (Chapel Hill, N.C., 1972), 326-334. Dunn finds sex ratios surprisingly balanced, but he also finds very high mortality, short marriages, and many orphans.

89. For a short discussion of this comparison see Menard, "Immigrants and Their Increase."

90. James K. Somerville has used Salem, Massachusetts, wills from 1660 to 1770 to examine women's status and importance within the home ("The Salem [Mass.] Woman in the Home, 1660-1770," *Eighteenth-Century Life*, I [1974], 11-14). See also Alexander Keyssar, "Widowhood in Eighteenth-Century Massachusetts: A Problem in the History of the Family," *Perspectives in American History*, VIII (1974), 83-119, which discusses provisions for 22 widows in 18th-century Woburn, Massachusetts. Both men find provisions for houseroom and care of the widow's property enjoined upon children proportionately far more

often than we have found in St. Mary's County, Maryland, where we found only five instances over 136 years. However, part of this difference may be a function of the differences in age at widowhood in the two regions. Neither Somerville nor Keyssar gives the percentage of widows who received a life interest in property, but their discussions imply a much higher proportion than we have found of women whose interest ended at remarriage or the majority of the oldest son.

❧ 3 ❧

BLACK WOMEN IN
COLONIAL PENNSYLVANIA

JEAN R. SODERLUND

Sometime before 1750, and perhaps as early as 1720, Rachel Pemberton, the wife of long-term assemblyman and Quaker leader Israel Pemberton, Sr., offered freedom to her slave Betty. The black woman refused the offer, preferring to remain with the family.[1] Later in the century, in the spring of 1776, another wealthy Quaker couple, provincial councilor William Logan and his wife Hannah, discussed freedom with their slave Dinah. In this case, however, the black woman broached the subject. According to William and Hannah, Dinah asked them to set her free. The Logans had already freed her daughter Bess, but they seem to have been saddened by Dinah's request because she had been in Hannah's family since she was a child and they considered her a part of their family. She was a grandmother and perhaps the Logans thought she should remain under their protection. But Dinah wanted the status of a free black, and in the end the Logans agreed to give her "full Liberty to go and live with whom & Where She may Chuse."[2] Dinah elected to stay in the household as a hired servant, though both Hannah and William Logan soon died, and she is the woman who is supposed to have saved Stenton, their Germantown mansion, from being burned by the British in 1777.[3]

The contrasting ways in which the Pembertons' slave Betty and the Logans' black woman Dinah faced the prospect of freedom, or indeed viewed their condition as slaves, may have resulted from individual differences. Betty was perhaps more timid or less skillful

Reprinted by permission, *Pennsylvania Magazine of History and Biography*.

than Dinah. Nevertheless, the periods of Pennsylvania history in which these two woman lived were likely to have influenced their decisions as well. Earlier on, when Betty turned down manumission, slavery was at its height in Philadelphia and very few free blacks lived in the city. By the time Dinah demanded her freedom, a substantial number of freed men and women resided in the town or nearby. Some owned property and married in the Anglican and Lutheran churches, and many had learned to read and write. While Betty's husband and children, if she had any, were almost certainly enslaved, we know that Dinah's daughter Bess, and perhaps other family members as well, were already free. Thus, leaving aside any personal differences, life as a free black woman in Philadelphia would have been much more problematic for Betty before 1740, than for Dinah in 1776.

Slavery had existed on the Delaware, and African women had lived in the region, since before William Penn came in 1682. The largest numbers of blacks were imported relative to the local population during the first two decades of the eighteenth century.[4] Some Pennsylvanians worried about this influx, especially after the New York slave revolt of 1712. The Pennsylvania Assembly in that year placed a prohibitive tariff of £20 on each black imported into the colony, but the Crown disallowed the law.[5] While during the years 1711-1716 Quakers from Chester County pressed the Philadelphia Yearly Meeting (the central body of Friends in the Delaware Valley) to prohibit members from buying imported blacks, the Yearly Meeting, influenced by Philadelphia merchants and other slaveholders, refused to do more than caution Friends not to buy blacks lately brought into the province.[6] In 1726, in order to control the relatively large local slave population and to discourage owners from freeing their slaves, the Assembly passed a black code that required a £30 surety bond for manumission, forbade intermarriage between whites and blacks, and restricted the freedom of both slaves and free blacks to travel, drink liquor, and carry on trade. The law also empowered justices to bind out free black children with or without the consent of their parents, boys until they reached the age of twenty-four years and girls until they were twenty-one.[7]

Unlike the sugar colonies of the West Indies and the tobacco regions of the Chesapeake, where plantation owners became increasingly dependent on black labor as the colonial period progressed, slaves remained a rather small proportion of the labor force in Philadelphia. Pennsylvania attracted large numbers of white immigrants after 1720; German and Scots-Irish servants and free laborers supplied much of the labor required by Pennsylvanians. Slavery reached a peak in Philadelphia around 1720 when slave prices were relatively low and white labor was quite scarce. With a more abundant supply of Europeans after 1720, however, Philadelphians who needed labor and wanted to avoid using slaves now had a greater choice. Thus slaveholding declined in Philadelphia after the second decade of the eighteenth century. Increasing numbers of Quakers and Presbyterians either manumitted their slaves or simply did not buy any. By the 1770s even several slave owners who were affiliated with the Church of England, the religion most resistant in Philadelphia to antislavery reform, freed their slaves. Abolitionism was strongest and earliest in the city among wealthy Quaker merchants and professionals who, because they used Africans and Afro-Americans mainly for personal service, could view involuntary bondage as a form of ostentation rather than as a necessary source of labor. Quaker craftsmen, in contrast, were much less willing to give up their blacks because they needed them to keep their shops going. Slaves became especially desirable once again during the Seven Years War when the supply of white servants dried up; but they were always valuable to craftsmen who invested a considerable amount of money and time to buy and train them. By the 1770s, however, slaveholding was much less common among all groups of philadelphians, even craftsmen. Poor economic conditions and a glut of free white workers after the end of the Seven Years War undercut the demand for slaves.[8]

In rural Pennsylvania, most slave owners were wealthy farmers, though some craftsmen and innkeepers also held blacks. Analysis of probate records for eastern Chester County, as well as tax lists for all of Chester, Philadelphia, and Lancaster counties, show that a much smaller percentage of rural inhabitants owned slaves than did Philadelphians throughout the period before 1770. Slavery, nevertheless, did not decline among Pennsylvania farmers after 1720 as it did among Philadelphia residents. To the contrary, in the 1770s the institution actually showed signs of growing in rural Pennsylvania. However, this expansion was retarded by the Pennsylvania Assembly's passage of the gradual abolition act of 1780 and by the decision of the Philadelphia Yearly Meeting in 1776 to disown all slave owners.[9]

Except in the kind of work they did, which for most was domestic service, black women in colonial Pennsylvania had a wide range of experiences depending on where and in what time period they lived. In Philadelphia, they were close to other blacks and had certain benefits, such as schooling, that the city could provide. On the other hand, most blacks in rural areas like eastern Chester County were thinly scattered across the countryside. The situation for all African and Afro-American women in Pennsylvania changed over time as increasing numbers achieved freedom. Thus, black women of the 1760s and 1770s had several advantages over their mothers and grandmothers who had lived thirty or forty years before; many of their owners were more amenable to arguments that they should be free and, if they lived in Philadelphia, they could rely on a fairly large community of free blacks for support.

Both of the slave women mentioned earlier, Betty and Dinah, worked for the families of rich Philadelphia Quaker merchants; their lives, therefore, were substantially different from the situation of sisters living in the plantation areas to the south or even of black women working in rural Pennsylvania. In the West Indies, South Carolina, and the Chesapeake, the large majority of black women worked from sunup to sundown in the fields growing sugar, rice, tobacco, and grain. In the West Indies, most lived on large plantations with fifty or more slaves. But even though many blacks lived in close proximity to one another on the islands, their family life was disrupted because mortality was high and women on average had few children. In Virginia and Maryland, the mean number of laborers on plantations was smaller than in the West Indies: most blacks lived in slave groups of fifteen or more. Though many planters transferred husbands and teenaged children to other quarters or separated families by sale, blacks in the pre-Revolutionary Chesapeake usually lived near their immediate families and kin.[10]

In Philadelphia, throughout the colonial period, owners held an average of only about 2.4 slaves.[11] This meant that entire black families, including the mother, father, and several children, rarely lived under the same roof. While the sex ratio of adult blacks was fairly even in the city, according to the probate inventories, at most only two in five black women lived in the same household with an adult black man (see Table 1). Only three percent were listed in the probate records with men who were described specifically as their husbands. The relationship of the rest of the men to the women is unknown; they could have been husbands or mates, prospective mates or friends, men to whom the women had no attachment, or men whom they detested or feared. Records of black marriages in Christ Church and St. Peter's Church, Philadelphia, also indicate that relatively few slave married couples lived together. Between 1727 and 1780, sixty-four black couples were married at the Anglican churches (all but eight after 1765). In one-quarter of these marriages, both partners were free, and another 14% were marriages between a free black and a slave. Twenty-nine (45.3%) were marriages in which both the husband and wife were slaves; of these slave couples, fewer than one-fourth (seven of the twenty-nine) were owned by the same master.[12]

That so few of Philadelphia's black women lived in the same households with their husbands was perhaps less disruptive of family life than it seems, because most husbands probably lived close by. Phila-

TABLE 1 Black Women and Men in Philadelphia, 1682-1780

	Sex Ratio	Black Women				Black Men		
No. Inventories	Adult Men per Adult Woman	No.	% Listed with Black Man	% Listed with Child Specified as Theirs	% Listed with Child who could be Theirs	No.	% Listed with Black Woman	% Listed with Child who could be Theirs
1682-90	22	1.40	5	100.0%	0%	20.0%	7	71.4%	42.8%
1691-1700	77	.88	8	37.5%	50.0%	0%	7	42.8%	42.8%
1701-10	104	1.05	21	33.3%	9.5%	33.3%	22	31.8%	22.7%
1711-20	165	1.33	24	37.5%	50.0%	4.2%	32	28.1%	46.9%
1721-30	182	.61	18	16.7%	33.3%	22.2%	11	27.3%	36.4%
1731-40	207	.93	27	33.3%	25.9%	14.8%	25	36.0%	36.0%
1741-50	353	1.11	46	39.1%	28.3%	19.6%	51	35.3%	35.3%
1751-60	378	1.33	43	48.8%	27.9%	18.6%	57	36.8%	26.3%
1761-70	512	1.17	66	48.5%	25.8%	21.2%	77	41.6%	36.4%
1771-80	401	.90	40	45.0%	30.0%	15.0%	36	50.0%	33.3%
1682-1780	2401	1.09	298	41.9%	28.5%	18.1%	325	38.5%	34.5%

(28.5% and 18.1% bracketed together: 46.6%)

Source: Probate Inventories

delphia, which as late as the 1770s reached only as far back from the Delaware as 7th Street,[13] had a fairly large black population throughout the eighteenth century. For instance, in 1750 when the population of Philadelphia was about 15,000, as many as 1500, or one-tenth, of the city's residents were black.[14] Evidence from other sources suggests that the number of blacks living in the city was large enough to make white Philadelphians uneasy. The whites complained on a number of occasions about slaves and free blacks gathering in groups in the evenings and on Sundays. In 1696, the Philadelphia Yearly Meeting urged its members to restrain their slaves "from Rambling abroad on First Days or other Times."[15] The Pennsylvania Assembly passed a law in 1706 prohibiting blacks from meeting together "in great companies," but this statute evidently had limited effect because a number of Philadelphians, seemingly unaware that this law was on the books, petitioned in 1723 for a similar ban. In 1750, another petition from inhabitants of Philadelphia County protested to the Assembly about the custom of shooting off guns at New Year's; they complained that such revelry was introduced into the country by immigrant Germans and was now practiced by servants and blacks. The behavior they found disagreeable included excessive drinking, firing guns into houses, and throwing lighted wadding into houses and barns.[16] And the historian Edward Turner claimed (albeit without giving the source of his information) that as many as a thousand blacks gathered for festivals on the outskirts of town.[17] Thus, while few black woman lived in the same house with their husbands, there was a large slave population living in what we would now consider a small city, and hence there was a good chance that their mates lived nearby.

Of course even this tenuous link between family members could be broken at any time by the owner. Slave-owning fathers sometimes gave a young slave to their children when they married,[18] and most testators either divided their blacks among the heirs or directed that the slaves be sold upon their deaths.[19] While the white family members who received the blacks might live fairly close together, an owner's demise could being about a painful separation for slaves. No testators stipulated that their slaves be sold together.[20] Philadelphia newspaper advertisements also provide evidence that many owners sold husbands away from wives, and children away from their parents; most indicated no concern about the consequences for the slaves. Merle G. Brouwer found in his survey of newspaper advertisements of slaves for sale in Pennsylvania that masters rarely specified that a slave should be kept in the neighborhood of his or her kin. Indeed, runaway notices indicate that slave families were broken up, and husbands or wives taken to other colonies. The first place masters thought to look for their runaway slaves was in the vicinity of their former residence and with the family from whom they had been separated.[21]

While slave women throughout Pennsylvania faced the prospect of being cut off from their families by sale or by the death of the master, Philadelphia black women were even less likely to live with their children than were adult females in rural areas. According to the probate inventories, which show the slaves' lives at only one point in time, only 28.5% of slave women in Philadelphia had children described as their own living in the same household (see Table 1). In most cases a woman had only one child who was specifically described as hers. Another eighteen percent (for a combined total of almost one-half) were listed on their owners' inventories with black children who *could* have been theirs but were not described as such. The number of city women who actually lived in the same household with their children was almost certainly lower than Table 1 suggests. Some of the children listed on their owners' inventories, especially those over age five, were hired out to other families.[22]

Rural black women in Pennsylvania were much more likely to live with their families than were urban slaves. In eastern Chester County (now Delaware County), seventy percent of the women were listed on inventories with black children who were theirs or who could have been, and as many as 48% lived with adult men (see Table 2).[23] Life was more difficult for Chester County women in another way, however, because many fewer blacks lived there and the distances between plantations on which other slaves lived were quite far. The situation for men in eastern Chester County was especially bad in the years from 1721 to 1740 and in the 1770s because, according to the inventories, men outnumbered women at those times by a considerable margin. Over the colonial period, at most only a third of the black men in Chester lived with a black woman, and even fewer lived with a black child (see Table 2).[24] Some blacks in Chester apparently conquered their loneliness by establishing sexual partnerships with whites. In the 1760s and 1770s, 13.5% of the slaves listed in Chester area inventories were mulattos. By contrast, in Philadelphia, where the chance of obtaining a black companion was better, only 3.2% of the slaves listed in inventories during those decades had mixed parentage. Data from Quaker manumissions show a similar pattern. Mulattos were 30% of the slaves freed by members of four Chester County meetings, but only 5.4% of those emancipated by Philadelphia Friends.[25] Almost 16% of the slaves registered by Chester County slaveholders in 1780 were mulattos.

Two factors may explain why fewer black women in Philadelphia

TABLE 2 Black Women and Men in Eastern Chester County, 1682-1780

		Sex Ratio	Black Women				Black Men		
	No. Inventories	Adult Men per Adult Woman	No.	% Listed with Black Man	% Listed with Child Specified as Theirs	% Listed with Child who could be Theirs	No.	% Listed with Black Woman	% Listed with Child who could be Theirs
1682-90	6	–	0	–	–	–	0	–	–
1691-1700	10	1.00	2	100.0%	100.0%	0%	2	100.0%	100.0%
1701-10	18	.67	3	33.3%	66.7%	0%	2	50.0%	50.0%
1711-20	30	0	1	0%	0%	100.0%	0	–	–
1721-30	42	6 to 0	0	–	–	–	6	0%	0%
1731-40	55	1.80	5	60.0%	20.0%	60.0%	9	33.3%	33.3%
1741-50	82	1.00	4	50.0%	25.0%	25.0%	4	50.0%	25.0%
1751-60	84	1.00	6	50.0%	0%	16.7%	6	50.0%	0%
1761-70	104	1.00	5	20.0%	40.0%	40.0%	5	20.0%	40.0%
1771-80	79	1.86	7	57.1%	57.1%	28.6%	13	30.8%	40.0%
1682-1780	510	1.42	33	48.5%	39.4%	30.3%	47	34.0%	29.8%

} 69.7%

Source: Probate Inventories

than in Chester lived with children. One reason is that infant mortality in the city was very high. Susan E. Klepp found in her study of white families that almost one-half of the children born to mothers in colonial Philadelphia died before they reached age fifteen; one-fourth died during their first year. No one has done an equivalent study of infant mortality in Chester County, but evidence from elsewhere in colonial America suggests that mortality among the total population was lower in rural areas than in the cities.[26] The other reason is that owners sold black children to other families. Raising a child could be expensive, especially when food had to be purchased, and her or his service was possibly less useful to a city family than on a farm. Black girls and boys in Philadelphia were more likely to be the only slaves living in their households than were children in Chester. According to the probate inventories, 20.1% of girls and 27.5% of boys in Philadelphia were their owners' only slaves, while just 9.1% of girls and 22.2% of boys in Chester lived apart from other blacks.

The evidence on the kinds of work black women performed suggests that most did domestic labor. While there are a few references to slave women working in shops, such as one woman listed in the "still house," even these women could have performed menial tasks usually assigned to females. Also, a few Pennsylvania owners kept as many as ten or fifteen blacks on their plantations; women in these groups were more likely to work in the fields.[27] Like most adult female slaves in Philadelphia, the Pembertons' Betty and the Logans' Dinah belonged to men who were merchants, shopkeepers, or craftsmen.[28] These two women probably worked under the supervision of their owners' wives. Although black men also worked as domestics in Philadelphia, the kinds of slaves owned by persons of various occupations suggest that the roles of men and women were dissimilar. As shown on Table 3, based on the Philadelphia inventories, innkeepers and widows, whose slaves would do mostly domestic labor, owned more women than men when they died. Craftsmen, professionals, and merchants owned more men. Husbands and fathers, in dividing their estates among heirs, often left a black woman or girl to their wives and daughters. If the woman married, her slave normally became the property of her husband under the law of coverture,[29] but the black woman probably continued to work for the wife. Israel Pemberton clearly regarded Betty as his wife's slave, but she was his legally and he made provision for her in his will. Hannah Logan had a definite interest in Dinah, and both she and her husband signed the manumission.[30]

Most black women in colonial Philadelphia did housework. They cooked, cleaned, washed and ironed laundry, kept fires, gardened,

TABLE 3   Gender and Age of Blacks Owned by Women and Men of Various Occupations in Philadelphia, 1682-1780

| | No. Blacks Owned | Percentage of Blacks | | | | | |
		Women	Men	Girls	Boys	Unkown	Total
Widows and Single Women	96	39.6%	21.9%	17.7%	10.4%	10.4%	100.0%
Innkeepers	37	35.2%	24.3%	13.5%	18.9%	8.1%	100.0%
Mariners	78	30.8%	26.9%	10.3%	17.9%	14.1%	100.0%
Craftsmen	287	27.2%	36.9%	11.1%	18.5%	6.3%	100.0%
Merchants and Shopkeepers	282	24.5%	30.1%	12.1%	21.6%	11.7%	100.0%
Gentlemen and Professionals	89	23.6%	36.0%	14.6%	23.6%	2.2%	100.0%

Source: Probate Inventories

looked after children, and served as maids. Some also sewed and made cloth. For instance, one fourteen-year-old girl knew housewifery, knitting, sewing, and could read.[31] Black women lived in their masters' houses and generally slept in garrets, kitchens, or rooms near kitchens. Merchants and professionals sometimes hired women and girls out by the year or by indenture;[32] and women could be lent or hired out for shorter periods to help tend the sick, put in gardens, preserve food, and wait on tables for special occasions. Girls were sometimes apprenticed to learn a trade, presumably housewifery or spinning.[33] Black women continued to do domestic labor even after they were freed, working as servants and laundrywomen.[34] In Chester County, most women also did housework, though here they would have tended larger gardens, raised poultry, milked cows, produced cloth, and helped in the fields (especially at harvest) as well.[35]

While the life conditions of slave women in Philadelphia remained essentially unchanged between 1720 and 1776 in several respects— notably in the fact that few lived with their families under one roof and in terms of the work they did—nevertheless, the situation of the Philadelphia black population as a whole altered sufficiently by 1776 that a woman like Dinah sought her freedom. Most importantly, a significant number of free blacks lived in the city and its environs by the 1770s. Back in the 1720s or 1730s, when Betty refused her freedom, most of the blacks in Pennsylvania had been recently imported. Few white Americans, in Pennsylvania or elsewhere, thought that slavery was wrong. Evidence of manumissions from wills, which thus far is the only source we have before the Quakers began recording manumissions in the 1770s, indicates that only nine slaves were freed by will by Philadelphians before 1720. Another nine were freed in the 1720s, and three more in the 1730s.[36] Perhaps others were released during their masters' lifetimes, but relatively few blacks were freed before 1740. The Assembly further demonstrated the pro-slavery climate in Pennsylvania in the 1720s when in response to a number of petitions they passed the black code of 1726. The act stated that "'tis found by experience that free negroes are an idle, slothful people and often prove burdensome to the neighborhood and afford ill examples to other negroes."[37]

In the decades after 1740, in contrast, antislavery opinion grew in Philadelphia, especially among Quakers and Presbyterians. In 1754, the Philadelphia Yearly Meeting issued *An Epistle of Caution*, its first forthright statement that slavery was wrong; and in 1758 Quakers forbade all members from importing or buying slaves, and appointed a committee to encourage Friends throughout the Delaware Valley to give up their blacks.[38] Though by no means all Quakers agreed with the

Yearly Meeting's decisions, many Friends freed their slaves in their wills after 1740, and others emancipated their blacks during their lives. Philadelphia Presbyterians, influenced by the religious egalitarianism of the Great Awakening, began manumitting their slaves by the 1760s, and even some Anglicans freed their blacks.[39] Between 1741 and 1770, Philadelphians emancipated at least seventy-five slaves in their wills.[40] Others freed their blacks before their deaths.[41] In the 1770s, the Philadelphia Monthly Meeting recorded manumissions for hundreds of slaves freed by Friends and non-Friends.[42] Gary B. Nash found a significant decrease in the number of slaves owned by Philadelphia taxpayers between the years 1767 and 1775. My study of probate records indicated the same decline, as the percentage of inventoried decedents owning slaves dropped from over 20 percent in the 1760s to 13 percent in the 1770s.[43] Most likely much of the decrease resulted from manumission and by 1776 a substantial free black population was living in or near the city. Given this large-scale move towards emancipation, Dinah's request for freedom should not have been too great a surprise for the Logans.

In the early nineteenth century, Philadelphia was the center of both the white and black abolitionist movements in America. The source of white antislavery reform has been linked to the eighteenth-century Quakers; Delaware Valley Friends move from ridding their meeting of slaveholding to helping to establish the Pennsylvania Abolition Society and lobbying for abolition in society at large. Historians have not yet traced the roots of the united and vocal black community of early-nineteenth-century Philadelphia back to the colonial period. Instead, they have focused on the founding of the Free African Society and separate churches by Richard Allen and Absolem Jones, and on James Forten's opposition to the movement for colonization of free blacks in Africa. No one has looked for the colonial beginnings on which these later developments rested.[44] Actually, Philadelphia became the center of the black abolitionist movement of America after 1790 because already in the 1770s a relatively large and sophisticated free black population lived there. Many could read and write and had learned trades. They married at the Anglican and Lutheran churches, and attended Quaker meetings (though they could not join the Society).[45] While the majority held menial jobs and few free blacks are noted on the tax lists, at least some owned property, and most supported themselves and their families in freedom.

Both the Society of Friends and the Anglican Church took an interest in educating Africans and Afro-Americans. Antislavery Quakers hoped to train blacks to be useful and moral citizens. As early as 1696, the Philadelphia Yearly Meeting urged its members to bring their slaves to meetings, and to watch over their behavior. Beginning in the 1750s, the Yearly Meeting continually reminded slave owners to teach blacks to read and write, to educate them in the principles of Christianity, and to train them in an occupation in preparation for freedom.[46] Most local meetings believed that their members were not doing enough in these respects, but quite a few blacks did learn to read and write.[47] John Woolman mentioned in 1762 that many slaves could read, and the Shrewsbury Monthly Meeting in East Jersey found in 1775 that at least five of the twenty-four slaves still held in bondage by meeting members, including two adults and three children, had been taught to read.[48] Many testators who directed that their young slaves be freed at a future date specified that they be apprenticed to a trade first.[49]

Several schools opened in Philadelphia to educate blacks. A "Mr. Bolton" was taken to court for teaching them in his school in 1740; Rev. William Sturgeon, assistant to Dr. Robert Jenney, the rector of Christ Church, started catechizing Afro-Americans in 1747; and in 1750 Anthony Benezet began holding evening classes for blacks in his home. In 1758, Bray's Associates opened a school at Christ Church for free blacks, and in 1770 Benezet convinced the Philadelphia Monthly Meeting to open an "African's School" of their own. The first class included twenty-two girls and boys, evenly divided in gender. Later, older black men and women also came. All of the children studied reading, writing, and arithmetic. The girls learned sewing and knitting from a mistress, while boys did more advanced academic work. Though the school had trouble keeping schoolmasters and also had difficulty in maintaining regular attendance of pupils who often had to help support their families, a total of 250 black students received some instruction between 1770 and 1775.[50]

Not very much is known about the economic status of free blacks in the late colonial period, but we do have a few clues. According to the Quaker committees who in the late 1770s and early 1780s checked on the welfare and behavior of blacks freed by meeting members, most freed men and women were able to support themselves. A committee of the Concord Monthly Meeting in Chester County, in a report that was more detailed than those of other meetings, found only two families who had economic problems: a mother with two young children whose husband was still a slave, and an aged couple who needed their daughter's help at home but could not provide for her education or training. It is unclear how many free black families lived in the Concord area in the 1770s, but the Quakers seemed pleased with their condition. The Friends inspected and settled accounts between the blacks and their employers, and encouraged freed men and women with large families to bind out their children as apprentices in order to relieve their financial burdens.[51] Quakers in other places also found that their ex-slaves prospered in freedom. Wilmington Friends were pleased that most of their liberated blacks could provide for themselves and their families "with frugallity," while members of a New Garden committee reported that most of the freed blacks continued to live among Friends and were successful in finding jobs. Quakers of the Philadelphia Quarterly Meeting, on the other hand, were disappointed that few free blacks asked for their help or advice; blacks in the city and its environs apparently had the resources to help one another over rough periods and thus avoided the paternalistic scrutiny to which Friends generally subjected recipients of their aid.[52]

Several free black women living in the Philadelphia area were quite successful. In Pennsylvania, unlike New Jersey and New York, blacks could own real property.[53] Three free black women died before 1780 leaving wills that have survived. The first was Jane Row, deceased in 1766. She held real estate on 4th Street in Philadelphia and in Southwark and owned two slaves, whom she wanted to be sold to reasonable and good masters. Row lived with but never married a man named Henry Hainy who had fathered two of her sons, John and Thomas Hainy. She had possibly been married earlier because another of her sons was William Row. A fourth son, John Miller, was a free mulatto. Like so many male testators who used the same phrase in bequeathing personalty to their wives, Row willed Hainy a bed and furniture as a token of her "love and esteem." Ann Elizabeth Fortune, a single woman, owned personal property and a black woman Jane, whom she freed. The third woman, Jane Linkhorn Woodby, was a widow; she had married her deceased husband Emanuel in 1756 at Christ Church. She directed that her lot and buildings in Spring Garden be sold and the money invested for the support and education of her daughter Jane.[54] While the numbers of black women owning property in colonial Philadelphia is unknown, these three wills suggest that at least some blacks were able to amass considerable estates. Jane Row, especially, appears to have lived with a forceful independence. She certainly took advantage of the lack of societal pressure on blacks to marry.

The names Pennsylvania blacks adopted also provide insight into their relationships with whites and into the way in which they identified themselves within the larger white society.[55] Evidence from manumissions, marriage records, and wills indicates that before emancipation at least some slaves used surnames which were at best grudgingly recognized by their masters. Most significantly, they never chose the surname of their latest owner.[56] Several examples from Quaker manumissions illustrate these points. Joseph Pratt of Edgmont

Township, Chester County, freed "a certain Negro woman named Susanna, otherwise called Susanna Cuff," and John Hoopes of nearby Goshen Township freed a "Negro man named Jo, otherwise called Joseph Samuel." George Brinton, also of Chester County, referred to his slave as "Mordica" or "Mott," but admitted that the man used an "allias," calling himself George Brown.[57] Mulattos were more likely to use surnames than were slaves listed as "Negroes," and more enslaved men than women held recognized last names. Of fifty-three mulattos freed by Quakers in ten monthly meetings, twenty-eight (52.8%) were listed with first and last names. Surnames were given for only 61 of 383 (15.9%) freed "Negroes."[58] In the Christ Church marriage records for 1709 to 1780, 20% of the male slaves being married had last names, but only one (2.6%) of thirty-eight female slaves had a surname given. Over 80% of both the free black men and women were listed with last names.[59]

Historians have known for a long time that slavery evolved differently in colonial Pennsylvania than in the plantation areas of the American South and the West Indies. However, paucity of evidence stretching over the entire colonial period has hindered full understanding of the role slavery played in the Pennsylvania economy and society. New information from probate inventories places tax list and census data available for the late colonial period in better perspective. Philadelphians relied heaviest on black slave labor early in the eighteenth century; they turned to whites as European immigration increased and as abolitionism took hold. Slavery was only one of several kinds of labor that Pennsylvanians employed; and even those who chose to own slaves held relatively few. On average, slave masters in both urban and rural areas held fewer than three slaves each.

The limited nature of the institution in Pennsylvania and the spread of antislavery thought had a profound influence on the lives of both urban and rural black women. Though the work Pennsylvania women performed varied little over time or by geographic area, other circumstances of their lives differed considerably. In Philadelphia, rather few lived in the same house with their husbands and children, but their families probably lived close by. In rural areas like Chester County, more women lived with their families, but the total black population was sparse. Though women in both places had a better chance to achieve freedom as time went by, blacks in the city had an added advantage by the 1770s because they could look to a substantial free black community for support. Many free black women, men, and children in Philadelphia could read and write and had learned trades or occupations. At least some owned property, including houses and lots in or near the city. Thus, the Logans might have anticipated that Dinah would ask for her freedom in 1776; probably many blacks throughout the province approached their owners with the same request. Serving as someone's slave in a city or area where friends, neighbors, and relatives were free must have angered and hurt quite a number of blacks. As many proslavery apologists predicted, including the Pennsylvania assemblymen of 1726 drafting their slave code, the presence of free blacks in a community had a pernicious influence on the willingness of other blacks to remain slaves.

NOTES

*The author is grateful to P.M.G. Harris, Department of History, Temple University, for his encouragement and helpful criticism, and to the Philadelphia Center for Early American Studies for financial support while she did much of the research for this article.

1. Philadelphia Recorded Wills, Israel Pemberton, 1754, Bk. K, 143; the original will has been lost. Original manuscript wills and inventories (Phila. Wills and Admins.) and books of recorded wills for Philadelphia County are located in the Register of Wills office in the basement of City Hall Annex, Philadelphia. The Chester County probate records cited below (Chester Wills) are housed in the Chester County Archives, Chester County Court House, West Chester, although most of the wills and inventories before 1715 are included with the Philadelphia records.

2. Manumission Book for the Three Philadelphia Monthly Meetings, 1772-1796, (Phila. MM mans.), Arch Street Meeting House, Philadelphia; Phila. Wills, James Logan, 1752, Bk. I, No. 314; Sarah Logan, 1754, Bk. K, No. 121; William Logan, 1776, Bk. Q, No. 324; Hannah Logan, 1777, Bk. Q, No. 339.

3. John F. Watson, *Annals of Philadelphia in the Olden Time*, revised ed. (Philadelphia, 1905), II, 480.

4. My analysis of all 2401 surviving probate inventories, 1682-1780, for the city of Philadelphia, where a large proportion of blacks in Pennsylvania lived throughout the colonial period, showed that the relative frequency of slave ownership peaked among decendents in the second decade of the eighteenth century. Jean Ruth Soderlund, "Conscience, Interest, and Power: The Development of Opposition to Slavery among Quakers in the Delaware Valley, 1688-1780" (Ph.D. diss., Temple University, 1981), 169-81. Population estimates in U.S. Bureau of the Census, *Historical Statistics of the United States, Colonial Times to 1970* (Washington, D.C., 1975) pt. 2, 1168, and burial statistics cited by Gary B. Nash ("Slaves and Slaveowners in Colonial Philadelphia," *The William and Mary Quarterly* [*WMQ*], ser. 3, XXX [April, 1973], 226-27, 230-31) show that as a percentage of the total population, blacks were more numerous in this region around 1720 than at any other time in the colonial period. Increased importation of Africans

and West Indian blacks also occurred in the Chesapeake and New York in the years just after 1700. *Historical Statistics*, pt. 2, 1172-73; Paul G.E. Clemens, *The Atlantic Economy and Colonial Maryland's Eastern Shore* (Ithaca, 1980), 60-61.

5. Darold D. Wax, "Negro Import Duties in Colonial Pennsylvania," *Pennsylvania Magazine of History and Biography (PMHB)*, XCVII (January, 1973), 23-24.

6. Soderlund, "Conscience, Interest, and Power," 57-61.

7. James T. Mitchell and Henry Flanders, comps., *The Statutes at Large of Pennsylvania from 1682 to 1801* (Harrisburg, 1896-1915), IV, 59-64.

8. Soderlund, "Conscience and Controversy: The Problem of Slavery in the Quaker City" (Paper presented at the Annual Meeting of the Organization of American Historians, Philadelphia, April 3, 1982); Nash, "Slaves and Slaveowners," 229-56; Billy G. Smith, "The Material Lives of Laboring Philadelphians, 1750-1800," *WMQ*, ser. 3, XXXVIII (April, 1981), 163-202.

9. Evidence from 510 surviving probate inventories, 1682-1780, for nine townships in eastern Chester County (Chester, Upper and Nether Providence, Aston, Middletown, Edgmont, Ridley, Springfield, and Marple) indicates that fewer than 17 percent of inventoried decedents held slaves during the years from 1701 to 1770. Thirty percent owned slaves when they died in the decade 1691-1700, and 19 percent were slave owners in the 1770s. Soderlund, "Conscience, Interest, and Power," 181-204. See also Nash, "Slaves and Slaveowners," 244-45; and Alan Tully, "Patterns of Slaveholding in Colonial Pennsylvania: Chester and Lancaster Counties, 1729-1758," *Journal of Social History*, VI (Spring, 1973), 284-305.

10. Richard S. Dunn, "Servants and Slaves: The Recruitment and Employment of Labor in Colonial America" (Paper presented at the Conference on Colonial America at Oxford, August, 1981); Allan Kulikoff, "The Beginnings of the Afro-American Family in Maryland," in Aubrey C. Land, Lois Green Carr, and Edward C. Papenfuse, eds., *Law, Society, and Politics in Early Maryland* (Baltimore, 1977), 171-96.

11. This average includes blacks listed in the probate inventories of decedents who had lived in the city of Philadelphia (not including Southwark and the Northern Liberties) during the years from 1682 to 1780. I have not included blacks who are specifically noted as living outside the city. The actual mean number of blacks in each household was lower because some masters had more than one house and because they often hired out their slaves. According to the Philadelphia constables' returns of 1780 (Philadelphia City Archives, City Hall Annex), only 1.4 blacks lived in each slaveholding household.

Much of the evidence for the discussion that follows comes from my analysis of probate wills and inventories for Philadelphia and for the nine townships in eastern Chester County, 1682-1780. It is assumed that the slaves listed in the probate records, aggregated by decade, represent an approximate cross section of the black population. See Soderlund, "Conscience, Interest, and Power," Appendix 2, for a discussion of the potential problems in using probate data.

12. Records of Christ Church, Philadelphia, Marriages, 1709-1800, Genealogical Society of Pennsylvania (GSP) transcripts, housed at the Historical Society of Pennsylvania (HSP).

13. Sam Bass Warner, Jr., *The Private City: Philadelphia in Three Periods of Its Growth* (Philadelphia, 1968), 11.

14. Billy G. Smith, "Death and Life in a Colonial Immigrant City: A Demographic Analysis of Philadelphia," *The Journal of Economic History*, XXXVII (December, 1977), 863-89. Blacks probably comprised 8 to 10 percent of Philadelphia's population at mid-century. My estimate is based upon data from the bills of mortality analyzed by Gary Nash ("Slaves and Slaveowners," 226-27, 230-31), which show that 13.8 percent of the burials in Philadelphia in 1722 were of blacks, 19.2 percent in 1729-1732, 10.9 percent in 1738-1742, 11.3 percent in 1743-1748, 7.7 percent in 1750-1755, 9.2 percent in 1756-1760, 8.1 percent in 1761-1765, 9.2 percent in 1766-1770, and 7.4 percent in 1771-1775. My estimate would be wrong if blacks had a higher mortality rate than the total population. However, while the black death rate may have been somewhat above that of whites, especially during periods of high importation in the early eighteenth century, in the 1730s, and in the early 1760s, the difference was probably minimized by the fact that immigrants (who had higher than average death rates) made up a large segment of the white Philadelphia population. For example, the percentage of decedents who were black, according to the mortality statistics, in the period 1750-1755 (7.7 percent) probably represents a low figure because the early 1750s was a time when few slaves were imported, but was the peak period of German immigration; close to 35,000 Germans arrived in Philadelphia during the years 1749-1754. Darold Duane Wax, "The Negro Slave Trade in Colonial Pennsylvania" (Ph.D. diss., University of Washington, 1962), 46; Marianne Wokeck, "The Flow and the Composition of German Immigration to Philadelphia, 1727-1775," *PMHB*, CV (July, 1981), 267.

15. Philadelphia Yearly Meeting (Men's), Minutes (PYM mins.), 23/7th mo./1696. These minutes and those of other Quaker meetings cited below are available on microfilm at the Friends Historical Library, Swarthmore College.

16. *Statutes at Large*, II, 236; Gertrude MacKinney, ed., *Pennsylvania Archives*, 8th ser. (Harrisburg, 1931), II, 1464; IV, 3396-97.

17. Edward R. Turner, *Slavery in Pennsylvania* (Baltimore, 1911), 32-33, 42.

18. For example, George Emlen gave Dinah to his daughter Hannah Logan during his lifetime; Phila. Wills, William Logan, 1776, Bk. Q, No. 324.

19. For examples, see Phila. Wills, Geroge Claypoole, 1731, Bk. E, No. 175; Henry Dexter, 1750, Bk. I, No. 139.

20. No wills were found in which the testators directed their executors to keep black families together when they were sold. Masters who cared that much about their slaves' needs either emancipated them or provided for their support by giving them small farms, houses, or tools. Some owners showed little concern about the consequences of separation for their blacks. Elizabeth Fishbourn of Chester, for example, directed that a young black boy be taken from his mother as soon as he was weaned (Phila. Wills, Bk. C, No. 141), while others wanted their slaves sold to the highest bidders.

21. Merle G. Brouwer, "Marriage and Family Life Among Blacks in Colonial Pennsylvania," *PMHB*, IC (July, 1975), 368-72.

22. Though William Masters was hardly a typical Philadelphia slave owner—he held thirty-three blacks at his death—his inventory provides valuable information on the practice of binding out black children. Of seventeen children listed in his inventory, eleven were bound out, one as far away as Wilmington. Phila. Wills, William Masters, Bk. M, No. 27.

23. Analysis of the Chester County Slave Register of 1780, which includes blacks registered in response to the gradual abolition act of 1780 by their owners from throughout Chester County, yielded somewhat similar results. Over 64 percent of the black women were listed with black children, and as many as 42 percent lived with a black man. Chester County Slave Register, 1780, Pennsylvania Abolition Society Papers, Reel 24, HSP. The author is indebted to Gary B. Nash for this reference.

24. The Chester County Slave Register of 1780 indicated an almost even adult sex ratio; thus 43 percent of the men were listed with a black woman, about the same as the percentage of women who were listed with men. The register also listed more men with children than did the inventories—as many as 44 percent—but still this percentage was considerably lower than the percentage of women living with black children. The discrepancy between data from the slave register and the probate inventories may have resulted from the fact that different geographic areas were covered, or because the Chester probate data for the 1770s are too small to represent the black population reliably.

25. Chester Monthly Meeting, Manumissions, 1776-1780; Concord Monthly Meeting, Manumissions Book, 1777-1789; Goshen Monthly Meeting, Manumissions, recorded in the monthly meeting minutes, 1775-1777; Kennett Monthly Meeting, Manumissions, 1776-1780; all located at Friends Historical Library, Swarthmore; Phila. MM mans. Only those emancipated slaves who lived in the vicinity of the monthly meeting are counted.

26. Susan E. Klepp, "Social Class and Infant Mortality in Philadelphia, 1720-1830" (Paper presented to the Philadelphia Center for Early American Studies Seminar, Philadelphia, November 6, 1981), 17-18; Smith, "Death and Life," 887-89.

27. For examples, Phila. Admins., John Knight, 1729, No. 19; Phila. Wills, John Jones, 1708, Bk. C, No. 83.

28. According to the Philadelphia probate inventories, 1682-1780, men in the these occupations owned 57.7 percent of all adult black women.

29. Marylynn Salmon, "Trust Estates and Marriage Settlements" (Paper presented at the Philadelphia Center for Early American Studies Seminar, November, 1979).

30. Phila. Wills, Israel Pemberton, 1754, Bk. K, 143; Phila. MM mans.

31. Pennsylvania Gazette, 22 January 1767; "Record of Indentures of Individuals Bound Out as Apprentices, Servants, Etc., and of German and Other Redemptioners in the Office of the Mayor of the City of Philadelphia, October 3, 1771, to October 5, 1773," The Pennsylvania-German Society Proceedings and Addresses, XVI (1907), 70-71; Carole Shammas, "Mammy and Miss Ellen in Colonial Virginia?" (Paper presented at the Conference on Women in Early America, November 5-7, 1981, Williamsburg, Va.); Mary Beth Norton, Liberty's Daughters: The Revolutionary Experience of American Women, 1750-1800 (Boston, 1980), 12-23.

32. Phila. MM mans.; Phila. Wills, Thomas Lloyd, 1694, Bk. A, No. 105; "Record of Indentures, 1771-1773."

33. Phila. Wills, Clement Plumstead, 1745, Bk. G, No. 163; William Coleman, 1769, Bk. O, No. 235-36.

34. Phila. Wills, James Bright, 1769, Bk. O, No. 254; Lloyd Zachary, 1756, Bk. K, No. 307; James White, 1770, Bk. O, No. 352; James Young, 1779, Bk. R, No. 162; Phila. MM mans.

35. Soderlund, "Conscience, Interest, and Power," 188-90; Norton, *Liberty's Daughters*, 13-15.

36. Phila. Wills, 1682-1739.

37. *Pennsylvania Archives*, 8th ser., II, 1462, 1735; *Statutes at Large*, IV, 59-64.

38. PYM mins., 14-19/9th mo./1754; 23-29/9th mo./1758.

39. Soderlund, "Conscience, Interest, and Power," ch. 6.

40. Phila. Wills, 1740-1770.

41. For several mentioned in wills, see Phila. Wills, Samuel Preston, 1743, Bk. G, No. 41; Nathaniel Allen, 1757, Bk. L, No. 28; John Jones, 1761, Bk. M, No. 82; Benjamin Trotter, 1769, Bk. O, No. 164.

42. Phila. MM mans.

43. Nash, "Servants and Slaves," 236-37; Soderlund, "Conscience, Interest, and Power," 171-81.

44. Benjamin Quarles, *Black Abolitionists* (London, 1969), 3-8; Winthrop D. Jordan, *White Over Black: American Attitudes Toward the Negro, 1550-1812* (Chapel Hill, 1968), 422-26.

45. Henry J. Cadbury, "Negro Membership in the Society of Friends," *The Journal of Negro History*, XXI (April, 1936), 151-213.

46. PYM mins., 23/7th mo./1696, 14-19/9th mo./1754, and 20-26/9th mo./1755.

47. In my survey of the minutes of most monthly meetings in the Philadelphia Yearly Meeting, I found that meetings generally reported in response to the query of the Yearly Meeting on slavery that their members treated their slaves decently but did not educate them as well as the meeting desired.

48. *The Journal and Major Essays of John Woolman*, ed. Phillips P. Moulton (New York, 1971), 117-18; Shrewsbury Monthly Meeting (Men's), Minutes, 7/8 mo./1775.

49. For example, John Jones (d. 1761), a Quaker cordwainer who freed his slaves, directed in his will that Phyllis (aged 13 years) remain bound to Joseph Morris, a Philadelphia merchant, until she reached age 15 and that she be sent to school long enough to learn to read well. Jones wanted his black boy James (aged 7 years) to go to school to learn to read and write and to be apprenticed to a light trade such as that of joiner. Phila. Wills, John Jones, 1781, Bk. M, No. 82. Boys were more frequently bound out to trades before freedom than were girls, and they were apprenticed to occupations such as cordwainer, tailor, and house carpenter. Phila. Wills, Elizabeth Holton, 1757, Bk. K, No. 324; Robert Cross, 1766, Bk. O, No. 7; Anthony Fortune, 1779, Bk. R, No. 232.

50. Nancy Slocum Hornick, "Anthony Benezet and the Africans' School: Toward a Theory of Full Equality," *PMHB*, IC (October, 1975), 399-421; Richard I. Shelling, "William Sturgeon, Catechist to the Negroes of Philadelphia and Assistant Rector of Christ Church, 1747-1766," *Historical Magazine of the Episcopal Church*, VIII (December, 1939), 388-401.

51. Concord Monthly Meeting (Men's), Minutes, 4/8th mo./1779. According to the Concord MM mans., members of the Concord meeting freed at least eleven

adult slaves during the period 1776-1779; other free blacks, who had been released earlier, certainly lived in the area as well.

52. Wilmington Monthly Meeting (Men's), Minutes, 14/7 mo./1779; New Garden Monthly Meeting (Men's), Minutes, 5/5th mo./1781. Phila. Quarterly Meeting (Men's), Minutes, 2/8th mo./1779.

53. William M. Wiecek, "The Statutory Law of Slavery and Race in the Thirteen Mainland Colonies of British America," *WMQ*, ser. 3, XXXIV (April, 1977), 279.

54. Phila. Wills, Jane Row, 1766, Bk. N, No. 255; Ann Elizabeth Fortune, 1768, Bk. O, No. 196, Jane Woodby, 1773, Bk. P, No. 333; Emanuel Woodby, 1773, Bk. P, No. 282; Records of Christ Church, Marriages, GSP, 4247.

55. See Herbert G. Gutman, *The Black Family in Slavery and Freedom 1750-1925* (New York, 1976), 230-56, on the use of surnames by 18th- and 19th-century slaves.

56. This generalization is drawn from the minority of slaves whose surnames are given in the manumission and church records cited below; a few mentioned in wills also had last names. Further research linking freed blacks to their former masters (for example, use of the Pennsylvania Abolition Society records) might reveal that some did adopt the names of their last owners.

57. Goshen Monthly Meeting (Men's), Minutes, 11/8th mo./1775 and 9/5th mo./1777; Concord MM mans., George Brinton, 1781.

58. See manumission records cited in n. 25, above, and Bucks Quarterly Meeting, Manumissions Book, 1776-1793; Chesterfield Monthly Meeting, Manumissions, 1774-1796; and Exeter Monthly Meeting, Manumissions, 1777-1787; all in Friends Historical Library, Swarthmore; and Abington Monthly Meeting, Manumissions, 1765-1784, Quaker Collection, Haverford College; Burlington Monthly Meeting, Manumission Book, 1771-1781, Burlington County Historical Society, Burlington, N.J.

59. Records of Christ Church, Marriages, GSP.

～4～

THE ILLUSION OF CHANGE: WOMEN AND THE AMERICAN REVOLUTION

JOAN HOFF WILSON

Since the 1920s an increasing number of historians have argued that during the colonial period women enjoyed a less sex-stereotyped existence than at any time until recently, despite the absence of any significant number of organized or individual feminists. This argument is largely an exaggeration based on inadequate samplings of the small group of women who worked outside the home, or the few who actually appeared in probate records, paid taxes, wrote wills, or asserted their legal and political rights through petitions and occasional voting.

It is true, however, for most of the period up to 1750 that conditions *out of necessity* increased the functional independence and importance of all women. By this I mean that much of the alleged freedom from sexism of colonial women was due to their initial numerical scarcity and the critical labor shortage in the New World throughout the seventeenth and eighteenth centuries. Such increased reproductive roles (economic as well as biological) reflected the logic of necessity and *not any fundamental change* in the sexist, patriarchal attitudes that had been transplanted from Europe. Based on two types of scarcity (sex and labor), which were not to last, these enhanced functions of colonial women diminished as the commercial and agricultural economy became more specialized and the population grew.

A gradual "embourgeoisement" of colonial culture accompanied this preindustrial trend toward modern capitalism. It limited the number of high status roles for eighteenth-century American women just as it had for seventeenth-century English and European women. Alice Clark, Margaret George, Natalie Zemon Davis, and Jane Abray have all argued convincingly that as socioeconomic capitalist organization takes place, it closes many opportunities normally open to women both inside and outside of the family unit in precapitalist times. The decline in the status of women that accompanied the appearance of bourgeois modernity in England, according to Margaret George, "was not merely a relative decline. Precapitalist woman was not simply relatively eclipsed by the great leap forward of the male achiever; she suffered rather, an absolute setback."[1]

In the New World this process took longer but was no less debilitating. Before 1800 it was both complicated and hindered by the existence of a severe labor shortage and religious as well as secular exhortations against the sins of idleness and vanity. Thus, colonial conditions demanded that all able-bodied men, women, and children work, and so the ornamental, middle-class woman existed more in theory than in practice.

The labor shortage that plagued colonial America placed a premium on women's work inside and outside the home, particularly during the war-related periods of economic dislocation between 1750 and 1815. And there is no doubt that home industry was basic to American development both before and after 1776. It is also true that there was no sharp delineation between the economic needs of the community and the work carried on within the preindustrial family until after the middle of the eighteenth century. Woman's role as a household manager was a basic and integral part of the early political economy of the colonies. Hence she occupied a position of unprecedented importance and equality within the socioeconomic unit of the family.[2]

As important as this function of women in the home was, from earliest colonial times, it nonetheless represented a division of labor based on sex-role stereotyping carried over from England. Men normally engaged in agricultural production; women engaged in domestic gardening and home manufacturing—only slave women worked in the fields. Even in those areas of Massachusetts and Pennsylvania that originally granted females allotments of land, the vestiges of this practice soon disappeared, and subsequently public divisions "simply denied the independent economic existence of women." While equality never extended outside the home in the colonial era, there was little likelihood that women felt useless or alienated because of the importance and demanding nature of their domestic responsibilities.[3]

In the seventeenth and eighteenth centuries spinning and weaving were the primary types of home production for women and children (of both sexes). This economic function was considered so important that legal and moral sanctions were developed to insure it. For example, labor laws were passed, compulsory spinning schools were established "for the education of children of the poor," and women were told that their virtue could be measured in yards of yarn.[4] So from the beginning there was a sex, and to a lesser degree a class and educational, bias built into colonial production of cloth, since no formal apprenticeship was required for learning the trade of spinning and weaving.

It has also been recognized that prerevolutionary boycotts of English goods after 1763 and later during the war increased the importance of female production of textiles both in the home and in the early piecework factory system. By mid-1776 in Philadelphia, for example, 4,000 women and children reportedly were spinning under the "putting out system" for local textile plants.[5]

The importance of those few women who fulfilled other economic roles *in addition to* their household activities is not so readily demonstrable. The documentation about bonafide female entrepreneurs remains highly fragmentary and difficult, if not impossible, to analyze with statistical accuracy.[6] Many, if not most, appear to be the widows of "men who had been less affluent." If we take Philadelphia as representative of greater urban specialization and utilization of female workers due to the shortage of labor,[7] we find a significant number of women in only three entrepreneurial occupations up to 1776: shopkeeping, innkeeping, and crafts-making. The first two were obviously sex-role based in that most of the early retail stores and taverns were located in private homes and simply represented an extension of normal household duties. Although craftswomen also often sold their products directly from their individual dwellings, their work was not always related to traditional domestic tasks. Thus, Philadelphia women engaged in roughly thirty different trades ranging from essential to luxury services. They included female silversmiths, tinworkers, barbers, bakers, fish picklers, brewers, tanners, ropemakers, lumberjacks, gunsmiths, butchers, milliners, harnessmakers, potash manufacturers, upholsterers, printers, morticians, chandlers, coachmakers, embroiderers, dry cleaners and dyers, woodworkers, staymakers, tailors, flour processors, seamstresses, netmakers, braziers, and founders.[8]

It is this impressive array of female artisans in Philadelphia and other colonial towns that has led to the conclusion that work for women was much less sex-stereotyped in the seventeenth and eighteenth centuries than it was to become in the nineteenth. The validity of this claim has yet to be documented by a comparative analysis of female artisans in different areas. On the one hand, women found themselves in these essential and nonfamilial roles because they were substituting for dead or absent husbands; on the other hand, it was not considered "inappropriate" according to prevailing socioeconomic norms for women to engage in this wide variety of occupations, carry on the family business if widowed, or become a skilled artisan while still married. Single and married women operating their own shops and taverns were an even more common fact of colonial life.[9]

From tavern licenses issued in Philadelphia, for example, it is clear that between 1762 and 1776 no less than 17 percent, and even as much as 22 percent, of all tavern operators were women,[10] and these figures do not include those women who may have been operating illegally without licenses.[11] Such fragmentary evidence shows there were at least ninety-four female shopkeepers operating in Philadelphia between 1720 and 1776, and that in 1717 nine out of twenty-eight, or 32 percent, of all shopkeepers taking out "freedoms" were women. None of these businesswomen seem to have been given any special attention or consideration—not even the six who signed the nonimportation agreement of 25 October 1765. At the moment there is no way of knowing how representative these figures on innkeepers or "she-merchants" are for other colonial towns on the eve of the American Revolution.[12]

The increasing commercial and agricultural specialization prior to 1776,[13] affected all Americans, but particularly women, whether they were the vast rural majority who engaged in home production or the few who became entrepreneurs in the cities and towns. Probably the most significant changes were an erratic rise in the standard of living and a substantial increase in the number of landless proletarians in the major urban areas. There is now evidence that the uneven and unequal distribution of wealth as shown for Boston existed as well in Philadelphia, Newport, and New York City. Any amount of economic inequality was particularly devastating for widows, who often had dependents to support. The economic plight of the increasingly large number of widows also led to an expansion of their legal rights before 1776, so that they could convert real property into capital for personal support or investment purposes.[14]

American living standards fluctuated with the unequal prosperity that was especially related to wars. Those engaging in craft production and commerce were particularly hard hit after 1750, first by the deflation and depression following the French and Indian War (1754–1763), and then by the War for Independence. In fact, not only were the decades immediately preceding and following the American Revolution ones of economic dislocation, but the entire period between 1775 and 1815 has been characterized as one of "arrested social and economic development." These trends, combined with increased specialization, particularly with the appearance of a nascent factory system, "initiated a decline in the economic and social position of many sections of the artisan class." Thus with the exception of the innkeeping and tavern business, all of the other primary economic occupations of city women were negatively affected by the periodic fluctuations in the commercial economy between 1763 and 1812.[15]

Women artisans and shopkeepers probably suffered most during times of economic crisis because of their greater difficulty in obtaining credit from merchants. Although research into their plight has been neglected, the documents are there—in the records of merchant houses showing women entrepreneurs paying their debts for goods and craft materials by transferring their own records of indebtedness, and in court records showing an increased number of single women, especially widows sued for their debts, or in public records of the increased number of bankrupt women who ended up on poor relief lists or in debtors' prisons or who were forced to become indentured servants or earn an independent living during hard times.[16]

It was also a difficult time for household spinners and weavers, about whom a few more facts are known. First, this all-important economic function increasingly reflected class distinctions. In 1763 one British governor estimated that only the poor wore homespun clothes, while more affluent Americans bought English imports. Second, it was primarily poor women of the northern and middle colonies who engaged in spinning and weaving for pay (often in the form of credit rather than cash), while black slave women and white female indentured servants performed the same function in the South. Naturally women in all frontier areas had no recourse but to make their own clothing. Beginning with the first boycotts of British goods in the 1760s, women of all classes were urged to make and wear homespun. Several additional "manufactory houses" were established as early as 1764 in major cities specifically for the employment of poor women. Direct appeals to patriotism and virtue were used very successfully to get wealthier women to engage in arduous home-spinning drives, but probably only for short periods of time.[17]

Thus all classes of women were actively recruited into domestic textile production by male patriots with such pleas as, "In this time of public distress you have each of you an opportunity not only to help to sustain your families, but likewise to call your mite into the treasury of the public good." They were further urged to "cease trifling their time away [and] prudently employ it in learning the use of the spinning wheel."[18] Beyond any doubt the most well-known appeal was the widely reprinted 9 November 1767 statement of advice to the "Daughters of Liberty" which first appeared in the *Massachusetts Gazette*. It read in part:

First then throw aside your high top knots of pride
Wear none but your own country linen.
Of economy boast. Let your pride be the most
To show cloaths of your make and spinning.

Peak periods in prerevolutionary spinning and weaving were reached during every major boycott from 1765 to 1777. But the war and inflation proved disruptive. For example, we know that the United Company of Philadelphia for Promoting American Manufactures, which employed 500 of the city's 4,000 women and children spinning at home, expired between 1777 and 1787, when it was revived. The record of similar organizations elsewhere was equally erratic.[19]

It is common for developing countries with a labor shortage to utilize technological means to meet production demands. After the war, the new republic proved no exception, as the inefficiency and insufficiency of household spinners became apparent. Ultimately the "putting out" system was replaced entirely by the factory that employed the same women and children who had formerly been household spinners. It took the entire first half of the nineteenth century before this process was completed, and when it was, it turned out to be at the expense of the social and economic status of female workers.[20]

At the beginning of this process, however, the early cotton mills in the last quarter of the eighteenth century utilized skilled immigrants of both sexes. In fact, according to one recent study, the years between 1763 and 1812 constituted the "non-verbal period of industrial technology" in American history. During this time English technological "know-how" was transferred to the United States primarily through artificers who either owned, could build, or could operate the latest "labour-saving machines." In July 1788, for example, the Pennsylvania Society located a woman who owned a twisting mill and immediately employed her "on the best Terms." How many of these migrating artisans were women is not yet precisely known.[21]

Direct employment in these early cotton textile mills was the final way, therefore, in which changing economic conditions affected women. Such employment did not represent a new economic function for women—it simply shifted their place of work from the home to the factory. Economic nationalists like Secretary of the Treasury Alexander Hamilton recognized the contributions of women in the production of cloth under the traditional "domestic system." At the same time he recommended, in his well-known *Report on Manufacturers* of 1791, that women and children be utilized in the factory production of cotton goods. All economic nationalists, both Federalist and Republican, openly recognized that the labor of women and children would have to be exploited if the nation were to industrialize.[22]

The position was reinforced in the 1790s by male moralists who preached that poor women who did not take up factory work would be "doomed to idleness and its inseparable attendants, vice and guilt." Through at least the War of 1812, this unholy alliance temporarily prolonged the pragmatic colonial idea that "woman's place was ... not in the home, ... but wherever her 'more important' work was."[23] Now, however, this idea became the basis for making a class distinction between women that had not been possible throughout most of the preindustrial colonial period. In other words, the potential economic contribution of women to the new textile industry contrasted sharply with the propagandistic rhetoric of the 1780s and the 1790s, which portrayed them as preservers of republican virtue, exclusively within the home as patriotic wives and educators.

Each role could be (and was) justified in the name of nationalism. But each projected distinctly different future tasks for women, depending upon their socioeconomic status. One led to the dual capitalist exploitation of women as a reserve supply of cheap labor in industry and the home, without any increase in their economic power or personal status; the other led to a less functional and isolated position of women within the modern, middle-class nuclear family, whose domestic duties and responsibilities gradually declined until they consisted primarily of improving male manners and nurturing children. Both were necessary for rapid industrialization in the nineteenth century.

While the industrialization that the War of 1812 stimulated did more to hasten these class distinctions (as well as the low status and alienating features of women's work inside and outside of the home) than did the American Revolution, the latter set the stage for what was to follow both in the attitudes toward women it fostered and the requirements it set for economic growth.

Before, during, and after the Revolution, American women were experiencing important demographic changes that ultimately contributed to their socioeconomic subordination in the modern world. These demographic factors were of such an evolutionary nature, however, that few seem to have been directly affected by the Revolution itself, save for the temporary disruption of the nuclearity of family life, as men left home to participate in political or military activities, and for the lowering of sexual and moral standards that normally accompany wars.

To date most social demographers have concentrated on the seventeenth and early eighteenth centuries rather than the revolutionary period. Nonetheless, much can be inferred from recent studies of family reconstitution about the condition of women on the eve of the American Revolution. While regional differences remain to be studied,[24] significant strides have been taken with vital statistics from about a half dozen small New England communities, which suggest trends for the colonial household in that area. Since such figures could not be obtained from traditional literary sources, earlier assumptions about mortality rates, domestic stability, family size, child raising, education, male-female sex roles, and even remarriage rates are now being questioned.[25]

In general, living conditions in New England (but not in the South) appear to have been more stable and healthy, especially in the seventeenth century, than they were in England and Europe. Thus, there is evidence of increased longevity for adults, decreased deaths from childbirth, and lower mortality rates for infants and adolescents. And contrary to what was commonly thought, the duration of first marriages was quite high— ranging from between twenty and twenty-five years in some New England towns—while remarriage of widows was less likely than once assumed.[26]

Even the much heralded and first significant demographic fact about colonial women, namely their scarcity, has been cast into a new light by social demographers. It is true, for example, that men outnumbered women by three to one in the initial immigration to New England, and by six to one in the early Virginia settlements. Nevertheless, this extreme imbalance in the sex ratio soon succumbed to the high fertility level among colonial women and to lower mortality rates in the New England colonies at the beginning of the eighteenth century. In the middle and southern colonies fertility was also high, but so were mortality rates. Consequently, in these areas immigration continued to play an important role not only in maintaining population growth but also in contributing to a sex imbalance. In colonies like Virginia and Maryland, for example, there were still about three men for every two women in 1700. Even though women colonists in the South showed a greater resistance than men to disease during the "seasoning" process, they remained scarce for the next twenty or thirty years. In contrast, by 1700 the larger New England coastal towns and small eastern settlements actually experienced a surplus of unmarried women, which continued to increase and whose significance has yet to be evaluated by historians.[27]

By 1750, at least northern colonial America could no longer be considered a "paradise on earth for women," where every free, white female could marry and where a stable, parental dominated marriage system or family of orientation (birth) prevailed. It was in the throes of a "demographic crisis." Among other things, this meant that the age gap narrowed between men and women at the time of their first marriages, with men generally marrying slightly earlier and women slightly later. In addition to facing the possibility of not being able to marry, or remarry, in the case of widows, by the time of the Revolution women had been gradually adjusting to changing courtship and marriage patterns, loosened sexual mores, smaller family size, and (among the wealthier, better educated) to more permissive theories from foreign authors about child raising, romantic love, and sex-stereotyped definitions of feminity.[28] All of these demographic alterations were part of the process of family modernization—that is, the evolution from the family of orientation to the family of procreation. This transition was most pronounced in the late eighteenth and early nineteenth centuries, and is therefore coincidentally connected but not substantially affected by the Revolution.

It was the changing position of women within this gradually evolving conjugal household and its declining socioeconomic importance in general that posed the most serious demographic problems for the revolutionary generation of women—not the exact size or structure of the family unit, which continued to vary from region to region and within local communities. In other words, except for the actual years in which the war was fought, colonial women found more and more of their traditional familial duties and responsibilities syphoned off as the economy became more commercially specialized and as other social institutions such as schools became more commonplace. Only women living in the most isolated frontier areas escaped this experience of declining importance and function within the family unit, and their position was far from enviable because of the physical and mental harshness of frontier life.[29]

The difficult task of documenting this trend toward modernization of the conjugal household through family reconstitution analysis is far from complete. But we do know, for example, that there was no dramatic shift from the so-called extended family structure to a nuclear one. Through the seventeenth and early eighteenth centuries New World households appear to have been largely nuclear in structure, with women of completed fertility producing an average of seven to eight children. The number of children borne by New England women declined in the last half of the eighteenth century to five or six. Once mortality rates and other factors are considered, however, the average number of free persons in each household varied from a crowded 9.3 in Boston to 6.7 in some of the interior counties of Massachusetts in 1764 to an average of around 5.8 (or 6.1 if slaves are included) per household by 1790. Despite this slight decrease both in the number of children borne and in household size in the course of the eighteenth century, average American families were still larger than those in England and Europe. No drastic decline in marital fertility rates and household size occurred in the United States until after 1850.[30]

Nonetheless, even this relatively small decline prior to 1800 is interesting both for what it did and did not represent. First, it should be noted that it occurred in urban and rural areas and among all religious groups (including the Quakers). With few exceptions it is doubtful that this can be considered conscious family limitation, yet for reasons not yet clear American parents were beginning to consider large families a liability after 1760. But they did not generally have the modern, small target families in mind. Second, there is some, albeit far from conclusive, evidence from letters and diaries that fewer children and smaller family units produced more intimate, sentimental, and affectionate relationships. This in turn is said to have contributed to the growth of individualism, modern concepts of self and ego development among children, and romantic love ties between husbands and wives. By and large, however, the more permissive, less authoritarian child-centered family of procreation simply had not evolved by 1776, as some scholars have claimed. While there are isolated private examples of a more sentimental view of children and a tendency to glorify motherhood, neither became an established practice until after 1800 in the United States. The same is true of the concept of romantic love that finally led to marriage as a "free act" of the couple involved rather than a parentally controlled affair.[31]

It appears that most eighteenth-century women, even those who had read Locke and Rousseau, were still primarily occupied with how to conquer the wills of their children rather than with the development of individual independence. If anything, the slightly smaller household usually meant that mothers, often weakened or ill from frequent pregnancies, were placed in greater direct contact with their children, since there were fewer relatives or servants present. This led at least upperclass colonial women (and aristocratic foreigners who visited them) in the last half of the century to complain about the recalcitrance of American children and the personal burden they had become. "You can not conceive how my time is taken up," Ester Edwards Burr, the mother of Aaron Burr, confided to her journal in 1756. "Sometimes I never sit down a whole day unless to vittles." Pamela Sedgwick of Massachusetts confided to a spinster friend that she no sooner would "snatch a moment from a crying infant," than two or three of her other "ungoverned children" would begin to make noise the like of which was "as distracting to the brain as a confused din of arms to a timid soldier." She finally wrote her often-absent husband Theodore Sedgwick, in 1790, that she was "tired of living a widow and being at the same time a nurse." Poorer women had neither the time nor the literacy to record their impressions of child raising, but it is doubtful that they were any less strict or less burdened than their better educated counterparts by the late eighteenth century.[32]

A much better indication of the transitional stage of the American family on the eve of the Revolution can be found in the general decline of parental economic control over the marriages of their children. Once again, this generalization applies more to the wealthier than the poorer segment of colonial society. During the seventeenth and up to the middle of the eighteenth century parental control had been exercised largely through delayed property inheritance or the need to support a widowed mother. Such authority was undermined, however, as the legal rights of widows were gradually expanded to make them less economically dependent on their male children, and as primogeniture became less feasible as a means of controlling the marital pattern of eldest sons—it actually made the younger ones, according to Thomas Jefferson, "independent of, and disobedient to their parents."[33]

In the case of women, the increase in those who remained unmarried or who married out of normal sibling sequence was an early indication of the decline in parental authority, and hence a weakening of the family of orientation. Another indication of the gradual separation of girls from their family of birth can be found in the significant drop in the percentage of mother-daughter name-sharing. Before 1700, in Hingham, Massachusetts, 98.5 percent of all families with three or more daughters named one after the mother. By 1780 this had dropped to 53.2 percent, and the practice was to decrease even more by the end of the nineteenth century, although less rapidly for boys than girls because of the potential inheritance value of having the same name as one's father or other close male relative.[34]

Probably the most important, yet often overlooked, of all the indices of changing family patterns was the unprecedented increase in premarital pregnancies among white Americans in the last half of the eighteenth century. A peak in the number of so-called "short-term" babies conceived before marriage was reached between 1761 and 1800, when 16.7 percent of all first babies were born under six months of marriage, 27.2 percent under eight and one-half months, and 33 percent under nine months. The overall figure of 30 percent for premarital pregnancies just before and after the American Revolution was not approximated again until the 1960s. Both high periods reflect more than a simple breakdown in sexual mores encouraged by such external factors as wars, the religious revivalism of the mid-eighteenth century, or the counterculture of the last decade.[35]

Instead, premarital pregnancies are perhaps the strongest demographic indication we have of the family in a period of transition and hence unable to enforce conventional controls over sexual behavior. They represent "a collision between an unchanging and increasingly antiquated family structure and a pattern of individual behavior which is more a part of the past than a harbinger of the future." In other words, a dramatic rise in premarital relations does not mean that all other traditional patterns of the established family in any given time period are also abruptly changed or abandoned. Indeed, premarital pregnancies were no more condoned in the last half of the eighteenth century than they are today, but in both instances they do symbolize a generational conflict and a revolt of the young that presage changing power relationships within conjugal households, which may or may not be liberalizing.[36]

In the case of this first peak period, the process of family change was not completed until the 1820s and 1830s, with the appearance of the established nuclear family of procreation. This new family pattern was not only characterized by the sentimentalization of children and the glorification of motherhood, but also ideally by more consensus, affection, and contractual relations than had existed in the more authoritarian family of orientation. Nonetheless, it was within this newly established, child-oriented household that the socioeconomic functions of women were severely limited and from which sexual restrictions and inhibitions emanated, culminating finally in the excessive sexual repression of the late nineteenth century.[37]

This is not to say that any class of women of the revolutionary generation understood what was happening to the family in the last half of the eighteenth century. In such periods of transition it is common that discrepancies increase between familial attitudes (thought) and behavior (function). It must be remembered that they were accustomed to relying upon external, primarily religious and economic, controls over sexual behavior. As the authority of all orthodox religion began to break down, premarital relations assumed class and gender overtones that had not previously existed. What has been called "a sexually permissive subculture" thus emerged more quickly among poorer groups as colonial society became more economically stratified. Most important, it was encouraged or at least passed on intergenerationally from lower-class mothers to their daughters largely through the practice of bundling. While women like Abigail Adams and Mercy Warren worried over how best to instill virtue in their offspring, at the other end of the social scale young girls were told that bundling was "no sin nor shame, for we your mothers did the same."[38]

At the same time we find male patriots quickly capitalizing on the popularity of the political analogy that symbolized the colonies as children in revolt against the "monstrous" mother country. Yet it is equally evident that they did not want to contribute any further to the generational conflict already in progress or to the generally ambiguous, if not actually contradictory, state of the family of orientation by 1776.[39] Nonetheless, it is difficult to imagine that such antiparental, antifemale rhetoric did not further undermine the existing precarious position of family life during the revolutionary years. It would not be until the first quarter of the nineteenth century, however, that lower-class premarital practices would merge with upper-class theories on permissive child raising and romantic love and courtship to complete the breakdown of the family of orientation and replace it with the family of procreation. Even the best educated women could not realize that they were demographically on their way toward modernization within the family of procreation that offered them the "cult of true womanhood" in place of collective validation and a sense of individual worth. Nor could they be expected to have anticipated other "double standard" limitations associated with this new family pattern, such as increased vicarious fulfillment through their husbands or male children and the psychic burden of the permissive child-centered household that epitomized individualism and modern ego development—for men.[40] Assuming that the rhetoric of the Revolution and the trauma of war had not temporarily obfuscated their view of the future, it is doubtful if the most perspicacious women of this generation could have discerned the degree to which demography, and not the separation from England, would determine the destiny of their daughters and grandchildren.

NOTES

1. Margaret George, *One Woman's "Situation": A Study of Mary Wollstonecraft* (Urbana: University of Illinois Press, 1970), p. 16; idem, "From 'Goodwife' and 'Mistress'," pp. 155–56; Natalie Zemon Davis, "Women on Top: Sexual Inversion and Political Disorder in Early Modern Europe," in *Society and Culture in Early Modern France: Eight Essays* (Stanford, Calif.: Stanford University Press, 1975), p. 126; Jane Abray, "Feminism and the French Revolution," *AHR* 80 (February 1975): 44; Alice Clark, *Working Life of Women in the Seventeenth Century* (New York: Augustus M. Kelley, 1968; reprint of the original 1919 Cass edition), pp. 9–13, 93–149.

2. Edith Abbott, *Women in Industry: A Study in American Economic History* (New York: Source Book Press, 1970; reprint of original 1910 Appleton edition), pp. viii, 11–12; Meta Stern Lilienthal, *From Fireside to Factory* (New York: Rand School of Social Science, 1916), pp. 7–15; Mary P. Ryan, *Womanhood in America: From Colonial Times to the Present* (New York: New Viewpoints, 1975), pp. 21–22, 26, 32, 64.

3. Herbert B. Adams, "Allotments of Land in Salem to Men, Women and Maids," *Essex Institute Historical Collections* 19 (1882): 167–75; Ryan, *Womanhood in America*, p. 35; Edmund S. Morgan, *American Slavery—American Freedom: The Ordeal of Colonial Virginia* (New York: W. W. Norton, 1975), pp. 235, 310.

4. Miriam Schnier, "Women in the Revolutionary Economy," paper delivered April 1975, Organization of American Historians Convention, pp. 2–3; Cotton Mather, *Ornaments for the Daughters of Zion, or the Character and Happiness of a Virtuous Woman* (London: Thomas Parkhurst, 1694), pp. 6–7; Abbott, *Women in Industry*, pp. 20–34; Marcus Wilson Jernegan, *Laboring and Dependent Classes in Colonial America, 1607–1783* (New York: Frederick Ungar Publishing Co., 1931), pp. 84–128; Leonard, *Dear-Bought Heritage*, pp. 156–87; Morgan, *American Slavery—American Freedom*, pp. 321–24. The primary purpose of compulsory education in the colonies was to teach a trade to prevent pauperism and only secondarily to educate for literacy.

5. Frances May Manges, "Women Shopkeepers, Tavernkeepers and Artisans in Colonial Philadelphia" (Ph.D. diss., University of Pennsylvania, 1958), p. 35; Henretta, *Evolution of American Society*, p. 194.

6. Mary Beth Norton, "Eighteenth-Century American Women: The Loyalists as a Test Case," paper delivered at Second Berkshire Conference on the History of Women, 27 October 1974, p. 10. This study of a cross section of female Loyalists indicates only 9.2 percent worked outside the home. Whether these figures are representative of most late eighteenth-century women remains to be documented.

7. For examples of the expansion of female services and functions in port towns, ranging from paid domestic servants, wet nurses, and prostitutes to that of a small group of wealthy women consumers, see Ryan, *Womanhood in America*, pp. 73, 86–87, 91–99; Virginia Bever Platt (Bowling Green State University), "The Working Women of Newport, Rhode Island," paper delivered at 1975 Conference on Women in the Era of the American Revolution. According to Platt's figures, female laborers in Newport (whether free, indentured, or hired-out as slaves, and regardless of race) were paid approximately 30 percent less than the lowest paid unskilled, free, white male workers and 20 percent less than hired-out male slaves.

8. Abbott, *Women in Industry*, pp. 13–20, 149–56; Manges, "Women Shop-keepers, Tavernkeepers and Artisans," pp. xxxi–xxxii, 40–41, 44(n. 101), 69–117(n. 290); Carl Bridenbaugh, *The Colonial Craftsman* (Chicago: University of Chicago Press, Phoenix Books, 1961; reprint of original 1950 New York University Press edition), pp. 105–8; Earle, *Colonial Dames and Good Wives*, pp. 45–87; Carl Holliday, *Women's Life in Colonial Days* (New York: Frederick Ungar Publishing Co., 1922), pp. 291–312; Elisabeth Anthony Dexter, *Colonial Women of Affairs: Women in Business and the Professions in America before 1776*, 2d ed., rev. (Boston: Houghton Mifflin Co., 1931), passim; Ryan, *Womanhood in America*, pp. 34, 92–94.

9. Daniel Scott Smith, "Family Limitation, Sexual Control and Domestic Feminism in Victorian America," *Feminist Studies* 1 (Winter-Spring 1973): 46; Manges, "Women Shopkeepers, Tavernkeepers and Artisans," pp. xii–xxiii, 40–115, 118–119; Page Smith, *Daughters of the Promised Land* (Boston: Little, Brown and Co., 1970), p. 54; Carl N. Degler, *Out of Our Past: Forces that Shaped Modern America* (New York: Harper and Brothers, 1959), pp. 59–60; Mary R. Beard, *Women as Force in History*, pp. 78–80, 106–21. For more details about the socio-economic activities of colonial women, see Julia Cherry Spruill, *Women's Life and*

Work in the Southern Colonies (New York: W. W. Norton & Co., 1972; reprint of original 1938 University of North Carolina Press edition), pp. 255-313, 340-66; Earle, *Colonial Dames and Good Wives*, pp. 45-87; Holliday, *Woman's Life in Colonial Days*, pp. 291-312; Elisabeth Anthony Dexter, *Career Women of America, 1776-1840* (Clifton, N.J.: Augustus M. Kelley Publishers, 1972; reprint of original 1950 Houghton Mifflin edition), passim; Leonard, *Dear-Bought Heritage*, pp. 118-236; Abbott, *Women in Industry*, pp. 10-47; Helen Campbell, *Women Wage Earners: Their Past, Their Present, and Their Future* (New York: Arno Press, 1972; reprint of original 1893 Roberts Brothers edition), pp. 57-76; Annie Nathan Meyer, *Woman's Work in America* (New York: Henry Holt and Co., 1891), passim; Benson, *Women in Eighteenth-Century America*, pp. 34-78, 100-35.

10. Manges, "Women Shopkeepers, Tavernkeepers and Artisans," p. xxiii. Manges's figures indicate that the low of 17 percent was recorded from July 1763 to July 1764 when 52 women were granted licenses out of a total of 308. The high of 22 percent was recorded from July 1770 to July 1771 when 60 women were granted licenses out of a total of 284. Between 1762 and 1776 the average number of years that each woman held a tavern license was 3.8, according to my analysis of her figures. For Boston taverns, see Carl Bridenbaugh, *Cities in Wilderness: The First Century of Urban Life in America, 1624-1742* (New York: Alfred A. Knopf, 1955) p. 72; idem, *Colonial Craftsmen*, pp. 121-22.

11. Manges, "Women Shopkeepers, Tavernkeepers and Artisans," pp. xxiii, 71, 75, 76, 78-81 (n. 205), 96, 116, 118.

12. Elisabeth Anthony Dexter's widely quoted statement that approximately 10 percent of all colonial shop managers or "she-merchants" in Boston were women is obviously based on an inadequate sampling of newspaper advertisements. On the other hand she provides evidence for the relative decline in women shop-keepers in the post-revolutionary period and their almost exclusive relegation to the sale of dry goods and clothes for their own sex. See Dexter, *Colonial Women of Affairs*, pp. 34-35, 37-38, 162-65; idem, *Career Women of America*, p. 139.

13. See Bernard Bailyn, *The New England Merchants in the Seventeenth Century* (New York: Harper & Row, Harper Torchbook, 1964; reprint of original 1955 Harvard University Press edition), passim; Richard B. Morris, *Government and Labor in Early America* (New York: Columbia University Press, 1946), pp. 1-54; Thomas C. Cochran, *Business in American Life*, pp. 28-57; idem, "The Business Revolution," *The American Historical Review* 79 (December 1974); 1449-66; Samuel Rezneck, "The Rise and Early Development of Industrial Consciousness in the United States, 1760-1830," *Journal of Economic and Business History* 4 (August 1932): 784-86; David J. Jeremy, "British Textile Technology Transmission to the United States: The Philadelphia Region Experience, 1770-1820," *Business History Review* 47 (Spring 1973): 24-29; Henretta, *Evolution of American Society*, pp. 95-112, 714-200; Manges, "Women Shopkeepers, Tavernkeepers and Artisans," pp. 8, 14-15, 17, 20, 25, 33, 37, 38, 42, 118.

14. James Henretta, "Economic Development and Social Structure in Colonial Boston," *William and Mary Quarterly* 22 (January 1965): 80-83, 85; Philip J. Greven, Jr., *Four Generations: Population, Land and Family in Colonial Andover, Massachusetts* (Ithaca: Cornell University Press, 1970), pp. 281-82; Richard L. Bushman, *From Puritan to Yankee: Character and the Social Order in Connecticut, 1690-1765* (Cambridge: Harvard University Press, 1967), pp. 267-88; Burrows and Wallace, "American Revolution," pp. 255-67; Jacob M. Price, "Economic

Function and the Growth of American Port Towns in the Eighteenth Century," *Perspectives in American History* 8 (1974): 130–37; Allan Kulikoff, "The Progress of Inequality in Revolutionary Boston," *William and Mary Quarterly* 28 (July 1971): 376, 378, 380, 383–84, 388–89, 406–9; James T. Lemon and Gary B. Nash, "The Distribution of Wealth in Eighteenth Century America: A Century of Changes in Chester County, Pennsylvania, 1693–1802," *Journal of Social History* 2 (1968–1969): 9–12; Kenneth Lockridge, "Land, Population and the Evolution of New England Society, 1630–1790," *Past and Present*, no. 39 (April 1968), pp. 62–80; Alexander Keyssar, "Widowhood in Eighteenth-Century Massachusetts: A Problem in the History of the Family," *Perspectives in American History* 8 (1974): 100–101, 114–15, 117–18; Platt, "Working Women of Newport," pp. 8, 11.

15. Henretta, *Evolution of American Society*, pp. 42, 72, 159, 188–89; idem, "Economic Development and Social Structure in Colonial Boston," pp. 72–92.

16. Henretta, *Evolution of American Society*, p. 196; Morris, *Government and Labor*, pp. 188–207, 354–63; *AFC*, 4:258; Manges, "Women Shopkeepers, Tavernkeepers and Artisans," pp. 34–35, 69; F. T. Carlton, "Abolition of Imprisonment for Debt in the United States," *Yale Review* 17 (1908): 339–44; Spruill, *Women's Life and Work*, pp. 338–39; Keyssar, "Widowhood in Eighteenth-Century Massachusetts," pp. 112–13; Kulikoff, "The Progress of Inequality in Revolutionary Boston," pp. 383–84, 408–9.

17. Platt, "Working Women of Newport," pp. 9–10; William R. Bagnall, *The Textile Industries of the United States* (New York: Augustus M. Kelley, 1971; reprint of the original 1893 Riverside Press edition), pp. 28–88; Rolla M. Tryon, *Household Manufactures in the U.S., 1640–1860* (Chicago: University of Chicago Press, 1917), pp. 58–59, 100–107, 112–15; Victor S. Clark, *History of Manufactures in the United States*, vol. 1, *1607–1860* (New York: Peter Smith, 1949; reprint of the original 1929 Carnegie Institution edition), pp. 116, 117, 188–91; Jernegan, *Laboring and Dependent Classes*, p. 18; Caroline Gilman, ed., *Letters of Eliza Wilkinson* (New York: Arno Press, 1969; reprint of original 1839 Samuel Colman edition), p. 105; Schneir, "Women in the Revolutionary Economy," p. 8, passim; Leonard, *Dear-Bought Heritage*, pp. 188–99.

18. Quoted from the *Pennsylvania Packet*, 7 August 1775 and 19 December 1774.

19. Jeremy, "British Textile Technology Transmission," pp. 28–29; Abbott, *Women in Industry*, pp. 36–37; Herbert Heaton, "The Industrial Immigrant in the United States, 1783–1812," *Proceedings of the American Philosophical Society* 95 (1951): 522–23; Rezneck, "Industrial Consciousness," pp. 786–90, 795–96; Cometti, "Women in American Revolution," pp. 332–33; Bagnall, *Textile Industries*, pp. 79–88; Leonard, *Dear-Bought Heritage*, pp. 199–203.

20. Cochran, "Business Revolution," pp. 1455, 1465; Abbott, *Women in Industry*, pp. 37–47; Jeremy, "British Textile Technology Transmission," pp. 31, 47; Manges, "Women Shopkeepers, Tavernkeepers and Artisans," pp. 27, 35, 37, 44–70, 119–20; Gerda Lerner, "The Lady and the Mill Girl: Changes in the Status of Women in the Age of Jackson," in *Our American Sisters*, eds. Jean E. Friedman and William G. Shade (Boston: Allyn and Bacon, 1973), pp. 89–90; Leonard, *Dear-Bought Heritage*, pp. 203–7; Elizabeth Faulkner Baker, *Technology and Women's Work* (New York: Columbia University Press, 1964), pp. 12–13; Abbott, *Women in Industry*, pp. 95–97, 109–47.

21. Jeremy, "British Textile Technology Transmission," pp. 24–52, 53–56 (quotations from pp. 29–30); Heaton, "Industrial Immigrant," p. 519; Mildred Campbell,

"English Emigration on the Eve of the American Revolution," *The American Historical Review* 61 (October 1955): 4, 6–7. Campbell's study showed that out of 6,000 emigrants to the New World from December 1773 to April 1776, 12 percent or 720 of these were adult females, of whom 23 percent or 165 "were working women with some skill or occupation" outside of that of housewife. Hopefully, the study in progress by David J. Jeremy will reveal a clearer picture of their contribution to the transmission of textile skills and technology between Britain and America.

22. Abbott, *Women in Industry*, pp. 46, 47, 88; Jeremy, "British Textile Technology Transmission," p. 36; Jacob E. Cooke, ed., *The Reports of Alexander Hamilton* (New York: Harper and Row, 1964), pp. 130–31. For the ways in which economic nationalists rationalized the exploitation of female labor, see Rezneck, "Industrial Consciousness," pp. 790–99.

23. Cochran, "Business Revolution," p. 1465; Baker, *Technology and Women's Work*, pp. 6–7. For earlier Puritan references to the "sin of idleness," see n. 61 below.

24. For demographic studies of the southern colonies see Lorena S. Walsh and Russell R. Menard, "Death in the Chesapeake: Two Life Tables for Men in Early Colonial Maryland," *Maryland Historical Magazine* 69 (Summer 1974): 211–27; Wesley Frank Craven, *White, Red, and Black: The Seventeenth-Century Virginian* (Charlottesville, Va: University of Virginia Press, 1971); Russell R. Menard, "Immigration to the Chesapeake Colonies in the Seventeenth Century: A Review Essay," *Maryland Historical Magazine* 68 (1973): 323–29; Irene W. D. Hecht, "The Virginia Muster of 1624/5 as a Source for Demographic History," *William and Mary Quarterly* 30 (1973): 65–92.

25. I am referring here to recent works on demography and social structure by John Demos, Philip J. Greven, James Henretta, Kenneth A. Lockridge, Robert V. Wells, Daniel Scott Smith, Darrett Rutman, Alexander Keyssar, and Richard Alterman that question some of the earlier prescriptive conclusions reached by Bernard Bailyn, Edmund Morgan, Oscar Handlin, Arthur W. Calhoun, Perry Miller, and Thomas Johnson based on research into literary sources.

26. Henretta, *Evolution of American Society*, pp. 12–13; Greven, *Four Generations*, pp. 21–40, 29, 110–11, 192–94; David E. Stannard, "Death and the Puritan Child," *American Quarterly* 26 (December 1974): 463–66; Keyssar, "Widowhood in Eighteenth-Century Massachusetts," pp. 88–94, 108–9; Walsh and Menard, "Death in the Chesapeake," pp. 222–27; Maris A. Vinovskis, "Mortality Rates and Trends in Massachusetts Before 1860," *Journal of Economic History* 32 (March 1972); 184–89, 190–91, 194–203, 212–13; John Demos, "Notes on Life in Plymouth Colony," *William and Mary Quarterly* 22 (1965): 271–72.

27. Daniel Scott Smith, "The Demographic History of Colonial New England," *Journal of Economic History* 32 (March 1972): 170–73; Herbert Moller, "Sex Composition and Correlated Culture Patterns of Colonial America," *William and Mary Quarterly* 2 (April 1945): 118, 124–25; Henretta, *Evolution of American Society*, p. 172; Greven, *Four Generations*, pp. 121–22; John Demos, "Families in Colonial Bristol, Rhode Island: An Exercise in Historical Demography," in *Quantitative History*, eds. D. K. Rowney and J. Q. Graham, Jr. (Homewood, Ill: Dorsey Press, 1969), pp. 301, 305; Keyssar, "Widowhood in Eighteenth-Century Massachusetts," pp. 95–97. Between 1721 and 1760 as many as 15 percent of all adult women remained unmarried at least until the age of 45 in certain towns in Massachusetts and Rhode Island.

28. Moller, "Sex Composition," p. 140; Demos, "Life in Plymouth," pp. 272–73, 275–76; Henretta, *Evolution of American Society*, p. 132; Bruce E. Steiner, "Demographic Studies," *New England Quarterly* 43 (September 1970), 482–89; Daniel Scott Smith, "Parental Power and Marriage Patterns: An Analysis of Historical Trends in Hingham, Massachusetts," *Journal of Marriage and the Family* 35 (August 1973): 419–28; Ryan, *Womanhood in America*, pp. 106–111; Greven, *Four Generations*, pp. 272–75; Smith and Hindus, "Premarital Pregnancy," pp. 561–64.

29. Smith, "Parental Power and Marriage Patterns," p. 427; Keyssar, "Widowhood in Eighteenth-Century Massachusetts," pp. 117–18; Ryan, *Womanhood in America*, pp. 86–91. Since none of the new demographic studies have dealt with actual frontier conditions I see no reason to deny the validity of the axiom that "the frontier was great for men and dogs, but hell for horses and women." There is a tendency among some historians who have recently rediscovered the functional importance of women within the seventeenth century colonial household to confuse conditions in newly settled coastal areas with those of frontier America, which continued well into the nineteenth century. The former were generally organized efforts characterized by the immediate establishment of stable family life and kinship networks, while the latter were often isolated and unplanned or poorly planned ventures into the wilderness where male dominance reigned supreme and where isolated women, whether they were there as status symbols, slaves, civilizers, or prostitutes, had no institutionalized protection (such as the proximity of their families of orientation) from the physical hardships imposed both by the environment and the men. It appears that this dominance diminished to some degree as the first elements of law and order were introduced and small communities with more balanced sex ratios developed—only to return when these settlements became fully "civilized" and well within the cultural and economic standards set by the older coastal towns. By saying this, I do not want to diminish the socio-economic importance of the western frontier woman; but at the same time I do not want to romanticize it.

30. Smith, "Parental Power and Marriage Patterns," pp. 421, 427; idem, "Demographic History of Colonial New England," pp. 165 (n. 2), 170–73; Greven, *Four Generations*, 14–16, 30, 111–13, 118–23, 261–68; Wilson H. Grabill, Clyde V. Kiser, and Pascal K. Whelpton, "A Long View," in *The American Family in Social-Historical Perspective*, ed. Michael Gordon (New York: St. Martin's Press, 1973), pp. 375, 379; idem, eds. *The Fertility of American Women* (New York: John Wiley and Sons, 1958), pp. 9–10; Philip J. Greven, Jr., "The Average Size of Families and Households in the Province of Massachusetts in 1764 and in the United States in 1790: An Overview," in *Household and Family in Past Time*, ed. Peter Laslett (London: Cambridge University Press, 1972), pp. 551, 556, 557–58, 559; Demos, "Families in Colonial Bristol," pp. 297, 299, 305.

31. J. William Frost, *The Quaker Family in Colonial America* (New York: St. Martin's Press, 1973), pp. 70, 86–88; Robert V. Wells, "Family Size and Fertility Control in Eighteenth-Century America: A Study of Quaker History," *Population Studies* 25 (1971): 73–82; idem, "Demographic Change and the Life Cycle of American Families," *Journal of Interdisciplinary History* 2 (Spring 1975): 743–49; Smith, "Parental Power and Marriage Patterns," pp. 421, 426; idem, "Demographic History of Colonial New England," pp. 166, 178, 179 (n. 17), 180 (n. 19), 182–83; Grabill, Kiser, and Whelpton, "A Long View," pp. 383–84; Ryan, *Womanhood in America*, pp. 48, 62, 121, 124–35; Lawrence Stone, "The Massacre of

the Innocents," *New York Review of Books*, 14 November 1974, p. 31; Greven, *Four Generations*, pp. 279–84; Bushman, *Puritan to Yankee*, pp. 183–95, 235–66; Burrows and Wallace, "American Revolution," pp. 255–67, 283–89; Gordon S. Wood, "Rhetoric and Reality in the American Revolution," *William and Mary Quarterly* 23 (1966): 25–31; John J. Waters, Jr., *The Otis Family in Provincial and Revolutionary Massachusetts* (Chapel Hill: University of North Carolina Press, 1968), pp. 128–34; David J. Rothman, "A Note on the Study of the Colonial Family," in *Education in American History*, ed. Michael B. Katz (New York: Praeger Publishers, 1973), pp. 22–28; Steiner, "Demographic Studies," pp. 482–89. All statements, even those as qualified as Greven's (p. 282), about the transition taking place in the family unit being complete in 1776, must be viewed with caution especially when Burrows and Wallace suggest (p. 283), "families provide the political system with the personality type it requires."

32. John F. Walzer, "Eighteenth-Century American Childhood," in *The History of Childhood*, ed. Lloyd deMause (New York: The Psychohistory Press, 1974), pp. 352–53, 358, 360–75, 378 (n. 50); Ann Hulton, *Letters of a Loyalist Lady* (Cambridge: Harvard University Press, 1927), pp. ix, 37, 49–50, 63; Spruill, *Women's Life and Work*, pp. 55–63; Stewart Mitchell, ed., *New Letters of Abigail Adams, 1788–1801* (Boston: Houghton Mifflin Co., 1947), pp. xxviii–xxix, 35–36, 109, 129, 130–31, 174; Philip J. Greven, Jr., ed., *Child-Rearing Concepts, 1628–1861* (Ithaca, Ill.: F. E. Peacock Publishers, 1973), pp. 1–6, 46–51, passim. Also see n. 14 for the child-rearing views of Abigail Adams and Mercy Warren.

33. Keyssar, "Widowhood in Eighteenth-Century Massachusetts," pp. 87–91, 100–101, 114, 117, 118; Smith, "Parental Power and Marriage Patterns," pp. 420–24; Greven, *Four Generations*, pp. 72–99, 280–86; Demos, "Notes on Life in Plymouth Colony," pp. 273–75; idem, *Little Commonwealth*, pp. 149–70; (on pages 169–70 Demos appears to contradict some of his own evidence and Greven's by denying "that parents deployed their ownership of property so as to maintain effective control over their grown children" in the seventeenth century); Paul Leicester Ford, ed., *The Words of Thomas Jefferson* (New York: G.P. Putnam's Sons, 1904), 2:269.

34. Joseph E. Illick, "Child-Rearing in Seventeenth-Century England and America," in *History of Childhood*, pp. 324–25; Smith, "Parental Power and Marriage Patterns," pp. 425–26 (n. 9).

35. Smith and Hindus, "Premarital Pregnancy," pp. 537, 561, passim; Daniel Scott Smith, "The Dating of the American Sexual Revolution: Evidence and Interpretation," in *American Family in Social-Historical Perspective*, p. 323; Moller, "Sex Composition," pp. 142–45; Arthur W. Calhoun, *A Social History of the American Family* (New York: Barnes and Noble, 1917), vol. 1; *Colonial Period*, pp. 51–64; Greven, *Four Generations*, pp. 113–16; Demos, "Families in Colonial Bristol, R. I.," p. 306; Henretta, *Evolution of American Society*, pp. 132–33.

36. Smith and Hindus, "Premarital Pregnancy," pp. 537–41, 549, 553 (quotation), 555–60.

37. Ibid., Greven, *Child-Rearing Concepts*, pp. 4–5. See also nn. 48 and 50 above.

38. Smith and Hindus, "Premarital Pregnancy," pp. 547–51. Bundling has been described by these two authors as "an eighteenth century compromise between persistent parental control and pressures of the young to subvert traditional familial authority" (p. 556). See n. 14 for views of Adams and Warren on virtue.

39. Ibid., p. 557; Michael Paul Rogin, *Fathers and Children* (New York: Alfred A.

Knopf, 1975), pp. 30, 34. See n. 50 above and section on education for confirmation of conservative views about the family held by the Founding Fathers.

40. Rogin, *Fathers and Children*, pp. 63–64, 70–71. For representative examples of the general submissiveness and the vicarious aspects of the lives of the middle- and upper-class women in the late eighteenth century which ultimately led to a culmination of the double standard in the cult of idleness and "true womanhood," see Linda Grant De Pauw, "The American Revolution and the Rights of Women: The Feminist Theory of Abigail Adams," paper delivered at the 1975 meeting of the Organization of American Historians; Hulton, *Letters of a Loyalist Lady*, p. 6; Woody, *History of Women's Education,* 1:133–34; Alice Morse Earle, ed., *Diary of Anna Green Winslow: A Boston School Girl of 1771* (Detroit: Singing Tree Press, 1970; reprint of the original 1894 Houghton Mifflin edition), passim; Eliza Southgate Bowne, *A Girl's Life Eighty Years Ago* (New York: Charles Scribner's Sons, 1887), pp. 15–19, 50–51; Ethel Armes, ed., *Nancy Shippen: Her Journal Book: The International Romance of a Young Lady of Fashion of Colonial Philadelphia with Letters to Her and About Her* (Philadelphia: J. B. Lippincott, 1935), pp. 41–42, passim; AFC, 2:407; 3:xxxiii; 4:210, 221, 258; Keith Thomas, "The Double Standard," *Journal of the History of Ideas* 20 (April 1959): 195–216; E. Willett Cunington, *Feminine Attitudes in the Nineteenth Century* (New York: MacMillan and Co., 1936), pp. 201–35; Barbara Welter, "The Cult of True Womanhood: 1820–1860," *American Quarterly* 18 (Summer 1966): 151–74; Ryan, *Womanhood in America*, pp. 137–91.

∾ 5 ∾

Daughters of Columbia: Educating Women for the Republic, 1787–1805

Linda K. Kerber

"I expect to see our young women forming a new era in female history," wrote Judith Sargent Murray in 1798.[1] Her optimism was part of a general sense that all possibilities were open in the post-Revolutionary world; as Benjamin Rush put it, the first act of the republican drama had only begun. The experience of war had given words like "independence" and "self-reliance" personal as well as political overtones; among the things that ordinary folk had learned from wartime had been that the world could, as the song had it, turn upside down. The rich could quickly become poor, wives might suddenly have to manage family businesses; women might even, as the famous Deborah Gannett had done, shoulder a gun. Political theory taught that republics rested on the virtue of their citizens; revolutionary experience taught that it was useful to be prepared for a wide range of unusual possibilities.[2]

A desire to explore the possibilities republicanism now opened to women was expressed by a handful of articulate, urban, middle-class men and women. While only a very few writers—Charles Brockden Brown, Judith Sargent Murray, Benjamin Rush—devoted extensive attention to women and what they might become, many essayists explored the subject in the periodical literature. In the fashion of the day, they concealed their identity under pseudonyms like "Cordelia," "Constantia," or, simply, "A Lady." These expressions came largely from Boston, New York, and Philadelphia: cities which were the centers of publishing. The vitality of Philadelphia, as political and social capital, is well known; the presence of so many national legislators in the city, turning up as they did at dances and dinner parties, was no doubt intellectually invigorating, and not least for the women of Philadelphia. In an informal way, women shared many of the political excitements of the city. Philadelphia was the home of the Young Ladies' Academy, founded in 1786, with explicitly fresh ideas about women's education, and an enrollment of more than a hundred within two years; Benjamin Rush would deliver his "Thoughts upon Female Education" there. The first attempt at a magazine expressly addressed to women was made by the Philadelphia *Lady's Magazine and Repository.* Two of the most intense anonymous writers—"Sophia" and "Nitidia"—wrote for Philadelphia newspapers. And after the government moved to Washington, Joseph Dennie's *Port Folio* solicited "the assistance of the ladies," and published essays by Gertrude Meredith, Sarah Hall, and Emily Hopkinson. Boston and New York were not far behind in displaying similar interests: in New York, Noah Webster's *American Magazine* included in its prospectus a specific appeal for female contributors; the *Boston Weekly Magazine* was careful to publish the speeches at the annual "Exhibition" of Susanna Rowson's Young Ladies' Academy.

Most journalists' comments on the role and functions of women in the republic merged, almost imperceptibly, into discussions of the sort of education proper for young girls. A pervasive Lockean environmentalism was displayed; what people were was assumed to be dependent on how they were educated. "Train up the child in the way he should grow, and when he is old he will not depart from it"; the biblical injunction was repeatedly quoted, and not quoted idly. When Americans spoke of what was best for the child they were also speaking—implicitly or explicitly—of their hopes for the adult. Charles Brockden Brown, for example, is careful to provide his readers with brief accounts of his heroines' early education. When we seek to learn the recipe for Murray's "new era in female history" we find ourselves reading comments on two related themes: how young women are to be "trained up," and what is to be expected of them when they are old.

If the republic were to fulfill the generous claims it made for the liberty and competence of its citizens, the education of young women would have to be an education for independence rather than for an upwardly mobile marriage. The periodicals are full of attacks on fashion, taking it for an emblem of superficiality and dependence. The Philadelphia *Lady's Magazine* criticized a father who prepared his daughters for the marriage market: "You boast of having given your daughters an education which will enable them 'to shine in the first circles.' . . . They sing indifferently; they play the harpsichord indifferently; they are mistresses of every common game at cards . . . they . . . have just as much knowledge of dress as to deform their persons by an awkward imitation of every new fashion which appears. . . . Placed in a situation of difficulty, they have neither a head to dictate, nor a hand to help in any domestic concern."[3] Teaching young girls to dress well was part of the larger message that their primary lifetime goal must be marriage; in this context, fashion became a feature of sexual politics. "I have sometimes been led," remarked Benjamin Rush, "to ascribe the invention of ridiculous and expensive fashions in female dress entirely to the gentlemen in order to divert the ladies from improving their minds and thereby to secure a more arbitrary and unlimited authority over them."[4] In the marriage market, beauty, flirtatiousness, and charm were at a premium; intelligence, good judgment, and competence (in short, the republican virtues) were at a discount. The republic did not need fashion plates; it needed citizens— women as well as men—of self-discipline and of strong mind. The contradiction between the counsel given to young women and their own self-interest, as well as the best interests of the republic, seemed obvious. The marriage market undercut the republic.[5]

Those who addressed themselves to the problem of the proper education for young women used the word "independence" frequently. Sometimes it was used in a theoretical fashion: How, it was asked, can women's minds be free if they are taught that their sphere is limited to clothing, music, and needlework? Often the context of independence is economic and political: it seemed appropriate that in a republic women should have greater control over their own lives. "The *dependence* for which women are uniformly educated" was deplored; it was pointed out that the unhappily married woman would quickly discover that she had "neither liberty nor property."[6]

The idea that political independence should be echoed by a self-reliance which would make women as well as men economically independent appears in its most developed form in a series of essays Judith Sargent Murray published in the *Massachusetts Magazine* between 1792 and 1794, and collected under the title *The Gleaner* in 1798. Murray insisted that instruction in a manual trade was especially appropriate in a republic, and decried the antiegalitarian habit of assuming that a genteel and impractical education was superior to a vocational one. She was critical of fathers who permitted their sons to grow up without knowing a useful skill; she was even more critical of parents who "pointed their daughters" toward marriage and dependence. This made girls' education contingent on a single event; it offered them a single image of the future. "I would give my daughters every accomplishment which I thought proper," Murray wrote, "and to crown all, I would early accustom them to habits of industry and order. They should be taught with precision the art economical; they should be enabled to procure for themselves the necessaries of life; independence should be placed within their grasp." Repeatedly Murray counseled that women should be made to feel competent at something: "A woman *should reverence herself.*"[7]

Murray scattered through the *Gleaner* essays and brief fictional versions of self-respecting women, in the characters of Margaretta, Mrs. Virgilius, and Penelope Airy. In his full-length novel *Ormond,* published in 1799, Charles Brockden Brown imagined a considerably more developed version of a competent woman. Constantia Dudley is eminently rational. When her father is embezzled of his fortune she, "her cheerfulness unimpaired," sells "every superfluous garb and trinket," her music and her books; she supports the family by needlework. Constantia never flinches; she can take whatever ill fortune brings, whether it is yellow fever or the poverty that forces her to conclude that the only alternative to starvation is cornmeal mush three times a day for three months. Through it all, she resists proposals of marriage, because even in adversity she scorns to become emotionally dependent without love.[8]

Everything Constantia does places her in sharp contrast to Helena Cleves, who also "was endowed with every feminine and fascinating quality." Helena has had a genteel education; she can paint, and sing, and play the clavichord, but it is all fashionable gloss to camouflage a lack of real mental accomplishment and self-discipline. What Brown called "exterior accomplishments" were acceptable so long as life held no surprises, but when Helena meets disaster, she is unprepared to maintain her independence and her self-respect. She falls into economic dependence upon a "kinswoman"; she succumbs to the "specious but delusive" reasoning of Ormond, and becomes his mistress. He takes advantage of her dependence, all the while seeking in Constantia a rational woman worthy of his intelligence; eventually, in despair, Helena kills herself.[9]

The argument that an appropriate education would steel girls to face adversity is related to the conviction that all citizens of a republic should be self-reliant. But the argument can be made independent of explicit republican ideology. It may well represent the common sense of a revolutionary era in which the unexpected was very likely to happen; in which large numbers of people had lived through reversals of fortune, encounters with strangers, physical dislocation. Constantia's friend Martinette de Beauvais has lived in Marseilles, Verona, Vienna, and Philadelphia; she had dressed like a man and fought in the American

Revolution; after that she was one of the "hundreds" of women who took up arms for the French.[10] Constantia admires and sympathizes with her friend; nothing in the novel is clearer than that women who are not ready to maintain their independence in a crisis, as Constantia and Martinette do, risk sinking, like Helena, into prostitution and death.

The model republican woman was competent and confident. She could ignore the vagaries of fashion; she was rational, benevolent, independent, self-reliant. Writers who spoke to this point prepared lists of what we would now call role models: heroines of the past offered as assurance that women could indeed be people of accomplishment. There were women of the ancient world, like Cornelia, the mother of the Gracchi; rulers like Elizabeth of England and the Empress Catherine of Russia; a handful of Frenchwomen: Mme. de Genlis, Mme. Maintenon, and Mme. Dacier; and a long list of British intellectuals: Lady Mary Wortley Montagu, Hannah More, Elizabeth Carter, Mrs. Knowles (the Quaker who had bested Dr. Johnson in debate), Mary Wollstonecraft, and the Whig historian Catharine Macaulay.[11] Such women were rumored to exist in America; they were given fictional embodiment by Murray and Brown. Those who believed in these republican models demanded that their presence be recognized and endorsed, and that a new generation of young women be urged to make them patterns for their own behavior. To create more such women became a major educational challenge.

Writers were fond of pointing out that the inadequacies of American women could be ascribed to early upbringing and environmental influences. "Will it be said that the judgment of a male of two years old, is more sage than that of a female of the same age?" asked Judith Sargent Murray. "But . . . as their years increased, the sister must be wholly domesticated, while the brother is led by the hand through all the flowery paths of science." The *Universal Asylum* published a long and thoughtful essay by "A Lady" which argued that "in the nursery, strength is equal in the male and female." When a boy went to school, he immediately met both intellectual and physical challenge; his teachers instructed him in science and language, his friends dared him to fight, to run after a hoop, to jump a rope. Girls, on the other hand, were "committed to illiterate teachers, . . . cooped up in a room, confined to needlework, deprived of exercise." Thomas Cooper defined the problem clearly: "We first keep their minds and then their persons in subjection," he wrote. "We educate women from infancy to marriage, in such a way as to debilitate both their corporeal and their mental powers. All the accomplishments we teach them are directed not to their future benefit in life but to the amusement of the male sex; and having for a series of years, with much assiduity, and sometimes at much expense, incapacitated them for any serious occupation, we say they are not fit to govern themselves."[12]

Schemes for the education of the "rising generation" proliferated in the early republic, including a number of projects for the education of women. Some, like those discussed in the well-known essays of Benjamin Rush and Noah Webster, were theoretical; others took the form of admitting girls to boys' academies or establishing new schools for girls. There were not as many as Judith Sargent Murray implied when she said: "Female academies are everywhere establishing," but she was not alone in seeing schools like Susanna Rowson's Young Ladies' Academy and the Young Ladies' Academy of Philadelphia as harbingers of a trend. One pamphlet address, written in support of the Philadelphia Academy, expressed the hope that it would become "a great national seminary" and insisted that although "stubborn prejudices still exist . . . we must (if open to conviction) be convinced that *females* are fully capable of sounding the most profound depths, and of attaining to the most sublime excellence in every part of science."[13]

Certainly there was a wide range of opinion on the content and scope of female education in the early republic. Samuel Harrison Smith's essay on the subject, which won the American Philosophical Society's 1797 prize for the best plan for a national system of education, began by proposing "that every male child, without exception, be educated."[14] At the other extreme was Timothy Dwight, the future president of Yale, who opened his academy at Greenfield Hill to girls and taught them the same subjects he taught to boys, at the same time and in the same rooms.[15] But Dwight was the exception. Most proposals for the education of young women agreed that the curriculum should be more advanced than that of the primary schools but somewhat less than that offered by colleges and even conventional boys' academies. Noah Webster thought women should learn speaking and writing, arithmetic, geography, belles-lettres; "A Reformer" in the *Weekly Magazine* advocated a similar program, to which practical instruction in nursing and cooking were added. Judith Sargent Murray thought women should be able to converse elegantly and correctly, pronounce French, read history (as a narrative substitute for novels, rather than for its own interest or value), and learn some simple geography and astronomy.[16] The best-known proposal was Benjamin Rush's; he too prescribed reading, grammar, penmanship, "figures and bookkeeping," geography. He added "the first principles of natural philosophy," vocal music (because it soothed cares and was good for the lungs) but not instrumental music (because, except for the most talented, it seemed a waste of valuable time), and history (again, as an antidote to novel reading).

Rush offered his model curriculum in a speech to the Board of Visitors of the Young Ladies' Academy of Philadelphia, later published and widely reprinted under the title "Thoughts upon Female Education Accommodated to the Present State of Society, Manners and Government in the United States of America." The academy claimed to be the first female academy chartered in the United States; when Rush spoke, on July 28, 1787, he was offering practical advice to a new school. Rush linked the academy to the greater cause of demonstrating the possibilities of women's minds. Those who were skeptical of education for women, Rush declared, were the same who opposed "the general diffusion of knowledge among the citizens of our republics." Rush argued that "female education should be accommodated to the state of society, manners, and government of the country in which it is conducted." An appropriate education for American women would be condensed, because they married earlier than their European counterparts; it would include bookkeeping, because American women could expect to be "the stewards and guardians of their husbands' property," and executrices of their husbands' wills. It would qualify them for "a general intercourse with the world" by an acquaintance with geography and chronology. If education is preparation for life, then the life styles of American women required a newly tailored educational program. [17]

The curriculum of the Young Ladies' Academy (which one of the Board of Visitors called "abundantly sufficient to complete the female mind") included reading, writing, arithmetic, English grammar, composition, rhetoric, and geography. It did not include the natural philosophy Rush hoped for (although Rush did deliver a dozen lectures on "The Application of the Principles of Natural Philosophy, and Chemistry, to Domestic and Culinary Purposes"); it did not include advanced mathematics or the classics. [18]

In 1794 the Young Ladies' Academy published a collection of its graduation addresses; one is struck by the scattered observations of valedictorians and salutatorians that reading, writing, and arithmetic were not enough. Priscilla Mason remarked in her 1793 graduation address that while it was unusual for a woman to address "a promiscuous assembly," there was no impropriety in women's becoming accomplished orators. What had prevented them, she argued, was that "our high and mighty Lords . . . have denied us the means of knowledge, and then reproached us for the want of it. . . . They doom'd the sex to servile or frivolous employments, on purpose to degrade their minds, that they themselves might hold unrivall'd, the power and pre-eminence they had usurped." Academies like hers enabled women to increase their knowledge, but the forums in which they might use it were still unavailable: "The Church, the Bar, and the Senate are shut against us."[19]

So long as the propriety of cultivating women's minds remained a matter for argument, it was hard to press a claim to public competence; Priscilla Mason was an exception. Rush had concluded his advice to the Young Ladies' Academy by challenging his audience to demonstrate "that the cultivation of reason in women is alike friendly to the order of nature and the private as well as the public happiness." But meeting even so mild a challenge was difficult; "bluestocking" was not a term of praise in the early republic. "Tell me," wrote the Philadelphian Gertrude Meredith angrily, ". . . do you imagine, from your knowledge of the young men in this city, that ladies are valued according to their mental acquirements? I can assure you that they are not, and I am very confident that they never will be, while men indulge themselves in expressions of contempt for one because she has a *bare elbow,* for another because she . . . never made a *good pun, nor smart repartee.* . . . [Would they] not titter . . . at her expense, if a woman made a Latin quotation, or spoke with enthusiasm of Classical learning?"[20] When Gertrude Meredith visited Baltimore, she found that her mildly satirical essays for the *Port Folio* had transformed her into a formidable figure: "Mrs. Cole says she should not have been more distressed at visiting Mrs. Macaulay the authoress than myself as she had heard I *was so sensible,* but she was very glad to find I was so free and easy. You must allow," she concluded dryly, "that this compliment was elegantly turned." A similar complaint was made by an essayist whom we know only as "Sophia":

> A woman who is conscious of possessing, more intellectual power than is requisite in superintending the pantry, and in adjusting the ceremonials of a feast, and who believes she, in conforming to the will of the giver, in improving the gift, is by the wits of the other sex denominated a learned lady. She is represented as disgustingly slovenly in her person, indecent in her habits, imperious to her husband, and negligent of her children. And the odious scarecrow is employed, exactly as the farmer employs his unsightly bundle of rags and straw, to terrify the simple birds, from picking up the precious grain, which he wishes to monopolize. After all this, what man in his sober senses can be astonished, to find the majority of women as they really are, frivolous and volatile; incapable of estimating their own dignity, and indifferent to the best interests of society. . . ?[21]

These women were not creating their own paranoid images of discouragement. The same newspapers for which they wrote often printed other articles insisting that intellectual accomplishment is inappropriate in a woman, that the intellectual woman is not only invading a male province, but must herself somehow be masculine. "Women of masculine minds," wrote the Boston minister John Sylvester John Gardiner, "have generally masculine manners, and a robustness of person ill calculated to inspire the tender passion." Noah Webster's *American Magazine,* which in its prospectus had made a special appeal to women writers and readers, published the unsigned comment: "If we picture to ourselves a woman . . . firm in resolve, unshaken in conduct, unmoved by the delicacies of situation, by the fashions of the times, . . . we immediately change the idea of the sex, and . . . we see under the form of a woman the virtues and qualities of a man." Even the *Lady's Magazine,* which had promised to demonstrate that "the FEMALES of Philadelphia are by no means deficient in *those talents,* which have immortalized the names of a *Montagu,* a *Craven,* a *More,* and a *Seward,* in their inimitable writings," published a cautionary tale, whose moral was that although "learning in men was the road to preferment . . . consequences very opposite were the result of the same quality in women." Amelia is a clergyman's only daughter; she is taught Latin and Greek, with the result that she becomes "negligent of her dress," and "pride and pedantry grew up with learning in her breast." Eventually she is avoided by both sexes, and becomes emblematic of the fabled "white-washed jackdaw (who, aiming at a station from which nature had placed him at a distance, found himself deserted by his own species, and driven out of every society)." For conclusion there was an explicit moral: "This story was intended (at a time when the press overflows with the productions of female pens) . . . to admonish them, that . . . because a few have gained applause by studying the dead languages, all womankind should [not] assume their Dictionaries and Lexicons; else . . . (as the Ladies made rapid advances towards manhood) we might in a few years behold a sweepstakes rode by women, or a second battle at Odiham, fought with superior skill, by Mesdames Humphries and Mendoza."[22]

The prediction that accomplishment would unsex women was coupled with the warning that educated women would abandon their proper sphere; the female pedant and the careful housekeeper were never found in the same person. The most usable cautionary emblem for this seems to have been Mary Wollstonecraft, whose life and work linked criticism of women's status with free love and political radicalism. Mary Wollstonecraft's *Vindication of the Rights of Women* was her generation's most coherent statement of what women deserved and what they might become. The influence of any book is difficult to trace, and although we know that her book was reprinted in Philadelphia shortly after its publication in 1792, it would be inaccurate to credit Wollstonecraft with responsibility for raising in America questions relating to the status of women. It seems far more likely that she verbalized effectively what a larger public was already thinking or was willing to hear; "In very many of her sentiments," remarked the Philadelphia Quaker Elizabeth Drinker, "she, as some of our friends say, *speaks my mind.*"[23]

Wollstonecraft's primary target was Rousseau, whose definition of woman's sphere was a limited one: "The empire of women," Rousseau had written, "is the empire of softness, of address, of complacency; her commands are caresses; her menaces are tears." Wollstonecraft perceived that to define women in this way was to condemn them to "a state of perpetual childhood"; she deplored the "false system of education" which made women "only anxious to inspire love, when they ought to cherish a nobler ambition, and by their abilities and virtues exact respect." Women's duties were different from those of men, but they similarly demanded the exercise of virtue and reason; women would be better wives and mothers if they were taught that they need not depend on frivolity and ignorance. Wollstonecraft ventured the suggestion that women might study medicine, politics, and business, but whatever they did, they should not be denied civil and political rights, they should not have to rely on marriage for assurance of economic support, they should not "remain immured in their families groping in the dark."[24]

If, in some quarters, Mary Wollstonecraft's work was greeted as the common sense of the matter, in others it was met with hostility. The *Vindication* was a popular subject of satire, especially when, after the author's death in childbirth in 1797, William Godwin published a *Memoir* revealing that she had lived with other men, and with Godwin himself before her pregnancy and their marriage. Critics were then freed to discount her call for reform as the self-serving demand of a woman of easy virtue, as Benjamin Silliman did throughout his *Letters of Shahcoolen.* Timothy Dwight, who had taken the lead in offering young women education on a par with young men, shuddered at Wollstonecraft and held "the female philosopher" up to ridicule in "Morpheus," a political satire which ran for eight installments in the *New-England Palladium.*[25] Dwight called Wollstonecraft "an unchaste woman," "a sentimental lover," "a strumpet"; as Silliman had done, he linked her radical politics to free love. " 'Away with all monopolies,' " Dwight has her say. " 'I hate these exclusive rights; these privileged orders. I am for having everything free, and open to all; like the air which we breathe. . . .' "

" 'Love, particularly, I suppose, Madam [?]' "

" 'Yes, brute, love, if you please, and everything else.' "[26] Even Charles Brockden Brown's feminist tract *Alcuin* concluded with a long gloss on the same theme: to permit any change in women's status was to imply the acceptance of free love. Alcuin, who has been playing the conservative skeptic, concludes that once it is established that marriage "has no other criterion than custom," it becomes simply "a mode of sexual intercourse." His friend Mrs. Carter protests energetically that free love is not at all what she wanted; " 'because I demand an equality of conditions among beings that equally partake of the same divine reason, would you rashly infer that I was an enemy to the institution of marriage itself?' " Brown lets her have the last word, but he does not make Alcuin change his mind.[27]

Dwight had one final charge to make against Wollstonecraft; he attacked her plea that women emerge from the confines of their families. " 'Who will make our puddings, Madam?' " his protagonist asks. When she responds: " 'Make them yourself,' " he presses harder: " 'Who shall nurse us when we are sick?' " and, finally, " 'Who shall nurse our children?' " The last question reduces the fictional Mary to blushes and silence.[28]

It would not, however, reduce Rush, or Murray, or Brown, to blushes and silence. (Nor, I think, would it have so affected the real Mary Wollstonecraft.) They had neither predicted that women would cease their housewifely duties nor demanded that women should. Priscilla Mason's demand that hitherto male professions be opened to women was highly unusual, and even she apologized for it before she left the podium. There were, it is true, some other hints that women might claim the privileges and duties of male citizens of the republic. In *Alcuin,* Mrs. Carter explains her intense political disappointment through the first two chapters, arguing that Americans had been false to their own revolutionary promises in denying political status to women. "If a stranger questions me concerning the nature of our government, I answer, that in this happy climate all men are free: the people are the source of all authority; from them it flows, and to them, in due season, it returns . . . our liberty consists in the choice of our governors: all, as reason requires, have a part in this choice, yet not without a few exceptions . . . females . . . minors . . . the poor . . . slaves. . . . I am tired of explaining this charming system of equality and independence." St. George Tucker, commenting on Blackstone, acknowledged that women were taxed without representation; like "aliens . . . children under the age of discretion, idiots, and lunatics," American women had neither political nor civil rights. "I fear there is little reason for a compliment to our laws for their respect and favour to the female sex," Tucker concluded. As Tucker had done, John Adams acknowledged that women's experience of the republic was different from men's; he hesitantly admitted that the republic claimed the right "to govern women without their consent." For a brief period from 1790 to

1807, New Jersey law granted the franchise to "all free inhabitants," and on occasion women exercised that right; it is conceivable that New Jersey might have stood as a precedent for other states. Instead, New Jersey's legislature rewrote its election law; the argument for political competence was taken no further.[29]

All of these were hesitant suggestions introduced into a hostile intellectual milieu in which female learning was equated with pedantry and masculinity. To resist those assumptions was to undertake a great deal; it was a task for which no one was ready; indeed, it is impossible to say that anyone really wanted to try. Instead, the reformers would have been quick to reply, with Brown's Mrs. Carter, that they had no intention of abandoning marriage; that they had every intention of making puddings and nursing babies; that the education they demanded was primarily to enable women to function more effectively within their traditional sphere, and only secondarily to fulfill demands like Priscilla Mason's that they emerge from it. People were complaining that American women were boring, frivolous, spending excessive amounts of money for impractical fashions; very well, a vigorously educated woman would be less likely to bore her husband, less likely to be a spendthrift, better able to cope with adverse fortune. Judith Sargent Murray versified an equation:

> Where'er the maiden Industry appears,
> A thrifty contour every object wears;
> And when fair order with the nymph combines,
> Adjusts, directs, and every plan designs,
> Then Independence fills her peerless seat,
> And lo! the matchless trio is complete.

Murray repeatedly made the point that the happiness of the nation depended on the happiness of families; and that the "felicity of families" is dependent on the presence of women who are "properly methodical, and economical in their distributions and expenditures of time." She denied that "the present enlarged plan of female education" was incompatible with traditional notions of women's duties: she predicted that the "daughters of Columbia" would be free of *"invidious and rancorous passions"* and "even the semblance of pedantry"; "when they become wives and mothers, they will fill with honour the parts allotted them."[30]

Rarely, in the literature of the early Republic, do we find any objection to the notion that women belong in the home; what emerges is the argument that the Revolution had enlarged the significance of what women did in their homes. Benjamin Rush's phrasing of this point is instructive; when he defined the goals of republican women, he was careful not to include a claim to political power: "The equal share that every citizen has in the liberty and the possible share he may have in the government of our country make it necessary that our ladies should be qualified to a certain degree by a peculiar and suitable education, *to concur in instructing their sons in the principles of liberty and government.*" The Young Ladies' Academy promised "not wholly to engross the mind" of each pupil, "but to allow her to prepare for the duties in life to which she may be destined." Miss P.W. Jackson, graduating from Mrs. Rowson's Academy, explained what she had learned of the goals of the educated woman: "A woman who is skilled in every useful art, who practices every domestic virtue ... may, by her precept and example, inspire her brothers, her husband, or her sons, with such a love of virtue, such just ideas of the true value of civil liberty ... that future heroes and statesmen, who arrive at the summit of military or political fame, shall *exaltingly declare, it is to my mother I owe this elevation.*" By their household management, by their refusal to countenance vice, crime, or cruelty in their suitors and husbands, women had the power to direct the moral development of the male citizens of the republic. The influence women had on children, especially on their sons, gave them ultimate responsibility for the future of the new nation.[31]

This constellation of ideas, and the republican rhetoric which made it convincing, appears at great length in the Columbia College commencement oration of 1795. Its title was "Female Influence"; behind the flowery rhetoric lurks a social and political message:

> Let us then figure to ourselves the accomplished woman, surrounded by a sprightly band, from the babe that imbibes the nutritive fluid, to the generous youth just ripening into manhood, and the lovely virgin. . . . Let us contemplate the mother distributing the mental nourishment to the fond smiling circle, by means proportionate to their different powers of reception, watching the gradual openings of their minds, and studying their various turns of temper. . . . Religion, fairest offspring of the skies, smiles auspicious on her endeavours; the Genius of Liberty hovers triumphant over the glorious scene. . . . Yes, ye fair, the reformation of a world is in your power. . . . Reflect on the result of your efforts. Contemplate the rising glory of confederated America. Consider that your exertions can best secure, increase, and perpetuate it. The solidity and stability of the liberties of your country rest with you; since Liberty is never sure, 'till Virtue reigns triumphant. . . . Already may we see the lovely daughters of Columbia asserting the importance and the honour of their sex. It rests with you to make this retreat [from the corruptions of Europe] doubly peaceful, doubly happy, by banishing from it those crimes and corrup-

tions, which have never yet failed of giving rise to tyranny, or anarchy. While you thus keep our country virtuous, you maintain its independence. . . .[32]

Defined this way, the educated woman ceased to threaten the sanctity of marriage; the bluestocking need not be masculine. In this awkward—and in the 1790s still only vaguely expressed—fashion, the traditional womanly virtues were endowed with political purpose. A pivotal political role was assigned to the least political inhabitants of the Republic. Ironically, the same women who were denied political identity were counted on to maintain the republican quality of the new nation. "Let the ladies of a country be educated properly," Rush said, "and they will not only make and administer its laws, but form its manners and character."[33]

When Americans addressed themselves to the matter of the role of women, they found that those who admired bluestockings and those who feared them could agree on one thing: in a world where moral influences were fast dissipating, women as a group seemed to represent moral stability. Few in the early republic demanded, in a sustained way, substantial revisions in women's political or legal status; few spoke to the nascent class of unskilled women workers. But many took pride in the assertion that properly educated republican women would stay in the home and, from that vantage point, would shape the characters of their sons and husbands in the direction of benevolence, self-restraint, and responsible independence. They refuted charges of free love and masculinization; in doing so they created a justification for woman as household goddess so deeply felt that one must be permitted to suspect that many women of their generation were *refusing* to be household goddesses.[34] They began to make the argument for intelligent household management that Catharine Beecher, a generation later, would enshrine in her *Treatise on Domestic Economy* as woman's highest goal. The Daughters of Columbia became, in effect, the Mothers of the Victorians. Whether Judith Sargent Murray, Charles Brockden Brown, or Benjamin Rush would have approved the ultimate results of their work is hard to say.

NOTES

1. *The Gleaner,* III (Boston, 1798), 189.
2. Montesquieu's comment that republics differed from other political systems

by the reliance they placed on virtue is explored in Howard Mumford Jones, *O Strange New World* (New York, 1964), p. 431.

3. August 1792, pp. 121–123.

4. "Thoughts upon Female Education, Accommodated to the Present State of Society, Manners, and Government in the United States of America" (Philadelphia and Boston, 1787). Reprinted in Frederick Rudolph, ed., *Essays on Education in the Early Republic* (Cambridge, Mass., 1865), p. 39.

5. "The greater proportion of young women are trained up by thoughtless parents, in ease and luxury, with no other dependence for their future support than the precarious chance of establishing themselves by marriage: for this purpose (the men best know why) elaborate attention is paid to external attractions and accomplishments, to the neglect of more useful and solid acquirements. . . . [Marriage is the] *sole* method of procuring for themselves an establishment." *New York Magazine*, August 1797, p. 406. For comment on the marriage market, see letter signed "A Matrimonial Republican" in Philadelphia *Lady's Magazine*, July 1792, pp. 64–67; "Legal Prostitution, Or Modern Marriage," Boston *Independent Chronicle*, October 28, 1793. For criticism of fashion, see *American Magazine*, December 1787, p. 39; July 1788, p. 594; *American Museum*, August 1788, p. 119; *Massachusetts Mercury*, August 16, 1793; January 16, 1795.

6. *New York Magazine*, August 1797, p. 406; Philadelphia *Universal Asylum and Columbian Magazine*, July 1791, p. 11.

7. Murray, *Gleaner*, I, 168, 193.

8. Charles Brockden Brown, *Ormond; Or the Secret Witness*, ed. by Ernest Marchand (New York, 1799; reprinted 1937, 1962), p. 19.

9. *Ibid.*, pp. 98–99.

10. "It was obvious to suppose that a woman thus fearless and sagacious had not been inactive at a period like the present, which called forth talents and courage without distinction of sex, and had been particularly distinguished by female enterprise and heroism." *Ibid.*, p. 170.

11. For examples of such lists, see: Murray, *Gleaner*, III, 200–219; John Blair Linn, *The Powers of Genius: A Poem in Three Parts* (Philadelphia, 1802); Philadelphia *Weekly Magazine*, August 4, 11, 1798; *Port Folio*, February 12, 1803; September 27, 1806; Philadelphia *Minerva*, March 14, 1795. For the admiration expressed by Abigail Adams and Mercy Otis Warren for Catharine Macaulay, see Abigail Adams to Isaac Smith, Jr., April 20, 1771; Abigail Adams to Catharine Sawbridge Macaulay, n.d., 1774; Mercy Otis Warren to Abigail Adams, January 28, 1775; in L. H. Butterfield, ed., *Adams Family Correspondence*, I (Cambridge, Mass., 1963), 76–77, 177–179, 181–183. For the circle of English "bluestockings," in the 1780s, see M. G. Jones, *Hannah More* (Cambridge, 1952), pp. 41–76.

12. *Massachusetts Magazine*, II (March 1790), 133; *Universal Asylum and Columbian Magazine*, July 1791, p. 9; Thomas Cooper, "Propositions Respecting the Foundation of Civil Government," in *Political Arithmetic* (Philadelphia [?], 1798), p. 27. See also *Boston Weekly Magazine*, May 21, 1803, pp. 121–122; *American Museum*, January 1787, p. 59; Philadelphia *Lady's Magazine*, June 1792.

13. J. A. Neale, "An Essay on the Genius and Education of the Fair Sex," Philadelphia *Minerva*, April 4, March 21, 1795.

14. *Remarks on Education: Illustrating the Close Connection between Virtue and Wisdom* (Philadelphia, 1798), reprinted in Rudolph, *Essays on Education*, p. 211.

Smith did acknowledge that female instruction was important, but commented that concepts of what it should be were so varied that he feared to make any proposals, and despaired of including women in the scheme he was then devising. "It is sufficient, perhaps, for the present, that the improvement of women is marked by a rapid progress and that a prospect opens equal to their most ambitious desires" (p. 217). The other prizewinner, Samuel Knox, proposed to admit girls to the primary schools in his system, but not to the academies or colleges. Knox's essay, "An Essay on the Best System of Liberal Education," may be found in Rudolph, *Essays on Education,* pp. 271–372.

15. Charles E. Cunningham, *Timothy Dwight: 1752–1817: A Biography* (New York, 1942), pp. 154–163.

16. Noah Webster, "Importance of Female Education," in *American Magazine,* May 1788, pp. 368, 369. This essay was part of his pamphlet *On the Education of Youth in America* (Boston, 1790), conveniently reprinted in Rudolph, *Essays on Education,* pp. 41–78. *Weekly Magazine,* April 7, 1798; Murray, *The Gleaner,* I, 70–71.

17. Benjamin Rush, "Thoughts upon Female Education," in Rudolph, *Essays on Education,* pp. 25–40. See also the comments of the Reverend James Sproat, a member of the Board of Visitors, June 10, 1789, in *The Rise and Progress of the Young Ladies' Academy of Philadelphia; Containing an Account of a Number of Public Examinations and Commencements; the Charter and Bye-Laws; Likewise, a Number of Orations delivered by the Young Ladies, and several by the Trustees of Said Institution* (Philadelphia, 1794), p. 24.

18. Benjamin Say, "Address," December 4, 1789, in *Rise and Progress of the Young Ladies' Academy,* p. 33; Benjamin Rush, *Syllabus of Lectures, Containing the Application of the Principles of Natural Philosophy . . .* (Philadelphia, 1787). Rush, of course, was waging his own crusade against the classics as inappropriate in a republic; he argued elsewhere that to omit Latin and Greek would have the beneficial effect of diminishing "the present immense disparity which subsists between the sexes, in the degrees of their education and knowledge." When his contemporaries omitted the classics from the female curriculum it was usually because they thought women's minds were not up to it. Rush, "Observations upon the Study of the Latin and Greek Languages," in *Essays, Literary, Moral and Philosophical* (Philadelphia, 1798), p. 44.

19. Priscilla Mason, "Oration," May 15, 1793, in *Rise and Progress of the Young Ladies' Academy,* pp. 90–95. See also the valedictory oration by Molly Wallace, June 12, 1792, *ibid.,* pp. 73–79.

20. Letter signed M.G., "American Lounger," *Port Folio,* April 7, 1804.

21. Gertrude Meredith to David Meredith, May 3, 1804, Meredith Papers, Historical Society of Pennsylvania; Philadelphia *Evening Fireside,* April 6, 1805.

22. *New-England Palladium,* September 18, 1801; *American Magazine,* February 1788, p. 134; *Lady's Magazine,* January 1793, pp. 68–72. (The "battle at Odiham" refers to a famous bare-knuckle prize fight, one of the earliest major events in the history of boxing, fought in 1788 by Daniel Mendoza and Richard Humphries in Hampshire, England.) Other attacks on female pedantry, which express the fear that intellectual women will be masculine, are found in the *American Magazine,* March 1788, pp. 244–245 ("To be lovely you must be content to be women . . . and leave the masculine virtues, and the profound researches of study to the province of the other sex"); *New-England Palladium,* September 4, 18, December 4,

1801, March 5, 9, 1802; Benjamin Silliman, *Letters of Shahcoolen, a Hindu Philosophy, Residing in Philadelphia; To His Friend, El Hassan, an Inhabitant of Delhi* (Boston, 1802), pp. 23–24, 62; *American Museum,* December 1788, p. 491; *Boston Weekly Magazine,* March 24, 1804, p. 86 ("Warlike women, learned women, and women who are politicians, equally abandon the circle which nature and institutions have traced round their sex; they convert themselves into men").

23. *Extracts from the Journal of Elizabeth Drinker, from 1759 to 1807, A.D.,* ed. by Henry D. Biddle (Philadelphia, 1889), p. 285. The entry is dated April 22, 1796.

24. Mary Wollstonecraft, *A Vindication of the Rights of Woman, With Strictures on Political and Moral Subjects* (New York, 1891), pp. 23, 149–156.

25. *New-England Palladium,* November 24, 27, December 8, 11, 15, 1801; March 2, 5, 9, 1802. Identification of Dwight as author is made by Robert Edson Lee, "Timothy Dwight and the Boston *Palladium,*" *New England Quarterly,* XXXV (1962), 229–239.

26. *New-England Palladium,* March 9, 1802.

27. Charles Brockden Brown and Lee R. Edwards, *Alcuin: A Dialogue* (New York, 1971), pp. 44–88.

28. *New-England Palladium,* March 9, 1802.

29. Brown, *Alcuin,* pp. 32–33; St. George Tucker, *Blackstone's Commentaries: With Notes of Reference, to the Constitution and Laws, of the Federal Government of the United States, and of the Commonwealth of Virginia,* II (Philadelphia, 1803), 145, 445; John Adams to James Sullivan, May 26, 1776, in *The Works of John Adams,* ed. by Charles Francis Adams, IX (1856), 375–379; Edward Raymond Turner, "Women's Suffrage in New Jersey: 1790–1807," *Smith College Studies in History,* I (1916), 165–187. Opposition to woman suffrage apparently surfaced after women voted as a bloc in an unsuccessful attempt to influence the outcome of an Essex County election in 1797.

30. *Gleaner,* I, 161, 12, 29, 191, 190.

31. Rush, "Thoughts upon Female Education," in Rudolph, *Essays on Education,* p. 28 (my italics); "On Female Education," *Port Folio,* May 1809, p. 388; *Boston Weekly Magazine,* October 29, 1803.

32. *New York Magazine,* May 1795, pp. 301–305.

33. Rush, "Thoughts upon Female Education," in Rudolph, *Essays on Education,* p. 36.

34. See, for example, *Boston Weekly Magazine,* December 18, 1802; *Weekly Magazine,* March 3, 1798; *Port Folio,* February 12, 1803, March 3, 1804, April 20, 1805.

Suggested Readings for Part I

Akers, Charles. *Abigail Adams*. Boston: Little, Brown & Co., 1979.

Benson, Mary Sumner. *Women in Eighteenth Century America*. New York: Columbia University Press, 1935.

Block, Ruth H. "American Feminine Ideals in Transition: The Rise of the Moral Mother, 1785-1815." *Feminist Studies* 4 (1978): 101-26.

Buel, Joy D., and Buel, Richard, Jr. *The Way of Duty: A Woman and Her Family in Revolutionary America*. New York: Norton, 1984.

Chambers-Schiller, Lee Virginia. *Liberty A Better Husband: Single Women in America: The Generation of 1780-1840*. New Haven: Yale University Press, 1984.

Cott, Nancy, "Eighteenth Century Family and Social Life Revealed in Massachusetts Divorce Records." *Journal of Social History* 10 (1976): 20-43.

Cowing, Cedric B. "Sex and Preaching in the Great Awakening." *American Quarterly* 30 (1968): 624-44.

Demos, John. *Entertaining Satan: Witchcraft and the Culture of Early New England*. New York: Oxford University Press, 1982.

Gladwin, Lee A. "Tobacco and Sex: Some Factors Affecting Non-Marital Sexual Behavior in Colonial Virginia." *Journal of Social History* 12 (1978): 57-75.

Greven, Philip J. *Four Generations: Population, Land and Family in Colonial Andover, Massachusetts*. Ithaca: Cornell University Press, 1970.

Hoffer, Peter, and Hull, N.E.H. *Murdering Mothers: Infanticide in England and New England*. New York: Oxford University Press, 1981.

Kerber, Linda. *Women of the Republic*. Chapel Hill: University of North Carolina Press, 1980.

Keyssan, Alexander. "Widowhood in Eighteenth-Century Massachusetts: A Problem in the History of the Family." *Perspectives in American History* 8 (1974): 83-119.

Koehler, Lyle. *A Search for Power: The "Weaker Sex" in Seventeenth-Century New England*. Urbana: University of Illinois Press, 1980.

Kulikoff, Alan. "The Beginnings of the Afro-American Family in Maryland." In *Law, Society and Politics in Early Maryland*, edited by A.C. Land, L.G. Carr, and E.G. Papenfuse. Baltimore: The Johns Hopkins University Press, 1977.

Lewis, Jan. *The Pursuit of Happiness: Family and Values in Jefferson's Virginia*. New York: Cambridge University Press, 1983.

Lindemann, Barbara S. " 'To Ravish and Carnally Know': Rape in Eighteenth Century Massachusetts." *Signs* 10 (Autumn 1984): 63-82.

Lockridge, Kenneth A. *Literacy in Colonial New England*. New York: W.W. Norton & Co., 1974.

Masson, Margaret W. "The Typology of the Female Model for the Regenerate: Puritan Preaching, 1690-1730." *Signs* 2 (1976): 304-315.

Meehan, Thomas R. " 'Not Made Out of Levity': Evolution of Divorce in Early Pennsylvania." *Pennsylvania Magazine of History and Biography* 42 (1968): 441-464.

Mills, Gary B. "Coincoin: An Eighteenth Century 'Liberated' Woman." *Journal of Southern History* 42 (1976): 205-222.

Morgan, Edmund S. *The Puritan Family.* Boston: Boston Public Library, 1944.

_____. "The Puritans and Sex." *New England Quarterly* 15 (1942): 591-607.

Mullin, Gerald W. *Flight and Rebellion: Slave Resistance in Eighteenth Century Virginia.* New York: Oxford University Press, 1972.

Norton, Mary Beth. "The Evolution of White Women's Experience in Early America." *American Historical Review* 89 (June 1984): 593-619.

_____. *Liberty's Daughters: The Revolutionary Experiences of American Women, 1750-1800.* Boston: Little, Brown & Co., 1980.

_____. "Eighteenth Century Women in Peace and War: The Case of the Loyalists." *William and Mary Quarterly* 33 (1976): 386-409.

Salmon, Marylynn. "Women and Property in South Carolina: The Evidence From Marriage Settlements, 1730 to 1830." *William and Mary Quarterly* 39 (October 1982): 654-85.

Scholten, Catherine. " 'On the Importance of the Obstetrik Art': Changing Customs of Childbirth in America, 1790-1825." *William and Mary Quarterly* 34 (1977): 425-45.

Shammas, Carole. "The Domestic Environment in Early Modern England and America." *Journal of Social History* 14 (1980-81): 3-24.

_____. "The Female Social Structure of Philadelphia in 1775." *Pennsylvania Magazine of History and Biography* 107 (1983):69-84.

Smith, Daniel B. *Inside the Great House: Planter Family Life in Eighteenth Century Chesapeake Society.* Ithaca: Cornell University Press, 1980.

Smith, Daniel Scott and Hindus, Michael S. "Premarital Pregnancy in America, 1640-1971: An Overview and Interpretation." *Journal of Interdisciplinary History* 5 (1975): 535-70.

Spruill, Julia Cherry. *Women's Life and Work in the Southern Colonies.* Chapel Hill: University of North Carolina Press, 1938.

Stone, Lawrence. *The Family, Sex and Marriage in England, 1500-1800.* New York: Harper & Row, 1977.

Thompson, Roger. *Women in Stuart England and America.* London: Routledge and Kegan Paul, 1974.

Ulrich, Laurel Thatcher. "Virtuous Women Found: New England Ministerial Literature, 1668-1735." *American Quarterly* 28 (1976): 20-40.

_____. *Good Wives: Image and Reality in the Lives of Women in Northern New England 1650-1750.* New York: Oxford University Press, 1982.

_____. " 'A Friendly Neighbor': Social Dimensions of Daily Work in Northern Colonial New England." *Feminist Studies* 6 (Summer 1980): 392-405.

Wright, Mary C. "Economic Development and Native Women in the Early Nineteenth Century." *American Quarterly* 33 (1981): 525-36.

~2~

VICTORIAN IMAGES

Nineteenth-century Americans were haunted by the prospect that unprecedented change in the nation's economy would bring social chaos. In the years following 1820, after several decades of relative stability, the American economy entered a period of sustained and extremely rapid growth that continued to the end of the nineteenth century. Accompanying this growth was a structural change that featured increasing economic diversification and a gradual shift in the nation's labor force from agriculture to manufacturing and other non-agricultural pursuits.

Although the birth rate continued to decline from the high level of the colonial period, the population roughly doubled every generation during the century. As the population grew, its makeup also changed. Massive waves of immigration brought new ethnic groups into the country. Geographic and social mobility—downward as well as upward—touched almost everyone. Local studies indicate that nearly three-quarters of the population—in the North and South, in the emerging cities of the Northeast, and in the restless rural counties of the West—changed their residence each decade. As a consequence, David Donald has written, "social atomization affected every segment of society," and it seemed to many Americans that "all the recognized values of orderly civilization were gradually being eroded."

Rapid industrialization and increased geographic mobility in the nineteenth century had special implications for American women because these changes reinforced the social distinctions that had become manifest in the post-Revolutionary period. In the context of extreme competitiveness and dizzying social change, the household lost many of its earlier functions and the Victorian "home" came to serve as a haven of tranquillity and order. As the size of American families decreased, the roles of husband and wife became more clearly differentiated than ever before. In the middle class especially, men participated in the productive economy while women ruled the home and served as the custodians of civility and culture. The intimacy of colonial marriage was rent, and a gulf that at times seemed unbridgeable was created between husbands and wives.

Along with the heightened understanding of male and female spheres of influence, the life styles of middle-class women became increasingly distinct from those of their lower-class sisters. Gerda Lerner focuses upon the ways in which social and economic change in the early nineteenth century affected the status of women of different classes in "The Lady and the Mill Girl." Medicine, law, business, and science—all areas in which women had played at least modest roles in the colonial period—became increasingly professional. Consequently, they were closed to middle-class women, who were expected to conform to the Victorian model of true womanhood—the gracious lady. At the same time, lower-class women were being forced out of their homes and into the expanding factory system, creating a second social type—the mill girl. "In the urbanized and industrialized Northeast the life experience of middle-class women was different in almost every respect from that of lower-class women."

The Victorian idealization of womanhood continued an earlier trend, the consequences of which are difficult to weigh. The position of the middle-class woman in the nineteenth century was indeed ambiguous, and it typifies the paradoxical role women have played throughout American history. Women became objects of both adoration and domination. Their moral superiority to the brutish and materialistic male was readily acknowledged, but their sphere of influence was confined to the family and the home. Women were accorded the power of intuition in a world that paid homage to reason; they were given a monopoly on piety, purity, and submissiveness in a society that increasingly trivialized these virtues. Although they gained greater control over their sexual lives, causing the birth rate to decline, women paid for this boon with their own desexualization. Denial of women's sexual pleasure and glorification of the womb symbolized female sexuality in the nineteenth century. Mary Ryan has stated bluntly, "Once active sexual desire and the organ of sexual pleasure, the clitoris, had been all but eradicated from female physiology, the nineteenth century gynecologist proceeded to elevate a woman's reproductive system to a position of biological hegemony."

However, the Victorian image was a malleable one; it could be manipulated to justify often conflicting life styles and be made to serve the interests of both reaction and reform. Ronald Hogeland has shown that the Victorian conception of womanhood could accommodate at least four distinct life styles, which he refers to as ornamental, romanticized, evangelical, and radical, each generating different forms of political behavior. The attitudes underlying the "cult of true womanhood" that characterized increasingly industrial, bourgeois New England differed in emphasis, if not content, from the values that idealized ladylike gentility in the plantation South. Men shaped each of these life styles and defined the proper sphere of women's activity in a limited fashion that assured male domination of society, politics, and the economy. Yet the association of women with the moral welfare of society allowed them to find within what the abolitionist Sarah M. Grimke ironically called, "the bonds of womanhood," a certain identity and sense of purpose that served many of their own needs.

The culture of Victorian America, which generated the "cult of true womanhood," was dominated by a form of evangelical Protestantism that led to what Ann Douglas termed the "feminization of American culture" in the nineteenth century. Americans had long distinguished between the faculties of the head and the heart, and at this time these faculties became increasingly defined as respectively masculine and feminine. Piety became a uniquely female response; and women, by their sheer numbers in the churches, molded the nature of Victorian religion. Disestablishment (deprivation of the status and privileges of the Church) had made ministers more dependent upon their congregations for support, and they turned to the growing number of women parishioners as natural allies. Sympathetic to women's frustrations, the clergy encouraged them to take an active role in religious activities. A wide variety of church-related voluntary organizations grew up in the early nineteenth century to support missions, education, and moral reform.

In the selection "Religion and the Bonds of Womanhood," Nancy F. Cott examines the feminization of religion in New England. She illustrates the increasing tendency of ministers to associate a religious temperament with femininity as women "flocked into the churches and church-related organizations." Cott shows, however, that, for the women involved, adherence to evangelical Christianity brought opportunity for legitimate self-expression and was a source of identity and purpose as part of a "community of peers." In reality, women found modest ways to benefit from the restricting Victorian image of true womanhood.

For no one did the contradiction between the image and the reality stand out more sharply than for the Southern lady, about whom Anne F. Scott has written so eloquently. In no other section of the country did the "ornamental" style of womanhood become so much a part of the sustaining myths of the society. In contrast to the image of the somewhat frivolous Southern belle sweeping about the plantation in an imported gown, exuding virtue, charm, and accomplishment, most Southern ladies assumed many burdensome tasks related to the domestic administration of the plantation system. In her essay "Women's Perspective on the Patriarchy of the 1850s," Scott supplements her earlier work by showing how the realities of life for the Southern lady conflicted with the "domestic metaphor" that underlay the Southerner's conception of an organic and patriarchal society. Although there is good reason to doubt that these women coldly resisted the pleasures of the flesh, the conflict between the ideal of motherhood and the attendant dangers of pregnancy and childbirth was one of the greatest sources of unhappiness for Southern women. Combined with the gnawing sense of betrayal derived from knowledge of their husbands' sexual relations with slave women, the conditions of Southern life helped to create discontent among "the female portion of the population" within what pro-slavery propagandist Langdon Cheves predicted would be "the most splendid empire upon which the sun has ever shown."

No organized women's movement, however, appeared in the antebellum South. When the Southern states seceded, women gave the rebellion their hearty support, supplying food and clothing for Confederate soldiers, nursing the sick and wounded, and assuming many tasks on the home front that had formerly been performed by men. Although women did benefit from the radical Reconstruction governments, many were more adamant than were Southern men in their opposition to Reconstruction. Eliza Frances Andrews's diary bristles with hostility toward the self-righteous "crack-brained fanatic" Yankees. "They have placed our people in the most humiliating position possible to devise," she wrote in 1865, "where we are obliged either to submit to the insolence of our own servants or appeal to our Northern masters for protection, as if we were slaves ourselves—and that is what they are trying to make us."

Of course, most women in nineteenth-century America could not afford to aspire to the bourgeois definition of true womanhood. Recent studies support the slaveholders' contention that the conditions of the free blacks were miserable and indicate that in the North as well as the South they were plagued by declining economic status and increased family disorganization in the decades preceding the Civil War. But the most obvious contradiction to the Victorian stereotype was presented by the nearly two million black women held in bondage within the fifteen slave states of antebellum America. The patriarchal image of the contented slave is no more accurate than that of the contented Southern lady serving her appointed master.

In many ways slavery bore more heavily upon women than upon men. The abolitionists—particularly female abolitionists—emphasized the degradation of women and the destruction of the family inherent in the economic and social relations structured by the "peculiar institution." Most scholars have repeated the abolitionists' depiction of slavery, but they have ignored the ways in which the abolitionist perspective reflected the Victorian image of womanhood. Two themes were prevalent in this indictment: slavery destroyed the family through the sale of children and through the refusal to legalize the marriage bond; and slavery encouraged the sexual exploitation of slave women by masters and their white retainers.

Recent studies suggest that claims of the total brutalization of women under slavery have been exaggerated, since resistance took many forms. Family ties among the slaves were far stronger than previous accounts have suggested. These intimate family relationships helped the slaves come to terms with the system. Historians such as Herbert Gutman have convincingly demonstrated the dominance of the two-parent household in the slave quarters. Refuting the white myth of licentious and promiscuous blacks, enslaved yet free of social constraint, he has shown that prenuptial sex coexisted with marital fidelity, as in many premodern societies. Within the slave community sexual behavior followed a well-structured pattern determined by the experience of slavery and cultural predisposition rather than by the dictates of white society. This is best illustrated by the slaves' taboo against marrying blood-cousins, which went unnoticed by whites and which stood in stark contrast to planter practices. Sale of slaves undoubtedly did not break up as many families as the abolitionists believed, although every black woman knew that her "chill'n could be sold away. . . ." Critics have claimed that abolitionists' views of the sexual exploitation of enslaved black women were warped by the extreme sexual repression within their own lives. However, documentary evidence clearly supports the widespread belief that miscegenation was rampant and that it was a central element of the society that scarred the lives of both black and white women.

While the most exciting recent work on women in slavery has focused on the question of the slave family, Jacqueline Jones attempts to broaden our focus in "My Mother Was Much of a Woman." Clearly the title reflects the vitality of the black family under slavery, but Jones emphasizes the trials of women living under the double burden of race and gender in a patriarchal society. She reminds her readers that ultimately slavery meant hard work and a rather tenuous control over one's life and body. The various structures within the covert slave community undoubtedly mitigated the plight of the female slave, but did not entirely eradicate sexually defined roles. What E. Franklin Frazier called "motherhood in bondage," involved numerous burdens and very few rewards.

Yet, in the wake of the Civil War black women desired to establish the legitimacy of their marriages and to provide the necessary basis for a stable family life. Although black men often attempted to emulate the Victorian ideal, black women, of necessity, continued to play the important role they had assumed under slavery. Until they were undermined by economic and political discrimination, such attempts to establish stable family ties were surprisingly successful.

Most working women in nineteenth-century America were not black, and the plight of those whom Lerner has associated with the image of the "mill girl" was an arduous one. The vast majority of adult women married and continued to work within their homes, meeting the multitude of demands placed upon them as farm women or attempting to master the fundamentals of "domestic science" detailed in the plethora of housekeeping manuals directed to middle-class women in the mid-nineteenth century. Ironically, as social and economic change created conditions that generated the cult of domesticity, an increasing number of unmarried women moved out of the home and into the ranks of paid labor. The most common job open to such women—that of domestic servant—represented little more than an extension of their former occupational role. Although the majority of working women continued to be domestics at the end of the century, the factory system employed large numbers of women because of their low labor cost and the relative scarcity of male workers. A handful of errant romantics have extolled the "freedom of the factory," but the women in the factories were generally secondary earners working to supplement a meagre family income.

At its inception, the Waltham or "boarding house" system of labor organization compared more closely to the idyllic view of the factory and did not conflict directly with the Victorian conception of true womanhood. In contrast to the Rhode Island or "family" system which, as its name suggests, was based upon the employment of whole families, the key feature of the Waltham system was the exploitation of young women, mostly with rural origins. For relatively short periods of time, they lived in company-owned boarding houses supervised by matronly housemothers. Generally these young women worked in order to send a brother to school or to provide themselves with an adequate trousseau. As the most famous of their number, Lucy Larcom, said in her autobiography, they were "happy in the knowledge that, at the longest, our employment was only to be temporary."

However, reality never conformed completely to the portrait of the Waltham system sketched in the pages of the *Lowell Offering*, a periodical written by mill girls and actively supported by mill owners, who wished to popularize a favorable image of their factories. In the two decades before the Civil War, that reality was changing and the Waltham system was deteriorating. During these years, wages in the textile industry, which had always been low, began to decline relative to wages paid by other jobs employing mostly women. Mill owners successfully resisted employee demands for improved working conditions and shorter hours. As a result, more children were drawn into the mills, and native-born women were increasingly replaced by the incoming flood of Irish and other immigrants. A few highly skilled women imported from Scotland were sufficiently well paid to save a portion of their earnings and to use their jobs in the mills to improve their lot. But thousands of unskilled immigrant women, who endured long hours and low pay in the textile mills of New England and the sweatshops of New York and Philadelphia, barely survived. In her essay "The Origins of the Sweatshop," Christine Stansell deals with the neglected subject of women's work in the industrializing metropolis. New York was not a small and planned mill town like Lowell and yet, it was "the foremost manufacturing center of America." It had a complex, multi-tiered economy that tended to continue to employ women as outside workers. In fact Stansell shows that "outside work had become the prevalent form of women's employment" in New York during the mid-nineteenth century spurt of industrialization. In the trades there continued to be a sexual division of labor which mirrored, in a refracted way, the middle-class Victorian conception of "separate spheres." Yet, while "women's domesticity became a practical necessity of industrial capitalism," these women remained poor and irregularly employed—at best, part of a struggling member of a family economy, and at worst, alone. By 1865, New York City had nearly 75,000 women workers struggling at the edge of poverty. Consequently, prostitution was extremely widespread.

Throughout the nineteenth century, a minority of women left the confines of their middle-class homes to join the vast array of reform movements that characterized the period. Early in the century, they became involved in the work of a growing number of benevolent societies, and by the 1840s the outlines of what would become "the woman movement" was clear. American feminism was part of the general ferment of humanitarian reform that appeared in the antebellum period. Religious enthusiasm attracted increasing numbers of women to antislavery, temperance, pacifism, prison reform, and other causes.

Although women constituted a majority of the supporters of abolition and temperance, they were generally denied leadership positions within these movements and often found men objecting to their activity on the grounds that it was inappropriate for women to speak publicly. Even among the radical abolitionists the question of women's participation was a divisive issue. Criticism of women who would assume "the place and tone of man as a public reformer" prompted Sarah Grimke to write her *Letters on the Equality of the Sexes* in defense of her reform activities. Other women reformers considered separate action to secure civil and political rights equal to those of men. After being barred from taking their seats at the World Anti-Slavery Convention in 1840 simply because of their sex, Lucretia Mott and Elizabeth Cady Stanton moved increasingly toward a more vigorous assertion of women's rights. In 1848 they called together a convention at Seneca Falls, New York, which issued its own declaration of independence proclaiming that "all men and women are created equal." This launched the struggle "to secure to themselves their sacred right to the elective franchise."

In "Women's Rights before the Civil War," Ellen C. DuBois traces the emergence of the women's rights movement. Like other writers on the subject, she finds the origins of women's activism in evangelical religion and political abolitionism. DuBois, however, emphasizes the problems faced in the infancy of the women's movement and the importance of factional splits within the abolition movement over the issue of women's participation. She also argues that the demand for the vote which came to be the focus of the women's movement was essentially radical and feminist, because in the context of nineteenth-century political theory it implied a challenge to the concept of a separate woman's sphere of influence and "the assumption of male authority over women."

Although the Civil War raised feminists' expectations of success in their battle for the vote, the passage of the Fifteenth Amendment granting black men the right to vote created a crisis in feminist ranks. Women had contributed in many ways to the Northern war effort. Mary Livermore was one of the leaders of the United States Sanitary Commission that employed thousands of women who distributed food and medical supplies; Dorothea Dix served as the superintendent of women nurses for the Army; and Elizabeth Stanton and Susan B. Anthony formed the National Women's Loyal League to support the Thirteenth Amendment that abolished slavery. Because of the work of these women and others such as "Mother" Bickerdyke and Harriet Tubman, feminists assumed that reformers would rally to the cause of women's suffrage. However, most Radical Republicans, who felt that black male suffrage was vital for the freedmen, thought that tying it to women's suffrage would mean inevitable defeat. Although Northern Democrats mocked women's suffrage and tried to use it along with the shibboleth of miscegenation to defeat the Fifteenth Amendment, most feminists refused to sacrifice women's suffrage to the cause of the black male. They consequently broke with those who insisted that it was "the Negro's hour."

Subsequently, the suffrage movement split into two groups. The National Woman Suffrage Association, led by Stanton and Anthony, concerned itself with a variety of reform causes and was decidedly the more radical of the two groups. The more conservative American Woman Suffrage Association, headed by Lucy Stone and her husband Henry Blackwell, stuck more closely to the single issue of the vote. In subsequent years, both groups agitated for women's suffrage with little success.

While recent historians have disputed the consequences of this split for the development of feminism in America, few would deny that the majority of women reformers in the years following the Civil War were at best "social feminists" who built their reform activities upon the idea of women's moral superiority. Their efforts were limited to such issues as social purity and temperance, which were designed to relieve women and society of the worst consequences of vulgar masculinity. Even when women did secure the vote, as they did in Wyoming in 1869, it was often the product of social forces over which women in general, and the Eastern feminist movement in particular, had little control. The suffrage victory in Wyoming was the product of an effort to reestablish Eastern ideas of order, refinement, and culture in the West.

Thus even the success of women's suffrage in the western states, which were the first to allow women to vote, reaffirmed the pervasiveness of the Victorian image of women as the guardians of culture and civilization. Throughout this period, most Americans, women as well as men, treated feminist demands with apathy or disgust. In his book *Sex and Education*, E.M. Clarke argued that college education would "desex" women. Opponents of equal suffrage insisted that it would undermine the family and endanger the entire social order. Women such as Eliza Francis Andrews agreed that a woman's "business is to refine and elevate society. . . Her mission is moral rather than intellectual, domestic, rather than political." The feminine intellect was deemed incapable of dealing with civic affairs. Until the twentieth century, the advocates of women's suffrage scored few successes because opposition from their own sex encouraged the hostility of men.

⧸6⧸

THE LADY AND THE MILL GIRL: CHANGES IN THE STATUS OF WOMEN IN THE AGE OF JACKSON

GERDA LERNER

The period 1800–1840 is one in which decisive changes occurred in the status of American women. It has remained surprisingly unexplored. With the exception of a recent, unpublished dissertation by Keith Melder and the distinctive work of Elisabeth Dexter, there is a dearth of descriptive material and an almost total absence of interpretation.[1] Yet the period offers essential clues to an understanding of later institutional developments, particularly the shape and nature of the women's rights movement. This analysis will consider the economic, political and social status of women and examine the changes in each area. It will also attempt an interpretation of the ideological shifts which occurred in American society concerning the "proper" role for women.

Periodization always offers difficulties. It seemed useful here, for purposes of comparison, to group women's status before 1800 roughly under the "colonial" heading and ignore the transitional and possibly

Reprinted from *Midcontinent American Studies* Journal, Volume 10, Number 1; © 1969 Mid-American Studies Association. Used by permission.

Research for this article was facilitated by a research grant provided by Long Island University, Brooklyn, N.Y., which is gratefully acknowledged.

   The generalizations in this article are based on extensive research in primary sources, including letters and manuscripts of the following women: Elizabeth Cady Stanton, Susan B. Anthony, Abby Kelley, Lucretia Mott, Lucy Stone, Sarah and Angelina Grimke, Maria Weston Chapman, Lydia Maria Child and Betsey Cowles. Among the organizational records consulted were those of the Boston Female Anti-Slavery Society, the Philadelphia Female Anti-Slavery Society, Anti-Slavery Conventions of American Women, all the Woman's Rights Conventions prior to 1870 and the records of various female charitable organizations.

atypical shifts which occurred during the American Revolution and the early period of nationhood. Also, regional differences were largely ignored. The South was left out of consideration entirely because its industrial development occurred later.

The status of colonial women has been well studied and described and can briefly be summarized for comparison with the later period. Throughout the colonial period there was a marked shortage of women, which varied with the regions and always was greatest in the frontier areas.[2] This (from the point of view of women) favorable sex ratio enhanced their status and position. The Puritan world view regarded idleness as sin; life in an underdeveloped country made it absolutely necessary that each member of the community perform an economic function. Thus work for women, married or single, was not only approved, it was regarded as a civic duty. Puritan town councils expected single girls, widows and unattached women to be self-supporting and for a long time provided needy spinsters with parcels of land. There was no social sanction against married women working; on the contrary, wives were expected to help their husbands in their trade and won social approval for doing extra work in or out of the home. Needy children, girls as well as boys, were indentured or apprenticed and were expected to work for their keep.

The vast majority of women worked within their homes, where their labor produced most articles needed for the family. The entire colonial production of cloth and clothing and partially that of shoes was in the hands of women. In addition to these occupations, women were found in many different kinds of employment. They were butchers, silversmiths, gunsmiths, upholsterers. They ran mills, plantations, tan yards, shipyards and every kind of shop, tavern and boarding house. They were gate keepers, jail keepers, sextons, journalists, printers, "doctoresses," apothecaries, midwives, nurses and teachers. Women acquired their skills the same way as did the men, through apprenticeship training, frequently within their own families.[3]

Absence of a dowry, ease of marriage and remarriage and a more lenient attitude of the law with regard to woman's property rights were manifestations of the improved position of wives in the colonies. Under British common law, marriage destroyed a woman's contractual capacity; she could not sign a contract even with the consent of her husband. But colonial authorities were more lenient toward the wife's property rights by protecting her dower rights in her husband's property, granting her personal clothing and upholding pre-nuptial contracts between husband and wife. In the absence of the husband, colonial courts granted women "femme sole" rights, which enabled them to conduct their husband's business, sign contracts and sue. The relative social freedom of women and the esteem in which they were held was commented upon by most early foreign travelers in America.[4]

But economic, legal and social status tell only part of the story. Colonial society as a whole was hierarchical, and rank and standing in society depended on the position of the men. Women did not play a determining role in the ranking pattern; they took their position in society through the men of their own family or the men they married. In other words, they participated in the hierarchy only as daughters and wives, not as individuals. Similarly, their occupations were, by and large, merely auxiliary, designed to contribute to family income, enhance their husbands' business or continue it in case of widowhood. The self-supporting spinsters were certainly the exception. The underlying assumption of colonial society was that women ought to occupy an inferior and subordinate position. The settlers had brought this assumption with them from Europe; it was reflected in their legal concepts, their willingness to exclude women from political life, their discriminatory educational practices. What is remarkable is the extent to which this felt inferiority of women was constantly challenged and modified under the impact of environment, frontier conditions and a favorable sex ratio.

By 1840 all of American society had changed. The Revolution had substituted an egalitarian ideology for the hierarchical concepts of colonial life. Privilege based on ability rather than inherited status, upward mobility for all groups of society and unlimited opportunities for individual self-fulfillment had become ideological goals, if not always realities. For men, that is; women were, by tacit consensus, excluded from the new democracy. Indeed their actual situation had in many respects deteriorated. While, as wives, they had benefitted from increasing wealth, urbanization and industrialization, their role as economic producers and as political members of society differed sharply from that of men. Women's work outside of the home no longer met with social approval; on the contrary, with two notable exceptions, it was condemned. Many business and professional occupations formerly open to women were now closed, many others restricted as to training and advancement. The entry of large numbers of women into low status, low pay and low skill industrial work had fixed such work by definition as "woman's work." Women's political status, while legally unchanged, had deteriorated relative to the advances made by men. At the same time the genteel lady of fashion had become a model of American femininity and the definition of "woman's proper sphere" seemed narrower and more confined than ever.

Within the scope of this article only a few of these changes can be more fully explained. The professionalization of medicine and its impact on women may serve as a typical example of what occurred in all the professions.

In colonial America there were no medical schools, no medical journals, few hospitals and few laws pertaining to the practice of the healing arts. Clergymen and governors, barbers, quacks, apprentices and women practiced medicine. Most practitioners acquired their credentials by reading Paracelsus and Galen and serving an apprenticeship with an established practitioner. Among the semi-trained "physics," surgeons, and healers, the occasional "doctoress" was fully accepted and frequently well rewarded. County records of all the colonies contain references to the work of the female physicians. There was even a female Army surgeon, a Mrs. Allyn, who served during King Philip's war. Plantation records mention by name several slave women who were granted special privileges because of their useful service as midwives and "doctoresses."[5]

The period of the professionalization of American medicine dates from 1765, when Dr. William Shippen began his lectures on midwifery in Philadelphia. The founding of medical faculties in several colleges, the standardization of training requirements, and the proliferation of medical societies intensified during the last quarter of the eighteenth century. The American Revolution dramatized the need for trained medical personnel, afforded first hand battlefield experience to a number of surgeons and brought increasing numbers of semi-trained practitioners in contact with the handful of European-trained surgeons working in the military hospitals. This was an experience from which women were excluded. The resulting interest in improved medical training, the gradual appearance of graduates of medical colleges and the efforts of medical societies led to licensing legislation. In 1801 Maryland required all medical practitioners to be licensed; in 1806 New York enacted a similar law, providing for an examination before a commission. By the late 1820's all states except three had set up licensing requirements. Since most of these laws stipulated attendance at a medical college as one of the prerequisites for licensing, women were automatically excluded.[6] By the 1830's the few established female practitioners who might have continued their practice in the old ways had probably died out. Whatever vested interest they had had was too weak to assert itself against the new profession.

This process of preemption of knowledge, institutionalization of the profession and legitimation of its claims by law and public acceptance is standard for the professionalization of the sciences, as George Daniels has pointed out.[7] It inevitably results in the elimination of fringe elements from the profession. It is interesting to note that women had been pushed out of the medical profession in sixteenth-century Europe by a similar process.[8] Once the public had come to accept licensing and college training as guarantees of up-to-date practice, the outsider, no matter how well qualified by years of experience, stood no chance in the competition. Women were the casualties of medical professionalization.

In the field of midwifery the results were similar, but the process was more complicated. Women had held a virtual monopoly in the profession in colonial America. In 1646 a man was prosecuted in Maine for practicing as a midwife.[9] There are many records of well trained midwives with diplomas from European institutions working in the colonies. In most of the colonies midwives were licensed, registered and required to pass an examination before a board. When Dr. Shippen announced his pioneering lectures on midwifery, he did it to "combat the widespread popular prejudice against the man-midwife" and because he considered most midwives ignorant and improperly trained. [10]

Yet he invited "those women who love virtue enough, to own their Ignorance, and apply for instruction" to attend his lectures, offering as an inducement the assurance that female pupils would be taught privately. It is not known if any midwives availed themselves of the opportunity.[11]

Technological advances, as well as scientific, worked against the interests of female midwives. In sixteenth-century Europe the invention and use of the obstetrical forceps had for three generations been the well-kept secret of the Chamberlen family and had greatly enhanced their medical practice. Hugh Chamberlen was forced by circumstances to sell the secret to the Medical College in Amsterdam, which in turn transmitted the precious knowledge to licensed physicians only. By the time the use of the instrument became widespread it had become associated with male physicians and midwives. Similarly in America, introduction of the obstetrical forceps was associated with the practice of male midwives and served to their advantage. By the end of the eighteenth century a number of male physicians advertised their practice of midwifery. Shortly thereafter female midwives also resorted to advertising, probably in an effort to meet the competition. By the early nineteenth century male physicians had virtually monopolized the practice of midwifery on the Eastern seaboard. True to the generally delayed economic development in the Western frontier regions, female midwives continued to work on the frontier until a much later period. It is interesting to note that the concepts of "propriety" shifted with the prevalent practice. In seventeenth-century Maine the attempt of a man to act as a midwife was considered outrageous and illegal; in mid-nineteenth century America the suggestion that women should train as midwives and physicians was considered equally outrageous and improper.[12]

Professionalization, similar to that in medicine with the elimination of women from the upgraded profession, occurred in the field of law. Before 1750, when law suits were commonly brought to the courts by the plaintiffs themselves or by deputies without specialized legal training, women as well as men could and did act as "attorneys-in-fact." When the law became a paid profession and trained lawyers took over litigation, women disappeared from the court scene for over a century.[13]

A similar process of shrinking opportunities for women developed in business and in the retail trades. There were fewer female storekeepers and business women in the 1830's than there had been in colonial days. There was also a noticeable shift in the kind of merchandise handled by them. Where previously women could be found running almost every kind of retail shop, after 1830 they were mostly found in businesses which served women only.[14]

The only fields in which professionalization did not result in the elimination of women from the upgraded profession were nursing and teaching. Both were characterized by a severe shortage of labor. Nursing lies outside the field of this inquiry since it did not become an organized profession until after the Civil War. Before then it was regarded peculiarly as a woman's occupation, although some of the hospitals and the Army during wars employed male nurses. These bore the stigma of low skill, low status and low pay. Generally, nursing was regarded as simply an extension of the unpaid services performed by the housewife—a characteristic attitude that haunts the profession to this day.

Education seems, at first glance, to offer an entirely opposite pattern from that of the other professions. In colonial days women had taught "Dame schools" and grade schools during summer sessions. Gradually, as educational opportunities for girls expanded, they advanced just a step ahead of their students. Professionalization of teaching occurred between 1820–1860, a period marked by a sharp increase in the number of women teachers. The spread of female seminaries, academies and normal schools provided new opportunities for the training and employment of female teachers.

This trend which runs counter to that found in the other professions can be accounted for by the fact that women filled a desperate need created by the challenge of the common schools, the ever-increasing size of the student body and the westward growth of the nation. America was committed to educating its children in public schools, but it was insistent on doing so as cheaply as possible. Women were available in great numbers and they were willing to work cheaply. The result was another ideological adaptation: in the very period when the gospel of the home as woman's only proper sphere was preached most loudly, it was discovered that women were the natural teachers of youth, could do the job better than men and were to be preferred for such employment. This was always provided, of course, that they would work at the proper wage differential—30–50% of the wages paid male teachers was considered appropriate. The result was that in 1888 in the country as a whole 63% of all teachers were women, while the figure for the cities only was 90.04%.[15]

It appeared in the teaching field, as it would in industry, that role expectations were adaptable provided the inferior status group filled a social need. The inconsistent and peculiar patterns of employment of black labor in the present-day market bear out the validity of this generalization.

There was another field in which the labor of women was appreciated and which they were urged to enter—industry. From Alexander Hamilton to Matthew Carey and Tench Coxe, advocates of industrialization sang the praises of the working girl and advanced arguments in favor of her employment. The social benefits of female labor particularly stressed were those bestowed upon her family, who now no longer had to support her. Working girls were "thus happily preserved from idleness and its attendant vices and crimes" and the whole community benefitted from their increased purchasing power.[16]

American industrialization, which occurred in an underdeveloped economy with a shortage of labor, depended on the labor of women and children. Men were occupied with agricultural work and were not available or willing to enter the factories. This accounts for the special features of the early development of the New England textile industry: the relatively high wages, the respectability of the job and relatively high status of the mill girls, the patriarchal character of the model factory towns and the temporary mobility of women workers from farm to factory and back again to farm. All this was characteristic only of a limited area and of a period of about two decades. By the late 1830's the romance had worn off; immigrants had supplied a strongly competitive, permanent work force willing to work for subsistence wages; early efforts at trade union organization had been shattered and mechanization had turned semiskilled factory labor into unskilled labor. The process led to the replacement of the New England-born farm girls by immigrants in the mills and was accompanied by a loss of status and respectability for female workers.

The lack of organized social services during periods of depression drove ever greater numbers of women into the labor market. At first, inside the factories distinctions between men's and women's jobs were blurred. Men and women were assigned to machinery on the basis of local need. But as more women entered industry the limited number of occupations open to them tended to increase competition among them, thus lowering pay standards. Generally, women regarded their work as temporary and hesitated to invest in apprenticeship training, because they expected to marry and raise families. Thus they remained untrained, casual labor and were soon, by custom, relegated to the lowest paid, least skilled jobs. Long hours, overwork and poor working conditions would characterize women's work in industry for almost a century.[17]

Another result of industrialization was in increasing differences in life styles between women of different classes. When female occupations, such as carding, spinning and weaving, were transferred from home to factory, the poorer women followed their traditional work and became industrial workers. The women of the middle and upper classes could use their newly gained time for leisure pursuits: they became ladies. And a small but significant group among them chose to prepare themselves for professional careers by advanced education. This group would prove to be the most vocal and troublesome in the near future.

As class distinctions sharpened, social attitudes toward women became polarized. The image of "the lady" was elevated to the accepted ideal of femininity toward which all women would strive. In this formulation of values lower class women were simply ignored. The actual lady was, of course, nothing new on the American scene; she had been present ever since colonial days. What was new in the 1830's was the cult of the lady, her elevation to a status symbol. The advancing prosperity of the early nineteenth century made it possible for middle class women to aspire to the status formerly reserved for upper class women. The "cult of true womanhood" of the 1830's became a vehicle for such aspirations. Mass circulation newspapers and magazines made it possible to teach every woman how to elevate the status of her family by setting "proper" standards of behavior, dress and literary tastes. *Godey's Lady's Book* and innumerable gift books and tracts of the period all preach the same gospel of "true womanhood"—piety, purity, domesticity.[18] Those unable to reach the goal of becoming ladies were to be satisfied with the lesser goal—acceptance of their "proper place" in the home.

It is no accident that the slogan "woman's place is in the home" took on a certain aggressiveness and shrillness precisely at the time when increasing numbers of poorer women *left* their homes to become factory workers. Working women were not a fit subject for the concern of publishers and mass media writers. Idleness, once a disgrace in the eyes of society, had become a status symbol. Thorstein Veblen, one of the earliest and sharpest commentators on the subject, observed that it had become almost the sole social function of the lady "to put in evidence her economic unit's ability to pay." She was "a means of conspicuously unproductive expenditure," devoted to displaying her husband's wealth.[19] Just as the cult of white womanhood in the South served to preserve a labor and social system based on race distinctions, so did the cult of the lady in an egalitarian society serve as a means of preserving class distinctions. Where class distinctions were not so great, as on the frontier, the position of women was closer to what it had been in colonial days; their economic contribution was more highly valued, their opportunities were less restricted and their positive participation in community life was taken for granted.

In the urbanized and industrialized Northeast the life experience of middle class women was different in almost every respect from that of the lower class women. But there was one thing the society lady and the mill girl had in common—they were equally disfranchised and isolated from the vital centers of power. Yet the political status of women had not actually deteriorated. With very few exceptions women had neither voted nor stood for office during the colonial period. Yet the spread of the franchise to ever wider groups of white males during the Jacksonian age, the removal of property restrictions, the increasing numbers of immigrants who acquired access to the franchise, made the gap between these new enfranchised voters and the disfranchised women more obvious. Quite naturally, educated and propertied women felt this deprivation more keenly. Their own career expectations had been encouraged by widening educational opportunites; their consciousness of their own abilities and of their potential for power had been enhanced by their activities in the reform movements of the 1830's; the general spirit of upward mobility and venturesome entrepreneurship that pervaded the Jacksonian era was infectious. But in the late 1840's a sense of acute frustration enveloped these educated and highly spirited women. Their rising expectations had met with frustration, their hopes had been shattered; they were bitterly conscious of a relative lowering of status and a loss of position. This sense of frustration led them to action; it was one of the main factors in the rise of the woman's rights movement.[20]

The women, who in 1848 declared boldly and with considerable exaggeration that "the history of mankind is a history of repeated injuries and usurpations on the part of man toward woman, having in direct object the establishment of an absolute tyranny over her," did not speak for the truly exploited and abused working woman.[21] As a matter of fact, they were largely ignorant of her condition and, with the notable exception of Susan B. Anthony, indifferent to her fate. But they judged from the realities of their own life experience. Like most revolutionaries, they were not the most downtrodden but rather the most status-deprived group. Their frustrations and traditional isolation from political power funneled their discontent into fairly utopian declarations and immature organizational means. They would learn better in the long, hard decades of practical struggle. Yet it is their initial emphasis on the legal and political "disabilities" of women which has provided the framework for most of the historical work on women. For almost a hundred years sympathetic historians have told the story of women in America from the feminist viewpoint. Their tendency has been to reason from the position of middle class women to a generalization concerning all American women. This distortion has obscured the actual and continuous contributions of women to American life.[22] To avoid such a distortion, any valid generalization concerning American women after the 1830's should reflect a recognition of class stratification.

For lower class women the changes brought by industrialization were actually advantageous, offering income and advancement opportunities, however limited, and a chance for participation in the ranks of organized labor. They, by and large, tended to join men in their struggle for economic advancement and became increasingly concerned with economic gains and protective labor legislation. Middle and upper-class women, on the other hand, reacted to actual and fancied status deprivation by increasing militancy and the formation of organizations for women's rights, by which they meant especially legal and property rights.

The four decades preceding the Seneca Falls Convention were decisive in the history of American women. They brought an actual deterioration in the economic opportunities open to women, a relative deterioration in their political status and a rising level of expectation and subsequent frustration in a privileged elite group of educated women. The ideology still pervasive in our present-day society regarding woman's "proper" role was formed in those decades. Later, under the impact of feminist attacks this ideology would grow defensive and attempt to bolster its claims by appeals to universality and pretentions to a history dating back to antiquity or, at least, to *The Mayflower*. Women, we are told, have always played a restricted and subordinate role in American life. In fact, however, it was in mid-nineteenth-century America that the ideology of "woman's place is in the home" changed from being an accurate description of existing reality into a myth. It became the "feminine mystique"—a longing for a lost, archaic world of agrarian family self-sufficiency, updated by woman's consumer function and the misunderstood dicta of Freudian psychology.

The decades 1800–1840 also provide the clues to an understanding of the institutional shape of the later women's organizations. These would be led by middle class women whose self-image, life experience and ideology had largely been fashioned and influenced by these early, transitional years. The concerns of middle class women—property rights, the franchise and moral uplift—would dominate the women's rights movement. But side by side with it, and at times cooperating with it, would grow a number of organizations serving the needs of working women.

American women were the largest disfranchised group in the nation's history, and they retained this position longer than any other group. Although they found ways of making their influence felt continuously, not only as individuals but as organized groups, power eluded them. The mill girl and the lady, both born in the age of Jackson, would not gain access to power until they learned to cooperate, each for her own separate interests. It would take almost six decades before they would find common ground. The issue around which they finally would unite and push their movement to victory was the "impractical and utopian" demand raised at Seneca Falls—the means to power in American society—female suffrage.

NOTES

1. Keith E. Melder, "The Beginnings of the Women's Rights Movement in the United States: 1800–1840" (Diss. Yale, 1963). Elisabeth A. Dexter, *Colonial Women of Affairs: Women in Business and Professions in America before 1776* (Boston, 1931); *Career Women of America: 1776–1840* (Francestown, N.H., 1950).

2. Herbert Moller, "Sex Composition and Corresponding Culture Patterns of Colonial America," *William and Mary Quarterly,* Ser. 3, II (April, 1945), 113–153.

3. The summary of the status of colonial women is based on the following sources: Mary Benson, *Women in 18th Century America: A Study of Opinion and Social Usage* (New York, 1935); Arthur Calhoun, *A Social History of the American Family,* 3 vols. (Cleveland, 1918); Dexter, *Colonial Women;* Dexter, *Career Women;* Edmund S. Morgan, *Virginians at Home: Family Life in the 18th Century* (Williamsburg, 1952); Julia C. Spruill, *Women's Life and Work in the Southern Colonies* (Chapel Hill, 1938).

4. E. M. Boatwright, "The political and legal status of women in Georgia: 1783–1860," *Georgia Historical Quarterly,* XXV (April, 1941). Richard B. Morris, *Studies in the History of American Law* (New York, 1930), Chap. 3. A summary of travelers' comments on American women may be found in: Jane Mesick, *The English Traveler in America: 1785–1835* (New York, 1922), 83–99.

5. For facts on colonial medicine the following sources were consulted: Wyndham B. Blanton, *Medicine in Virginia,* 3 vols. (Richmond, 1930); N. S. Davis, M.D.,

History of Medical Education and Institutions in the United States. . . . (Chicago, 1851); Dexter, *Career Women;* K. C. Hurd-Mead, M.D., *A History of Women in Medicine: from the Earliest Times to the Beginning of the 19th Century* (Haddam, Conn., 1938); Geo. W. Norris, *The Early History of Medicine in Philadelphia* (Philadephia, 1886); Joseph M. Toner, *Contributions to the Annals of Medical Progress in the United States before and during the War of Independence* (Washington, D.C., 1874). The citation regarding Mrs. Allyn is from Hurd-Mead, *Women in Medicine,* 487.

6. Fielding H. Garrison, M.D., *An Introduction to the History of Medicine* (Philadelphia, 1929). For licensing legislation: Davis, 88–103.

7. George Daniels, "The Professionalization of American Science: the emergent period, 1820–1860," paper delivered at the joint session of the History of Science Society and the Society of the History of Technology, San Francisco, December 28, 1965.

8. Hurd-Mead, *Women in Medicine,* 391.

9. *Ibid.,* 486.

10. Betsy E. Corner, *William Shippen Jr.: Pioneer in American Medical Education* (Philadelphia, 1951), 103.

11. *Ibid.*

12. Benjamin Lee Gordon, *Medieval and Renaissance Medicine* (New York, 1959), 689–691. Blanton, *Medicine,* II, 23–24; Hurd-Mead, *Women in Medicine,* 487–88; Annie Nathan Meyer, *Woman's Work in America* (New York, 1891). Harriot K. Hunt, M.D., *Glances and Glimpses or Fifty Years Social including Twenty Years Professional Life* (Boston, 1856), 127–140. Eleanor Flexner, *Century of Struggle: The Woman's Rights Movement in the United States* (Cambridge, Mass., 1959), 115–119.

13. Sophie H. Drinker, "Women Attorneys of Colonial Times," *Maryland Historical Society Bulletin,* LVI, No. 4 (Dec., 1961).

14. Dexter, *Colonial Women,* 34–35, 162–165.

15. Harriet W. Marr, *The Old New England Academies* (New York, 1959), Chap. 8; Thomas Woody, *A History of Women's Education in the United States,* 2 vols. (New York, 1929) H, 100–109, 458–460, 492–493.

16. Matthew Carey, *Essays on Political Economy* . . . (Philadelphia, 1822), 459.

17. The statements on women industrial workers are based on the following sources: Edith Abbot, *Women in Industry* (New York, 1910), 66–80; Edith Abbot, "Harriet Martineau and the Employment of Women in 1836," *Journal of Political Economy,* XIV (Dec., 1906), 614–626; Matthew Carey, *Miscellaneous Essays* (Philadelphia, 1830), 153–203; Helen L. Sumner, *History of Women in Industry in the United States,* in *Report on Condition of Women and Child Wage-Earners in the United States,* 19 vols. (Washington, D.C., 1910), IX. Also: Elizabeth F. Baker, *Technology and Woman's Work* (New York, 1964), Chaps. 1–5.

18. Emily Putnam, *The Lady: Studies of certain significant Phases of her History* (New York, 1910), 319–320. Barbara Welter, "The Cult of True Womanhood: 1820–1860," *American Quarterly,* XVIII, No. 2, Part I (Summer, 1966), 151–174.

19. Veblen generalized from his observations of the society of the Gilded Age and fell into the usual error of simply ignoring the lower class women, whom he dismissed as "drudges . . . fairly content with their lot," but his analysis of women's role in "conspicuous consumption" and of the function of women's fashions is

unsurpassed. For references see: Thorstein Veblen, *The Theory of the Leisure Class* (New York, 1962, first printing, 1899), 70–71, 231–232. Thorstein Veblen, "The Economic Theory of Woman's Dress," *Essays in Our Changing Order* (New York, 1934), 65–77.

20. Like most groups fighting status oppression women formulated a compensatory ideology of female superiority. Norton Mezvinsky has postulated that this was clearly expressed only in 1874; in fact this formulation appeared in the earliest speeches of Elizabeth Cady Stanton and in the speeches and resolutions of the Seneca Falls Conventions and other pre-Civil War woman's rights conventions. Rather than a main motivating force, the idea was a tactical formulation, designed to take advantage of the popularly held male belief in woman's "moral" superiority and to convince reformers that they needed the votes of women. Those middle class feminists who believed in woman's "moral" superiority exploited the concept in order to win their major goal—female equality. For references see: Norton Mezvinsky, "An Idea of Female Superiority," *Midcontinent American Studies Journal*, II, No. I (Spring, 1961), 17–26. E. C. Stanton, S. B. Anthony and M. J. Gage, eds., *A History of Woman Suffrage*, 6 vols. (New York, 1881–1922), I, 72, 479, 522, 529 and *passim*. Alan P. Grimes, *The Puritan Ethic and Woman Suffrage* (New York, 1967), Chaps. 2 and 3.

21. Stanton *et al*, *History of Woman Suffrage*, I, 70.

22. Mary R. Beard, *Woman as Force in History: A Study of Traditions and Realities* (New York, 1946).

∽ 7 ∽

RELIGION AND THE BONDS
OF WOMANHOOD

NANCY F. COTT

Woman was "fitted by nature" for Christian benevolence, announced a Presbyterian minister in Newburyport, Massachusetts, in 1837— "religion seems almost to have been entrusted by its author to her particular custody." As he saw it, Christianity had performed a unique service for women by bringing them social advantages as well as spiritual hope, and women had incurred a corresponding obligation.[1] The numbers and activity of women in New England churches suggest that they found benefits indeed in their religious devotion—but did their perception of the benefits and the minister's exactly coincide?

The Puritans who settled Massachusetts Bay worshipped a patriarchal God, but as early as the mid-seventeenth century women outnumbered men in the New England churches. While the church hierarchy remained strictly male the majority of women in their congregations increased, and ministers felt compelled to explain it.[2] "As there were three Marys to one John, standing under the Cross of our Dying Lord," Cotton Mather wrote in 1692, "so still there are far more Godly Women in the World, than there are Godly Men; and our Church Communions give us a Little Demonstration of it." Mather offered two explanations for the persistent pattern. Because of Eve's sins God had decreed that woman's lot would include subjection to man, and pain in childbirth; but he had mercifully converted these curses into blessings. The trials that women had to endure made them "tender," made them seek consolation, and thus turned them toward God and piety. Mather also thought that women had more opportunity and

From *The Bonds of Womanhood: "Woman's Sphere in New England, 1780-1835*. (New Haven: Yale University Press, 1977). Reprinted by permission of Yale University Press.

time to devote to "soul-service" than men had because they were ordinarily at home and had little "Worldly Business." Two decades later, when the Reverend Benjamin Colman praised women for showing "more of the Life & Power of Religion" than men, he discerned similar causes: women's "natural Tenderness of Spirit & Your Retiredness from the Cares & Snares of the World; so more especially in Your Multiplied Sorrows the curse pronounc'd upon our first Mother Eve, turn'd into the greatest blessing to Your Souls." Writers later in the eighteenth century dropped the references to Mother Eve and focused instead on the religious inclination "naturally" present in female temperament. In the British work *A Father's Legacy to his Daughters,* which was widely reprinted in New England after 1775, Dr. John Gregory maintained that women were more "susceptible" to religion because of their "superior delicacy," "modesty," "natural softness and sensibility of . . . dispositions," and "natural warmth of . . . imagination." (Men, he assumed, naturally had harder hearts and stronger passions, and were more dissolute and resistant to religious appeal because of the greater freedom they enjoyed.) Gregory also thought that women needed the consolations of religion, since they suffered great difficulties in life yet could "not plunge into business, or dissipate [them]selves in pleasure and riot" (as men might) for diversion. An influential British Evangelical named Thomas Gisborne made a similar appraisal of women's religious inclinations at the turn of the century, giving more weight, however, to women's distress and fear in childbirth as motivations of their piety.[3]

By the early nineteenth century New England ministers took for granted that women were the majority among Christians. They had assimilated the eighteenth-century argument that "women are happily formed for religion" by means of their "natural endowments" of sensibility, delicacy, imagination, and sympathy.[4] It testified how far New England Protestantism had become a matter of "the heart" rather than "the head" between the seventeenth and the nineteenth century — just as it had become a religion chiefly of women rather than men—that such characteristics manifested a "religious" temperament.[5] Recalling Christ's blessing of the meek and merciful, the Reverend Joseph Buckminster asked a Boston women's organization in 1810 if it was "surprising, that the most fond and faithful votaries of such a religion should be found among a sex, destined by their very constitution, to the exercise of the passive, the quiet, the secret, the gentle and humble virtues?" Men, the "self-styled lords of Creation," pursued wealth, politics or pleasure, but "the dependent, solitary female" sought God. Because of their softheartedness women were attuned to Christianity, Buckminster thought, and they appreciated Christianity because it valued domestic life. He summed up dramatically, "I believe that if Christianity should be compelled to flee from the mansions of the great, the academies of the philosophers, the halls of legislators, or the throng of busy men, we should find her last and purest retreat with women at the fireside; her last altar would be the female heart; her last audience would be the children gathered around the knees of a mother; her last sacrifice, the secret prayer, escaping in silence from her lips, and heard perhaps only at the throne of God."[6] Christianity was essentially female, his pronouns revealed.

Buckminster and his colleagues developed a powerful rationale for women's special obligations to Christianity. They reasoned that women's devotion to the religion was only fair recompense for the gospel's service in elevating them to their "proper" rank. Only Christianity, they claimed, made "men willing to treat females as equals, and in some respects, as superiors"; only Christianity "exalt[ed] woman to an equal rank with man in all the felicities of the soul, in all the advantages of religious attainment, in all the prospects and hopes of immortality"; only Christianity redeemed human nature from the base passions and taught reverence for domestic relations.[7] Drawing comparisons from history and from other cultures (readily at hand because of the foreign-mission movement), ministers affirmed that New England women owed their social rank to the progress of Christian civilization. This was an omnipresent theme.[8]

Contrasts between the condition of women in New England and in the countries to which missionaries traveled made it plausible that the Christian gospel had "civilized" men's attitudes to women. To appeal to a female charitable society for funds in 1829, the male trustees of the New Hampshire mission society asserted that "heathen" women were "ignorant—degraded—oppressed—enslaved. They are never treated by the other sex as companions and equals. They are in a great measure outcasts from society. They are made to minister to the *pleasures* of man; they are made to do the *work* of men; but, admitted to the enjoyment of equal rights, and raised to the respecta-bility and happiness of free and honourable social intercourse, they are not." New Hampshire women by contrast were respected and free, and had access to knowledge.[9] Rebeccah Lee, wife of the pastor in Marlborough, Connecticut, urged this point of view on the members of several female societies there. "To the Christian religion we owe the rank we hold in society, and we should feel our obligations," she declared.

It is that, which prevents our being treated like beasts of burden—which secures us the honourable privilege of human companionship in social life, and raises us in the domestic relations to the elevated stations of wives and mothers. Only seriously reflect upon the state of our sex, in those regions of the globe unvisited and unblessed with the light of Christianity; we see them degraded to a level with the brutes, and shut out from the society of lordly *man*; as if they were made by their Creator, not as the companions, but as the slaves and drudges of domineering masters. . . . Let each one then ask herself, how much do I owe?[10]

The "feminization" of Protestantism in the early nineteenth century was conspicuous.[11] Women flocked into churches and church-related organizations, repopulating religious institutions. Female converts in the New England Great Awakening between 1798 and 1826 (before the Methodist impact) outnumbered males by three to two.[12] Women's prayer groups, charitable institutions, missionary and education societies, Sabbath School organizations, and moral reform and maternal associations all multiplied phenomenally after 1800, and all of these had religious motives. Women thus exercised as fully as men the American penchant for voluntary association noted by Tocqueville in the 1830s, but women's associations before 1835 were *all* allied with the church, whereas men's also expressed a variety of secular, civic, political, and vocational concerns.[13]

This flowering of women's associational activities was part of the revival movement of the early nineteenth century in which Protestants tried to counteract religious indifference, rationalism, and Catholicism and to create an enduring and moral social order. Ministers were joined by lay persons, often (not always) of wealthy and conservative background, in giving the Awakening its momentum. They interpreted the aftermath of the French Revolution in the 1790s as proof of the dangers of a "godless" society, and feared that the American republic, with its growing urban populations, its Catholic immigrants, its Western inhabitants far from New England culture and clergy, might fall victim to similar "godless" influence. They saw religious education not only as a means to inculcate true faith but as a route to salvation on this earth, since it could teach the restraints demanded for an orderly society. The lay activities of the revival intended education, religious conversion, and the reformation of individual character whether they took the form of distributing bibles and tracts among the urban poor and Western frontier residents, raising money to train ministers or missionaries to evangelize the unchurched, setting up Sabbath schools for children to begin the business of Christian training early, or other myriad forms.[14]

Ministers' religious and denominational aims, conservatives' manipulation of religious benevolence for social control, humanitarians' perceptions of the needs of the poor, and women's orientation toward religious and gender-group expression all contributed to the proliferation of Christian women's societies. Since the prayer meetings called during religious revivals were often sex-segregated, they could serve as prototypes of religious organizations exclusively for women. The British Evangelical movement also supplied explicit models of charitable and humanitarian efforts by women.[15] These several motives and predispositions help to explain the extraordinarily swift rise and geographical dispersion of women's religious benevolent associations. Under the combined forces of local ministers, agents of national benevolent organizations and individual women who took to heart their obligations, female religious and charitable societies were established in all the larger cities of New England shortly after the turn of the century—in Middlebury and Montpelier, Concord and Portsmouth, Portland and Eastport, Providence and Newport, Hartford and New Haven, Boston, Salem, and Newburyport. Small towns in Vermont such as Jericho Center, Danville, Cornwall, Thetford, and Castleton had female religious and missionary societies before 1816. Scores of religious charitable societies were formed among New Hampshire women in rural towns between 1804 and 1814. With the encouragement of agents of the New Hampshire Bible Society, women founded local affiliates in 138 towns between 1820 and 1828. Women belonged to dozens of female charitable societies and "education" societies (which raised funds to educate ministers) in Connecticut towns by 1815; and societies for prayer, for propagation of the gospel, for missionary and charitable purposes were even more numerous in Massachusetts. The Boston Female Society for Missionary Purposes corresponded with 109 similar societies in 1817–18.[16]

Why did women support religion so faithfully? Perhaps Cotton Mather's and Benjamin Colman's reasoning deserves some credence. The specter of death in childbirth repeatedly forced women to think on the state of their souls. And women's domestic occupations may have diverted them from piety less than the "snares" of the world did men; besides, ministers and pious women made every effort to conflate domestic values with religious values. Domestic occupations offered women little likelihood of finding a set of values and symbols to rival the ones proposed by evangelical Christianity. For women at home in New England society, Christian belief had a self-perpetuating force that was not likely to be disrupted by experience that would provide alternative and equally satisfying explanations.[17] Yet women whose occupations took them outside the home, and single women generally, were prominent in the female religious community. Early factory workers participated in revivals, as Catherine Sedgwick, a Unitarian opposed to evangelical fervor, reported to her brother in

1833: "We have had the religious agitators among us lately—They have produced some effect on the factory girls & such light & combustible materials."[18] Perhaps the eighteenth-century reasoning about women's temperament suiting them for Christian faith had a deeper truth. Characteristics expected in women and in Christians—those of the "tender heart"—increasingly coincided during the eighteenth century, because women supported Christianity more consistently than men, and became ministers' major constituency.[19] By the early nineteenth century, the clergy claimed that women supported (or should support) Christianity because it was in the interest of their sex to do so; that reassured the faithful, whether or not it accurately described their motives.

It is less than satisfying, however, to attribute New England women's religiosity to their mortal risks in childbirth or to a socialization process that inculcated domestic piety and "Christian" temperament in them. Skeptics at the time suggested other reasons. Harriet Martineau, a witty and politically astute British visitor who criticized hypocrisies in American women's expected roles, noticed that "in New England, a vast deal of [women's] time is spent in attending preachings, and other religious meetings: and in paying visits, for religious purposes, to the poor and sorrowful." She even found it plausible "that they could not exist without religion," but considered that an unhealthy circumstance. Women were "driven back upon religion as a resource against vacuity," in her view.[20]

(Although Martineau seems to have meant vacuity of *mind* rather than *time*, some evidence suggests that women without pressing demands on their time were indeed the *most* devoted to religion. Single women or childless wives not responsible for the whole of their own support were the most likely to record their religious musings unfailingly. Abigail Brackett Lyman began a journal of that sort in her teens when she made a public profession of faith, and continued, as she reflected several years later, "to inscribe nothing in my journal but devotional exercises from the period abovementioned till some time after my marriage when cares increasing & being obliged to entertain considerable company I found it impossible to continue this laudable practice." Another ardent convert remarked plaintively, while she was still single, "Most of my associates were settled in life but I saw that those who had been zealous and devoted before their marriage had mostly declined in piety when pressed with the domestic cares of a family. I said to myself Why is it so? It cannot be because there is anything in that state subversive of piety for it is of Divine appointment."[21])

Martineau's insight was still more piercing. She said women "pursue[d] religion as an occupation" because they were constrained from exercising their full range of moral, intellectual, and physical powers in other ways. With an extension of her allusion religious activities can be seen as a means used by New England women to define self and find community, two functions that wordly occupations more likely performed for men. Traditionally, of course, religion had enlightened individuals of both sexes about their identity and placed them in a like-minded community; but women's particular needs and the configuration of religious institutions at this time enhanced those social functions. In an era when Protestantism was a "crusade," when ministers presented evangelical Christianity as embattled and yet triumphant, religious affiliation announced one's identity and purpose. "I made religion the principal business of my life," Nancy Thompson summarized the effect of her conversion at nineteen. Abigail Lyman exhorted herself in 1800 (before the Second Great Awakening had progressed widely) "to Live up to the Professions of Religion I had made—to dare to be singular in this day when iniquity abounds."[22]

Religion stretched before the convert a lifetime of purposeful struggle holding out heartening rewards. It provided a way to order one's life and priorities. The evangelical theology of the early nineteenth century made that process of ordering amenable to personal choice. "The salvation of our precious souls is not to be effected independent of our exertions," Lyman wrote in her journal, "—we are free agents and as such should work out our salvation with fear and trembling. . . . We may believe and rely on the faith of Revelation—and form our actions and tempers by its pure and perfect precepts—or we may resist the truth—appose [sic] its influence & harden our hearts in sin—either the one or the other all are constantly doing." Yet an individual made the religious choice in submission to God's will rather than through personal initiative. The morphology of religious conversion echoed women's expected self-resignation and submissiveness while it offered enormously satisfying assurance to converts. Nancy Meriam, a devout young woman of Oxford, Massachusetts, recorded in her religious notes of 1815, "There is sweetness in committing ourselves to God which the world knows nothing of. The idea that I am intirely [sic] in the hands of God fills my mind with a secret pleasure which I cannot describe."[23]

Yet religious identity also allowed women to assert themselves, both in private and in public ways. It enabled them to rely on an authority beyond the world of men and provided a crucial support to those who stepped beyond accepted bounds—reformers, for example. Women dissenters from Ann Hutchinson to Sarah Grimké displayed the subversive potential of religious belief. Religious faith also allowed women a sort of holy selfishness, or self-absorption, the result of the self-examination intrinsic to the Calvinist tradition. In contrast to the self-abnegation required of women in their domestic vocation, religious commitment required attention to one's own thoughts, actions, and prospects. By recording their religious meditations women expressed their literacy and rising self-consciousness in a sanctioned mode. Vigilance for their souls and their conformity to God's requirements compelled them to scrutinize their lives. And the more distinctly Christianity appeared a preserve of *female* values, the more legitimate (and likely) it became for religious women to scrutinize their gender-role. If the popular sales of the published memoirs of female missionaries are any guide, that model of religious commitment, which proposed a submission of self that was simultaneously a pronounced form of self-assertion, had wide appeal. Time and again women who made note of little reading except the Bible read the memoirs of Mrs. Newell, missionary to Burma (1814), and responded perhaps as a young matron of Woodmont, Connecticut, did: "O that I could feel as she did . . . , it appears to me as though I had ought to feel willing to contribute freely to spread the gospel among the heathen."[24]

No other avenue of self-expression besides religion at once offered women social approbation, the encouragement of male leaders (ministers), and, most important, the community of their peers. Conversion and church membership in the era of the Second Great Awakening implied joining a community of Christians. As historians have noted, the individual convert in the revival entered "a community of belief in which he [or she] was encouraged to make a decision that would be a positive organizing principle for his [or her] own life." During these decades the sacramental dimension of the church faded in the light of a new conception, "a voluntary association of explicitly convinced Christians for the purpose of mutual edification in the worship of God and the propagandization of the Christian faith as the group defined it." Because the vigor of religion had sunk during the late eighteenth century, the "awakened" Christian community defined itself to an unusual extent by its adversary and evangelical relation to the outside world, as well as by its intramural purposes. "He that is not with us said the Saviour is against us," Abigail Lyman reiterated.[25]

Being a Christian in this period meant becoming a member of a voluntary community not only in a psychological but in a literal sense, for piety implied group evangelical activity. Associative activity flowed naturally from church membership. The motive to advance personal piety and the cause of Christianity, together with the desire to act cooperatively, and (often) the local minister's support, influenced women to form associations even before they had specific aims. The process of organization of the Female Religious and Cent Society in Jericho Center, Vermont, seems to have been typical. In 1805 a number of women joined together because they wished to "do good" and aid the cause of religion, but they did not know what path to take. They began meeting for prayer. (This was the simplest form religious association took, and probably the most widespread, but also the most difficult to find record of.[26]) With their minister's assistance they formed a society and began to raise money for the missionary movement. The articles of their society proclaimed in 1806 that they would meet fortnightly "for social prayer and praise and religious instruction and edification." They also pledged mutual support and group intimacy, resolving that "all persons attending the meeting shall conduct themselves with seriousness and solemnity dureing [sic] the Exercises nor shall an Illiberal remark be made respecting the performance of any of the members, neither shall they report abroad any of the transactions of the society to the prejudice of any of its members." The society prospered. In 1816, when it joined with a Young Ladies' Society that had been formed in 1812 under another minister's guidance, and founded the Female Cent Society of Jericho, the new group had seventy members.[27]

Women's diaries reveal the efforts, and the high esteem, given to religious associations. As a young matron in Greenfield, Massachusetts, in 1815 Sarah Ripley Stearns joined a group of "youthful females" who hoped to improve themselves in piety. The same year she helped found a female charitable society, with the goal of aiding destitute children to attend school and church. She noted when the "band of associated females" met at her house, and remarked that their "Benevolent Institution" was one of her chief sources of enjoyment. In 1816 she endeavored to found a maternal association, a "Juvenile Institution," and a "heathen school society." She carried on these activities during the years in which she bore three children, despite her laments that household cares left her little time for diary writing, pious reading, or church attendance.[28]

Sarah Connell Ayer of Maine involved herself even more thoroughly. Although her youth had been frivolous, the deaths of four infants during her first five years of marriage turned her increasingly to religion and its community of consolation. (The deaths of children, in these years, may have given women more powerful motivation toward religiosity than ever did fears of their own mortality in childbirth.) By the time Sarah Ayer was twenty-four she saw nothing more pleasant "than to spend an evening in conversation with a few pious friends." In early 1816 she belonged to a female missionary society, prayer meeting, and donation society in Portland, and was devoted to her orthodox Congregationalist minister. After giving birth to two children who survived, she joined the Maternal Association and found its meetings "profitable." In 1822 her husband's appointment as surveyor of the port induced the family to move to Eastport. There Mrs. Ayer found the Congregationalist minister too Unitarian for her taste, and missed her Portland friends greatly. "We loved to meet together, to talk of Heaven as our final home, Christ as our Saviour; we shared each others joys and sorrows, and found the one heightened and the other alleviated by sympathy. Ah! how prone am I to murmur when things go contrary to my own inclinations," she wrote in her diary. Soon, however, she reestablished comparable activities in Eastport. At first she discovered a compatible community among the Baptists, and then worked with a small group of orthodox Congregationalists—seventeen women and three men—to set up a church to her preference. By the late 1820s she participated in a maternal association, a female prayer society, a benevolent society, and Sabbath School class.[29]

The ease with which women moved among evangelical societies, and participated in several at once, suggests that associating under the ideological aegis of evangelical Christianity mattered more to them than the specific goals of any one group. The founding members of the Female Religious Biographical and Reading Society (or "Berean Circle") associated in 1826 because they were "convinced of the importance and utility of the benevolent associations of the present day, and wish[ed] to unite our efforts in the same worthy objects, and also desir[ed] to improve and impress our own minds by obtaining religious instructions."[30] The occurrence of such associations in virtually every Protestant church implied that professing faith had come to include participating in group activity. Whether local ministers, state organizations, or pious individuals launched them, such associations created peer groups which became part of their members' definition of Christian piety.

The chosen Christian community also entered into a woman's self-definition. Rachel Willard Stearns, who set herself off from her Congregational family by converting to Methodism, exemplified that effect in a pronounced way. She appreciated the Methodist small-group meetings, she said, because "if we have been gay or trifling, or anger or revenge have had a place in our hearts, we do not wish to go, if we stay away, then the others will think there is something wrong. . . . I am thankful that I have placed myself under the watch-care and discipline of a church, where when I do wrong they will tell me of it. . . ."[31] Stearns's Methodism brought her to an especially intense religious self-concept; but religion performed an analogous social function for women in traditional denominations.

Within their Christian peer groups women examined their own behavior, weighed the balance between self and sacrifice in their lives, and sought appropriate models. In October 1828 the Berean Circle discussed the question, "Can an individual who is more strongly activated by selfish motives than by a view to the glory of God be a Christian?" They recorded their conclusions: "If their *habitual prevailing* motives are selfish they cannot; for the most important point in conversion is the change from selfishness to benevolence. We are not required to be so disinterested as to leave our own *chief* happiness out of view. This subject led to much interesting conversation." Several years later the group was engaged in similar topics, pursuing such questions as "Is an ungoverned temper, proof of an unsanctified heart?" Women's remarks in diaries suggest unanimously the deep satisfaction derived from occasions for discussion. One recorded that her meeting provided "much pleasure," another that it was "instructive and entertaining," a third that "I returned much refreshed in spirit."[32]

A shift in ministers' views also encouraged women's religious activities. The seventeenth-century clergy had tended to stress Eve's legacy, and hence to focus on woman being the "first in transgression." During the eighteenth century, ministers turned their attention from Eve to other promising models of female character in the Bible, in order to justify the idea that women could bear the standard of the religious community.[33] From the 1790s to the 1820s ministers of several denominations endorsed the view that women were of conscientious and prudent character, especially suited to religion. Drawing often on the text of Proverbs 31, they showed the model Christian woman to be a modest and faithful wife, an industrious and benevolent community member, and an efficient housekeeper who did not neglect the refinements of life. Fervently they described how pious women could influence others in the community and in their own families. From Baptists to Unitarians, clergymen agreed that family religion communicated from parents to children was the natural, divinely approved, most effective means of reproducing true Christian character.[34] By the pastors' own admission, mothers had more impact on children in this regard than fathers did. The reasoning of a Wolfborough, New Hampshire, Sabbath School convention reiterated the pervasive idea that mothers (and by extension, all women) propagated religion best. They resolved in 1834: "Whereas the influence of females on little children ordinarily determines their future character and eternal destiny, and as it has been most effectually exerted in bringing them to Christ, therefore, *Resolved,* that it is the sacred duty of all females to use every effort to promote the cause of Sabbath Schools."[35]

No other public institution spoke to women and cultivated their loyalty so assiduously as the churches did. Quickened by religious anxiety and self-interest, the clergy gave their formulations of women's roles unusual force. They pinned on women's domestic occupation and influence their own best hopes. Their portrayal of women's roles grew in persuasive power because it overlapped with republican commonplaces about the need for virtuous citizens for a successful republic. It gained intensity because it intersected with new interest in early childhood learning. Ministers declared repeatedly that women's pious influence was not only appropriate to them but crucial for society. "We look to you, ladies," said Joseph Buckminster, "to raise the standard of character in our own sex; we look to you, to guard and fortify those barriers, which still exist in society, against the encroachments of impudence and licentiousness. We look to you for the continuance of domestick purity, for the revival of domestick religion, for the increase of our charities, and the support of what remains of religion in our private habits and publick institutions."[36]

Ministers addressed women as a sex and, at the same time, as an interest group in the polity that had special civil and social responsibilities and special powers to defend its interests. "I address you as a class," said a Boston pastor to the mothers of the Mount Vernon Maternal Association, "because your duties and responsibilities are peculiar."[37] Ministers viewed women's sex-role as a social role, in other words. It meant no lessening of women's consciousness of the responsibilities borne to them by gender that the interests and obligations proposed to them were the ministers' own interests, and that the latter looked ahead to a rising generation of sons (the *men* who would lead society). Under ministers' guidance women could conclude that their sex shared not simply a biological but a social purpose. They were entrusted with the morals and faith of the next generation. According to prevailing conceptions of republican virtue, this was a task having political impact.[38]

NOTES

1. Jonathan Stearns, *Female Influence, and the True Christian Mode of Its Exercise: A Discourse delivered in the 1st Presbyterian Church in Newburyport, July 30, 1837* (Newburyport: John G. Tilton, 1837), p. 11. He had to qualify his assertion with "almost," I assume, in order to encourage male church-goers and also to account for the exclusion of women from the ministry.

2. Women's majority did not increase in a linear fashion from the seventeenth to the nineteenth centuries because during the Great Awakening of the 1740s proportionally more men converted than during nonrevival years. On the sex ratio among church members during the seventeenth century see Edmund S. Morgan, "New

England Puritanism: Another Approach," *WMQ* 3d ser., 18 (1961):236–42; Darrett Rutman, "God's Bridge Falling Down–'Another Approach' to New England Puritanism Assayed," *WMQ* 3d ser., 19 (1962):408–21; on the early eighteenth century see Cedric Cowing, "Sex and Preaching in the "Great Awakening," *AQ* 20 (1968):625–34; J. Bumsted, "Religion, Finance and Democracy in Massachusetts: The Town of Norton as a Case Study," *JAH* 57 (1971):817–31; James Walsh, "The Great Awakening in the First Congregational Church of Woodbury, Connecticut, *WMQ* 3d ser., 28 (1971):543–52; Gerald F. Moran, "Conditions of Religious Conversion in the First Society of Norwich, Connecticut, 1718–1744," *JSH* 5 (1972):331–43; Philip J. Greven, Jr., "Youth, Maturity, and Religious Conversion: A Note on the Ages of Converts in Andover, Massachusetts, 1711–1749," *Essex Institute Historical Collections* (April 1972):119–34; on the early nineteenth century see Nancy F. Cott, "Young Women in the Second Great Awakening" *FS* 3 (1975): 15–29; Donald Mathews, "The Second Great Awakening as an Organizing Process," *AQ* 21 (1969), esp. p. 42; Whitney R. Cross, *The Burned-Over District* (New York: Harper Torchbooks, 1965), esp. pp. 84–89; and Barbara Welter, "The Feminization of Religion in Nineteenth-Century America," in Mary Hartman and Lois Banner, eds., *Clio's Consciousness Raised* (New York: Harper Torchbooks, 1973).

3. Cotton Mather, *Ornaments for the Daughters of Zion* (Cambridge, Mass., 1692), pp. 44–45; Benjamin Colman, *The Duty and Honour of Aged Women* (Boston, 1711), pp. ii–iii; Dr. John Gregory, *A Father's Legacy to his Daughters* (London: John Sharpe, 1822), pp. 11–12; Thomas Gisborne, *An Enquiry into the Duties of the Female Sex* (London, reprinted Philadelphia: James Humphreys, 1798), pp. 182–83. I cite these English works because of the evidence that they were read in New England; on this, see Nancy F. Cott, "In the Bonds of Womanhood: Perspectives on Female Experience and Consciousness in New England, 1780–1830" (Ph.D. diss., Brandeis University, 1974), pp. 225–27.

4. Quotation from Daniel Chaplin, *A Discourse Delivered before the Charitable Female Society in Groton [Massachusetts], October 19, 1814* (Andover, Mass., 1814), p. 9.

When I speak of "New England ministers' views" in what follows, my opinions primarily derive from my reading of 65 sermons concerning or addressed to women between 1792 and 1837, of which 54 were written between 1800 and 1820, and 57 were delivered to meetings of female associations in New England towns and cities. The denomination best represented were the trinitarian Congregationalists, who contributed at least a third of the sermons, while Unitarian Congregationalists, Presbyterians, Episcopalians, Baptists, and others together gave the rest. Denominational differences did not perceptibly vary ministers' assessments of women's roles, however. But note that I am not dealing here with the Methodist contribution or the influence of Charles G. Finney's revivalism, which occurred chiefly after 1835 in New England. I have presented the ministers' views in greater detail in "In the Bonds of Womanhood," chap. 3.

5. Jonathan Edwards was, of course, a central figure in this transformation.

6. Joseph Buckminster, "A Sermon Preached before the Members of the Boston Female Asylum, September 1810," hand-copied and bound with other printed sermons to the BFA, pp. 7–9, BPI.

7. Chaplin, *A Discourse*, p. 12; Pitt Clarke, *A Discourse Delivered before the Norton Female Christian Association on . . . June 13, 1818* (Taunton, Mass., 1818), p. 11; Samuel Worcester, *Female Love to Christ* (Salem, Mass., 1809), pp. 12–13.

8. E.g., see Daniel Clark, *The Wise Builder, a Sermon Delivered to the Females of the 1st Parish in Amherst, Mass.* (Boston, 1820), pp. 17-18, 23-24; John Bullard, *A Discourse, delivered at Pepperell, September 19, 1815, before the Charitable Female Society* (Amherst, N.H., 1815), pp. 9-10; Benjamin Wadsworth, *Female Charity an Acceptable Offering* ...(Andover, Mass., 1817), pp. 27-28; David T. Kimball, *The Obligation and Disposition of Females to Promote Christianity* ... (Newburyport, 1819), p. 4.

9. *16th Annual Report on the concerns of the Female Cent Institution, New Hampshire* (Concord, N.H., 1829), pp. 3-4 (quotation), 4-6.

10. Mrs. Rebeccah Lee, *An Address, Delivered in Marlborough, Connecticut, September 7, 1831* (Hartford, 1831), p. 4. She also noted, "There is not a town or village in our country, perhaps, where females are not actively engaged in this good cause, and from us much is expected in the present day."

11. The term is Barbara Welter's, in "The Feminization of Religion."

12. See Ebenezer Porter, *Letters on Revivals of Religion* (Andover, Mass.: The Revival Association, 1832), p. 5; and Cott, "Young Women in the Second Great Awakening." Beginning in 1830 Methodist evangelism under Charles G. Finney encouraged women's religious activity, particularly their public praying, more vigorously than other denominations. On the contribution of Methodist practice to Congregational and Presbyterian revival measures in the northeast before Finney, see Richard Carwardine, "The Second Great Awakening in the Urban Centers: An Examination of Methodism and the 'New Measures'," *JAH* 59 (1972):327-41.

Studies of many individual communities will be necessary before the precise impact of the revivals of the sex ratio among church members can be ascertained. Recent historical research on the Second Great Awakening suggests that the proportion of men among the converts was greater during revival years than ordinary years, but only large enough to reduce the female majority somewhat, not to undermine it. See Mary P. Ryan, "A Woman's Awakening: Revivalist Religion in Utica, New York, 1800-1835," paper delivered at the Third Berkshire Conference on the History of Women, Bryn Mawr, Pa., June 10, 1976, and Paul E. Johnson, "A Shopkeeper's Millennium: Society and Revivals in Rochester, N.Y., 1815-1837" (Ph.D. diss., University of California at Los Angeles, 1975).

13. See Alexis de Tocqueville, *Democracy in America,* ed. Phillips Bradley (New York: Vintage Books, 1945), 1:198-205, 2:114-18, 123-28. Cf. Richard D. Brown, "The Emergence of Voluntary Associations in Massachusetts, 1760-1830," *Journal of Voluntary Action Research* 2 (1973), esp. 68-70.

14. See Clifford S. Griffin, "Religious Benevolence as Social Control, 1815-1860," *MVHR* 44 (1957), esp. 440-42; Charles I. Foster, *An Errand of Mercy: The Evangelical United Front, 1790-1837* (Chapel Hill, N.C.: University of North Carolina Press, 1960). A recent critique by Lois Banner, "Religious Benevolence as Social Control: A Critique of an Interpretation," *JAH* 60 (1973):23-41, stresses the organizational dynamics of the Protestant denominations and the sincere educational and humanitarian aims of proponents.

15. Merle Curti, "American Philanthropy and the National Character," *AQ* 10 (1958):425. The first female charitable institution in the United States, the Society for the Relief of Poor Widows and Small Children, was founded in 1796 in New York by a newly arrived Scotswoman, Isabella M. Graham, on the model of a London institution for poor relief.

16. The formation of the national benevolent societies, such as the American Bible Society, the American Sabbath School Association, etc., did not occur until 1815 and after. Documentation of the existence of women's associations occurs in the titles of ministers' sermons, in printed constitutions and reports and manuscript records of the societies themselves, in women's diaries and letters, and in local histories. In addition to titles listed in the Suggested Readings, see documents from the Jericho Center Female Religious Society, Cent Society, and Maternal Association, and constitution and rules of the Maternal Association in Dorchester, Mass., Dec. 25, 1816, CL; documents of the Charitable Female Society in the 2d parish in Bradford, 1815–21, of the West Bradford Female Temperance Society, 1829–34, of the Female Religious, Biographical, Reading Society (Berean Circle), 1826–32, of the Belleville Female Benevolent Society, or Dorcas Society, 1839–40, and of the Hamilton Maternal Association, 1834–35, EI; *Report on the Concerns of the New Hampshire Cent Institution* (Concord, 1814, 1815, 1816); *The Rules, Regulations, Etc. of the Portsmouth Female Asylum* (Portsmouth, 1815); Edward Aiken, *The First Hundred Years of the New Hampshire Bible Society* (Concord, 1912), p. 66; Mrs. L. H. Daggett, ed., *Historical Sketches of Women's Missionary Societies in America and England* (Boston, n.d.), p. 50; *Annual Reports of the Education Society of Connecticut and the Female Education Society of New Haven* (New Haven, 1816–26); *An Account of the Rise, Progress, and Present State of the Boston Female Asylum* (Boston, 1803); *Constitution of the Salem Female Charitable Society, Instituted July 1st, 1801* (printed circular, 1801); *Reminiscences of the Boston Female Asylum* (printed, Boston, 1844); *Account of the Plan and Regulations of the Female Charitable Society of Newburyport* (Newburyport, 1803); *A Brief Account of the Origin and Progress of the Boston Female Society for Missionary Purposes, with extracts from the reports of the society in May 1817 and 1818* (Boston, 1818); *Report of the Boston Female Society for Missionary Purposes* (Boston, 1825); *Constitution of the Female Samaritan Society instituted in Boston, Nov. 19, 1817 and revised 1825* (Boston, 1833); *Constitution of the Female Society of Boston and the Vicinity for Promoting Christianity among the Jews, instituted June 5, 1816* (Boston, n.d.); *Constitution of the Fragment Society, Boston, founded 1817* (Boston, 1825); *Constitution of the Female Philanthropick Society, instituted Dec. 1822* (Boston, 1823); *Boston Fatherless and Widows Society, founded 1817, Annual Report* (Boston, 1836); *Second Annual Report, Third Annual Report, of the Boston Female Moral Reform Society* (Boston, 1837, 1838); *Constitution of the Maternal Association of Newburyport* (printed, 1815); *Constitution of the Maternal Association of the 2d Parish in West-Newbury, adopted Sept. 1834* (printed, n.d.); *Constitution of the Maternal Association* (Dedham, Mass., n.d.); *Constitution of the Maternal Association of the New Congregational Church in Boston, Mass., organized Oct. 6, 1842* (Boston, 1843); *Diary of Sarah Connell Ayer* (Portland, Me., 1910), pp. 213–15, 226, 228, 237, 285–307; diary of Mary Hurlbut, Feb. 10, 1833, CHS. See also Keith Melder, " 'Ladies Bountiful': Organized Women's Benevolence in Early Nineteenth-Century America," *New York History* 48 (1967): 231–54; Mary B. Treudley, "The Benevolent Fair: A Study of Charitable Organizations Among Women in the First Third of the Nineteenth Century," *Social Service Review* 14 (1940):506–22.

17. This line of argument was suggested to me by Gordon Schochet's reasoning about patriarchalism in the seventeenth century in "Patriarchalism, Politics, and Mass Attitudes in Stuart England," *Historical Journal* 12 (1959), esp. 421–25.

18. Catherine Sedgwick to Robert Sedgwick, Sept. 15, 1833, Sedgwick Collection, MHS. See also the diary of Mary Hall, a Lowell operative, NHHS; and Almond H. Davis, ed., *The Female Preacher, or Memoir of Salome Lincoln* (Providence, R.I., 1843).

19. Lonna Malmsheimer suggests that the numerical predominance of women in New England churches forced adjustments in ministers' views of their character during the eighteenth century, in "New England Funeral Sermons and Changing Attitudes toward Women, 1672-1792" (Ph.D. diss., University of Minnesota, 1973).

20. Harriet Martineau, *Society in America* (New York: Saunders and Otley, 1837), 2:255-57, 229, 363. Martineau strenuously objected to women working to raise money to educate young clerics (as they did in "education" societies); see pp. 363, 415-20.

21. Journal of Abigail Brackett Lyman, Jan. 1, 1800, in Helen Roelker Kessler, "The Worlds of Abigail Brackett Lyman" (M.A. thesis, Tufts Univ., 1976), appendix A; "A Short Sketch of the life of Nancy Thomson [*sic*]," autobiographical fragment in the diary of Nancy Thompson (Hunt), c. 1813, CHS. See also the journal of Mary Treadwell Hooker, 1795-1812, CSI.

22. "Short Sketch," diary of Nancy Thompson, c. 1808; journal of Abigail Brackett Lyman, Jan. 30, 1800; see also diary of Lucinda Read, March 30, 1816, MHS.

23. Journal of Abigail Brackett Lyman, Oct. 3, 1802; Nancy Meriam, "Religious Notes, 1811-15," April 9, 1815, WHS; also see Cott, "Young Women in the Second Great Awakening," on this theme. William McLoughlin summarizes the idea of "compliance with the terms of salvation" thus: "The process of conversion . . . became a shared act, a complementary relationship. Man striving and yearning; God benevolent and eager to save; the sinner stretching out his hands to receive the gift of grace held out by a loving God. This belief in man's free will or his partial power to effect his own salvation had in earlier Calvinist days been condemned as the heresy of Arminianism. For this reason most nineteenth-century ministers preferred to call themselves Evangelicals." *The American Evangelicals 1800-1900* (New York: Harper Torchbooks, 1968), p. 10.

24. Diary of Mrs. S. Smith, March 29, 1825, CSL. See also the diary of Mary Treadwell Hooker; diary of Sarah Ripley Stearns, May 1, 1814, and March 19, 1815, Stearns Collection, S.L.; correspondence between Almira Eaton and Weltha Brown, 1812-22, Hooker Collection, SL.

25. Richard D. Birdsall, "The Second Great Awakening and the New England Social Order," *Church History* 39 (1970):357; Sidney E. Mead, "The Rise of the Evangelical Conception of the Ministry in America, 1607-1850," in H. Richard Niebuhr and Daniel L. Williams, eds., *The Ministry in Historical Perspective* (New York: Harper and Bros., 1956), p. 224; journal of Abigail Brackett Lyman, Oct. 3, 1802. Historians of religion consistently maintain that during the last two decades of the eighteenth century American churches "reached a lower ebb of vitality . . . than at any other time in the country's religious history," in the words of Sydney E. Ahlstrom, *A Religious History of the American People* (New Haven: Yale University Press, 1972), p. 365. Douglas Sweet protests that consensus in "Church Vitality and the American Revolution," *Church History* 45 (1976):341-57. The Second Great Awakening, beginning in the late 1790s, decisively changed the religious climate. Estimates for New England, which generally was the region of highest church affiliation, are unavailable, but Winthrop S. Hudson estimates that church members in the United States as a whole increased from 1

out of 15 in the population in 1800, to 1 out of 8, in 1835, raising the churches' "constituency" from 40 percent to 75 percent of the population; *Religion in America: An Historical Account* (2d ed., New York: Scribners, 1973), pp. 129–30.

26. Mary Orne Tucker mentions her attendance at such a meeting in her diary, April 12, 1802, EI; see also *The Writings of Nancy Maria Hyde of Norwich, Conn.* (Norwich, 1816), pp. 182–83, 189–90, 192–93, 201–02, 203–05.

27. Documents of the Jericho Center, Vermont, Female Religious Society, Cent Society, and Maternal Associations. By 1824 the Cent Society had 120 subscribers.

28. Sarah Ripley Stearns diary, 1814–17, esp. Dec. 24, 1815, March 2, March 31, July 14, Oct. 13, 1816, June 1817.

29. *Diary of Sarah Connell Ayer 1805–1835,* pp. 209, 211, 213, 214, 215, 225, 226, 228, 231–33, 236–37, 239–40, 254, 278, 282–305. There is a gap in the diary between 1811 and 1815, the years in which Ayer bore and buried her first four children.

30. Record book of the Female Religious, Biographical, Reading Society (the Berean Circle), 1826–32, EI. The society was probably located near Newburyport, though its exact location is not clear.

31. Diary of Rachel Willard Stearns, July 19, 1835, Stearns Collection, SI.

32. Record book of the Berean Circle, Oct. 15, 1828, Jan. 17, 1832; Mary Orne Tucker diary, April 12, 1802; *The Writings of Nancy Maria Hyde*, pp. 189–90; diary of Nancy Meriam, May 12, 1819, WHS.

33. See Malmsheimer, "New England Funeral Sermons."

34. See, for example, Amos Chase, *On Female Excellence* (Litchfield, Conn., 1792); John C. Ogden, *The Female Guide* (Concord, N.H., 1793); George Strebeck, *A Sermon on the Character of the Virtuous Woman* (New York, 1800); William Lyman, *A Virtuous Woman the Bond of Domestic Union and the Source of Domestic Happiness* (New London, Conn., 1802); Nathan Strong, *The Character of a Virtuous and Good Woman* (Hartford, 1809); Ethan Smith, *Daughters of Zion Excelling* (Concord, N.H., 1814); Daniel Clark, *The Wise Builder* (Boston, 1820); and Cott, "In the Bonds of Womanhood," pp. 105–15.

35. Quoted by Henry C. Wright in his journal, 6:135, June 18, 1834, HCL.

36. Buckminster, "A Sermon Preached . . . 1810," pp. 24–25.

37. Pastor's address appended to *Constitution of the Maternal Association of the New Congregational Church* (Boston, 1843), p. 5.

38. E.g., Ward Cotton told the women of Boylston, Massachusetts, that bringing domestic missionaries to unchurched Western residents would be "the means not only of the salvation of their souls, but also of the political salvation of our country." *Causes and Effects of Female Regard to Christ* (Worcester, 1816), p. 13.

≈ 8 ≈

WOMEN'S PERSPECTIVE ON THE PATRIARCHY IN THE 1850S

ANNE FIROR SCOTT

Southern women were scarcely to be seen in the political crisis of the 1850s. Historical works dealing with that crucial decade seldom mention a woman unless it is in a footnote citing a significant letter from a male correspondent. In women's own diaries and letters the burgeoning conflict between the North and South almost never inspired comment before John Brown's raid and rarely even then.

At the same time, women were a crucial part of one southern response to the mounting outside attack on slavery. The response was an ever more vehement elaboration of what has been called the "domestic metaphor," the image of a beautifully articulated, patriarchal society in which every southerner, black or white, male or female, rich or poor, had an appropriate place and was happy in it. "The negro slaves of the South are the happiest, and, in some sense, the freest people in the world," George Fitzhugh wrote, describing the happy plantation on which none were oppressed by care. "Public opinion," he stoutly maintained, "unites with self-interest, domestic affection, and municipal law to protect the slave. The man who maltreats the weak and dependent, who abuses his authority over wife, children, or slaves is universally detested." Slavery, Fitzhugh thought, was an admirable education system as well as an ideal society.[1]

What Fitzhugh argued in theory many planters tried to make come true in real life. "My people" or "my black and white family" were phrases that rolled easily from their tongues and pens. "I am friend and

From *Journal of American History* 61 (June 1974). Reprinted by permission.

well wisher both for time and eternity to every one of them . . ." a North Carolinian wrote to his slave overseer upon the death of a slave, expressing sorrow that he could not be present for the funeral.[2] This letter was one in a series of fatherly letters to that particular slave, and the writer, a bachelor, offered similar fatherly guidance to his grown sisters, as he doled out their money to them.

Even as planters tried to make the dream come true, they could not hide their fear and doubt. "It gave me much pleasure to see so much interest manifested," one wrote his wife, reporting that the slaves had inquired about her health and welfare, "and I am convinced that much of it was sincere."[3] Quick panic followed rumors of insurrection, and when the war came many planters took the precaution of moving their slaves as Yankee armies approached. For those who enjoy poetic justice there is plenty to be found in the pained comments of loving patriarchs when their most pampered house servants were the first to depart for Yankee camps.

Women, like slaves, were an intrinsic part of the patriarchal dream. If plantation ladies did not support, sustain, and idealize the patriarch, if they did not believe in and help create the happy plantation, which no rational slave would exchange for the jungle of a free society, who would? If women, consciously or unconsciously, undermined the image designed to convince the doubting world that the abolitionists were all wrong, what then?

Some southern men had doubts about women as well as slaves. This is clear in the nearly paranoid reaction of some of them to the pronouncements and behavior of "strong-minded" women in the North. Southern gentlemen hoped very much that no southern lady would think well of such goings-on, but clearly they were not certain.[4] Their fears had some foundation, for in the privacy of their own rooms southern matrons were reading Margaret Fuller, Madame de Stael, and what one of them described as "decided women's rights novels."[5]

Unlike the slaves, southern women did not threaten open revolt, and when the war came they did not run to the Yankees. Instead they were supportive, as they worked to feed and clothe civilians and the army, nurse the sick, run the plantations, supervise the slaves, and pray for victory. Yet even these activities were partly an indirect protest against the limitations of women's role in the patriarchy. Suddenly women were able to do business in their own right, make decisions, write letters to newspaper editors, and in many other ways assert themselves as individual human beings. Many of them obviously enjoyed this new freedom.[6]

Even before the war women were not always as enthusiastic in their support of the patriarchy as slavery's defenders liked to believe. To the assertion that "The slave is held to *involuntary service;*" an Alabama minister responded:

> So is the wife. Her relation to her husband, in the immense majority of cases, is made for her, and not by her. And when she makes it for herself, how often, and how soon . . . would she throw off the yoke if she could! O ye wives, I know how superior you are to your husbands in many respects—not only in personal attraction . . . in grace, in refined thought, in passive fortitude, in enduring love, and in a heart to be filled with the spirit of heaven. . . . I know you may surpass him in his own sphere of boasted prudence and worldly wisdom about dollars and cents. Nevertheless, he has authority, from God, to rule over you. You are under service to him. You are bound to obey him in all things. . . . you cannot leave your parlor, nor your bed-chamber, nor your couch, if your husband commands you to stay there![7]

The minister was speaking to a northern audience and intended, no doubt, to convince northern women that they should not waste energy deploring the servitude of the slave since their own was just as bad, but surely this Alabama man shaped his understanding of married life in his home territory.

The minister's perception is supported in a little volume entitled *Tales and Sketches for the Fireside,* written by an Alabama woman for the purpose of glorifying southern life and answering the abolitionists. Woman's influence, she wrote,

> is especially felt in the home circle; she is the weaker, physically, and yet in many other respects the stronger. There is no question of what she can bear, but what she is obliged to bear in her positions as wife and mother, she has her troubles which man, the stronger, can never know. Many annoying things to woman pass unnoticed by those whose thoughts and feelings naturally lead them beyond their homes.

The writer added that since men were so restless, God in his wisdom designed women to be "the most patient and untiring in the performance . . . of duties." Weariness almost leaps from her pages. Not only is she bitter about the burdens of woman's lot, she also feels keenly the one-sidedness of those burdens and the failure of men even to notice.[8]

Personal documents provide even more detailed evidence of female discontent in the South of the 1850s. Unhappiness centered on women's lack of control over many aspects of their own sexual lives and the sexual lives of their husbands, over the institution of slavery which they could not change, and over the inferior status which kept them so powerless.[9]

The most widespread source of discontent, since it affected the majority of married women, was the actuality of the much glorified institution of motherhood. Most women were not able to control their own fertility. The typical planter's wife was married young, to a husband older than herself, and proceeded to bear children for two decades. While conscious family limitation was sometimes practiced in the nineteenth century, effective contraception was not available, and custom, myth, religion, and men operated to prevent limitation. With the existing state of medical knowledge it was realistic to fear childbirth and to expect to lose some children in infancy.[10]

The diary of a Georgia woman shows a typical pattern of childbearing and some reactions to it. Married in 1852 at the age of eighteen to a man of twenty-one, she bore her first child a year later. In the summer of 1855, noting certain telltale symptoms, she wrote "I am again destined to be a mother . . . the knowledge causes no exhilirating feelings . . . [while] suffering almost constantly . . . I cannot view the idea with a great deal of pleasure."[11] The baby was born but died in a few weeks, a circumstance which she prayed would help her live more dutifully in the future. A few months later she was happily planning a trip to the North because "I have no infant and I cannot tell whether next summer I will be so free from care . . . ."[12] but in four days her dreams of travel vanished abruptly when morning nausea led her to wonder whether she was "in a peculiar situation, a calamity which I would especially dread this summer."[13] Her fears were justified, and she had a miscarriage in August. There was no rest for the weary. By January 1857 she was pregnant again, and on her twenty-fourth birthday in April 1858 she was pregnant for the fifth time in six years, though she had only two living children. Diary volumes for the next two years are missing, but in December 1862 she recorded yet another pregnancy, saying "I am too sick and irritable to regard this circumstance as a blessing *yet awhile.*"[14] A year later with the house being painted and all in confusion she jotted the illuminating comment: "I don't wonder that men have studys which . . . I imagine to be only an excuse for making themselves comfortable and being out of the bustle and confusion of . . . housekeeping . . . and children."[15] She also expressed bitter opposition to the practice of sending pregnant slaves to work in the fields. By February 1865, after four years of war, she was writing "unfortunately I have the prospect of adding again to the little members of my household. . . . I am sincerely sorry for it."[16] When the child was born prematurely in June the mother thanked God that it did not live. By 1869, this woman had managed to relegate her husband to a separate bedroom, and, for good measure, she kept the most recent infant in her bed, as effective a means of contraception as she could devise.[17] Later she reflected that she had never "been so opposed to having children as many women I know."[18]

The difference between the male and female angle of vision is illustrated in the life of a South Carolina woman, a niece of James L. Petigru, married to a cousin ten years her senior. She gave birth to six children in the first nine years of her marriage, and her uncle—normally a wise and perceptive human being—wrote to the young woman's mother: "Well done for little Carey! Has she not done her duty . . . two sons and four daughters and only nine years a wife? Why the Queen of England hardly beats her. . . ."[19] If the uncle had had access to the correspondence between "little Carey" and her planter husband he might not have been so quick to congratulate her. It seems likely from the evidence of these letters that her three-month sojourns with her mother in the summers were partly motivated by a desire to prolong the time between babies, but no sooner did her lonesome husband come to visit than she was pregnant again.[20]

This woman had a faithful family doctor who moved into her household when time for her confinement drew near, but even his comforting presence did not prevent her fears of death each time. Mrs. Thomas, writer of the first diary, relied on a slave midwife, her mother, and a town doctor. Both these women loved their children and cared for them, though with ample assistance before the war. Yet each privately insisted that she would have preferred a much longer time between babies. As the Alabama minister quoted earlier suggested, however, a woman could not leave her bedchamber or her couch without her husband's permission.[21]

Women's private feelings about constant childbearing provide one example of unhappiness which was masked by the cheerful plantation image. The behavior of the patriarchs themselves in other realms of sexual life was another source of discontent. The patriarchal ideal which called for pure, gentle, pious women also expected a great deal of men: that they should be strong, chaste, dignified, decisive, and wise. Women who lived in close intimacy with these men were aware of the gap between the cavalier of the image and the husband of the reality, and they were also aware that those who had the greatest power were also—by women's standards—the most sinful. A diarist summarized an afternoon of sewing and conversation in Richmond County, Georgia:

> We were speaking of the virtue of men. I admitted to their general depravity, but considered that there were some noble exceptions, among those I class my own husband. . . .[22]

The entry revealed a certain uneasiness even about the noble exception, since the writer added that if her faith in her husband should be destroyed by experience her happiness on earth would end, and added

"between husband and wife this is (or should be) a forbidden topic."
She was twenty-two.

This notation parallels one in a more familiar dairy. Observing the goings-on of the low-country aristocracy, Mary Boykin Chesnut wrote: "Thank God for my country women, but alas for the men! They are probably no worse than men everywhere, but the lower their mistresses the more degraded they must be. . . ."[23] Chesnut's comment revealed the dual nature of male depravity: sexual aberration in general and crossing the racial barrier in particular. Concern on this topic was an insistent theme in the writings of southern women and continued to be so long after emancipation. It may be significant that they did not blame black women, who might have provided convenient scapegoats. The blame was squarely placed on men. "You have no confidence in men," wrote one husband; "to use your own phrase 'we are all humbugs,' " adding that he himself was a great sinner though he did not specify his sin.[24]

Miscegenation was the fatal flaw in the patriarchal doctrine. While southern men could defend slavery as "domestic and patriarchal," arguing that slaves had "all the family associations, and family pride, and sympathies of the master," and that the relationship between master and slave secured obedience "as a sort of filial respect," southern women looked askance at the fact that so many slaves quite literally owed their masters filial respect.[25] "There is the great point for the abolitionists . . . ," one wrote.[26] While some southern reviewers blasted "the fiend in petticoats" who wrote Uncle Tom's Cabin, southern women passed copies of the book from hand to hand.

Impressive evidence of the pervasiveness of interracial sex and its effects on the minds and spirits of white women, gathered thirty years ago, has recently found its way into print. James Hugo Johnston examined 35,000 manuscript petitions to the Virginia legislature. Among these documents were many divorce petitions in which white women named slave women as the cause of their distress. In some petitions wives told the whole story of their marriages, throwing much light on what could happen to the family in a slave society. One testified that her husband had repeated connection with many slaves, another protested several black mistresses who had been placed in her home and had treated her insolently. Yet another recounted a complicated story in which her brother had tried to force her husband to send away his black mistress, without success. In several cases the husband's attention to his mulatto children, sometimes in preference to his legitimate children, was offered in evidence. The stories run on and on until one is surfeited with pain and tragedy from the white woman's point of view, pain which could doubtless be matched from the black woman's point of view if it had been recorded. Many petitioners candidly described their husbands' long attachment to black mistresses, and their reluctance to give them up. Johnston also adduced evidence of the tortured efforts white men made to provide for their mulatto children, efforts corroborated by Helen Catterall's compilation of legal cases dealing with slavery.[27]

If so much evidence found its way into the official records of the state of Virginia, how much is there yet unexamined in the records of other slave states, and how much more was never recorded because women suffered in silence rather than go against religion, custom, and social approval to sue for divorce by a special act of the legislature? Johnston, from his close acquaintance with the documents, surmised that there must have been many women who calmly or sullenly submitted to becoming "chief slave of the master's harem," a phrase attributed to Dolley Madison.[28]

Even apart from miscegenation, the general sexual freedom society accorded to men was deeply resented by women. A thread of bitterness runs through letters describing marital problems, the usual assumption being that male heartlessness could be expected. The double standard was just one more example of how unfairly the world was organized:

> As far as a womans being forever 'Anathema . . .' in society for the same offence which in a man, very slightly lowers, and in the estimation of some of his own sex rather elevates him. In this I say there appears to be a very very great injustice. I am the greatest possible advocate for womans purity, in word, thought or deed, yet I think if a few of the harangues directed to women were directed in a point where it is more needed the standard of morality might be elevated.[29]

Ten years later the same woman had not changed her mind: "it occurs to me that if virtue be the test to distinguish man from beast the claim of many Southern white men might be questionable. . . ."[30]

In addition to the widely prevailing skepticism with which women viewed the pretensions of their lords and masters (a label often used with a measure of irony), there was widespread discontent with the institution of slavery. "I never met with a lady of southern origin who did not speak of Slavery as a sin and a curse—the burden which oppressed their lives," Harriet Martineau observed in her autobiography.[31]

In Virginia, after the Nat Turner rebellion, twenty-four women joined in a petition to the legislature, noting that though "it be unexampled, in our beloved State, that females should interfere in its political concerns," they were so unhappy about slavery that they were willing to break the tradition. They urged the legislature to find a way to abolish slavery.[32]   An overseer of wide experience told Chesnut in 1861 that in all his life he had met only one or two women who were not abolitionists.[33]   William Gilmore Simms, reviewing *Uncle Tom's Cabin* in the *Southern Quarterly Review,* made clear his understanding of the opposition to slavery among southern women.[34]

Of course Martineau and the overseer exaggerated to make a point, and the Virginia petitioners were unusual. Women of slaveholding families responded ambiguously to the life imposed on them. Some accepted it without question. Others, complaining of the burden of slavery, nevertheless expected and sometimes got a degree of personal service which would have been inconceivable to women in the free states.[35]   It was also true that few were philanthropic enough to give up a large investment for a principle. It is further clear that most southern women accepted, with a few nagging questions, the racial assumptions of their time and place.

Even with these conditions many women of the planter class had strong doubts about either the morality or the expediency of slavery, as the following statements indicate. "Always I felt the moral guilt of it, felt how impossible it must be for an owner of slaves to win his way into Heaven."[36]   "But I do not hesitate to say ... that slavery was a curse to the South—that the time had come in the providence of God to give every human being a chance for liberty and I would as soon hark back to a charnel house for health inspiration as to go to the doctrines of secession, founded on the institution of slavery, to find rules and regulations. ..."[37]   "When the thunderbolt of John Brown's raid broke over Virginia I was inwardly terrified, because I thought it was God's vengeance for the torture of such as Uncle Tom."[38]   "I will confess that what troubles me more than anything else is that I am not certain that *Slavery is right.*"[39]   "When will it please our God to enfranchise both the holders and the slaves from bondage? It is a stigma, a disgrace to our country. ..."[40]   "In 1864 I read Bishop Hopkins' book on slavery. He took the ground that we had a right to hold the sons of Ham in bondage. ... Fancy a besotted, grinding, hardfisted slave driver taking up a moral tone as one of God's accredited agents!!"[41]

One doubter suggested that she would happily pay wages to her house servants if her husband would agree, and another thought slaves ought to be permitted to choose their own masters. Still another devoted all her time to teaching slaves to read and write, even though to do so was illegal, and to providing a Sunday school for slave children.[42]

Moral doubts were further complicated by strong personal attachments between white and black women. A South Carolina woman went into mourning in 1857 when her favorite slave died, and her sister wrote that "She loved Rose better than any other human being."[43]

Another member of the same family insisted that her brother and brother-in-law keep promises made to slaves whom she had sold within the family. A Virginia woman, seeking permission to free her slave woman and keep her in the state, contrary to the law, testified to her "strong and lasting attachment to her slave Amanda."[44] Such phrases were not uncommon among southern women.

For every woman who held slavery to be immoral, or who simply loved individual slaves, there were dozens who hated it for practical reasons. "Free at last," cried one white woman when she heard of the Emancipation Proclamation. "If slavery were restored and every Negro on the American continent offered to me," wrote another, "I should spurn them. I should prefer poverty rather than assume again the cares and perplexities of ownership. . . ."[45] Such quotations could be multiplied. They are typified by a diary entry in the fall of 1866 expressing relief "that I had no Negro clothes to cut out this fall O what a burden, like that of Sinbad the Sailor, was the thought of 'Negro clothes to be cut out.'"[46]

Motherhood, happy families, omnipotent men, satisfied slaves—all were essential parts of the image of the organic patriarchy. In none of these areas did the image accurately depict the whole reality.

For women as for the slaves, open revolt was made difficult by many constraints. Though women had complaints, they shared many of the assumptions of men, and, at least intermittently, enjoyed the role and status of the landholding aristocracy. Discontent does not automatically lead to a clear idea of alternatives, and few, if any, southern women in the 1850s had visions of a multiracial society based on freedom, much less equality. Nor did they conceive of fundamental change in the patterns of marriage and family which bound them so tight. Some, to be sure, found widowhood a liberating experience.[47]

The ideology of woman's liberation, which was being worked out in the North by Sarah Grimké, Margaret Fuller, Elizabeth Cady Stanton, and others, had only begun to take shape in the minds of southern women, but signs of change can be found. A letter written from Yazoo, Mississippi, in 1849 to the Southern Ladies Companion complained about an article which seemed to imply that only men were part of mankind:

> Woman is not, or ought not to be, either *an article* to be turned to good account by the persons who compose "this life" [men] nor a plaything for their amusement. She ought to be regarded as forming a part of mankind herself. She ought to be regarded as having as much interest or proprietorship in "this life" as anyone else. And the highest compliment to be paid her is that she is useful to herself—that in conjunction with the rest of mankind, in works of virtue, religion and morality, the sum of human

happiness is augmented, the kingdom of the Savior enlarged and the glory of God displayed.[48]

By the 1850s some echoes of the woman's rights debate which had erupted in the North in 1848 began to reach southern ears. A violent attack on the Woman's Rights Convention held in Worcester, Massachusetts, in 1851 appeared in the *Southern Quarterly Review,* written by a distinguished southern woman, Louisa Cheves McCord.[49] A closer look at McCord's own history is instructive with respect to built-in constraints. Daughter of Langdon Cheves, she was outstandingly able both as a writer and as an administrator. Yet she used her ability to defend the whole southern domestic metaphor, including slavery. One has only to imagine her born in Boston instead of Charleston to find in Louisa McCord all the makings of a Margaret Fuller or an Elizabeth Cady Stanton.

What was the significance of this widespread discontent? Public decisions are rooted in private feelings, and the psychological climate in any society is one of the most important things a social or political historian needs to understand. The South by 1860 was in a high state of internal tension, as feelings of guilt and fear of the future mounted. The part played by slaves themselves, as well as by women, in exacerbating these tensions is just now beginning to be examined. Speaking of the American Revolution, Charles Francis Adams once remarked that it "drew its nourishment from the sentiment that pervaded the dwellings of the entire population," and added, "How much this home sentiment did then, and does ever, depend upon the character of the female portion of the people, will be too readily understood by all to require explanation."[50] What Adams called "the home sentiment" was in the South of 1860 an unstable and hence explosive mixture of fear, guilt, anxiety, and discontent with things as they were. How much this stemmed from the unhappiness of "the female portion of the population" is not yet well understood, but it is worth a good deal of study.

NOTES

1. George Fitzhugh, *Cannibals All! or Slaves Without Masters* (Cambridge, Mass., 1960), p. 18.

2. William Pettigrew to Mose, July 12, 1856, Pettigrew Family Papers (Southern Historical Collection, University of North Carolina).

3. Charles Pettigrew to Caroline Pettigrew, Oct. 18, 1857, *ibid.*

4. Anne Firor Scott, *The Southern Lady: From Pedestal to Politics 1830–1930* (Chicago, 1970), 20–21.

5. *Corinne,* Madame de Stael's famous feminist novel, appeared often in lists of books read by southern women. Even Mary Wollstonecraft was not entirely unknown in the South. See William R. Taylor, *Cavalier and Yankee: The Old South and the American National Character* (New York, 1961), 162–67, for discussion of a pervasive malaise among ante bellum southern women.

6. See H. E. Sterkx, *Partners in Rebellion: Alabama Women in the Civil War* (Rutherford, N.J., 1970), for the most recent collection of evidence concerning the extraordinary vigor and range of southern women's activities during the war. It is important to note that this essay does not treat all classes of women. There were eight million southerners in 1860, of whom the largest part were ordinary farmer folk, slaves, and free blacks. This majority was ruled, politically, economically, and socially, by a small top layer, the large and medium-sized plantation owners who had money, or at least credit, slaves, and power. From their ranks came the proslavery philosophers, the mythmakers, the leaders of opinion. From their ranks came the most visible southerners, the minority which the rest saw and heard. It was members of this minority who consciously or unconsciously clung to the idea of the beautiful organic society so well described in George Fitzhugh, *Sociology for the South: or the Failure of Free Society* (Richmond, 1954). It was women of this minority who were called upon to play the appropriate role, to live up to the image of the southern lady. Other women, farmer's wives and daughters and illiterate black women, were part of society and in some inarticulate way doubtless helped to shape it, but historians have just begun to forge tools which may permit an examination of their role. For insights into southern society, see Steven A. Channing, *Crisis of Fear: Secession in South Carolina* (New York, 1970).

7. Fred A. Ross, *Slavery Ordained of God* (Philadelphia, 1859), 54–56.

8. R. M. Ruffin, *Tales and Sketches for the Fireside* (Marion, Ala., 1858).

9. For other sources of women's unhappiness, especially the desire for education, see Scott, *Southern Lady.* This essay concentrates on areas of complaint directly related to the patriarchal myth. Of course the education some women hoped for, had it been available, would have indirectly undermined the patriarchy.

10. See *Annual Report to the Legislature of South Carolina Relating to the Registration of Births, Deaths and Marriages for the Year Ending December 13, 1856* (Columbia, S. C., 1857). Though the report acknowledges grave deficiencies in its fact gathering, this early venture into vital statistics supports generalizations suggested here. For comparative purposes the report includes some statistics from Kentucky which are also supportive. Of the deaths recorded in South Carolina in 1856, nearly one half were children under the age of five and nearly one fourth were children under one year. Of marriages in the same year, 5.7 percent were of men under twenty, while 40.4 percent of the women were under that age. Nearly one half of the men and three fourths of the women who married in 1856 were under twenty-five. One fourth of the men but only 9.4 percent of the women married between the ages of twenty-five and thirty. A cohort analysis of selected groups of southern women patterned on Robert V. Wells' study of Quakers might be useful, if data could be found. See Robert V. Wells, "Demographic Change and the Life Cycle of American Families," *Journal of Interdisciplinary History,* II (Autumn 1971), 273–82. Analysis of the biographical sketches of 150 low-country

planters prepared by Chalmers Gaston Davidson provides further evidence of the age gap between husbands and wives. Davidson's study is based on 440 South Carolinians who had 100 or more slaves on a single estate. (Although fifty of the planters were women—a somewhat startling fact—his information is always about the men these women married.) The majority of the men were one to ten years older than their wives in first marriage. For second marriages the age difference increased, as it did for third and fourth marriages. In cases where the woman was older than her husband (twenty-three in all), the age gap was usually up to five years, though three women were more than ten years older than their husbands. Chalmers Gaston Davidson, *The Last Foray: The South Carolina Planters of 1860: A Sociological Study* (Columbia, S. C., 1971), 170–267.

11. E. G. C. Thomas Diary, June 26, 1855 (Department of Manuscripts, Duke University).

12. *Ibid.*, May 26, 1856.

13. *Ibid.*, June 1, 1856.

14. *Ibid.*, Dec. 1862.

15. *Ibid.*, Dec. 31, 1863.

16. *Ibid.*, Feb. 12, 1865.

17. *Ibid.*, Jan. 29, 1869.

18. *Ibid.*, Nov. 29, 1870.

19. James Petigru Carson, *Life, Letters and Speeches of James Louis Petigru: The Union Man of South Carolina* (Washington, 1920), 441.

20. Letters of Charles and Caroline Pettigrew, 1856–1861, Pettigrew Family Papers.

21. The degree to which maternity shaped women's lives emerges from any random examination of family histories. For example, Charles and Mary Pratt Edmonston of North Carolina had their first child in 1812, their last in 1833. During those twenty-one years Mrs. Edmonston bore eleven children, four of whom died in infancy. Mrs. Andrew McCollum of Louisiana bore ten children between 1840 and 1855, including one set of twins. Three died in infancy. During 180 months of married life, she spent ninety in pregnancy and seventy in nursing babies, since she did not use wet nurses. Thus in all her married life there was one month when she was neither pregnant nor nursing a baby. Margaret Ann Morris Grimball, wife of South Carolinian John B. Grimball, married at twenty and had a child every two years for eighteen years. At seventeen Varina Howell of Mississippi married Jefferson Davis who was thirty-five and a widower. Children were born in 1852, 1855, 1857, 1861, and 1864. Georgian David Crenshaw Barrow married Sarah Pope who bore him nine children in seventeen years, then died. John Crittenden's wife bore seven children in thirteen years. Robert Allston of South Carolina married Adele Petigru, ten years his junior. She bore ten children in seventeen years of whom five lived to maturity. Examples could be multiplied indefinitely, but far more useful would be a careful demographic study of selected southern counties, tidewater and upcountry, to give a firm underpinning to this kind of impressionistic evidence.

22. Thomas Diary, April 12, 1856.

23. Mary Boykin Chesnut, *Diary from Dixie,* Ben Ames Williams, ed. (Boston, 1949), 21–22.

24. Charles Pettigrew to Caroline Pettigrew, July 10, 1856, Pettigrew Family Papers.

25. Quoted in Severn Duvall, *"Uncle Tom's Cabin:* The Sinister Side of the Patriarchy," *New England Quarterly,* XXXVI (March 1963), 7–8. This perceptive article deserves serious attention from social historians.

26. Thomas Diary, Jan. 2, 1858.

27. James Hugo Johnston, *Race Relations in Virginia & Miscegenation in the South 1776–1860* (Amherst, 1970); Helen Tunnicliff Catterall, *Judicial Cases concerning American Slavery and the Negro* (2 vols., Washington, 1926). See also Guion Griffis Johnson, *Ante-Bellum North Carolina: A Social History* (Chapel Hill, 1937), 221, for evidence that cohabitation with a Negro was the second most important cause for divorce in North Carolina.

28. Johnston, *Race Relations in Virginia,* 237.

29. Thomas Diary, Feb. 9, 1858.

30. *Ibid.,* May 7, 1869.

31. Harriet Martineau, *Harriet Martineau's Autobiography: With Memorials by Maria Weston Chapman* (3 vols., London, 1877), II, 21.

32. Augusta County Legislative Petitions, 1825–1833 (Virginia State Library, Richmond).

33. Chesnut, *Diary from Dixie,* 169.

34. William Gilmore Simms, review of *Uncle Tom's Cabin, Southern Quarterly Review,* VIII (July 1853), 216, 233.

35. Their expectations may be illustrated by the E. G. C. Thomas family in its poverty-stricken postwar phase still requiring, so they thought, a person to cook, a person to clean, a person to wash and iron, one to do the chores, and a carriage driver. See Thomas Diary, 1868–1869, as Mrs. Thomas details her search for reliable domestic help among the freed people. One complication was that it was considered unethical to hire fine servants who had once belonged to friends.

36. John Q. Anderson, ed., *Brokenburn: The Journal of Kate Stone 1861–1868* (Baton Rouge, 1955), 8.

37. Rebecca L. Felton, "The Subjection of Women," pamphlet 19, Rebecca L. Felton Papers (Manuscript Division, University of Georgia).

38. Mrs. Burton [Constance Cary] Harrison, *Recollections Grave and Gay* (New York, 1912), 42.

39. Thomas Diary, Sept. 23, 1854.

40. Martha E. Foster Crawford Diary, Feb. 7, 1853, Feb. 3, 1854 (Department of Manuscripts, Duke University).

41. Hope Summerell Chamberlain, *Old Days in Chapel Hill, being the Life and Letters of Cornelia Phillips Spencer* (Chapel Hill, 1926), 93.

42. John Q. Anderson, "Sarah Anne Ellis Dorsey," Edward T. James and others, eds., *Notable American Women 1607–1950: A Biographical Dictionary* (3 vols., Cambridge, Mass., 1971), I, 505–06. There were southern men who opposed slavery, too, but theirs was usually an economic, not a moral critique.

43. Jane P. North to Caroline Pettigrew, Nov. 16, 1857, Pettigrew Family Papers.

44. J. H. Easterby, ed., *The South Carolina Rice Plantation as Revealed in the Papers of Robert F. W. Allston* (Chicago, 1945), 149.

45. Caroline Merrick, *Old Times in Dixie* (New York, 1901), 19. Mary A. H. Gay of Georgia, quoted in Matthew Page Andrews, *Women of the South in Wartime* (Baltimore, 1920), 334.

46. Thomas Diary, Sept. 20, 1866.

47. A study of planter's widows would be interesting. Many of them conducted plantations with considerable success, and as they necessarily came in contact with the outside world in business they began to develop more forceful personalities and interest in politics as well. For example, Jane Petigru North, sister of the famous James L. Petigru, was widowed early and ran one plantation owned by her brother and then another owned by her son-in-law, Charles L. Pettigrew. She did not hesitate to take full responsibility, and like her brother she was an outspoken supporter of the Union down to the moment of secession.

48. *Southern Ladies Companion,* II (1848), 45.

49. [Louisa Cheves McCord] L. S. M., *Southern Quarterly Review,* V (April 1852), 322–41. See also Margaret Farrand Thorp, "Louisa Susannah Cheves Mc-Cord," James and others, eds., *Notable American Women,* II, 451–52.

50. Charles Francis Adams, *Letters of Mrs. Adams with an Introductory Memoir by her grandson* (Boston, 1848), xix.

❧ 9 ❧

"MY MOTHER WAS MUCH OF A WOMAN": BLACK WOMEN, WORK, AND THE FAMILY UNDER SLAVERY

JACQUELINE JONES

"Ah was born back due in slavery," says Nanny to her granddaughter in Zora Neale Hurston's novel, *Their Eyes Were Watching God,* "so it wasn't for me to fulfill my dreams of whut a woman oughta be and to do." Nanny had never confused the degrading regimen of slavery with her own desires as they related to work, love, and motherhood: "Ah didn't want to be used for a work-ox and a brood-sow and Ah didn't want mah daughter used dat way neither. It sho wasn't mah will for things to happen lak they did." Throughout her life, she had sustained a silent faith in herself and her sisters that was permitted no expression within the spirtual void of bondage: "Ah wanted to preach a great sermon about colored women sittin' on high, but they wasn't no pulpit for me," she grieved.[1]

Nanny's lament offers a challenge to the historian who seeks to understand American slave women—their unfulfilled dreams as well as their day-in, day-out experiences. Despite recent scholarly interest in the relationship between women's work and family life on the one hand and Afro-American culture on the other, a systematic analysis of the roles of slave women is lacking. In her pioneering article entitled "Reflections on the Black Woman's Role in the Community of Slaves" (published over a decade ago), Angela Davis made a crucial distinction between the work that women were forced to perform for a master and the domestic labor that they provided for their own families. But

From *Feminist Studies*, Volume 8, No. 2 (Summer 1982): 235-269, by permission of the publisher *Feminist Studies,* Inc., c/o Women's Studies Program, University of Maryland, College Park, MD 20742.

her emphasis on the political implications of nurturing under slavery has not received the in-depth consideration it deserves.[2]

For example, a few scholars have explored the roles of the bond-woman as devoted wife and mother, physically powerful fieldworker, and rebellious servant. Herbert G. Gutman has illuminated the strength of kin ties within the slave community, and Eugene D. Genovese has furthered our understanding of black-white, male-female relations on the antebellum plantation. However, most historians continue to rely on the gender-neutral term "slave"—which invariably connotes "male"—and race supersedes sex as the focal point of their discussions. Consequently, questions related to the sexual division of labor under slavery and the way in which task assignments in the fields, the "Big House," and the slave quarters shaped the experiences of black women have gone unanswered—and unasked.[3]

Moreover, historians primarily concerned with the status of American women have examined the effects of patriarchy on various classes and ethnic groups over time; in the process they have highlighted variations on the theme of women's distinctive work patterns as determined by changing economic conditions, combined with traditional cultural assumptions about women's domestic responsibilities. Yet within the context of current feminist scholarship, slave women as a group remain for the most part neglected, perhaps because they existed outside the mainstream of the industrial revolution and (together with their menfolk) had few opportunities to put into practice their own ideas about appropriate work for women and men. According to this view, slave women were something of a historical aberration, a "special case" that has little relevance to current theoretical and methodological perspectives on women's work.[4]

The purpose of this article is to suggest that the burdens shouldered by slave women actually represented in extreme form the dual nature of all women's labor within a patriarchal, capitalist society: the production of goods and services and the reproduction and care of members of a future work force. The antebellum plantation brought into focus the interaction between notions of women *qua* "equal" workers and women *qua* unequal reproducers; hence a slaveowner just as "naturally" put his bondwomen to work chopping cotton as washing, ironing, or cooking. Furthermore, in seeking to maximize the productivity of his entire labor force while reserving certain domestic tasks for women exclusively, the master demonstrated how patriarchal and capitalist assumptions concerning women's work could reinforce one another. The "peculiar institution" thus involved forms of oppression against women that were unique manifestations of a more universal condition. The following discussion focuses on female slaves in the

American rural South between 1830 and 1860—cotton boom years that laid bare the economic and social underpinnings of slavery and indeed all of American society.[5]

Under slavery, blacks' attempts to maintain the integrity of family life amounted to a political act of protest, and herein lies a central irony in the history of slave women. In defiance of their owners' tendencies to ignore gender differences in making work assignments in the fields, the slaves whenever possible adhered to a strict division of labor within their own households and communities. This impulse was exhibited most dramatically in patterns of black family and economic life after emancipation. Consequently, the family, often considered by feminists to be a source (or at least a vehicle) of women's subservience, played a key role in the freed people's struggle to resist racial and gender oppression, for black women's full attention to the duties of motherhood deprived whites of their power over these women as field laborers and domestic servants.[6]

Interviewed by a Federal Writers Project (FWP) worker in 1937, Hannah Davidson spoke reluctantly of her experiences as a slave in Kentucky: "The things that my sister May and I suffered were so terrible . . . . It is best not to have such things in our memory." During the course of the interview, she stressed that unremitting toil has been the hallmark of her life under bondage. "Work, work, work," she said; it had consumed all her days (from dawn until midnight) and all her years (she was only eight when she began minding her master's children and helping the older women with their spinning). "I been so exhausted working, I was like an inchworm crawling along a roof. I worked till I thought another lick would kill me." On Sundays, "the only time they had to themselves," women washed clothes, and some of the men tended their small tobacco patches. As a child she loved to play in the haystack, but that was possible only on "Sunday evening, after work."[7]

American slavery was an economic and political system by which a group of whites extracted as much labor as possible from blacks through the use or threat of force. A slaveowner thus replaced any traditional division of labor that might have existed among blacks before enslavement with a work structure of his own choosing. All slaves were barred by law from owning property or acquiring literacy skills, and although the system played favorites with a few, black females and males were equal in the sense that neither sex wielded economic power over the other. Hence property relations—"the basic determinant of the sexual division of labor and of the sexual order" within most societies[8]—did not affect male-female interaction among the slaves themselves. To a considerable extent, the types of jobs slaves did, and the amount and regularity of labor they were forced to devote to such jobs, were all dictated by the master.

For these reasons the definition of slave women's work is problematical. If work is any activity that leads either directly or indirectly to the production of marketable goods, then slave women did nothing *but* work.[9] Even their efforts to care for themselves and their families helped to maintain the owner's work force, and to enhance its overall productivity. Tasks performed within the family context—childcare, cooking, and washing clothes, for example—were distinct from labor carried out under the lash in the field or under the mistress's watchful eye in the Big House. Still, these forms of nurture contributed to the health and welfare of the slave population, thereby increasing the actual value of the master's property (that is, slaves as both strong workers and "marketable commodities"). White men warned prospective mothers that they wanted neither "runts" nor girls born on their plantations, and slave women understood that their owner's economic self-interest affected even the most intimate family ties. Of the pregnant bondwomen on her husband's expansive Butlers Island (Georgia) rice plantation, Fanny Kemble observed, "they have all of them a most distinct and perfect knowledge of their value to their owners as property," and she recoiled at their obsequious profession obviously intended to delight her: "Missus, tho' we no able to work, we make little niggers for Massa." One North Carolina slave woman, the mother of fifteen children, used to carry her youngest with her to the field each day, and "when it get hungry she just slip it around in front and feed it and go right on picking or hoeing...," symbolizing in one deft motion the equal significance of the productive and reproductive functions to her owner.[10]

It is possible to divide the daily work routine of slave women into three discrete types of activity. These involved the production of goods and services for different groups and individuals, and included women's labor that directly benefited first, their families, second, other members of the slave community, and third, their owners. Although the master served as the ultimate regulator of all three types of work, he did not subject certain duties related to personal sustenance (that is, those carried out in the slave quarters) to the same scrutiny that characterized fieldwork or domestic service.

The rhythm of the planting-weeding-harvesting cycle shaped the lives of almost all American slaves, 95 percent of whom lived in rural areas. This cycle dictated a common work routine for slaves throughout the South, though the staple crop varied from tobacco in the Upper South to rice on the Georgia and South Carolina Sea Islands, sugar in

Louisiana, and the "king" of all agricultural products, cotton, in the broad swath of "Black Belt" that dominated the whole region. Of almost four million slaves, about one-half labored on farms with holdings of twenty slaves or more; one-quarter endured bondage with at least fifty other people on the same plantation. In its most basic form, a life of slavery meant working the soil with other blacks at a pace calculated to reap the largest harvest for a white master.[11]

In his efforts to wrench as much field labor as possible from female slaves without injuring their capacity to bear children, the master made "a noble admission of female equality," observed one abolitionist sympathizer with bitter irony. Slaveholders had little use for sentimental platitudes about the delicacy of the female constitution when it came to grading their "hands" according to physical strength and endurance. Judged on the basis of a standard set by a healthy adult man, most women probably ranked as three-quarter hands; yet there were enough women like Susan Mabry of Virginia, who could pick four or five hundred pounds of cotton a day (one hundred and fifty to two hundred pounds was considered respectable for an average worker), to remove from a master's mind all doubts about the ability of a strong, healthy, woman fieldworker. As a result, he conveniently discarded his time-honored Anglo-Saxon notions about the types of work best suited for women, thereby producing many "dreary scenes" like the one described by northern journalist Frederick Law Olmsted: during winter preparation of rice fields on a Sea Island plantation, a group of black women, "armed with axes, shovels and hoes . . . all slopping about in the black, unctuous mire at the botton of the ditches." Although pregnant and nursing women suffered from temporary lapses in productivity, most slaveholders apparently agreed with the (in Olmsted's words) "well-known, intelligent, and benevolent" Mississippi planter who declared that "labor is conducive to health; a healthy woman will rear [the] most children." In essence, the quest for an "efficient" agricultural work force led slaveowners to downplay gender differences in assigning adults to field labor.[12]

Dressed in coarse osnaburg gowns; their skirts "reefed up with a cord drawn tightly around the body, a little above the hips" (the traditional "second belt"); long sleeves pushed above the elbows and kerchiefs on their heads, female field hands were a common sight throughout the antebellum South. Together with their fathers, husbands, brothers, and sons, black women were roused at four A.M. and spent up to fourteen hours a day toiling out of doors, often under a blazing sun. In the cotton belt they plowed fields; dropped seed; and hoed, picked, ginned, and sorted cotton. On farms in Virginia, North Carolina, Kentucky, and Tennessee, women hoed tobacco; laid worm fences; and threshed, raked, and bound wheat. For those on the Sea Islands and in coastal areas, rice culture included raking and burning the stubble from the previous year's crop; ditching; sowing seed; plowing, listing, and hoeing fields; and harvesting, stacking, and threshing the rice. In the bayou region of Louisiana, women planted sugarcane cuttings, plowed, and helped to harvest and gin the cane. During the winter, they performed a myriad of tasks necessary on nineteenth-century farms of all kinds: repairing roads, pitching hay, burning brush, and setting up post and rail fences. Like Sara Colquitt of Alabama, most adult females "worked in de fields every day from 'fore daylight to almost plumb dark." During the busy harvest season, everyone was forced to labor up to sixteen hours at a time—after sunset by the light of candles or burning pine knots. Miscellaneous chores occupied women and men around outbuildings regularly and indoors on rainy days. Slaves of both sexes watered the horses, fed the chickens, and slopped the hogs. Together they ginned cotton, ground hominy, shelled corn and peas, and milled flour.[13]

Work assignments for women and men differed according to the size of a plantation and its degree of specialization. For example, on one Virginia wheat farm, the men scythed and cradled the grain, women raked and bound it into sheaves which children then gathered and stacked. Thomas Couper, a wealthy Sea Island planter, divided his slaves according to sex and employed men exclusively in ditching and women in moting [cleaning] and sorting cotton. Within the two gender groups, he further classified hands according to individual strength so that during the sugarcane harvest three "gangs" of women stripped blades (medium-level task), cut them (hardest) and bound and carried them (easiest). However, because cotton served as the basis of the southern agricultural system, distinct patterns of female work usually transcended local and regional differences in labor-force management. Stated simply, most women spent a good deal of their lives plowing, hoeing, and picking cotton. In the fields, the notion of a distinctive "women's work" vanished as slaveholders realized that "women can do plowing very well and full well with the hoes and equal to men at picking."[14]

To harness a double team of mules or oxen and steer a heavy wooden plow was no mean feat for any person, and yet a "substantial minority" of slave women mastered these rigorous activities. White women and men from the North and South marvelled at the skill and strength of female plow hands. Emily Burke of eastern Georgia saw women and men "promiscuously run their ploughs side by side, and day after day . . . and as far as I was able to learn, the part the women sustained in this masculine employment, was quite as efficient as that of the more athletic sex." In his travels through Mississippi, Olmsted watched as women "twitched their plows around on the headland, jerking their reins, and yelling to their mules, with apparent ease, energy, and rapidity." He saw no indication that "their sex unfitted them for the occupation."[15]

On another estate in the Mississippi Valley, Olmsted observed forty of the "largest and strongest" women he had ever seen; they "carried themselves loftily, each having a hoe over the shoulder, and walking with a free, powerful swing, like *chasseurs* on the march." In preparing fields for planting, and in keeping grass from strangling the crop, women as well as men blistered their hands with the clumsy hoe characteristic of southern agriculture. "Hammered out of pig iron, broad like a shovel," these "slave-time hoes" withstood most forms of abuse (destruction of farm implements constituted an integral part of resistance to forced labor). Recalled one former slave of the tool that also served as pick, spade, and gravedigger: "Dey make 'em heavy so dey fall hard, but de bigges' trouble was liftin' dem up." Hoeing was backbreaking labor, but the versatility of the tool and its importance to cotton cultivation meant that the majority of female hands used it a good part of the year.[16]

The cotton-picking season usually began in late July or early August and continued without interruption until the end of December. Thus for up to five months annually, every available man, woman, and child was engaged in a type of work that was strenuous and "tedious from its sameness." Each picker carried a bag fastened by a strap around her neck and deposited the cotton in it as she made her way down the row, at the end of which she emptied the bag's contents into a basket. Picking cotton required endurance and agility as much as physical strength, and women frequently won regional and inter-farm competitions conducted during the year. Pregnant and nursing women usually ranked as half-hands and were required to pick an amount less than the "average" one hundred and fifty or so pounds per day.[17]

Slaveholders often reserved the tasks that demanded sheer muscle power for men exclusively. These included clearing the land of trees, rolling logs, and chopping and hauling wood. However, plantation exigencies sometimes mandated women's labor in the area, too; in general, the smaller the farm, the more arduous and varied was women's fieldwork. Lizzie Atkins, who lived on a twenty-five-acre Texas planta-tion with only three other slaves remembered working "until slam dark every day"; she helped to clear land, cut wood, and tend the livestock in addition to her other duties of hoeing corn, spinning thread, sewing clothes, cooking, washing dishes, and grinding corn. One Texas farmer, who had his female slaves haul logs and plow with oxen, even made them wear breeches, thus minimizing outward differences between the sexes. Still, FWP interviews with former slaves indicate that blacks considered certain jobs uncharacteristic of bondwomen. Recalled Louise Terrell of her days on a farm near Jackson, Mississippi: "The women had to split rails all day long, just like the men." Nancy Boudry of Georgia said she used to "split wood jus' like a man." Elderly women reminisced about their mothers and grandmothers with a mixture of pride and wonder. Mary Frances Webb declared of her slave grand-mother, "in the winter she sawed and cut core wood just like a man. She said it didn't hurt her as she was strong as an ox." Janie Scott's description of her mother implied the extent of the older woman's emotional as well as physical strength: she was "strong and could roll and cut logs like a man, and was much of a woman."[18]

Very few women served as skilled artisans or mechanics; on large estates, men invariably filled the positions of carpenter, cooper, wheel-wright, tanner, blacksmith, and shoemaker. At first it seems ironic that masters would utilize women fully as field laborers, but reserve most of the skilled occupations that required manual dexterity for men. Here the high cost of specialized and extensive training proved crucial in determining the division of labor; although women were capable of learning these skills, their work lives were frequently interrupted by childbearing and nursing; a female blacksmith might not be able to provide the regular service required on a plantation. Too, masters frequently "hired out" mechanics and artisans to work for other employers during the winter, and women's domestic responsibilities were deemed too important to permit protracted absences from the quarters. However, many young girls learned to spin thread and weave cloth because these tasks could occupy them during confinement.[19]

The drive for cotton profits induced slaveowners to squeeze every bit of strength from black women as a group. According to the esti-mates of Roger L. Ransom and Richard Sutch, in the 1850s at least 90 percent of all female slaves over sixteen years of age labored more than 261 days per year, eleven to thirteen hours each day. Few overseers or masters had any patience with women whose movements in the field were persistently "clumsy, awkward, gross, [and] elephan-tine" for whatever reasons—malnutrition, exhaustion, recalcitrance. As Hannah Davidson said: "If you had something to do, you did it or got whipped." The enforced pace of work more nearly resembled that of a factory than a farm; Kemble referred to female field hands as "human hoeing machines." The bitter memories of former slaves merely suggest the extent to which the physical strength of women was exploited. Eliza Scantling of South Carolina, only sixteen years old at the end of the Civil War, plowed with a mule during the coldest months of the year: "Sometimes me hands get so cold I jes' cry." Matilda Perry of Virginia "Use to wuk fum sun to sun in dat ole terbaccy field. Wuk till my back felt lak it ready to pop in two."[20]

At times a woman would rebel in a manner commensurate with the work demands imposed upon her. "She'd git stubbon like a mule and quit." Or she took her hoe and knocked the overseer "plum down" and "chopped him right across his head." When masters and drivers "got rough on her, she got rough on them, and ran away in the woods." She cursed the man who insisted he "owned" her so that he beat her "till she fell" and left her broken body to serve as a warning to the others: "Dat's what you git effen you sass me." Indeed, in the severity of punishment meted out to slaves, little distinction was made between the sexes: "Beat women! Why sure he [master] beat women. Beat women jes' lak men." A systematic survey of the FWP slave narrative collection reveals that women were more likely than men to engage in "verbal confrontations and striking the master but not running away," probably because of their family and childcare responsibilities.[21]

Family members who perceived their mothers or sisters as particularly weak and vulnerable in the fields conspired to lessen their work load. Frank Bell and his four brothers, slaves on a Virginia wheat farm, followed his parents down the long rows of grain during the harvest season. "In dat way one could help de other when dey got behind. All of us would pitch in and help Momma who warn't very strong." The overseer discouraged families from working together because he believed "dey ain't gonna work as fast as when dey all mixed up," but the black driver, Bell's uncle, "always looked out for his kinfolk, especially my mother." James Taliaferro told of his father, who counted the corn rows marked out for Aunt Rebecca ("a short-talking woman that ole Marsa didn't like") and told her that her assignment was almost double that given to the other women. Rebecca indignantly confronted the master, who relented by reducing her task, but not before he threatened to sell James's father for his meddling. On another plantation, the hands surreptitiously added handfuls of cotton to the basket of a young woman who "was small and just couldn't get her proper amount."[22]

No slave women exercised authority over slave men as part of their work routine, but it is uncertain whether this practice reflected the sensibilities of the slaveowners or of the slaves themselves. Women were assigned to teach children simple tasks in the house and field and to supervise other women in various facets of household industry. A master might "let [a woman] off fo' de buryings 'cause she know how to manage de other niggahs and keep dem quiet at de funerls," but he would not install her as a driver over people in the field. Many strong-willed women demonstrated that they commanded respect among males as well as females, but more often than not masters perceived this as a negative quality to be suppressed. One Louisiana slaveholder complained bitterly about a particularly "rascally set of old negroes"—"the better you treat them the worst they are." He had no difficulty pinpointing the cause of the trouble, for "Big Lucy, the leader, corrupts every young negro in her power." On other plantations, women were held responsible for instigating all sorts of undesirable behavior among their husbands and brothers and sisters. On Charles Colcock Jones's Georgia plantation, the slave Cash gave up going to prayer meeting and started swearing as soon as he married Phoebe, well-known for her truculence. Apparently few masters attempted to co-opt high-spirited women by offering them positions of formal power over black men.[23]

In terms of labor-force management, southern slaveowners walked a fine line between making use of the physical strength of women as productive workers and protecting their investment in women as childbearers. These two objectives—one focused on immediate profit returns and the other on long-term economic considerations—at times clashed, because women who spent long hours picking cotton, toiling in the fields with heavy iron hoes, and walking several miles a day sustained damage to their reproductive systems immediately before and after giving birth. For financial reasons, slaveholders might have "regarded pregnancy as almost holy," in the words of one medical historian. But they frequently suspected their bondwoman (like "the most insufferable liar" Nora) of shamming illness—"play[ing] the lady at your expense," as one Virginia planter put it. These fears help to account for the reckless brutality with which owners forced women to work in the fields during and after pregnancy.[24]

Work in the soil thus represented the chief lot of all slaves, female and male. In the Big House, a division of labor based on both gender and age became more apparent, reflecting slaveowners' assumptions about the nature of domestic service. Although women predominated as household workers, few devoted their energies full time to this kind of labor; the size of the plantation determined the degree to which the tasks of cleaning, laundering, caring for the master's children, cooking, and ironing were specialized. According to Eugene Genovese, as few as 5 percent of all antebellum adult slaves served in the elite corps of house servants trained for specific duties. Of course, during the harvest season all slaves, including those in the house, went to the fields to make obeisance to King Cotton. Thus the lines between domestic service and fieldwork blurred during the day and during the lives of slave women. Many continued to live in the slave quarters, but rose early in the morning to perform various chores for the mistress—"up wid de fust light to draw water and help as a house girl"—before heading for the field. James Claiborne's mother "wuked in de fiel' some, an' aroun' de house sometimes ..." Young girls tended babies and waited on tables until they were sent outside—"mos' soon's" they could work—and returned to the house years later, too frail to hoe weeds, but still able to cook and sew. The circle of women's domestic work went unbroken from day to day and from generation to generation.[25]

Just as southern white men scorned manual labor as the proper sphere of slaves, so their wives strove (often unsuccessfully) to lead a life of leisure within their own homes. Those duties necessary to maintain the health, comfort, and daily welfare of white slaveholders were considered less women's work than black women's and black children's work. Slave mistresses supervised the whole operation, but the sheer magnitude of labor involved in keeping all slaves and whites fed and clothed (with different standards set according to race, of course) meant that black women had to supply the elbow grease. For most slaves, housework involved hard, steady, often strenuous labor as they juggled the demands made by the mistress and other members of the master's family. Mingo White of Alabama never forgot that his slave mother had shouldered a work load "too heavy for any one person." She served as personal maid to the master's daughter, cooked for all the hands on the plantation, carded cotton, spun a daily quota of thread, wove and dyed cloth. Every Wednesday she carried the white family's laundry three-quarters of a mile to a creek, where she beat each garment with a wooden paddle. Ironing consumed the rest of her day. Like the lowliest field hand, she felt the lash if any tasks went undone.[26]

Although mistresses found that their husbands commandeered most bondwomen for fieldwork during the better part of the day, they discovered in black children an acceptable alternative source of labor. Girls were favored for domestic service, but a child's sex played only a secondary role in determining household assignments. On smaller holdings especially, the demands of housework, like cotton cultivation, admitted of no finely honed division of labor. Indeed, until puberty, girls and boys shared a great deal in terms of dress and work. All children wore a "split-tail shirt," a knee-length smock slit up the sides: "Boys and gals all dress jes' alike .... They call it a shirt iffen a boy wear it and call it a dress iffen the gal wear it." At the age of six or so, many received assignments around the barnyard or in the Big House from one or more members of the master's family. Mr. and Mrs. Alex Smith, who grew up together, remembered performing different tasks. As a girl she helped to spin thread and pick seeds from cotton and cockle burrs from wool. He chopped wood, carried water, hoed weeds, tended the cows, and picked bugs from tobacco plants. However, slave narratives contain descriptions of both girls and boys elsewhere doing each of these things.[27]

Between the ages of six and twelve, black girls and boys followed the mistress's directions in filling woodboxes with kindling, lighting fires in chilly bedrooms in the morning and evening, making beds, washing and ironing clothes, parching coffee, polishing shoes, and stoking fires while the white family slept at night. They fetched water and milk from the springhouse and meat from the smokehouse. Three times a day they set the table, helped to prepare and serve meals, "minded flies" with peacock feather brushes, passed the salt and pepper on command and washed the dishes. They swept, polished, and dusted, served drinks and fanned overheated visitors. Mistresses entrusted to the care of those who were little more than babies themselves the bathing, diapering, dressing, grooming, and entertaining of white infants. In the barnyard black children gathered eggs, plucked chickens, drove cows to and from the stable and "tended the gaps" (opened and closed gates). (In the fields they acted as human scarecrows, toted water to the hands, and hauled shocks of corn together.) It was no wonder that Mary Ella Grandberry, a slave child grown old, "disremember[ed] ever playin' lack chilluns do today."[28]

In only a few tasks did a sexual division of labor exist among children. Masters always chose boys to accompany them on hunting trips and to serve as their personal valets. Little girls learned how to sew, to milk cows and churn butter, and to attend to the personal needs of their mistresses. As tiny ladies-in-waiting, they did the bidding of fastidious white women and of girls not much older than they. Cicely Cawthon, age six when the Civil War began, called herself the mistress's "little keeper"; "I stayed around, and waited on her, handed her water, fanned her, kept the flies off her, pulled up her pillow, and done anything she'd tell me to do." Martha Showvely recounted a nightly ritual with her Virginia mistress. After she finished her regular work around the house the young girl would go to the woman's bedroom, bow to her, wait for acknowledgment, and then scurry around as ordered, lowering the shades, filling the water pitcher, arranging towels on the washstand, or "anything else" that struck the woman's fancy. Mary Woodward, only eleven in 1865, was taught to comb her mistress's hair, lace her corset, and arrange her hoop skirts. At the end of the toilet Mary was supposed to say, "You is served, mistress!" Recalled the former slave, "Her lak them little words at de last."[29]

Sexual exploitation of female servants of all ages (described in graphic detail by Harriet Jacobs in Lydia Maria Child's *Incidents in the Life of a Slave Girl*) predictably antagonized white women. Jealousy over their husbands' real or suspected infidelities resulted in a propensity for spontaneous violence among many. Husbands who flaunted their adventures in the slave quarters increased the chance that their wives would attack a specific woman or her offspring. Sarah Wilson remembered being "picked on" by the mistress, who chafed under her husband's taunts; he would say, "Let her alone, she got big, big blood in her, and then laugh."[30]

A divorce petition filed with the Virginia legislature in 1848 included a witness's testimony that the master in question one morning told his slave favorite to sit down at the breakfast table "to which Mrs. N[his wife] objected, saying. . . that she (Mrs. N.) would have her severely punished." Her husband replied "that in that event he would visit her (Mrs. N.) with a like punishment. Mrs. N. then burst into tears and asked if it was not too much for her to stand." This husband went to extreme lengths to remind his spouse of slave-mistress Mary Chesnut's observation that "there is no slave, after all, like a wife." In the black woman the mistress saw not only the source of her own degradation, she saw herself—a woman without rights, subject to the impulses of an arrogant husband-master.[31]

To punish black women for minor offenses, mistresses were likely to attack with any weapon available—a fork, butcher knife, knitting needle, pan of boiling water. Some of the most barbaric forms of punishment resulting in the mutilation and permanent scarring of female servants were devised by white mistresses in the heat of passion. As a group they received well-deserved notoriety for the "veritable terror" they unleashed upon black women in the Big House.[32]

Interviews with former slaves suggest that the advantages of domestic service (over fieldwork) for women have been exaggerated in accounts written by whites. Carrying wood and water, preparing three full meals a day over a smoky fireplace or pressing damp clothes with a hot iron rivaled cotton picking as back-breaking labor. Always "on call," women servants often had to snatch a bite to eat whenever they could, remain standing in the presence of whites, and sleep on the floor at the foot of their mistress's bed (increasing the chances that they would sooner or later be bribed, seduced, or forced into sexual relations with the master). To peel potatoes with a sharp knife, build a fire, or carry a heavy load of laundry down a steep flight of stairs required skills and dexterity not always possessed by little girls and boys, and injuries were common. Chastisement for minor infractions came with swift severity; cooks who burned the bread and children who stole cookies or fell asleep while singing to the baby suffered every conceivable form of physical abuse, from jabs with pins to beatings that left them disfigured for life. The master's house offered no shelter from the most brutal manifestations of slavery.[33]

For any one or all of these reasons, black women might prefer fieldwork to housework. During his visit to a rice plantation in 1853, Olmsted noted that hands "accustomed to the comparatively unconstrained life of the negro-settlement detest the close control and careful movements required of the house servants." Marriage could be both a means and an incentive to escape a willful mistress. Jessie Sparrow's mother wed at age thirteen in order "to go outer de big house. Dat how come she to marry so soon. . ." Claude Wilson recalled many years later that "his mother was very rebellious toward her duties and constantly harassed the 'Missus' about letting her work in the fields with her husband until finally she was permitted to make the change from the house to the fields to be near her man." Other women, denied an alternative, explored the range of their own emotional resources in attempting to resist petty tyranny; their "sassiness" rubbed raw the nerves of mistresses already harried and high-strung. A few servants simply withdrew into a shell of "melancholy and timidity."[34]

The dual status of a bondwoman—a slave and a female—afforded her master a certain degree of flexibility in formulating her work assignments. When he needed a field hand, her status as an able-bodied slave took precedence over gender considerations, and she was forced to toil alongside her menfolk. At the same time, the master's belief that most forms of domestic service required the attentions of a female reinforced among slave women the traditional role of woman as household worker.

The authority of the master in enforcing a sexual division of labor was absolute, but at times individual women could influence his decisions to some extent. In certain cases, a woman's preferences for either fieldwork or domestic service worked to her advantage. For example, the rebelliousness of Claude Wilson's mother prompted her removal from the Big House to the field, a change she desired. Similarly, masters might promise a woman an opportunity to do a kind of work she preferred as a reward for her cooperation and diligence. On the other hand, a slave's misbehavior might cause her to lose a position she had come to value; more than one prized cook or maid was exiled to the fields for "sassing" the mistress or stealing. A system of rewards and punishments thus depended on the preferences of individual slaves, and a servant determined to make life miserable for the family in the Big House might get her way in any case.[35]

In the field and Big House, black women worked under the close supervison of whites (the master, overseer, or mistress) at a forced pace.

The slaves derived few, if any, tangible benefits from their labor to increase staple-crop profits and to render the white family comfortable (at least in physical terms). However, their efforts to provide for their own health and welfare often took place apart from whites, with a rhythm more in tune with community and family life. For slave women, these responsibilities, although physically arduous, offered a degree of personal fulfillment. As Martha Colquitt remarked of her slave grandmother and mother who stayed up late to knit and sew clothes "for us chillun": "Dey done it 'cause dey wanted to. Dey wuz workin' for deyselves den." Slave women deprived of the ability to cook for their own kinfolk or discipline their own children felt a keen sense of loss; family responsibilities revealed the limited extent to which black women (and men) could control their own lives. Furthermore, a strict sexual division of labor in the quarters openly challenged the master's opportunistic approach to slave women's work.[36]

A number of activities were carried out either communally or centrally for the whole plantation by older women. On smaller farms, for example, a cook and her assistants might prepare one or all of the meals for the other slaves each day except Sunday. Similarly, an elderly woman, with the help of children too young to work in the fields, often was assigned charge of a nursery in the quarters, where mothers left their babies during the day. To keep any number of little ones happy and out of trouble for up to twelve to fourteen hours at a time taxed the patience of the most kindly souls. Slave children grew up with a mixture of affection and fear for the "grandmothers" who had dished out the licks along with the cornbread and clabber. Other grannies usurped the position of the white physician (he rarely appeared in any case); they "brewed medicines for every ailment," gave cloves and whiskey to ease the pain of childbirth, and prescribed potions for the lovesick. Even a child forced to partake of "Stinkin' Jacob tea" or a concoction of "turpentine an' castor oil an' Jerusalem oak" (for worms) would assert years later that "Gran'mammy was a great doctor," surely a testimony to her respected position within the slave community, if not to the delectability of her remedies.[37]

On many plantations, it was the custom to release adult women from fieldwork early on Saturday so that they could do their week's washing. Whether laundering was done in old wooden tubs, iron pots, or a nearby creek with batten sticks, wooden paddles, or washboards, it was a time-consuming and difficult chore. Yet this ancient form of women's work provided opportunities for socializing "whilst de 'omans leaned over de tubs washin' and a-singin' dem old songs." Mary Frances Webb remembered wash day—"a regular picnic"—with some fondness;

it was a time for women "to spend the day together," out of the sight and earshot of whites.[38]

Much of the work black women did for the slave community resembled the colonial system of household industry. Well into the nineteenth century throughout the South, slave women continued to spin thread, weave and dye cloth, sew clothes, make soap and candles, prepare and preserve foods, churn butter, and grow food for the family table. Slave women mastered all these tasks with the aid of primitive equipment and skills passed on from grandmothers. Many years later, blacks of both sexes exclaimed over their slave mothers' ability to prepare clothing dye from various combinations of tree bark and leaves, soil and berries; make soap out of ashes and animal skins; and fashion bottle lamps from string and tallow. Because of their lack of time and materials, black women only rarely found in these activities an outlet for creative expression, but they did take pride in their resourcefulness and produced articles of value to the community as a whole.[39]

Black women's work in home textile production illustrates the ironies of community labor under slavery, for the threads of cotton and wool bound them together in both bondage and sisterhood. Masters (or mistresses) imposed rigid spinning and weaving quotas on women who worked in the fields all day. For example, many were forced to spin one "cut" (about three hundred yards) of thread nightly, or four to five cuts during rainy days or in the winter. Women of all ages worked together and children of both sexes helped to tease and card wool, pick up the loom shuttles, and knit. In the flickering candlelight, the whirr of the spinning wheel and the clackety-clack of the loom played a seductive lullabye, drawing those who were already "mighty tired" away from their assigned tasks.[40]

As the "head spinner" on a Virginia plantation, Bob Ellis's mother was often sent home from fieldwork early to prepare materials for the night's work; "She had to portion out de cotton dey was gonna spin an' see dat each got a fair share." Later that evening, after supper, as she moved around the dusty loom room to check on the progress of the other women, she would sing:

> Keep yo' eye on de sun,
> See how she run
> Don't let her catch you with you work undone,
> I'm a trouble, I'm a trouble,
> Trouble don' las' always.

With her song of urgency and promise she coaxed her sisters to finish their work so they could return home by sundown: "Dat made de women all speed up so dey could finish fo' dark catch 'em, 'cause it mighty hard handlin' dat cotton thread by fire-light."[41]

In the quarters, group work melded into family responsibilities, for the communal spirt was but a manifestation of primary kin relationships. Here it is possible only to outline the social dynamics of the slave household. The significance of the family in relation to the sexual division of labor under slavery cannot be overestimated; out of the mother-father, wife-husband nexus sprang the slaves' beliefs about what women and men should be and do. Ultimately, the practical application of those beliefs (in the words of Genovese) "provided a weapon for joint resistance to dehumanization."[42]

The two-parent, nuclear family was the typical form of slave cohabitation regardless of the location, size, or economy of a plantation; the nature of its ownership; or the age of its slave community. Because of the omnipresent threat of forced separation by sale, gift, or bequest, this family was not "stable." Yet, in the absence of such separations, unions between husbands and wives and parents and children often endured for many years. Marital customs, particularly exogamy, and the practice of naming children after the mother's or father's relatives (the most common pattern was to name a boy after a male relative) revealed the strong sense of kinship among slaves. Households tended to be large; Herbert G. Gutman found families with eight living children to be quite common. Out of economic considerations, a master would encourage his work force to reproduce itself, but the slaves welcomed each new birth primarily as "a social and familial fact." A web of human emotions spun by close family ties—affection, dignity, love—brought slaves together in a world apart from whites.[43]

In their own cabins, the blacks maintained a traditional division of labor between the sexes. Like women in almost all cultures, slave women had both a biological and a social "destiny." As part of their childbearing role, they assumed primary responsibility for childcare (when a husband and wife lived on separate plantations, the children remained with their mother and belonged to her master). Women also performed operations related to daily household maintenance—cooking, cleaning, tending fires, sewing and patching clothes.[44]

Fathers shared the obligations of family life with their wives. In denying slaves the right to own property, make a living for themselves, participate in public life, or protect their children, the institution of bondage deprived black men of access to the patriarchy in the larger economic and political sense. But at home women and men worked together to support the father's role as provider and protector. In the evenings and on Sundays, men collected firewood; made shoes; wove baskets; constructed beds, tables, and chairs; and carved butter paddles, ax handles, and animal traps. Other family members appreciated a father's skills; recalled Molly Ammonds, "My pappy make all de funiture dat went in our house an' it were might' good funiture too," and Pauline Johnson echoed, "De furn'chure was ho-mek, but my daddy mek it good an' stout." Husbands provided necessary supplements to the family diet by hunting and trapping quails, possums, turkeys, rabbits, squirrels, and raccoons, and by fishing. They often assumed responsibility for cultivating the tiny household garden plots allotted to families by the master. Some craftsmen, like Bill Austin's father, received goods or small sums of money in return for their work on nearby estates; Jack Austin, "regarded as a fairly good carpenter, mason, and bricklayer," was paid in "hams, bits of corn-meal, cloth for dresses for his wife and children, and other small gifts; these he either used for his small family or bartered with other slaves."[45]

These familial duties also applied to men who lived apart from their wives and children even though they were usually allowed to visit only on Saturday night and Sunday. Lucinda Miller's family "never had any sugar, and only got coffee when her father would bring it to her mother" during his visits. The father of Hannah Chapman was sold to a nearby planter when she was very small. Because "he missed us and us longed for him," she said many years later, he tried to visit his family under the cover of darkness whenever possible. She noted, "Us would gather 'round him an' crawl up in his lap, tickled slap to death, but he give us dese pleasures at painful risk." If the master should happen to discover him, "Us could track him de nex' day by de blood stains," she remembered.[46]

Hannah McFarland of South Carolina well remembered the time when the local slave patrol attempted to whip her mother, "but my papa sho stopped dat," she said proudly. Whether or not he was made to suffer for his courage is unknown; however, the primary literature of slavery is replete with accounts of slave husbands who intervened, at the risk of their own lives, to save wives and children from violence at the hands of white men. More often, however, fathers had to show their compassion in less dramatic (though no less revealing) ways. On a Florida plantation, the Minus children often rose in the morning to find still warm in the fireplace the potatoes "which their father had throughfully roasted and which [they] readily consumed." Margrett Nickerson recalled how her father would tenderly bind up the wounds inflicted on her by a maniacal overseer; in later years, her crippled legs preserved the memory of a father's sorrow intermingled with her own suffering.[47]

The more freedom the slaves had in determining their own activities the more clearly emerged a distinct division of labor between the sexes. During community festivities like log rollings, rail splittings, wood choppings, and corn shuckings, men performed the prescribed labor while women cooked the meals. At times, male participants willingly "worked all night," for, in the words of one former slave, "we had the 'Heavenly Banners' (women and whiskey) by us." A limited amount of primary evidence indicates that men actively scorned women's work, especially cooking, housecleaning, sewing, washing clothes, and intimate forms of childcare (like bathing children and picking lice out of their hair). Some slaveholders devised forms of public humiliation that capitalized on men's attempts to avoid these tasks. One Louisiana cotton planter punished slave men by forcing them to wash clothes (he also made chronic offenders wear women's dresses). In *This Species of Property*, Leslie Howard Owens remarks of men so treated, "So great was their shame before their fellows that many ran off and suffered the lash on their backs rather than submit to the discipline. Men clearly viewed certain chores as women's tasks, and female slaves largely respected the distinction."[48]

The values and customs of the slave community played a pre-dominant role in structuring work patterns among women and men within the quarters in general and the family in particular. Yet slave-holders affected the division of labor in the quarters in several ways; for example, they took women and girls out of the fields early on Saturdays to wash the clothes, and they enforced certain task assignments related to the production of household goods. An understanding of the social significance of the sexual division of labor requires at least brief mention of West African cultural preferences and the ways in which the American system of slavery disrupted or sustained traditional (African) patterns of women's work. Here it is important to keep in mind two points. First, cotton did not emerge as the South's primary staple crop until the late eighteenth century (the first slaves on the North American continent toiled in tobacco, rice, indigo, and corn fields); and second, regardless of the system of task assignments imposed upon antebellum blacks, the grueling pace of forced labor represented a cruel break from the past for people who had followed age-old customs related to subsistence agriculture.[49]

Though dimmed by time and necessity, the outlines of African work patterns endured among the slaves. As members of traditional agricultural societies, African women played a major role in producing the family's food as well as in providing basic household services. The sexual division of labor was more often determined by a woman's child-care and domestic responsibilities than by any presumed physical weakness. She might engage in heavy, monotonous fieldwork (in some tribes) as long as she could make provisions for nursing her baby; that often meant keeping an infant with her in the field. She cultivated a kitchen garden that yielded a variety of vegetables consumed by the family or sold at market, and she usually milked the cows and churned butter.[50]

West Africans in general brought with them competencies and knowledge that slaveowners readily exploited. Certain tribes were familiar with rice, cotton, and indigo cultivation. Many black women had had experience spinning thread, weaving cloth, and sewing clothes. Moreover, slaves often used techniques and tools handed down from their ancestors—in the method of planting, hoeing, and pounding rice, for example. Whites frequently commented on the ability of slave women to balance heavy and unwieldly loads on their heads, an African trait.[51]

The primary difficulty in generalizing about African women's part in agriculture stems from the fact that members of West African tribes captured for the North American slave trade came from different hoe-culture economies. Within the geographically limited Niger Delta region, for example, women and men of the Ibo tribe worked together in planting, weeding, and harvesting, but female members of another prominent group, the Yoruba, helped only with harvest. In general, throughout most of sub-Saharan Africa (and particularly on the west coast) women had primary responsibility for tilling (though not clearing) the soil and cultivating the crops; perhaps this tradition, combined with work patterns established by white masters in this country, reinforced the blacks' beliefs that cutting trees and rolling logs was "men's work." In any case it is clear that African women often did fieldwork. But because the sexual division of labor varied according to tribe, it is impossible to state with any precision the effect of the African heritage on the slaves' perceptions of women's agricultural work.[52]

The West African tradition of respect for one's elders found new meaning among American slaves; for most women, old age brought increased influence within the slave community even as their economic value to the master declined. Owners, fearful lest women escape from "earning their salt" once they became too infirm to go to the field, set them to work at other tasks—knitting, cooking, spinning, weaving, dairying, washing, ironing, caring for the children. (Elderly men worked as gardeners, wagoners, carters, and stocktenders.) But the imperatives of the southern economic system sometimes compelled slaveowners to extract from feeble women what field labor they could. In other cases they reduced the material provisions of the elderly—housing and allowances of food and clothing—in proportion to their decreased productivity.[53]

The overwhelming youth of the general slave population between 1830 and 1860 (more than one-half of all slaves were under twenty years of age) meant that most plantations had only a few old persons— the 10 percent over fifty years of age considered elderly. These slaves served as a repository of history and folklore for the others. Harriet Ware, a northern teacher assigned to the South Carolina Sea Islands, reported in 1862, " 'Learning' with these people I find means a knowl-edge of medicine, and a person is valued accordingly." Many older women practiced "medicine" in the broadest sense in their combined role of mid-wife, root doctor, healer, and conjurer. They guarded ancient secrets about herbs and other forms of plant life. In their interpretation of dreams and strange occurrences, they brought the real world closer to the supernatural realm and offered spiritual guidance to the ill, the troubled, and the lovelorn.[54]

For slaves in the late antebellum period, these revered (and some-times feared) women served as a tangible link with the African past. Interviewed by an FWP worker in 1937, a Mississippi-born former slave, James Brittian, recalled his own "grandma Aunt Mary" who had lived for 110 years. A "Molly Gasca [Madagascar?] negro," she was plagued by a jealous mistress because of her striking physical appear-ance; "Her hair it was fine as silk and hung down below her waist." Ned Chaney's African-born Granny Silla (she was the oldest person anyone knew, he thought) commanded respect among the other slaves by virtue of her advanced age and her remarkable healing powers: "Ever'body set a heap of sto' by her. I reckon, because she done 'cumullated so much knowledge an' because her head were so white." When Granny Silla died, her "little bags" of mysterious substances were buried with her because no one else knew how to use them. Yet Chaney's description of his own mother, a mid-wife and herb doctor, indicates that she too eventually assumed a position of at least informal authority within the community.[55]

As a little girl in Georgia, Mary Colbert adored her grandmother, a strong field hand, "smart as a whip," "I used to tell my mother that I wished I was named Hannah for her, and so Mother called me Mary Hannah," she recalled. Amanda Harris, interviewed in Virginia when she was ninety years old, looked back to the decade before the war when her grandmother was still alive: "Used to see her puffin' on dat ole pipe o' her'n, an' one day I ast her what fun she got outen it. 'Tain't no fun, chile,' she tole me. 'But it's a pow'ful lot o' easment. Smoke away trouble, darter. Blow ole trouble an' worry 'way in smoke.' " Amanda started smoking a pipe shortly before her grandmother died, and in 1937 she declared, "Now dat I'm ole as she was I know what she mean." In the quiet dignity of their own lives, these grandmothers preserved the past for future generations of Afro-American women.[56]

Within well-defined limits, the slaves created—or preserved—an explicit sexual division of labor based on their own preferences. Wives and husbands and mothers and fathers had reciprocal obligations toward one another. Together they worked to preserve the integrity of the family. Having laid to rest once and for all the myth of the slave matriarchy, some historians suggest that relations between the sexes approximated "a healthy sexual equality."[57] Without private property, slave men lacked the means to achieve economic superiority over their wives, one of the major sources of inequality in the ("free") sexual order. But if female and male slaves shared duties related to household maintenance and community survival, they were nonetheless reduced to a state of powerlessness that rendered virtually meaningless the concept of equality as it applies to marital relations.

Developments during the turbulent postwar years, when the chains of bondage were loosened but not destroyed, made clear the significance of black women's work in supporting the southern staple-crop economy. They also revealed the connection between patterns of women's work and black family life—a connection that had, at least to some degree, remained latent under slavery. Black women did their part in helping to provide for their families after the war. Female household heads had a particularly difficult time, for under the "free labor" system, a mother working alone rarely earned enough to support small children who were themselves too little to make any money. Relatives in a better financial situation often "adopted" these children, or took the whole family under their care.[58]

After the war, black women continued to serve as domestic servants, but large numbers stopped going to the fields altogether, or agreed to work only in harvest time. Indeed, from all over the South came reports that "the negro women are now almost wholly withdrawn from field labor." Ransom and Sutch, in their study of the economic consequences of emancipation, estimate that between one-third and one-half of all the women who worked in the fields under slavery provided proportionately less agricultural labor in the 1870s. This decline in overall female productivity was the result of two factors: many wives stayed home, and the ones who did continue to labor in the fields (like black men) put in shorter hours and fewer days each year than they had as slaves. Crop output in many locales dropped accordingly, and white landowners lamented their loss, "for women were as efficient as men in working and picking cotton."[59]

In their speculation about the sources of this "evil of female loaferism," whites offered a number of theories, from the pernicious influence of northern schoolteachers to the inherent laziness of the black race. Actually, black women and men responded to freedom in a manner consistent with preferences that had been thwarted during slavery. Husbands sought to protect their wives from the sexual abuse and physical punishment that continued to prevail under the wage system of agricultural labor. Wives wanted to remain at home with their children, as befitted free and freed women; many continued to contribute to the family welfare by taking in washing or raising chickens.[60]

By 1867, freed people who wanted to assert control over their own productive energies had reached what some historians term a "compromise" with white landowners anxious to duplicate antebellum crop levels. This "compromise" came in the form of the sharecropping system, a family organization of labor that represented both a radical departure from collective or "gang" work characteristics of slavery and a rejection of the wage economy so integral to the (North's) fledgling industrial revolution. Freed families moved out of the old slave quarters into cabins scattered around a white man's plantation; they received "furnishings" (tools and seed) and agreed to pay the landlord a share of the crop—usually one-half of all the cotton they produced—in return for the use of the land and modest dwelling. Under this arrangement, black husbands assumed primary responsibility for crop management, and their wives devoted as much attention as possible to their roles as mothers and homemakers. During the particularly busy planting or harvesting seasons, a woman would join her husband and children at work in the field. In this way she could keep an eye on her offspring and still put to use her considerable strength and skills unmolested by white men.[61]

The Reconstruction South was not the best of all worlds in which to foster a new order between the races—or the sexes. Faced with persistent economic exploitation and political subservience within white-dominated society, black men sought to assert their authority as protectors of their communities and families. Outwardly, they placed a premium on closing ranks at home. This impulse was institutionalized in the freed people's churches ("Wives submit yourselves to your husbands" was the text of more than one postbellum sermon) and political organizations. One searches in vain for evidence of female participants in the many black conventions and meetings during this period, although this was perhaps in part attributable to the fact that women did not have the right to vote. Black women remained militantly outspoken in defense of their families and property rights, but they lacked a formal power base within their own communities. And in an atmosphere fraught with sexual violence, where freedwomen remained at the mercy of white men and where "the mere suggestion" that a black man was attracted to a white woman was "enough to hang him," a black husband's resentment might continue to manifest itself in his relations with those closest to him. A Sea Island slave folktale offered the lesson that "God had nebber made a woman for the head of a man." In the struggle against white racism this often meant that black women were denied the equality with their men to which their labor—not to mention justice—entitled them.[62]

The sexual division of labor under slavery actually assumed two forms—one system of work forced upon slaves by masters who valued women only as work-oxen and brood-sows, and the other initiated by the slaves themselves in the quarters. Only the profit motive accorded a measure of consistency to the slaveholder's decisions concerning female work assignments; he sought to exploit his "hands" efficiently, and either invoked or repudiated traditional notions of women's work to suit his own purposes. In this respect, his decision-making process represented in microcosm the shifting priorities of the larger society, wherein different groups of women were alternately defined primarily as producers or as reproducers according to the fluctuating labor demands of the capitalist economy.[63]

Within their own communities, the slaves attempted to make work choices based on their African heritage as it applied to the American experience. Their well-defined sexual division of labor contrasted with the calcualted self-interest of slaveowners. Slave women were allowed to fulfill their duties as wives and mothers only insofar as these responsibilities did not conflict with their masters' demands for field or domestic labor. As sharecroppers, freed people sought to institutionalize their resistance to the whites' conviction that black women should be servants or cotton pickers first, and family members only incidentally. In working together as a unit, black parents and children made an explicit political statement to the effect that their own priorities were inimical to those of white landowners.

To a considerable extent, the freed family's own patriarchal tendencies—fathers took care of "public" negotiations with the white landlord while mothers assumed primary responsibiity for childcare—resulted from the black man's desire to protect his household in the midst of a violently racist society. The postbellum black nuclear family never duplicated exactly the functions of the white middle-class model, which (beginning in the late eighteenth century) drew an increasingly rigid distinction between masculine and feminine spheres of activity characteristic of commercial-industrial capitalism. Clearly, the peculiar southern way of life suggests that an analysis of black women's oppression should focus not so much on the family as on the dynamics of racial prejudice. However, black women and men in the long run paid a high price for their allegiance to a patriarchal family structure, and it is important not to romanticize this arrangement as it affected the status and opportunities of women, even within the confines of black community life. Women continued to wield informal influence in their roles as herb doctors and "grannies," but men held all positions of formal political and religious authority. Ultimately, black people's "preferences" in the postwar period took shape within two overlapping caste systems—one based on race, the other on gender. Former slaves were "free" only in the sense that they created their own forms of masculine authority as a counter to poverty and racism.

The story of slave women's work encapsulates an important part of American history. For here in naked form, stripped free of the pieties often used in describing white women and free workers at the time, were the forces that shaped patriarchal capitalism—exploitation of the most vulnerable members of society, and a contempt for women that knew no ethical or physical bounds. And yet, slave women demonstrated "true womanhood" in its truest sense. Like Janie Scott's mother who was "much of a woman," they revealed a physical and emotional strength that transcended gender and preached a great sermon about the human spirit.

NOTES

The author would like to acknowledge the helpful suggestions and comments provided by Rosalind Petchesky and other members of the *Feminist Studies* editorial board and by Michael P. Johnson. Research for this project (part of a full-length study of black women, work, and the family in America, 1830-1980) was funded by a grant from the National Endowment for the Humanities.

1. Zora N. Hurston, *Their Eyes Were Watching God* (London: J.M. Dent and Sons, 1938), pp. 31-32. Novelist, folklorist, and anthropologist, Hurston (born 1901, died 1960) had collected a massive amount of primary data on the culture and folklore of Afro-Americans before she began work on *Their Eyes Were Watching God*. In 1938 she served as supervisor of the Negro Unit of the Florida Federal Writers Project which compiled interviews with former slaves. Her various writings are finally receiving long-overdue literary attention and critical acclaim. See Robert E. Hemenway, *Zora Neale Hurston: A Literary Biography* (Urbana: University of Illinois Press, 1977); and a recent anthology; Zora N. Hurston, *I Love Myself When I Am Laughing . . . And Then Again When I Am Looking Mean and Impressive*, ed. Alice Walker (Old Westbury, N.Y.: Feminist Press, 1980).

2. Angela Davis, "Reflections on the Black Woman's Role in the Community of Slaves," *The Black Scholar* 3 (December 1971): 3-15. For other works that focus on slave women, see Mary Ellen Obitko, "'Custodians of a House of Resistance': Black Women Respond to Slavery," in *Women and Men: The Consequences of Power*, ed. Dana V. Hiller and Robin Ann Sheets (Cincinnati: Office of Women's Studies, University of Cincinnati, 1977), pp. 256-59; Deborah G. White, "Ain't I A Woman? Female Slaves in the Antebellum South" (Ph. D. dissertation, University of Illinois-Chicago Circle, 1979). White's work examines several important themes related to slave women's work and family life, but her study lacks a coherent theoretical framework. She asserts that slave women gained considerable "self-confidence" because they achieved "equality" with men of their race, and even suggests that emancipation resulted in a "loss" of women's "equality"; freedom amounted to "a decline in the status of black women" (p. 51). When used in this context, the concepts of equality and status lose all meaning and relevance to the complex issues involved; White's arument obscures the subtleties of black female-male relations under bondage and after emancipation.

The volume edited by Gerda Lerner, *Black Women in White America: A Documentary History* (New York: Randam House, 1972), includes material on the history of slave women.

3. Herbert G. Gutman, *The Black Family in Slavery and Freedom, 1750-1925* (New York: Pantheon Books, 1976); Eugene D. Genovese, *Roll, Jordan, Roll: The World the Slaves Made* (New York: Randam House, 1974); Leslie Howard Owens, *This Species of Property: Slave Life and Culture in the Old South* (New York: Oxford University Press, 1976); John D. Blassingame, *The Slave Community: Planatation Life in the Old South* (New York: Oxford University Press, 1972); Paul A. David et al., *Reckoning With Slavery: A Critical Study in the Quantitative History of American Negro Slavery* (New York: Oxford University Press, 1976); Paul D. Escott, *Slavery Remembered: A Record of Twentieth-Century Slave Narratives* (Chapel Hill: University of North Carolina Press, 1978).

In some specialized studies, women are largely excluded from the general analysis and discussed only in brief sections under the heading "Women and Children." See, for example, Robert S. Starobin, *Industrial Slavery in the Old South* (New York: Oxford University Press, 1970); and Todd L. Savitt, *Medicine and Slavery: The Diseases and Health Care of Blacks in Antebellum Virginia* (Urbana: University of Illinois Press, 1978).

4. For examples of studies of specific groups of women and the relationship between their work and family life, see Nancy F. Cott, *The Bonds of Womanhood: 'Woman's Sphere' in New England, 1780-1835* (New Haven: Yale University Press, 1977); Thomas Dublin, *Women at Work: The Transformation of Work and Community in Lowell, Massachusetts, 1826-1860* (New York: Columbia University Press, 1979); Milton Cantor and Bruce Laurie, ed., *Class, Sex, and the Woman Worker* (Westport, Conn.: Greenwood Press, 1977); Virginia Yans McLaughlin, "Patterns of Work and Family Organization: Buffalo's Italians," *Journal of Interdisciplinary History* 2 (Autumn 1971): 297-314; Leslie Woodcock Tentler, *Wage-Earning Women: Industrial Work and Family Life in the United States, 1900-1930* (New York: Oxford University Press, 1979).

General overviews and theoretical formulations that fail to take into account the experiences of slave women include Patricia Branca, "A New Perspective on Women's Work: A Comparative Typology," *Journal of Social History* 9 (Winter 1975): 129-53; W. Elliot Brownlee, "Household Values, Women's Work, and

Economic Growth, 1800-1930," *Journal of Economic History* 39 (March 1979): 199-209; Maurine Weiner Greenwald, "Historians and the Working-Class Woman in America," *International Labor and Working-Class History,* no. 14/15 (Spring 1979): 23-32; Alice Kessler-Harris, "Women, Work, and the Social Order," in *Liberating Women's History: Theoretical and Critical Essays,* ed. Berenice A. Carroll (Urbana: University of Illinois Press, 1976), pp. 330-43.

5. On women's "productive-reproductive" functions and the relationship between patriarchy and capitalism, see Joan Kelly, "The Doubled Vision of Feminist Theory: A Postscript to the 'Women and Power' Conference," *Feminist Studies* 5 (Spring 1979): 216-27; Heidi Hartmann, "Capitalism, Patriarchy, and Job Segragation by Sex," and Zillah Eisenstein, "Developing a Theory of Capitalist Patriarchy and Socialist Feminism," and "Some Notes on the Relations of Capitalist Patriarchy," in *Capitalist Patriarchy and the Case for Social Feminism,* ed. Zillah R. Eisenstein (New York: Monthly Review Press, 1979); Annette Kuhn and AnnMarie Wolpe, "Feminism and Materialism" and Veronica Beechey, "Women and Production: A Critical Analysis of Some Sociological Theories of Women's Work," both in *Feminism and Materialism: Women and Modes of Production,* ed. Annette Kuhn and AnnMarie Wolpe (London: Routledge and Kegan Paul, 1978).

Several scholars argue that the last three decades of the antebellum period constituted a distinct phase in the history of slavery. Improved textile machinery and a rise in world demand for cotton led to a tremendous growth in the American slave economy, especially in the Lower South. A marked increase in slave mortality rates and family breakups (a consequence of forced migration from Upper to Lower South), and a slight decline in female fertility rates indicate the heightened demands made upon slave labor during the years 1830-60. See David, et al., *Reckoning With Slavery,* pp. 99, 356-57; Jack Erickson Eblen, "New Estimates of the Vital Rates of the United States Black Population During the Nineteenth Century," *Demography* 11 (May 1974): 307-13.

6. For example, see Kelly, "Doubled Vision," pp. 217-18, and Eisenstein, "Relations of Capitalist Patriarchy," pp. 48-52, on the regressive implications of family life for women. But Davis notes that the slave woman's "survival-oriented activities were themselves a form of resistance" ("Reflections on the Black Woman's Role," p. 7).

7. Interviews with former slaves have been published in various forms, including George P. Rawick, ed., *The American Slave: A Composite Autobiography,* 41 vols., Series 1 and 2, supp. Series 1 and 2 (Westport Conn.: Greenwood Press, 1972, 1978, 1979); Social Science Institute, Fisk University, *Unwritten History of Slavery: Autobiographical Accounts of Negro Ex-Slaves* (Washington, D.C.: Microcards Editions, 1968); Charles L. Perdue, Jr., Thomas E. Borden, and Robert K. Phillips, *Weevils in the Wheat: Interviews with Virginia Ex-Slaves* (Charlottesville: University Press of Virginia, 1976); John B. Cade, "Out of the Mouths of Ex-Slaves." *Journal of Negro History* 20 (July 1935): 294-337.

The narratives as a historical source are evaluated in Escott, *Slavery Remembered,* pp. 3-18 ("the slave narratives offer the best evidence we will ever have on the feelings and attitudes of America's slaves . . ."); Martia Graham Goodson, "An Introductory Essay and Subject Index to Selected Interviews from the Slave Narrative Collection" (Ph.D. dissertation, Union Graduate School, 1977); and C. Vann Woodward, "History from Slave Sources," *American Historical Review* 79 (April 1974): 470-81.

The Davidson quotation is from Rawick, ed., *American Slave*, Ohio Narrs., Series 1, vol. 16, pp. 26-29. Hereafter, all references to this collection will include the name of the state, series number, volume, and page numbers. The other major source of slave interview material taken from the FWP collection for this paper—Perdue, et al.—will be referred to as *Weevils in the Wheat.*

8. Joan Kelly-Gadol, "The Social Relations of the Sexes: Methodological Implications of Women's History," *Signs* 1 (Summer 1976): 809-10, 819.

9, For discussions of women's work and the inadequacy of male-biased economic and social scientific theory to define and analyze it, see Joan Acker, "Issues in the Sociological Study of Women's Work," in *Working Women: Theories and Facts in Perspective*, ed., Ann H. Stromberg and Sherley Harkess (Palo Alto, Calif.: Mayfield Publishing Co. 1978), pp. 134-61; and Judith K. Brown, "A Note on the Division of Labor by Sex," *American Anthropologist* 72 (October 1970): 1073-78.

10. Miss. Narrs., supp. Series 1, pt. 2, vol. 7, p. 350; Okla. Narrs., supp. Series 1, vol. 12, p. 110; Davis, "Reflections on the Black Woman's Role," p. 8; Frances Anne Kemble, *Journal of a Residence on a Georgian Plantation in 1838-1839* (London: Longman, Green, 1863), pp. 60, 92.

11. Owens, *This Species of Property*, pp. 8-20.

12. Kemble, *Journal of a Residence*, p. 28; Lewis Cecil Gray, *History of Agriculture in the Southern United States*, vol. 1 (Washington, D.C.: Carnegie Institution, 1933), pp. 533-548; *Weevils in the Wheat*, p. 199; Fla. Narrs., Series 1, vol. 17, p. 305; Charles S. Sydnor, *Slavery in Mississippi* (Gloucester, Mass.: P. Smith, 1965), p. 20; Frederick Law Olmsted, *A Journey in the Seaboard Slave States* (New York: Dix and Edwards, 1856), p. 470; Frederick Law Olmsted, *A Journey in the Back Country* (New York: Mason Brothers, 1860), p. 59.

13. Olmsted, *A Journey in the Searboard Slave States*, p. 387; Ala. Narrs., Series 1, vol. 6, p. 87. Work descriptions were gleaned from the FWP slave narrative collection (*American Slave* and *Weevils in the Wheat*) and Gray, *History of Agriculture*. Goodson ("Introductory Essay") has indexed a sample of the interviews with women by subject (for example, "candlemaking," "carding wool," "field work," "splitting rails.").

For pictures of early twentieth-century black women of St. Helena's Islands, South Carolina, wearing the second belt, see photographs in Edith M. Dabbs, *Face of an Island: Leigh Richmond Miner's Photographs of St. Helena's Island* (New York: Grossman, 1971). The caption of one photo entitled "Woman with Hoe" reads: "Adelaide Washington sets off for her day's work in the field. The second belt or cord tied around the hips lifted all her garments a little and protected the long skirts from both early morning dew and contact with the dirt . . . [according to] an African superstition . . . the second cord also gave the wearer extra strength" (no. pp.). Olmsted, *Slave States*, p. 387, includes a sketch of this form of dress.

14. *Weevils in the Wheat*, p. 26; Gary, *History of Agriculture*, p. 251; planter quoted in Owens, *This Species of Property*, p. 39.

15. Genovese, *Roll, Jordan, Roll*, p. 495; Burke quoted in Gray, *History of Agriculture*, p. 549; Olmsted, *A Journey in the Back Country*, p. 81. For former slaves' descriptions of women who plowed, see Okla. Narrs., Series 1, vol. 7, p. 314; Fla. Narrs., Series 1, vol. 17, p. 33.

16. Olmsted quoted in Sydnor, *Slavery in Mississippi*, p. 68; *Weevils in the Wheat*,

p. 77. Of the women who worked in the South Carolina Sea Islands cotton fields, Harriet Ware (a northern teacher) wrote, "they walk off with their heavy hoes on their shoulders, as free, strong, and graceful as possible." Elizabeth Ware Pearson, ed., *Letters from Port Royal Written at the Time of the Civil War* (Boston: W.B. Clarke, 1906), p. 52.

17. Stuart Bruchey, ed., *Cotton and the Growth of the American Economy: 1790-1860* (New York: Harcourt, Brace & World, 1967), p. 174. See the documents under the heading "Making Cotton" and "The Routine of the Cotton Year," pp. 171-80. For examples of outstanding female pickers see Ala. Narrs., Series 1, vol. 6, p. 275 ("Oncet I won a contest wid a man an' made 480 pounds."); *Weevils in the Wheat*, p. 199.

18. Texas Narrs., supp. Series 2, pt. 1, vol. 2, pp. 93-94; Miss. Narrs., supp. Series 1, pt. 1, vol. 6, pp. 235-36, and pt. 2, vol. 7, p. 404; Tex. Narrs., Series 1, pt. 3, vol. 5, p. 231; Ind. Narrs., Series 1, vol. 6, p. 25; Ga. Narrs., Series 1, pt. 1, vol. 12, p. 113; Okla. Narrs., Series 1, vol. 7, p. 314; Ala. Narrs., Series 1, vol. 6, p. 338.

19. For a general discussion of slave artisans in the South see Gray, *History of Agriculture*, pp. 548, 565-67; Sydnor, *Slavery in Mississippi*, p. 9. Roger L. Ransom and Richard Sutch, in *One Kind of Freedom: The Economic Consequences of Emancipation* (Cambridge: Cambridge University Press, 1977) discuss "Occupational Distribution of Southern Blacks: 1860, 1870, 1890" in app. B, pp. 220-31. The works of Starobin *(Industrial Slavery)*, and James H. Brewer, *The Confederate Negro: Virginia's Craftsmen and Military Laborers, 1861-1865* (Durham: Duke University Press, 1969), focus almost exclusively on male slaves. See also Herbert Gutman and Richard Sutch, "Victorians All? The Sexual Mores and Conduct of Slaves and their Masters," in David, et al., *Reckoning With Slavery*, p. 160; Gutman, *Black Family*, pp. 599-600. The "hiring out" of men and children frequently disrupted family life.

20. Ransom and Sutch, *One Kind of Freedom*, p. 233; Olmsted, *Slave States*, p. 388; Ohio Narrs., Series 1, vol. 16, p. 28; Kemble, *Journal*, p. 121; S.C. Narrs., Series 1, pt. 4, vol. 3, p. 78; *Weevils in the Wheat*, pp. 223-24. Genovese describes the plantation system as a "halfway house between peasant and factory cultures" (*Roll, Jordan, Roll*, p. 286). For further discussion of the grueling pace of field-work see Herbert G. Gutman and Richard Sutch, "Sambo Makes Good, or Were Slaves Imbued with the Protestant Work Ethic?" in David, et al., *Reckoning With Slavery*, pp. 55-93.

21. Ala. Narrs., Series 1, vol. 6, p. 46; Fla. Narrs., Series 1, vol. 17, p. 185; *Weevils in the Wheat*, pp. 259, 216; Va. Narrs., Series 1, vol. 16, p. 51; Escott, *Slavery Remembered*, pp. 86-93. Escott includes an extensive discussion of resistance as revealed in the FWP slave narrative collection and provides data on the age, sex, and marital status of resisters and the purposes and forms of resistance. Gutman argues that the "typical runaway" was a male, aged sixteen to thirty-five years (*Black Family*, pp. 264-65). See also Obitko, "Custodians of a House of Resistance,"; Owens, *This Species of Property*, pp. 38, 88, 95.

22. *Weevils in the Wheat*, pp. 26, 282, 157. According to Gutman, plantation work patterns "apparently failed to take into account enlarged slave kin groups, and further study may show that a central tension between slaves and their owners had its origins in the separation of work and kinship obligations" (*Black Family*, p. 209.).

23. Fla. Narrs., Series 1, vol. 17, p. 191; Bennet H. Barrow quoted in Gutman,

Black Family, p. 263, Robert S. Starobin, ed., *Blacks in Bondage: Letters of American Slaves* (New York: New Viewpoints, 1974), p. 54.

In his recent study, *The Slave Drivers: Black Agricultural Labor Supervisors in the Antebellum South* (Westport, Conn.: Greenwood Press, 1979), William L. Van DeBurg examines the anomalous position of black (male) drivers in relation to the rest of the slave community.

24. Savitt, *Medicine and Slavery*, pp. 115-20; planter quoted in Owens, *This Species of Property*, pp. 38-40; planter quoted in Olmsted, *A Journey in the Seaboard Slave States*, p. 190; Kemble, *Journal of a Residence*, p. 121. Cf. White, "Ain't I A Woman?" pp. 77-86, 101, 155-60.

25. Genovese, *Roll, Jordan, Roll*, pp. 328, 340; Ala. Narrs., Series 1, vol. 6, p. 273; Miss. Narrs., supp. Series 1, pt. 2, vol. 7, p. 400; Tex. Narrs., Series 1, pt. 3, vol. 5, p. 45. Recent historians have emphasized that the distinction between housework and fieldwork was not always meaningful in terms of shaping a slave's personality and self-perception or defining her or his status. See Owens, *This Species of Property*, p. 113; Escott, *Slavery Remembered*, pp. 59-60.

26. Ala. Narrs., Series 1, vol. 6, pp. 416-17. In her study of slave mistresses, Anne Firor Scott gives an accurate description of their numerous supervisory duties, but she ignores that most of the actual manual labor was performed by slave women. See *The Southern Lady: From Pedestal to Politics, 1830-1930* (Chicago: University of Chicago Press, 1970), p. 31.

27. Tex. Narrs., Series 1, pt. 4, vol. 5, p. 11; Ind. Narrs., Series 1, vol. 6, p. 83. See also Miss. Narrs., supp. Series 1, pt. 1, vol. 6, pp. 54-55, 216, 257, 365, 380-81.

28. The FWP slave narrative collection provides these examples of children's work, and many more. Ala. Narrs., Series 1, vol. 6, p. 157; Genovese, *Role, Jordan, Roll*, pp. 502-19; Owens, *This Species of Property*, p. 202.

In early adolescence (ages ten to fourteen), a child would normally join the regular work force as a half-hand. At that time (or perhaps before), she or he received adult clothing. This *rite de passage* apparently made more of an impression on boys than girls, probably because pants offered more of a contrast to the infant's smock than did a dress. Willis Cofer attested to the significance of the change: "Boys jes' wore shirts what looked lak dresses 'til dey wuz 12 years old and big enough to wuk in de field . . . and all de boys wuz mighty pround when dey got big enough to wear pants and go to wuk in de fields wid grown folkses. When a boy got to be man enough to wear pants, he drawed rations and quit eatin' out of de trough [in the nursery]." Ga. Narrs., Series 1, pt. 1, vol. 12, p. 203. For other examples of the significance of change from adults' to children's clothing, see Tex. Narrs., Series 1, pt. 3, vol. 5, pp. 211, 275; p. 4, pp. 109-110, Ga. Narrs., Series 1, pt. 1, vol. 12, p. 277; Genovese, *Roll, Jordan, Roll*, p. 505.

29. Ga. Narrs., supp. Series 1, pt. 1, vol. 3, p. 185; *Weevils in the Wheat*, pp. 264-65; S.C. Narrs., Series 1, pt. 4, vol. 3, p. 257.

30. Okla. Narrs., Series 1, vol. 7, p. 347; White "Ain't I A Woman?" pp. 210-15; L. Maria Child, ed., *Incidents in the Life of a Slave Girl, Written By Herself* (Boston: L. Maria-Child, 1861).

31. James Hugo Johnston, *Race Relations in Virginia and Miscegenation in the South, 1776-1860* (Amherst: University of Massachusetts Press, 1970), p. 247; Mary Boykin Chesnut, *A Diary From Dixie*, ed. Ben Ames Williams (Cambridge, Mass.: Harvard University Press, 1980), p. 49.

32. Fla. Narrs., Series 1, vol. 17, p. 35. For specific incidents illustrating these

points, see *Weevils in the Wheat*, pp. 63, 199; Okla. Narrs., Series 1, vol. 7, pp. 135, 165-66; Tenn. Narrs., Series 1, vol. 16, p. 14. Slave punishment in general is discussed in Escott, *Slavery Remembered*, pp. 42-46; Owens, *This Species of Property*, p. 88; Savitt, *Slavery and Medicine*, pp. 65-69; Gutman and Sutch, "Sambo Makes Good," pp. 55-93; Frederick Douglass, *Narrative of the Life of Frederick Douglass, An American Slave* (Cambridge: Harvard University Press, 1960), pp. 60-61. These examples indicate that Anne Firor Scott is a bit sanguine in suggesting that although southern women were sensitive to the "depravity" of their husbands, "It may be significant that they did not blame black women, who might have provided convenient scapegoats. The blame was squarely placed on men." See Anne Firor Scott, "Women's Perspectives on the Patriarchy in the 1850s," *Journal of American History* 61 (June 1974): 52-64.

33. Genovese, *Roll, Jordan, Roll*, pp. 333-38. See, for example, the document entitled "A Seamstress is Punished" in Lerner, ed., *Black Women in White America*, pp. 18-19.

34. Olmsted, *A Journey in the Seaboard Slave States*, p. 421; S.C. Narrs., Series 1, pt. 4, vol. 3, p. 126; Fla. Narrs., Series 1, vol. 14, p. 356; Escott, *Slavery Remembered*, p. 64; Kemble, *Journal of a Residence*, p. 98; Genovese, *Roll, Jordan, Roll*, pp. 346-47.

35. Fla. Narrs., Series 1, vol. 17, p. 356; Gutman and Sutch, "Sambo Makes Good," p. 74; Kemble, *Journal of a Residence*, p. 153; Gray, *History of Agriculture*, p. 553; Owens, *This Species of Property*, p. 113.

36. Ga. Narrs., Series 1, pt. 1, vol. 12, p. 243; Davis, "Reflections on the Black Woman's Role," pp. 4-7. For general discussions of women's work as it related to slave communal life see also Owens, *This Species of Property*, pp. 23, 225; and White, "Ain't I A Woman?." Polly Cancer recalled that, when she was growing up on a Mississippi plantation, the master "wudn't let de mammies whip dey own chillun [or "do dey own cookin'"] ... ef he cum 'cross a 'ooman whuppin' her chile he'd say, 'Git 'way 'ooman; dats my bizness...'" Miss. Narrs., supp. Series 1, p. 2, vol. 7, pp. 340-41.

37. Gray, *History of Agriculture*, p. 563; Olmsted, *A Journey in the Seaboard Slave States*, pp. 424-25, 697-98; Owens, *This Species of Property*, p. 47; Fla. Narrs., Series 1, vol. 17, p. 175; Ala. Narrs., Series 1, vol. 6, p. 216; Miss. Narrs., supp. Series 1, pt. 1, vol. 6, pp. 10, 23, 25, 123; Ga. Narrs., supp. Series 1, pt. 1, vol. 3, p. 27. Savitt (*Slavery and Medicine*) includes a section on "Black Medicine" (pp. 171-84) and confirms Rebecca Hook's recollection that "on the plantation, the doctor was not nearly as popular as the 'granny' or midwife." Fla. Narrs., Series 1, vol. 17, p. 175.

38. Ga. Narrs., Series 1, pt. 1, vol. 12, p. 70; Okla. Narrs., Series 1, vol. 7, pp. 314-15; White, "Ain't I A Woman?" pp. 22-23; Tex. Narrs., Series 2, pt. 1, vol. 2, p. 98.

39. The FWP slave narrative collection contains many descriptions of slaves engaged in household industry. Alice Morse Earle details comparable techniques used by white women in colonial New England in *Home Life in Colonial Days* (New York: MacMillan Co., 1935).

40. See, for example, S.C. Narrs., Series 1, pt. 3, vol. 3, pp. 15, 218, 236; Tex. Narrs., Series 1, pt. 3, vol. 5, pp. 20, 89, 108, 114, 171, 188, 220; Miss. Narrs., supp. Series 1, pt. 1, vol. 6, p. 36.

41. *Weevils in the Wheat*, pp. 88-89. George White of Lynchburg reported that

his mother sang a similar version of this song to women while they were spinning (p. 309).

42. Genovese, *Roll, Jordan, Roll*, p. 319.

43. Gutman, *Black Family*, p. 75. Escott points out that masters and slaves lived in "different worlds" (*Slavery Remembered*, p. 20). This paragraph briefly summarizes Gutman's pioneering work.

44. Davis, "Reflections on the Black Woman's Role," p. 7.

45. Ala. Narrs., Series 1, vol. 6, p. 9; Tex. Narrs., supp. Series 2, p. 5, vol. 6, pp. 2036-37; Fla. Narrs., Series 1, vol. 17, pp. 22-23; White, "Ain't I A Woman?," pp. 30-31, 65.

46. Gutman, *Black Family*, pp. 142, 67-68, 267-78; Genovese, *Roll, Jordan, Roll*, pp. 318, 482-94; S.C. Narrs., Series 1, pt. 3, vol. 3, p. 192; Miss. Narrs., supp. Series 1, pt. 2, vol. 7, pp. 380-81.

47. Okla. Narrs., Series 1, vol. 7, p. 210; Escott, *Slavery Remembered*, pp. 49-57, 87; Owens, *This Species of Property*, p. 201.

48. Gutman and Sutch, "Sambo Makes Good," p. 63; Owens, *This Species of Property*, p. 195; Miss. Narrs., supp. Series 1, pt. 1, vol. 6, pp. 59-60. For mention of corn shuckings in particular, see Genovese, *Roll, Jordan, Roll*, p. 318; Miss. Narrs., Series 1, vol. 7, p. 6; Okla. Narrs., Series 1, vol. 7, p. 230. In the context of traditional female-male roles, what Genovese calls the "curious sexual division of labor" that marked these festivities was not "curious" at all (p. 318).

49. Unfortunately, much of the data about precolonial African work patterns must be extrapolated from recent findings of anthropologists. The author benefited from conversations with Dr. M. Jean Hay of the Boston University African Studies Center concerning women's work in precolonial Africa and methodological problems in studying this subject.

50. For a theoretical formulation of the sexual division of labor in preindustrial societies, see Brown, "A Note on the Division of Labor By Sex."

51. Peter Wood, *Black Majority: Negroes in Colonial South Carolina From 1670 Through the Stono Rebellion* (New York: Alfred A. Knopf, 1974), pp. 59-62; P.C. Lloyd, "Osi takunde of Ijebu," in *Africa Remembered: Narratives by West Africans from the Era of the Slave Trade,* ed. Philip D. Curtin (Madison: University of Wisconsin Press, 1967), p. 263; Marguerite Dupire, "The Position of Women in a Pastoral Society," in *Women of Tropical Africa*, ed. Denise Paulme (Berkeley: University of California Press, 1963), pp. 76-80; Olaudah Equiano, "The Life of Olaudah Equiano or Gustavus Vassa the African Written by Himself," in *Great Slave Narratives,* ed. Arna Bontemps (Boston: Beacon Press, 1969), pp. 7-10; Kemble, *Journal of a Residence*, p. 42; Pearson, ed., *Letters from Port Royal*, pp. 58, 106.

52. Melville J. Herskovits, *The Myth of the Negro Past* (New York: Harper & Bros., 1941), pp. 33-85; Wood, *Black Majority*, pp. 179, 250; Hermann Baumann, "The Division of Work According to Sex in African Hoe Culture," *Africa* 1 (July 1928): 289-319.

On the role of women in hoe agriculture, see also Leith Mullings, "Women and Economic Change in Africa," in *Women in Africa: Studies in Social and Economic Change*, ed. Nancy J. Hafkin and Edna G. Bay (Stanford: Stanford University Press, 1976), pp. 239-64; Sylvia Leith-Ross, *African Women: A Study of the Ibo of Nigeria* (New York Frederick A. Praeger, 1965), pp. 84-91; Ester Boserup, *Woman's Role in Economic Development* (New York: St. Martin's Press,

1970), pp. 156-36; Jack Goody and Joan Buckley, "Inheritance and Women's Labour in Africa," *Africa* 63 (April 1973), 108-21. No tribes in precolonial Africa used the plow.

53. Olmsted, *A Journey in the Seaboard Slave States*, p. 433; Gray, *History of Agriculture*, p. 548; Kemble, *Journal of a Residence*, pp. 164, 247; Douglass, *Narrative*, pp. 76-78. According to Genovese, the ability of these elderly slaves "to live decently and with self-respect depended primarily on the support of their younger fellow slaves" (*Roll, Jordan, Roll*, p. 523); White "Ain't I A Woman?" p. 49; Miss. Narrs., supp. Series 1, pt. 1, vol. 6, p. 242.

54. Eblen, "New Estimates," p. 306; Pearson, ed. *Letters from Port Royal*, p. 25; Genovese, *Roll, Jordan, Roll*, pp. 522-23; Eliza F. Andrews, *The War-Time Journal of a Georgia Girl, 1864-1865* (New York: D. Appelton & Co., 1908), p. 101; Escott, *Slavery Remembered*, pp. 108-09; Owens, *This Species of Property*, p. 140; Gutman, *Black Family*, p. 218. For specific examples, see Ala. Narrs., supp. Series 1, pt. 1, vol. 6, p. 217; pt. 2, vol. 7, pp. 369-73. See also White, "Ain't I A Woman?" pp. 107-112.

55. Miss. Narrs., Supp. Series 1, pt. 1, Vol. 6, p. 217; pt. 2, Vol. 7, pp. 369-73. See also White "Ain't I A Woman?" pp. 107-112.

56. Ga. Narrs., Series 1, pt. 1, vol. 12, p. 214; *Weevils in the Wheat*, p. 128.

57. Genovese, *Roll, Jordan, Roll*, p. 500. See also White, "Ain't I A Woman?" pp. 3-20, 51-54; and Davis, "Reflections on the Black Woman's Role," p. 7.

58. This section summarizes material in an essay by the author entitled "Freed Women?: Black Women, Work, and the Family During the Civil War and Recon- struction," Wellesley Center for Research on Women Working Paper No. 61 (Wellesley, Mass., 1980). '"My Mother'" and "Freed Women" constitute the first two chapters of a book on Afro-American women, work, and the family, 1830-1980 (forthcoming).

59. Robert Somers, *The Southern States Since the War, 1870-1* (London: MacMillan & Co., 1871), p. 59; Ransom and Sutch, *One Kind of Freedom*, p. 233; Francis W. Loring and C.F. Atkinson, *Cotton Culture and the South Considered with Reference to Emigration* (Boston: A. Williams, 1869), pp. 4-23. Other primary works that include relevant information are Frances Butler Leigh, *Ten Years on a Georgia Plantation Since the War* (London: R. Bentley, 1883); Charles Nordhoff, *The Cotton States in the Spring and Summer of 1875* (New York: D. Appleton & Co., 1876); George Campbell, *White and Black: The Outcome of a Visit to the United States* (London: Chatto and Windus, 1879).

60. Freedmen's Bureau official quoted in Gutman, *Black Family*, p. 167.

61. The transition from wage labor to the sharecropping system is examined in Ralph Shlomowitz, "The Origins of Southern Sharecropping," *Agricultural History* 53 (July 1979): 557-75, and his "The Transition From Slave to Freedman Labor Arrangements in Southern Agriculture, 1865-1870," *Journal of Economic History* 39 (March 1979): 333-36; Jay R. Mandle, *The Roots of Black Poverty: The Southern Plantation Economy After the Civil War* (Durham, N.C.: Duke University Press, 1978); Joseph D. Reid, Jr., "White Land, Black Labor, and Agricultural Stagnation: The Causes and Effects of Sharecropping in the Postbellum South," *Explorations in Economic History* 16 (January 1979): 31-55; Ransom and Sutch, *One Kind of Freedom*.

Jonathan Wiener suggests that blacks' rejection of gang labor and preference for family share units "represented a move away from classic capitalist organizations." See "Class Structure and Economic Development in the American South, 1865-1955," *American Historical Review* 84 (October 1979): 984.

62. Elizabeth Hyde Botume, *First Days Amongst the Contrabands* (Boston: Lee & Shepard, 1893), p. 166; Campbell, *White and Black*, pp. 172, 344, 364; tale entitled "De Tiger an' de Nyung Lady" quoted in Owens, *This Species of Property*, p. 144. See Leon Litwack, *Been in the Storm So Long: The Aftermath of Slavery* (New York: Alfred A. Knopf, 1979), pp. 502-56, for a detailed discussion of various freedmen's conventions held throughout the South.

63. For an analysis of the ways in which the household responsibilities of women are defined and redefined to alter the supply of available wage-earners, see Louise A. Tilly and Joan Scott, *Women, Work, and Family* (New York: Holt, Rinehart & Winston, 1978).

THE ORIGINS OF THE SWEATSHOP: WOMEN AND EARLY INDUSTRIALIZATION IN NEW YORK CITY

CHRISTINE STANSELL

Between 1820 and 1860, New York City became the foremost manufacturing center of America, a rise to eminence which, as in all industrializing situations, entailed massive disruptions for the city's working
people. Antebellum New Yorkers were well aware of the poverty and
suffering of their own laboring classes, but contemporaries agreed
that of those pulled into the new wage-labor relations, women workers
were the most precariously situated of all. In 1830, for instance,
labor reformer Matthew Carey called women's wages and working
conditions "harrowing truths."[1] Carey was referring to the outside
workers, those women who worked for wages in their own households,
"outside" a shop or factory. Thirty years later, exploitation had
become more deeply entrenched; indeed, the ladies of one women's
charity declared with uncharacteristic vehemence that the outworker's
wage *"does not decently support life."*[2] By mid-century, low wages,
underemployment, and overwork were the rule for outside workers,
and outside work had become the prevalent form of women's employment in America's leading industrial city.

The development of the outside system as the dominant form of
female wage-labor affected the segmentation of the work force, the
segregation of the labor movement, and the formation of class and
gender consciousness in one of America's most radical cities. Through
the outside system, metropolitan industry turned to its own uses the
ties of poor women to their families and households. The core of its

From *Working Class America*, Michael H. Frisch and Daniel J. Walkowitz, eds., 1983, 78-103.
Reprinted by permission of University of Illinois Press.

labor force was comprised of female heads of household who did not leave their homes because of responsibilities to kin—although as the system expanded, it also incorporated young single women more independent of domestic duties. Instead of pulling these women out of their households, as did, for example, the factories of rural New England, urban manufacturing converted their tenement homes into workshops. On the one hand, this allowed women to do their part as wives, mothers, and daughters, the domestic labor that deteriorating conditions of life in these years made all the more important. On the other, it made them vulnerable to the most severe exploitation as workers and limited their means of redress through collective organizing. Homework had a double edge: the very woman who stayed home, "keeping a house together," as one woman put it,[3] placed herself in the way of the worst abuses of the New York labor market. Through the outside system, the requirements of industrial capitalism meshed with the needs of the working-class family and thus incorporated gender roles into an expanding system of economic exploitation.

To understand the importance of women to "metropolitan industrialization," as Sean Wilentz had termed it,[4] we must first rethink older conceptions of the role of outwork. Historians and economists have usually viewed outwork as a transition, a precursor to the prototypical industrial form of the factory. Eric Hobsbawm, for instance, in 1965 spoke of domestic manufactures as transitional devices which employers utilized to overcome the great social obstacles to industrialization.[5] The dispersed work force and handicraft technology intrinsic to outwork made the system too cumbersome to allow capital accumulation, so the argument goes; as soon as technological innovation occurred and it become possible to centralize the labor force, such wasteful and irrational forms of production disappeared. It is important to understand, however, that although outwork was only a precursor to factories in some settings, it remained at the heart of the industrializing process in many of the great cities. In New York, the outside system flourished through the nineteenth century and into the twentieth: the infamous sweatshops of turn-of-the-century New York were variants on the antebellum form. A similar process occurred in London, Paris, and other metropolitan manufacturing centers in Europe. In late-nineteenth-century Holland, outwork actually superseded factory production: employers shifted industrial wagework from the factory into the home.[6]

In New York City, material conditions did not favor the rise of factories, but in other ways conditions for manufacturing were propitious. Of great advantage to employers were the city's proximity to the port and, most important, the enormous pool of cheap labor which existed from the first wave of immigration following the end of the War of 1812. By expanding their markets and tapping this labor pool, employers transformed the handicraft system from within. In many trades, manufactures developed without the benefit of any new mechanization.[7] In the clothing trade, for instance, until the advent of the sewing machine in the 1850s, clothing was sewn in the same way it had been made in private households and tailors' shops. The outside system was crucial to this kind of labor-intensive industrialization: it gave employers the capacity to expand production outside their shop walls in much the same way as machinery allowed factory owners to increase production inside theirs.

In the commercial port setting of New York, then, the kind of cumbersome enterprise which utilized outwork was at the forefront of industrialization for the first half of the century. We must adjust our notions of class formation accordingly. The female workers of the outside system were not marginal to the industrial proletariat, an auxiliary of wives and daughters, as historians have often believed. Despite the fact that they remained in their households, they found themselves in new relations which were at the center of industrialization and class development. Analogously, the outside system had great significance for the development of new gender relations within the working class: the creation of new modes of wifehood, motherhood, and daughterhood. If employers in some settings utilized outwork only until they overcame the barriers to women working outside the home, New York employers capitalized upon and profited from those very obstacles. Through the outside system, the immobility and apparent marginality of women workers became institutionalized and formalized in urban industrial capitalism.

I

The outside system replicated the gender divisions of the household in the new setting of metropolitan industry. A sexual division of labor developed between branches of New York manufactures, based primarily on outwork; trades like clothing that relied on put-out work became women's trades, while those that did not mostly remained closed to women. The consequence was a segmentation of industry that limited women in the city to a few trades; by 1860, three or four dozen industries employed over 90 percent of the city's workwomen. In the manufactures of paper boxes, hoopskirts, shirts and collars, millinery, artificial flowers, and ladies' cloaks, over 85 percent of the employees were female.[8] The crowding of women into a few industries increased competition for work and thereby made them more vulnerable than men to wage-cutting, overwork, and casualization.

Before 1820, women's wagework had been marginal to the New York economy. Poor women worked mostly in the customary female employments of domestic service and street selling. Commodity production, still centered in artisan shops, had not developed to the point where it could incorporate large numbers of women. Shipping and commerce employed men of the laboring poor as seamen, dock laborers, and road-builders, and there was seasonal work for them on farms in New Jersey, Connecticut, and New York State. But this kind of heavy labor was mostly closed to women. When Mayor Edward Livingston proposed a scheme of employment for the poor in 1803, he suggested work programs for men in street construction, farm labor, and public works, but he could prescribe nothing more concrete for women than a large workroom where they might work at unspecified tasks "suited to their strength."[9]

Some women found work at the turn of the eighteenth century in the putting-out system, the progenitor of outside work. In the period after the Revolution, city merchants and village storekeepers along the northeastern seaboard began "putting out" raw materials to women to work up at home into ready-made goods. Wage payments were given for flax- and wool-spinning, straw-braiding, weaving, glove-making, stocking-knitting, and shoe-binding: all crafts which women also practiced in their own domestic work.[10] Although putting-out appears to have flourished mostly in rural New England, it also provided some opportunities for New York women: work at shoe-binding was available from a number of cordwainers in the early years of the century, and spinning was one of the handful of remunerative employments the Society for the Relief of Poor Widows could encourage among its almoners.[11] Between 1814 and 1819, several hundred poor women found work in given-out crafts at the House of Industry, a charity founded to alleviate destitution among the honest female poor. The House gave out flax and wool to spin, stockings to knit, and gloves and a few fine linen shirts to sew. Although its managers modified putting-out by centralizing some of the work on the premises, the ties of wagework to domestic activity and family life were still evident. One mother brought her youngest children with her, a young widow spun with her baby on her lap, and old women knit stockings, much as they would have done in households were they lived as dependent grandmothers and great-aunts.[12]

In the next decade, manufacturing on both sides of the Atlantic would take over the production of given-out crafts: women like the

Widow Hammel, who applied to a charity in 1817 for money to repair her spinning wheel, would have a hard time finding work.[13] Because of the advent of the textile mills, spinning, the staple of the putting-out system, would disappear as handiwork by 1820, although traces of it appeared in the city well into the antebellum years; as late as 1839, the managers of an asylum for old women voted to give one resident a flax wheel to spin sewing thread for the others; "it seems quite necessary for her comfort that she should be employed, and it is the only thing she can do."[14] In New England, spinning mills provided the means for capitalists to utilize female labor beyond the given-out system, but since mills were impracticable in Manhattan, employers there as yet had no way to capitalize systematically on the poverty of women like those who had spun for the House of Industry. Even the stern gentlemen of the Society for the Prevention of Pauperism, ever vigilant against an idle poor, granted in 1821 that "there is often a defect of profitable employment for women and children of indigent families."[15]

It was the outside system which opened up this labor market for profitable employment. After the War of 1812, conditions for other manufacturing besides textiles were beneficial. Because of the thriving port economy, the city was already a major center of capital, and its merchants were seeking new investments for their profits from the war years. The advent of regular trans-Atlantic and coastal shipping lines put New York producers in a favored position over competitors elsewhere to buy raw materials and sell finished goods, and the federal tariff of 1816 gave domestic industry much-needed protection from British goods. The postwar wave of immigration brought to the city highly skilled British artisans, familiar with the most advanced technology, as well as thousands of unskilled workers who would form the first of New York's many armies of cheap labor.[16]

Master and merchant tailors were the first in these advantageous circumstances to hire large numbers of women; the clothing trade would continue to be the leading employer of female labor in New York throughout the nineteenth century.[17] By 1860, the federal census reported 25,000 women working in manufacturing—one-quarter of the entire labor force; two-thirds of them working in the clothing trades.[18] Garment manufacture would also prove typical of women's industries in its dependence on outwork. Initially, its employers depended almost entirely on home workers, and even as they began to set up factories in the 1840s, they maintained the outside system in tandem with factory labor, or "inside work" as they called it. The outside system allowed employers to cut costs to the bone. There were minimal expenses for overhead, and they could easily hold down wages by taking on and letting go workers according to their needs of the moment. Thus seasonality and casualization became the hallmarks of outwork. When female employment extended to other industries, employers emulated the successful clothing manufacturers in mixing factory work and homework.

Before 1812, there had been virtually no ready-made clothing in America. Except for the poor, who bought their clothes secondhand, Americans had their garments made by artisans—tailors, tailoresses, and seamstresses—and by wives, daughters, and female servants. There was a rough division of labor between the household and the artisan shop. Women at home did the plain sewing; artisans, the garments that required more skill and fitting. So women made most of their own everyday clothes, their children's, and the simpler men's garments—shirts and everyday "pantaloons," or loose trousers. Dressmakers helped them with fancy dresses; seamstresses, with children's clothes, mending, and particularly artful tasks. Thus an eighteenth-century seamstress advertised her deftness in turning old clothes into new: "she will as usual graft Pieces to knit Jackets and Breeches not to be discerned, also to graft and foot Stockings, and Gentlemen's Gloves, Mittens, or makes Children's Stockings out of Old ones."[19] Where tailors were concerned instead of tailoresses and dressmakers, there was a stricter division of labor. Tailors would not touch most women's work—shirts, dresses, children's clothes, and mending. Their province encompassed those men's garments which were closely fitted, like breeches and vests, and cumbersome to sew, like coats and capes.[20] This eighteenth-century division of labor between women and tailors would have important ramifications in the development of clothing manufacture, since industrialization occurred first in the making of *men's* clothes, which tailors had traditionally monopolized, thus introducing female wageworkers as competition.

The only ready-made clothing in the eighteenth century was for sailors. Crews docking in New York needed to outfit themselves quickly and cheaply for the next voyage. By 1805, "slop-shops" by the waterfront catered to their needs with ready-made pants, shirts, and jackets; "slop-work" was the tailors' term for cheap garments made with little care and no fitting. Army uniforms were the other souce of slop-work, since during the Revolution and the War of 1812 there had been a great demand for new uniforms which persisted, although much diminished, into peacetime. Between the two, a small but steady trade in slops was established in New York before 1820. Journeymen tailors turned to it in the winter, the slack season for custom orders, while masters put out some of the plainer slop-work—shirts and pantaloons—to women they employed the year round.[21]

The garment trades prospered in the 1820s, as city merchants captured the lucrative "Southern trade" in slave clothing from the British. The tariff of 1816 and cheap textiles from New England mills allowed New York merchants to undercut British prices.[22] With an assured market for slops, employers began to take on more women to sew the work which journeymen preferred to do only in their slow seasons. By the 1830s, some shops employed as many as 500 women, and coarse "Negro cottons," as they were called, were regular cargo on southern-bound packets.[23] From slave clothing, the trade diversified into a luxury trade in fine linen shirts and vests for southern planters, and firms also began to keep high quality ready-mades in stock for local customers, travelers, and gentlemen visiting the city on business. When the Erie Canal connected the city with midwestern and upstate customers, a "Western trade" developed in dungarees, hickory and flashy figured shirts, and flannel drawers; in 1849, the gold rush gave the impetus for a "California trade" in overalls and calico shirts for the thousands of men who had no women to outfit them.[24] By 1860, two-thirds of the garments made in New York went south and the rest were shipped to a nationwide market. "Scarcely a single individual thinks of having his shirts made at home," averred an observer of fashion.[25] He neglected the farm families who continued to make their own clothes well into the late 1800s, but he was right about city people and townsfolk across the country, whose sense of style in men's clothes was already attuned to New York ready-mades by the 1840s: "Everywhere throughout the country, New-York-made clothing is popular over all others."[26]

The clothing trade was one New York business that did offer workingmen and immigrants a path from employment to proprietorship. The market was usually dependable and the profit margin always high—an estimated 500 percent markup in the early 1830s.[27] Most important, a man needed very little money to set up shop, since the outside system allowed him to take advantage of the city's cheap labor while minimizing overhead costs. Rents in the business district of lower Manhattan were too high for any but large proprietors to afford the space for an inside shop, and even they limited their overhead by employing a host of outworkers. In 1860, the renowned Brooks Brothers employed 70 workers inside and 2,000 to 3,000 on the outside, and another of the largest concerns employed 500 and 800 workers on the inside and outside respectively.[28] The smallest proprietors, tailors themselves, did not keep shop at all but contracted out goods from the large shops, cut them at home, and put them out, thus passing along all the costs of space, light, fuel, needles, and thread to their home workers.[29]

If the trade offered the common man an entrée to entrepreneurship, however, it did not necessarily bring him affluence. By mid-century, economic pressures on employers were rigorous. The trade operated on a dense network of credit, and the search to maximize credit was the driving force behind operations at every level. Profits could be high, but they seldom appeared in cash. At its most complex, the trade involved a jobber or merchant, a master tailor, his inside workers, one or even two levels of subcontractors, and their out-workers. The jobber/merchant bought the cloth and sold the finished merchandise, the master cut the goods and gave them to his workers and subcontractors, and the subcontractors put out the goods to their outside workers. Since profit at every level came from the difference between the fixed payment received and costs paid out for labor and overhead, there was heavy pressure to cut wages. All down the line, too, goods were passed along on credit and payment was postponed until the finished work was returned; credit extended to sales as well, to the planters and country storekeepers who visited Manhattan every spring to buy their stock for the year. As a result, there was little cash on hand at any given moment at any level of the trade, the reason that business depressions were calamitous for employers large and small: in both 1837 and 1857 the trade was the first in the city to go under and the last to recover. Dependence on credit was also the factor that above all others bred what were universally acknowledged to be among the worst abuses of workers in the North. As one historian has written, by the 1850s, "hardly a period known for its sentimentality in business," the hardest-boiled contemporaries acknowledged the sewing trade to be unscrupulous.[30]

The economic pressures on small shop-owners at mid-century were one factor which explains the plethora of complaints then about wage-cutting, rate-busting, underpayment, and withholding wages. "The worst features," maintained Horace Greeley, "are its hopelessness and its constant tendency from bad to worse."[31] Women living with a man's support were not so adversely affected, but single women and their dependents could suffer terribly. In the 1855 census report for two neighborhoods on the Lower East Side, nearly 60 percent of 600 workingwomen sampled had no adult male in the household.[32] In their case—that of the majority of New York's female wageworkers, if this sample is indicative—there can be no doubt that Victorian sentimentalizations of the starving seamstress reflected a real situation. Two stories make the point, both from 1855, a depression year "When flour was so high last winter as to place it beyond the reach of the provident poor," the secretary of the Society for the Relief of Poor Widows related, "One of the Managers visited a respectable

Widow, who had maintained herself and her three little girls by sewing." The eldest had just died from what the ladies delicately termed "disease aggravated by improper food," and the second child was also sick with the same malady. When the visitor inquired about the family's needs, the woman asked for flour: "'But you have thought before that meal would answer,' said the Manager, 'and you know we hardly think it right to give flour at its present price.' 'Yes,' said the woman, bursting into tears, 'we have lived on meal this winter, but the Doctor says it killed Mary and now Katy is getting in the same way, and I cannot let her die, too.'"[33] The response of a second mother in the same situation—one of her eight children sick with a chest complaint—was less suited to the terms of Victorian pathos. "Perhaps it will please the Lord to take him," she replied matter-of-factly to the manager's solicitude; "if it would please the Lord to take them all, I should be glad, then I'd know they were well off; but how I shall support them all another year in this world I am sure I can't tell."[34] These were not extreme cases: these were the hardships of a *class*— and a particular group within it—not of isolated individuals.

The outworkers' most pressing problem was underpayment. Like employment in many metropolitan trades, seasonal work peaked in October and April, when orders for winter and summer stock were rushed out. The pattern was sufficiently predictable for women to meet the slack seasons with some forethought: farm labor was an alternative for the mobile in the slow summer months, a sojourn in the almshouse an option for the nonrespectable in winter. Some women pieced together a sequence of employment from other trades; a seamstress could combine sewing with straw-sewing, for instance, which peaked in January.[35] Married women and mothers with grown sons could dovetail employment with their men: the busy season for day labor, to give one instance, was the warm weather, when the clothing trades were slow. But there were also fluctuations week to week that were impossible to foresee; to be out of work one or two days every week was common for outside workers. There was no guarantee that when a seamstress returned her sewing to the shop she would get more, and if she did, it was not necessarily a full week's work. This meant that self-supporting women had to shift about from one shop to another for enough work to live on, a feature of the trade which workwomen protested with particular bitterness. For women on their own, labor time was precious, and they keenly felt the waste in spending hours seeking work, waiting for work, and returning work.[36]

"Small as are the earnings of these seamstresses, they constantly tend to diminish," Horace Greeley observed.[37] Small employers were notorious for vicious rate-cutting, especially the German Jews of Chatham Street slop shops, the perennial target of denunciations which were always laced with anti-Semitism. "A class of beings in human form," angry seamstresses called them after a wage cut in 1831, and two decades later a journalist sympathetic to the seamstresses conjured up the stereotype of the avaricious Jew, the "shop-keeping, penny-turning genius."[38] More prosperous businessmen liked to see themselves as superior to the immigrant entrepreneurs in benevolence and moral scruples and were quite content to see issues of ethnicity obscure those of class. In actuality, their firms—respectable concerns like Brooks Brothers—profited equally from rate-cutting, although its practice was less visible. They kept their hands clean, in a sense, because they did not set the piece rates for their outside workers but left it to the contractors, men who were the worst gougers in the trade.

Because there were so many women competing for work, there was little that needlewomen could do to prevent wage-cutting. "I have heard it said, and even by benevolent men, in justification of this hideous state of things, that these women do not complain," wrote a nettled Matthew Carey in 1830. "True. It would answer no purpose. If the price of shirts were brought down to six cents (as it sometimes is . . .), they would accept it, and thankfully too. Their numbers and their wants are so great, and the competition so urgent, that they are wholly at the mercy of their employers."[39]

Seamstresses were more militant in posing their grievances in the ensuing years: there were turnouts in 1831, 1836, and 1845, as well as strikes in Philadelphia and Boston. But organization never succeeded in securing their wage demands. In this respect, they were much worse off than their closest male counterparts, the day laborers, who earned about twice as much as fully employed needlewomen throughout the period. Day laborers managed to enforce a customary wage of around a dollar a day, sometimes, it seems, through turning out.[40] Outside workers were never able to use the turnout effectively; there were too many women in the city who would undercut them by taking work at any price. In 1839, for instance, an employer "sought up emigrants, or went to the almshouse, to have his work done; if he could find no women in his neighborhood willing to undertake it . . . so that he forced them to come to his own terms."[41] Three decades later, in the first month of the Panic of 1857, women who were turned away from the failing regular shops had no recourse but to take out work at the lowest prices going from Chatham Street, leading a journalist to infer that the numbers of women living from hand to mouth were more than he had supposed.[42]

The most unscrupulous practice of employers in the moral code of mid-century, and the one which outside workers protested most bitterly, was that of withholding wages. It was not uncommon for employers, especially small proprietors and subcontractors, to postpone paying a woman when she returned to work, to require alterations before they paid her, to refuse to pay her at all, and to hold back the deposits that they required for taking out work. A visitor to New York described one of these transactions in 1852: "He takes the bundle, unrolls it, turns up his nose, as if he had smelt a dead rat, and remarks, in the crossest manner possible, 'You have ruined the job,' makes the whole lot up together, and contempuously throws it under the counter. . . . She then asks for her money back, but only receives a threat in return, with a low, muttering grumble, that 'you have damaged us already eight or ten dollars, and we will retain your dollar, as it is all we shall ever get for our goods, which you have spoilt!'"[43]

In 1855, the outworker Margaret Byrnes took her grievances to the mayor's court when she encountered this treatment. She had taken finished shirts back three times to Davis & Company, suppliers to the western and southern trades; on each occasion the proprietors demanded more alterations, refused to pay for the shirts they did accept, held back her deposit, and finally tried to coerce her into paying them for the sewing they rejected. Soon after Byrnes went to court, Mary Gilroy of Five Points joined the fray with her own charges against the Davises, who had also refused to settle with her and had fleeced her out of a deposit. Clearly not a woman to take foul play sitting down, Gilroy had retaliated by taking out a dozen Davis shirts to hold for ransom. Neither woman, it should be said, seems to have secured much satisfaction in the end despite favorable publicity and testimony from the Davises that could hardly have been more damning: Margaret Byrnes won back her deposit but not her wages, and Mary Gilroy, as far as the record shows, must have taken her hostage shirts to the grave.[44] While the trial shows that the nonpayment of women's wages was an open scandal, the practice would not be systematically challenged until after the Civil War, with the formation of the Workingwoman's Protection Union.[45] Meanwhile, the party who reaped the most benefits from this particular confrontation was Tammany mayor Fernando Wood, whom the press showered with praise for "redressing the wrongs of the unfriended toiler."[46]

Proprietors like the Davises provided the material out of which middle-class investigators sympathetic to the seamstresses fashioned the figure of the villainous employer, a stock figure in so many Victorian renderings of the outside system. "There sat the proprietor in his shirt-sleeves, a vulgar-looking creature, smoking a cigar." "He can browbeat, and haggel with, and impose upon a poor, weak, sickly, industrious work-girl to more purpose, and more to his own advantage than any body else."[47] These images of iniquity so dominate the historical evidence that it is difficult to look at the situation analytically: why, we can ask, should these employers have been so particularly abusive and dishonest? The Victorian accounts certainly do not falsify the situation, although they do obliterate its complexities: as unsentimental an observer as the southerner William Bobo described the typical clothing employer as "a sour, crabbed, ill-gained foreigner, or blue-skinned Yankee, (just as bad,) that has no more feeling of kindness towards his fellow-creatures than a savage."[48] But from the small employer's point of view, what seemed villainy to others was a way to cope with the cutthroat economics in which he operated. "The clothing makers for the southern trade are generally the target of popular hostility on account of low wages, and there can be no doubt that many of them are gripers," the *Tribune* acknowledged. The paper was the self-proclaimed champion of the needlewomen, but its editor Horace Greeley was never a man to get his mind around the imperatives of capitalism, and here his paper pointed out simple economic fact: "If they were all the purest philanthropists, they could not raise the wages of their seamstresses to anything like a living price. Necessity rests as heavily upon them as upon the occupant of the most contracted garret. They can only live by their business so long as they can get garments made here low enough to enable them to pay cost, risk and charges and undersell. . . . If they were compelled to pay living wages for their work, they must stop it altogether."[49]

When proprietors put off paying a workwoman as the Davises did, they were not always lying when they claimed they had no cash on hand. Nor was the issue of flawed work necessarily a sham. For all the extraordinary advantages the outside system gave employers, it was not the most technically efficient and economically rational organization of work, and one of its drawbacks was nonstandardized work—that is, garments sewn too differently from each other to be sold for a unit price.[50]

In the 1850s, employers hard pressed by growing competition took steps to solve the problem of standardization by introducing the sewing machine, which standardized the stitch, and by putting out detail work instead of whole garments. Home workers sewed pieces of the garment—cuffs, buttonholes, sleeves—which were then assembled in an inside shop. In the shop, employers could maximize their supervision of the assemblage, the step in production where the mark of the individual worker was most conspicuous. Hanford & Brothers, reputedly the largest firm in the country, put out shirt wristbands, collars, and bosoms separately; the finished pieces were then sewn together in the factory.[51] New methods of production increased the pressure on small employers, who did not have the resources to shift to such an organization but still had to offer standardized merchandise in order to compete. Consequently, when these men niggled over alterations, they could be genuinely concerned with the quality of their stock as well as covertly engaged in driving down the wage.

For seamstresses, wage-cutting and underemployment bred overwork. When piece rates fell, they could only do more work for the income needed, a principle which Henry Mayhew elucidated in his investigations of London slop-workers.[52] Since work was not always available, they had to work as much as they could when they did find employment. In the 1830s, Matthew Carey had found that seamstresses without male support worked from sunrise to nine or ten at night; in the 1850s, the sewing machine drove piece rates so low that fifteen- to eighteen-hour workdays were not uncommon. "Those who make at the lowest prices appear to have no other mission on earth but to sew up bleached muslin into shirts," maintained Virginia Penny, self-styled Mayhew of New York's working women. "In some instances we have been informed, that where there are two or three or more women or girls engaged in this enterprise of making shirts to enable gentlemen to appear respectable in society, they absolutely divide the night season into watches."[53] To be sure, these stints were intermittent because employment was not steady. But when we consider that the days without work brought mostly anxiety and the search for more employment, it becomes clear that there was little leisure in these women's lives to ease the strain.

To fully comprehend the hardships of outside workers, however, we must understand the nature of the labor itself. Hand-sewing strained the eyes and cramped the back and neck so much that a practiced observer like Virginia Penny could recognize a seamstress on the street by her peculiar stooped carriage: "the neck suddenly bending forward, and the arms being, even in walking, considerably bent forward, or folded more or less upward from the elbows."[54] The curvature came from bending over the sewing in badly lit rooms: most were too dark in the daytime to read without artificial light, and seamstresses had to economize in their use of candles. The tiny backstitch which they used was painstakingly slow; it took about twelve hours to make one shirt. There was, moreover, a multitude of chances to make mistakes. A shirt bosom could be too full, the sleeves too short, and the wristbands too long, and the man who examined the garments—the employer or his "piece master," as the foreman of outside workers was called in large shops—might return the work for alterations on any of these counts. Even a clearheaded woman could easily botch the piecing, but a tired one who had been working for hours was that much more likely to make a mistake that would cost hours to repair, to sew in a sleeve backward or embroider a buttonhole out of line. The doggerel beat of Thomas Hood's "Son of the Shirt," a favorite propaganda piece of seamstresses and their supporters, captures something of the drudgery of the work itself:

> *Work-work-work!*
> *Till the brain begins to swim;*
> *Work-work-work!*
> *Till the eyes are heavy and dim!*
> *Seam, and gusset, and band,*
> *Band, and gusset, and seam,*
> *Till over the buttons I fall asleep*
> *And sew them on in a dream.*[55]

The sewing machine, as it was used in the context of nineteenth-century capitalism, did little to lighten the labor. From the perspective of the operatives, machine-sewing was as taxing as hand-sewing; it only shifted the strain from the arms to the lower torso. Women working the machines suffered chronic pain in their hips, nervous disorders from the jarring of the mechanism, and eyestrain from following the long lines of stitching.[56]

In their appeals for help, seamstresses and their supporters stressed the high rate of mortality and disease associated with their trade, what we could call in retrospect the biological experience of class. A doctor in 1860 guessed that a thousand women a year died of causes related to sewing in the outside system.[57] Malnutrition, fatigue, cold, and bad ventilation in the tenements bred pneumonia and consumption, the major killers of nineteenth-century cities. A newspaper investigator in 1853 heard that the hardest-working women could squeeze as much as double the average earnings out of the piece rates, but the extra money usually went to medicines.[58] "Will the men of New-York allow the unfortunate Shirt Sewers to stitch their own shrouds?" one seamstresses' broadside rhetorically inquired.[59]

II

The outside system of metropolitan industry was grafted onto women's domestic work, and the victimization of women as outside workers was tied to their role as family members and household laborers. Under the pressures of early industrialism, family labor became both the means by which women met their own household needs and the instrument of their exploitation within the work force: to put it another way, it was the source of both respectability and alienation. Outside workers were at the bottom of the city's labor force not only because they were women—the explanation that historians of industrialization have favored; they were there because they were wives, mothers, and daughters with family responsibilities.[60]

By 1860, the outside system had branched out from the clothing trade into other women's industries. The 1840s saw the emergence of a new middle-class market for a panoply of consumer goods: embellishments and adornments to grace the Victorian home and person. Artificial-flower-making, fringe- and tassel-making, embroidery, mantua-making, fancy book-binding, and parasol-making flourished, along with all manner of other fancy worked, burnished, and gilded manufactures. Light and easily transported, most of these goods could be put out; requiring deftness and delicacy in their assemblage, they were considered suitable for female hands. Shoebinding, the female employment that had been second to sewing at the turn of the century, also continued to provide work for women. Although the cordwainers of Lynn, Massachusetts, had captured much of the national market by 1815, New York shoemakers went on making slop shoes for the poor and the military along with luxury slippers for wealthy customers. In all these industries, the organization of outside work was similar to that of the clothing trade.

Throughout the entire system, women turned family labor to the purposes of wagework as well as housework. As they divided up domestic chores with their children, so they divided up homework. Family labor helped them combat the effect of wage-cutting by allowing them to increase the amount of work they could do. In box-making, children helped with the easier parts of cutting and gluing; in matchstick-making, the lowliest of put-out employments, young children dipped the matchheads while mothers and older siblings cut out the sticks. In families of seamstresses, children as young as five could do the simple task of pulling bastings, and at ten years or so, daughters were nimble fingered enough to sew straight seams and attach buttons. Most important, children who knew their way about the streets could save their mothers valuable time by carrying work back and forth from the shop.[61]

In the families of some artisans, an older pattern of outside work persisted in which the entire family worked along with the craftsman. This had been a common practice in the eighteenth century, and it continued—although in a greatly altered context—in the households of fur-sewers, shoemakers, and tailors, in the form of the "family shop."[62] A sample from the 1855 census shows that in one poor working-class neighborhood in the Fourth Ward near the waterfront, 16 percent of seamstresses were living with male kin who worked in the tailoring trade: such households were probably family shops.[63] The men did the most skilled work, negotiated with employers, and integrated the different operations, while women and children worked at the preparatory and subsidiary tasks. In the 1850s, piece rates were too low for journeymen tailors to make a living without family labor: "A tailor is nothing without a wife, and very often a child," went a maxim of German craftsmen.[64]

The family shop was a unit laboring for its own subsistence, dependent on the cooperation of all. From the perspective of our own more fragmented time, such families evoke images of solidarity and mutuality, attachments which we assume such intimate reciprocity would have fostered. Indeed, within the metropolitan economy, family shops did function as cooperative units, but it is important to see that within each group, relations were hierarchical, not egalitarian: men were at the top, children at the bottom. The hierarchical structure may not have been especially important while the family unit was intact, as it was in the eighteenth century, each person working for the common good and sharing more or less equally in the earnings. But it did become significant when each individual earned wages, for then wage differentials developed between men, women, and children, and then it became profitable for adults, especially men, to replicate familial arrangements among non-kin as well as kin. In other words, traditions of family labor became a means of exploitation in the nineteenth century as well as a way for working people to support themselves through cooperation.[65]

In New York, new forms of outside work that replicated the family hierarchy developed out of family labor. Women and girls, for instance, began to work in the 1850s for unmarried journeymen in the same capacities as wives and daughters assisted tailors in their own homes. The journeymen mediated between piece masters and the home shop and took the largest portion of earnings. Poor as these men were, they were still employers and women were their workers: they paid the women fixed wages and took the small profits for themselves.[66] Women also put themselves at the top of this type of arrangement in the "learning" system. Learning was a debased form of apprenticeship which corresponded to the relation of parents and children in family labor. In exchange for the crudest training, girls worked for tailors, seamstresses, dressmakers, and milliners either for their keep or for a few pennies a day. Journeymen also used this system: adults made their profit by taking out work at regular piece rates and paying employees either lower rates or nothing at all to make it up. "Learning" proliferated in the 1850s along with the family shop and its variants as a way for individuals to combat the effects of the sewing machine. Like all child laborers, learners were the humblest of the trade, but since their employers themselves were so poor, the learners' condition was especially lowly. In 1853 a *Herald* reporter found a learners' garret near the waterfront where four tennage girls worked for an Irish seamstress every day except Sunday in exchange for their board; they paid for rent, clothes, and Sunday's food by prostituting themselves to sailors.[67]

All forms of outside work merged with sweating, which spread through the poor districts in the 1850s as trade flourished. There were many levels of sweaters: journeymen tailors, piece masters themselves (who contracted work from their employers), garret masters and mistresses. The journeymen who took out work for their wives were engaged in a kind of sweating, although in the sweating system proper, the contractor invested no labor of his own but took his earnings from the "sweat" of others. So in the case of tailors who contracted out work: "The hands hired by the Journeymen do not generally get more than $3.50 or $4 per week, while the Journeyman receives his $6.25 for every Coat from the employer. . . . Sometimes, also, the same principle is applied in another way: the Journeyman letting out his work by the piece to the lowest bidder and thus making more or less profit on every garment given him by the Cutter—for which, of course, the proprietor of the shop is charged full price."[68]

The use of the sewing machine encouraged sweating, since very few women workers (and few tailors, too) could afford their own but neither could they afford to work without one. Several inventors had taken out patents on sewing machines in the 1840s, but the stitches unraveled too easily and the power came from an unwieldly hand crank. In 1846, Elias Howe devised a lockstitch which imitated the handsewers' sturdy backstitch and, in 1850, Issac Singer replaced the crank with a foot treadle and devised other improvements which made the machine practicable for the first time.[69] Employers could push the sewing machine relatively easily upon a system in which small-scale production predominated and workers had been forced to absorb overhead costs for several decades. A German-born New York tailor told the story well. "The bosses said: 'We want you to use the sewing-machine, you have to buy one,'" he recalled. "Many of the tailors had a few dollars in the bank, and they took the money and bought machines. Many others had no money . . . so they brought their stitching . . . to the other tailors who had sewing machines, and paid them a few cents for the stitching. Later, when the money was given out for the work, we found out that we could earn no more than we could without a machine.''[70] Since seamstresses were less able to save money than tailors, few could purchase their own machines, and the shift to machine work made it more necessary for them to work for some kind of sweater.

Between 1815 and 1860 the outside system incorporated increasing numbers of male as well as female workers in the city. Nonetheless, there were crucial differences between the experiences of men and women in outwork, differences which would shape the history of labor-organizing in New York. The bonds between male workers were evident in their everyday relations in the outside workplace. In some work situations, masculine associations were immediately felt: there were tailors' and shoemakers' boardinghouses, for instance, where single journeymen worked on goods which the proprietors contracted out to them.[71] But even when a man worked with his family rather than other men, he sustained the bonds of his trade, bonds which were exclusively masculine. His sense of fellowship with other artisans remained alive. He fraternized with other men on the basis of their shared trade, and carried with him a history of work associations with men dating back to his apprenticeship. Trade societies sustained and vivified these associations, and every wave of trade-union militance strengthened the ties; tailors, to take one group of male outworkers, were among the most highly organized artisans in the city.

Women's situation in outwork was less structured by same-sex relations. Most often, women probably worked alone. To be sure, they also worked with other women in garrets, sweatshops, and tenement rooms, and single women sometimes sewed together in units resembling a family shop. Virginia Penny encountered such groups, young seamstresses who rented rooms and worked together in twos and threes.[72] Most commonly, however, these workplace associations were family- rather than gender- or trade-based, as men's were. Rather than female peers, workmates in collective groups could be children and husbands, sisters and mothers,[73] unlike men's, women's network of wage-labor associations did not transcend their domestic world. They did not fraternize with other women on the basis of a shared history in a trade but on the basis of family, neighborliness, and household concerns. A journeyman brought a sense of himself as a man bound to other men to whatever other work relations he had in a sweater's garret or his own home; a woman brought her identity as a mother or daughter, a woman bound to men and children, to her work relations with other women. The psychological associations of the household as well as the actual working relations there made it unlikely that women could develop a sense of a collectivity comprised solely of other women, associated through their common self-interest in the labor market.[74]

The confinement of women workers to their households gave rise to a specific psychology of female subordination in their relations with employers as well as to a particular organization of labor. The outside system masked women's involvement in wage labor; they appeared to be peripheral to industrial production and their identity as workers seemed secondary to their roles as wives and mothers. In actuality, their wagework was not marginal, either in their own lives or in the development of metropolitan industry. But shut away as they were from the primary confrontations of labor and capital, they had little chance to develop a sense of themselves as active in the struggle. In the interstices of the outside system, a plebeian variant of the bourgeois woman's sphere appeared which shut away women from a comprehension of the economy equal to that of the men with whom they lived. In the family shop, after all, it was the man who mediated between the world of the market and the world of the household.

Employers capitalized upon this construction of women as "outside" the economy, lacking acumen about the world outside their doors. "Our employers set up the most frivolous pretexts for reducing our wages," a former seamstress remembered. "Some of them were so transparently false that I wondered how any one could have the impudence to present them." She concluded that they could because they "considered a sewing-woman as either too dull to detect the fallacy, or too timid to expose and resent it."[75] This was a psychology of heterosexuality as well as one of class; likewise, when piece masters used derision in order to drive down a woman's wage: "He pulls at each seam, at each button, from end to end, and over every part of it his keen eye wanders in search of a flaw. Ha! he has found one . . . in a gruff, sharp tone, he asks her: 'Do you call this work?'" "Are they not well done?" replied the timid workwoman in this journalist's sketch. "I'm sure I did my best." "Well done, Woman, well done indeed, why they're blown together." He implied that she had no idea what constituted decent sewing; what she thought was "well done" was in actuality "blown together." With his claim to objective judgment, based on his knowledge of the business, he drove the woman back on the subjective—"I'm sure I did my best"—a meager defense in the world of the marketplace. By revealing her ignorance, he dramatized his own business acumen and effectively undermined any protest she might have made when he lowered her wage: "There, take that," he snapped when he paid her less than the price he promised. "No one shall say I deal hardly with my work people, but I must be just."[76] He had demonstrated his comprehension of value and fair exchange, and in so doing he placed himself above arbitrariness and guile; his claim to meting out justice rested on firm psychological ground. He was a man schooled in the abstract justice of commodity exchange, impatient with a woman who at every turn showed her ignorance of the laws of the marketplace.

Through the outside system, women's domesticity became a practical necessity of industrial capitalism. By the 1850s, employers (should they have been asked) could have agreed with evangelical reformers that the place of women was in the home, the poor not excluded. For the women themselves, outwork reinforced their ties to the domestic world at the same time as the necessities of their lives pushed them more entirely under the rule of the marketplace. As the line between family labor and wage labor was blurred, so was the boundary between their sense of themselves as workers for their families and their sense of themselves as wage laborers. In the long run, this limited their consciousness of themselves as workers: there was little room in the emerging plebeian woman's sphere for women to develop a sense of themselves as individuals bound to like individuals through common self-interest in the workplace. Their loyalties and priorities there were so entangled with children, husbands, and kin: how could the more abstract solidarity of sex replace the felt unity of family? Home workers were literally "outside" the arena of public life where working men were developing the mutual associations which were the basis for a new kind of politicized community in the Victorian city.

NOTES

1. Matthew Carey, "Essays on the Public Charities of Philadelphia," *Miscellaneous Essays* (Philadelphia: Carey & Hart, 1830), p. 154.

2. Society for the Relief of Poor Widows, Minutes, Nov. 1859, New York Historical Society, New York.

3. New York Children's Aid Society, *Second Annual Report* (New York, 1855), pp. 38-39.

4. See Sean Wilentz's essay in this collection; also his "Class Conflict and the Rights of Man: Artisans and the Rise of Labor Radicalism in New York City" (Ph.D. dissertation, Yale University, 1980).

5. Eric Hobsbawm, "The Formation of the Industrial Working Classes: Some Problems," *3e Conférence Internationale d'Histoire Economique, Congrès et Colloques,* vol. 1 (The Hague, 1965), pp. 176-77. Marx speaks of domestic manufactures as peripheral to the central tendency of industrialization "to conversion to the factory system proper." *Capital,* trans. Samuel Moore and Edward Aveling (Moscow: Progress Publishers, n.d.), vol. 1, p. 445. See also Sidney Pollard, *The Genesis of Modern Management* (Cambridge, Mass.: Harvard University Press, 1965), pp. 34-35.

6. In 1910, Helen L. Sumner noted that the factory system in the clothing trade "has only recently made headway." See her *History of Women in Industry in the United States* in U.S. Congress, Senate, *Report on Condition of Women and Child Wage-Earners in the United States,* S. Doc. 645, 61st Cong., 2d Sess. (Washington, D.C., 1910), vol. 9, p. 116, hereafter cited as Sumner, *History of Women.* On London, see Sally Alexander, "Women's Work in Nineteenth-Century London: A Study of the Years 1820-1850," in *The Rights and Wrongs of Women,* ed. Juliet Mitchell and Ann Oakley (Harmondsworth, Eng.: Penguin Books, 1976), pp. 63, 65; for Paris, Henriette Vanier, *La Mode et Ses Metiers: Frivolités et Luttes des Classes, 1830-1870* (Paris: Armand Colin, 1960); for Holland, Selma Leydesdorff, "Women and Children in Home Industry" (paper presented at the International Conference in Women's History, University of Maryland, Nov. 16, 1977).

7. For a general discussion of the importance of hand technology to industrialization, see Raphael Samuel, "The Workshops of the World: Steam Power and Hand Technology in Mid-Victorian Britain," *History Workshop,* 3 (Spring 1977), 6-72.

8. Carl Degler, "Labor in the Economy and Politics of New York City, 1850-1860: A Study of the Impact of Early Industrialism" (Ph.D. dissertation, Columbia University, 1952), pp. 106, 124.

9. Edward Livingston to James Warner, President of the General Society of Mechanics and Tradesmen, *New York Evening Post,* Feb. 24, 1803. Mary Ryan describes the absence of female employment in the entire Northeast in *Womanhood in America from Colonial Times to the Present* (New York: Franklin Watts, 1975), pp. 100-101.

10. Edith Abbott, *Women in Industry: A Study in American Economic History* (New York: D. Appleton & Company, 1924), pp. 19-20, 42, 70-78; Nancy Cott, *Bonds of Womanhood: "Woman's Sphere" in New England, 1780-1835* (New Haven, Conn.: Yale University Press, 1977), pp. 25, 39-40.

11. Sumner, *History of Women,* p. 167. Sumner also mentions spinning manufactories for poor New York women in the late eighteenth century. Ibid., pp. 53, 124. See also Society for the Relief of Poor Widows, Minutes, Feb. 21, 1803.

12. *Evening Post,* Oct. 27, Nov. 29, 1819.

13. Society for the Relief of Poor Widows, Minutes, Nov. 17, 1817.

14. Association for the Relief of Respectable, Aged and Indigent Females in New York City, Visitor's Book, Feb. 6, 1839, New York Historical Society, New York. For the demise of spinning, see Victor S. Clark, *History of Manufactures in the United States,* 3 vols. (New York: McGraw-Hill Book Company, 1929), vol. 1, p. 531. I should note that the interruption of commerce during the War of 1812 revivified hand-spinning for a short time. *Ibid.,* pp. 563-64.

15. Society for the Prevention of Pauperism in the City of New York, *Fifth Annual Report* (New York, 1821), p. 12.

16. An important component of this pool of cheap labor was the high number of women. See David Montgomery's suggestion that seaport cities in the early nineteenth century had an advantage over other centers of population in America in economic growth because of their surplus of women. "It may be that the westward movement of men created a labor surplus in the East, a surplus of women . . . perhaps . . . one of the major advantages that a city would have had at this time. Women were coming into the labor market in large numbers as widows, as orphans or as single women. You notice that the age bracket in which the women were available, the marrying age, 16 to 25, was where they outnumbered men." In David T. Gilchrist, ed., *The Growth of the Seaport Cities 1790-1825. Proceedings of a Conference Sponsored by the Eleutherian Mills-Hagley Foundation, March 17-18, 1966* (Charlottesville: University of Virginia Press, 1966), pp. 100-101.

In her study of the Sixth Ward, Carol Groneman found a large number of widows with dependents. She attributes this to the high death rate among foreign-born male workers in New York in the prime of life. "'She Earns as a Child—She Pays as a Man': Women Workers in the Mid-Nineteenth-Century New York Community," in *Class, Sex, and the Woman Worker*, ed. Milton Cantor and Bruce Laurie (Wesport, Conn.: Greenwood Press, 1977), pp. 93-96.

Among whites in the city, the sex ratio was balanced until 1830, when women began to outnumber men. In 1830, there were 106 women for every 100 men; in 1840, 108; in 1850, 102; in 1860, 125. These calculations are based on population data from Franklin B. Hough, *Statistics on the Population of the City and County of New York* (New York: New York Printing Company, 1866).

17. Indeed clothing manufacture was the leading employer of women in the city well into the twentieth century. I have traced it in the U.S. census for manufactures as far as 1940, when it still far outstripped any other industry in this regard.

18. *Manufactures of the United States in 1860; Compiled from the Original Returns of the Eighth Census* (Washington, D.C., 1865); calculated from returns for New York County, pp. 380-85.

Precisely because of the prevalence of outwork among women wageworkers, we can only take these census statistics as rough estimates of the number of women in the labor force. Any discussion of female labor-force participation in industrializing countries must take account of this serious problem of under-enumeration. For the same point about women's wagework in England and Holland, respectively, see Alexander, "Women's Work in Nineteenth-Century London," pp. 59, 111, and Leydesdorff, "Women and Children in Home Industry."

19. Quoted in Alexander C. Flick, gen. ed., *History of the State of New York*, 10 vols. (New York: Columbia University Press, 1933-37), vol. 3, *Whig and Tory*, pp. 297-98.

20. Abbott, *Women in Industry*, p. 217; Egal Feldman, *Fit for Men: A Study of New York's Clothing Trade* (Washington, D.C..: Public Affairs Press, 1960), pp. 1-2.

21. For sailors' slops, see Feldman, *Fit for Men*, pp. 1-2; Edwin T. Freedley, ed., *Leading Pursuits and Leading Men* (Philadelphia: Edward Young, 1856), p. 89. For uniforms, see Flick, *History of the State of New York*, vol. 3, *Whig*

and Tory, p. 315. In 1819 the ladies of the House of Industry acquired a contract for navy blankets and uniforms to avert insolvency. *Evening Post*, Nov. 29, 1819. For journeymen sewing slops, see Feldman, *Fit for Men*, pp. 77-78; Jesse Eliphalet Pope, *The Clothing Industry in New York* (Columbia: University of Missouri Press, 1905), p. 11. For mentions of women sewing slops, see Ezra Stiles Ely, *Visits of Mercy; Being the Journal of the Stated Preacher to the Hospital and Almshouse in the City of New York, 1811* (New York: Whiting & Watson, 1812), p. 32; Society for the Relief of Poor Widows, Minutes, 1798, Jan. 10, 1803, Apr. 8, 1807.

22. Feldman, *Fit for Men*, p. 3; Sumner, *History of Women*, p. 122.

23. Freedley, *Leading Pursuits*, p. 89.

24. Chauncey M. Depew, *One Hundred Years of American Commerce* (New York: D.O. Haynes & Company, 1895), p. 565; *New York Herald*, Oct. 25, 1857.

25. *Herald*, Oct. 25, 1857. See John C. Golbright, *The Union Sketch-Book: A Reliable Guide ... of the Leading Mercantile and Manufacturing Firms of New York* (New York: Rudd & Carleton, 1861), pp. 40-41, for the national market.

26. Gobright, *Union Sketch-Book*, p. 40.

27. Sumner, *History of Women*, p. 138.

28. Virginia Penny, *The Employments of Women: An Encyclopedia of Women's Work* (Boston: Walker, Wise, & Co., 1863), p. 113.

29. For the attractions of the clothing trade for immigrants, see Robert Ernst, *Immigrant Life in New York City 1825-1863* (New York: Columbia University Press, 1949), p. 93. After 1835, when the commercial district was rebuilt after the great fire of that year, rents soared in lower Manhattan. For the expansion of homework in London under similar pressures of high rents, see Gareth Stedman Jones, *Outcast London: A Study in the Relationship between Classes in Victorian Society* (London: Oxford University Press, 1971), p. 23.

Sidney Pollard stresses the importance of subcontracting in early industrial capitalist enterprises in England. The large entrepreneur could thereby reduce his supervisory activities and to some degree stablize his cost structure by paying the subcontractor a fixed price. *Genesis of Modern Management*, pp. 38-39.

30. Degler, "Labor in the Economy and Politics of New York City," p. 111. See also Freedley, *Leading Pursuits*, pp. 126-27, for the difficulties of small manufacturers. I am indebted to Sean Wilentz for discussions which have elucidated the structure of the clothing trade.

31. Quoted in Sumner, *History of Women*, p. 136.

32. New York State Census, 1855, Population Schedules, Ward 4, Electoral District 2, and Ward 17, Electoral District 3, mss at County Clerk's Office, New York City. I selected these two neighborhoods for sampling because they represented two strata of the laboring classes: the Seventeenth Ward was a new neighborhood for recent arrivals, while the Fourth Ward was an old, extremely poor neighborhood of day laborers and sailors.

33. Society for the Relief of Poor Widows, Minutes, No. 15, 1855.

34. *Ibid.*

35. *Herald*, June 7, 1853.

36. For the importance of dovetailing employment in a casualized labor market, see Jones, *Outcast London*, pp. 39-41. For mention of both weekly and seasonal

unemployment, see Carey, "Report on Female Wages," *Miscellaneous Essays*, p. 267; Shirt Sewers' Cooperative, "Circular of the Shirt Sewers' Association," Broadsides Collection, New York Historical Society, New York; *Daily Tribune*, June 8, 1853; Society for the Relief of Poor Widows, Minutes, Nov. 16, 1854; Penny, *Employments of Women*, pp. 114-15.

37. Quoted in Sumner, *History of Women*, p. 136.

38. *Working Man's Advocate* (New York), Sept. 6, 1831; George C. Foster, *New York in Slices: By an Experienced Carver* (New York: William H. Graham, 1849), p. 13.

39. Carey, "Report on Female Wages," *Miscellaneous Essays*, p. 280.

40. Little is known about day laborers in New York except their wages, which are alluded to throughout the reform and charity literature. I have garnered my impressions about turnouts from examining the cases of the New York County Court of General Sessions, New York County Courthouse.

41. *Working Man's Advocate*, Sept. 11, 1830.

42. *Herald*, Oct. 21, 1857.

43. William M. Bobo, *Glimpses of New York City, by a South Carolinian* (Charleston: J.J. McCarter, 1852), p. 109; see also pp. 107-10. Other references can be found in the *Herald*, June 7, 1853, Oct. 25, 1857; *Daily Tribune*, Aug. 7, 1849, June 8, 1853; *Working Man's Advocate*, Apr. 6, 1844; William W. Sanger, *The History of Prostitution* (New York: Harper & Brothers, 1859), p. 527; *Jonathan's Whittlings of War*, Apr. 22, 1854, pp. 102-3.

44. *New York Daily Times*, Feb. 24, 27, Mar. 1, 1855. A third seamstress sued her employer in court on Mar. 1.

45. The union was founded in 1863, apparently by middle-class men, who comprised its board of directors in the 1870s. Among them, interestingly enough, was police chief George Matsell. Workingwomen's Protective Union, *Twelfth Annual Report* (New York, 1876).

46. *Daily Times*, Mar. 1, 1855.

47. "Needle and Garden. The Story of a Seamstress Who Laid Down Her Needle and Became a Strawberry Girl," *Atlantic Monthly*, 15 (1865), 170; *Jonathan's Whittlings*, Apr. 22, 1854, p. 102.

48. Bobo, *Glimpses of New York City*, p. 109.

49. *Daily Tribune*, Mar. 7, 1845.

50. Penny, *Employments of Women*, pp. 111, 114, 356. See also Pollard, *Genesis of Modern Management*, pp. 33-34. The inefficiency of putting-out is also discussed in Ivy Pinchbeck, *Women Workers and the Industrial Revolution 1750-1850* (1930; reprint ed., New York: Augustus M. Kelley Publishers, 1969), p. 137.

The other drawback of the outside system was the opportunity it gave workers to embezzle goods. Stephen Marglin has argued that embezzlement was widely practiced by English cottage workers in the eighteenth and early nineteenth centuries. He believes that embezzlement was the most serious of many problems of labor discipline which led capitalists to factory organization: not because factories were initially technologically superior to outwork but because such refractory practices could be better controlled by direct supervision. "What Do Bosses Do? The Origins and Functions of Hierarchy in Capitalist Production," *Review of Radical Political Economics*, 6 (Summer 1974), 33-35.

There is some evidence of embezzlement among New York workers. One employer told Penny that he had taken serious losses from nonreturned work: "On inquiry at the place where the women said they lived, they would find they had never been there." Another mentioned a blacklist of women who did not return their work, and a third corroborated the existence of a blacklist but claimed that he himself had never had any problems with embezzlement: "If they [the women] should keep them, they would soon be known at the different establishments, and have no place to go for work." Penny, *Employments of Women*, pp. 112, 115, 352. There were arrests of tailors for embezzlement during the tailors' strike of 1850, and one employer raised it as a general problem. See *Daily Tribune*, July 26, Aug. 14, 1850. There was an extensive network of illicit trade in New York, comprised of secondhand and pawnshops. If women did not embezzle goods, it would be interesting to know why, given the accessibility of that network and the frequency with which they went to pawnshops.

51. *Herald*, June 11, 1853; Freedley, *Leading Pursuits*, p. 130.

52. Letter subtitled "Over-work makes under-pay" and "Under-pay makes over-work," in Eileen Yeo and E.P. Thompson, *The Unknown Mayhew* (New York: Pantheon Books, 1971), pp. 384-88.

53. Penny, *Employments of Women*, pp. 350-51; evidence on the length of the workday is in Carey, "Essays on the Public Charities of Philadelphia," *Miscellaneous Essays*, p. 167; "Address of the Shirt Sewers' Cooperative," Broadsides Collection, New York Historical Society, New York; Penny, *Employments of Women*, p. 356.

54. Penny, *Employments of Women*, p. 310.

55. Reprinted in "Circular of the Shirt Sewers' Association"; a more accessible reprinting is in Alan Bold, ed., *The Penguin Book of Socialist Verse* (Harmondsworth, Eng.: Penguin Books, 1970), pp. 66-68.

56. Penny, *Employments of Women*, p. 311.

57. Ibid. p. 356.

58. *Herald*, June 7, 1853.

59. "Circular of the Shirt Sewers' Associations."

60. In the 1855 sample from the Fourth and Seventeenth Wards, 200 (69.9 percent) of the 286 women who appeared to work "outside" were residing with husbands, parents, children, or kin. New York State Census, 1855, Population Schedules, Ward 4, Electoral District 2; Ward 17, Electoral District 3.

61. There are allusions to family labor in waged employment throughout the case histories of the New York House of Refuge Papers, Case Histories 1825-1860, New York State Library, Albany, and the published reports of the Children's Aid Society. For other references see "Needle and Garden," p. 91; *Daily Tribune*, Aug. 28, 1845; *The New-York Cries in Rhyme* (New York: Mahlon Day, 1832), p. 18; *Herald*, June 11, 1853.

62. Abbott, *Women in Industry*, pp. 2211-22. For contemporary references see Penny, *Employments of Women*, pp. 114, 310-11, 312-14, 355; Freedley, *Leading Pursuits*, p. 129; *Daily Tribune*, Sept. 5, 9, 1845; *Working Man's Advocate*, July 27, 1844.

63. New York State Census, 1855, Population Schedules, Ward 4, Electoral District 2. The sample includes all women (*N* = 142) enumerated as seamstresses in this electoral district. Carol Groneman reached a similar conclusion with her data from the Sixth Ward. "'She Earns as a Child,'" p. 93.

64. Conrad Carl, a New York tailor, testifying before a Senate investigatory committee, cited this proverb. U.S. Congress, Senate, Committee on Education and Labor, *Testimony as to the Relations between Labor and Capital*, 48th Cong., 1885, p. 414.

65. Pinchbeck, *Women Workers and the Industrial Revolution*, p. 2, makes this point about the effect on women of the breakup of the family unit of employment, although she does not extend it to the development of new forms of exploitation and an entire system of wage differentials.

66. *Working Man's Advocate*, July 27, 1844; Penny, *Employments of Women*, pp. 113-14.

67. Penny refers to the learning system throughout *Employments of Women*. See also *Herald*, Oct. 21, 1857. For the Irish garret-mistress, see *Herald*, June 8, 1853.

68. *Daily Tribune*, Nov. 12, 1845. References to the many different kinds of sweaters can be found in the following: *Daily Tribune*, Nov. 15, 1845; Penny, *Employments of Women*, pp. 112, 312, 342-43, 356, 452. In *Hunt's Merchant Magazine*, Jan. 1849, is the very interesting piece of information that piece masters in the large establishments of New York made anywhere from $25 to $150 a week, an indication that they were engaged in quite lucrative subcontracting. George C. Foster mentions sweaters and under-sweaters in *New York Naked* (New York: R.M. DeWitt [185?]), pp. 137-38.

69. Depew, *One Hundred Years of American Commerce,* p. 525; Feldman, *Fit for Men*, pp. 106-7; most important, see the fascinating account of the invention of the sewing machine in Ruth Brandon, *A Capitalist Romance: Singer and the Sewing Machine* (Philadelphia: J.B. Lippincott Company, 1977), pp. 42-89.

70. U.S. Congress, Senate, Committee on Education and Labor, *Relations between Labor and Capital*, pp. 413-14. A machine in the early 1850s was quite expensive ($100-$150) but by 1858 the price had dropped to $50 and there was a substantial secondhand trade. Feldman, *Fit for Men*, pp. 108-9. For another account (from Philadelphia) of how the machine encouraged sweating, see "Needle and Garden," pp. 173-75.

71. Carol Groneman Pernicone found forty tailors' and shoemakers' boarding-houses in the Sixth Ward in the 1850s. "The 'Bloudy Ould Sixth': A Social Analysis of a New York City Working-Class Community in the Mid-Nineteenth Century" (Ph.D. dissertation, University of Rochester, 1973), p. 105.

72. Penny, *Employments of Women*, p. 112.

73. In the 1855 sample, I located forty-five households containing what appeared to be all-female work groups. Eighty percent of these were based on kin relations. New York State Census, 1855, Population Schedules, Ward 4, Electoral District 2, and Ward 17, Electoral District 3.

74. I was helped in my reasoning on this point by Heidi Hartmann's speculations about the reasons for men's "superior organizational ability" in the transition to industrial capitalism in "Capitalism, Patriarchy, and Job Segregation by Sex," in *Capitalist Patriarchy and the Case for Socialist Feminism*, ed. Zillah R. Eisenstein (New York: Monthly Review Press, 1979). pp. 216-17. See also Alexander, "Women's Work in Nineteenth-Century London," for a picture of the mingling of waged and domestic labor in a similar metropolitan economy. Mary McDougall, writing on industrialization in Europe, makes a point similar to mine about a particular vulnerability of women to sweating: "While the overall number of

domestic workers declined in the process of industrialization, mainly men gave it up, leaving behind a preponderance of women." "Working Class Women during the Industrial Revolution, 1780-1914," in *Becoming Visible: Women in European History,* ed. Renate Bridenthal and Claudia Koonz (Boston: Houghton Mifflin Company, 1977), p. 266.

75. "Needle and Garden," p. 173.

76. *Jonathan's Whittlings*, Apr. 22, 1854, p. 102.

～11～
WOMEN'S RIGHTS BEFORE THE CIVIL WAR

ELLEN CAROL DUBOIS

For many years before 1848, American women had manifested consider-able discontent with their lot. They wrote and read domestic novels in which a thin veneer of sentiment overlaid a great deal of anger about women's dependence on undependable men. They attended female academies and formed ladies' benevolent societies, in which they pursued the widest range of interests and activities they could imagine without calling into question the whole notion of "woman's sphere." In such settings, they probed the experiences that united and restrained them—what one historian has called "the bonds of womanhood."[1] Yet women's discontent remained unexamined, implicit, and above all, disorganized. Although increasing numbers of women were questioning what it meant to be a woman and were ready to challenge their tradi-tional position, they did not yet know each other.

The women's rights movement crystallized these sentiments into a feminist politics. Although preceded by individual theorists like Margaret Fuller, and by particular demands on behalf of women for property rights, education, and admission to the professions, the women's rights movment began a new phase in the history of feminism. It introduced the possibility of social change into a situation in which many women had already become dissatisfied. It posed women, not merely as beneficiaries of change in the relation of the sexes, but as agents of change as well. As Elizabeth Cady Stanton said at the meeting that inaugurated the movement, "Woman herself must do the work."[2]

The pioneers of women's rights pointed the way toward women's discontent organized to have an impact on women's history.

The women's rights movement developed in the dozen years before the Civil War. It had two sources. On the one hand, it emerged from women's growing awareness of their common conditions and grievances. Simultaneously, it was an aspect of antebellum reform politics, particularly of the antislavery movement. The women who built and led the women's rights movement combined these two historical experiences. They shared in and understood the lives of white, native-born American women of the working and middle classes: the limited domestic sphere prescribed for them, their increasing isolation from the major economic and political developments of their society, and above all their mounting discontent with their situation. Women's rights leaders raised this discontent to a self-conscious level and channeled it into activities intended to transform women's position. They were able to do this because of their experience in the antislavery movement, to which they were led, in part, by that very dissatisfaction with exclusively domestic life. Female abolitionists followed the course of the antislavery movement from evangelicism to politics, moving from a framework of individual sin and conversion to an understanding of institutionalized oppression and social reform. This development is what enabled them and other women's rights pioneers to imagine changing the traditional subservient status of women. Borrowing from antislavery ideology, they articulated a vision of equality and independence for women, and borrowing from antislavery method, they spread their radical ideas widely to challenge other people to imagine a new set of sexual relations. Their most radical demand was enfranchisement. More than any other element in the women's rights program of legal reform, woman suffrage embodied the movement's feminism, the challenge it posed to women's dependence upon and subservience to men.

The first episode of the women's rights movement was the 1848 Seneca Falls Convention, organized by Elizabeth Cady Stanton, Lucretia Mott, and several other women. As befitted an enterprise handicapped by the very injustices it was designed to protest, the proceedings were a mixture of womanly modesty and feminist militancy. When faced with the task of composing a manifesto for the convention, the organizers, in Stanton's words, felt "as helpless and hopeless as if they had been suddenly asked to construct a steam engine." Nor was any woman willing to chair the meeting, and the office fell to Lucretia Mott's husband. Yet the list of grievances which the organizers presented was comprehensive. In retrospect, we can see that their Declaration of Sentiments and Resolutions anticipated every demand of nineteenth-century feminism. To express their ideas about women's rights and wrongs, they chose to rewrite the Preamble of the Declaration of Independence around "the repeated injuries and usurpations on the part of man towards woman." On the one hand, this decision reflected their need to borrow political legitimacy from the American Revolution. On the other, it permitted them to state in the clearest possible fashion that they identified the tyranny of men as the cause of women's grievances.[3]

The Seneca Falls Convention was consciously intended to initiate a broader movement for the emancipation of women. For the women who organized the convention, and others like them, the first and greatest task was acquiring the skills and knowledge necessary to lead such an enterprise. In Elizabeth Cady Stanton's words, they had to transform themselves into a "race of women worthy to assert the humanity of women."[4] Their development as feminists, as women able to bring politics to bear on the condition of their sex, had as its starting point the experience they shared with other women. While many accounts of this first generation of feminist activists stress what distinguished them from other women—their bravery and open rebellion—it is equally important to recognize what they had in common with nonfeminists: lack of public skills; lives marked by excessive domesticity; husbands and fathers hostile to their efforts; the material pressures of housekeeping and child-rearing; and the deep psychological insecurity bred by all these factors. A movement is a process by which rebellion generates more rebellion. The women's rights pioneers did not begin their political activities already "emancipated," freed from the limitations that other women suffered. Many of the personal and political resources they drew on to challenge the oppression of women were developed in the course of mounting the challenge itself.

"THE INFANCY OF OUR MOVEMENT"

Even the most committed and militant of the first-generation women's rights activists hesitated on the brink of the public activity necessary to build a feminist movement. Although a successful writer, Frances Dana Gage was as homebound as other women, when she was asked to preside over a women's rights convention in Akron in 1851. She was reluctant, but accepted the responsibility. "I have never in my life attended a regular business meeting," she told her audience, whose vistas were even more circumscribed than hers.[5] When Clarina Nichols delivered the first women's rights address before the Vermont legislature in 1850, her voice broke and her supporters feared that she would fail.

Spurred on by "the conviction that only an eminently successful presentation of her subject could spike the enemy's batteries," she finished her speech, "though her voice was tremulous."[6] Daring to speak out at the first women's rights convention she had ever attended, in 1852, Matilda Joslyn Gage was inaudible to her audience and "trembling in every limb." The mother of four young children at the time, Gage did not plunge seriously into political work until after the war, when her children had grown and domestic responsibilities were less insistent.[7] Abigail Bush spoke for an entire generation of feminists committed to acquiring political skills in service to their sex. When the audience at a convention in Rochester in 1848 called down the women speakers with cries of "louder, louder!" Bush responded: "Friends, we present ourselves here before you, as an oppressed class, with trembling frames and faltering tongues, and we do not expect to be able to speak as to be heard by all at first, but we trust we shall have the sympathy of the audience, and that you will bear with our weakness now in the infancy of our movement. Our trust in the omnipotency of right is our only faith that we shall succeed."[8]

Compared to many other women, Antoinette Brown was relatively self-confident as she prepared herself for public life and women's rights leadership. For three years, she resisted Oberlin College's attempts to drive her from its theological course. Nonetheless, the objection of a respected mentor to her women's rights ideas "put me into such an agony . . . I did wish God had not made me a woman."[9] The opposition of men, particularly the fathers and husbands on whom they were dependent, reinforced women's lack of public experience to restrain their feminist activism. Excluded from the World's Anti-Slavery Convention in London in 1840, Mary Grew returned to Pennsylvania to circulate petitions for a married women's property act. Her abolitionist father, who had encouraged her to do similar work in behalf of the slave, vigorously opposed her.[10] Elizabeth Cady Stanton, who was singularly unafflicted with psychological insecurity, faced her greatest obstacles in her husband and her father. Henry Stanton stubbornly opposed his wife's desire to join in the 1855–1856 canvass of New York, and her father, whom she adored, temporarily disinherited her when she began public lecturing. Her convictions only deepened. "To think," she wrote, "that all in me of which my father would have felt a proper pride had I been a man, is deeply mortifying to him because I am a woman . . . has stung me to a fierce decision—to speak as soon as I can do myself credit. But the pressure on me just now is too great. Henry sides with my friends, who oppose me in all that is dearest to my heart. They are not willing that I should write even on the woman question. But I will both write and speak."[11]

During the late 1850's the focus of Stanton's "domestic bondage" shifted from the opposition of husband and father to the demands of her seven children. "I seldom have one hour undisturbed in which to sit down and write," she complained, while nursing her daughter. "Men who can, when they wish to write a document, shut themselves up for days with their thoughts and their books, know little of what difficulties a woman must surmount to get off a tolerable production."[12] By sharing both political and domestic work with Anthony, she was able to continue leading the women's rights movement for most of this period. But Stanton's last pregnancy was enough to undermine even her exceptional self-confidence and physical strength. "You need expect nothing from me for some time," she wrote to Anthony after the birth of 12½-pound Robert. "I can scarcely walk across the room . . . and have to keep my mind in the most quiet state in order to sleep. . . . He seems to take up every particle of my vitality, soul and body."[13] Four months later, she was still "in no situation to think or write," but succumbed to Anthony's blandishments to prepare a memorial for the New York State legislature. "We have issued bulls under all circumstances," she conceded. "I think you and I can do more even if you must make the pudding and carry the baby."[14]

Unlike Stanton, Lucy Stone and Antoinette Brown assumed domestic responsibilities after they had become prominent women's rights advocates. Stone married Henry Blackwell in 1855, and Brown married his brother Samuel a year later. Brown had seven children; Stone had one, which kept her out of political work for over a decade. "I wish I felt the old impulse and power to lecture . . . , but I am afraid and dare not trust Lucy Stone," Stone wrote to Brown, when her daughter was a year and a half old. "I went to hear E. P. Whipple lecture on Joan d'Arc. It was very inspiring and for the hour I felt as though all things were possible to me. But when I came home and looked in Alice's sleeping face and thought of the possible evil that might befall her if my guardian eye was turned away, I shrank like a snail into its shell and saw that for these years I can be only a mother."[15] Brown experienced this same dilemma. Unable even to keep up a political correspondence because of the press of household obligations, she wrote to Anthony, "This, Susan, is 'woman's sphere.' "[16] Anthony was unsympathetic to her comrade's preference for what she called "the ineffable joys of Maternity," and resentful of the political responsibilities that devolved on her. She wrote to Brown in frustration over Stone's preparations for an important debate: "A woman who *is* and *must* of necessity continue for the present at least the representative woman has no right to *disqualify* herself for such a *representative occasion*. I do feel that it is so foolish for her to put herself in the position of *maid of all work* and *baby tender*. What man would dream of going before the public on such an occasion as this one night-tired and worn from such a multitude of engrossing cares."[17] Indeed, even though Brown and Stone had foresworn marriage while young girls, Anthony was the only first-generation national women's rights leader who remained single. "Where are you Susan and what are you doing?" Stanton wrote when she hadn't heard from Anthony for some time. "Are you dead or married?"[18]

In the face of such obstacles, the major resource on which women's rights activists drew to support themselves and advance their cause was one another. Like many nineteenth-century women, they formed intense and lasting friendships with other women. Frequently these were the most passionate and emotionally supportive relationships that they had. While feminists' mutual relationships were similar to other female friendships in emotional texture, they were different in their focus on the public and political concerns that made their lives as women unique. The most enduring and productive of these friendships was undoubtedly that of Elizabeth Cady Stanton and Susan B. Anthony, which began in 1851. The initial basis of their inter-dependency was that Anthony gave Stanton psychological and material support in domestic matters, while Stanton provided Anthony with a political education. In an episode repeated often in their first decade together, Anthony called on Stanton when she found herself unable to write a speech for a New York teachers' convention: "For the love of me and for the saving of the reputation of womanhood, I beg you, with one baby on your knee, . . . and four boys whistling, buzzing, hallooing 'Ma, Ma,' set yourself about the work. . . . I must not and will not allow these schoolmasters to say, 'See, these women can't or won't do anything when we do give them a chance.'"[19]

Antoinette Brown and Lucy Stone were also bound by an intense friendship, formed when they were both students at Oberlin. They turned to each other to fortify their common feminism against the assaults of friends and teachers, and, as Brown remembered it, "used to sit with our arms around each other . . . and talk of our friends and our homes and of ten thousand subjects of mutual interest until both our hearts felt warmer and lighter."[20] Their relationship continued to sustain them after they left Oberlin and became abolitionists and women's rights agitators. When Stone was subject to particularly intense harassment for wearing bloomers, Brown offered her support. "Tonight I could nestle closer to your heart than on the night when I went through the dark and the rain and Tappan Hall and school rules—all to feel your arm around me," she wrote, "and to know that in all this wide world I was not alone."[21]

An important aspect of these relationships was overtly political. Given the strength of men's commitment to maintaining their political monopoly, the few women who were fortunate enough to have acquired a political education had to share their skills and knowledge with others. Stanton's contribution to Anthony's political development has already been noted. When Brown and Stone first met, they organized six other women students into "an informal debating and speaking society" to provide the oratorical experience they were denied in Oberlin's "ladies" course. They were so afraid of official intervention that they met in a black woman's home "on the outskirts of town," and occasionally in the woods, with a guard posted "against possible intruders." When Brown returned home to Michigan for a year, she organized another group to discuss women's sphere and women's rights. "We are exceedingly careful in this matter and all move on together step by step," she wrote to Stone. "Some will undoubtedly shrink back when they come to find where they stand and believe they must have been mistaken . . . and a few I hope and believe will go out into the world pioneers in the great reform which is about to revolutionize society."[22]

There were limits, however, to the support women's rights pioneers could offer one another. One such constraint was physical distance. As reformers they traveled to a degree unheard of among pre-Civil War women and, when unmarried, could scarcely be said to have a home. They were usually alone. In addition, the attacks on them for stepping outside women's sphere were constant, severe, and beyond the power of friends to halt or counteract. Brown described for Stone the response she elicited from the townspeople of Oberlin: "Sometimes they warn me not to be a Fanny Wright man, sometimes believe I am joking, sometimes stare at me with amazement and sometimes seem to start back with a kind of horror. Men and women are about equal and seem to have their mouths opened and their tongues loosed to about the same extent." Surrounded on all sides by hostility, women's rights agitators had to work most of the time without the companionship and sisterhood they so prized. "You know we used to wish sometimes that we could live on and have no need of the sympathy of anyone," Brown reminded Stone, after she had left Oberlin, "I have learned to feel so." "What hard work it is to stand alone!" she wrote a few years later. "I am forever wanting to lean over onto somebody but nobody will support me."[23]

In the face of such pressures, some women could not maintain their resolve to challenge women's sphere. One such woman was Letitia Holmes, who was Antoinette Brown's classmate at Oberlin and, like her, committed to becoming a religious teacher. Holmes married a minister, moved with him to Portsmouth, New Hampshire, and found herself in a role she had not anticipated, isolated from any source of support. "You know I have been looked upon as a pastor's wife with the incumbent duties to perform . . . ," she wrote to Brown. "I have been (I was going to say tired to death) receiving calls." An educated woman, she had ambitions beyond her sphere, which were not well received in Portsmouth. "There are but few here who think of women as anything more than slave or a plaything, and they think I am different from most women," she wrote. "I tell them I think not." Despite a sympathetic husband, she could not find an outlet for her talents or knowledge. Her long letter describing her situation to Brown, who was already achieving some prominence as a public lecturer, was a mixture of jealousy and a plea for help. Holmes regretted that she did not have another woman "who seems to be one of us you might say . . . another self of my own sex." She asked Brown for "a list of what books would be advantageous for me to read and study with a view to assist me in preparing for public duties." She also asked for Brown's lectures on women's rights, and offered a glimpse into the pressures operating against her Oberlin education and her strong-minded aspirations: "The thing is just this. I do not see it all as clearly as I should to explain to others and when they bring forward the scriptures I fear for myself." In the end, Holmes continued to believe that she would "go forth," which she never did, and could not understand why she was so "long in beginning."[24]

ABOLITIONIST POLITICS

The abolitionist movement provided the particular framework within which the politics of women's rights developed. From the 1837 clerical attack on the Grimké sisters, through the 1840 meeting of Lucretia Mott and Elizabeth Cady Stanton at the World's Anti-Slavery Convention, to the Civil War and Reconstruction, the development of American feminism was inseparable from the unfolding of the antislavery drama. In tracing the sources of the women's rights movement, Stanton and Anthony cited abolitionism "above all other causes." Mistaking political rhetoric for historical process, historians commonly identify the connection between the two movements as women's discovery of their own oppression through its analogy with slavery.[25] Certainly women's rights leaders made liberal use of the slave metaphor to describe women's oppression. Yet women's discontent with their position was as much cause as effect of their involvement with the antislavery movement. What American women learned from abolitionism was less that they were oppressed than what to do with that perception, how to turn it into a political movement. Abolitionism provided them with a way to escape clerical authority, an egalitarian ideology, and a theory of social change, all of which permitted the leaders to transform the insights into the oppression of women which they shared with many of their contemporaries into the beginnings of the women's rights movement.

Women's involvement in abolitionism developed out of traditions of pietistic female benevolence that were an accepted aspect of women's sphere in the early nineteenth century. The feminist militance of Sarah and Angelina Grimké and the women who succeeded them was rooted in this common soil. The abolitionist movement was one of the many religious reforms that grew out of evangelical Protestantism. For the movement's first half-decade, the role women had in it was consistent with that in other benevolent religious efforts such as urban missionary activities and moral reform. Women organized separate antislavery auxiliaries, in which they worked to support men's organizations and gave particular attention to the female victims and domestic casualties of slavery. The Grimkés entered abolitionism on these terms.[26] Unlike other pious activisms, however, abolition had an unavoidably political thrust and a tendency to outgrow its evangelical origins. As the movement became secularized, so did the activities of benevolent women in it. "Those who urged women to become missionaries and form tract societies . . . have changed the household utensil to a living, energetic being," wrote domestic author and abolitionist Lydia Maria Child, "and they have no spell to turn it into a broom again."[27]

The emergence of the Garrisonian wing of the abolitionist movement embodied and accelerated these secularizing processes. In 1837 William Lloyd Garrison was converted by utopian John Humphrey Noyes to the doctrine of perfectionism, which identified the sanctified individual conscience as the supreme moral standard, and corrupt institutions, not people, as the source of sin. In particular, Garrisonians turned on their churchly origins and attacked the Protestant clergy for its perversion of true Christianity and its support of slavery.[28] Garrisonians' ability to distinguish religious institutions from their own deeply-felt religious impulses was an impressive achievement for evangelicals in an evangelical age. The reformulation of antislavery strategy around these beliefs drew Hicksite Quakers, liberal Unitarians, ultraist come-outers, and a disproportionate number of women activists.

The clergy was the major force that controlled women's moral energies and kept pietistic activism from becoming political activism. Garrisonian anticlericalism was therefore critical to the emergence of abolitionist feminism and its subsequent development into the women's rights movement. This was clear in the 1837 confrontation between the Grimké sisters and the Congregational clergy of Massachusetts. In this episode, Garrisonian perfectionism and the limits of women's sphere were inseparable matters. Like women in moral reform and other pious activisms, the Grimkés had been led by their religious vocation to step outside their traditional role. At that point, like other benevolent women, they were confronted by clerical authority and ordered to return to more womanly pursuits. Yet the fact that they were Garrisonians enabled them to hold fast to their religious convictions, reject clerical criticism, and instead indict the churches for being institutional bulwarks of slavery and women's oppression.[29]

Against the power of clerical authority, which had long restrained women's impulses for a larger life, Garrisonian abolition armed women with faith in their own convictions. Although restrained by the fact that her husband was a political abolitionist, Elizabeth Cady Stanton's allegiances were with the Garrisonians. Throughout her young adulthood, she had wrestled unsuccessfully with religious orthodoxy from which Garrisonian anticlericalism liberated her.

> In the darkness and gloom of a false theology, I was slowly sawing off the chains of my spiritual bondage, when, for the first time, I met Garrison in London. A few bold strokes from the hammer of his truth, I was free! Only those who have lived all their lives under the dark clouds of vague, undefined fears can appreciate the joy of a doubting soul suddenly born into the kingdom of reason and free thought. Is the bondage of the priest-ridden less galling than that of the slave, because we do not see the chains, the indelible scars, the festering wounds, the deep degradation of all the powers of the God-like mind?[30]

Almost until the Civil War, conflict with clerical authority remained a central issue for the women's rights movement. The 1854 national convention resolved: "We feel it a duty to declare in regard to the sacred cause which has brought us together, that the most determined opposition it encounters is from the clergy generally, whose teachings of the Bible are intensely inimical to the equality of women with man." Representatives of the clergy pursued their fleeting authority onto the women's rights platform. However, Garrisonian women had learned the techniques of Biblical exegesis in numerous debates over the scriptural basis of slavery. They met clergymen on their own ground, skillfully refuting them quote for quote. "The pulpit has been prostituted, the Bible has been ill-used . . . ," Lucretia Mott contended at the 1854 convention. "The temperance people have had to feel its supposed denunciations. Then the anti-slavery, and now this reform has met, and still continues to meet, passage after passage of the Bible, never intended to be so used.''[31] When ministers with national reputations started to offer their support to the women's rights movement in the 1850's, the issue of clerical authority began to recede in importance. It was not a major aspect of postwar feminism, because of changes in both the movement and the clergy.

Women in the Garrisonian abolitionist movement not only absorbed its anticlericalism, but also drew on its principle of the absolute moral equality of all human beings. Because the Garrisonian abolitionists' target was Northern racial prejudice and their goal the development of white empathy for the suffering slave, they focused their arguments on convincing white people of their basic identity with black people. The weakness of this emphasis on the ultimate moral identity of the races was its inability to account for their historical differences. Garrisonians did not develop an explanation for the origins and persistence of racism, and as a result many abolitionists continued to believe that there were biological causes for the inferior position of black people. Instead, Garrisonian abolitionism stressed the common humanity of blacks and whites. Garrisonians formulated this approach as a moral abstraction, but its basis was the concrete demands of the agitational task they faced as abolitionists.[32]

Abolitionist feminists appropriated this belief and applied it to women. The philosophical tenet that women were essentially human and only incidentally female liberated them from the necessity of justifying their own actions in terms of what was appropriate to women's sphere. In other words, Garrisonianism provided an ideology of equality for women to use in fighting their way out of a society built around sexual difference and inequality. The degree to which abolitionist feminists ignored the demands of women's sphere is particularly remarkable because they did so at the same time that the ideology of sexual spheres was being elaborated by benevolent women, in other ways very much like them. To the Congregational clergy's demand that she return "to the appropriate duties and influence of women," Sarah Grimké responded: "The Lord Jesus defines the duties of his followers in his Sermon on the Mount . . . without any reference to sex or condition . . . never even referring to the distinction now so strenuously insisted upon between masculine and feminine virtues. . . . Men and women are CREATED EQUAL! They are both moral and accountable beings and whatever is right for man to do is right for woman.''[33] Her belief in sex equality took added strength from Hicksite Quaker doctrine and practices. The Grimkés were followed by other Garrisonian feminists who also refused to justify their efforts in terms of women's sphere. "Too much has already been said and written about woman's sphere," Lucy Stone said in 1854. "Leave women, then, to find their sphere." The 1851 women's rights convention resolved that: "We deny the right of any portion of the species to decide for another portion . . . what is and what is not their 'proper sphere'; that the proper sphere for all human beings is the largest and highest to which they are able to attain."[34]

Just as the Garrisonian emphasis on the moral equality of the races could not account for their historical inequality, the conviction that men and women were morally identical had serious analytical limitations. The women's rights belief in the moral irrelevance of sexual spheres ignored the reality of women's domestic confinement, which made them different from and dependent on men, and gave credence to the doctrine of spheres. Indeed, Garrisonian feminists ignored the question of women's sphere while simultaneously believing in its existence. A women's rights convention in Ohio in 1852 simultaneously resolved: "Since every human being has an individual sphere, and that is the largest he or she can fill, no one has the right to determine the proper sphere of another," and "In demanding for women equality of rights with their fathers, husbands, brothers, and sons, we neither deny that distinctive character, nor wish them to avoid any duty, or to lay aside that feminine delicacy which legitimately belongs to them as mothers, wives, sisters, and daughters."[35] Like other women, women's rights activists believed in the particular suitability of their sex for domestic activities and did not protect a reorganization of the division of labor within the home. They believed that domestic activities were as "naturally" female as childbearing, and as little subject to deliberate social manipulation.[36] The abstract quality of their belief in the moral identity of the sexes did not help them to confront this contradiction in their feminism. Indeed, while permitting the prewar women's rights movement to establish sexual equality as its goal, Garrisonian premises simultaneously held it back from the critical task of examining the sources of sexual inequality.

Along with a philosophical basis, Garrisonian abolitionism provided the women's rights movement with a theory and practice of social change, a strategy that gave direction to its efforts for female emancipation. The core of Garrisonian strategy was the belief that a revolution in people's ideas must precede and underlie institutional and legal reform, in order to effect true social change. "Great political changes may be forced by the pressure of external circumstances, without a corresponding change in the moral sentiment of a nation," Lydia Maria Child wrote in 1842, "but in all such cases, the change is worse than useless; the evil reappears, and usually in a more exaggerated form."[37] Some historians, notably Stanley Elkins and Gilbert Barnes, have mistaken this radical and democratic approach to reform as an anarchistic disregard for the institutional structures of social reality.[38] Garrisonians were not indifferent to institutions, but it is true that they did not specify how changes in popular ideology could be translated into institutional reform. They left this up to the politicians. Instead, they saw themselves as agitators concentrating their energies on provoking public sentiment. While Garrisonian agitation did not develop political mechanisms for ending slavery, it was well suited to the early years of the antislavery movement when the primary problem was overcoming public apathy.

Faced with an equally stubborn and widespread indifference to the oppression of women, women's rights leaders drew on this abolitionist precedent and formulated their task as the agitation of public sentiment. "Disappointment is the lot of woman," Lucy Stone wrote in 1855. "It shall be the business of my life to deepen this disappointment in every woman's heart until she bows down to it no longer."[39] Ernestine Rose described the work as "breaking up the ground and sowing the seed."[40] To Lucy Stone and Susan B. Anthony, both of whom were paid agents of the American Anti-Slavery Society, the role of itinerant feminist agitator came quite naturally. However, it was Elizabeth Cady Stanton who developed the strategy of women's rights agitation most fully, and this was one of the bases of her leadership. Throughout her long political career, she consistently believed that anything that focused public attention on women's oppression was desirable. She wrote in her diary in 1888, "If I were to draw up a set of rules for the guidance of reformers . . . I should put at the head of the list: 'Do all you can, *no matter what*, to get people to think on your reform, and then, if the reform is good, it will come about in due season.' "[41] She did not care whether her efforts generated sympathy or antipathy, as long as they undermined public apathy. Nor did she believe that translating agitation into reform was her function. "I am a leader in thought, rather than numbers," she wrote late in her life, when her methods had become alien to young feminists.[42]

Garrisonian agitation was built around the demand for unconditional, immediate abolition. The intention was both to achieve a concrete reform and to launch an ideological attack on the slaveholding mentality. With this program Garrisonians were able to work simultaneously for the legal abolition of slavery and a revolution in the racial consciousness of whites to give abolition meaning. As Aileen Kraditor has interpreted it, immediate abolition was both the means and the end for Garrisonian antislavery.[43] The demand for woman suffrage functioned in a similar fashion in the women's rights movement. It aimed at both a concrete reform in women's legal status and the education of public opinion to the principle of the equal humanity of the sexes.

The goal was necessarily twofold because, like unconditional abolition, woman suffrage was a radical idea, acknowledged inside and outside the movement as the capstone of women's emancipation.

THE DEMAND FOR WOMAN SUFFRAGE

From the beginning, gaining the franchise was part of the program of the women's rights movement. It was one of a series of reforms that looked toward the elimination of women's dependent and inferior position before the law. The women's rights movement demanded for married women control over their own wages, the right to contract for their own property, joint guardianship over their children, and improved inheritance rights when widowed. For all women, the movement demanded the elective franchise and the rights of citizenship. Compared to legal reforms in women's status articulated before 1848, for instance equal right to inherit real property, the women's rights program was very broadly based, and intentionally so.[44] In particular, the right to control one's earnings and the right to vote were demands that affected large numbers of women—farm women, wives of urban artisans and laborers, millgirls and needlewomen.

While part of this general reform in women's legal status, the demand for woman suffrage was always treated differently from other women's rights. In the first place, it initially met with greater opposition within the movement than other demands did. At the Seneca Falls Convention, Elizabeth Cady Stanton submitted a resolution on "the duty of the women of this country to secure to themselves the sacred right to the elective franchise." Lucretia Mott thought the resolution a mistake, and tried to dissuade her from presenting it. Mott's position may have been based on her Garrisonian objections to involvement in the world of electoral politics, but surely others recoiled from the woman suffrage demand because it seemed too radical. Although the convention passed all other motions unanimously, it was seriously divided over the suffrage. Frederick Douglass, who, himself disfranchised, appreciated the importance of membership in the political community, was Stanton's staunchest supporter at Seneca Falls. The woman suffrage resolution barely passed.[45]

Soon, however, woman suffrage was distinguished from other reforms by being elevated to a preeminent position in the women's rights movement. After the Seneca Falls Convention, there is no further evidence of reluctance within the movement to demand the vote. On the contrary, it quickly became the cornerstone of the women's rights program. A resolution passed at the 1856 national convention may be taken as representative: "Resolved, that the main power of the woman's rights movement lies in this: that while always demanding for woman better education, better employment, and better laws, it has kept steadily in view the one cardinal demand for the right of suffrage: in a democracy, the symbol and guarantee of all other rights."[46]

In keeping with the truth of this resolution, the demand for woman suffrage also generated much more opposition outside the movement. Public opinion and politicians were more sympathetic to feminists' economic demands than to their political ones. In the mid-1850's, state legislatures began to respond favorably to women's lobbying and petition efforts for reforms in property law. By 1860, fourteen states had passed some form of women's property rights legislation. Encouraged by these victories, the movement escalated its demands and shifted its emphasis from property rights to the suffrage. This was clearest in the case of New York. Initially, to gain maximum support for the less controversial demand, activists there circulated separate petitions for property rights and for the vote. As the movement gained strength, however, they included both economic and political demands on a single petition, and, in 1857, presented a unified program to the legislature.[47] Three years later, the New York legislature passed the most comprehensive piece of women's rights legislation in the United States, the Married Women's Property Act. This law granted New York women all the economic rights they demanded, but still refused women the right to vote.[48]

To both opponents and advocates of women's rights, therefore, the demand for woman suffrage was significantly more controversial than other demands for equality with men. Why was this the case? Like the overwhelming majority of their contemporaries, nineteenth-century feminists believed that the vote was the ultimate repository of social and economic power in a democratic society. They wanted that power for women and relied on well-developed natural rights arguments and the rhetorical traditions of the American Revolution and the Declaration of Independence to make their demand. "In demanding the political rights of woman," the 1853 national convention resolved, "we simply assert the fundamental principle of democracy—that taxation and representation should go together, and that, if the principle is denied, all our institutions must fall with it."[49]

The widespread belief in the importance of the ballot which feminists drew on to make their case for woman suffrage is a somewhat elusive aspect of the American political tradition because the extension of the franchise to the masses of white men had been such a gradual process. No organized political movement was required as Chartism had been in Britain. As a result, what the vote meant and promised to antebellum American men was not formalized into an explicit ideological statement, and is that much harder for us to assess in retrospect. However, American white working men seem to have attached considerable importance to their franchise. Even though they did not have to organize to win the vote, they did form working men's parties in every northern state to protect it and give it power. Believing that the vote "put into our hands the power of perfecting our government and securing our happiness," they organized against obstacles to its use, such as indirect elections and caucus nominations.[50] In addition, working men saw the democratic franchise, divested of property qualifications, as a victory against privilege. As a British Chartist put it in 1834, "With us Universal suffrage will begin in our lodges, extend to the general union, embrace the management of trade, and finally swallow up political power."[51] To the degree that organized working men believed that universal white manhood suffrage established the necessary preconditions for social democracy, they looked to their own shortcomings for their failure to achieve such a society. "Our fathers have purchased for us political rights and an equality of privileges," a July Fourth orator chastised the trade unions of Boston in 1834, "which we have not yet had the intelligence to appreciate, nor the courage to protect, nor the wisdom to employ."[52]

Yet these general ideas about the power and importance of the ballot are not sufficient to explain the special significance of the suffrage issue for women. The ideas of democratic political theory were not systematically applied to women until feminist leaders, anxious to challenge the subservient position of women, appropriated those ideas and demanded the vote. Like black men, women were excluded from the actual expansion of the suffrage in the late eighteenth and early nineteenth centuries, but the exclusion of women from political life went even further. Women were so far outside the boundaries of the antebellum political community that the fact of their disfranchisement, unlike that of black men, was barely noticed. The French and American Revolutions greatly intensified awareness of the educational, economic, and social inequality of the sexes, but few Revolutionary leaders considered the inclusion of women in the franchise, and even fewer—perhaps only Condorcet—called for it.[53] Further back in the democratic political tradition, the radical Levellers of seventeenth-century England made the same distinction between women's civil and moral rights, which they advocated, and women's political rights, which they never considered.[54] In large part, the awareness that women were being excluded from the political community and the need to justify this disfranchisement came after women began to demand political equality. Prior to the women's rights movement, those who noticed and commented on the disfranchisement of women were not advocates of woman suffrage, but anti-democrats, who used this exception to disprove the natural right of people to self-government.[55]

On what basis were women excluded from any consideration in the distribution of political power, even when that power was organized on democratic principles? At least part of the answer seems to lie in the concept of "independence," which was the major criterion for enfranchisement in classical democratic political theory, and which acted to exclude women from the political community. Even the radical Tom Paine thought that servants should not have the vote because they were economically and socially dependent on their masters, and "freedom is destroyed by dependence."[56] A contemporary political theorist, C.B. Macpherson, has defined the core of this concept of "independence" as self-ownership, the individual's right to possess his own person: "The essential humanity of the individual consisted in his freedom from the will of other persons, freedom to enjoy his own person and to develop his own capacities. One's person was property not metaphorically, but essentially; the property one had in it was the right to exclude others from its use and enjoyment."[57] Women's traditional relationships to men within their families constituted the essence of dependence. When John Adams considered the question, "Whence arises the right of men to govern the women without their consent?" he found the answer in men's power to feed, clothe, and employ women and therefore to make political decisions on their behalf.[58] Not only were eighteenth- and early nineteenth-century women prohibited from owning real property or controlling wealth; they could not be said even to hold property in themselves. Law and custom granted the husband ownership, not only of his wife's labor power and the wages she earned by it, but of her physical person as well, in the sexual rights of the marriage relation. No people, with the exception of chattel slaves, had less proprietary rights over themselves in eighteenth- and early nineteenth-century America than married women.[59] Until the emergence of feminism, the dependent status that women held was considered natural, and if not right, then inescapable.

Thus, the demand that women be included in the electorate was not simply a stage in the expansion and democratization of the franchise. It was a particularly feminist demand, because it exposed and challenged the assumption of male authority over women. To women fighting to extend their sphere beyond its traditional domestic limitations, political rights involved a radical change in women's status, their emergence into public life. The right to vote raised the prospect of female autonomy in a way that other claims to equal rights could not. Petitions to state legislatures for equal rights to property and children were memorials for the redress of grievances, which could be tolerated within the traditional chivalrous framework that accorded women the "right" to protection. In 1859 the *New York Times* supported the passage of the New York Married Women's Property Act by distinguishing the "legal protection and fair play to which women are justly entitled" from "the claims to a share of political power which the extreme advocates of Women's Rights are fond of advancing."[60] By contrast, the suffrage demand challenged the idea that women's interests were identical or even compatible with men's. As such, it embodied a vision of female self-determination that placed it at the center of the feminist movement. "While we would not undervalue other methods," the 1851 national women's rights convention resolved, "the Right of Suffrage for Women is, in our opinion, the cornerstone of this enterprise, since we do not seek to protect woman, but rather to place her in a position to protect herself."[61]

The feminist implications of the suffrage demand are further evident in the reverberations it sent through the ideology of sexual spheres, the nineteenth-century formulation of the sexual division of labor. Most obviously, woman suffrage constituted a serious challenge to the masculine monopoly of the public sphere. Although the growing numbers of women in schools, trades, professions, and wage-labor were weakening the sexual barriers around life outside the family, most adult women remained at home, defined politically, economically, and socially by their family position. In this context, the prospect of enfranchisement was uniquely able to touch all women, offering them a public role and a relation to the community unmediated by husband or children. While the suffrage demand did not address the domestic side of the nineteenth-century sexual order directly, the connections between public and private spheres carried its implications into the family as well. In particular, the public honor of citizenship promised to elevate women's status in the home and raised the specter of sexual equality there. Women's rights leaders were relatively modest about the implications of the franchise for women's position in the family, anticipating reform of family law and improvement in the quality of domestic relations. Their opponents, however, predicted that woman suffrage would have a revolutionary impact on the family. "It is well known that the object of these unsexed women is to overthrow the most sacred of our institutions . . . ," a New York legislator responded to women's rights petitions. "Are we to put the stamp of truth upon the libel here set forth, that men and women, in the matrimonial relation, are to be equal?"[62] In the introduction to the *History of Woman Suffrage*, Elizabeth Cady Stanton penetrated to the core of this antisuffrage response. "Political rights, involving in their last results equality everywhere," she wrote, "roused all the antagonism of a dominant power, against the self-assertion of a class hitherto subservient."[63]

OBSTACLES TO GROWTH

The process by which women's rights ideas were spread was a highly informal one. As the first activists reached the small towns of New York, Massachusetts, Ohio, and Indiana, their example drew local women out of their isolation. A speech by Lucy Stone impelled two Rockland, Maine, women to become printers.[64] Olympia Brown was brought into the movement when, still a student at Antioch College, she heard author and abolitionist Frances Gage. "It was the first time I had heard a woman preach," she recalled, "and the sense of victory lifted me up."[65] Frances Ellen Burr, who went on to lead suffrage forces in Connecticut, attended a women's rights convention in Cleveland when she was twenty-two. She was surprised at how attracted she was to the militance of the speakers and noted in her diary, "Never saw anything of the kind before." "Lucy Stone . . . is independent in manner and advocates woman's rights in the strongest terms," she wrote; "scorns the idea of *asking* rights of man, but says she must boldly assert her own rights, and *take* them in her own strength."[66] Reports of the Seneca Falls Convention stirred Emily Collins to gather fifteen neighbors into an equal rights society, and draw up a petition to the legislature. "I was born and lived almost forty years in South Bristol, Ontario County—one of the most secluded spots in Western New York," she explained,

> but from the earliest dawn of reason I pined for that freedom of thought and action that was then denied to all womankind. I revolted in spirit against the customs of society and the laws of the State that crushed my aspirations and debarred me from the pursuit of almost every object worthy of an intelligent, rational mind. But not until that meeting at Seneca Falls in 1848, of the pioneers in the cause, gave this feeling of unrest form and voice, did I take action.[67]

Of all the pre-Civil War activists, Susan B. Anthony was the most deliberate about introducing new women to women's rights. Between 1854 and 1860 she made several canvasses of New York. In the innumerable small towns she visited, she tried to locate the people most sympathetic to women's rights. She particularly cultivated the women, encouraging the boldest of them by asking them to preside over the meetings she organized or by staying in their homes overnight.

Occasionally, she discovered a genuinely strong-minded woman, waiting for the women's rights movement to take her up. In Aurora, she found three women wearing bloomers, one of whom she asked to conduct the meeting. "It does my heart good to see them," she wrote in her diary.[68]

Nonetheless, the movement grew slowly. As Stone rationalized after a particularly disappointing lecture tour, "I sell a great many of the tracts, so seed is being scattered that will grow *sometime*."[69] In the wake of their lectures and conventions, Stone, Anthony, and others left a trail of strong-minded women behind them. Sarah Burger attended a women's rights convention in 1853, when she was sixteen. What she heard there convinced her that the University of Michigan should be opened to women and "that women themselves should move in the matter." She located twelve other girls to join with her and in 1858 petitioned the university for admission. She continued her campaign for several years, and, although she had to attend a normal school, the University of Michigan finally admitted women in 1869.[70] Two Ellsworth, Maine, women organized a lecture series on women's rights. Despite threats to the livelihood of one of them, they persisted and the lectures were held.[71] Other local activists, more than we may ever know, launched their own protests, but often the women's rights movement was too small and weak to sustain them. In 1859, Mary Harrington of Claremont, New Hampshire, refused to pay her taxes because she was disfranchised. The tax collector seized her furniture and the local newspaper editor attacked her in print. She was too isolated to do anything more, and her rebellion went underground for the time being. "Such unjust treatment seemed so cruel that I sometimes felt I could willingly lay down my life," she wrote later, "if it would deliver my sex from such degrading oppression. I have, every year since, submissively paid my taxes, humbly hoping and praying that I may live to see the day that women will not be compelled to pay taxes without representation."[72]

Prewar women's rights agitation had an impact on a large number of women who were not ready to speak or act publicly but were convinced that the position of their sex demanded reform. A friend of her sister's invited Antoinette Brown to visit her "to introduce you to my friends here and let them see that you have not got horns. . . . I think I see more and more clearly that the Lord has a work for females to do that they have not understood," she continued, "and I am glad that there are some that are willing to learn and to do what He requires of them."[73] Anthony reported to Stanton that she had been to dinner with Mrs. Finney, the wife of the president of Oberlin. After her husband denounced women's rights, "Mrs. Finney took me to another seat and with much earnestness inquired all about what we were doing and the growth of our movement. . . . Said she you have the sympathy of a large proportion of the educated women with you. In my circle I hear the movement much talked of and earnest hopes for its spread expressed—but these women dare not speak out their sympathy."[74] Women's rights agitators barely knew how many women they were affecting, much less how to encourage their halting sympathies.

Ironically, the Garrisonian politics and abolitionist alliance that had enabled the women's rights movement to develop in the first place were beginning to restrain its continued growth. Like the abolitionists before them, women's rights activists saw themselves as agitators, stirring up discontent. However, they had no way to consolidate the feminist sentiment that their agitation was beginning to create. Once the level of their discontent was raised, there was nothing for most women to do with it. Women's rights activities were organized around a small group who were politically skilled, willing to shoulder the opprobrium of "strongmindedness," and able to commit a great deal of their energies to the movement. Women who were just beginning to develop political skills and sensibilities could not normally find an active role to play. The limitations to growth inherent in the agitational focus of prewar women's rights were embodied in the movement's organizational underdevelopment. There were no national or state organizations. Annual conventions were planned by an informal and constantly changing coordinating committee. Speaking tours and legislative campaigns were highly individualistic matters, which put a premium on personal initiative and bravery. The movement's close political relationship with abolitionism further restrained its organizational growth, in that its ability to rely on the organizational resources of the American Anti-Slavery Society meant that it did not develop its own. Women's rights articles were published in antislavery newspapers, and its tracts were printed with antislavery funds. The surrogate political coherence that abolitionism provided women's rights permitted the movement's leaders to indulge their propensities for individualism without risking the entire women's rights enterprise. The 1852 national convention rejected a proposal for a national women's rights society on the grounds that formal organizations "fetter and distort the expanding mind."[75]

Above all, the prewar women's rights movement depended on abolitionism for its constituency. It is impossible to estimate how many women were touched by women's rights, and how many of these were abolitionists. Still, the movement's strongest, most reliable, and most visible support came from abolitionist ranks, particularly from the women. This dependence on an organized constituency borrowed from abolitionism was particularly marked on the national level. The call for the first national women's rights convention was timed to coincide with the annual meeting of the American Anti-Slavery Society.[76] Abolitionist women provided women's rights with an audience well suited to its first, highly controversial years. Their antislavery activity had already put them outside the pale of respectable womanhood, where they were less likely to be frightened by public hostility. However, the availability of an audience among antislavery women kept feminist leaders from a systematic effort to reach the many women who were not reformers. At the worst, it gave them a kind of disdain for the nonpolitical preoccupations of most women. The fearlessness of female abolitionists sheltered the women's rights movement from a confrontation with the very real fears of male opposition and public disapproval that lay between it and the mobilization of large numbers of women.

Although primarily a source of strength, the relation of women's rights to abolitionism was thus a potential liability as well. The partnership was unequal, with women's rights dependent on abolitionism for essential resources and support. The basic precepts, strategic methods, and organizational forms of Garrisonian abolitionism had sustained the women's rights movement through its first dozen years. On this basis, feminist leaders were able to transform insights into the oppression of women that they shared with many other women into a social movement strong enough to have a future. This achievement raised other political problems—the extent of the movement's reforming ambitions, the nature of its constituency, the organizational form it would take, and above all, its relation to abolitionism. The resolution of these matters was interrupted by the outbreak of the Civil War. Women's rights activists subordinated all other interests to the fate of slavery, and suspended feminist activity for the length of the war. When they returned, four years later, to consider the future of women's rights, the political context within which they did so had been completely altered.

NOTES*

1. Nancy F. Cott, *The Bonds of Womanhood: "Woman's Sphere" in New England, 1780–1835* (New Haven, 1977). On the early nineteenth century, see also Kathryn Kish Sklar, *Catharine Beecher: A Study in American Domesticity* (New Haven,

*Here *HWS* refers to *History of Woman Suffrage*, ed. by Elizabeth Cady Stanton, Susan B. Anthony, Matilda Joslyn Gage, et al. (Rochester: Susan B. Anthony; New York; National American Woman Suffrage Association, 1881–1922), 6 vols.

1973); Carroll Smith Rosenberg, "Beauty, the Beast and the Militant Woman: A Case Study in Sex Roles and Social Stress in Jacksonian America," *American Quarterly*, 23 (1971), 562–584; and Keith Melder, "The Beginnings of the Woman's Rights Movement in the United States, 1800–1840" (doctoral diss., Yale University, 1964).

2. As quoted in Flexner, *Century of Struggle*, p. 77.

3. On the Seneca Falls convention, see *HWS*, I, 68–73.

4. Stanton to Gerrit Smith, January 3, 1856, *Stanton Letters*, p. 64.

5. *HWS*, I, 111.

6. *HWS*, I, 174.

7. Elizabeth B. Warbasse, "Matilda Joslyn Gage," *NAW*, II, 4.

8. *HWS*, I, 76.

9. Antoinette Brown Blackwell, "Autobiography," unpublished manuscript, 1909, SL, p. 117.

10. Ira V. Brown, "Mary Grew," *NAW*, II, 91.

11. Stanton to Anthony, September 10, 1855, *Stanton Letters*, pp. 59–60. Also see Stanton to Elizabeth Smith Miller, September 20, 1855, *ibid.*, pp. 60–62.

12. Stanton to Anthony, December 1, 1853, *ibid.*, p. 55.

13. Stanton to Anthony, April 2, 1859, Autograph Collection, Vassar College Library.

14. Stanton to Anthony, July 15, 1859, *ibid.*

15. Stone to Antoinette Brown Blackwell, February 20, 1859, Blackwell Family Papers, SL.

16. Antoinette Brown Blackwell to Anthony, October 25, 1859, as quoted in Blackwell, "Autobiography," p. 228.

17. Anthony to Martha Coffin Wright, June 6, 1856, Garrison Family Papers, Sophia Smith Collection (Women's History Archive), Smith College Library; Anthony to Antoinette Brown Blackwell, April 22, 1858, as quoted in Blackwell, "Autobiography," p. 223.

18. Stanton to Anthony, January, 1856, Autograph Collection, Vassar College Library.

19. Anthony to Stanton, June 5, 1856, *Stanton Letters*, pp. 64–65. See Carroll Smith Rosenberg, "The Female World of Love and Ritual: Relations between Women in Nineteenth-Century America," *Signs: Journal of Women in Culture and Society*, 1 (1975), 1–29.

20. Brown to Stone, sometime in 1848, as quoted in A. B. Blackwell, "Autobiography," p. 128.

21. Brown to Stone, February 18, 1854, as quoted in *ibid.*, p. 172.

22. *Ibid.*, pp. 54 and 119.

23. *Ibid.*, pp. 127 (1848), 129 (1848), and 137 (August 4, 1852).

24. Holmes to Brown, March 9, 1851, SL.

25. *HWS*, I, 52. Women's antislavery activities are surveyed in Alma Lutz, *Crusade for Freedom: Women of the Antislavery Movement* (Boston, 1968). Andrew Sinclair locates the origins of women's discontent in the abolitionist movement in *The Emancipation of the American Woman* (New York, 1966),

p. 37. Also see Flexner, *Century of Struggle*, p. 40. The most notable exception to this approach is Melder, "Beginnings of the Woman's Rights Movement."

26. On the evangelical origins of abolitionism, see Bertram Wyatt-Brown, *Lewis Tappan and the Evangelical War against Slavery* (Cleveland, 1969), and Ronald G. Walters, *The Antislavery Appeal: American Abolitionism after 1830* (Baltimore, 1976). On women's early antislavery benevolence, see Keith Melder, "Ladies Bountiful: Organized Women's Benevolence in Early Nineteenth Century America," *New York History*, 48 (1967), 231–254. On the Grimké sisters, see Gerda Lerner, *The Grimké Sisters from South Carolina: Rebels against Slavery* (Boston, 1967).

27. Child, July 23, 1841, *The Liberator*, as reprinted in Aileen S. Kraditor, *Means and Ends in American Abolitionism: Garrison and His Critics on Strategy and Tactics, 1834–1850* (New York, 1967), p. 47. Kraditor is excellent on the emergence of the women's rights issue within abolitionist circles in the late 1830's.

28. Wyatt-Brown, *Lewis Tappan,* and Lewis Perry, *Radical Abolitionism: Anarchy and the Government of God in Antislavery Thought* (Ithaca: Cornell University Press, 1973).

29. Lerner, *Grimké Sisters*, chap. 12. The 1837 Pastoral Letter of the Massachusetts Congregational clergy and the Grimkés' responses are excerpted in *Up from the Pedestal: Selected Writings in the History of American Feminism*, ed. Aileen S. Kraditor (Chicago, 1968), pp. 50–66. For the restraining influence that clerical authority had on women's protofeminism, see Sklar, *Catharine Beecher*, chap. 3.

30. Stanton, "Speech to the 1860 Anniversary of the American Anti-Slavery Society," Elizabeth Cady Stanton Papers, LC.

31. *HWS*, I, 383 and 380.

32. Kraditor, *Means and Ends, passim*, esp. p. 59.

33. Sarah Grimké, *Letters on the Equality of the Sexes and the Condition of Woman: Addressed to Mary S. Parker* (Boston, 1837), p. 16.

34. *HWS*, I, 165 and 826.

35. *HWS*, I, 817.

36. For an account of how these domestic beliefs affected the life of one abolitionist-feminist, see Ellen DuBois, "Struggling into Existence: The Feminism of Sarah and Angelina Grimké," *Women: A Journal of Liberation*, 1 (1970), 4–11.

37. Child, "Dissolution of the Union," *Liberator*, May 20, 1842, as quoted in Kraditor, *Means and Ends*, p. 23. Kraditor provides an excellent analysis of the Garrisonians' agitational approach to social change.

38. Elkins, *Slavery* (Chicago, 1959), and Barnes, *The Antislavery Impulse, 1830–1844* (New York, 1964).

39. *HWS*, I, 165.

40. *HWS*, I, 693.

41. Diary entry, August 20, 1888, *Stanton Letters*, p. 252.

42. Stanton to Olympia Brown, May 8, 1888, Olympia Brown Willis Papers, SL.

43. Kraditor, *Means and Ends, passim*.

44. For an excellent account of the pre-Seneca Falls efforts to improve women's legal position see Margaret M. Rabkin, "The Silent Feminist Revolution: Women and the Law in New York State from Blackstone to the Beginnings of American Women's Rights Movement" (doctoral diss., State University of New York at Buffalo, 1975).

45. On the Seneca Falls Convention see *HWS*, I, 63–75, and Elizabeth Cady Stanton, *Eighty Years and More: Reminiscences, 1815–1897* (New York, 1899), pp. 143–154. In 1849, Lucretia Mott publicly supported woman suffrage, while very clearly maintaining her distance from electoral politics: "Far be it from me to encourage women to vote or take an active part in politics in the present state of our government. Her right to the elective franchise, however, is the same, and should be yielded to her, whether she exercise that right or not" (*HWS*, I, p. 372).

46. *HWS*, I, 634.

47. *HWS*, I, 588–589 and 676–677. The fourteen states were: Massachusetts, Vermont, New Hampshire, Rhode Island, Ohio, Illinois, Indiana, Wisconsin, Connecticut, Texas, Maine, Iowa, Kansas, and Alabama.

48. *HWS*, I, 686–687.

49. *HWS*, I, 834. As one kind of evidence that woman suffrage was considered more radical than other women's rights demands, note that, in Ohio in 1850, a petition for "equal rights" for women received four times as many signatures as a petition for equal suffrage (*HWS*, I, 122). Similarly, at the 1853 National Women's Rights Convention, Clarina I. H. Nichols explained that "the propriety of woman voting" had been the last obstacle to her conversion to women's rights (*ibid.*, p. 355).

50. Frederick Robinson, "An Oration Delivered before the Trade Unions of Boston," (1834) in *Labor Politics: Collected Pamphlets*, ed. Leon Stein and Philip Taft, (New York, 1971), I, 28–29. Also see Walter Hugins, *Jacksonian Democracy and the Working Class: A Study of the New York Workingmen's Movement, 1829–1837* (Palo Alto, Calif., 1960). The one instance during the nineteenth century in which white men had to organize politically to get the vote was in Rhode Island. See Marvin Gettleman, *The Dorr Rebellion* (New York, 1973).

51. Ray Boston, *British Chartists in America, 1838–1900* (Manchester, 1971), p. 2.

52. Robinson, "Oration," p. 6.

53. Marguerite Fisher, "Eighteenth Century Theorists of Women's Liberation," in *"Remember the Ladies": New Perspectives on Women in American History,* ed. Carol V. R. George (Syracuse, N.Y., 1975), pp. 39–47.

54. C. B. Macpherson, *The Political Theory of Possessive Individualism: Hobbes to Locke* (London, 1962), p. 296.

55. See, for instance, Francis Bowman, "Recent Contest in Rhode Island (1834)," in Stein and Taft, *Labor Politics*, I, 421.

56. Eric Foner. *Tom Paine and Revolutionary America* (New York, 1976), pp. 142–144.

57. Macpherson, *Political Theory*, p. 153.

58. Cited in Scott and Scott, *One Half the People*, p. 4.

59. Rabkin, "The Silent Feminist Revolution," *passim.*

60. "Property of Married Women," *New York Times*, April 8, 1859, p. 4.

61. *HWS*, I, p. 825.

62. *HWS*, I, 613.

63. *HWS*, I, 16.

64. Alice Stone Blackwell, *Lucy Stone: Pioneer of Women's Rights* (Boston, 1930), pp. 101–102.

65. Lawrence L. Graves, "Olympia Brown," *NAW*, I, 257, and Olympia Brown Willis, *Acquaintances Old and New among Reformers* (Milwaukee, 1911), p. 10.

66. *HWS*, III, 335.

67. Collins, "Reminiscences," *HWS*, I, 88.

68. Diary entry, January, 1855. Susan B. Anthony Papers, SL.

69. Stone to Susan B. Anthony, November 8, 1855, Blackwell Family Collection, LC.

70. *HWS*, III, 527.

71. *HWS*, III, 365.

72. *HWS*, III, 373–374.

73. Unknown correspondent to Antoinette Brown, November 5, 1852, SL.

74. Anthony to Stanton, May 26, 1856, Elizabeth Cady Stanton Papers, Vassar College Library.

75. *HWS*, I, 540–542. The speaker was Angelina Grimké Weld.

76. *HWS*, I, 216.

Suggested Readings for Part II

Arrington, Leonard J. "Rural Life Among Ninteteenth Century Mormons: The Woman's Experience." *Agricultural History* 58 (July 1984): 238-246.

Banner, Lois. *Elizabeth Cady Stanton.* Boston: Little, Brown & Co., 1979.

Barker-Benfield, G.J. *The Horrors of the Half-Known Life: Male Attitudes Toward Women and Sexuality in Nineteenth-Century America.* New York: Harper & Row Inc., 1976.

———. "The Spermatic Economy: A Nineteenth Century View of Sexuality." *Feminist Studies* 1 (1972): 45-74.

Basch, Norma. *In the Eyes of the Law: Women, Marriage, and Property in Nineteenth Century New York.* Ithaca: Cornell University Press, 1982.

———. "Invisible Woman: The Legal Fiction of Marital Unity in Nineteenth Century America." *Feminist Studies* 8 (1979): 346-366.

———. "Equity vs. Equality: Emerging Concepts of Women's Political Status in the Age of Jackson." *Journal of the Early Republic* 3 (Fall 1983): 297-318.

Berg, Barbara. *The Remembered Gate: Origins of American Feminism—The Woman and the City.* New York: Oxford University Press, 1978.

Blassingame, John. *The Slave Community: Plantation Life in the Ante-bellum South.* New York: Oxford University Press, 1972.

Brown, Steven E. "Sexuality and the Slave Community." *Phylon* 42 (Spring 1981): 1-10.

Boylan, Anne M. "Women in Groups: An Analysis of Women's Benevolent Organizations in New York and Boston, 1797-1840." *Journal of American History* 71 (December 1984): 497-523.

Censer, Jane T. "Smiling through Her Tears: Antebellum Southern Women and Divorce." *American Journal of Legal History* 25 (January 1981): 24-47.

Clinton, Catherine. *The Plantation Mistress: Woman's World in the Old South.* N.Y.: Pantheon, 1982.

Conrad, Susan P. *Perish the Thought: Intellectual Women in Romantic America, 1830-1860.* New York: Oxford University Press, 1976.

Cott, Nancy F. "Passionlessness: An Interpretation of Victorian Sexual Ideology, 1790-1850." *Signs* 4 (1978): 219-36.

De Graaf, Lawrence B. "Race, Sex and Region: Black Women in the American West, 1850-1920." *Pacific Historical Review* 49 (May 1980): 285-313.

Douglas, Ann. *The Feminization of American Culture.* New York: Alfred A. Knopf, 1977.

Dublin, Thomas. *Women at Work: The Transformation of Work and Community in Lowell, Massachusetts, 1826-1860.* New York: Columbia University Press, 1979.

———. "Women Workers and the Study of Mobility." *Journal of Interdisciplinary History* 10 (1979): 647-665.

Dudden, Faye E. *Serving Women: Household Service in Nineteenth Century America.* Westport, CT: Wesleyan, 1983.

Duntey, Julie. "'Living the Principle' of Plural Marriage: Mormon Women, Utopia and Female Sexuality in the Nineteenth Century." *Feminist Studies* 10 (Fall 1984): 523-36.

Eckhardt, Celia Morris. *Fanny Wright: Rebel in America.* Cambridge: Harvard University Press, 1984.

Epstein, Barbara. *The Politics of Domesticity: Women, Evangelism, and Temperance in Nineteenth-Century America.* New York: Wesleyan University Press, 1981.

Faragher, John Mack. *Women and Men on the Overland Trail.* New Haven: Yale University Press, 1979.

_____, and Stansell, Christine. "Women and their Families on the Overland Trail to California and Oregon, 1842-1867." *Feminist Studies* 2 (1975): 150-66.

Fogel, Robert W. and Engerman, Stanley. *Time on the Cross: The Economics of American Negro Slavery.* Boston: Little, Brown & Co., 1974.

Frazier, E. Franklin. *The Negro Family in the United States.* Chicago: University of Chicago Press, 1939.

_____. *Family and Divorce in California, 1850-1890: Victorian Illusions and Everyday Reality.* Albany: State University of New York Press, 1982.

Genovese, Eugene. *Roll, Jordan, Roll: The World the Slaves Made.* New York: Pantheon Books, 1974.

Ginger, Ray. "Labor in a Massachusetts Cotton Mill, 1853-1860." *Business History Review* 28 (1954): 67-81.

Gitelman, Howard M. "The Waltham System and the Coming of the Irish." *Labor History* 8 (1967): 227-53.

Goldin, Claudia. "Female Labor Force Participation: The Origin of Black and White Differences, 1870 and 1880." *Journal of Economic History* 37 (March 1977): 87-108.

Goldin, Claudia and Sokoloff, Kenneth. "Women, Children and Industrialization in the Early Republic: Evidence from the Manufacturing Censuses." *Journal of Economic History* 42 (December 1982): 741-74.

Griswold, Robert L. "Apart But Not Adrift: Wives, Divorce, and Independence in California, 1850-1890." *Pacific Historical Review* 49 (May 1980): 265-83.

Groneman, Carol. "Working-Class Immigrant Women in Mid-Nineteenth Century New York: The Irish Woman's Experience." *Journal of Urban History* 4 (1978): 255-74.

Gutman, Herbert G. *The Black Family in Slavery and Freedom.* New York: Pantheon Books, 1976.

Hagler, D. Harland. "The Ideal Woman in the Antebellum South: Lady or Farmwife?" *Journal of Southern History* 46 (1980): 405-18.

Haller, John S., and Haller, Robin M. *The Physician and Female Sexuality in Nineteenth Century America.* Urbana: University of Illinois Press, 1974.

Hardesty, Nancy A. *Women Called to Witness: Evangelical Feminism in the Nineteenth Century.* Nashville, TN: Abingdon, 1984.

Hersh, Blanche Glassman. *The Slavery of Sex.* Urbana: University of Illinois Press, 1978.

Hewitt, Nancy A. *Women's Activism and Social Change: Rochester, New York, 1822-1872.* Ithaca: Cornell University Press, 1984.

Hogeland, Ronald W. "The Female Appendage: Feminine Life-Styles in America, 1820-1860." *Civil War History* 17 (1971): 101-114.

Jeffrey, Julie Roy. *Frontier Women.* New York: Hill & Wang, 1979.

Johnson, James Hugo. *Race Relations in Virginia and Miscegenation in the South, 1776-1860.* Amherst: University of Massachusetts Press, 1970.

Kaminer, Wendy. *Women Volunteering: The Pleasure, Pain, and Politics of Unpaid Work from 1830 to the Present.* Garden City, NY: Doubleday, 1984.

Kelley, Mary. *Private Woman, Public Stage: Literary Domesticity in Nineteenth Century America.* New York: Oxford University Press, 1984.

Kelley, Mary, ed. *Woman's Being, Woman's Place: Female Identity and Victorian American History.* Boston: G.K. Hall, 1979.

Johnson, Michael P. "Smothered Slave Infants: Were Slave Mothers at Fault?" *Journal of Southern History* 21 (1979): 439-52.

Kaser, David. "Nashville's Women of Pleasure in 1860." *Tennessee Historical Quarterly* 23 (1964): 379-82.

Katzman, David. *Seven Days a Week: Women and Domestic Service in Industrializing America.* New York: Oxford University Press, 1978.

Kleinberg, Susan. "Technology and Women's Work: The Lives of Working Class Women in Pittsburgh, 1870-1900." *Labor History* 17 (1976): 58-72.

Kraditor, Aileen S. *Means and Ends in American Abolitionism: Garrison and His Critics on Strategy and Tactics, 1834-1850.* New York: Pantheon Books, 1969.

Lapsansky, Emma J. "Friends, Wives, and Strivings: Networks and Community Values among Nineteenth Century Philadelphia Afro-American Elites." *Pennsylvania Magazine of History and Biography* 108 (January 1984):

Larson, T.A. "Emancipating the West's Dolls, Vassals and Hopeless Drudges! The Origins of Woman Suffrage in the West." In *Essays in Western History in Honor of T.A. Larson,* edited by Roger Daniels. Laramie: University of Wyoming, 1971.

Leashore, Bogart R. "Black Female Workers: Live-in Domestics in Detroit, Michigan, 1860-1880." *Phylon* 45 (June 1984): 111-120.

Lebsock, Susan D. "Radical Reconstruction and the Property Rights of Southern Women." *Journal of Southern History* 63 (1977): 195-216.

————. "Free Black Women and the Question of Matriarchy: Petersburg, Virginia, 1784-1820." *Feminist Studies* 8 (Summer 1982): 271-91.

————. *The Free Women of Petersburg: Status and Culture in a Southern Town, 1784-1860.* New York: Norton, 1984.

Lerner, Gerda. *The Grimke Sisters from South Carolina: Rebels Against Slavery.* Boston: Houghton Mifflin, 1967.

Lumpkin, Katharine DuPre. *The Emancipation of Angelina Grimke.* Chapel Hill: University of North Carolina Press, 1974.

Marable, Manning. "Groundings with my Sisters: Patriarchy and the Exploitation of Black Women." *Journal of Ethnic Studies* 11 (Summer 1983): 1-39.

Marti, Donald B. "Sisters of the Grange: Rural Feminism in the Late Nineteenth Century." *Agricultural History* 58 (1984): 247-61.

Massy, Mary Elizabeth. *Bonnet Brigades.* New York: Alfred A. Knopf, 1966.

McGraw, Judith A. "'A Good Place to Work': Industrial Women and Occupational Choice." *Journal of Interdisciplinary History* 10 (1979): 227-48.

McPherson, James. "Abolitionists, Woman Suffrage and the Negro, 1865-1869." *Mid-America* 47 (1965): 40-47.

Melder, Keith E. *Beginnings of Sisterhood: The American Woman's Rights Movement, 1800-1850.* New York: Schocken Books, 1977.

Mills, Gary B. "Miscegenation and the Free Negro in Antebellum 'Anglo' Alabama: A Reexamination of Race Relations." *Journal of American History* 68 (1981): 16-34.

Mintz, Steven. *A Prison of Expectations: The Family in Victorian Culture.* New York: New York University Press, 1983.

Mohr, James C. *Abortion in America: The Origins and Evolution of National Policy.* New York: Oxford University Press, 1978.

Mott, Frank L. "Portrait of an American Mill Town: Demographic Response in Mid-Nineteenth Century Warren, Rhode Island." *Population Studies* 26 (1972): 147-57.

Morantz, Regina. "Making Women Modern: Middle Class Women and Health Reform in 19th Century America." *Journal of Social History* 10 (1976-77): 490-507.

Morantz, Regina M. and Zschoche, Sue. "Professionalism, Feminism and Gender Roles: A Comparative Study of Nineteenth Century Medical Therapeutics." *Journal of American History* 67 (December 1980): 568-88.

Muncy, Raymond Lee. *Sex and Marriage in Utopian Communities: Nineteenth Century America.* Bloomington: University of Indiana Press, 1974.

O'Neill, William L. *The Woman Movement: Feminism in the United States and England.* Chicago: Quadrangle Books, 1971.

Pivar, David J. *Purity Crusade: Sexual Morality and Social Control, 1868-1900.* Westport, Conn.: Greenwood Press, 1973.

Pleck, Elizabeth. "The Two-Parent Household: Black Family Structure in Late Nineteenth-Century Boston." *Journal of Social History* 6 (1972): 1-31.

————. "A Mother's Wages: Income Earning Among Married Italian and Black Women, 1896-1911." In *The American Family in Social-Historical Perspective,* edited by Michael Gordon, pp. 490-510. New York: St. Martin's Press, 1978.

Riley, Glenda. *Frontierswoman: The Iowa Experience.* Ames: Iowa State University Press, 1981.

————. "Women in the West." *Journal of American Culture* 3 (Summer 1980):

Ripley, C. Peter. "The Black Family in Transition: Louisiana, 1860-65." *Journal of Southern History* 41 (1975): 869-80.

Rosenberg, Charles E. "Sexuality, Class and Role in 19th-Century America." *American Quarterly* 25 (1973): 131-53.

Ryan, Mary. *Cradle of the Middle Class Family: Oneida County, New York, 1780-1865.* Cambridge: Cambridge University Press, 1980.

————. "A Woman's Awakening: Evangelical Religion and the Families of Utica, N.Y., 1800-1840." *American Quarterly* 30 (1978): 602-23.

————. "The Power of Women's Networks: A Case Study of Female Moral Reform in Antebellum America." *Feminist Studies* 5 (1979): 66-85.

Scott, Anne F. *The Southern Lady: From Pedestal to Politics, 1830-1930.* Chicago: University of Chicago Press, 1970.

Sklar, Kathryn Kish. *Catherine Beecher: A Study in Domesticity*. New Haven: Yale University Press, 1973.

Smith, Daniel Scott. "Family Limitation, Sexual Control, and Domestic Feminism in Victorian America." *Feminist Studies* 1 (1973): 40-57.

Smith-Rosenberg, Carroll. "Beauty, the Beast and the Militant Woman: A Case Study of Sex Roles and Social Stress in Jacksonian America." *American Quarterly* 23 (1971): 562-84.

_____. "The Female World of Love and Ritual: Relations Between Women in Nineteenth Century America." *Signs* 1 (1975): 1-29.

_____, and Rosenberg, Charles E. "The Female Animal: Medical and Biological Views of Women in Nineteenth-Century America." *Journal of American History* 60 (1973): 332-56.

Stansell, Christine. "Women, Children and the Uses of the Streets: Class and Gender Conflict in New York City, 1850-1860." *Feminist Studies* 8 (Summer 1982): 309-35.

Steckel, Richard H. "Slave Marriage and the Family." *Journal of Family History* 5 (Winter 1980): 406-21.

Sterkx, H.E. *Partners in Rebellion: Alabama Women in the Civil War*. Teaneck, N.J.: Fairleigh Dickinson University Press, 1970.

Stowe, Steven M. "The Thing Not Its Vision: A Woman's Courtship and Her Sphere in the Southern Planter Class." *Feminist Studies* 9 (Spring 1983): 113-130.

Suitor, Jill. "Husbands' Participation in Childbirth: A Nineteenth Century Phenomenon." *Journal of Family History* 6 (Fall 1981): 278-93.

Sutherland, Daniel E. *Americans and Their Servants: Domestic Service in the United States from 1800 to 1920*. Baton Rouge, Louisiana State University Press, 1981.

Taylor, William R. and Lasch, Christopher. "Two 'Kindred Spirits': Sorority and Family in New England, 1839-1846." *New England Quarterly* 36 (1963): 23-41.

Walker, Altina L. *Reverend Beecher and Mrs. Tilton: Sex and Class in Victorian America*. Amherst: University of Massachusetts Press, 1982.

Walters, Ronald G. "The Erotic South: Civilization and Sexuality in American Abolitionism." *American Quarterly* 25 (1973): 177-201.

Ware, Caroline. *Early New England Cotton Manufacture*. Boston: Houghton Mifflin, 1931.

Weiner, Nella F. "On Feminism and Birth Control Propaganda (1790-1840)." *International Journal of Women's Studies* 3 (September/October 1980): 411-30.

Weiss, Janice. "Educating for Clerical Work: The Nineteenth Century Private Commercial School." *Journal of Social History* 14 (Spring 1981): 407-23.

Welter, Barbara. *Dimity Convictions: The American Woman in the Nineteenth Century*. Athens: Ohio University Press, 1976.

White, Deborah G. "Female Slaves: Sex Roles and Status in the Antebellum Plantation South." *Journal of Family History* 8 (Fall 1983): 248-61.

Wiley, Bell Irwin. *Confederate Women*. Westport, Conn.: Greenwood Press, 1975.

Wood, Ann Douglas. "The War Within a War: Women Nurses in the Union Army." *Civil War History* 18 (1972): 197-212.

Yans-McLaughlin, Virginia. *Family and Community: Italian Immigrants in Buffalo, 1880-1930*. Ithaca: Cornell University Press, 1977.

―――. "Patterns of Work and Family Organization: Buffalo's Italians." *Journal of Interdisciplinary History* 2 (1971): 299-314.

~3~

THE PROGRESSIVE IMPULSE

Throughout the latter part of the nineteenth century and into the twentieth, expansion, urbanization and industrialization proceeded at an ever-increasing pace. Women followed the general migration pattern from country to city, from farm to factory. At all economic levels, women were breaking out of the confines of the home and entering the public arena. For new immigrants and for lower-class women in general, this process brought the dubious emancipation of jobs outside the home in domestic service, sweatshops, and shirtwaist factories. For their wealthier sisters, increased leisure time and education created opportunities to enter the professions and to invest their energies in the cause of social justice. Women became a major element in the Progressive reform coalition, creating a growing tangle of organization that confronted a wide range of social issues from pornography and prostitution to world peace. This female "response to industrialism" took many forms that stretched, but failed to fundamentally alter, traditional sex roles.

One element of the Progressive impulse is represented by the Agrarian Revolt of the farmers of the South and West in which women played a notable part. Late nineteenth-century America was still based upon agricultural production. It was not until 1920 that the census revealed more people living in urban than in rural areas. The largest single group of adult women in the nineteenth century were farmwives. This was true in every section of the country, and in the agricultural press the image of the farmwife challenged that of the lady as the ideal woman. Frontier women have been portrayed in a variety of ways: the "gentle tamers" who brought civilization to the wild west; the "sunbonneted help-mates" who worked next to their husbands in the fields; and the "bad women" who were dancehall queens, prostitutes, and outlaws. Most frontier women were simply farmwives, and although most farmwives did not live on the frontier, they performed similar roles from Maine to Missouri. Providing meals, caring for the sick, raising children and burying the dead were all in women's hands. One can easily understand why the Granger movement, established immediately following the Civil War, appealed to women seeking social contact and release from the drudgery of farm life.

For thousands of farmwives the populist movement of the 1880s and 1890s provided an opportunity to become involved in reforms that could alter their traditional role. The expanding progressive impulse even touched the women of the "New South." In "Women in the Southern Farmers Alliance," Julie Roy Jeffrey details the various ways in which North Carolina women participated in the activities of the Alliance. The farmwives she discusses hardly fit the model of the pious, virtuous, and submissive Southern lady who was "the delight and charm of every circle" in which she moved. They were practical, hardworking women well aware of the sexual barriers erected against them. The Populists offered a "spirited attempt to work out a new place for [women] both in theory and practice," but even these male reformers were wary of women's direct participation in politics.

Elsewhere the plight of the growing and increasingly embattled working class provided an impetus for reform. By the 1890s, the non-agricultural work force equalled the number of farmers and included a sizable number of women. In "Working Class Women in the Gilded Age," Daniel J. Walkowitz examines a specific group of mid-nineteenth-century mill girls, the cotton textile workers of Cohoes in upstate New York. As elsewhere, immigrants, including the Irish and, to a lesser degree, the French Canadians, were displacing native-born women workers. Walkowitz traces the effect of work in the mills on the lives of women of different ethnic groups and emphasizes the way in which patterns of marriage and family structure varied along ethnic lines. Although mill girls shared a collective experience in their encounter with the "dark satanic mills," their responses to this situation and its effect upon their lives can only be fully understood in terms of the ethnic differences that characterized their society.

During the nineteenth century, women's protests against low wages and horrid working conditions seldom provided the basis for long-term organization. The American Federation of Labor vacillated and was generally unsympathetic to the problem. However, attempts to organize working women were made by the Daughters of St. Crispin and later by the Knights of Labor. Like the Populists, the Knights tried to accommodate traditional ideas about gender within a radical economic program. As Susan Levine notes in "Labor's True Woman," women's wage labor was a central feature of the Gilded Age economy and one accepted by the Knights. Neither men nor women, however, were willing to give up the idea of domesticity. Women used it to advance their own interests as they became "a small, but significant force within the labor movement." The Knights welcomed women and extended modest positions of power, but were essentially oriented toward traditional conceptions of the family. Labor's image of the true woman's role—like the Populists' "farmwife"—was not far from the middle-class ideal although similarly moulded to class needs. The distance between reality and symbol is clear in the image of "Mother Jones", the "Miners' Angel", who led the children's crusade. Like Mary Lease, the "Kansas Pythoness" who told the farmers to "Raise less corn and more Hell," these women were activists, propagandists, and vigorous speakers. Levine shows the myriad ways in which images of "true womanhood" were manipulated in the nineteenth century by many diverse groups.

At a time when the sex/gender system seemed most firmly entrenched, these outspoken working women shared traditional ideas about sex roles. The Knights embraced the Temperance movement both as an agent of mobility and as a feminist issue. Drunken men were poor providers, sexually inadequate husbands, and were violent to both wives and children. In their efforts to slay the dragon of corruption and, through cooperation, to revive the values of hearth and home, the Knights saw the Saloon as representing a gathering of the forces of evil. Much of their message infused the Progressive impulse that glorified women and children and did battle against the forces that would undermine traditional family values.

Although the conditions of children and working women were ameliorated through the activities of such women as Florence Kelley, the executive secretary of the National Consumers' League, and Elizabeth Gurley Flynn and Rose Schneiderman, who struggled in the interest of the working classes, women workers remained generally unorganized and outside the mainstream of the feminist movement. Feminism and labor radicalism never came together, which prevented working-class women from contributing further to Progressive reform.

Although the percentage of women in industry gradually declined, the number of working women increased with each census. By 1900 working women represented 20 percent of the total female population over sixteen years of age. For the most part, they worked as domestic servants or farm workers, and many still labored in the textile mills. Increasing numbers, however, worked in new white-collar jobs as telephone and telegraph operators and secretaries. The lot of most working women was a hard one that improved little until the enactment of Progressive reforms setting minimum wages and controlling hours and conditions of labor. In 1910 the Bureau of Labor reported that most working women were "paid very low wages—wages in many cases inadequate to supply a reasonable standard of living for women dependent upon their own earnings for support."

Only a few women in select areas, such as the garment industry, moved into the labor movement. After 1903 the Women's Trade Union League, organized by Mary Kenny O'Sullivan, attempted with limited success to bring women into the trade union movement. The idea behind the WTUL was to join working-class women and their middle-class female allies in a single organization to improve the wages and working conditions of laboring women. Nancy Schrom Dye illustrates some of the problems within the New York WTUL in her essay,

"Creating a Feminist Alliance." Class and ethnic differences among these women undermined a sense of sorority. The League also failed to develop "an analysis which came to terms with both facets of women workers' situation," that is, one that synthesized class and gender in a meaningful explanation.

In the face of adversity, the WTUL did score a few modest successes. They gave crucial support to the New York shirtwaist-makers' strikes of 1909-1910, and were primarily responsible for the establishment of the Women in Industry Division of the Department of Labor during World War I, which eventually became the Woman's Bureau under the direction of Mary Anderson in 1920. The career of the WTUL illustrates both the immense problems involved in organizing women due to the opposition of male workers and the limitations of the women's movement of the Progressive era. As so often in the American Woman Suffrage Association (NAWSA) under the presidency of Elizabeth Cady Stanton. From 1890 to 1910, the new organization their sex.

The latter part of the nineteenth century also witnessed major changes in thought and behavior that ushered in an era of reform. Among the new generation of reformers were the reform Darwinists, who scathingly criticized nearly all elements of Victorian thought and emphasized "coming to grips with life, experience, process, growth, context and function." Their emphasis on the economic context of social order promised immense benefits to women. Although these thinkers failed to seriously confront many aspects of the nineteenth-century definition of a woman, they challenged the sanctity of social and economic institutions that confined women to a limited sphere of influence. In "Loving Courtship or the Marriage Market?" Sondra R. Herman compares the traditional nineteenth-century view of marriage with the anxious orthodoxy of the social purity movement and the critical analyses of five leading reform Darwinists, including Charlotte Perkins Gilman, one of the era's most interesting feminists. At the heart of Gilman's brilliant polemic, *Women and Economics*, which emphasized the economic basis of women's subordination to men, was a radical assault on the inequalities and inefficiencies of contemporary marriage. She agreed with radical men like Edward Bellamy and Lester Frank Ward that only a fundamental change in the economic specialization of the sexes could reorient the relationship between husband and wife to make true social progress possible.

At the same time that radical critics were challenging the sanctity of traditional marriage, major shifts were occurring in sexual and marital practices. Urban conditions, including the shrinking dimensions of the household, the growing autonomy of middle-class women due to expanded educational opportunities, and increased employment of women outside the home, produced new patterns of behavior. A startling rise in the rates of illegitimacy and premarital intercourse, which had been falling throughout the nineteenth century, indicated increased sexual activity. Although marriage and childbirth continued to characterize the average woman's life, in the final two decades of the nineteenth century larger numbers of women chose not to marry than at any other time in American history. Those who did were, on the average, older when they decided to marry, and a greater percentage of married women chose not to have children. More startling to contemporaries, however, was the rapid increase in the number of women who sought release from unhappy marriages through divorce. As the percentage of women marrying returned to "normal" after the turn of the century, the United States had the anomalous distinction of both marriage and divorce rates that ranked among the highest in the world.

Expanded opportunities for education drew middle-class women out of the home and into some professions. Under the leadership of Emma Willard and Catherine Beecher, secondary education was increasingly available to women during the years before the Civil War. In 1837 Mary Lyon founded Mount Holyoke Female Seminary, which set an example for the rapid expansion of women's colleges after the war: in 1865, Vassar was established; Smith and Wellesley in 1875; and Bryn Mawr in 1885. Coeducation on the college level emerged first in the Midwest when Oberlin College in Ohio opened its doors to women in the 1830s. After the Civil War, a growing number of state universities followed Oberlin's example.

By the end of the century, over 5,000 women were graduating yearly from the nation's colleges, and the majority moved into the labor force. The number of women doctors increased as medical education (in sexually segregated classes) became available to more women. Through the dogged efforts of women such as Myra Bradwell and Belva Lockwood, who ran for president in 1884 and 1888, resistance to women in the legal profession was gradually eroded. However, most women were excluded from these professions and confined to teaching, nursing, and library work, occupations characterized by low status and low pay.

This unique group, whom Vida D. Scudder termed "the first-generation of college women," became the nucleus of a burgeoning reform movement. Horrified by multiplying slums, contaminated food and water, and unhealthy conditions under which the poor, and particularly poor women, labored, they devoted themselves to serving others in missions overseas and in settlement houses within the urban ghettos. The activities of Lillian Wald and Jane Addams are well known, but the women's organizations that appeared in increasing numbers after 1890 were more typical of the Progressive era. These organizations, which often shared members and sometimes worked together, ranged from the numerous women's clubs that focused on civic improvement—loosely united after 1901 under the aegis of the General Federation of Women's Clubs (GFWC)—to older political groups like the Women's Christian Temperance Union (WCTU).

As women who wished to reform the social order increasingly felt their disfranchisement a great handicap, women's suffrage became the focus of the women's movement. In 1890 the warring factions in the suffrage movement made peace and banded together in the National American Woman Suffrage Association (NAWSA) under the presidency of Elizabeth Cady Stanton. From 1890 to 1910, the new organization continued to follow the strategy of securing women's suffrage on a state-by-state basis. Although these women had remarkable success in opening school board and municipal elections to women, only a handful of states provided for equal suffrage.

In this century a new generation of suffrage leaders, represented by Dr. Anna Howard Shaw and Carrie Chapman Catt, led the NAWSA to its final victory. Under the direction of Catt, NAWSA swelled to nearly two million members and concentrated on the enactment and ratification of the Nineteenth Amendment. However, it was not until after 1910 that major strides were made. In quick succession, five far-western states joined with Kansas and Illinois in giving women the vote. Then in 1912, the Progressive party included a women's suffrage plank in its platform. Suffragists waged major campaigns in the populous states of the Midwest and East during 1915, and, although these attempts failed, the results indicated that the possibility of future success was excellent.

At about the same time, the campaign for an amendment to the Constitution was revived through the vigrous action of Alice Paul, a young Quaker woman who had been deeply influenced by her work with the militant English feminists. On returning to the United States, she organized the Congressional Union, which was at first affiliated with the NAWSA but eventually became the basis for the independent Woman's Party. Until 1917 the two groups maintained an uneasy alliance.

It does not diminish the achievement of Catt to argue that the final success of women's suffrage depended not only upon a few heroic national leaders, but also upon the vigorous activity of the rank and file who struggled within the complex web of state politics. In "Leadership and Tactics in the American Suffrage Movement," Sharon Hartman Strom focuses on the campaign for the vote in Massachusetts and the relationship between feminism and progressivism. Strom explains how the suffrage movement, which seemed to have been stymied by a defeat in the Massachusetts referendum of 1895, was revitalized after the turn of the century and grew in power until it swept the ratification of the Nineteenth Amendment before it. She emphasizes the importance of the rank and file to other Progressive reforms and the incorporation by suffragists of some of the radical tactics employed by their English sisters. Strom's study is detailed and complex; it shows once again that differences in ethnicity, religion, and class hindered the unity of the women's movement. She highlights to a greater extent than any previous scholar the intricate political maneuvering between suffragists and Progressives, which led to the final success of the suffrage amendment.

Ironically the Nineteenth Amendment was finally recommended by President Woodrow Wilson as a wartime measure—in response to American women's wholehearted support of World War I. Women had traditionally made up a sizable element of the American peace movement, and, at first, organizations such as NAWSA joined with the radical Woman's Peace Party to oppose American entrance into the war. But once war was declared, the majority of women supported the administration. Anna Howard Shaw, former president of NAWSA, served as head of the National Women's Committee of the Council of National Defense during the war. Although their efforts had little effect on the government, NAWSA worked through state and local branches, rolling bandages for the Red Cross and providing food and clothing for the soldiers. Many other women took over men's jobs in factories and in civil service and worked in Europe with the U.S. Army Corps of Nurses, the Red Cross, and the Salvation Army. Such activities drew wide praise and contributed to women's attainment of suffrage.

By 1920 women reformers had reason to be proud of their accomplishments and to be optimistic about the future. The two major reforms for which women organized and worked during the nineteenth century had been achieved with the enactment of the constitutional amendments providing for prohibition and women's suffrage. Organized women had played an important role in securing protective legislation for child labor, pure food and drugs, and conservation. They also influenced Progressive measures in two other areas traditionally of interest to women—reform of divorce laws and the curbing of prostitution. This impressive body of legislative success in the interest of women has led one scholar to term the Progressive era "the greatest age in the history of American women." However, the achievement of these reforms was not without cost to the women's movement.

As success became a possibility, the increasing concern for tactics undermined the idealism of the movement. In order to gain the unity necessary for effective political pressure, the major women's organizations had to disavow their more militant elements, such as Alice Paul's Women's Party, and ignore the needs and desires of black women. Blacks were involved in the Progressive movement: Ida B. Wells-Barnett led the crusade against lynching, and Mary Church Terrill organized the National Association of Colored Women. A few white women did take a special interest in racial equality. Mary White Ovington, for example, was one of the founders of the National Association for the Advancement of Colored People. But for the most part, the interests of black women were sacrificed to attain southern support. The CFWC and the WCTU were built upon sectional reconciliation and were strong in the South, but even NAWSA, whose roots stretched back into the abolitionist movement, tolerated racist arguments and gave in to the racist demands of its southern members. During World War I attempts were made to enlist the support of black women. The efforts of Alice Dunbar Nelson and the Committee on Women's Defense Work created an unusual cooperation between southern white and black women that extended beyond the Committee's original goals into other areas of reform. Black women, however, continued to be overwhelmingly poor and victims of double discrimination. Throughout most of these years, the majority remained in the South and were mired in the sharecropping system. Those who in increasing numbers "escaped" to the North were excluded from factory jobs and concentrated in domestic service.

Aside from class, racial, and ethnic divisions within the movement, feminism was plagued by ideological inconsistencies. In the 1890s the basis of the suffrage argument shifted from natural rights to expediency. Suffragists increasingly related other reform measures to their demand for the vote. They insisted that a purification of the political process would follow the entrance of women into the polling place. Alice Stone Blackwell, the activist daughter of Lucy Stone, believed that "in the main, suffrage and prohibition have the same friends and the same enemies" and urged clergymen to support suffrage because it would augment the power of the churches in "the warfare against the liquor traffic, and the white slave traffic, child labor, impure food, and many other existing evils."

In "Women Reformers and American Culture, 1870–1930," Jill Conway emphasizes the failure of reformers to question basic aspects of traditional sexual stereotypes and their emphasis on the distinctive moral qualities of women. Women like Jane Addams and Lillian Wald "worked within the tradition which saw women as civilizing and moralizing forces within the society." They conceived of women as temperamentally suited to the task of social housekeeping. Because women alone possessed the virtues extolled in Victorian sexual stereotypes, Addams and Wald urged women to move out of the home into efforts for social justice and the reform of politics. Even Charlotte Gilman, who questioned almost every aspect of the subordination of women, believed that motherhood was the biological destiny of women and that women were by nature more peaceful, even-tempered, and less competitive than men. The success of the major progressive reforms was based upon "not the image of women as equals . . . but the image of women as victims."

❧ 12 ❧

WOMEN IN THE SOUTHERN FARMERS' ALLIANCE: A RECONSIDERATION OF THE ROLE AND STATUS OF WOMEN IN THE LATE NINETEENTH-CENTURY SOUTH

JULIE ROY JEFFREY

In the spring of 1891, Mrs. Brown, secretary of the Menola Sub-Alliance in North Carolina, welcomed an audience of delegates to the quarterly meeting of the Hertford County Farmers' Alliance. After introductory remarks to both the women and men in the audience, Brown addressed her female listeners directly.

> Words would fail me to express to you, my Alliance sisters, my apprecia-
> tion of woman's opportunity of being co-workers with the brethren in
> the movement which is stirring this great nation. Oh, what womanly
> women we ought to be, for we find on every hand, fields of usefulness
> opening before us. Our brothers ... are giving us grand opportunities to
> show them, as Frances E. Willard says, that "Drudgery, fashion and
> gossip are no longer the bounds of woman's Sphere."

So enthusiastically was Brown's speech received, that the County Alliance unanimously requested its publication in the official paper of the Farmers' Alliance, the *Progressive Farmer*.[1] In a similar fashion, the Failing Creek Alliance asked the *Progressive Farmer* later that year to reprint a speech Katie Moore had delivered to them. Moore had also spoken before an audience of women and men, and she too had had some special words for the women. " 'Tis not enough that we should be what our mothers were," she told them. "We should be more, since our advantages are superior. . . . This is the only order that allows us equal privileges to the men; we certainly should appreciate the privilege and prove to the world that we are worthy to be considered on an equal footing with them"[2]

From *Feminist Studies* 2 (Fall 1975). Reprinted by permission of the publisher, Feminist Studies, Inc., Women's Studies Program, University of Maryland, College Park, Maryland 20742. Roy Jeffrey first appeared in *Feminist Studies*, 2, no. 2/3 (Fall 1975): 72–91.

That the two audiences had approved of these speeches to the point of urging their wider circulation was not surprising. For the slogan of the Southern Farmers' Alliance itself was, "Equal rights to all, special privileges to none." As one Alliance publication explained, "The Alliance has come to redeem women from her enslaved condition, and place her in her proper sphere. She is admitted into the organization as the equal of her brother . . . the prejudice against woman's progress is being removed."[3]

Such statements about the condition of Alliance women were important, for they came from an organization which had millions of members and which was a significant force on the regional and national level in the 1880s and 1890s. In part, the Alliance was a rural protest against the inferior social, economic, and political position its members felt farmers occupied in the emerging urban-industrial society. But, like civil service reformers and other protest groups in the Gilded Age, the Farmers' Alliance argued that the finely balanced two-party system responded only to the demands of special interest groups and political machines rather than to the needs of the people. Alliance members first tried to change this situation by pressing at the state level for control of monopolies and other unfriendly interests and for favorable legislation. Better public schools for rural children, state agricultural colleges, colleges for women, laws controlling the railroads, better prices for farm products were some of the goals the Alliance sought to enable rural classes to survive within a new world. As this strategy proved frustrating, about half of the Alliance membership moved into the Populist party which ran its first presidential candidate in 1892. Although the Populist party ultimately failed, it offered the most serious challenge to the two-party system in the late nineteenth century and contributed to the reshaping of the American political system.[4]

These exhortations and demands emphasizing female equality and opportunity were important, then, because the Alliance was important, but they have an unfamiliar ring in the context of what has generally been known about sex roles and relationships in the post-Civil War South. The accepted interpretation of late nineteenth-century southern society has argued that the model of the southern lady, submissive and virtuous, "the most fascinating being in creation . . . the delight and charm of every circle she moves in," still marked the parameters of appropriate behavior for middle-class women, though the model had been predictably weakened by the traumatic experience of civil war. As for lower-class women, this interpretation suggests, they were "not much affected by role expectations," although "farmers' wives and daughters and illiterate black women . . . in some inarticulate way doubtless helped to shape [society]" and its standards.[5]

Yet an investigation of the Farmers' Alliance in North Carolina, where the Alliance had great success, indicates this explanation does not hold true for that state. If the North Carolina experience is at all typical of other southern Alliance states, and there is little reason to think it is not, the reality of southern attitudes toward women was more complex than recent analyses have allowed.[6] The Civil War had been the initial catalyst for women entering new areas of activities; after the war, poverty and loss of fathers, brothers, husbands, and other male relatives forced many women to run farms, boarding houses, to become seamstresses, postmistresses, and teachers.[7] As the traditional view of woman's sphere crumbled under the impact of the post-war conditions, at least one alternative to the older view emerged in the South—one exemplified by the case of North Carolina. Responsive to social changes stemming from war and defeat, the Alliance in the 1880s and 1890s urged women to adopt a new self-image, one that included education, economic self-sufficiency, one that made a mockery of all false ideas of gentility. The activities and behavior that the Alliance sanctioned were not only considered appropriate for middle-class women but for women on all social levels.[8] Although evidence on the social class composition of the Alliance is limited, recent work suggests that approximately 55 percent of the North Carolina membership owned their land, about 31 percent were tenants, and 14 percent rural professionals. Since many wives and daughters joined the Alliance, it seems reasonable to assume that female membership, like male membership, crossed class lines.[9] Certainly, the new female role was applicable to all of them. Finally, although it was not actually created by Alliance women, the new cultural model was consciously elaborated by some of them, thus offering one way of understanding how middle-class farming women, later deemed "inarticulate" because they left so few written records, perceived and shaped their social role.

Furthermore, a case study of the North Carolina Farmers' Alliance shows that the Alliance also offered numerous rural women the rare privilege of discussing important economic and political issues with men and of functioning as their organizational equals. Few southern institutions offered women similar opportunities. The political party barred them altogether. The Methodist and Baptist churches, which with the Presbyterian claimed a majority of church members, still supported the traditional view that women ought to remain at home although they had allowed women a new area of activity in establishing female missionary societies. This expansion of their sphere was considered to be "no compromise . . . [to] female modesty and refinement," although, in reality, women could and did acquire political experience and skills in them.[10] After 1883, North Carolina women also gained valuable organizational knowledge through their involvement in the Women's Christian Temperance Union. But the W.C.T.U., the church missionary societies and women's clubs of the 1880s were all-female organizations and thus did not offer women the chance to establish a pragmatic working relationship with men as the Alliance would do.[11]

One other rural organization in the South, the Grange, which reached its height of popularity in North Carolina between 1873 and 1875, admitted both sexes before the Alliance did so. Unlike the Alliance, however, the Grange made clear distinctions between most of the offices and ranks women and men could hold. Nevertheless, the Grange clearly provided women with some practical organizational experience with men and, presumably, offered some kind of rough equality. Still, partly because of its Northern origins, the impact of the Grange was limited in the South. In North Carolina, the Grange's total membership never surpassed the 15,000 mark, and by the 1880s, numbers had dwindled.[12] Moreover, since the Grange was primarily an educational body, it failed to provide the same kind of experience for southern women as the Alliance would in the 1880s and 1890s. Ostensibly apolitical, the Alliance was actually devoted to a discussion of the "science of economical government" and was deeply involved in political questions.[13] Within the North Carolina Alliance, the spheres of women and men drew closer as both sexes voted, held office, and discussed together the stirring issues of the day as they had rarely done before.

Within the framework of the Alliance, then, southern women had the opportunity to discuss pressing economic, political, and social questions, to try out ways of behaving in mixed groups and to gain confidence in newly acquired skills. One might expect that a group of women, and perhaps men, eventually emerged whose Alliance experiences would lead them ultimately to demand or sympathize with the greater expansion of woman's role that the organization officially supported. Yet this never happened. At the same time that the Alliance offered new roles and organizational possibilities for women, the meaning of equality for women was constricted by the organization's major goal of reviving southern agriculture. Political rights within the Alliance were not seen as the first step toward political rights outside of the Alliance. The career of the North Carolina Alliance and its inclusion of women in its membership thus offers another kind of study of the slow progress of the women's rights movement in North Carolina and perhaps gives additional clues for its uncertain course in the South as a whole.[14]

The evidence for this study comes from many sources. Most useful is the State Alliance paper, the *Progressive Farmer*,[15] whose policy it was to publish the views of the Alliance membership. Few of these rural correspondents provided the leading articles for the paper, but rather they contributed letters to the correspondence page. Since these long forgotten farm women and men left virtually no other personal records, their letters, some literary, most artless, provide a crucial insight into the grassroots level of the Alliance and an important view of their responses to the opportunities the Alliance held out to them.

Initial interest in a farmers' organization in North Carolina resulted from the depressed state of southern agriculture in the 1880s. By 1886, Colonel Leonidas Polk, editor of the new agricultural weekly, the *Progressive Farmer*, was vigorously urging the paper's readers to organize local farmers' clubs as the basis for a future state wide organization. From the beginning he visualized at least some women in the clubs, for he advised they could be "elected as honorary members." Yet farmers' clubs were not to have a long life in North Carolina. By May 1887 Alliance organizers from Texas, where the agricultural order had originated, had begun to establish local Alliances in North Carolina, while a Carolinian, J. B. Barry, also began recruiting. Polk, aware of the growth potential of the Alliance, joined one of Barry's Alliances in July 1887, and was soon meeting with Texas Alliance leaders to discuss a merger between the Alliance and his farmers' clubs. After the merger was made the North Carolina Alliance grew by leaps and bounds. In the summer of 1888 the membership stood at 42,000. By 1891 the Alliance claimed 100,000 members in over 2,000 local chapters.[16]

Requirements for membership in the Alliance, formalized in the state constitution adopted in October 1887, were far more positive to female members than Polk's farmers' clubs had been. Membership was open to rural white women and men over sixteen years of age who had a "good moral character," believed in "the existence of a Supreme Being," and showed "industrious habits." While men were to pay fifty cents as an initiation fee in addition to quarterly dues of twenty-five cents, women had no required fee or dues, no doubt a recognition of their marginal economic status and their desirablility as members.[17] Membership of both sexes was essential to Alliance goals as state Alliance president, Captain Sydenham B. Alexander, indicated. The purpose of the Alliance, Alexander wrote in 1887 was "to encourage education among the agricultural and laboring classes, and *elevate to higher manhood and womanhood* those who bear the burdens of productive industry."[18]

Alliance leaders did not leave the issue of female participation in the organization to chance but stressed it forcefully. Harry Tracy, a National Lecturer of the order, urged *the ladies to come out and hear him*," and warned Alliance members: "The ladies eligible must join the order before we can succeed." Despite emphatic support from the top, however, letters from local Alliances to the *Progressive Farmer*, now the official organ of the North Carolina Alliance, indicate some male resistance to the idea of female members. As the Secretary of the Davidson College Alliance explained: "I think that the ladies are best suited to home affairs." Verbal opposition to female members led one woman to comment, "They don't want us to join, and think it no place for us." Other, more subtle techniques of discouraging female membership seem to have existed. Holding meetings in places where women would be uncomfortable or feel out of place kept the number of female members down. As the correspondent from Lenoir Alliance noted, his Alliance had fifty men and one woman because meetings were held in the court house. As one frequent contributor to the *Progressive Farmer* who favored female members pointed out: "Each Sub-Alliance needs a hall. . . . We cannot urge the ladies to attend until we can seat them comfortably."[19]

Numerous questions addressed to Polk, now secretary of the state Alliance as well as editor of the *Progressive Farmer* indicated that even if not opposed to female membership, men were often hesitant and confused about the membership of women. A variety of questions focused on what women were eligible for membership and, if elected, what their rights should be. Were women, in fact, to have the same "rights and privileges of the male members"?[20] Over and over again Polk replied that women were to have equal rights and privileges; they were to vote on new members, participate in all Alliance business and to know "all the secret words and signs" of the order.[21]

If some men were unenthusiastic about female members, so too were some of the women. As one Allianceman explained: "Our female friends seem to repose great confidence in our ability to conduct the affairs of the Alliance without their direct union and assistance. Indeed, our wives, mothers and sisters have as much as they can do to attend their own business." Other letters from men more enthusiastic about female members agreed that women refused to join because they were "too modest, or think it out of their line."[22] There was even some outright female opposition to Alliance membership as one "bright and energetic young lady," the first woman to join the Alliance in Vance County, discovered when her friends ridiculed "the idea of young ladies joining."[23] The traditional view of woman's sphere, then, constituted a barrier to active female participation in the Alliance, and it was one which female members consciously tried to undermine. When Alliancewomen wrote to the *Progressive Farmer* they frequently urged the other women to overcome feelings of timidity. "Dear Sisters, go to work; don't stay home and die, then say I have something else to do; that will never do," wrote Addie Pigford. "Sisters, what are you doing?" asked Mrs. Carver. "There is work for us to do, and we shall not be found wanting. We can help in many ways, and we must do it."[24]

Opposition and hesitation on the subject of female members obviously existed as the reports of local and county Alliances and male and female correspondents to the *Progressive Farmer* show. But evidence suggests that the message that women were to be encouraged as vigorous participants of the Alliance eventually came through clearly to most local groups. By 1889, for example, the State Line Alliance reported it was planning to discuss the desirability of female members. Rather ruefully, the writer commented: "That indicates *how far we are behind*, but we do not intend to remain there."[25] Questions about membership requirements and privileges, membership breakdowns sent into the *Progressive Farmer*, and local minute books, indicate that women were presenting themselves for membership. Not only did the wives and daughters of male members join but so too did unattached women. As the Alliance grew so did the number of women in the organization. In some cases, women comprised one-third to one-half of local groups.[26] "We can work just as well as the brethren," pointed out one Alliance woman. "If we want to derive good from the Alliance, we must work in love and harmony with our fellow-man"[27]

As thousands of women responded to the Alliance's invitation to join "the great army of reform," there were hints that women felt increasingly at ease in their new organizational role. Although it is difficult to recover the perceptions of these rural women, their letters to the *Progressive Farmer* from 1887 through 1891 can serve as an imperfect measure for their thoughts and feelings about their participation in the Alliance.[28]

One of the most striking aspects of the women's correspondence is the initial hesitation about writing to a newspaper at all. Only one woman communicated to the editor in 1887. Gradually, however, women began to send letters, many of them conscious of departing from past patterns of behavior. "Being a farmer's wife, I am not in the habit of writing for the public prints," wrote the first female correspondent of 1888, a certain Mrs. Hogan who was concerned about stray dogs. Replied the second, "Mr. Editor:—I have never written anything for the public to read, but I feel just now, after reading Mrs. Hogan's trouble . . . that I want to tell her I truly sympathize with her."[29] Other correspondents in 1888 and 1889 often began their letters with the polite request for a "small space" for a few words from a farm woman or with the phrase, "I am but a female." "I suppose your many subscribers will not expect much from a female correspondent," wrote one corresponding secretary, "and if so, they will not be disappointed when they read this article, but if I can be of any service to the Alliance by putting in my little mite, I am willing to do what I can."[30] By 1890 such protestations and expressions of humility had disappeared. A series of letters from Evangeline Usher exemplifies the growing confidence on the part of women that their letters and reports on Alliance activities were appropriate and acceptable. In an early letter, Usher urged other women to write to the paper, with the typical hope that Polk would "give us a little space somewhere." Describing herself as fearful that her letter would go into the wastebasket, she further explained that her feelings of delicacy would prevent her from contributing her Alliance's news regularly. "I already imagine I see Brother 'R' smiling ludicrously at the idea." Within a few months, however, Usher wrote again, confessing "a kind of literary pride in seeing my name in print." By 1889, she could begin her letter, "I feel like I must intrude again, and as I am quite independent of all disfavor, I do not care whether you like the intrusion or not."[31] Though Usher was unusually outspoken, her growing boldness correlates with the straightforward and secure tone women gradually adopted in writing to the paper and suggests their greater feelings of confidence within the organization.[32]

Local reports, letters, and records also give information on another crucial consideration concerning women's involvement in the Alliance. If women only sat on the back benches during Alliance meetings, listening silently while men discussed the great economic and political issues of the day, their membership would have been insignificant. If, on the other hand, women actually helped to run the organization and helped contribute to its success, even if they were not equal in every respect to men, then the Alliance was an important departure from the typical southern organization.

Although there is no indication that women were ever elected to the office of president of local Alliances, they were occasionally, at least, voted into important positions. The Jamestown Alliance Minute Book, for example, records that a year after the subject of female members was first discussed, a woman was elected as assistant secretary; she declined, but two months later was elected as treasurer.[33] Other women held the office of secretary, with the responsibility not only for making "a fair record of all things necessary to be written," but also for "receiving all moneys due" and for communicating with

Secretary Polk.[34] Still others became lecturers or assistant lecturers, both crucial positions since they were to give addresses, lead discussions, and furnish "the material of thought for the future consideration of the members."[35] Women as well as men read papers "on subjects of importance for the benefit of the order." In one Alliance, records show that women conducted the business on an Alliance meeting day.[36] At the county level where meetings were held quarterly, women were included in the membership count on which representation was based, were delegates, and at least one was elected vice-president. Others gave key addresses to large audiences.[37] Women could also be found at the annual meetings of the state Alliance. As the *Progressive Farmer* warmly replied to two women who had written to ask if they could go to the meeting, "You are not only *allowed*, but you will be most cordially welcomed to a seat."[38] Though such evidence is fragmentary, it does imply that many women took an active part in running Alliance affairs.

Women's participation in the Alliance is seen in a variety of other areas too. Several letters to the *Progressive Farmer* noted that women subscribed to the State Business Agency Fund, an important Alliance effort aimed at eliminating middlemen in purchasing fertilizers, groceries, and agricultural goods. Alliance leaders urged local groups to donate at least fifty cents a member to the fund. A few reports show women carrying their financial share. Women also sent in news to the paper, wrote articles, and worked to increase the subscription list, a job which Polk and other leaders saw as vital to Alliance success since they argued that earlier efforts to arouse farmers had foundered on ignorance and lack of proper information.[39]

If not all women were active members of the Alliance, enough were to be reported and praised in the *Progressive Farmer*. Clearly, many women welcomed the chance to work in the organization. Moreover, as their letters indicate, they shared men's interest in the compelling subjects of the day: agricultural cooperation, the role of combines and trusts in creating the farming crisis, the need to diversify southern agriculture, all standard themes for discussion and instruction in Alliance meetings and reading material.[40] But as much as women were involved with such topics, as much as they enjoyed the social conviviality of the Alliance, many must have agreed with the woman who reminded her Alliance, "This is the only order that allows us equal privileges to the man; we certainly should appreciate the privilege."[41]

North Carolina Alliance's support of "equal rights" for women within the organization and of the new role described for them outside it may seem startling, yet it corresponded to the reality of life for southern women in the late 1880s and early 1890s. It would have been surprising if the changes in southern society following the Civil War had failed to result in some ideological reconsideration of women's status. Yet the Alliance's stance was not merely a response to social change in the South. The National Alliance upheld the concept of equal rights. State leaders recognized that the farmer and his wife worked as an agricultural unit. It made sense to involve both in the Alliance for as one farmer pointed out, "We know we can scarcely dispense with the labor of our wives and children on the farm."[42] Furthermore, leaders reasoned that the Alliance could not count on continued enthusiasm and good attendance unless women as well as men came to meetings. "Meetings must be interesting" to spur membership and attendance, one pamphlet pointed out, "and the first step in this direction is to get more women and young people into the Order." At least one member agreed. The presence of women, he wrote, "cheers us on." Clearly, if the Alliance and its work were to prosper, both sexes would have to be involved.[43]

The social composition of the leadership suggests another important reason for the Alliance support for women. Although men like Colonel Polk and Sydenham Alexander, president of the state Alliance, had been or were farmers genuinely concerned with agricultural problems, they were also members of the rural upper-class. Polk had had a long career as planter, army officer, legislator, commissioner of agriculture, and editor. Alexander had headed the state Grange in the 1870s. Other leaders were teachers, doctors, and clergymen.[44] As members of North Carolina's elite, these men partially accepted the traditional view of woman as the beacon of social morality. "If our organization means anything," one prominent supporter of female members wrote, "it means a moral reformation, morality must be our guide. The ladies are and always have been the great moral element in society; therefore *it is impossible to succeed without calling to our aid the greatest moral element in the country.*"[45]

This was how Alliance leaders conceived of the role and importance of women within their organization. But women themselves had their own ideas about their role, as an examination of their letters to the *Progressive Farmer* reveal. The writers stressed their pride in farm life, the need to throw off female passivity, the vital importance of women to the Alliance effort. "While it has been remarked that women are a necessary evil," wrote Fannie Pentecost, "let us by our untiring energy, and zeal show them that it is a mistake. . . . We should devise plans and means by which we can assist those who have to bear the burdens of life." In the Alliance, another woman pointed out, women had the unique opportunity of helping men "in the thickest of the fight" by encouragement, prayers, self-denial, and endurance. Some correspondents clearly saw their role as one of moral support, but others visualized a more active role, using words like helpmate or companion to describe how they saw themselves.[46] One woman shaped the female role curiously: "Let us all put our shoulders to this great wheel, the Alliance. We, as sisters of this Alliance may feel we are silent factors in this work; we know we constantly need something to lean upon. . . . Let us so entwine ourselves around our brothers that *should we be taken away* they will feel they are *tottering*." Here, encouragement and support had become the vital activity for women. So, too, one woman from Fair Grove commented that women must be "ready to hold the hands of the strong, should they become weak."[47]

That women perceived themselves occasionally as the major support for men corresponds with the way in which Alliance leaders visualized them. But there was a sharp edge to the role of moral guide as some correspondence revealed. Again, Evangeline Usher provides an insight into this kind of thinking. In a letter of September 1890, Usher wrote that someone had recently sent her a compliment, "saying they were just as strong an Alliance boy as I was an Alliance girl." Evangeline's rather surprising comment was "Brother . . . I only hope you are, for I am one that believes in working and not talking." Other letters and articles convey a similar scepticism of men. "Why," asked assistant lecturer Lizzie Marshburn, "is it that the farmer and laboring class generally, have got no self-will or resolution of their own? . . . as a general rule they have been ever ready to link their destinies with any political aspirant who can get up and deliver a flowerly address of misrepresentation." Allie Marsh told her audience at a Randolph County meeting, "We come to these meetings with an unwritten agreement to take things as they are." Women, she said, were "perfectly content" that men exercise political rights "as long as you are vigilant in making [the ballot box] as efficient as possible." Yet the remainder of her speech suggested that she had found the men "wanting." A letter from still another woman acidly observed, "Some men can't see beyond their nose."[48]

Although most women and men probably agreed upon the function of women's participation within the Alliance, it appears that some Alliance women saw the matter differently and that they suspected that the commonly accepted view of women as the quiet impetus behind male reformers was inadequate. Their letters convey misgivings about the ability of men to persist in their support of reform and implicitly suggest that these women perceived themselves as steadier leaders than the men. As one Alliance woman explained: "My sisters, this is something we should know, that our names are on this list [of reformers] and [we should] regret we could not be allowed this opportunity years ago, for no doubt our country would be in a much better condition to-day had we taken this step." Added another, apparently filled with misgivings about men: "I would earnestly *beg the brethren* when they put their hands to the plow *not to look back . . . if they do,* they will not reap the harvest we all desire. *We must work* and *wait,* and not grow discouraged."[49] Yet, despite these indications that women suspected that they rather than men were possibly the most steadfast and reliable leaders of reform, they were hardly ready to challenge openly the Alliance's basic assumptions because of the positive support the Alliance was already providing for southern women in many areas of life.

Indeed, women's rights within the organization was only part of the Alliance's reformulation of women's status. A woman's role in the Alliance was understood to parallel the more significant role the Alliance suggested women could enjoy in society at large. The *Progressive Farmer*'s policy of reporting on the achievements of women who were doctors, surgeons, journalists, lawyers, government workers, even pastors, indicated the wide range of possibilities beyond the conventional one of marriage and motherhood.[50] These career options, of course, depended on educating women, a goal that the Alliance and its official newspaper consistently supported as part of the general attempt to improve all educational facilities for "farmers and laborers."[51]

"The ability of girls," the *Progressive Farmer* stated flatly, "has been found equal to that of boys." As the resolutions of the 1890 State Alliance meeting show, the Alliance went on record that year not only in favor of public schools for boys and girls but also in support of "ample [state] appropriations [for] the training and higher education of females." The paper explained, "The lopsided system of education in North Carolina . . . provides for the education of men and neglects that of women. Gentlemanly instinct, to say nothing of justice and mercy, requires that women should be given as good a chance for education as men possess. . . . Give the noble girls of the State—those who are not able to go to our expensive colleges a chance to get an education," the paper urged. Responding to pressure from the Alliance and other interested groups, the legislature of 1891 appropriated $10,000 a year to establish a normal and industrial training school for girls.[52]

The reason for the Alliance's concern with women's education becomes obvious in the *Progressive Farmer*'s discussions of private girls' schools. Traditionally, these schools had stressed teaching female accomplishments to the would-be southern lady of means. But now, the *Progressive Farmer* enthusiastically reported, Salem Female Academy had expanded its offering by establishing a business course featuring music, telegraphy, phonography (shorthand), typing and bookkeeping. Such a course, the *Progressive Farmer* pointed out, was most desirable with its "studies of a practical character, fitting the learners for active avocations when required to depend upon their own efforts in the battle of life." Other schools, the paper urged, ought to follow Salem Academy's example. The fundamental point, the paper emphasized, was that *all* young women of *all* social classes should be prepared for jobs. It was true, of course, that education would help poor girls by enabling them "to make an honest living," but all women ought to learn to be self-sufficient and self-supporting.[53]

Women themselves stressed the importance of economic self-sufficiency. They did not want to "be entirely dependent upon the bounties of others" if they lost their protectors. And, as an additional point in favor of education, one Alliance woman brought up the important question of marriage. Self-sufficiency would allow women to marry because they wanted to, not because they needed financial support. Thus education of a certain kind would help women avoid the "fatal blunder," incompatibility in marriage.[54]

Alliance support for practical education for women was based on a rejection of the concept of gentility which had been such a fundamental component of the idea of the southern lady.[55] The search for a "pale and delicate" complexion, the interest in elaborate clothing and accomplishments were all denounced in the pages of the *Progressive Farmer*. These traditional female concerns were misguided since they undermined the importance of hard work and, thus, the opportunities for female independence. The idea that labor was degrading, the *Progressive Farmer* reminded its readers, was just another unfortunate remnant of slavery, and, in fact, contributed in an important way to poverty itself. True Alliance men and women wanted young people "to see that it is no disgrace, but a high honor, to know how to work and to be able to do it." The feminine ideal was the woman who was independent and practical, educated either to support herself or to marry wisely.[56]

Better education for both sexes was an issue with which many Alliance members sympathized, hoping their children's future would be more promising than their own. Yet the Alliance could not concern itself exclusively with the new options for young women who still had their lives ahead of them. With so many adult female members, the Alliance also considered how to reshape life styles for those women who would never leave the farm for school or a job. "Is the life of the Farmer's wife under present systems, calculated to give her virtue and intelligence full play?" asked the Southern Alliance paper, the *National Economist*. "Is she not a slave and a drudge in many cases?" The

Progressive Farmer gave the answer: there were "thousands and tens of thousands" of farmers' wives "worked to their graves."[57] Improving this dreary situation necessitated a multipronged approach. First, the paper's scientific articles on housekeeping and cooking could show the farmwife how to lighten her work load. Then, too, her husband was to be prodded into helping her out. As one correspondent to the *Progressive Farmer* explained, men needed tough words. "Our Lecturer, in trying to discuss the social feature [of the Alliance], handles husbands quite roughly, but it is received in the proper spirit. If country life is ever made more attractive, there must be more congeniality in spirit and aggressiveness between the one that follows the plow handles and the one of all beings earthly that acts as a helpmeet to man." What were "the conveniences for the good and faithful wife?" asked Colonel Polk. How far did she have to walk to the woodpile or the spring? Had the bloom on her cheeks faded prematurely? These were the subjects, he urged, that ought to be discussed in Alliance circles so that "new life, new energy, new action . . . and new views of life and living" might emerge for both sexes.[58]

The Alliance's concern with helping hard working farmwomen fused with the order's major objective, the overall improvement of agricultural life. To this end, the Alliance sought to discover "a remedy for every evil known to exist and afflict farmers and other producers."[59] The remedy of improved farming methods was especially important as the number of articles in the *Progressive Farmer* attest. The paper argued that the one-crop system was the obvious and basic cause of the state's agricultural depression. Over and over again, the paper and Alliance meetings focused on the need to farm properly and to stay out of debt. Consider the two kinds of farmers, the *Progressive Farmer* urged. One raised cotton on his land, bought milk, bread, hay and fertilizers on credit. The other chose the Alliance route and would prosper. And "his wife, dear devoted woman, instead of wearing out her life in cooking for a lot of negroes to work cotton, has time to look after the adornment and the beautifying of her home, to attend to her milk and butter, eggs, garden, bees, chickens and other poultry, and with all this they have a little time to spare socially with their neighbors and to go to church."[60]

The *Progressive Farmer* might describe the tasks of the wise farmer's wife enthusiastically, but the list of her activities highlights a crucial problem in the Alliance's approach to women. Although the Alliance supported expanding women's rights and privileges, its overall objective was to put farmers on an economic, social, and political parity with other occupations. To do so, or to try to do so, had definite implications for women's lives and shaped the Alliance's conception of equality. If the home was to be made attractive enough to discourage children from abandoning farm life, if it was to be "a place of rest, of comfort, of social refinement and domestic pleasure," then women would have to make it so.[61] If the farm was to stay out of debt, if the farmer was to remain free of the supply merchant by raising as many of his necessities as he could, his wife must help. Woman's "judgement and skill in management may be essential to the success of her husband," one article reminded Alliance readers. "And this responsibility . . . continues to the close of her life."[62]

The Alliance proposed a position for women that embodied an equality of sorts, the economic equality of a diligent coworker. In its recognition of the importance and difficulty of woman's work, the role model differed from that of the southern lady. Nor did the model merely update the characters of the yeoman farmer's family. The Alliance's concern with diversifying southern agriculture, with eliminating the disastrous dependency on the one-crop system, was not an attempt to recreate the small farm and agricultural myth of an idealized past but to create a new kind of farm and a new cast of characters. Agricultural reform, in fact, was seen as part of a modernizing process, and it was favored not only by the Alliance but also by leaders of the New South movement. Spokesmen for each group agreed that the South had to end its colonial status both through substantial industrial growth and through agricultural diversification.[63]

But what were the implications of such a view for women? "The housewife, who, by her industry, transforms the milk from her dairy into butter . . . is as truly a manufacturer as the most purse-proud mill-owner of Britain," explained the *National Economist*. Labeled manufacturers or helpmates, women were to carry a heavy burden in creating the new order.[64] The truth was that even though the Alliance talked of a variety of opportunities available for women, most women in North Carolina would continue to live on the farm, and Alliance leaders thought this right in terms of the world they wished to create. Farm women were important for they would share in the task of restoring agriculture to its rightful position in the economy. Even the Alliance's interest in women's education was partially tied to this goal. If women were to become efficient, modern coworkers in the task of agricultural reconstruction, they needed an education. As Polk explained: "The great and imperative need of our people and our time, is the practical education of the masses. . . . It will be a glorious day for the South when her young ladies, educated in all the higher and refined arts of life, shall boast and without blushing of equal proficiency in the management of the household and the flower-garden."[65]

Moreover, women needed to be educated so that, in turn, they could teach Alliance children, first at home and then at school. Rural children, many Alliance members were convinced, needed a special kind of education, one that embraced "the moral, physical and industrial, as well as the mental training of our children." By providing such an education, women could offer an "invaluable service." For "this system will strengthen the attachment of these classes [to agricultural life] instead of alienating [them] from it . . . it will better qualify them for success and happiness in life . . . increase the opportunity and inclination to adorn the home and practice the social virtues."[66]

Other pragmatic considerations led to the support of women's education. Education could provide poor girls with the opportunity "to make an honest living." Most, but not all, women would marry. To prepare for the possibility of spinsterhood, every careful mother must see not only that daughters were trained in their domestic and spiritual responsibilities, but would also "have them taught a trade or profession and thus equip them fully to 'face the world' if this need shall come to them."[67] No one, not even a woman, ought to be an economic drain on the others. Teaching provided one means of support. So too would factory work, which the Alliance leaders, like spokesmen of the New South movement, hoped would be a growing field of employment. North Carolina's piedmont region, the *Progressive Farmer* enthusiastically suggested, should be covered with factories. "Then we could have money because our boys and girls and women who are now consumers would find constant, honorable and remunerative employment and would thus become self-supporting." Women not only had the option but, indeed, the duty of being self-supporting and of adding "to the general wealth of the place." The more educated and useful women became, "the better for them and for our State."[68]

The part that the Alliance encouraged women to play in southern life was more expansive than the traditional role of the southern lady at the same time that it had definite limitations. Women need no longer cultivate the appearance of genteel passivity; they required education as the preparation for a useful life. But the Alliance defined utility in terms of the organization's over-all objectives, the profitability of agriculture, the prosperity of the state. Thus, it was vital that women learn to be skilled managers or teachers. Whether spinsters or widows, women must never be parasites on their families or on their state. Beneath the rhetoric, the lifestyle the Alliance supported for women was one of constant hard work and low wages, if women were to be paid for their labor at all. These limitations, harsh though they seem, were realistic both in terms of the Alliance's major goals and in terms of available options in the South. As one northern observer testified, "There is yet no rapid development of opportunity for profitable labor for young white women in the South."[69]

There may be yet another reason for the contradictory meaning of equality that the Alliance proposed for women. Despite the support the Alliance gave to an expanded life style for women, Alliance leaders were affected by the circumstances of time, place, and class. Like other well-born Southerners, they had not rejected the traditional view of women as the source of morality and goodness. Because of their moral qualities, women had to participate in the Alliance, but it is doubtful whether North Carolina Alliance leaders would have supported enlarging women's sphere in any way that might threaten their own social or political position.[70]

As the *Progressive Farmer* firmly acknowledged, it had no sympathy with "that spirit which could encourage class feeling or class prejudice. . . . It is . . . *subversive of the social order*."[71] Leaders wanted changes, but not at the expense of social stability. Thus women might share in a kind of social and economic equality with men but they would hardly be offered political rights.

There are few indications that this strategy was unacceptable to the majority of Alliance women. Most letters from women indicate that the new parameters for female behavior were thankfully welcomed. Only occasionally can one discern an undercurrent of unrest, when women remarked on men's failure to be vigorous Alliance fighters or when they pointed out how much better a place the world would be had women, long ago, taken a more active part in shaping it.[72] Then, too, a few women dared to write on political matters, giving their own opinions and urging men to take notice.[73] At least one woman realized how far she had stepped out of her place. After mocking Alliance men who were "willing to wave Alliance principles and swallow the whole Democratic party," she observed, "I could say a good deal more on this line, but will stop, for fear some fool will ask: 'Are you a woman?' "[74]

The *Progressive Farmer* not surprisingly steered away from the explosive issue of women's participation in politics.[75] In two unusual references to the question of women's political rights, however, it is clear that the issue had come up in local meetings. At one county rally, the lecturer told the women, "He did not invite them to suffrage, though it was gaining rapidly in public favor and if they had the ballot they would drive out the liquor traffic of this country and other evils." In Almance County, the Alliance lecturer warned his female listeners, "Do not spend your time in longing for opportunities that will never come, but be contented in the sphere the Lord hath placed you in. If the Lord had intended you for a preacher or lawyer He would have given you a pair of pantaloons."[76]

But the desire to maintain the *status quo* did not automatically succeed. Though Alliance leaders delineated definite boundaries to the theoretical and actual position women might occupy in the world, the fact that suffrage was mentioned at all may indicate a turbid undercurrent of half conscious challenge to the leadership. The way the two Alliance speakers spoke of the suffrage issue suggests that some Alliance circles had discussed it. A few letters to the *Progressive Farmer* and other fragmentary evidence point to the same conclusion. On a visit to North Carolina in 1893, for example, a Mrs. Virginia Durant who had established a suffrage organization in South Carolina, reported she found "suffrage sentiment" of an unfocused kind in the state. Perhaps she sensed incipient interest among those women exposed to the Alliance.[77]

Yet there is not enough evidence to resolve the issue. If there were some support for the further expansion of women's activities through the Alliance, however, it never had the time to grow strong and vocal. For although the Alliance lingered on into the twentieth century, by the mid-1890s it had ceased to be an institution of importance. The failure of Alliance cooperative economic ventures, continued hard times, and a split within the organization over the support of the Populist party all contributed to a decline in membership. A changing political climate brought new issues, new questions to the fore; many of them would have conservative implications.[78] By the end of the decade, the shape of southern life would be set. After the Populist challenge, franchise for both poor whites and blacks would be limited and the question of political participation closed. Voting was a privilege, not a right. "Equal rights for all, special privileges for none" was a slogan best forgotten.[79]

Though the Alliance did not survive long enough to dislodge the traditional ideas of woman's sphere, its spirited attempt to work out a new place for her both in theory and practice shows greater complexity in late nineteenth-century attitudes and behavior with respect to sex roles than previously recognized, and suggests that there may have been other attempts to create new roles for women in the South. The Alliance alternative, it is true, fell short of offering women equality in all spheres of life. Primary Alliance goals and the nature of the leadership limited the meaning of equal rights for women. Yet to expect the Alliance to propose full equality for women would be to ignore the influence of both time and place and to expect consistency of thought and action when such consistency rarely exists.

NOTES

1. *Progressive Farmer*, June 23, April 21, 1891.

2. *Progressive Farmer*, December 22, 1891.

3. Nelson A. Dunning, ed., *The Farmer's Alliance History and Agricultural Digest* (Washington: The Alliance Publishing Co., 1891), pp. 309-310. See also *National Economist*, June 6, 1891.

4. For general information on the Alliance see John D. Hicks, *The Populist Revolt: A History of the Farmers' Alliance and the People's Party* (Minneapolis: University of Minnesota Press, 1931), pp. 105, 146; Theodore Saloutos, *Farmer Movements in the South: 1865-1933* (Berkeley: University of California Press, 1960), pp. 85, 123, 282-83; Hugh Talmage Lefler and Albert Ray Newsome, *The History of A Southern State: North Carolina* (Chapel Hill: University of North Carolina Press, 1963), p. 513; John M. Dobson, *Politics in the Gilded Age: A New Perspective on Reform* (New York: Praeger, 1972), pp. 172-75, 183-86.

5. Quoted in Anne Firor Scott, *The Southern Lady: From Pedestal to Politics, 1830-1930* (Chicago: University of Chicago Press, 1970), pp. 4-5, x-xi, and Anne Firor Scott, "Women's Perspective on the Patriarchy in the 1850s," *Journal of American History* 61 (June 1974): 54, note 4.

6. Other areas in the South were more radical in their views about women than North Carolina. See *National Economist*, May 4, May 25, September 1, 1889; March 1, June 14, July 12, July 26, October 25, 1890; June 6, July 25, November 12, 1892. See also Annie L. Diggs, "The Women in the Alliance Movement," *The Arena* 6 (June 1892): 163; Dunning, *Farmer's Alliance*, pp. 308-309; A. D. Mayo, "Southern Women in the Recent Educational Movement in the South," *Bureau of Education Circular of Information*, no. 1 (Washington, D.C.: G.P.O., 1892), pp. 54, 124; Josephine K. Henry, "The New Woman of the New South," *The Arena* 11 (February 1895): 353-62; Saloutos, *Farmer Movements*, chapters 5-7.

7. Scott, *Southern Lady*, chapters 4 and 5.

8. Robert Carroll McMath, Jr., "The Farmer's Alliance in the South: The Career of an Agrarian Institution" (Ph.D. dissertation, University of North Carolina at Chapel Hill, 1972), pp. 88-89; Robert Carroll McMath, Jr., "Agrarian Protest at the Forks of the Creek: Three Subordinate Farmers' Alliances in North Carolina," *The North Carolina Historical Review* 51 (January 1974): 47; Philip Roy Muller, "New South Populism: North Carolina, 1884-1900," (Ph.D. dissertation, University of North Carolina at Chapel Hill, 1971), pp. 33-37, 148-54.

9. McMath, "Farmers' Alliance," pp. 88-89.

10. Quoted in Hunter Dickinson Farish, *The Circuit Rider Dismounts: A Social History of Southern Methodism, 1865-1900* (Richmond: Dietz Press, 1938), pp. 327, 325-26; Scott, *Southern Lady,* pp. 137-41; Anne Firor Scott, "Women, Religion and Social Change in the South, 1830-1930, in *Religion and the Solid South*, ed., Samuel S. Hill, Jr. (Nashville: Abingdon Press, 1972), pp. 93-115; Marjorie Stratford Mendenhall, "Southern Women of a 'Lost Generation,'" *South Atlantic Quarterly* 33 (October 1937): 339-41; Emory Stevens Bucke, ed., *The History of American Methodism* (Nashville: Abingdon Press, 1964), vol. 2, pp. 291-92.

11. Daniel J. Whitener, *Prohibition in North Carolina, 1715-1935* (Chapel Hill: University of North Carolina Press, 1945), pp. 104-105; Scott, *Southern Lady*, pp. 139-52. Men were admitted as honorary members to the W. C. T. U. Another organization that included both women and men was the International Order of The King's Daughters and Sons, established in 1886. As in the W. C. T. U., men played little part in the organizational activities of the charitable group. Easdale Shaw, *The History of the North Carolina Branch of the International Order of The King's Daughters and Sons* (Raleigh: Capital Printing Co., 1929), pp. 3-4.

12. Solon Justus Buck, *The Granger Movement: A Study of Agricultural Organization and Its Political, Economic and Social Manifestations: 1870-1880* (Cambridge: Harvard University Press, 1913), pp. 41-43, 381; Saloutos, *Farmer Movements*, pp. 30-33, 42; Stuart Noblin, *The Grange in North Carolina 1929-1954: A Story of Agricultural Progress* (Greensboro: The North Carolina State Grange, 1954), pp. 2, 3.

13. Saloutos, *Farmer Movements*, pp. 32, 42; Roy V. Scott, *The Reluctant Farmer: The Rise of Agricultural Extension to 1914* (Urbana: University of Illinois Press, 1970), pp. 42-46; *National Economist*, March 14, 1889, June 7, 1890; *Progressive Farmer*, December 1, 1887, January 28, 1890. In 1889, the North Carolina State Alliance decided all political demands were to be sent to local Alliances for their approval. See "Official Circular No. 6," May 27, 1892, John R. Osborne Papers, Duke University, where Alliance secretaries are ordered to present the State Alliance resolution in favor of a secret ballot to their Sub-Alliances "for discussion and ratification."

14. In other parts of the country, the Alliance did radicalize some women and men. O. Gene Clanton, *Kansas Populists: Ideas and Men* (Lawrence: University of Kansas Press, 1969), *passim*. But for the story of the slow-moving suffrage campaign in North Carolina, see A. Elizabeth Taylor, "The Woman Suffrage Movement in North Carolina," *The North Carolina Historical Review* 38 (January and April 1961): 45-62, 173-89; Virginius Dabney, *Liberalism in the South* (Chapel Hill: University of North Carolina Press, 1932), chapter 19.

15. Although major Alliance manuscript collections and records were utilized for this study, the most useful source for it was the official newspaper of the North Carolina Alliance, the *Progressive Farmer*. The weekly paper served as one of the major means of communication between the state Alliance and local and county groups, publishing reports, orders, and instructions for Alliance members and, in turn, including letters and reports from the membership. Its paid circulation, the largest of any North Carolina newspaper of the time, had reached 18,240 by 1891. Actually, the paper reached more readers than this figure indicates since it was passed on and often read aloud at Alliance meetings. See McMath, "The Farmers' Alliance," pp. 200-204; Stuart Noblin, *Leonidas LaFayette Polk: Agrarian Crusader* (Chapel Hill: University of North Carolina Press, 1949), p. 210. Letters and articles for 1886, the year before the Alliance officially adopted the paper are also used since they do not differ in content or tone from what was published later. The *Progressive Farmer* is the best source for this study of Alliance thought and practice not only because of its central role in disseminating and reflecting Alliance views, but because local Alliance records are skimpy, leaders were often concerned with the "major" issues, and few of the women and men left any lasting remains at all aside from their letters to the paper. The *National Economist*, official journal of the Southern Alliance between 1889 and 1893,

also proved helpful as a supplement and contrast to the *Progressive Farmer*, as did other Alliance books and pamphlets.

16. *Progressive Farmer*, March 31, 1886; McMath, "Farmers' Alliance," pp. 82–83; John D. Hicks, "The Farmers' Alliance in North Carolina," *The North Carolina Historical Review* 2 (April 1925): 169. It is difficult precisely to estimate membership in the Southern Alliance or its North Carolina branch. The organization claimed a total membership of 362,970 in July 1888, just a year after recruiting began. Of these, 42,496 or 12 percent were women. By 1890, the Alliance reported it had 3,000,000 members, a figure that some believe was inflated (Saloutos, *Farmer Movements*, p. 77). In North Carolina, the Farmers' Alliance *Daybook*, North Carolina State Archives, Raleigh, notes that the number of local Alliances had reached 2,000 in February 1890. See also *Minutes* of the Farmers' State Alliance, 1887–1893, August 14, 1888, North Carolina State Archives, Raleigh; McMath, "Farmers' Alliance," p. 139.

17. *Minutes*, Farmers' State Alliance, October 4, 1887, August 16, 1888.

18. Reprinted in *Progressive Farmer*, December 8, 1887; my italics.

19. *Progressive Farmer*, July 9, 1889, February 25, 1890, June 23, 1891. *The Sub Alliance and What It Can Accomplish: Report of the Program Committee of the North Carolina Farmers State Alliance* (no date, North Carolina State Archives, Raleigh) emphatically makes the point that female membership is a necessity. See also *Progressive Farmer*, June 11, 1889; July 10, May 22, 1888; July 30, 1889; February 25, 1890; April 8, 1890; June 25, 1889.

20. *Progressive Farmer*, December 18, June 12, December 4, June 12, July 24, 1888, May 14, 1889.

21. Ibid.; also *Progressive Farmer*, March 13, 1888, March 5, 1889.

22. *Progressive Farmer*, May 22, 1888; October 7, 1890. See also July 30, August 6, 1889, September 23, October 7, 1890.

23. *Progressive Farmer*, February 18, 1890, April 17, 1888.

24. *Progressive Farmer*, December 16, March 25, 1890. See also July 24, 1888, June 11, August 6, October 1, 1889; February 11, September 23, 1890; September 22, December 22, 1890; *National Economist*, June 6, 1891. Of course, men were also encouraged to be more vigorous in their support of the Alliance.

25. *Progressive Farmer*, June 11, November 19, 1889.

26. For membership ratios, see the Bethany Alliance Minute Book, John R. Osborne Papers, Duke University, Jamestown Alliance Minute Book, Duke University, and the Mt. Sylvan Alliance Minute Book, North Carolina State Archives, Raleigh. See also the Account Book of Wake City Alliance, Roll Book of L. L. Polk, Sub Alliance No. 2254, Wake County, Polk Papers, in the Southern Historical Collection, University of North Carolina Library, Chapel Hill, and the *Progressive Farmer, passim*. The Wake County Alliance Account Book, which gives membership figures for about 45 local Alliances in that County, indicates that 36 percent of the County's membership in September 1890 were women. A year later this percentage of women had risen to 38 percent.

27. *Progressive Farmer*, February 11, 1890; August 7, May 15, December 11, 1888; August 13, 1889.

28. *Progressive Farmer*, March 10, 1891. There is, of course, the possibility that any woman writing to the newspaper was atypical.

29. *Progressive Farmer*, January 19, 1887; February 16, March 13, 1888.

30. *Progressive Farmer*, April 16, April 30, 1889; October 1, 1889.

31. *Progressive Farmer*, July 24, December 11, 1888; September 23, 1889; see also her letter of March 19, 1889, and February 25, 1890. Interestingly enough, Polk saved a letter from Usher that can be found in his papers. Evangeline Usher to L. L. Polk, December 25, 1889, Polk Papers, in the Southern Historical Collection, University of North Carolina Library, Chapel Hill.

32. A letter from a Kansas woman, Mrs. S. V. P. Johnson to L. L. Polk, April 1, 1892, Polk Papers, in the Southern Historical Collection, University of North Carolina Library, Chapel Hill discusses in detail the difficulties of throwing off female hesitancy, the opportunities she felt the Alliance offered her, and her lack of confidence.

33. Jamestown Alliance Minute Book. She subsequently left this office. "Organizers Report," November 13, 1889, Polk Papers, in the Southern Historical Collection, University of North Carolina Library, Chapel Hill, notes Mrs. J. M. E. Midget as treasurer. Unfortunately, inadequate records make it impossible to discover how many women held office. There are enough casual references to women in office, however, to suggest that female office holders were not unusual.

34. *National Farmers' Alliance and Industrial Union Ritual* (Washington, D.C.: National Economist Publishing Co., 1891). *Progressive Farmer*, May 28, October 1, 1889; September 23, October 7, 1890.

35. *Ritual; Progressive Farmer*, August 6, September 24, 1889. President Alexander stressed the crucial importance of the lecturer's position in characterizing it as "more important than any of the others" (*Minutes*, Farmers' State Alliance, August 13, 1889).

36. *Progressive Farmer*, September 11, 1888; March 31, December 22, 1891.

37. *Progressive Farmer*, June 23, 1891; July 17, October 23, 1888; April 21, 1891. There was clearly some confusion about counting women for representation. W. M. Koonts, secretary of the Davidson County Alliance, wrote to the Bethany Alliance secretary, "You are only entitled to delegates for the *male* members clear on the books." But the previous year Polk, in answer to a question on this very point, had announced that both sexes were to be counted (S. M. Koonts, to John R. Osborne, December 27, 1889, John R. Osborne papers, Duke University, *Progressive Farmer*, July 17, 1888.

38. *Progressive Farmer*, July 9, 1889.

39. "Circular No. 3, North Carolina Farmers' Alliance Business Agency Fund," November 22, 1890, Richard Street Papers, North Carolina State Archives, Raleigh; *Progressive Farmer*, August 13, 1889, July 24, 1888, September 8, 1887; S.B. Alexander to L. L. Polk, November 14, 1885, Polk Papers, Southern Historical Collection, University of North Carolina Library, Chapel Hill; *Progressive Farmer*, May 28, October 1, 1889; Circular, "Important to Sub-Alliances: Please Read at Next Meeting," L. Polk Denmark Collection, North Carolina State Archives, Raleigh.

40. Women reported on crop information and expressed interest in a wide variety of subjects. See *Progressive Farmer*, August 14, November 6, 1888; February 26, April 30, July 9, 1889 for examples.

41. *Progressive Farmer*, December 22, 1891.

42. *Progressive Farmer*, September 11, 1888.

43. *Progressive Farmer*, June 25, 1889. For a similar view, but from Texas, see *National Economist*, September 1, 1889. *The Sub-Alliance and What It Can Accomplish*, pp. 3, 4; *National Economist*, June 7, 1890; *Progressive Farmer*, June 11, 1889.

44. See Noblin, *Polk, passim*; Noblin, *The Grange*, p. 3; McMath, "Farmers' Alliance," pp. 84–88; Muller, "New South Populism," pp. 33–37, 148–54.

45. *Progressive Farmer*, July 9, 1889; March 31, 1891; June 25, 1889; November 12, 1888. The Pleasant Garden Alliance Minute Book, William D. Hardin Papers, Duke University, shows the importance members attributed to moral and orderly conduct at meetings. *Progressive Farmer*, March 24, 1891.

46. *Progressive Farmer*, June 11, 1889; June 23, 1891; for similar views from other southern women, see *National Economist*, July 12, July 26, 1889; October 25, 1890; July 25, 1891.

47. *Progressive Farmer*, July 24, 1888, my italics; *Progressive Farmer*, June 4, 1889.

48. *Progressive Farmer*, September 23, 1890; September 24, 1889; January 22, 1889; February 25, 1890.

49. *Progressive Farmer*, September 22, 1891; December 10, 1889, my italics.

50. These items are generally given without any editorial comments, as were the other items of general interest. For examples, see *Progressive Farmer*, May 18, July 21, October 29, November 17, 1886; February 2,. May 8, June 12, July 3, November 6, 1888; August 20, 1889.

51 *Progressive Farmer*, November 10, 1887.

52. *Progressive Farmer*, February 10, 1891; *Minutes*, Farmers' State Alliance, August 14, 1890; *Progressive Farmer*, January 20, 1891 and August 19, 1890; February 18, 1889; Virginia Terrell Lathrop, *Educate a Woman: Fifty Years of Life at the Woman's College of the University of North Carolina* (Chapel Hill: University of North Carolina Press, 1942), pp. xi–xiii.

53. *Progressive Farmer*, June 19, 1888, June 23, 1887, January 12, 1888; February 19, 1889. The objectives of the Normal and Industrial School for girls were "(1) to give young women such education as shall fit them to teach; (2) to give instruction in drawing, telegraphy, typewriting, stenography, and such other arts as may be suitable to their sex and conducive to their usefulness." (quoted in Lathrop, *Educate a Woman*, p. xii).

54. *Progressive Farmer*, June 25, 1889; December 16, 1890.

55. Scott, *Southern Lady*, pp. 4–8.

56. *Progressive Farmer*, March 10, June 30, 1886; April 21, 1887; February 26, June 11, 1889; July 7, February 10, 1886; February 2, 1887; November 20, 1888; September 4, 1888; March 24, 1886.

57. *National Economist*, May 4, 1889. See also W. Scott Morgan, *History of the Wheel and Alliance and the Impending Revolution* (Fort Scott: J. H. Rice & Sons, 1889), pp. 197–99; *Progressive Farmer*, June 2, 1886; September 4, 1888.

58. *Progressive Farmer*, January 19, 1887; June 30, 1886; June 5, 1888; February 28, 1888; December 8, 1886. For another southern view, see *National Economist*, June 14, 1890.

59. Dunning, *The Farmers' Alliance*, p. 257; Saloutos, *Farmer Movements*, p. 85.

60. *Progressive Farmer*, March 26, 1889.

61. *Progressive Farmer*, March 10, April 21, 1886. See *National Economist*, May 25, 1889, in which one of the Alabama Alliance's goals is to "adorn and beautify our homes, and render farm life more attractive."

62. *Progressive Farmer*, January 19, 1887; June 2, 1886; May 28, 1889; May 5, 1887. See also *The Sub-Alliance and What It Can Accomplish*, p. 6.

63. Richard H. Abbott, "The Agricultural Press Views the Yeoman: 1819-1859," *Agricultural History* 42 (January 1968): 35-48, suggests that historians have over-estimated the importance of the myth of the yeoman farmer. See also, Muller, "New South Populism," p. 23; Paul M. Gaston, *The New South Creed: A Study in Southern Mythmaking* (New York: Alfred A. Knopf, 1970), pp. 64-68, 107-108.

64. *National Economist*, April 5, 1889.

65. *Progressive Farmer*, January 12, 1888; May 12, July 7, October 13, 1886; September 15, 1887; November 20, 1888.

66. *Progressive Farmer*, November 10, 1887; *Minutes*, Farmers' State Alliance, August 11, 1892; *Progressive Farmer*, February 19, 1889.

67. *Progressive Farmer*, July 2, and April 21, 1887.

68. *Progressive Farmer*, March 2, 1887; December 8, 1886; July 28, 1887; December 3, 1889.

69. Mayo, "Southern Women," p. 170.

70. As Muller, "New South Populism," notes, p. 149, only men qualified as members of the elite.

71. *Progressive Farmer*, February 2, 1888. See Muller, "New South Populism," pp. 56-57, 177-85, for discussions of the social conservatism of Alliance leaders, pp. 104-105.

72. *Progressive Farmer*, September 22, 1891.

73. *Progressive Farmer*, June 3, September 16, December 23, 1890; July 7, December 15, 1891.

74. *Progressive Farmer*, November 4, 1890.

75. For suffrage discussions, see *National Economist*, March 1, July 12, October 18, October 25, 1890; March 5, November 12, December 24, 1892; January 21, February 18, March 11, 1893.

76. *Progressive Farmer*, September 15, 1891; December 3, 1889. There were occasionally other references to suffrage; see January 22, 1889, for example.

77. Quoted in Taylor, "Woman Suffrage," p. 46.

78. Saloutos, *Farmer Movements*, pp. 122-26; McMath, "Agrarian Protest," pp. 56-63.

79. Gerald Henderson Gaither, "Blacks and the Populist Revolt: Ballots and Bigotry in the New South (Ph.D. dissertation, University of Tennessee, 1972), pp. 151, 201-209; Gaston, *The New South*, pp. 38-39; J. Morgan Kousser, "The Shaping of Southern Politics: Suffrage Restriction and the Establishment of the One Party South, 1880-1910," (Ph.D. dissertation, Yale University, 1971), pp. 139-43; Guion Griffis Johnson, "The Ideology of White Supremacy, 1876-1910," in Fletcher Melvin Green, ed., *Essays in Southern History* (Chapel Hill: University of North Carolina Press, 1949), p. 133.

⇜ 13 ⇝

WORKING-CLASS WOMEN IN THE GILDED AGE: FACTORY, COMMUNITY, AND FAMILY LIFE AMONG COHOES, NEW YORK, COTTON WORKERS

DANIEL J. WALKOWITZ

In much of the recent work characterized as the "New Urban History," sociologists and historians have focused on the relationship between social mobility and behavior within the nineteenth-century working class.[1] To a large extent this scholarship has tried to grapple with the question often posed by the New Left: "Whatever happened to the revolution?" Two alternative arguments have generally been put forth concerning working-class oppression and united or individual efforts towards social amelioration. In the first case, the oppressed working class organized and struggled—even violently—to gain some affluence and security through the labor movement. In the second case, workers individually achieved some mobility, and consequently little or no united effort was made to win a social revolution.[2] Something, however, of both these views may be correct: workers lived and worked under oppressive conditions, but workers achieved some significant

This is an expanded version of a paper read at the annual meeting of the American Historical Association in Boston, December 30, 1970. Data for the paper were compiled from the United States manuscript census schedules for the city of Cohoes, Albany County, New York: Census Office, 8th Census of Population, 1860; Census Office, 8th Census of Manufactures 1860; Census Office, 10th Census of Population, 1880; and, 10th Census of Manufactures, 1880. Especially helpful also was Arthur Masten, *History of Cohoes, New York, From its Earliest Settlement to the Present Time* (Albany, 1877).

measure of social mobility. Furthermore, considerable violence did occur in labor struggles, but no social revolution occurred.

These seeming paradoxes hinge on the contrast between working-class mobility as it was perceived by the members of the working class themselves and the attempt to make some "objective" assessment of the parameters of that mobility. This essay intends to examine the ways in which the cultural experience of the predominantly immigrant working class might have distorted their view of their social conditions and impaired their ability to focus on the origins of their oppression. Consequently, working-class violence, rather than being directed at the manufacturer, was directed at the ranks of the unemployed ready to claim their jobs. In this way, the working class did not engage in aggressive violence to win a social revolution so much as it fought defensive struggles to protect its modest gains.

Working-class behavior is not merely a response to objective social conditions but is fundamentally shaped by the *perception* of those conditions. Historians have correctly emphasized the poverty and fragility of working-class economic and social existence during the Gilded Age. For instance, a New York State Assembly Committee investigating laboring conditions declared that the testimony of 17 randomly selected employees of the Harmony cotton mills in Cohoes, New York, "very clearly establishes . . . [that] very few families are enabled to save money, while a majority of them barely manage to make both ends meet at the close of the year."[3] But these harsh social realities must be viewed in the context of the expectations—the social dream—and the alternatives open to the working-class community. While violence marked the struggle to control the conditions of industrial life, the equation between poverty and violent social behavior is not precise. The history of the Cohoes cotton worker community is a case in point.

Cohoes, New York, is a small city located eight miles north of Albany on the west bank of the Hudson River at the confluence of that river and the Mohawk River. The cotton mills of Cohoes provided job opportunities in light industry for female laborers, opportunities that helped to create an unusual social community: the mills attracted a high percentage of working women and almost one quarter of the cotton worker families was headed by a woman. Confronted by the values of Puritan America, subjected to the social paternalism of the Harmony Corporation and sensitive to the demands of their own ethnic traditions, these women were immersed in a patriarchal culture. What kind of security and status, then, could Cohoes offer these women and their families? And, equally important, how did security and status function? The history of Cohoes' cotton workers demonstrates that the factory and the community helped both to sustain the mill operatives and to secure some social mobility for them. However, the small degree of status and security they attained did not liberate them from economic and social worries; rather, these modest gains restricted their field of vision and alienated them from their own social reality. It is within this context that we must view labor violence that erupted in Cohoes during the early 1880s.

During the 1870s, in the midst of a national economic storm that produced many financial failures, bitter strikes and violence, the Harmony Mills had offered relative industrial calm—with the not inconsiderable financial security and stability that this represented, especially for the immigrant working-class family. The depression compelled the Harmony Mills to close only one month during that entire decade; and while wages fell, the workers never struck. However, the tone and temper of Cohoes industrial life changed suddenly in 1880. In that year, and in 1882, extended strikes were fought. The strikes and lockouts began usually over further wage reductions, but at their core was a conflict over union recognition and power. These struggles culminated in violent mob scenes where angry women cotton workers and their children confronted imported Swedish "scab" workers and their police bodyguards.

Why was the Cohoes labor movement dormant during the 1870s, and why did disorder and violence erupt after 1880? If as E.P. Thompson suggests,[4] class is a relationship between people, a shared consciousness, what then were the dominant needs and values that influenced working-class behavior? What institutions were most valuable to them? And what effect did the industrial experience have on the position and attitudes of women in nineteenth-century Cohoes? Did it permit them some measure of independence; did it give them some role in community life; did they suffer a loss of status by having to leave the home to work? Central to our concern is the relationship between the factory, the community and the cotton worker and her family.

Since the Industrial Revolution, woman as worker has been seen as a contradiction in terms, as some sort of sin against nature. This attitude underlay the widely held belief that for women to work would, as Richard Ely wrote in 1893, mean "the scattering of the members of the family and the breakdown of the home. . . ."[5] Carroll D. Wright, writing in the Tenth United States Census in 1880 identified the factory as the culprit: "The factory system necessitates the employment of women and children to an injurious extent, and consequently its tendency is to destroy family life and ties and domestic habits, and ultimately the home."[6] Wright's implications were clear: since the factory system removed mother from the home, it destroyed the family; therefore, remove women from the factory and the family would be saved.

Although they have disagreed on the causes, many historians have accepted the view that the working-class family was disorganized. Oscar Handlin has suggested, for example, that the urban industrial slum, "the disorganizing pressure of the environment," and not the factory, weakened the family.[7] In this way, the city, the factory and the immigrant experience, each have received the blame for the disorganization of the working-class family.

The history of the Cohoes, New York, cotton worker community, suggests the need to reconsider the impact of the factory and the city on the lives of the cotton worker and her family. Quite early in its history Cohoes had one distinct feature: by 1860 it had become a company town. Although both wool and cotton mills gave the city its title as the Spindle City, the Harmony Mills Company dominated the city, and by 1864 monopolized the town's cotton industry. But the Harmony Company controlled much more than Cohoes' cotton industry. In association with the wool manufacturers, company officials constituted an interlocking directorate that held virtually every major political and financial post in the city throughout this period.[8] And lastly, the company maintained considerable economic influence over the working-class community. The company built and rented the more than 800 brick tenement houses and five boarding houses that spread over Harmony Hill, the city's first ward where the cotton workers all lived. In addition, Harmony Mill paternalism oversaw the workers' lives from the child's attendance at the Sabbath School to the family's weekly food purchased from the Company Store. Consequently, strike issues included not only wages and hours, but also such complaints as the credit system under which the cotton workers bought their food and the rent deducted from the family's pay.

The cotton mills, led by the Harmony Company, more than kept pace with the growth of the overwhelmingly working-class inhabitants of Cohoes, whose population numbered only 1,850 residents in 1840, 8,800 in 1860 and 19,416 in 1880. Consequently, while approximately one out of every four Cohosiers worked as a cotton hand in 1860, the ratio had risen to almost one in three in 1880. Most important, 60 percent of these cotton workers were women, and in 1860 more than half were immigrant Irish, while in 1880 four out of every five cotton workers were either first or second generation Irish or French-Canadian immigrants.

The experience of Cohoes suggests, however, that the factory and the working-class community play a more ambiguous part in the life of workers and their families than is traditionally thought. The cotton workers organized in response to this corporative omnipresence, and their activities touched all aspects of social life in the Harmony Hill community. The working class organized around the factory. Led by the skilled male spinners and female weavers, cotton workers organized unions which struck and won a wage advance in the Harmony Mills in 1858. During and immediately after the Civil War, the union activity waned, but the cotton workers did participate in the Short Hour Movement, the Workingman's Party and in the Workingman's Cooperative Store. Since working-class culture on Cohoes' Harmony Hill was also ethnic culture, mass strike rallies were addressed in both French and English to help unite the Irish and French Canadians around their common problems and needs. For certain issues involved social conditions which these people experienced together. So, to their laboring, political and ethnic activities must be added their role within the Harmony Hill community. For almost all cotton workers and their families lived on the Hill. There these workers had constructed a full and complex network of fraternal, religious and political clubs and institutions that offered them entertainment, security and some cultural nourishment. Usually several members of each family and occasionally whole families worked in the mills. These workers were not concerned only with narrow economic questions, but saw union activity as vital to the security of their family and community, security some had traveled as much as 3,000 miles to achieve. Thus, we have to view the working-class woman in the full context of her community. But before we can begin to understand behavior within the working-class community, we need to identify the workers and their families and see what changes took place in the Harmony Hill community between 1860 and 1880.

For Lucy Larcom[9] and her fellow workers in the 1830s, the cotton mill might have seemed like a boarding school for young ladies; but in Cohoes in 1857 the image of the factory and the factory girl had drastically changed. In reply to a series of letters from "A Factory Girl" in the local newspaper, a town teacher explains why she held these girls in contempt: "I *do* claim to be superior to the vulgar herd with which our factories are stocked, and I *do* consider them unfit to associate with me, or to move in the same society to which I belong. Such, too, is the sentiment of all 'Upper Tendom.' "[10] For the "elite" of Cohoes society who may well have spent their own girlhood in the mills, factory life had lost status. But it remains to be seen whether it had lost status for the large masses of Cohosiers who now worked in the mills.

The manuscript United States Census of Population for Cohoes in 1860 does not distinguish between cotton and wool workers,[11] but the average textile worker in the town was not a native American by birth.[12] Factory life had become predominantly an immigrant experience. More than one half the employees in 1860 were either Irish immigrants or their children, only one quarter were native Americans, while English and French-Canadian hands each constituted less than one tenth of the workers. The typical cotton worker had more than a single social and cultural identity: this worker was both Irish and female. Moreover, the Harmony Mills cotton hand was most likely an unskilled and unmarried woman between the ages of 15 and 25. Four out of every five Irish women between the ages of 15 and 19 worked in the mills in 1860 (Table 3).

Although fewer women and young men were employed among the other ethnic groups, they followed a common pattern: children entered the mills in their early teens and left increasingly in their twenties. Women then married and men found employment outside the mills. Only English males remained in the mills. Usually married and of middle-age they worked as skilled spinners, weavers, dressers and carders. The husbands of other cotton mill workers found other jobs. Americans established themselves in trades or business outside the factory, while the Irish and French-Canadians became unskilled day laborers on the Erie and Champlain canal network or on the factory maintenance staff.[13]

Thus, even before the Civil War, immigrant Irish families had found work for their children in the Harmony Mills. While the Irish clearly dominated the mills, they were joined by a sizable number of native American workers. Other ethnic groups also moved readily into the mills in numbers equal to their relative share of the city's population. Finally, the factory did not draw mothers away from their families. When they married and began raising families women did not work. Their children worked. The additional income especially from unmarried daughters could be put to good advantage. As Stephan Thernstrom discovered among the Newburyport Irish, income provided by the children enabled the family to gain some small measure of the security Ireland had not afforded—property. Similarly in the Cohoes working-class community of 1860, it was mainly a few families headed by Irish cotton workers who accumulated property: 11 percent of these Irishmen owned property in 1860, compared to only 5.9 percent of the Englishmen, 1.8 percent of the Americans and none of the French Canadians.

Cohoes differed from the early New England textile town. Not only did young immigrant Irishwomen dominate the Cohoes cotton mills in 1860, but also by this time weaving remained the only skilled trade in which women still readily found employment: slightly more than half

TABLE 1 Factory (Textile) Workers (FW) and Ethnicity, 1860, and Cotton Workers (CW) and Ethnicity, 1880

1860*	Male	Female	Total	Percent of Population	FW† (%)
All Textile Workers	778	1103	1881	28.3	100.0
(Ten and Over)	41.4%	58.6%			
Native American	197	293	490	22.8	26.0
	40.2%	59.8%			
Irish	377	617	994	31.6	52.8
	37.9%	62.1%			
English	101	74	175	30.0	9.3
	57.7%	42.3%			
Fr. Canadian	50	74	124	26.2	6.5
	40.3%	59.7%			
*1880**					
All Cotton Workers	1280	1964	3244	21.3	100.0
(Ten and Over)	39.5%	60.5%			
Native American	136	148	284	9.1	8.8
	47.9%	52.1%			
Irish	514	958	1472	26.8	45.4
	34.9%	66.1%			
English	151	111	262	19.2	8.1
	57.6%	42.4%			
Fr. Canadian	435	674	1109	24.6	34.2
	39.2%	60.8%			

*Manuscript Census of Population data.

†Percentages of ethnic groups do not total 100% because small numbers of Scottish and German workers are omitted.

the Cohoes weavers in 1860 were women. The number of skilled workers distinguished by the census leaves much to be desired. But while the English filled skilled positions in the mills considerably in excess of their relatively small numbers in the town, Irishmen and women held skilled as well as unskilled positions (Table 2). This evidence shows the Irishmen did more than dig ditches and lay railroad track and Irishwomen worked in other than domestic services.[14] While the relative concentration of female English weavers was six times that of the Irish, in Civil War Cohoes, Irishwomen held as many skilled posts as weavers as did workers of American and English extraction. Native Americans still held about one quarter of the jobs, but by 1860 Cohoes' cotton mills had become largely Irish "institutions."

Between 1860 and 1880, Cohoes' Harmony Mills expanded greatly. New hands were needed to operate her spinning mules and looms. But

TABLE 2 Percentage and Relative Concentration* of Skilled and Unskilled Cotton Workers in Ethnic Groups, 1860 and 1880

1860	Unskilled Males	Unskilled Females	Skilled Males	Skilled Females	Spinners (Males)	Dressers Carders (Males)
USA	25.3%	26.5%	2.4%	32.6%	16.6%	46.1%
	80	84	8	103	52	145
IRE	48.4%	55.9%	36.6%	32.6%	25.0%	7.6%
	107	114	81	67	55	17
ENG.	12.9%	6.7%	46.3%	32.6%	50.0%	30.7%
	130	86	468	418	505	310
FR. CAN	6.4%	6.7%	0.0%	0.0%	0.0%	7.6%
	86	97	0	0	0	103
N:	778	1103	41	46	12	13
1880						
USA	10.6%	7.5%	11.1%	2.0%	0.0%	9.0%
	53	37	58	10	0	44
IRE	40.2%	48.8%	44.4%	72.9%	60.0%	54.5%
	117	139	127	200	175	159
ENG	11.8%	5.7%	11.1%	14.5%	33.3%	22.7%
	122	70	117	177	342	233
FR. CAN	34.0%	34.3%	0.0%	4.1%	0.0%	4.5%
	121	114	0	14	0	16
N:	1280	1964	9	48	30	22

*Proportion among gainful workers in all occupations = 100.

how had the characteristics of the average cotton worker and her family changed during these decades? And again, in what ways did these changes reflect the absence of union activity and relative quiescence of the Cohoes' cotton worker then?

During the two decades in question, the most dramatic change in the mill labor force involved the native American and French-Canadian ethnic groups. Whereas one out of every four unskilled textile workers in Cohoes in 1860 had been of native American extraction, and less than one in ten had been of French Canadian origin, by 1880 the percentages were virtually reversed (Table 1). The Harmony Mills population had doubled, but the number of native American workers was almost one half its 1860 figure. The 124 French-Canadian textile workers counted in 1860, for instance, had increased by 1880 ninefold to 1,109 in the cotton mills alone; the number of native Americans dropped 42 percent during this period from 490 to 284. Almost half the workers were still Irish, but better than one in three unskilled cotton hands were of French-Canadian ancestry. Native American and English workers now comprised less than one in ten of each group. Even under the pressure represented by the influx of large numbers of

TABLE 3 Percentage of Cohoes Men and Women of an Age and Ethnic Group Employed as Cohoes Factory (Textile) Workers, 1860

Ethnicity	Age 10–14	15–19	20–29	30–39	40+
American	5.4%	57.2%	34.8%	13.3%	6.9%
Irish	14.7%	81.9%	47.7%	13.7%	6.2%
Females					
English	11.5%	50.8%	31.8%	21.8%	9.2%
French Canadian	11.1%	77.0%	26.0%	12.1%	0.0%
American	6.4%	50.3%	24.9%	13.7%	7.4%
Irish	16.4%	67.6%	29.4%	18.1%	8.8%
Males					
English	3.6%	40.5%	52.1%	44.3%	23.6%
French Canadian	7.8%	58.0%	27.1%	25.0%	10.7%

"cheap" employable French-Canadian immigrant laborers, the Irish found additional employment in the mills. Similarly, the French Canadians found Harmony Hill to be a hospitable textile center. It is true that almost all teenage members of the family had to work for subsistence wages and everyone in the community depended heavily on company paternalism. The Harmony Mills, however, offered these people steady employment, solid brick-construction housing and a steady though meagre income. The French Canadian had found a home and, with friends, had established a community.

Although each ethnic group had distinct work patterns that reflected its separate cultural background, there were similarities among them. Two out of every three cotton workers in 1880 were female. The Irish and French Canadians maintained this ratio, while in contrast, the number of American-born men and women was almost even, and the number of English male workers continued as in 1860 to exceed the number of females in the mills. Native Americans had left the mills: 22.8 percent of the native population age ten and over labored in the textile mills in 1860, but by 1880 the percentage had dropped to 9.1 percent. Otherwise, among each of the three large immigrant ethnic groups—the Irish, French Canadians and English—the percentage of cotton workers remained about one out of every four or five "adults." Finally, as in 1860, the English continued to show a work pattern different from the other groups: the average English cotton hand was more likely to be a married male who was older than was his Irish, French-Canadian or native-American counterpart.

Thus, the typical unskilled cotton hand in 1880 was probably an Irish or French-Canadian woman. Not only was she a young unmarried woman, but the reverse was equally true: if one was a young Irish or

French-Canadian girl growing up in Cohoes, the chance that she once worked, still worked or would shortly work in the Harmony Mills was most probable. It was also likely that she started work in the mills at an earlier age in 1880 than she would have in 1860, especially if she was of French-Canadian extraction (Table 4).

The percentage of workers under twenty remained at about 50 percent in both census years, but the percentage of children under 14 employed tripled between 1860 and 1880 from 7.4 percent of the entire work force in 1860 to 24.1 percent in 1880. And while the increase was more marked among boys than girls, both vastly increased; and children from all ethnic groups worked. The average age of the workers remained fairly constant, at approximately 20. However, the average age of the women *did* vary with ethnicity: for instance, two out of every three female French-Canadian cotton workers were *under* 20, while the same percentage of English were *over* 20. These differences suggest different attitudes toward the child's role in the family and the birth rate among the different ethnic groups. A higher number of English women did not work. The key here is that fewer English children worked. Married Englishwomen did not flock to the mills; rather, they appear to have remained at home and to have kept their daughters home or in school. This decision might have been motivated by a variety of concerns. The desire of the English to educate or protect their daughters, cultural animosities and the fear of loss of status through association with the mass of mostly Irish and French-Canadian cotton workers may serve as explanations. For the Irish and newly arrived French-Canadian family, there was much more to be gained than lost by working in the mills. Children increasingly could and had to work the exhausting 72 hour week under frequently dangerous conditions at absurdly low salaries; but their income enabled mother to stay home with the youngest children. For a young Irish woman or man the mills also offered the prospect of some occupational mobility.

TABLE 4 Percentage of Female Factory (Textile) Workers, 1860, and Cotton Workers, 1880, in Selected Ethnic Groups Who Are under Twenty Years Old

	Age	U.S.A.	Ire.	Eng.	Fr. Can.
1860	0–14	2.7%	7.1%	10.5%	6.4%
	15–19	36.5	48.5	38.2	63.5
	Under 20	39.2	55.6	48.7	69.9
1880	0–14	16.7	15.6	13.5	27.3
	15–19	27.5	32.5	24.3	38.7
	Under 20	44.2	48.1	37.8	66.0

Achievement therefore related to the fortunes of the family. Many Irish appeared to have become skilled weavers and spinners as early as 1860. And by 1880 the Irish filled a majority of the skilled cotton mill positions. Irishwomen comprised 72.9 percent of the female weavers, and their sons and husbands fared equally well. Skilled Irishmen constituted 60 percent of the spinners and 54.5 percent of the dressers, carders and loom harness makers in 1880.

Consequently, while young girls of English and native-American origin may no longer have found factory work desirable, Irish and French-Canadian families wanted and easily obtained employment for their teenage daughters and sons and unmarried young women. So how may we evaluate the economic gains and social mobility experienced by the average cotton worker and her family between 1860 and 1880? High costs and low incomes made steady employment essential, and the Harmony Mills provided it.[15] The hours were long, the work among the whirling machines dangerous, but the Irish family procured work for as many children, relatives and neighbors as might turn up, and gained skilled positions. A few even translated money earned into some small property holdings. In this way, the history of Cohoes' working-class Irish and French Canadians suggests the need to reconsider Thernstrom's conclusion that the nineteenth-century working class did not exhibit the economic and social mobility celebrated in the American success myth.[16]

Thernstrom measured mobility in industrial and economic terms: occupational mobility and change in real estate and personal estate holdings. But these useful indices are too narrow. To grasp more fully the significance and character of social mobility in America, historians need to consider the goals and aspirations of the worker and her family on the one hand, and the form and function of status and power on the other. We can then assess the impact of technology, economic pressures and attitudes toward women. Might it not, for example, be the full realization of a social dream for the cotton worker family, freshly arrived in the new country with memories of famine still vivid, to find ample and steady employment in the mills, to maintain the security of the tenement home and to develop community fellowship? Cohoes' Irish found full employment in the Harmony Mills, and during the 20 years they increasingly dominated the skilled crafts. Life was not easy. But unlike many other factories during the depression, the Harmony Mills continued to provide regular monthly pay checks throughout the 1870s. The Company also maintained some unusually fine living conditions: well constructed apartments, paved streets, even some garbage collection and manicured lawns with room for a small garden. Compared to what one saw and heard of English manufacturing districts, and relative to the sorry conditions that impelled them to leave either Ireland or Quebec, it is easy to understand their desire to defend this small but for them not insignificant measure of security. Moreover, a woman had only to look at her Irish neighbors on the other side of town who worked at more menial service jobs—housekeepers and washerwomen—to recognize her preferred status. As the local newspaper noted, Cohoes' textile mills' employment of women made it "next to impossibility [sic] to get competent, reliable girls, who are willing to do housework at any price." The women had "the feeling that as operatives in the mills they take a higher place in the social scale than is accorded them when they do housework. The fact is, they don't like the idea of being servants, or being treated as such, and unless compelled by lack of the employment of their choice they avoid it with scorn."[17] So by 1880, as far as she was concerned, the cotton worker had achieved some measure of both status and security.

But what impact did the factory have on the cotton worker family? Did the company town tear the family apart? While there were considerable economic strains on the Cohoes cotton worker families, it is significant that working-class marriage patterns strikingly resembled the nonfactory family Richard Sennett described in the middle-class community of Union Park in Chicago during this same period. Except for the important presence of child labor among the working class, there appear to be surprisingly few structural differences between these working-class and middle-class families.

Whatever differences did exist between the marriage patterns of Union Park middle-class families and Cohoes cotton worker families seem to have arisen as much from the various ethnic cultural experiences as from disparities in economic position. For example, the percentage of married workers in the Harmony Mills follows the same pattern found in middle-class Union Park.[18] The average cotton worker couple married only when the husband had reached his early thirties, most likely when he felt somewhat more financially secure (Table 5). For the vast majority of the couples, no wide age difference separated the wife and husband (Table 6). In more than 80 percent of the marriages, the wife was less than ten years younger than the husband. And only Englishwomen married younger men with any frequency. Among 15.6 percent of all couples the wife was older than her husband, but among English couples the percentage was 25.3 percent. Women usually left the mills when they were married to assume the role of wife, mother and homemaker. But what of the relative size of the working-class and middle-class family? Once the family formed, conventional wisdom has it that the working class multiplied while the middle class exercised some reproductive restraint. Quoting Sennett on Union

TABLE 5 Percentage Married Within an Age Group, 1880, Among Cohoes Cotton Workers and Chicago's Union Park

Age	Workers	Middle Class Union Park Chicago*	Age
15–19	0.8%	3.5%	15–19
20–29	16.2%	20.4%	20–24
		43.0%	25–29
30–39	61.8%	60.3%	30–34
		60.3%	35–39
40–49	74.2%	70.7%	40–44
		72.0%	45–49
50–59	89.3%		

Percentage Married Within an Age Group by Sex and Ethnicity, 1880, Among Cohoes Cotton Workers

	Age	Ire.	Fr. Can.	Ethnicity Eng.	USA	Total
Females	20–29	8.0%	11.5%	13.0%	25.0%	10.3%
	30–39	44.2%	31.4%	83.3%	17.6%	41.0%
Males	20–29	24.0%	32.3%	39.3%	52.5%	29.1%
	30–39	80.7%	78.5%	91.6%	76.9%	90.6%

*Sennett, *Families Against the City,* 105.

Park, "A host of sexual taboos and the prohibition of child labor in this middle-class community made abstinence not only possible but a compelling necessity."[19] Cohoes, however, suggests again that the most important variable in terms of family size was ethnicity. The ratio of children under ten to the adult population in each ethnic group in 1860 (the "survival rate") demonstrates that family planning crossed class lines: the English and Irish couples averaged 30 percent and the French Canadians almost 50 percent more children than the couples of native-American extraction.[20] Finally, intermarriage figures between persons of different ethnic background demonstrate further the impact of ethnic culture. Almost 40 percent of the working-class English and native Americans who married wed outside of their own ethnic group. In contrast, French Canadians and Irish almost never married outside their ethnic community.[21] The reasons for this low rate of intermarriage would seem to be twofold: the Catholic injunction against marriage outside the religion, and the exclusiveness of both *Canadien* and Irish nationalist culture. In sum, working-class marriage patterns shared

TABLE 6   Age Differences Between Husbands and Wifes of Cotton Worker Families, 1880

	Marriages (N)	Wife Older (%)	Husbands 0–9 yr. older (%)	Wife less than 5 yr. older Husbands; 0–9 yr. older (%)
Ir.	303	15.8	69.7	81.6
Fr. Can.	105	11.6	80.0	87.7
U.S.A.	50	12.0	72.0	80.0
Eng.	75	25.3	65.4	82.7
Other	18	16.7	66.6	77.7
Total	601	15.6	71.9	83.0

many of the same concerns for tradition, security and stability as the middle-class marriage. Each ethnic group, however, expressed these concerns in different forms of behavior.

Working-class households on Harmony Hill in 1880 again resembled those in Union Park. As in that middle-class community, working-class Cohosiers predominantly lived in nuclear families. By contemporary standards, however, cotton worker families experienced considerable disorganization. In a culture that celebrated a traditional two-parent family and the guiding role of the father, one-parent families, especially when headed by a woman, were considered incomplete and hence "disorganized." But it is crucial to examine the origins and dimensions of this "disorganization." Three quarters of the Irish and English male- or female-headed households were nuclear families (Table 7). These households, composed of first and second generation immigrants, were nuclear after the 3,000-mile migration. Households headed by native Americans or French Canadians had a percentage of families augmented by both relatives and boarders almost twice that of the other two groups. But it was the high percentage of one-parent families that distinguished the cotton worker family from other working-class and Chicago middle-class families.

One out of every four Cohoes cotton worker families on Harmony Hill was a "broken" family—a family headed by one parent. One-parent Irish families had raised the percentage considerably: 28.8 percent of the Irish families were "broken," compared to only about 14 percent of the families of other ethnic groups. Furthermore, almost all of these "broken" families were female-headed. Thus, almost one-quarter of the Harmony Hill families were headed by a "widow"—a woman whose husband had either left her or died. Family structure among the iron workers of Troy, New York, across the river, suggests that this extra-

TABLE 7 Cotton Worker Household and Family Structure in Cohoes, 1880—Ward One, Harmony Hill

Households	Ire.	Can.	USA	Eng.	Other	Total
Nuclear	323	125	35	63	18	564
	72.7%	67.9%	60.3%	77.8%	81.8%	71.5%
Extended	42	20	6	8	2	78
	9.5%	10.9%	10.3%	9.9%	9.1%	9.9%
Augmented	65	38	15	10	2	130
	14.6%	20.7%	25.9%	12.3%	9.1%	16.5%
Mixed Adult Group* (MAG) & Single	14	1	2	0	0	17
	3.2%	0.5%	3.5%	0.0%	0.0%	2.2%
	444	184	58	81	22	789
*Families**						
Whole	302	157	47	71	17	594
	68.0%	85.3%	81.0%	87.7%	77.3%	75.3%
"Broken"	128	26	9	10	5	178
	28.8%	14.1%	15.5%	12.3%	22.7%	22.6%
Percentage of "broken" families headed by a female	89.8%	88.5%	88.9%	80.0%	80.0%	88.8%
Average No. Cotton Wkers/ Family†	2.75	3.63	1.67	2.04	–	2.79

*The two boarding houses are not included.

**MAG & Singles not included.

†Based on first 250 families enumerated in Ward One.

ordinary rate of family "disorganization" reflected conditions peculiar to the textile industry more than it did the general character of working-class life. Sennett found 10.9 percent of the Union Park families to be without one parent. Troy's iron workers, both skilled and unskilled, lived in "broken" homes to about the same extent.[22]

Differences did occur, however, *between* ethnic groups. In Troy and Cohoes the rate of one-parent Irish families outdistanced the other groups. Combining skilled and unskilled Troy iron workers, approximately 15 percent of the Irish, 6 percent of the English, and 10 percent of the native Americans lived in "broken" homes. Thus working-class and middle-class household and family structure strongly resembled one another: both were nuclear families with two parents. Differences were ethnic and industrial—in our case, especially among the Irish and the cotton industry. Why were so many of the cotton worker families one-parent in structure? Widowed women may have taken their families to Cohoes where their children could find employment in the Harmony Mills' light industry. Almost all the widows were over 40 years old with teenage children, and the cotton mills made it possible for mother to stay home with the youngest children while the older children earned the family's income.

Thus Cohoes' cotton worker families were more "disorganized" than Troy's iron worker families. But the high incidence of nuclear families suggests a problem with the term "disorganization." The term exposes the historical prejudice against the one-parent family and ignores the tensions that may have wracked many two-parent families. In addition, the cotton mill may have provided employment and a financial refuge for the widowed family. Thus Sennett's categories may be inadequate to understand the pressures on the nineteenth-century working-class family. In fact almost nine of every ten non-Irish cotton worker families were two-parent headed. Sennett is correct, however, when he insightfully suggests the importance of the stable family in a changing and complex industrial city. According to Sennett, "The family was enshrined out of a sense of its peril in the city."[23] For Sennett, fear that the stability and security of the family would not be maintained became a "guiding force" in the history of the nineteenth-century American city. The middle class clung to the family as the one stable institution in the midst of a rapidly changing world. Although the pressures on the family were immense, the family did not constitute the workers' single supportive institution. On the contrary, the factory and community also structured their social life. Thus, the working class, and the Irish in particular, made an effort to get their daughters and sons unskilled and skilled jobs in the mills and membership in the network of city fraternal and religious associations.

Why, however, was the Irish family so distinctly scarred? In her pioneering study of working-class Irish in mid-nineteenth-century London, Lynn Lees showed the continued dominance of the nuclear family in the Irish household, noted the similarity between the Irish and the English working-class family and concluded that the Irish had not suffered any unusual breakdown.[24] Lees, however, failed to adequately distinguish between families headed by two parents and those in which only one parent was present. In this regard, we were not told whether or not the Irish in London differed from the English. The evidence in both Troy and Cohoes suggests that the Irish family structure—though not household structure—differed from that of the other major ethnic groups present in these two cities. Statistics compiled by the United States Immigration Commission in 1910 corroborate this evidence: the Commission *Reports* listed 12.4 percent of the immigrant cotton workers born in Ireland as widowed, compared to percentages of 5.9 percent of the French Canadians and 7.1 percent for the English.[25] Significantly, these *Reports* suggested that this difference largely disappeared within one generation. For the second generation immigrant family—the first born in the United States—the percentage of Irish widows more nearly approximates the percentages for the other groups: the percentages for the American-born Irish, English and Canadian respectively are 5.9 percent, 4.8 and 3.8 percent. So, though some of the distinctions between the family structure of the Irish and other ethnic groups appear at face value to have diminished with a generation of acclimation, acculturation and without a 3,000-mile migration, the situation of the immigrant Irish family remains somewhat unique. The fragile Irish family reflected the problems that worried the immigrant in industrial America, i.e., considerable prejudice, high mortality and the intense pressures of industrial capitalism. But the higher number of one-parent Irish families may also have reflected distinct ethnic values. We may offer some preliminary suggestions for this. Peasant, semifeudal Irish cultural traditions celebrated Irish community life and kinship and then were patriarchal. Beyond this, though, the Irish families' willingness to allow young girls out of the home and into the factory during adolescence suggests that the Irish husband subscribed to a set of traditional family values distinctly different from those held by men of Protestant English and American origins. Lastly, the Irish peasants' culture had unregimented preindustrial work rhythms. Adjustment required by factory life, with its highly disciplined work patterns, made the Irish industrial experience disruptive and alienating.[26] Although more work needs to be done in this area, we see the importance of ethnic culture in shaping working-class experience.

What then can we say about the cotton workers and their families, their community and their adjustment to factory life during the Gilded Age? The history of Patrick Dillon and his family illustrates the life of one representative cotton worker family in Cohoes.[27] Patrick Dillon probably left Ireland with his wife Ellen and their six children during the potato famine. They arrived in New York around 1850, and by 1860 had added three more children to their family. At the outbreak of the Civil War the now 11-member family lived in a four- or five-room company tenement at 4 Willow Street in the heart of the Harmony Hill Community. The family had managed to save approximately 300 dollars, but it had not been easy; four members of the family worked full time. Every morning the 45-year-old head of the household left home before six for work as a day laborer. The two eldest sons, Michael and William, age 20 and 18 respectively, answered the call of the Harmony Mills' bell, and walked down the street to the mill for a six-o'clock start, too. And Patrick, the 16-year-old son, joined his father as a day laborer. The father and son possibly worked on one of the canal or railroad labor gangs involved in area construction. They may well, however, have also worked for the Harmony Company—building new tenements or enlarging the newly acquired Ogden Mills. Mother, meanwhile, had her hands full at home. Matthew, age 14, and the 12-year-old twin girls did not yet work and only six-year-old James attended school. In addition, not only was Mrs. Dillon pregnant, but the baby, Bridget, who had only just celebrated her first birthday, and Margaret, age three, must have required considerable attention.

Meanwhile the men came home for lunch on their 40-minute noon break and then returned to the mills. At half past six the bell rang to close the mills for another day. For these 12 hours of work an adult common laborer received $0.75, while a skilled mule spinner received as much as $1.50. Women and especially children who labored in the mills received considerably less: an unskilled "back boy," for example, received $0.30 for his 12-hour day. When the monthly pay day arrived, the tenement house rent of between $5 and $7 was simply deducted from the salary.[28]

What happened to the Dillons during the next two decades? Did the family unit survive intact, did the family remain financially solvent and did they remain to establish themselves within the Cohoes' community? Patrick Dillon, Sr., had died late in the 1860s, but his widow continued to maintain the home on Willow Street. Family economics required that Mrs. Dillon open her small home to another family—John Kanal, his wife and two children—and to a boarder. Of her children, Patrick, Jr., died suddenly in 1870 at the age of 26 (shortly after his marriage) and James died September 15, 1874, at the age of 19—both from causes that are undisclosed. Michael and Matthew reappear periodically in the city directory as operatives in the Harmony Mills. Finally, while the older girls had most likely married, William, the second eldest son 20 years earlier, by 1880 had become head of the family, still located in their Willow Street tenement. The family once again sustained itself without boarders. William Dillon's first wife had died but he had remarried. His second wife, Elizabeth, was 15 years his junior, and was only nine years older than his son Patrick, now 15.[29] William now ran a "saloon" but his three youngest sisters, now 19, 20 and 22 years old, together with Patrick worked in the Harmony Mills, much as the family had for the past 20 years. Over the years the Dillon family had secured a place within the community for its remaining numbers but there had been many deaths in the family and most at relatively young ages.

Work in the mills had hardly changed. Wages for the now ten and a half to 11-hour day had dropped back from the high level maintained between 1867 and 1875 to their 1864 level: for a day's work a common laborer now received $1.12½, a skilled spinner $1.75, and a back boy $0.42. The Harmony Company continued throughout this period to play a central part in the life of the Dillon family: the Willow Street tenement remained a focus for the family, and the mills continuously employed the teenagers and adult Dillons and so helped to sustain the family. In fact, five of the seven members of the family in 1880 worked—four of them in the cotton mills. And, five years later the Dillons evidently felt secure enough to permit young Patrick, now 20 years old, to leave the mills and return to school. While living at home, Patrick Dillon—the grandson of his namesake who arrived in American almost 40 years earlier—had become a "student," with the considerable occupational and social mobility American society afforded the educated man. Though for many of his relatives, mobility had been only from the mills to the grave, young Patrick had achieved an avenue both he and the dominant American culture could celebrate.

Like other families in Cohoes, the lives of the Dillon family extended beyond the factory and was fuller and richer than this industrial portrait suggests. On Cohoes' Harmony Hill, the Irish and French-Canadian cotton workers like the Dillons had established by 1880 a diverse and full community replete with ethnic, religious, social and political club life. There were separate Irish and French Catholic churches; the Irish organized the Fenians and the Land League, and the French formed the St. Jean Baptiste Society; a French newspaper, *La Patrie Nouvelle,* was begun in the city in 1876; each ethnic group formed benevolent societies; and while Cohoes Irishmen usually voted Democratic, it was not uncommon for French Republican groups to form before the fall elections.

Carl Wittke has emphasized the competition between the Irish and the French Canadians. This competition supposedly stemmed from the French-Canadian support of the Republican Party and their reluctance to organize.[30] There were, however, certain fundamental similarities in their experience as well. Whether the workers were Irish like the Dillons, or French Canadian, both were Catholic, both came to America in search of economic advancement. Both worked side by side in the mills and were neighbors on the Hill. And together both struggled against the manufacturers to preserve their jobs and to control their work conditions. Work for the women and children in the Mills was indeed taxing. But through the depression, families like the Dillons gained some security and status. There were openings in skilled positions and some families had even become property holders. The factory did not provide "pin money," especially in the case of the large number of widowed families. The factory offered women jobs and made it possible to hold the female-headed family together and to maintain a nuclear family. In this way, rather than destroying the family, for the cotton workers, the Harmony Mill helped to sustain it.

In addition, urban Harmony Hill did not necessarily alienate the family. While living conditions left something to be desired, the close relationships and organization of the community also helped sustain the cotton worker family. When the workers went out on strike, the whole city was affected. Community pressure helped to maintain the strike: some businessmen offered discounts and contributions to striking workers; one woman, for instance, complained to the local press that the family above her had been persecuting her family for working, and that the day before she had been hit on the head by a bottle thrown by one of them; various tenants who wanted to work complained of "bulldozing"—intimidation from striking neighbors. But community pressures weakened the strikers, too; many striking weavers would return to Cohoes to work because they and their girls were homesick. As Miss O'Brien wrote from Forestdale, R.I., "This [Forestdale] is a very pretty place, but not like home [Cohoes]."[31]

So, why did violence erupt in Cohoes in the early 1880s? This seemingly optimistic portrait was deceptive. The family, community life and occupational mobility in the factory were enclaves against a threatening and insecure urban industrial life. Cohoes cotton workers lived in poverty. That they could endure three wage reductions during the 1873–1877 depression demonstrates how their depressed lives had lowered their expectations. At least the Harmony Company had not closed. In this way, they felt they had gained some success and had established a home. But they continued to live on the edge of fear—low pay, technological changes in the industry and an always ample supply of surplus labor threatened to destroy the small part of the social dream they had been able to realize. In addition, the increasing competition of industrial capitalism demanded increased production, lower costs and greater efficiency. To secure and maintain their profits the Harmony Mill manufacturers felt it necessary to reduce wages and control all aspects of mill life. Unions stood in their way. When the cotton workers' wages were reduced for the fourth time in seven years, they saw their minimal success, status and security threatened. Central to the struggle was control. At issue were not simply salaries, but the survival of the entire community. When, after six months of strikes, the manufacturers brought in disciplined, Protestant, Swedish immigrant families to replace the strikers, the women and children cotton workers responded directly and vigorously. They gathered at the mill entrances to "greet" the Swedes with stones. Police were brought in to protect the "scabs," and violence ensued. Although the strike was crushed, the working-class community then united and two months later elected the strike leader to the State Assembly.

In conclusion, the behavior of the Cohoes cotton worker community suggests the need to understand the place of ethnic traditions in the context of working-class achievements and perception. Furthermore, we need to reassess the impact of the community and factory on the working-class family. Many working-class cotton mill families *were* broken. Child labor was necessary. Industrial capitalism divested the worker of control over work conditions and threatened the family's quest for social and economic security. Both the factory and the urban experience intensified the problems of adjustment for preindustrial peoples, subjecting them to new and alienating work and to the strange heterogeneity of the city. But it must be remembered that by 1880 both the factory and the community had come to sustain the cotton worker family, and especially the female-headed household, in important ways. Together the mills and community provided another avenue to social fulfillment and achievement for the Irish and French Canadians of Harmony Hill. Thus, ironically, the argument that urged women to be taken out of the factory did much to rob many families of their one vital source of income. For in the textile mills at least, the women who worked not only needed the money desperately, but were usually unmarried adolescents, not mothers. Lastly, the Cohoes cotton worker community illustrates the *embourgeoisement* of the working class; the working class had begun to acquire certain middle-class attitudes about the values of status, security, property and the privatized nuclear family. Thus the final irony of cotton worker mobility: on the road to success, the pressures of industrial capitalism had reduced the cotton worker and her family to perceptual cripples, alienated from and by their own conditions. Cohoes' working class did engage in violence, but the violence was defensive—an attempt to protect their modest social position. There is perhaps no greater testimony to how difficult these people's lives had been, how fragile their economic existence remained and how fearfully they faced the future, than the energetic manner in which the women of Cohoes' Harmony Hill cotton worker community defended and celebrated the modicum of status and security they had achieved. Enmeshed in this difficult, fragile and fearful existence, the working-class dream had become a nightmare.

NOTES

1. See Richard Sennett and Stephan Thernstrom, eds., *Nineteenth-Century Cities: Essays in the New Urban History* (New Haven: 1969).

2. There are, of course, variations on each theme. The first view is widespread in the literature of the labor movement. (One popular refinement of this view emphasizes the considerable oppression of the working class and argues that this suffocated its radicalization.) The second view is expressed by Stephan Thernstrom in the conclusion to his article in a New Left anthology. Stephan Thernstrom, "Urbanization, Migration, and Social Mobility in Late Nineteenth-Century America" in *Towards a New Past: Dissenting Essays in American History,* Barton J. Bernstein, ed. (New York: 1968), 158–75.

3. New York State Bureau of Statistics of Labor, *2nd Annual Report, 1884* Legislative Assembly Document 26 (1882), "Establishing the Fact of the Existence of Child Labor in the State," (Albany: 1885), 112.

4. Edward P. Thompson, *The Making of the English Working Class* (New York: 1963), 9–10.

5. Richard Ely, "Introduction," in Helen S. Campbell, *Women Wage-Earners* (Boston: 1893), n.p.

6. Carroll D. Wright, quoted in Campbell, 90.

7. Oscar Handlin, *The Uprooted* (New York: 1951), 167.

8. The biography of William E. Thorn, the agent and treasurer of the Harmony Company from 1867 to 1910, well exemplifies the social, financial and political institutions that Cohoes textile manufacturers controlled. Thorn was both the son-in-law of Commodore Cornelius Vanderbilt and the nephew of Thomas Garner, the owner of the Harmony Mills. After coming to Cohoes in 1867, Thorn served on the Board of Directors of the Cohoes Company (the water power company), was secretary and treasurer of the Cohoes Gas Light Company (both controlled by the Garner interests), was director and first president of the Manufacturers' Bank of Cohoes and was instrumental in organizing the Cohoes Mechanics' Savings Bank. Finally Thorn was elected mayor of Cohoes in 1878 and 1880 and served as a Republican Presidential elector in 1892. See James H. Manning, *New York State Men* (Albany: 1920).

9. Lucy Larcom, *A New England Girlhood* (New edition, New York: 1961). See Edith Abbott, *Women in Industry: A Study in American Economic History* (New York, 1918), 114–16. Abbott writes of the Lowell, Massachusetts, mills that "all operatives were required to live in the company boarding houses . . . organized to resemble . . . big boarding schools." And, "Lowell had a high reputation for good order, morality, piety, and all that was dear to the old-fashioned New Englander's heart."

10. "A Factory Girl" to the editor, *Cohoes Cataract,* April 18, 1857.

11. One encounters various problems working with census data. In Cohoes all mill hands are simply enumerated in the 1860 Census of Population as "Works in Factory." The Census of Manufactures, however, suggests that the cotton and wool worker situation did not vary much. The statistics from the Census of Population for textile workers closely approximates the Census of Manufactures data for the Harmony and other cotton mills in the city. Therefore, one must interpolate from the former to the latter. In 1880 cotton workers and sections of town are distinguished.

12. Unless otherwise indicated the father's place of birth is used to define ethnicity. Thus a native American is someone whose father was born in the United States.

13. The percentage of Irish and French-Canadian men in their thirties and forties who worked as laborers doubled and tripled respectively the percentage of those in their twenties. The actual number also rose markedly. For example, 49 Irishmen or 17.2 percent of those Irishmen in their twenties were laborers, but among those in their forties the number rose to 95 or 54.3 percent.

14. See Oscar Handlin, *Boston's Immigrants, 1790–1865: A Study in Acculturation* (Cambridge, Mass.: 1941), 61–75; Thomas N. Brown, *Irish-American Nationalism: 1870–1890* (Phila.: 1966), 18–19; William V. Shannon, *The American Irish* (New York: 1963), 28, 95; Carl Wittke, *The Irish in America* (Baton Rouge, La.: 1956).

15. In 1880, between four and five people worked in the average Irish and French Canadian household respectively; in contrast, only two or three people worked in the average English and American cotton worker household.

16. Stephan Thernstrom, *Poverty and Progress: Social Mobility in a Nineteenth Century City* (Cambridge, Mass.: 1964), 146.

17. *Cohoes Daily News,* May 11, 1881.

18. See Richard Sennett, *Families Against the City: Middle-Class Homes of Industrial Chicago, 1872–1890* (Cambridge, Mass.: 1970), 105.

19. Sennett, *Families Against the City,* 118.

20. Comparative birth rates for Cohoes in 1860 can be approximated by comparing the ratio between the adult population of each ethnic group and the number of children in that group below a given age. (I have chosen age ten, but the figure can be adjusted easily.) Multiplied by one thousand, the birth rate (actually a "survival rate") per thousand population in 1860 reads:

Native Americans	209
English	263
Irish	277
French Canadians	308

21. Only six of 298 French Canadians in Cohoes Harmony Hill (2.0 percent) married someone from another ethnic group. Forty-two of 596 Irish men or women (7.0 percent) intermarried.

22. Thirteen and eight-tenths percent and 12.2 percent of Troy's skilled and unskilled iron workers respectively lived in one-parent households. See Daniel J. Walkowitz, "Statistics and the Writing of Working-class Culture: The iron workers of Troy, New York, 1860–1880," forthcoming, 1972, in a book edited by Herbert G. Gutman.

23. Sennett, *Families Against the City,* 116–19.

24. Lynn Lees, "Patterns of Lower-class Life: Irish Slum Communities in Nineteenth-Century London," in *Nineteenth-Century Cities,* 359–85.

25. U.S. Immigration Commission, *Reports of the Immigration Commission to Congress,* 1910, 10, part 3, *Immigrants in Industries,* 154–55.

26. Thompson, 436–44.

27. This biographical sketch is based upon the original federal manuscript census schedules. Most important also was the *Troy Directory, also Cohoes...,* 1867–1885; Masten, *History of Cohoes;* and, Census Office, 10th Census, 1880, *Reports,* 20, "Statistics of Wages...," 361–63.

28. Caroline F. Ware, *The Early New England Cotton Manufacture,* 244, presents a picture of the wage structure in New England cotton towns that is sensitive to the dependence of the employee on meagre wages, the ways in which salary was tied to their total social condition through rent and store pay and the reduced wages of women and children.

29. This 15-year age difference between William Dillon and his second wife reflected the usual pattern. When widowers remarried there is almost always a larger age gap with the second wife than with the first. This suggests something of the poor odds against a widow's remarrying. For an extended discussion of this problem, see William J. Goode, *World Revolution and Family Pattern* (New York: 1963), 318–19.

30. Carl Wittke, *We Who Built America* (New York: 1940), 315–28.

31. *Cohoes Daily News,* August 15, 1882.

ᔖ 14 ᔘ

LABOR'S TRUE WOMAN: DOMESTICITY AND EQUAL RIGHTS IN THE KNIGHTS OF LABOR

SUSAN LEVINE

The language of domesticity with its sentimental attachment to hearth and home and its strict and limiting definition of the feminine sphere was a dominant feature of nineteenth-century American culture. But we must look more closely at the rhetoric of domesticity in the context of nineteenth-century women's lives to see just what the words meant to particular groups of women, especially those outside the middle class. In what way did the cult of domesticity enter the lives of working-class women? Did it simply trickle down into their consciousness making their lives a never ending struggle for middle-class respectability? Or did working-class women take up the rhetoric of domesticity on their own terms? It seems likely that the language of home, family, and femininity had special meanings for working-class women, particularly those whose experiences were shaped by the labor and reform movements of the Gilded Age. For an earlier era Ellen DuBois has convincingly related the very emergence of the women's rights movement to the development of a distinct woman's sphere. Recent work on the Women's Christian Temperance Union (WCTU) likewise demonstrates that Frances Willard harnessed contemporary domestic imagery to build a broad-based reform movement that ultimately challenged the assumptions of the domestic ideology itself. Domesticity, family, and womanhood are therefore not static, universal, or unchanging categories. This paper argues that the experience of working-class women in the Gilded Age labor movement

From *The Journal of American History* 70, 1983. Reprinted by permission.

allowed them to use the language of domesticity to criticize the competitive capitalist system that they saw encroaching upon their traditional rights, dignity, and comforts. Ideologically as far removed from modern-day feminism as from the Victorian cult of ladyhood, these late-nineteenth century women discovered a source of cultural support and political opportunity in the labor movement of their day.[1]

The Noble and Holy Order of the Knights of Labor, in particular, provided a powerful alternative to the growing popular image of true womanhood. Begun in 1869 as a secret trade union, the Knights emerged ten years later as the largest and most encompassing labor organization of the century. During the mid-1880s the Knights extended trade unionism and a tradition of republican egalitarian reform to the growing mass of immigrant, unskilled industrial laborers. Their compelling vision juxtaposed a cooperative, moral industrial order against the ravages of the competitive wage system. This system, it seemed, had only recently enveloped vast new numbers of American women.[2]

By the 1880s wage work for many women was a fact of life. From 1870 to 1910 the proportion of women "engaged in gainful occupations" steadily increased from 14 percent to over 20 percent. This general figure, however, masked the specific importance of women's work for particular communities or industries. In some areas, few if any women worked outside their own homes, while elsewhere the figures far exceeded the national average. In 1880, for example, women constituted 26 percent of Philadelphia's workers, 34 percent of the workers in Fall River, Massachusetts, and 35 percent of the work force in Atlanta, Georgia. Women's work-force participation depended largely on local employment opportunities. Areas with major concentrations of textile mills or clothing industries employed the largest numbers of women. In Philadelphia women made up 46 percent of the city's textile industry while in Fall River the figure approached 50 percent. Except for two textile cities, Lowell and Lawrence, Massachusetts, Atlanta had the highest percentage of employed women because of exceptional numbers of domestic servants, most of whom probably were black. In contrast, centers of heavy industry such as Chicago or Pittsburgh held fewer opportunities for women's employment. In Chicago women constituted only 19 percent of the work force, 42 percent of them working as servants and another 34 percent in the clothing industry. Clearly the significance of women's work varied according to local circumstances. Nonetheless, in particular communities and specific industries, women's wage work had become a central feature of Gilded Age life.[3]

When the Knights of Labor reached out to a mass constituency during the late 1870s and early 1880s female factory workers readily responded. The Knights' open principles of organization, their commitment to unskilled as well as skilled workers, and their early pledge to support both equal pay for equal work and women's suffrage made their organization particularly appealing to women. In 1881 when the organization officially opened its doors to women, they found many already organized into local unions or fledgling Knights' assemblies.[4] By 1883 one labor editor observed, "In almost every city where the Knights of Labor have an organization the women who work for wages have banned together and formed an assembly."[5]

Between 1881 and 1890 women formed a small but significant force within the labor movement. In 1887 Leonora M. Barry, the Knights' general investigator for women's work, estimated that about 65,000 women belong to the order. This figure represented about 10 percent of the Knights' total membership, just under the percentage of women in the work force generally. During the 1880s the Knights chartered over four hundred local assemblies that included women. Of these, two-thirds were "ladies' locals," while the others were mixed assemblies of men and women. Women also chartered both mixed-trade and single-trade assemblies.[6] For example, all the operatives in the Helping Hand Assembly worked in the Haverhill, Massachusetts, shoe factories, while Leonora M. Barry's Amsterdam, New York, assembly included "all female employees in the city; carpet and hosiery operatives, dressmakers, milliners and music teachers." The Zaneville, Ohio, Ladies of Labor invited "all who labor at any useful employment and especially . . . the ranks of those who earn their own livelihood" to join their assembly.[7]

The scope of women's activities within the order and the widespread support for their endeavors, including strikes, hint at both the significance of women for the order and the importance of the movement for the women themselves. During the 1880s women in mills and factories across the country spontaneously engaged in collective action in strikes, boycotts, and informal protests. The Knights and the labor press enthusiastically reported on the progress of organization among women. Many of the Knights' major industrial actions, including the great Mohawk Valley knit-goods strike in 1885 and the nationwide carpet weavers' strike lasting from 1884 until 1886, were initiated and organized by young women workers.[8] One labor editor praised the work being done by women and said, "they are the best men in the Order."[9] Kansas Knight, Hugh Cameron, the "Bard of the Bluff" dedicated one of his poems to women in the movement:

Her faith and patient industry
as willing, useful worker,
Will strengthen earnest workingmen,
check doubter, growler, shirker,
Here she's her brother's equal quite,
she votes as well as he,
Therefore our Order's rightly blessed,
with much prosperity.[10]

Cooperative production combined with industrial action provided a strategic focus for women in the Knights movement. Because women had traditionally been excluded from trade unions, cooperatives represented an especially important form of protection from the wage system. By taking seriously the Knights' goal of cooperation, women hoped not only to avoid the exploitation of "wage slavery" but also to alleviate the terrible conditions under which so many worked.[11] The blacklisted garment workers who founded Chicago's "Our Girls Co-Op" in 1886 wrote, "We, as wage workers, have been in the workshop for years ... and not wishing to be dependent upon a wage system we have formed a cooperative society." Under the banner of "CO-OP OR STARVE," their venture maintained itself for about two years.[12] In Indianapolis the Martha Washington Assembly initiated a cooperative underwear factory to "give employment to unemployed women and also to give to the laborers the profit of their labor."[13] Women's cooperatives were widespread although generally short lived. Lady Knights in Danville, Massachusetts, for example formed a cooperative underwear factory and urged men in the order to "help the noble women on to success." Massachusetts shoe stitchers formed a cooperative stitching room, as did their sisters in Philadelphia and in Binghamton, New York. In addition, Knights in many neighborhoods and towns formed consumer cooperatives designed to help members keep down the cost of living.[14]

The Knights viewed women activists in a fundamentally different way than did the middle-class press of the day. Local newspapers often referred to trade union women as "amazons" and question their right to the title of "lady."[15] During the 1885 Yonkers, New York, carpet weavers' strike, the local editor cautioned the women "to go to Sunday School and be good girls" so that they might "yet get good husbands and become honored members of society."[16] These same women were highly honored members of the labor movement's "society." The labor press praised them for their "strength and dedication as unionists."

Popular editor John Swinton bestowed the women with silver medals of honor and extolled them for their "self-denial in behalf of womanhood."[17]

Through their range of activity in the Knights' movement, women were encouraged to become informed and "improving" citizens. Women's columns in the labor press combined news of women's strikes and industrial conditions with lessons in cooperation, suggestions for self-education, and advice on domestic concerns. The "Labor Book News Agency" printed in every local labor newspaper recommended reading for local assemblies and offered books at discount rates, particularly to locals desiring to establish libraries or book exchanges. For women, the lists and libraries represented a crucial link to the Knights' movement, which expected them to be as educated in the "questions of the day" as their brothers. Mrs. L. Wright warned her sister readers: "Don't let your natural love for 'nice things' prevent you from sparing a little for books and papers from which to study the social and labor questions. A great deal of reading may be enjoyed for a small sum by exchanging with each other and will be a preparation for you to assist in the work which needs the united efforts of all earnest, thoughtful men and women—the emancipation of the workers from the thraldom of wage slavery."[18]

The Knights' lists included books on the woman question, such as August Bebel's *Women and Socialism*, Margaret Fuller's *Woman in the Nineteenth Century*, and the feminist lectures of Lillie Devereux Blake. The lists also suggested readings in political economy, science, and literature. Among the recommended authors were Karl Marx, Ferdinand LaSalle, Charles Darwin, George Eliot, and Samuel Taylor Coleridge.[19] One woman encouraged the readers of *John Swinton's Paper* to take their education seriously. "Human misery must be cured and not diminished," she wrote, "but in order to cure, one must know the cause of the malady. Think then, think hard, working girl! To find out the *cause*, and when you have done so, new duties, new obligations towards yourself and society are in store for you."[20]

The order's literary overtures lessened the isolation of women in the home and brought them into contact with contemporary political and cultural trends. Domestic advice in the columns of the labor press served a similar end. Suggestions on "Food for Hard Workers" were interspersed with reminders that "to organize is justly one of women's rights."[21] Another note informed women: "Fourteen states now grant the right to women to vote in school board elections. Demand this in your state." Lists of famous women appeared side by side with articles on painless childbirth, comments on food adulteration, and advice on child-rearing.[22]

By addressing housewives as well as wage earners, the Knights opened important options for working-class women. "Ladies' locals" encompassed both housewives and employed women—sometimes together, sometimes in distinct assemblies—and possessed full rights and privileges within the organization. Defining productive toil by a moral rather than a strictly economic yardstick, the Knights thus offered women a role in the movement not directly dependent upon their status in the labor market. One female correspondent to *John Swinton's Paper* referred to "the housekeeping wives of laboring men" as a "class of people." The conditions of this class—long hours, subsistence standard of living—were no better, she claimed, than that of female wage earners.[23] Another woman informed Chicago's Knights, "The wives of nine out of ten laboring men work more hours per day than you do."[24] Still another noted, "Housework is not mere physical labor, it requires as much hard work to keep a house successfully as to build a house successfully."[25]

A similar logic led the Knights to extend their efforts to domestic servants. For the first time women's major arena of employment was taken seriously within the ranks of the labor movement. Domestic workers—housewives, servants and housekeepers—represented fully one-quarter of all women's local assemblies.[26] Cooks, parlor maids, laundresses, and housekeepers as well as housewives joined the organization. In 1883 Shawnee, Ohio, housekeepers formed the Good Will Assembly, and in 1886 their counterparts in Wabash, Indiana, chartered the Martha Washington Assembly. Cooks in Georgia, black parlor maids in Arkansas, the housekeepers in Illinois all became lady Knights.[27] The order's recognition of work within the home as a vital part of the community's total production led them, in short, to a dramatic upgrading of women's role in the labor movement.

The Knights did not, however, reject the home as the proper sphere of women's activities. In fact, they hoped that by reforming the wage system they would elevate and, in some sense, extend that sphere. Some women in the organization did offer tentative proposals for reform within the domestic sphere that echoed the values of cooperative production. "Only cooperation," wrote one woman, "offers escape for the overtired housekeeper." She assured her readers that "there are many ways in which housemothers can help one another that will serve to lighten daily toil and increase happiness." One cooperative scheme called simply for "neighborly neighbors to work together: Let their bread making all be done one day and let them take turns at baking it, even including the making of it. One doing it one week, the other the next. It entails upon the one extra work for that week, but she finds compensation in being exempt from this duty the succeeding two, three or four weeks."[28] Following this suggestion, Toledo's Joan of Arc Assembly formed a home-baked-goods cooperative, and New York tenement women pooled their incomes to buy supplies in bulk. The New York women reported a saving of nearly 50 percent in their weekly budgets. "Why should there be as now," they asked, "in one block of dwellings from thirty to forty cooks with attending waste of materials and physical strength?"[29] In their discussions of cooperative housekeeping the women reflected the influence of many contemporary feminist writers.[30] Although the actual number of cooperative housekeeping ventures is impossible to determine, the principle formed part of an overall critique of the wage system and the beginnings of a critique of domestic arrangement within it.

The local assembly, the basic unit of Knights' organization, provided a crucial test site for the order's principles as they applied to women. Women were encouraged to attend local assembly meetings and even to bring their children. A Michigan Knight commented that in his area "the sisters had enough sense to take their babies along with them, thereby not being detained from the meeting."[31] A woman addressing the readers of the *Journal of United Labor* told women their presence in the local assembly would "tone up the meetings," and another encouraged women to join the movement "because it is a striving for a noble equality, join to help protect the chastity of the home."[32] George Bennie, an Erie, Pennsylvania, Knight, worried that if his wife joined the movement, she would be forced to "sit amongst a lot of men from half past seven until eleven in the evening." But General Master Terence Powderly assured him, "She does not unsex herself by going where her father, brother or lover goes in the evening. If the assembly is a bad place for a woman to go it is a bad place for the man to go."[33]

As a self-conscious microcosm of the society it was trying to build, the order ultimately extended its educational claims to the entire family. During the mid-1880s a number of labor newspapers that had been carrying women's columns initiated children's pages as well. The columns included games and stories as well as practical advice. The *Detroit Labor Leaf* advised all boys and girls, "Recollect when you hear of a strike that somebody's father is trying to make things easier for you and always remember to be honorable to union men and women."[34] The Knights' moral code strongly condemned any abuse of home or family. Along with embezzlement and slander, the Knights counted desertion, drunkenness, or wife beating as grounds for expulsion.[35]

The ideal of hearth and home provided a powerful ideological symbol for the Knights' movement. The *Journal of United Labor* approvingly quoted orator and free thinker Robert Ingersoll, who observed: "The family is the heart of all society. If we have no family we can have no community, no township, no state, no nation. The greatest patriots are those who seek to preserve the family intact; the most unpatriotic are those who disintegrate the family by compelling women and children to toil for scanty subsistence."[36] The Knights shared Ingersoll's concern for the family. To save it, however, would require reshaping of both work and community life. In the process family life itself would be significantly altered by becoming a more integral part of the public trust.

The Knights' ideal of equal rights within the movement and within the working-class community generally operated in tenuous balance with their romantic and sentimental domestic vision. A movement poet, A.M. Sheridan, expressed the combination of expectations for women in a poem dedicated to the striking Philadelphia carpet weavers.

> *We ask not your pity, we charity scorn,*
> *We ask but the rights to which we were born.*
> *For the flag of freedom has waved o'er our land,*
> *We justice and equality claim and demand.*
>
> *Then strive for your rights, O, sisters dear,*
> *And ever remember in your own sphere,*
> *You may aid the cause of all mankind,*
> *And be the true women that God designed.*[37]

The Knights' commitment to equal rights inherently challenged conventional notions of domesticity and woman's sphere. Yet the Knights simultaneously asserted industrial reform and social renewal in the name of domestic idealism. The order held two seemingly contradictory goals. One was the elimination of wage work for women—in Powderly's words, "to secure homes for the women."[38] "We place women on the same plane as men," he wrote, "we would exalt them even higher."[39] At the same time the order asserted its aim "to protect and elevate the laboring class irrespective of sex."[40] "The rights of the sexes are co-equal," Powderly said, "their privileges should be the same as I can see no reason why women should not be entitled to giving to the world its products as well as men ... the working women of America do not ask for the cooperation of men ... as a favor but as a right to which they are entitled by reason of the nobility of toil no matter by whom performed."[41]

Two women nationally prominent in the Knights' movement symbolized in their own lives and in their organizational roles the twin aspects of labor's "true woman." Leonora M. Barry, a knit-goods worker from Amsterdam, New York, who was the only woman to hold national office in the order, and Elizabeth Rodgers, a Chicago housewife who headed the organization's largest district assembly, each in her own way reflected the tension between the Knights' commitment to equal rights and its domestic idealism.

Elizabeth Rodgers represented the Knights' domestic ideal when she charmed the 1886 Richmond convention with her two-week-old daughter, her tenth child. She recalled, "I was the first woman in Chicago to join the Knights. They offered us the chance, and I said to myself, 'There must be a first one, and so I'll go forward.'"[42] The wife of an iron molder and labor activist, Elizabeth Rodgers was involved with the labor movement from a young age. Irish-born like many of her fellow Knights, she came to North America at the age of six, settling with her mother in London, Ontario. During the 1850s she grew up amidst an active labor community where she met and married union organizer George Rodgers. The two of them were black-listed "all over this western country," and for six years the couple was constantly on the move. Wherever they settled, Elizabeth Rodgers kept boarders in order to supplement or at times to provide the family income. Simultaneous commitment to the labor movement and to her family required great sacrifice from Elizabeth Rodgers. Several times during her married life she was forced to "sell all her furniture" and uproot her home and children. Beginning her own labor career during the severe depression of the early 1870s when the family settled permanently in Chicago, she became the presiding officer of the "first women's union." In 1877 she was elected one of the few female delegates to the Illinois state trades assembly. Despite the burden of housework and a growing number of children, she continued her labor activities and in 1882 became master workman of Chicago's Local Assembly No. 1789. She represented that body in the city's fifty-thousand-member District Assembly No. 24. In 1885 Powderly chartered her as a regular organizer, and in 1886 when the district master workman died, Elizabeth Rodgers took over the office as the order's first female district master workman.[43]

Elizabeth Rodgers displayed an undeviating commitment to both family and political concerns. When her husband once suggested that she resign her labor activities to concentrate on the family, she reminded him, "Women should do anything they liked that was good and which they could do well."[44] Her decision to remain active was an easy one, she said. "Knowing my duty to my sex I thought it was an opportunity to show our brothers how false the theories are that women are not good for anything."[45] Indeed, her public commitments went beyond the labor movement. She was active in Irish affairs and temperance politics as well. Perhaps the most striking feature of her career was her consistent devotion to family life. She bore twelve children, raised ten, and kept house for a workingman. She said proudly, "I do, and always have done, all my own work." Even when pregnant or nursing, she presided over regular meetings of three hundred or more and spent many hours at Knights of Labor duties. Temperance leader Willard once visited Elizabeth Rodgers in her "small, but comfortable . . . house." Willard was greeted at the door by "a woman . . . with sleeves rolled up and babe in arms." Her "healthful" complexion and "honest gray" eyes combined with a "round, clear voice, gentle and womanly," showed Willard a person with "her mental faculties . . . thoroughly well in hand." This warm and motherly woman defied the stictures on nineteenth-century womanhood by becoming an important figure in the public world.[46]

If Elizabeth Rodgers represented the Knights' domestic ideal by combining hearth and home with a commitment to the labor movement, Barry represented the order's ideal wage-earning woman. Barry was forced into wage work by necessity but immediately joined the Knights in an effort to ameliorate her condition. Barry was also more typical of later female labor activists. During her four-year tenure as general investigator, she devoted her life entirely to the labor movement.

A "tall commanding figure" with a "warm voice," Barry came to the labor movement late in her life.[47] She was born in Ireland in 1849 and settled with her family in upstate New York during the 1850s. There she became a rural school teacher. In 1871 she married William E. Barry, an itinerant painter and musician. The couple moved from town to town for ten years, during which time they had three children. In 1881 Barry lost both her husband and her only daughter to one of the persistent fevers of the time. Left to support herself and two boys, she attempted to maintain domestic life by taking in sewing but found the strain too great on her eyes. Living in Amsterdam, New York, the center of the nation's knit-goods industry, Barry then sought employment in one of the local mills.[48]

Barry's labor career began soon after she entered the factory. Women in Amsterdam had organized the Victory Assembly in early 1883, and within a year it claimed fifteen hundred members. Barry joined the local in 1884 and soon became master workman. The next year she went as a delegate to the district assembly, and in 1886 she joined Elizabeth Rodgers at the Knights' Richmond General Assembly, where she was elected general investigator for women's work.[49] In her acceptance speech Barry promised to "investigate the condition of working women, instruct and educate them in the Order, and organize female locals when it will not conflict with more important work."[50] She set up subcommittees in every district assembly and encouraged all lady Knights to "acquire a thorough knowledge of the condition of working women within their jurisdiction." Barry assured the women that "any abuse existing which a female local would be delicate in mentioning to the General Executive Board may be communicated to the president of the Committee on Women's Work."[51]

During her four years as general investigator, Barry effectively lived without a home. She spent most of those years on the road visiting local assemblies in almost every part of the country. Barry traveled all but two weeks of the year, staying in hotels or with friendly Knights of Labor families. She entered one son in a Philadelphia convent school and placed the other with her sister-in-law. Like many women who turned to labor activism, Barry found that the movement demanded a difficult choice between more traditional feminine concerns and a significant role in public life.[52]

The problems of organizing women became apparent during Barry's first year in office. She was charged with "investigation" but had no legal authority to enter factories or to act on violations she saw. In her first annual report she said, "I was obliged to refrain from going through establishments where the owners were opposed to our Order lest some of our members be victimized."[53] She did accompany various state factory inspectors and gave the Knights' General Assembly detailed reports on the condition of working women throughout the country. Her reports always emphasized the need for organization and protection through the Knights. But recognizing the limits of this route, Barry also became a strong advocate of state and federal protective legislation.

Unable to act on her investigative experience, Barry turned increasingly toward organizing through the order's educational activities. She became one of the Knights' most popular lecturers at public meetings as well as at private Knights' gatherings. She was "to the women of the Order," wrote one labor editor, "what Terence V. Powderly is to the men."[54] Barry made it her duty to publicize and raise funds for women's activities, including educational sessions and cooperatives. In 1888 Barry delivered a Fourth of July speech to over three thousand people in Rockford, Illinois. In her honor the women's local there renamed the holiday "Foremothers' Day."[55]

Barry's annual reports outlined two major obstacles facing women in their organizing efforts. The first was the undeniable persistence of male hostility to women in their organization. The second was women's own reluctance to take advantage of the movement. "While the cause of [women's] lack of interest in organized labor is largely due to their own ignorance of the importance of this step," she said, "yet much blame can be attached to the neglect and indifference of their brother toilers . . . who seem to lose sight of one inportant fact, that organization can never do the work it was intended to do until every competitor in the labor market can be taught its principles."[56] Barry warned the Knights, "If those who pledged themselves to the support of [equal pay] do not resolve to trample under foot their selfish personal ambition and for a time turn their attention to the poor down-trodden white slave, as represented by the women wage-workers of this country, then let us here and now withdraw the twenty-second plank out of our platform, and no longer make a farce of one of the grandest principles of our Order."[57]

In Barry's thought, as in her life experience, changing realities had forced a revision, albeit a reluctant one, of the premises of women's sphere. Equal rights, with all it implied for active citizenship, offered the crucial safeguard for women in a changing world of wage labor and disrupted households. When she retired as general investigator in 1889, Barry told the assembled Knights, "If it were possible, I wish that it were not necessary for women to learn any trade but that of domestic duties, as I believe it was intended that man should be the bread-winner." "But," she added, "as that is impossible under present conditions, I believe women should have every opportunity to become proficient in whatever vocation they choose or find themselves best fitted for."[58] Her most difficult task, she reflected, had been acquainting woman "with her own values and the important part she plays in the industrial and social welfare of our nation, and encouraging her in demanding and securing that which is her just right."[59] Barry warned women who "foolishly imagin[e] that with marriage their connection with and interest in labor matters end" that they would only find the "struggle" harder when forced to "work for two instead of one."[60] Another woman echoed Barry's cautions when she told the lady Knights, "as you doubtlessly have already or will soon pledge yourself to the man you love for better or worse, let me tell you that if you do not join him in his efforts to organize labor it will be all 'worse' and no 'better.'"[61]

Elizabeth Rodgers and Barry continued to be active in reform politics even after the Knights' decline in the late 1880s. Elizabeth Rodgers retired from the labor movement to take up Catholic reform work and temperance. She helped to organize the Women's Catholic Order of Foresters, a fraternal, insurance society, and she served as its head until 1908.[62] Barry quit the labor movement in 1890 and married Obadiah Read Lake, a St. Louis printer. She too remained active in Catholic charity work, temperance, and suffrage politics. During the 1890s she campaigned for suffrage in Colorado, worked for the WCTU, and served as an officer of the Catholic Total Abstinence Union of America. She became a widely sought speaker on the Chautauqua circuit and a lecturer for the famous agency of Redpath and Slayton. Sometimes known as "Mother Lake," Barry continued her dedication to labor reform, one of her most popular speeches being "The Dignity of Labor."[63] For these women as for numerous others, the Knights served as a crucial political and philosophical training ground.

Many early-twentieth-century labor and reform activists testified to the importance of the Knights in their early education. Mary Harris Jones ("Mother Jones"), the "Miners' Angel" who remained active until her death in the 1930s, recalled her experience in the order's early days. "The Knights of Labor was the labor organization of those days," she wrote. "I used to spend my evenings at their meetings, listening to splendid speakers."[64] Mary Elizabeth Lease, the well-known Populist organizer, began her career as a Knights' lecturer and in 1887 became master workman of one of Kansas's largest local assemblies.[65] Leonora O'Reilly, who served on the board of the Women's Trade Union League, recalled joining the Knights in 1886. She had accompanied her mother to "labor and radical meetings" and then turned to the Knights.[66] Agnes Nestor, also active in the Women's Trade Union League, was too young to join the order, but her father, a staunch Knight of Labor, taught her trade union principles.[67] Alzina P. Stevens, a "bright and brainy little woman" who taught herself the printing trade and became the first woman member of Toledo's Typographical Union No. 63, also used her experience in the Knights to become an active labor reformer and trade union advocate throughout the Populist era and into the twentieth century. Stevens joined the order during the early 1880s. She became master workman of Toledo's Joan of Arc Assembly No. 2341 and in 1886 was elected district master workman of the city's populous District Assembly No. 72. In 1890 Stevens was nominated to succeed Barry as general investigator, but by that time the Knights' movement was seriously on the wane. Stevens declined the nomination and turned instead to factory reform and Populist politics. During the 1890s Stevens became assistant factory inspector for the state of Illinois. She later joined Jane Addams at Hull House and became active in social work and juvenile reform.[68] Although scant records of lady Knights survive, those that we have attest to the impact of the order among working-class women of the Gilded Age and to the important part the Knights played in contributing to a wide range of reform concerns.

The career of Mrs. E.C. Williams Patterson, a Knights' organizer, reveals the broad range of issues that informed the experiences of women in the order. Born in the "burnt-over" district near Seneca Falls, New York, Patterson was one of fourteen children. Her French mother and Scottish father held an uncharacteristic belief in education for their daughters and sent her to a country school and a ladies' academy. When her schooling was completed, Patterson moved, probably with her new husband, to California, where she lived on a farm for several years. As a member of the Universalist church, Patterson began her lecturing career with speeches on spiritualism. She soon broadened her range to include temperance, suffrage, and "all kindred topics." She considered herself a "progressive spiritualist" and joined the Theantropic Society, under whose auspices she embarked on the professional lecture circuit. In 1885 Patterson joined San Francisco's Local Assembly No. 2999 and turned her energies to the labor movement. Her first lecture topic for the Knights was "Woman's Position as Related to the Labor Movement." This topic was "enthusiastically received," and she became one of the order's most widely sought speakers. Patterson reportedly delivered 129 lectures in two months' time and "held as many assembly talks." One newspaper claimed in 1886, "She has done more than any other woman in Illinois to organize factory girls and thus pave the way for them to receive equal pay for equal work with men." Patterson always considered herself a "firm believer in evolution." She was committed to women's rights as much as to the labor question and felt the order allowed her to be "free and frank to avow her belief upon any topic, claiming for her sex equal rights to every opportunity and condemning fearlessly every wrong action which debars her sex of these rights."[69]

The Knights of Labor supported women's rights in a broad sense and forged what might be termed a labor feminism. Women in the Knights insisted upon full equality with men, including equal pay, equal rights within the organization, and equal respect for their productive work whether in the home or factory. The lady Knights did not challenge the notion of a domestic sphere for women. Rather, like many nineteenth-century feminists, they believed in a particularly feminine sensibility, one that upheld the values of hearth and home and that could at the same time infuse the public world with a more moral, humane, and cooperative character. The broad reform vision of the Knights provided women with a link between their industrial concerns and the issues addressed by the contemporary women's movements, most notably suffrage and temperance.[70]

The Knights vocally supported women's suffrage and frequently welcomed speakers to their local assemblies and lecture platforms. "If women cannot be entrusted with the vote," wrote one lady Knight, "they cannot be trusted to raise boys who are future law makers."[71] Despite their support for the principle of suffrage, the lady Knights differed with the suffrage movement in important ways. Women in the order, like many trade union activists later, tended to see industrial problems as their major concerns, while the suffrage movement increasingly focused on the vote as the key to women's equality. In 1886 the Knights' Committee on Women's Work said there was "more important work for women to do before they are prepared to vote in the affairs of the nation."[72] A few months later the *Journal of United Labor* told its readers, "The enfranchisement of women means much more than the ballot, and while this advance step is imperatively called for, there are other reforms that rest on woman herself and need not wait for legislation, indeed, legislation can do little toward their accomplishment." The *Journal* focused on the central problem for working women when it observed, "In the matter of the individual relation of woman to her employer, while the ballot would doubtless make her an important factor in social and political economics, it does not touch the more important business relations."[73]

The issue that most clearly united lady Knights with the Gilded Age women's movement was temperance. The order enthusiastically embraced the temperance cause. The notions of sobriety and respectability easily complemented their vision of domesticity in a cooperative industrial community. Leading women from the temperance movement, most notably Willard of the WCTU, often spoke at Knights' events drawing the links between industrial reform and the issue of drink. Willard praised the order's stand on equal pay and temperance and observed: "I see that the Knights of Labor are also the Knights of the new chivalry. Who knows but these men shall bring in the new republic?"[74] For Gilded Age women the temperance movement represented the most inclusive critique of social and domestic arrangements. The organization of the WCTU, in particular, afforded women of varying class and ethnic backgrounds an opportunity for independent political action. Infused with the energy and vision of Willard's "do everything" strategy, the WCTU became perhaps the most significant women's movement of the century.[75]

For working-class women the issue of temperance held special importance. In many working-class communities the saloon was the traditional meeting place for trade unions as well as for political organizations. Lady Knights, and a significant number of men, argued that using the saloon as a meeting place not only gave support to the monopolistic brewing interests but also encouraged division within the family by separating the husband from his wife and children. The Knights proposed their own local assemblies as alternatives to saloon culture and posed their movement as the alternative focus for working-class community life.[76] Willard noted the success of this effort, saying, "The Local Assembly in every town and village draws young men away from the saloon, its debates help to make them better citizens, and that the mighty Labor movement has, by outlawing the saloon socially, done more for temperance than we who devote our lives to its propaganda have been able to achieve in the same period."[77]

The Gilded Age labor movement sought to define a working-class culture in opposition to the prevailing currents of individualist morality and corporate power. Domestic harmony, a cooperative workplace, and an active democratic citizenry defined an alternative industrial society for both women and men. The domestic ideal fundamentally motivated industrial reform and collective action. Yet the organization of women and their experiences within the movement implicitly and sometimes explicitly challenged the notion of woman's sphere. The Knights' commitment to equal rights upheld women's role as citizens.

But the extension of the domestic sphere was only possible within the context of a movement open to all and committed to broad social reform—one that within its own ranks sought to create a new social order. With the decline of the Knights' movement after 1890, the contours of domesticity for working-class women changed. Where the Knights had attempted to include women's concerns as integral to building the cooperative movement, the trade union movement afterwards assigned those concerns, and the women who held them, to an essentially auxiliary role. Domesticity, in short, returned to the kitchen, to the impoverishment of both home and union hall.

NOTES

1. On "true womanhood" and woman's sphere in the nineteenth century, see Barbara Welter, "The Cult of True Womanhood: 1820-1860," *American Quarterly*, 18 (Summer 1966), 151-74; Nancy F. Cott, *The Bonds of Womanhood: "Woman's Sphere" in New England, 1780-1835* (New Haven, 1977), 160-206; Carroll Smith-Rosenberg, "The Female World of Love and Ritual: Relations between Women in Nineteenth-Century America," *Signs*, 1 (Autumn 1975), 1-29. On the relationship of this ideology to women's politics in the nineteenth century, see Ellen Carol DuBois, *Feminism and Suffrage: The Emergence of an Independent Women's Movement in America, 1848-1869* (Ithaca, 1978), 15-52; Barbara Leslie Epstein,

The Politics of Domesticity: Women, Evangelism, and Temperance in Nineteenth-Century America (Middletown, Conn., 1981); and Mari Jo Buhle, *Women and American Socialism 1870-1920* (Urbana, Ill., 1981), 49-103. For a recent discussion of domestic ideology and women's work, see Alice Kessler-Harris, *Out to Work: A History of Wage-Earning Women in the United States* (New York, 1982), 45-72.

2. On the Knights of Labor, see Norman J. Ware, *The Labor Movement in the United States, 1860-1895: A Study in Democracy* (New York, 1929); Gerald N. Grob, *Workers and Utopia: A Study of Ideological Conflict in the American Labor Movement, 1865-1900* (Chicago, 1969), 11-78; and Leon Fink, *Workingmen's Democracy: The Knights of Labor and American Politics* (Champaign, Ill., 1983).

3. U.S. Department of the Interior, Census Office, *Compendium of the Ninth Census of the United States* (Washington, 1872), 594; U.S. Bureau of the Census, *Thirteenth Census of the United States Taken in the Year 1910*, vol. IV: *Population, 1910: Occupation Statistics* (Washington, 1914), 37; U.S. Department of the Interior, Census Office, *Tenth Census of the United States: 1880*, vol. I: *Statistics of the Population* (Washington, 1883), 862, 870, 877, 894, 895.

4. For an extended discussion of women's role in the Knights of Labor, see Susan Beth Levine, "Their Own Sphere: Women's Work, the Knights of Labor and the Transformation of the Carpet Trade, 1870-1890" (Ph.D. diss., City University of New York, 1979), 179-238.

5. *New York Voice of the People*, Feb. 11, 1883. See also *John Swinton's Paper*, April 11, 1886.

6. Leonora M. Barry's estimate appeared in *Detroit Advance and Labor Leaf*, Dec. 11, 1888. Information on female membership in the Knights of Labor is based on Jonathan Garlock and N.C. Builder, "Knights of Labor Data Bank: Users' Manual and Index to Local Assemblies," manuscript, 1973 (in Susan Levine's possession); John B. Andrews and W.D.P. Bliss, *A History of Women in Trade Unions* (Washington, 1911), 118-22; and an exhaustive list of women's and mixed-sex assemblies compiled from labor newspapers. For estimates of the Knights' total membership, see Ware, *Labor Movement in the United States*, 66.

7. *Journal of United Labor*, July 16, 1889.

8. See Levine, "Their Own Sphere," 50-114, 179-238.

9. *John Swinton's Paper*, April 26, 1885.

10. *Richmond Whig*, Oct. 6, 1866.

11. On cooperation in the Knights, see Ware, *Labor Movement in the United States*, 320-33. See also Clare A. Horner, "The Knights of Labor and Producers' Cooperation," typescript, 1979 (in Levine's possession).

12. *Chicago Knights of Labor*, Dec. 11, 1886; *John Swinton's Paper*, Jan. 9, 1887.

13. Catherine F. Kirn and Mary E. Armstead to Terence B. Powderly, Jan. 20, 1887, microfilm reel 20, Terence V. Powderly Papers (Catholic University of America Library, Washington).

14. See, for example, *Haverhill Laborer*, April 30, 1886; *Boston Labor Leader*, Jan. 1, 1887; *Philadelphia Inquirer*, Sept. 3, 1884; announcement for the Fannie Allyn Cooperative Fair sponsored by Cincinnati, Ohio, Local Assembly No. 4457, Feb. 28, 1886, microfilm reel 14, Powderly Papers.

15. *John Swinton's Paper*, June 27, 1886.

16. *Yonkers Statesman*, May 29, 1885.

17. *John Swinton's Paper*, June 6, June 14, 1885.

18. *Ibid.*, Dec. 12, 1885.

19. See, for example, *Philadelphia Tocsin*, Aug. 7, 1886. This issue advertised the "Knights of Labor Library," including "32 separate works by 28 authors" to be sent at the reduced price of five dollars to Knights of Labor local assemblies and other libraries. The list included works by August Bebel, Charles Darwin, Henry George, John Swinton, Marie Howland, and others. In *John Swinton's Paper*, March 2, 1884, the editor advertised "Swinton's Storyteller." A subscription of one dollar per year would yield the reader the works of Mark Twain and Edgar Allan Poe among others. In *John Swinton's Paper*, July 5, 1885, Swinton announced the "New York Labor Lyceum and Circulating Library." Included among the books offered were Margaret Fuller's *Woman in the Nineteenth Century* (1845), Lillie Devereaux Blake's *Woman's Place Today* (1883), assorted works of fiction, dictionaires, and copies of the Constitution of the United States.

20. *John Swinton's Paper*, March 1, 1885.

21. *Ibid.*, Dec. 13, 1885.

22. See, for example, *Journal of United Labor*, May 22, Nov. 25, 1887.

23. *John Swinton's Paper*, Dec. 19, 1886.

24. *Chicago Knights of Labor*, Sept. 11, 1886; see also *Detroit Labor Leaf*, Oct. 7, 1885; and *Journal of United Labor*, Oct. 8, 1887.

25. *Journal of United Labor*, Jan. 10, 1885.

26. For a detailed description of women's local assemblies, see Levine, "Their Own Sphere," 179-238.

27. *Ibid.* In my estimate of women's membership in the order, housewives, boardinghouse keepers, housekeepers, servants, laundresses, cooks, and parlor maids were all considered domestic workers. The Knights organization of black women was practically unique in the history of the American labor movement.

28. *Journal of United Labor*, Dec. 24, 1887.

29. *Ibid.*, April 2, 1887.

30. See, for example, William Leach, *True Love and Perfect Union: The Feminist Reform of Sex and Society* (New York, 1980), 202-12. See also Dolores Hayden, "Redesigning the Domestic Workplace," *Chrysalis*, 1 (1977), 19-29; Dolores Hayden, "Two Utopian Feminists and Their Campaigns for Kitchenless Houses," *Signs*, 4 (Winter 1978), 274-90.

31. *Journal of United Labor*, July 25, 1885.

32. *Ibid.*, Oct. 15, 1887.

33. George Bennie to Powderly, Jan. 24, 1887, microfilm reel 20, Powderly Papers; Powderly to Bennie, Jan. 28, 1887, *ibid.*

34. *Detroit Labor Leaf*, Oct. 7, 1885.

35. See, for example, list of grounds for expulsion from the Order, 1882, microfilm reel 5, Powderly Papers.

36. *Journal of United Labor*, March 10, 1885.

37. *Ibid.*, Jan. 10, 1885.

38. Terence Powderly, "Report of the General Master Workman," Nov. 1888, p. 12, microfilm reel 67, Powderly Papers.

39. Powderly to Bennie, Jan. 28, 1887, microfilm reel 20, *ibid.*

40. *New York Voice of the People*, Feb. 11, 1883.

41. Powderly, "Report of the General Master Workman," 13.

42. Frances E. Willard, *Glimpses of Fifty Years: The Autobiography of an American Woman* (Chicago, 1889), 523.

43. This account of Elizabeth Rodgers's life is taken from a detailed biography that appeared in the *Detroit Labor Leaf*, Dec. 29, 1886.

44. Willard, *Glimpses of Fifty Years*, 523.

45. *Chicago Knights of Labor*, March 5, 1887.

46. Willard, *Glimpses of Fifty Years,* 522-23. For additional information on Rodgers, see Edward T. James, Janet Wilson James, and Paul S. Boyer, eds., *Notable American Women, 1607-1950: A Biographical Dictionary* (3 vols., Cambridge, Mass., 1971), III, 187-88; and *Journal of United Labor*, Jan. 8, 1886.

47. *Detroit Advance and Labor Leaf*, Dec. 15, 1888.

48. James, James, and Boyer, eds., *Notable American Women*, I, 101-02.

49. *Journal of United Labor*, July 16, 1889.

50. Mary Hanifin, "Report of the Committee on Women's Work," Oct. 1886, p. 287, microfilm reel 67, Powderly Papers.

51. *Ibid.*

52. James, James, and Boyer, eds., *Notable American Women*, I, 101-02. Barry chronicled her travels and work schedule in her annual reports to the Knights' General Assembly. See, for example, Leonora M. Barry, "Report of the General Investigator," in *Proceedings of the General Assembly of the Knights of Labor of America, Eleventh Regular Session, Held at Minneapolis, Minnesota, October 4 to 19, 1887* (n.p.,, 1887), 1581-88. On the strains between union activism and personal life for women, see Alice Kessler-Harris, "Organizing the Unorganizable: Three Jewish Women and Their Union," *Labor History*, 17 (Winter 1976), 5-23.

53. Barry, "Report of the General Investigator" (1887), 1581.

54. *Detroit Advance and Labor Leaf*, Dec. 15, 1888.

55. Leonora M. Barry, "Report of the General Investigator of Women's Work," Nov. 1888, p. 6, microfilm reel 67, Powderly Papers.

56. Barry, "Report of the General Investigator" (1887), 1587.

57. *Ibid.*, 1581. The twenty-second plank called for equal pay for equal work for both sexes.

58. Leonora M. Barry, "Report of the General Instructor and Director of Woman's Work," in *Proceedings of the Thirteenth Regular Session of the General Assembly Held at Atlanta, Ga., 1889* (n.p., n.d.), 1. It is generally assumed that Barry's speech reflected her own motivation for retiring from the Knights when she remarried in 1890. There is evidence, however, that Barry was forced to retire her position and disband the women's committee under financial pressure from Terence B. Powderly. In July 1888 wrote a "strictly confidential" letter to Charles Lichtman, saying: "I have this day received a positive yes . . . from our GMW to retire from the lecture field. Of course he knows best and I obey. When my voice is lifted for the K of L again it will be under different circumstances than now exist." Lichtman replied: "I sympathize with you fully in what I know are your feelings. It seems to me that economy may be practical in other directions without clipping the only work being done in behalf of women." Lichtman then added: "The time will come

when we can speak with perfect freedom and satisfy our consciences at the same time. But more of this when we meet." Although this communication reveals some underlying tension between Barry and Powderly, in public she remained a Powderly supporter. Leonora Barry to Charles Lichtman, July 1888, microfilm reel 27, Powderly Papers; Lichtman to Barry, July 1888, *ibid.*

59. Barry, "Report of the General investigator of Women's Work" (1888), 15.

60. Barry, "Report of the General Instructor and Director of Woman's Work," 2.

61. *Journal of United Labor*, Oct. 15, 1887.

62. James, James, and Boyer, eds., *Notable American Women*, III, 187-88.

63. *Ibid.*, I, 101-02.

64. Mary Harris Jones, *The Autobiography of Mother Jones*, ed. Mary Field Parton (Chicago, 1976), 14; James, James, and Boyer, eds., *Notable American Women*, II, 287. Mary Harris Jones claims to have sought refuge in the Knights of Labor hall during the 1871 Chicago fire and to have joined the order shortly after, even though women were not officially granted membership for another decade.

65. James, James, and Boyer, eds., *Notable American Women*, II, 380-81; Henry Perry to Powderly, Feb. 7, 1888, microfilm reel 25, Powderly Papers.

66. James, James, and Boyer, eds., *Notable American Women*, II, 651-53.

67. *Ibid.*, 616.

68. *Ibid.*, III, 368; see also *Detroit Labor Leaf*, Dec. 22, 1886.

69. The account of Mrs. E.C. Williams Patterson is based on a biographical sketch that appeared in the *Dubuque Industrial Leader*, Aug. 13, 1887, clipping, microfilm reel 24, Powderly Papers.

70. For a discussion of nineteenth-century feminism, see Leach, *True Love and Perfect Union*, 133-212; and Buhle, *Women and American Socialism*, 214-87.

71. *Journal of United Labor*, June 11, 1887.

72. Hanifin, "Report of the Committee on Women's Work," 288.

73. *Journal of United Labor*, Nov. 25, 1886. See also Gregory S. Kealey, *Toronto Workers Respond to Industrial Capitalism, 1867-1892* (Toronto, 1980), 188. For a critical discussion of feminism, suffrage, and the labor movement, see DuBois, *Feminism and Suffrage*, 105-61.

74. *Enterprise* (Kans.) *Anti-Monopolist*, April 28, 1887.

75. See, for example, Epstein, *Politics of Domesticity*, 89-146. For a discussion of the Knights' attitudes on temperance see David Brundage, "The Producing Classes and the Saloon: Denver in the 1880s," typescript, 1979 (in Levine's possession).

76. *Journal of United Labor*, Sept. 6, 1888.

77. Willard, *Glimpses of Fifty Years,* 525.

❧ 15 ❧

CREATING A FEMINIST ALLIANCE:
SISTERHOOD AND CLASS CONFLICT IN THE
NEW YORK WOMEN'S TRADE UNION
LEAGUE, 1903–1914

NANCY SCHROM DYE

A "small band of enthusiasts who believed that the nonindustrial person could be of service to her industrial sister in helping her find her way through the chaos of industry"[1] formed the Women's Trade Union League of New York late in 1903. The organization's members—a unique coalition of women workers and wealthy women disenchanted with conventional philanthropic and social reform activities—dedicated themselves to improving female laborers' working conditions and their status in the labor movement.

The women who formed the core of the New York Women's Trade Union League's membership were both trade unionists and feminists. As unionists, they worked to integrate women into the mainstream of the American labor movement. As feminists, they tried to make the early twentieth-century women's movement relevant to working women's concerns. To these ends, the WTUL attempted to serve as a link between women workers and the labor movement and as a focal point for unorganized women interested in unionism. The League agitated among unorganized women workers in an effort to educate women to the importance of unionization. In addition, the organization made concerted efforts to change male trade unionists' negative attitudes

From *Feminist Studies* 2 2/3 (1975). Reprinted by permission of the publisher, Feminist Studies, Inc., c/o Women's Studies Program, University of Maryland, College Park, MD 20742.

This paper was originally presented at the Conference on Class and Ethnicity in Women's History, SUNY—Binghamton, September 1974.

toward women. The WTUL offered assistance to municipal labor organizations and often aided local unions during strikes. League members also worked as organizers and helped establish several dozen unions of unskilled and semiskilled women workers in New York City. Most notably, the New York League played an important role in building the shirtwaist makers' union (International Ladies' Garment Workers' Union Local 25) and the white goods workers' union (International Ladies' Garment Workers' Union Local 62). In a later period of its history, particularly during the 1910s and 1920s, the New York League abandoned its singleminded emphasis on union organizing in order to concentrate most of its efforts on the campaigns for woman suffrage and women's protective labor legislation.[2]

Women came to the League from a variety of backgrounds. Many members were young working women who learned of the WTUL through their unions or through League publicity campaigns. Other members were wealthy women. Often college-educated, allies, as upper-class members were called, usually came to the League with experience in charity organizations, social reform societies, or social settlements. The New York City Consumers' League, the working girls' clubs, and the Workingwomen's Society were among the groups dedicated to improving the women's position in the labor force. Such organizations as the Municipal League and the Young Women's Christian Association occasionally conducted investigations of women's working and living conditions. Residents of the city's settlement houses frequently took an interest in working women and in the rapidly growing trade union movement.

The WTUL, however, differed from these organizations in two important respects. First, the League stressed the importance of actual union organizing efforts rather than such customary reform activities as social investigations. Many women joined the League precisely because they were discouraged by the slow approach of social reform organizations or by the elitism of traditional charity work. As Gertrude Barnum, a leading upper-class member in the League's early years, explained,

> I myself have graduated from the Settlement into the trade union. As I became more familiar with the conditions around me, I began to feel that while the Settlement was undoubtedly doing a great deal to make the lives of working people less grim and hard, the work was not fundamental. It introduced into their lives books and flowers and music, and it gave them a place to meet and see their friends or leave their babies when they went out to work, but it did not raise their wages or shorten their hours. It began to dawn on me, therefore, that it would be more practical to turn our energies toward raising wages and shortening hours.[3]

Second, the Women's Trade Union League stressed the importance of cross-class cooperation between upper-class and working-class women, and it was the only early twentieth-century women's organization that attempted to build such an egalitarian, cross-class alliance into its organizational structure. New York League membership was open to any individual who professed her allegiance to the American Federation of Labor and who indicated her willingness to work to unionize New York's women workers. League members stressed that allies as well as workers could be dedicated trade unionists and effective labor organizers.

Examining the day-to-day relationships WTUL members established among themselves and studying the alignments on policy issues makes it possible to observe the dynamics of cross-class cooperation and conflict. Two questions are of particular importance: How successful was the League in establishing an egalitarian, cross-class alliance? What were the sources of conflict within the organization that undermined the alliance?

The success of the New York Women's Trade Union League depended upon maintaining harmony and a sense of purpose within its coalition of workers and allies. The individuals who founded the League did not expect the coalition's stability to be a problem. The first WTUL members—most of whom were settlement residents and social reformers—apparently anticipated few difficulties in relating to one another: women could, they believed, surmount social and ethnic differences and unite on the basis of their common femininity. In this respect, the Women's Trade Union League was typical of the early twentieth-century women's movement. A conviction that women could relate to one another across class lines in the spirit of sisterhood and an emphasis on the special qualities that women shared linked many League members to the larger feminist movement. One of the major ideological strains in American feminism at the turn of the century was that women were different, emotionally and culturally, from men. Unlike mid-nineteenth-century feminists who had inveighed against the notion of a separate sphere for women and who had argued that both sexes shared a common humanity, early twentieth-century feminists, suffragists, and social reformers stressed the importance of sex differences. As WTUL member Rheta Childe Dorr expressed this philosophy,

> Women now form a new social group, separate, and to a degree homogeneous. Already they have evolved a group opinion and a group ideal. . . . Society will soon be compelled to make a serious survey of the opinions and the ideals of women. As far as these have found collective expressions, it is evident that they differ very radically from the accepted opinions and ideals of men. . . . It is inevitable that this should be so.[4]

League members, like other feminists in the early twentieth century, were often vague when they tried to define women's sisterhood. They usually used the term to convey the idea that social class was less important than gender for understanding a woman's status. The primary social dichotomy was a sex distinction rooted in differences between women and men, not classes. Women, some League members argued, shared distinct emotional qualities: they were more gentle and moral than men, more sensitive and responsive to human needs. League members also argued that women, regardless of class, could empathize with one another because they belonged to an oppressed social group.[5] This belief in sisterhood provided the ideological impetus for the League's formation and helps explain why many women joined the organization.

In certain basic respects, members found that their ideal of sisterhood could be realized. As an organization in which both upper-class and working-class women played important roles, and in which working-class and upper-class women could gain knowledge and confidence from one another, the WTUL remained viable for several decades. And it is possible to document many examples of close personal and working relationships within the League that transcended class lines.

In many other respects, however, WTUL members discovered that it was considerably easier to make verbal assertions of sisterhood than it was to put the ideal into practice. In contrast to the League's public affirmation of sorority, the organization's internal affairs were rarely harmonious. Beyond a basic commitment to unionizing women workers and to the American Federation of Labor, there was little upon which women in the League could agree. Far from behaving in sisterly fashion in their day-to-day affairs, members were often at odds with one another over League objectives and policies: Who should be allowed to join the organization? How much money and energy should the League commit to labor organization, to educational activities, to suffrage agitation? Should the League support protective legislation for women? Personal animosity and rancor accompanied debates over WTUL priorities. Leading members frequently submitted resignations or threatened to resign. They wrote angry letters denouncing one another or defending themselves against others' attacks. In short, WTUL women were a contentious lot. "If we have failed in what might be our greatest usefulness to the workers," Leonora O'Reilly, a leading working-class member, concluded wearily in 1914, "it is just in proportion as we have exhausted the energy of our friends and ourselves . . . in periodical tiffs and skermishes [sic]."[6]

What accounted for the high level of animosity within the New York WTUL? It is tempting to single out class conflict as a blanket explanation for the League's factionalism, policy disputes, and difficult personal relationships. Without doubt, class conflict was a reality within the League and a factor which undercut members' attempts to create an egalitarian alliance. Allies and workers came to the organization with different conceptions of social class, different attitudes toward work, and, of course, radically different social, educational, and cultural backgrounds. The ideal of sisterhood notwithstanding, difficulties and misunderstandings between women from different social backgrounds were inevitable. Yet class conflict in and of itself is not an adequate explanation for the controversies that regularly shook the organization. Indeed, social relationships among League members sometimes tended to mitigate serious class conflict. More important, there were no simple class alignments on League issues. Clearly, factors in addition to class conflict were involved.

The women who made up the organization were never able to reconcile their dedication to women as an oppressed minority within the work force and their commitment to the labor movement as a whole. Belief in sisterhood, League members discovered, was not always compatible with a belief in the importance of class solidarity. In other words, League members were unable to develop a satisfactory solution to the problem of women's dual exploitation: were women workers oppressed because they were workers or because they were female? In effect, many controversies which characterized the organization were in large part a reflection of the League's struggle to synthesize feminism and unionism—a struggle that had personal as well as ideological ramifications for many WTUL members.[7]

Although differences in members' social backgrounds did not fully account for the conflicts within the League, they were an important contributing factor. In the organization's first years, from late 1903 through 1906, allies much more readily than working women joined the WTUL. During these years, when the League rarely had more than fifty members, upper-class women dominated the organization numerically. Although the League's first president was a working woman—Margaret Daly, a United Garment Workers organizer—she remained in the League for only a short time. She was succeeded by Margaret Dreier, an ally. With the exception of Daly, all of the WTUL's officers and a small majority of the executive board members were allies. References can be found to young working women who joined the League between 1903 and 1907, but their role in the organization was shadowy—few remained in the League for more than a year or took a vocal role in the organization's activities.[8]

To stem the tide of young college graduates and settlement residents who flocked to the League in its first years, Gertrude Barnum, an ally herself, suggested that the WTUL impose a quota system to limit the number of upper-class members and that prospective allies be required to endorse the principle of the closed shop as a measure of their commitment to the labor movement. The League did not implement either of these policies. The organization's major provision to guard against upper-class domination was contained in its constitution, which stipulated that working women were to hold the majority of executive board positions. In addition, positions of leadership on organizing committees were sometimes reserved for working women. Such safeguards, however, could not change the fact that in the first years allies dominated the organization numerically. Although no one questioned the desirability of large numbers of working-class members, the first members had difficulty recruiting them.

By 1907, the League had established itself and had begun to come to the attention of young working women through its organizing efforts and its support of labor activities. More workers joined the organization. Three of the League's five officers in 1907 were working women, as was a clear majority of the executive board. After the 1909 general shirtwaist strike, in which the WTUL played a central role, workers joined the League in greater numbers than at any time previously. The year after the strike, eight of the ten executive board members were working women. For the rest of the period under consideration, the League's total membership was several hundred individuals, and working women and allies were numerically balanced.[9]

Numerical equality, however, could not solve the more serious problem of upper-class cultural domination—a problem that was always with the WTUL. Most upper-class members were seemingly unconscious of the genteel atmosphere that permeated the League, despite its unpretentious headquarters in dingy Lower East Side flats. Allies apparently saw nothing incongruous about juxtaposing "interpretive dance recitals" with shop meetings or inviting women to stop by for an afternoon of "drinking tea and discussing unionism." For working women, however, the League had an aristocratic air about it. For example, Rose Schneiderman, a young Jewish capmaker who had grown up on the Lower East Side, recalled her amazement when she attended her first League meeting and watched the participants dance the Virginia Reel. She, like many workers, had to overcome initial reluctance to join an organization with so many wealthy, college-educated women. On a personal level, the League's gentility undermined workers' self-confidence and made them feel awkward; on an ideological level, the organization's aristocratic character was foreign and often suspect. "Contact with the Lady does harm in the long run," Leonora O'Reilly declared at one point. "It gives the wrong standard."[10]

Ideally, allies were to extirpate from themselves any trace of the "Lady with something to give to her sisters."[11] They were to make way for working-class members to take the initiative in labor affairs. In short, they were to learn about trade unionism, labor organizing, and working conditions from the women who had first hand experience in such matters. Despite the emphasis on egalitarian relationships between working-class and upper-class members, however, allies often took the lead in day-to-day affairs. In part, this might be explained by the fact that upper-class members had the advantages of good education and financial independence. Then, too, allies were, on the average, ten years older than working-class members, and their age may have given them additional confidence and authority in the League.[12]

The patronizing attitudes of certain allies toward working-class members were evident in the WTUL's educational work. Upper-class members occasionally assumed the self-appointed task of discovering and developing natural leaders among New York City working women. As Mary Beard confided to another League member, "It has been my dream to develop young women to be a help in the awakening of their class. . . ."[13] One young WTUL organizer recorded in her monthly work report that her scheduled activities included writing lessons. ". . . Miss Scott felt that I ought to practice my writing as I would have to do a great deal of it in the future. I put in several days at nothing else but writing. I had two lessons with Mrs. Charles Beard."[14] Instead of working-class members teaching allies to relate to women workers and to be effective organizers, the opposite was sometimes the case.

Such attitudes did not go ignored or uncriticized. Leonora O'Reilly, a working woman with long experience as a garment trades organizer and labor speaker and one of the original members of the League, was particularly vocal in expressing her dislike of college women who came to the labor movement with lofty ideals of feminism and solidarity but who knew nothing about the realities of labor organizing or of working for a living. She was determined that working-class members should not be intimidated by upper-class women's academic and financial advantages. More specifically, she carried on a running campaign against Laura Elliot, an older ally who joined the League in 1910. Elliot offered League members courses in singing, elocution, and art history; she organized a League chorus and took groups of young women workers to museums and concerts. Most members apparently regarded Elliot as an eccentric but harmless individual and paid her little mind. O'Reilly, however, found her ideas pernicious enough to attack. She harangued Elliot about her condescending attempts to save working women by filling them with useless and pretentious notions of culture.

Elliot was hurt and confused by O'Reilly's anger, but insisted that she had a contribution to make to the League.

> You cannot push me out and you cannot make me afraid of any working girl sisters or render me self-conscious before them, I refuse to be afraid to take them to the Metropolitan Museum and teach them and help them. . . . I feel no fear in putting my side of the proposition up to any working girl. I'm not afraid to tell her that I have something to bring her and I'm never afraid that she will misunderstand or resent what I say. She needs my present help just as the whole race needs her uprising. . . .[15]

Workers sometimes asserted that allies, despite good intentions, did not know how to appeal to working women: their experiences and backgrounds were simply too different from those of their constituents to bridge the gap. Pauline Newman, a young Jewish immigrant who joined the League during the 1909 shirtwaist strike, summarized her impressions of upper-class limitations in both the League and the suffrage campaign in her remark: "the 'cultured' ladies may be very sincere . . . I don't doubt their sincereity [sic] but because their views are narrow and their knowledge of social conditions limited, they cannot do as well as some of us can."[16]

Workers' frustration with the well-intentioned but sometimes inept efforts of their affluent colleagues was understandable. Allies, as the executive board admitted at one point, could be "trying."[17] Upper-class members were sometimes responsible for decisions which exasperated working women. On at least one occasion, for example, League officers scheduled a conference on Yom Kippur, despite Jewish members' protestations. In the League's book of English lessons, *New World Lessons for Old World People,* references to Jewish working girls going to church slipped by uncorrected. Only one League ally is known to have studied Yiddish. Some allies held stereotypic conceptions of immigrant women. Jewish women were often described as "dark-eyed," "studious," and "revolutionary" in League literature. Italians were usually "docile," "fun-loving," "submissive," and "superstitious."[18]

Overt class and ethnic conflict in the WTUL reached its peak during a 1914 presidential contest between Rose Schneiderman and Melinda Scott. At the time of the election, Rose Schneiderman was the WTUL's East Side or Jewish organizer. Scott, a skilled hat trimmer and president of an independent union in her trade, served as the League's organizer of American-born women in the neckwear and dressmaking industries. Although both candidates were workers, they represented widely divergent approaches to the problems of organizing women. Schneiderman had always emphasized the importance of reaching immigrant women. Scott was pessimistic about organizing immigrants and advocated a policy of concentrating on American-born workers. Thus, the election involved League attitudes and policies toward immigrants. Nevertheless, support for the two candidates divided along class lines: allies backed Scott while working women voted for Schneiderman.[19] When Scott won by four votes, Pauline Newman related the details to Schneiderman.

> Your vote, with the exception of three or four was a real trade Union vote. On the other hand, the vote for Linda was purely a vote of the social workers. People who have not been near the League for four or five years, came to vote . . . but they could not get the girls from the Union to vote against you. . . . So you see, that nothing was left undone by them to line up a vote for Linda on the ground that you were a socialist, a Jewes [sic] and one interested in suffrage.[20]

Part of the difficulty underlying clashes between allies and workers lay in the fact that the two groups had different conceptions of class. The importance of class differences was usually far more obvious to working women than it was to allies. Upper-class members were not as acutely aware of class antagonism within the League and often downplayed the importance of social background. Many were confused by the emphasis workers placed on class differences. As Laura Elliot wrote to Leonora O'Reilly, "Before I was unconscious about this class and that class and this stupid difference and that stupid difference. Girls were just girls to me, and now you people are putting all sorts of ideas in my head and making me timid and self-conscious."[21]

Many allies believed that with great effort an individual could transcend her social background. Social class was flexible, not immutable. When allies talked of transcending their backgrounds, they were referring to young women from wealthy families who became self-sufficient and who could relate to workers without self-consciousness. Helen Marot, an ally who came from a comfortably affluent Philadelphia family regarded herself as a worker because she worked as the League's secretary and supported herself on her earnings. In similar fashion, Violet Pike, a young woman who joined the League shortly after her graduation from Vassar in 1907, was included among the working women on the executive board because she performed some clerical duties and joined the Bookkeepers, Stenographers, and Accountants' union.[22] Maud Younger, a wealthy ally, was listed on the League's masthead as a representative of the Waitresses' Union because she conducted an investigation of waitresses' working conditions and attended meetings of the union. In a sense, these women were workers, and they were proud of being self-supporting and resisted being categorized in their fathers' class.

Allies and workers came to the League with different conceptions of work as well. Upper-class members frequently had romanticized views of poverty and often regarded self-sufficiency as a kind of luxury. Work meant liberation from the confines of proper femininity. This attitude contributed to allies' naivete concerning the role of work in the lives of female wage-earners. Because they idealized work and equated it with economic and emotional self-sufficiency, many allies never seemed to come to terms with the fact that most women were not independent laborers but part of a family economic unit in which work did not usually connote independent economic status.[23] "Thank God working girls have a chance to be themselves because they earn their own wage and nobody owns them," one typical League article began. "I am pretty sure you are somebody, because you are self-support-ing."[24]

That the New York League was characterized by personal, cultural and political strife there can be no doubt. But Pauline Newman's 1914 depiction of an organization sharply divided between "social workers" and "trade unionists" was overdrawn and simplistic. Although it is easy to document class conflict, it is also possible to document experiences that mitigated serious, sustained conflict between upper-class and working-class women. There were cohesive factors as well as divisive tendencies that operated within the League and enabled the organization to function.

League members' personal relationships with one another constituted one factor that undercut the class conflict inherent in the organization. Sisterhood sometimes became a tangible reality in friendships. Mary Dreier, the WTUL's president from 1907 through 1914, and Leonora O'Reilly, for example, maintained a warm personal relationship for many years that survived numerous political and cultural differences between the two women. "You say you wonder whether I would always trust you," Dreier wrote O'Reilly after some disagreement over League policy.

> There doesn't even seem to be such a word as trust necessary between thee and me. . . . I might not always understand, as you might not always understand my activities—but as to doubting your integrity of soul, or the assurance on which trust is built seems as impossible to me as walking on a sunbeam into the heart of the sun for any of us humans—a strange and beautiful mixture of personal and impersonal is my relationship to you and I love you.[25]

Such relationships were not uncommon among League women. Some, like that of Dreier and O'Reilly, cut across class lines. Other close friendships were established between women of the same social background.

It is not surprising that such relationships were common among League members. For many WTUL women, the organization was a full-time commitment, a way of life. Then, too, that League members should form their closest emotional ties with other women is not surprising in light of the social conventions that governed personal relationships in the pre-Freudian culture of the early twentieth century. Emotional attachments between individuals of the same sex were not viewed with the same suspicion that would characterize a later period. Intense relationships involving open expressions of tenderness and affection were accepted as natural.[26]

Then, too, the longer a working woman spent in the League, the more she had in common with an upper-class ally. Both groups of women were atypical in early twentieth-century American society: the majority were single at ages when most women were married, they prided themselves on being independent and self-supporting, and they lived in a gynaecentric environment in which other women were their closest companions, their working colleagues, and their sources of emotional support. Only an extremely mechanistic definition of social class could fail to take into account that these women shared many important life experiences.

Finally, class conflict is not an adequate explanation for the disagreements within the organization for the simple reason that a member's social background did not dictate her stand on League policies. On every important issue, alignments were unclear. Suffrage, traditionally regarded as a middle-class issue, was an important priority for many working-class members. Rose Schneiderman and Pauline Newman were the first members to devote themselves full-time to the suffrage campaign. Ally Helen Marot, on the other hand, resisted the League's growing emphasis on the importance of the vote. Protective labor legislation, an issue that was enormously important in the League's history during the 1910s and 1920s, was a more controversial issue than woman suffrage, but on that issue as well, there were no clear class alignments. Allies and workers could be found on both sides of the question. In short, one cannot argue that only upper-class League members supported such reform issues as protective legislation while only workers supported labor policies such as direct organizing. There is no evidence to support the view that working women saw the League as a labor union and allies viewed it as a social reform organization. Rather, it is clear that factors in addition to class conflict played a role in creating the controversies in which League members found themselves embroiled.[27]

League members, regardless of class background, viewed the WTUL both as a women's organization and as a labor organization. Therein lay the second and perhaps more pervasive source of discord. Members had difficulty reconciling their commitment to organized labor with their commitment to the women's movement. They could not agree on a solution to the problem of women workers' dual exploitation or find a way to reconcile their belief in sisterhood with their belief in the importance of working-class solidarity. If a woman dedicated herself to working for protective legislation or for suffrage, or if she advocated separate unions for women workers, she opened herself to the charge of dividing the working class. If, on the other hand, she stayed away from women's issues entirely, she was guilty of ignoring women's special problems in the work force. This dilemma was real, and neither the League nor the individuals in it fully resolved the question.

Some members felt strongly that dedication to the labor movement should override the League's feminist leanings. In their analysis, the problems of women workers were bound up inextricably with the problems of working men. Class, not gender, was the main concern. True, they said, women suffered discrimination in the labor movement, but such opposition was not insurmountable.

Other members found their primary orientation in the women's movement. Or, as happened more frequently, women first attempted to cooperate with organized labor but ultimately despaired of changing male unionists' attitudes. They dismissed the labor movement and turned to suffrage and protective legislation as ways to ameliorate women workers' conditions.

Helen Marot, the League's secretary and an organizer, epitomized the first, or "woman as worker" position. Although she was never an industrial worker, she never wavered from her conviction that the WTUL should be committed to organized labor as a whole and not to women as a separate group. Female workers, she emphasized, should be regarded as inseparable from male workers: to think otherwise was to impede class solidarity and to denigrate women's capabilities. Throughout her career in the League and in her book, *American Labor Unions*, Marot vigorously opposed any policy that smacked of caste-consciousness. She emphasized that women were difficult to organize because they were unskilled, not because they were female. She was vehement in her opposition to the minimum wage for women, despite the fact that the measure eventually won the approval of many working-class League members. "If women need state protection on the ground that they do not organize as men do," she told the New York State Factory Investigating Commission, "then also do the mass of unskilled, unorganized men who do not appreciate or take advantage of organization.... The reasons for trade unionists to oppose State interference in wage rates apply to women workers as they do to men."[28]

Harriot Stanton Blatch, a well-known suffragist, represented the other strain of the WTUL. Unlike Marot, her interest in women workers derived from her involvement in the women's movement, not from a concern with industrial problems. Unions for women were only one aspect of a multifaceted campaign for women's rights, not an end in themselves. For Blatch, any class-related issue was secondary to the vote. In part, expedient 'considerations motivated her participation in the League: she realized that working women's support was vital for the ultimate success of the suffrage movement, and the League offered an avenue by which to reach them. On another level, however, Blatch was convinced that political equality was a prerequisite for any other improvement in women's status. Thus, only when women could vote would they command the respect of the labor movement. And only with suffrage would women develop the confidence to fight for industrial equality. "I have . . . [been] working with the Women's Trade Union League and attending meetings of the women's locals on the E. Side," Blatch wrote Gompers in 1905. "Those young women need stirring up, need independence, and some fight instilled into them. . . . I am understanding of all that the vote would mean to them—[it] would help in the trade union work as nothing else could."[29]

Marot and Blatch were sure of their objectives and their ideological orientation. The problem of women's dual status was not so clearcut for the majority of League members, however. For working-class members, the problems posed by the WTUL's dual commitment to its constituents as women and as workers were particularly vexing. For them, the matter was not only a theoretical and political issue, but frequently a personal dilemma as well. On the one hand, workers identified with their class background. They came to the League with experience in organizing activities and committed to trade unionism. On the other hand, they, like allies, were also feminists. Although workers were less likely than allies to come to the WTUL with an interest in the women's movement and probably became acquainted with the ideas of organized feminism and with the goals of the women's movement through their relationships with allies, most became dedicated feminists. More important, by comparing their experiences in the League with their role in trade unions they often came to a realization that the WTUL offered more opportunities for women to fill autonomous, responsible positions than male-dominated unions did.

Leonora O'Reilly's career in the League provides a good example of working-women's difficulties. Her commitment to the League was always ambivalent. She was faced with what she regarded as a conflict between her class background and her work in a women's organization. This was aggravated by her conviction that any serious attempt to organize working women had to be a feminist as well as a labor effort. An outspoken feminist herself, she recognized the need for an organization such as the League to devote special attention to women. She knew from her own experience as a United Garment Workers' organizer that women could count on little assistance from male unions. For all that, O'Reilly never came to terms with her ambivalence. She vacillated between urging the League to refrain from interfering in union affairs and stressing that the League should implement its policies in an autonomous fashion.[30] Sometimes she exalted the ability of women to fend for themselves in the work force, independent of men. ". . . I want to say to my sisters," she once declared to a WTUL convention, "for mercy's sake, let's be glad if the men don't help us!"[31] From her days in the Working-women's Society in the 1890s, O'Reilly had stressed the importance of sisterhood. She was a dedicated suffragist. On a number of occasions she spoke of "women's real togetherness." "Personally," she wrote, "I suffer torture dividing the woman's movement into the Industrial Group and all the other groups. Women real women anywhere and everywhere are what we must nourish and cherish."[32] Yet at other times, O'Reilly denounced the League as an elitist organization that had no real concern for working-class people. "The League ought to die," she reportedly said at one point, "the sooner the better."[33] Her two resignations from the WTUL in 1905 and in 1914 indicated her continual difficulty in resolving the conflict. In both instances she emphasized that working women would have to organize themselves.[34]

Rose Schneiderman and Pauline Newman exhibited similar confusion and ambivalence about their role as working women in the League. On the one hand, they identified with the East Side immigrant working-class community in which they had grown up. On the other, they regarded themselves as feminists devoted to women's issues. Like O'Reilly, they frequently experienced enough conflict to consider resigning from the League.[35]

Both women were torn between working in the WTUL and devoting themselves to the East Side Jewish labor movement. Yet to work as an organizer for a Jewish union or for the International Ladies' Garment Workers' Union, as both women discovered, was often an isolated and lonely experience. If the WTUL was not sufficiently interested in the progress of the working class and did not sufficiently appreciate efforts and ability to reach immigrant women, the Jewish labor organizations ignored the special problems of women altogether and discriminated against the small number of women organizers. Newman, after several years of unhappy and unrewarding work as an ILGWU organizer concluded that League work was more desirable than she had thought originally: ". . . remember Rose that no matter how much you are with the Jewish people, you are still more with the people of the League and that is a relieff. [*sic*]"[36] It seems clear, therefore, that working women could compare the League favorably with trade unions. The WTUL offered women organizers considerably more autonomy and responsibility than unions did. What was more, the League provided the company of women who shared interests and experiences.

Still, both Schneiderman and Newman continually had difficulty reconciling the women's movement and the labor movement. On occasion, both women denounced the superficial efforts of upper-class philanthropists and reformers to improve industrial conditions. Yet they were the first WTUL members to work as full-time suffrage agitators. Later in the League's history, both were vocal supporters of women's protective legislation, especially of minimum wage statutes and maternity insurance, despite the fact that the labor movement frowned upon the principle of protective legislation in general and upon the minimum wage in particular. During Rose Schneiderman's presidency in the 1920s, the WTUL devoted itself almost exclusively to legislative activity.

The difficulties these women faced were not uncommon. Most League members experienced some conflict between feminism and unionism. The organization's policies also reflected this: during the first decade of its history, from 1903 to 1914, the WTUL downplayed women's special problems in the work force and concentrated on integrating women into the labor movement as workers, while during a later period its members worked hard to implement demands that were relevant only to women workers: suffrage and protective legislation. For League members, explanations for the oppression of working women were always couched in "either/or" terms: either a working woman was exploited as a worker or she suffered as a woman. What the League needed was an analysis which came to terms with both facets of women workers' situation. That analysis was never realized, and the League remained split. Caught between two alternatives, League members frequently were unable to define their purpose or their role.

In short, the Women's Trade Union League had only limited success in achieving its goal of an egalitarian cross-class alliance. Although the League went further than any other women's organization in establishing sustained relations with working women and in grappling with the problems a feminist alliance posed, its internal affairs were rarely harmonious. In part, the organization's difficulties can be attributed to conflict between allies and workers. Both groups' problems in resolving the WTUL's dual commitment to the labor movement and the women's movement also contributed to the difficulties in establishing a cross-class alliance.

NOTES

1. Mary Dreier, "Expansion Through Agitation and Education," *Life and Labor* 11 (June 1921): 163.

2. The New York Women's Trade Union League was an autonomous organization, but it was closely related to a larger body, the National Women's Trade Union League of America. The same individuals founded both organizations in late 1903.

3. *Weekly Bulletin of the Clothing Trades,* March 24, 1905, p. 2.

4. Rheta Childe Dorr, *What Eight Million Women Want* (Boston: Small, Maynard, 1910), p. 5. For a good discussion of the changes in American feminist ideology from the mid-nineteenth century to the early twentieth century, see Aileen Kraditor, *The Ideas of the Woman Suffrage Movement* (New York: Columbia University Press, 1965), Chapter 3.

5. See, for example, Gertrude Barnum, "The Modern Society Woman," *Ladies' Garment Worker* 2 (June 1911): 8. "All women before the laws of the country . . . are of equal rank or lack of rank, being classed without exception with children, idiots, and criminals. With a common sense of injustice, feminine descendents of Patrick Henry, Tom Paine, and Thomas Jefferson ignore social differences and march shoulder to shoulder in campaigns to secure their 'inalienable rights'—to secure the fullest possible social equality with man."

6. Leonora O'Reilly to the executive board, Women's Trade Union League of New York, January 14, 1914, Women's Trade Union League of New York Papers, New York State Labor Library, New York, New York (hereafter cited as WTUL of NY papers).

7. Some historians who have dealt briefly with the Women's Trade Union League have interpreted the discord within the organization and the shift from labor organizing to legislative activity as the result of class conflict between allies, or social reformers, and working women. William Chafe argues, for example, "Reformers viewed the WTUL's primary function as educational, and believed that the interests of the workers could best be served by investigating industrial conditions, securing legislative action, and building public support for the principle of trade unionism. Female unionists, on the other hand, insisted that organizing women and strengthening existing unions represented the League's principal purpose. One group perceived the WTUL as primarily an instrument of social uplift, the other as an agency for labor organization" (Chafe, *The American Woman, Her Changing Social, Economic, and Political Roles, 1920–1970* (New York: Oxford University Press, 1972), p. 71.

8. The New York League was never a large organization. Although it counted several hundred women among its dues-paying members in the years after 1907, few of these individuals played active roles in the League's day-to-day work. In the years from 1903 to 1914, about twenty women formed a core group of members. These women made League policies, served as League officers, organizers, and speakers, and set League priorities. Although the composition of this core group changed from year to year, most of these members devoted most of their time to the organization for at least several years. Using the lists of executive board members, officers, and committee members that are extant, it is possible to reach some conclusions about the changing class composition of the core membership

group. This discussion on membership is based on a more complete treatment in my doctoral dissertation, "The Women's Trade Union League of New York, 1903–1920," (University of Wisconsin, Madison, Wisconsin, 1974).

9. Women's Trade Union League of New York, *Annual Reports,* 1909–1910 to 1913–1914. For a more detailed discussion of membership, see Dye, "The Women's Trade Union League of New York, 1903–1920."

10. Letter to Leonora O'Reilly, 1908. O'Reilly's statement is in the form of a note written to herself on the back of the letter. Leonora O'Reilly Papers, Schlesinger Library, Cambridge, Massachusetts (hereafter cited as Leonora O'Reilly Papers).

11. William English Walling to Leonora O'Reilly, December 1903 (O'Reilly's handwritten note on the back of the letter), Leonora O'Reilly Papers.

12. This statement is based on the compilation of biographical information on the WTUL's core membership group. For more complete information, see Dye, "The Women's Trade Union League of New York."

13. Mary Beard to Leonora O'Reilly, July 21, 1912, Leonora O'Reilly Papers.

14. Report of the Organizer, October, 1915, Women's Trade Union League of New York, WTUL of NY Papers.

15. Laura Elliot to Leonora O'Reilly, March 1911, Leonora O'Reilly Papers.

16. Pauline Newman to Rose Schneiderman, July 16, 1912, Rose Schneiderman Papers, Tamiment Institute, New York University, New York, N.Y. (hereafter cited as Rose Schneiderman Papers).

17. Minutes, Executive Board, Women's Trade Union League of New York, January 25, 1906, WTUL of NY Papers.

18. See, for example, Violet Pike, *New World Lessons for Old World People* (New York: Women's Trade Union League of New York, 1912); Gertrude Barnum, "A Story with a Moral," *Weekly Bulletin of the Clothing Trades,* November 20, 1908, p. 6; Gertrude Barnum, "At the Shirtwaist Factory, A Story," *Ladies' Garment Worker,* 1 (June 1910): 4.

19. Pauline Newman recorded her impressions of the election in three letters to Rose Schneiderman. Pauline Newman to Rose Schneiderman, 1914, Rose Schneiderman Papers.

20. Ibid.

21. Laura Elliot to Leonora O'Reilly, March 1911, Leonora O'Reilly Papers.

22. Women's Trade Union League of New York, *Annual Reports,* 1910–1911, 1911–1912. In both years, Pike is listed as a union representative for the Bookkeepers, Steographers, and Accountants' Union.

23. U. S. Congress, Senate, *Report on Condition of Woman and Child Wage-Earners in the United States,* "Wage-Earning Women in Stores and Factories," S. Doc. 645, 61st Cong., 2d sess., 1910, 5: 18, 25, 144. Senate investigators pointed out that New York City had the smallest proportion of self-supporting women of all the major cities investigated.

24. Gertrude Barnum, "Women Workers," *Weekly Bulletin of The Clothing Trades,* July 13, 1906, p. 8.

25. Mary Dreier to Leonora O'Reilly, June 19, 1908, Leonora O'Reilly Papers.

26. Other historical studies have touched upon this phenomenon. See, for example, Christopher Lasch and William Taylor, "Two Kindred Spirits," *New England Quarterly* 36 (Winter 1963): 23–41.

27. This interpretation differs from brief accounts of the WTUL in other works. See, for example, Kraditor, *Ideas of the Woman Suffrage Movement,* Chapter 6, and Chafe, *American Woman,* Chapter 3.

28. New York, Factory Investigating Commission, *Fourth Report of the New York State Factory Investigating Commission, 1915* 1: 774; Helen Marot, *American Labor Unions, By a Member* (New York: Henry Holt, 1915), Chapter 5.

29. Harriot Stanton Blatch to Samuel Gompers, December 30, 1905, American Federation of Labor Papers, Wisconsin State Historical Society, Madison, Wisconsin; Harriot Stanton Blatch, *Challenging Years* (New York: Putnam, 1940).

30. See, for example, Leonora O'Reilly to executive board, Women's Trade Union League of New York, January 14, 1914, WTUL of NY Papers.

31. National Women's Trade Union League, *Proceedings of the Second Biennial Convention, 1909,* p. 26.

32. Leonora O'Reilly to Mary Hay, December 29, 1917, Leonora O'Reilly Papers.

33. Leonora O'Reilly's statement was quoted in a letter from Pauline Newman to Rose Schneiderman, 1914, Rose Schneiderman Papers. Newman wrote, "Mrs. Robins wanted Nora [Leonora O'Reilly] to tell her what she thought of the candidats [sic] but Nora said that, 'this you will never know, but I can tell you what I think of the League, it ought to die, and the sooner the better."

34. Minutes, Special Meeting, Executive Board, Women's Trade Union League of New York, November 19, 1915, WTUL of NY Papers.

35. See, for example, Pauline Newman to Rose Schneiderman, February 22, 1912, Rose Schneiderman Papers.

36. Pauline Newman to Rose Schneiderman, April 17, 1911, Rose Schneiderman Papers.

～16 ～

LOVING COURTSHIP OR THE MARRIAGE MARKET? THE IDEAL AND ITS CRITICS, 1871–1911

SONDRA R. HERMAN

During the last three decades of the 19th century and the first of the 20th, American feminists generally avoided discussion of marital and sexual issues. Fearful of disgracing the movement with scandal, particularly after the Victoria Woodhull affair, and sharing the sexually repressive standards of the age, feminists increasingly turned their attention to the suffrage and the supposed benefits it would bring all of society.

Yet in these same decades of repression a debate *did* arise over marital questions. If the implications of sexuality could not be considered freely, neither could the subject of marriage be avoided. More women were going to work; more were seeking a college education, particularly after the 1890s. More couples were moving to the city. Defenders of traditional marriage promulgated the old ideals of female domesticity, submissiveness and sexual purity in the face of what they thought were some dangerous trends. Critics of American marriage found that male domination, female uselessness and economic

From the *American Quarterly* 25 (May 1973). Copyright © 1973, American Studies Association.

A revised version of this paper was presented at the meeting of the Organization of American Historians, April 1972.

The author would like to thank all of the following individuals for helpful comments on an earlier version of this paper, although none should be associated with the positions I have taken in it: Carl N. Degler, Samuel Haber, Anne Sherrill, Carroll Smith-Rosenberg, Warren I. Susman.

dependency had distorted marital happiness. Both groups concentrated their attention on the processes of courtship, for here they perceived the sex roles they were either defending or challenging took on most obvious forms.

The debate centered on a peculiar question: Was American courtship a process of practical love-seeking or was it a marriage market? Since we have no evidence that American marriages were in fact marriages of convenience in the 1880s and 1890s any more than earlier, the critics' charge of materialism seemed in large measure a weapon in the battle for female independence. The defense of courtship as love-seeking similarly was part of an effort to keep women at home in an age known for the restlessness of its females.

Both defenders and critics realized that their evaluation of marriage was connected to their evaluations of the whole social order. In general the defenders of traditional marriage implied that America offered opportunity enough for men and contentment for wives if they would only be supportive. The critics of American marriage, at least the five treated here—Edward Bellamy, Lester Frank Ward, Charlotte Perkins Gilman, Thorstein Veblen and Theodore Dreiser—attacked traditional marriage as part of the general injustice of American society. Thus while the debate could not before 1910 take direct sexual terms, it took a social form—defense of or attack upon the social status quo.

The defenders of the status quo were most often Protestant, especially evangelical clergy, conservative women, and doctors who wrote books offering the most traditional marital advice. The critics were intellectuals who refused to acknowledge religious authority and who openly challenged the ideal of fixed sex roles contained in such works. Only toward the end of the era, after 1910 or so, did an actual rebellion against repressive notions of sexuality begin. The debate in the eighties and nineties, while occasionally hinting at discontent with sexual standards, focused on proper sex roles and on woman's economic dependency.

Writers of the marriage manuals frequently asserted that indissoluble matrimony was the foundation of the whole social order. It was a "duty binding upon all well-equipped people who cannot show some larger obligation that is inconsistent with this."[1] It was, first, essential to complete the humanity of each man and woman. The two sexes, more different from one another than alike, needed to enter a human trinity—man, woman, child, so that each could become more truly a self. Celibacy not only meant incompletion, it threatened a sinful life, especially for men. Marriage was essential, secondly, to fulfill the social obligation of parenthood.[2] Sex was an expression of love but essential for reproduction only.

Like the Puritan clergy generations earlier, the marital advisers of the late 19th century assumed that it was completely within the partners' capabilities to make or unmake their marriage. Marital happiness became a duty to be performed not only for the husband and wife's own benefit, but for the sake of the children and society.

Critics of American marriage, on the other hand, believed that marital happiness was deeply influenced by social conditions outside of marriage. They implied by the term "marriage market" that materialistic motives were necessarily present in most marriage choices. Young ladies presented themselves as merchandise for eager young men to marry. The girls, being dependent, had to do so in order to survive. Secondly, the term "market" suggested a terrible impersonality in the exchange of love for support. The harshness of the business world was invading the home itself. Home was no longer a refuge from the cold world, but rather its extension. To correct these conditions, the critics argued, a new social ethic was needed—more independence for women, more freedom to marry outside of one's class, more freedom to reject marriage altogether.

The audience for these strictures was an urban middle class who may have found marital choice freer and more difficult than ever before.[3] The sheer population of neighborhoods, the increasing opportunities for men and women to meet at work, made it virtually impossible for parents to know all the eligibles from whom a son or daughter would make a choice. Some resource had to replace the valuable gossip of the small town. The marriage advice books flowed into the gap. Some of these works, particularly those of doctors promising postnuptial sexual advice, as well as advice as to marital choice, were quite popular. *The Physical Life of Woman* by Dr. George Napheys sold 150,000 copies in its original 1869 edition and was reprinted in 1888. Others appeared to be collections of sermons circulating little further than the clergyman's parish, but clerical works sometimes ran to later editions as well.[4]

The marital advice books attempted to erect barriers against changing values. They cautioned against neglect of the church and against extravagant, worldly women. They upheld static definitions of role, relating these to the protection of the American home from declining moral standards. The major responsibility for creating a moral society, by building the foundations at home, lay with the wife. Unlike the critics, the nuptial guides viewed woman as relatively influential because they valued her role as moral guardian. Home was to provide a haven of tenderness in the cold world, and woman, by nature more emotional than man, was the source of that warmth. Her husband's success and therefore the economic well-being of the family, her children's character, and therefore the moral future of the republic, depended critically upon her patient strength. She, more than anyone else, upheld the ideals of sexual purity and family devotion.[5]

Given such conditions the ministers and doctors wrote fairly uniform descriptions of the good wife, and they castigated behavior that did not conform with their ideals. Men were advised to seek both character and performance in a wife. The prospective bride had to show she could become a thrifty, meticulous housekeeper. But prevalent female extravagance in dress made this requirement difficult to meet. The writers feared that idle wives who ministered only to their husbands' sensual needs were on the increase. Their families were not large enough to occupy them.[6] A wife, secondly, had to identify her future with her husband's completely, listen sympathetically to his plans and comfort him when they failed. And sympathy was needed by the husband. "I counsel the wife to remember in what a severe and terrific battle of life her husband is engaged," preached the Reverend DeWitt Talmage in 1886.[7] The independent college graduate, more in evidence in the next decade, evidently had to learn this submissive, traditional role. Above all, the wife had to be trustworthy, which meant both that she could be her husband's confidante, and that she was sexually pure. No hint of sexual interest should ever touch her manner or conversation. Her reputation, more than her husband's, became the reputation of the entire family. For the most part, the marriage advisers believed that this requirement would be easier to meet than the others. Most asserted or implied that woman's sexual drive was much weaker than man's, although some doctors emphasized that it was not absent altogether.[8] The fulfillment of these feminine ideals—tenderness, chastity, homemaking skills—came with maternity. The requirements of motherhood pervaded the advice literature which was often anti-birth-control literature as well.

Similarly, the prospective husband was regarded in his role as paterfamilias. If a woman's duty was to comfort and serve, a man's was to love and protect. Assuming that man's "animal nature" was much stronger than woman's (yet necessary for the propagation of the race), the doctors and clergy issued stern warnings about the average masculine morality. Women might exercise a softening influence, but they could never reform fundamental wrongs. The girls should avoid men much older than themselves, licentious men, drunkards, gamblers, cold-hearted tyrants, those whose work took them away from home frequently and "despisers of the Christian religion."[9] Of all the postnuptial failings, man's overabsorption in his business and in the attractions of hotel life were believed most common. Marriage advisers warned wives to stay neat and attractive.[10]

The wife's choice of a husband (but interestingly, not the husband's choice of a wife) was deemed fatal. Presumably the clergy's opposition to divorce would equalize the seriousness of choosing. It did not. Some writers acknowledged that a man could always escape to his club, but a woman had no escape. Was this an implied acknowledgment of the double standard? It is hard to say, for other advisers cautioned men against "lascivious actions which are a drain upon the whole system" and asked them to come to the marriage bed as virginal as their brides.[11]

One factor that increased the dangers of poor choice by the woman, her economic dependence, a major concern of critics, was rarely mentioned by the guides. They may have taken the husband's provider role for granted. Yet this avoidance of any discussion of money appeared to be related to the estimate of woman's weaker sex drive. When a man sought a girl he was following a powerful instinct. The girl, on the other hand, could judge a suitor more rationally.[12] Thus the clergymen avoided any statement implying ecclesiastical approval of women coldly evaluating prospective husbands in terms of earning power.

Having presented marriage as a sacred institution, and home as a refuge from the world's commercialism, the advisers could hardly allow commercial standards of judgment about marriage. To have acknowledged materialistic motives on a general scale would have been to admit precisely what the critics implied—the obligation to Christianize the social order, an order that had so corrupted matrimony. The marital advisers acted on the contrary assumption: the traditional marital relationship was pure. It did not need woman's economic independence to cure its materialism. On the contrary, when marriage was delayed in order to acquire the money for a respectable "establishment," it was the sinner's corruption, not society's. Woman's worship of fashion, man's "absurd social ambition," were individual evils, not symptoms of social disorder.[13]

After cautioning their readers about financial extravagance, the preachers presumed to tell lovers how to judge love. Their intentions were clear—to discourage matches of sudden passion and deceptive romance. Sudden falling in love they believed a myth fostered by too much novel reading. A marriage based upon passion was as dangerous as an overcalculating one. Instead, men and women should grow in love, that is, make reasonable and practical choices based upon secure knowledge of one another's characters. Above all, it was important to distinguish passion from love. The first was easily satiated and carnal, but love was at least partially spiritual and entirely unselfish, reasonable and tender. It could pass certain tests which lovers should make before they married. It had the constancy required for indissoluble marriage and responsible parenthood.[14] By emphasizing love's reasonableness, the nuptial counselors gave hardly any hint of the mysterious process by which men and women discovered their mutuality, nor of the possibilities of tragic choices. If one was sensible, the endings were happy. Love, true tender love, was essential to marriage. It was the greatest guarantee of marital and social stability.

Frequently, objections to romantic love merged with objections to marriage across class lines. Harmonious differences in temperament were considered healthy, but not marked differences in status. Cultural incompatibility would destroy such a marriage which might have been motivated by social climbing on the part of the poorer partner. As they feared such class mixtures (and certainly racial and religious mixtures were beyond the pale), so the advisers feared the drowning of an educated, Protestant, older American population in a sea of ignorant, immigrant poor. The urging of practical, compatible marriages some- times took place in this context.[15]

In spite of the pleas for class compatibility, the Cinderella ideal remained as popular as ever in short stories and plays. Writers usually sought a formula to prove that Cinderella was not a fortune-hunter. In one of the longest-run productions on the New York stage and on the road, Steel McKaye's *Hazel Kirke* (1880), the lovely, submissive miller's daughter fell in love with a titled Englishman, quite unaware of his position. When the inevitable obstacles arose in the form of previously promised marriages of convenience, the hero sacrificed fortune and position to keep Hazel—thereby equalizing their social positions. In most short stories, however, in the women's mass circulation magazines of the first decade of the 20th century, the fortune, hidden during courtship, was revealed and kept at the end as a reward for true love.[16] Although the fiction upheld the Cinderella ideal and the marriage manuals cautioned against it, together they constituted a success litera- ture. Both declared that chastity and virtuous courtship would win rewards—both spiritual and practical.

It is difficult to know just how seriously readers took the advice to marry within their class. Some middle-class families, perhaps chiefly those in the upper middle class, found that neighborhood acquaintance alone was not enough to maintain the lines. When Ethel Sturgis, daughter of the President of the Chicago, Northwestern Bank, became engaged to Francis Dummer, Vice President of the same bank in 1888, she wrote, "I almost tremble to think if love and duty had not coincided, what a struggle our two lives would have been." Ethel's father and Francis' sister had, however, pointed out the virtues of Ethel and Francis to each other.[17] In contrast, when a niece of the famous Doctors Blackwell, Elizabeth and Emily, pursued a young farmer in

Martha's Vineyard, the family placed every possible obstacle in the way of this "common" marriage. In spite of their niece's behavior the aunts assumed a lower moral standard went with the lower class.[18]

In this assumption, the Blackwells reflected an undercurrent of anxiety that ran through some of the purity campaigns of the 1890s and 1900s. The purity crusaders were a diverse group of women, doctors, prohibitionists, later progressives who launched a series of campaigns against prostitution and lax age-of-consent laws. They certainly wanted a single standard of sexual morality—but not only for both sexes, but for all classes as well. They resented society's "heartless discriminations in favor of the rich and the influential."[19] As Benjamin Flower, editor of the *Arena,* a vehicle for the movement, observed: "The immorality and degradation of rapid life among the mushroom aristocracy is matched by the grosser manifestations of immorality in the social cellar . . . [and] the great middle class absorbs the contagion from above and below."[20]

The purity advocates warned against social climbing in marriage, believing that ambitious marriages increased extramarital temptations. Avaricious parents led innocent sons and daughters into such marriages while corrupt churchmen ignored the social consequences.[21] As Nathan G. Hale has pointed out, the purity campaigns for sex education, their muckraking against white slavery, the whole drive for a break in the wall of silence they claimed protected vice, had very different results than they envisioned. The campaigns undermined the old repressive standards.[22] In spite of this contrast in effects, the campaigners upheld the same values as those of the churchmen whose protection of virtue they considered so inadequate. Their ideals remained: chastity, female domesticity, rational love and class compatibility.

The purity campaigners' emphasis upon the social injustices which they thought imperiled the home was one indication among many that Americans were, by the 1880s, more receptive to more radical analyses of their society. No stronger weapon existed in the radical armory than the charge that even the home, the supposed haven of warmth and love, was corrupted by materialism. All of the five critics—Bellamy, Ward, Gilman, Veblen and Dreiser—had reason to challenge the alliance of church, home and business. Edward Bellamy and Lester Frank Ward, for example, had early experienced crises of belief which left them with the idea that the church's repressive sexual standards and the guilt they induced were themselves a source of evil.[23] Economic insecurity had scarred the childhoods of Charlotte Perkins Gilman and Theodore Dreiser. Mrs. Gilman's father had deserted a family of four, offering only occasional financial, and no psychological support. Charlotte, seeing her mother's submissive suffering, could never play the traditional female role. Theodore Dreiser's family disintegrated altogether under the combined disasters of his father's obsessive moralism and frequent unemployment. Thorstein Veblen appeared to have learned his skepticism early by contrasting the life of the hard-working Norwegian American farmers with that of the Yankee middle class. By the time he attended Carleton College, he was a full-fledged rebel.[24] In various ways, then, these critics' early experiences led them to reject the conservative success ethos that shaped traditional marital standards.

Edward Bellamy, whose utopian novel, *Looking Backward* (1888) appealed both to intellectuals and to the general public as a solution to the ills of monopolistic capitalism, did not revolt against his own closely knit family, but first against the remnants of Calvinist dogma which crushed the individual conscience. The destructive sense of guilt, the haunting Nemesis of an evil fate, he considered more psychologically damaging than any evil deed. By the 1870s his vaguely transcendental Religion of Solidarity replaced the old religion and provided the philosophical ground of his utopia, being at once impersonal and social.[25]

While he was in his twenties, in the midst of this religious crisis, Bellamy *had* entertained profound doubts about marriage. Avoiding it himself, he argued that marriage became the grave of the creative man who had to prostitute his talents in order to support dependents. In an unpublished novel, *Eliot Carson*, he toyed with the monastic solution for artists. This could hardly answer for all of society. Bellamy himself finally found it unsatisfactory and married late in his thirties.[26] Yet the question remained: How could men have love and a home without the imprisoning economic dependency of women?

Only when Bellamy turned from his fiction of individual psychological transformation to his utopia of revolutionary social transformation did he find the answer. In *Looking Backward,* the hero Julian awoke in the year 2000 to find a society in which both men and women worked for the state until their forties, and all received state support throughout their lifetimes. Men had the delights of domesticity without its restrictive burdens; women, having simpler homes (and with much of the traditional domestic labor performed publicly), had the interest of working in the world. The price, unfortunately, was considerable regimentation, but Bellamy did not think this an obstacle.[27] Society was rid of inhumane poverty and inequality.

The economic equality of the year 2000 utterly destroyed the marriage market. Men and women married for love alone; there could be no other reasons. Class distinctions in marriage were gone as were the classes themselves. Bellamy believed that such a free marriage system had tremendous genetic implications: "For the first time in human history, the principle of sexual selection with the tendency to preserve and transmit the better types of the race . . . has unhindered operation. The necessity of poverty, the need of having a home, no longer tempt women to accept as fathers of their children men whom they can neither love nor respect. . . . The gifts of the person, mind, and disposition . . . are sure of transmission to posterity."[28]

Thus did Bellamy affirm one of the strongest values of the radical critics of American marriage—the goal of an improved future generation. This goal, which was also implicit in the marital guidebooks' concern for proper parenthood, took a different form in the critics' analysis. They thought about the development of future generations more in post-Darwinian terms. Bellamy had even for a time entertained the idea of stirpiculture.[29] The guides believed that a marriage system which preserved class divisions, and in which the educated produced more children than the poor and uneducated, promised the best future. The critics believed that a class society, and a society of economically dependent women, harmed the future generation. They valued instead what Veblen called the parental bent—concern not just for one's own children, but for all children and for their future.

Bellamy relied upon "nationalism" to destroy the marriage market and he claimed it would end such accompanying evils as female triviality, hypocrisy (induced by 19th century courtship) and the double standard. This last reflected sexual economics more than sexual morality. It protected the purity of dependent married women at a horrible cost in prostitution. Since true ethical behavior could originate only with free choice, and since neither prostitutes nor chaste women were free, true sexual morality could begin only when women were economically independent of men. Such free women could frankly confess their love to men. No longer compelled to please the average man, in order to catch a husband, each woman could develop her own interests and talents. Women would no longer pass on their "mental and moral slavery" to their offspring.[30]

In thus simplifying the problem in economic terms, Bellamy was deferring to the popular, sexually repressive opinion of his day. His brother Charles had offered in a utopian novel, *An Experiment in Marriage* (1889), solutions Edward eschewed—virtually complete communal living, easy divorce and frequent remarriage. Only this system preserved the freshness of love.[31] With his brother's ideals of frank courtship and female equality Edward agreed. But divorce he could not endorse publicly, and he certainly had reservations about the sensuality favored in *An Experiment in Marriage*. Under "nationalism" he suggested the sexual drive would be not more intense but more diffuse, "like light that passes through a prism . . . refracted into many shades and hues."[32] In place of the free divorce system he created in the story "To Whom This May Come" a society of mind readers who recognized their true loves at once (vitiating the need for sensual experimentation). And these mind readers' unions were, of course, more spiritual than passionate, affirming the Bellamy ideal of love—moderate rapture. Since men would not have to support women in the socialist state, intense passion would not be needed to induce marriage. As family relationships declined in intensity, everyone would be "a thousandfold more than now occupied with nature and the next steps of the race."[33]

Like Bellamy, Lester Frank Ward and Charlotte Perkins Gilman attacked the exaggerated sexual differentiation of lives in late 19th century America. While Ward deplored sexual repression, Mrs. Gilman, who had paid the high price of nervous depression, divorce and separation from her daughter to attain autonomy, felt that American marriages *over-emphasized* sensuality. She was never able to accept the freer standards of the war years. In the early seventies Ward launched attacks upon the church, whose doctrines of female submission and indissoluble marriage he held directly responsible for prostitution.[34] Yet he left off his attack as he turned his attention to evolutionary theory and only took up the defense of freer sexual expression in 1903. In the 1890s then both Ward and Gilman criticized American marriage in the only "acceptable" way it could be criticized—by challenging traditional notions of the female role.

Both asserted that female inferiority was not inherent, but developed in the processes of the marriage market. Both extended the discussion to include a naturalistic consideration of the mate-selection process. Ward outlined a woman-centered theory of evolution indicating how the female of the species had abandoned an initially superior status. In all subhuman species, he noted, it was the female, not the male, who transmitted the characteristics of the race. She selected the males with whom to mate. Eventually, however, the females began to select not only the strongest, but the most intelligent mates. At that point, just as primitive man evolved, a crucial transformation took place. The men perceived that it was easier to seize females for mating than to contest for their favors with stronger males, allowing the female to choose the victor. This seizure and rape process, male-dominated mate selection, was the germ of marriage. And men continued to dominate the marriage market until modern times.[35]

Charlotte Perkins Gilman added that this male domination of the market bred a race of frail, backward women. Men chose such women for wives, so the smarter, stronger ones did not reproduce their own kind. But there was an even more crucial reason for female inferiority. Once man had conquered woman and enslaved her, she could no longer hunt for her own food, or provide for her own young as female animals did. Man stood between woman and the challenging environment of the economic world. Women, thus, developed largely through their relationships with men. They developed those traits needed to catch a husband: conformity, flirtatiousness, sexual exaggeration and passivity.[36] Marriageable women, as much as prostitutes, were utterly dependent upon men and in essence sold themselves. "When we confront this fact boldly . . . in the open market of vice, we are sick with horror. When we see the same economic relation made permanent, established by law . . . sanctified by religion, covered with flowers and accumulated sentiment, we think it innocent, lovely, and right. The transient trade we think evil, the bargain for life we think good."[37]

Both Ward and Gilman saw signs, however, that the age of the marriage market was passing. As societies became more complex and more highly civilized, the most fastidious individuals, Ward believed, had difficulty choosing a mate, and tended to decline marriage altogether. This, and the burden of economically unproductive women, made the goal of one indissoluble marriage for each impossible of realization.[38]

Ward asserted that by the end of the 19th century male-dominated selection was fortunately declining. If men continued to select women for their frail, ephemeral beauty, the race would eventually be extinct. But modern men were selecting women for their mental and moral strengths as well as for beauty. By this process they happily increased female influence. More and more *mutual* selection took place. Ward identified this mutual selection with romantic love. Unlike most nuptial guides, he cherished and celebrated romance as not only beautiful for individuals, but beneficial for society. It was the highest form of man's noblest natural instinct—sexual love. When men and women fell in love, they advanced both the race and the civilization. By choosing mates of contrasting temperament and build, they acted out of a natural wisdom to produce well-balanced offspring. Thus the only sound eugenics was obedience to the law of love.[39] Ward, arguing in evolutionary terms, was using a powerful weapon against "practical" marriage advice.

Moreover, romantic love aided civilization just because it rarely ran smooth. For each couple it meant working, struggling, long denial. Out of this yearning struggle came man's deepest inspirations to create in the arts and sciences. And the struggle, unstable in itself, ended in fulfillment, with the onset of calm conjugal love. Society's standards, therefore, should not be sexually repressive. Love was a "higher law" that should prevail over social conventions. Free divorce should be allowed so that marriages contracted out of unromantic motives, loveless, practical marriages could be ended for the sake of romance and the next generation.[40] This combination of romantic idealism and evolutionary science constituted Ward's plea for greater sexual freedom.

Mrs. Gilman was distinctly less enthusiastic about sexual freedom, although she too wanted love unshackled from economic marriage. Her own experiences, her early allegiance to Bellamy's socialism, led her to emphasize the collective life of modern society which she wished women to enter. In her famous *Women and Economics* (1898) she demonstrated that the individualism of the marital relation contradicted and distorted economic relations which tended to collectivity as industries modernized. Man's selfishness for "the sake of the family" was no more reasonable in a cooperative world than woman's isolation at home or overspecialization as to sex. The traditional roles had to and would decay for the world's benefit. Already a complex economy was drawing women out of the home, ending their alienation from creative labor. Primitive household labor was becoming obsolete. Woman's very restlessness in the domestic role indicated a new social consciousness.[41]

Woman's economic independence would not threaten marriage itself, but would end the male-dominated marriage market. Marriage would no longer be a "sexuo-economic" relationship. Women would choose husbands, sublimating immediate sexual attractiveness to the demands of "right parentage." At the same time, female influence would counteract the aggressive tendencies of the man-made world with the values of "peaceful, helpful interservice." A new social environment, reinforcing industrial efficiency, would prevail, making the egalitarian changes in the marriage relationship permanent.[42]

Although he was less hopeful than Mrs. Gilman, Thorstein Veblen made a very similar identification between the peaceful primitive matriarchy of the past and a possible future industrial republic. Like Ward and Gilman he looked backward in order to criticize the present and reconstruct the future. His anthropological economics was so implicitly subversive that readers could only regard their own mores as vestiges of barbarism. In all the Veblenian lexicon the most barbaric institution of all was the patriarchal marriage.

The patriarchy originated when primitive tribes acquired an excess of goods and encountered hostile tribes. Seizing the conquered tribes' goods and women, they eventually made war a way of life. In the transformation into a barbaric society, private ownership, slavery and patriarchal marriage originated. Because only wives and slaves worked, labor was judged irksome. The patriarch displayed his wives as possessions, and he owned the products of their labor. Riches and status came together. "The ownership and control of women is gratifying evidence of prowess and high standing."[43]

When Veblen extended this argument into a work both popular and scholarly, *The Theory of the Leisure Class* (1899), he forged a weapon of considerable power against traditional sex roles. For in stating that the middle-class wife functioned only to display luxury and idleness as proof of her husband's social standing, he touched an area as sensitive with the conservative preachers as with the radical critics. America's traditional values could not encompass idleness or uselessness and Veblen knew this. Moreover, he answered a hopeful strain of the 1890s by stating that in spite of the interference of barbaric capitalism, the processes of modern technology would destroy the patriarchal marriage and allow a reemergence of "the most ancient habits of thought of the race."[44]

Veblen's economics implied goals very similar to those of Bellamy's utopia, Gilman's feminist analysis and Ward's naturalistic sociology. All viewed marriage as an institution distorted by late 19th century capitalistic culture. In its distorted form, in its competitive materialism, it was an impediment to a cooperative future. While the writers of marriage manuals viewed marriage as a sacred absolute, the critics thought it had the tinges of a modern slavery. Nevertheless, they too suggested an ideal marriage at the end of evolutionary change—a relationship personal yet more responsive to community needs, romantic because freed from the man's one-sided economic dominance and responsibilities. In place of the guides' values—home, purity, social order—they cherished woman's economic independence, creative and cooperative labor, romantic love and the parental bent. They grounded these values in a naturalistic Weltanschauung rather than in a traditionally Protestant one.

Only when the repressive sexual ethic met a direct challenge, however, would the revolt against the older morality be launched. Of course, changing behavior itself was such a challenge. But ideologically the challenge, out of a naturalistic framework, was issued by a "new man" with no loyalty to the older, small-town America, to its code or its optimism. Theodore Dreiser confronted the sexual code by depicting directly its everyday violations. His first two novels, *Sister Carrie* (1900) and *Jennie Gerhardt* (1911) grew out of his sister's experiences with the civilized morality. In those works, as in his others, Dreiser painted Americans as they actually stood—unprotected in the lonely urban world. His newspaper experience had told him a great deal about the city's real values in contrast to the small-town pieties.[45] But Dreiser's first lessons began at home.

After witnessing repeated contradictions between the standard 19th century moral conventions and his sisters' escape from poverty through illicit affairs, between his father's gloomy prudery and the life of pleasure his brother, songwriter Paul Dresser, led, Theodore compounded his own naturalistic religion to replace his father's Catholicism. He came to believe that sexual love, infused with the love of natural beauty, was *the* experience initiating men and women into nature's truth. Change was the law of life, and any static institutions or ideals of respectability had to be cast aside if they stood in the way of sheer survival.[46]

In *Sister Carrie* the heroine adapted to the urban world, first by a simple, hardly considered abandonment of virginity, then by a determined struggle and finally by developing into an actress. In choosing to become Drouet's mistress, rather than remain a cold, poorly paid, worn factory-hand, Carrie was taking the first step toward survival and success, rather than toward the traditional downfall and ruin. Her second lover, Hurstwood, destroyed himself not by stealing money or committing adultery, but in a futile effort to retain his middle-class respectability.[47] Carrie knew how to fight; Hurstwood gave up. That was all. Their sexual behavior brought neither punishment nor reward. That was what was most devastating about Dreiser's portraits—his refusal to pass any condemning judgments. Carrie trading her body outside of marriage appeared not a whit more materialistic than Hurstwood's wife trading within marriage, and offering her daughter Jessica in the marriage market.

In *Jennie Gerhardt* (1911) Dreiser drew the contrast between "the grasping legality of established matrimony" and the free flow of love most clearly. Jennie was that most ancient of literary heroines, the woman in love. Full of passionate tenderness, she seemed at one with nature itself. Lester Kane, her lover, heir to a manufacturing fortune, shared a passionate communion with Jennie. But he knew he need never marry her. She was a lower-class girl and marriage was a very practical arrangement. He had hoped to escape it altogether. When business interests and his family dictated otherwise, Kane left Jennie to marry an attractive, rich widow with whom he shared social and intellectual interests. Thus Dreiser portrayed man in the natural world of feeling, a world of great depth, and yet bound to the world of convention, if unable to pay the price of defiance. The conventional world upheld that static institution—marriage—and reversed the natural value of passionate love. That was reason enough for Dreiser's contempt for convention. Jennie, alone, having lost social acceptance, her love and her child, triumphed by sheer affirmation of natural love.[48]

By the time Dreiser wrote this defiance of the marriage market, the age of new sexual standards was beginning. *Jennie Gerhardt* was a critical and popular success. Although his subsequent struggle with *The Genius* (1915) indicated that Comstockery did not die all at once, the tide had turned. Perhaps for this very reason the revolt of the 1880s and 1890s seemed excessive to the new age. Dreiser's attack upon marriage, and especially upon the class divisions marriage upheld, was not repeated, although studies confirmed that Americans continued to marry those of similar wealth and status.[49] To the postwar generation there would be something anachronistic about Gilman's feminism, although American women had not achieved anything approaching her ideal of economic independence.

Above all, the critics' implicit association between marital discontent and the inequalities of late 19th century society seemed too radical for the war and postwar generations. Did social institutions require a thoroughgoing transformation for men and women to enjoy a healthier, franker relationship? In the age of Freud the younger generation doubted it. The double standard was withering, but women were receptive to a new ideology of domesticity. Yet the radicals of the 1880s and 1890s *did* connect social transformation with true freedom for romantic love. The sexually repressive standards of Gilman and Bellamy were distinctly Victorian. But in their attacks upon the home, upon women's economic dependency and upon exaggerated sexual differentiation of roles, the critics appear to speak more to our own generation than they did to the generations that directly succeeded them.

NOTES

1. Delos S. Wilcox, *Ethical Marriage: A Discussion of the Relation of Sex from the Standpoint of Social Duty* (Ann Arbor: Wood-Allen, 1900), p. 10; see also John L. Brandt, *Marriage and the Home* (Chicago: Laird & Lee, 1892), pp. 21–22, 57.

2. Caroline Corbin, *A Woman's Philosophy of Love* (Boston: Lee, Shepard, 1893), p. 13; Minot Judson Savage, *Man, Woman, and Child* (Boston: George Ellis, 1884), pp. 64, 136–37; George McLean, *The Curtain Lifted: Hidden Secrets Revealed* (Chicago: Lewis, 1887), pp. 165–67; James Reed, *Man and Woman: Equal but Unlike* (Boston: Nichols & Noyes, 1870), *passim;* Samuel R. Wells, *Wedlock* (New York: S. R. Wells, 1871), pp. 24–25; William H. Holcombe, *The Sexes Here and Hereafter* (Philadelphia: Lippincott, 1869), p. 166; and George H. Napheys, M.D., *The Physical Life of Woman* (Philadelphia: David McKay, 1888), pp. 57–58.

3. The author is indebted to Prof. Samuel Haber of the University of California, Berkeley for this observation and for pointing out that the very existence of many choices may have popularized the phrase "marriage market."

4. Napheys, *Physical Life*, preface, p. vii. Other doctor works include Henry Hanchett, *Sexual Health* (New York: Charles Harlburt, 1887); Henry Guernsey, *Plain Talks on Avoided Subjects* (Philadelphia: F. A. Davis, 1882); and H. S.

Pomeroy, *The Ethics of Marriage* (New York: Funk & Wagnalls, 1888), commended as an anti-birth-control work in Brevard Sinclair, *The Crowning Sin of the Age* (Boston: H. L. Hastings, 1892), p. 15, and in *Journal of the American Medical Association*, 2 (1888), 309–11. Clerical works or limited edition collections of sermons used as brides' books include: S. D. & Mary Kilgore Gordon, *Quiet Talks on Home Ideals* (New York: Fleming Revell, 1909); Robert F. Horton, *On the Art of Living Together* (New York: Dodd Mead, 1896); and F. B. Meyer, *Lovers Always* (New York: Fleming Revell, 1899). Examples of second editions in marital guide-books are: Wells, *Wedlock* (c. 1869, 1871 ed.); Mrs. E. B. Duffy, *The Relations of the Sexes* (New York: M. L. Holbrook, c. 1876, 1889 ed.); and James R. Miller, D.D., *The Wedded Life* (Presbyterian Board of Publication of Philadelphia, c. 1886, 1894 ed.).

5. Brandt, *Marriage and Home,* pp. 51, 210; Wells, *Wedlock,* p. 173; and Savage, *Man, Woman, and Child,* pp. 33, 37. The same assumptions cropped up in personal correspondence concerning courtships and betrothal. For example, when Austin Baldwin of Savannah became engaged to Louise Maynard of Massachusetts, Baldwin's brother wrote: "It is . . . not the man that makes his wife, but the wife that more often makes the man and I hope my new sister will prove a good advisor and helpmate. . . . If Lou is as good as she is handsome . . . you may date your success in life from the time you were married." T. J. Baldwin to A. Baldwin, May 15, 1872, Baldwin Family Papers, Schlesinger Archives, Radcliffe College. Similarly, Emily Blackwell wrote her sister Elizabeth: "I felt a great deal depended upon the woman he married. If she had been a girl whose ambition was for society . . . it would have spoiled him. Frances will be ambitious for him to choose a worthwhile career, and will support him in any serious work. I believe she will be an excellent influence in his life." Nov. 6, 1904, Blackwell Family Papers, Schlesinger Archives, Radcliffe College.

6. Cortland Myers, *The Lost Wedding Ring* (New York: Funk & Wagnalls, 1902), pp. 100–2; Elizabeth Blackwell, *Counsel to Parents on the Moral Education of their Children* (New York: Brentano, 1883), p. 75; Charles Frederick Goss, *Husband, Wife and Home* (Philadelphia: Vir Publishing, 1905), pp. 33–34; Brandt, *Marriage,* pp. 70–71, 81–85, 85–88; and Miller, *Wedded Life,* pp. 65–67.

7. *The Marriage Ring: A Series of Discourses in Brooklyn Tabernacle* (New York: Funk & Wagnalls, 1886), p. 62. See also Savage, *Man, Woman, and Child,* p. 38; and Miller, *Wedded Life,* pp. 20–21.

8. Napheys, *Physical Life,* pp. 96, 102; Hanchett, *Sexual Health,* p. 37; Brandt, *Marriage,* pp. 80–81. •

9. Talmage, *Marriage Ring,* pp. 24–25, 28–29; M. Salmonsen, *From the Marriage License Window* (Chicago: John Anderson, 1887), pp. 100, 103; Savage, *Man, Woman, and Child,* pp. 13–21; and Miller, *Wedded Life,* pp. 31–39, 42–49, 52–54 detail the masculine ideal.

10. Goss, *Husband, Wife, Homes,* pp. 50, 66–68; and Talmage, *Marriage Ring,* pp. 62–64, 66.

11. Guernsey, *Plain Talks,* p. 36; Brandt, *Marriage,* p. 111; Talmage, *Marriage Ring,* pp. 24–25; Myers, *Wedding Ring,* p. 84.

12. Frank N. Hagar, *The American Family: A Sociological Problem* (New York: University Publishing Soc., 1905), pp. 44–45.

13. McLean, *Curtain Lifted,* pp. 161–62; Kate Gannett Wells, "Why More Men Do

Not Marry," *North American Review*, 165 (July 1897), 124; George Shinn, *Friendly Talks About Marriage* (Boston: Jos. Knight, c. 1897), pp. 56–57.

14. Anthony W. Thorald, *On Marriage* (New York: Dodd Mead, 1896), p. 16; Pomeroy, *Ethics of Marriage*, p. 51; Sarah Grand, "Marriage Questions in Fiction: The Standpoint of a Typical Modern Woman," *Living Age*, 217 (Apr. 1898), 73; Corbin, *Woman's Philosophy*, pp. 38–41; Mary Wood-Allen, M.D., *What a Young Woman Ought to Know* (Philadelphia: Vir Publishing, 1893), pp. 200–4; Brandt, *Marriage*, pp. 41–42; and Wells, *Wedlock*, pp. 51–52.

15. Wilcox, *Ethical Marriage*, pp. 25–28; Thorald, *Marriage*, p. 25; Myers, *Wedding Ring*, p. 7; McLean, *Curtain Lifted*, pp. 161–62; Shinn, *Friendly Talks About Marriage*, pp. 31–32; Hagar, *American Family*, pp. 73–74; Sinclair, *Crowning Sin*, pp. 13, 17–18; and Wells, *Wedlock*, pp. 45, 47, 49.

16. Arthur Hobson Quinn, ed., *Representative American Plays* (New York: Appleton-Century, 1930) pp. 435–36, 439–40, 451, 453, 457, 465, 470; and Donald Makosky, "The Portrayal of Women in Wide Circulation Magazine Short Stories, 1905–1955," Diss. University of Pennsylvania 1966, pp. 139–40.

17. Ethel Sturgis to Francis Dummer, June 11, 1888. See also Dummer to Sturgis, Mar. 6, 1888; Mrs. Sturgis to F. Dummer, June 12, 1888; Katherine Dummer to Ethel Sturgis, June 12, 1888; and Katherine Dummer to Francis Dummer, June 12, 1888, Sturgis-Dummer Family Papers, Schlesinger Archives, Radcliffe College.

18. Emily Blackwell to Elizabeth Blackwell, Aug. 13, 1881, Oct. 2, 1881. For a contrasting view within the family see Alice Stone Blackwell to Kitty Barry Blackwell, July 23, 1882, Aug. 27, 1882, Blackwell Family Papers, Schlesinger Archives, Radcliffe College. The marriage took place nevertheless.

19. J. Bellanger, "Sexual Purity and the Double Standard," *Arena*, 11 (Feb. 1895), 373.

20. "Social Conditions as Feeders of Immorality," *Arena*, 11 (Feb. 1895), 410–11. For the way in which the purity movement shifted from an ecclesiastical to a scientific rationale for its positions, see David J. Pivar, "The New Abolitionism: The Quest for Social Purity, 1876–1900," Diss. University of Pennsylvania 1965.

21. Helen Gardiner, *Is This Your Son My Lord?* (Boston: Arena Publishing, 1890), *passim.*

22. *Freud and the Americans: The Beginnings of Psychoanalysis in the United States, 1876–1917* (New York: Oxford Univ. Press, 1971), pp. 252–54.

23. Joseph Schiffman, "Editor's Introduction," *Edward Bellamy: Selected Writings on Religion and Society* (New York: Liberal Arts Press, 1955), pp. xii–iii; Bellamy, *Dr. Heidenhoff's Process* (New York: c. 1880, Ams. Press, 1969), pp. 119–20, 138–39; Ward, "Revealed Religion and Human Progress," from *Iconoclast*, i (Nov. 1, 1870); *Glimpses of the Cosmos* (New York: Putnam, 1918), 1: 91–95; and "The Social Evil," *Iconoclast*, 2 (Aug. 1871), *Glimpses*, 1: 238–41.

24. Carl N. Degler, "Introduction to the Torchbook Edition," Gilman, *Woman and Economics* (New York: Harper & Row, 1966), pp. ix–x; Robert H. Elias, *Theodore Dreiser, Apostle of Nature* (Ithaca: Cornell Univ. Press, 1970), pp. 6, 11–13; and Henry Steele Commager, *The American Mind: An Interpretation of American Thought and Character Since the 1880's* (New Haven: Yale Univ. Press, 1959), pp. 238–39.

25. "The Religion of Solidarity" (1874) in Schiffman, *Bellamy, Religion and*

Society, pp. 15–17; Arthur E. Morgan, *Edward Bellamy* (New York: Columbia Univ. Press, 1955), p. 138.

26. Sylvia E. Bowman, *The Year 2000: A Critical Biography of Edward Bellamy* (New York: Bookman Associates, 1959), pp. 69–70, 279; and Morgan, *Edward Bellamy,* p. 55.

27. *New Nation,* 1 (Mar. 14, 1891), 110; (Apr. 4, 1891), 159.

28. *Looking Backward 2000–1887* (New York: Random House, n.d.), p. 218.

29. "Stirpiculture," *Springfield Daily Union* (Oct. 2, 1875), p. 4. The term, used by John Humphrey Noyes of the Oneida Community and briefly practiced there, meant arranged marriages to bring out the genetic strengths of the partners—the breeding of children. At the same time Bellamy was supporting "common-sense" in marriage which he occasionally identified with "like marrying like" in terms somewhat similar to those of the guides. He thought that marked class differences were accompanied by cultural differences, but he did not raise the objections of fortune hunting, etc. See "Literary Notices," *Springfield Daily Union* (Jan. 30, 1875), p. 6; and (Feb. 6, 1875), p. 6. *Looking Backward* then meant a considerable change in outlook.

30. *Equality,* 10th ed. (New York: Appleton, 1909), pp. 135–38, 140–41.

31. *An Experiment in Marriage: A Romance* (Albany: Albany Book, 1889), pp. 17, 24–25, 96–102, 116–17.

32. *New Nation,* 1 (1891), 298.

33. *The Blindman's World and Other Stories* (New York: Garrett, 1968), pp. 405–6, 408–9; papers B 2-7-10,11 quoted in Arthur E. Morgan, *The Philosophy of Edward Bellamy* (New York: Kings Crown, 1945), pp. 76–77. Bellamy's distrust of passion came early and remained with him; see Morgan, *Bellamy* (biography), p. 81.

34. "Revealed Religion and Human Progress" and "The Social Evil."

35. "Our Better Halves," *Forum,* 6 (Nov. 1888), 266–75: Speech Before the Six O'Clock Club, May 24, 1888, *Glimpses,* 4: 129: and *Dynamic Sociology* (New York: Appleton, 1883), 1: 617, 648.

36. *Our Androcentric Culture or the Man-Made World,* as serialized in *Forerunner,* 1 (Nov. 1909), 23–25; *Women and Economics,* pp. 61–63, 86–88.

37. *Women and Economics,* pp. 63–64.

38. *Dynamic Sociology,* 1: 624–26.

39. *Pure Sociology* (New York: Macmillan, 1903), pp. 381, 384, 398–99. In spite of Ward's appreciation for the importance of the sexual drive, Harriet Stanton Blatch thought he underestimated female sexuality, and even the "pretty clear physiological aim" of those mothers whom the world thought mercenary in pushing their daughters into the marriage market. Blatch to Ward, June 31, 1903, Sept. 2, 1903, Ward Collection, Brown University.

40. *Pure Sociology,* p. 398 n.; pp. 401–3.

41. *Woman and Economics,* pp. 105–7, 143, 154–57, 160; see also "All the World to Her," *Independent,* 55 (July 9, 1903), 1614 for the effects of woman receiving the world through her husband, and her overconcentration upon him.

42. "Man Made World," *Forerunner,* 1 (Dec. 1910), 22–24; (Dec. 1909), 14.

43. "The Barbarian Status of Women," *American Journal of Sociology,* 4 (Jan.

1899), 510; see also pp. 503–4 and "The Beginnings of Ownership" (Nov. 1898), pp. 364–65.

44. "Barbarian Status," p. 514. For Veblen's discussion of feminine beauty and dress in this regard see *The Theory of the Leisure Class* (New York: Modern Library, 1934), pp. 146–48, 179–82.

45. Dreiser, *Dawn* (New York: Liveright, 1931), pp. 173, 264; *A Book About Myself* (London: Constable, 1939), pp. 65–67, 70, 480, 488–89; Malcolm Cowley, "Sister Carrie Her Fall and Rise," *The Stature of Theodore Dreiser,* eds. Alfred Kazin and Charles Shapiro (Bloomington: Indiana Univ. Press, 1965), p. 174.

46. Maxwell Geismar, *Rebels and Ancestors: The American Novel, 1890–1915* (Boston: Houghton Mifflin, 1953), p. 291; John McAleer, *Theodore Dreiser: An Introduction and an Interpretation* (New York: Holt, Rinehart & Winston, 1968), pp. 34–35.

47. *Sister Carrie* (New York: New American Library, 1961), pp. 56, 61–62, 75–76, 84–88, 258, 267, 270–72, 315, 330–31, 421–22, 462.

48. *Jennie Gerhardt: A Novel* (New York: Harper, 1911), pp. 18, 128, 130, 215, 238, 313, 317, 322.

49. August Hollingshead, "Cultural Factors in Selection of Marriage Mates," in Marvin Sussman, ed., *Sourcebook in Marriage and the Family* (Cambridge: Riverside Press, 1955), pp. 43–50; and Richard Centers, "Occupational Endogamy in Marital Selection," ibid., pp. 56–61.

～17～

LEADERSHIP AND TACTICS IN THE AMERICAN WOMAN SUFFRAGE MOVEMENT: A NEW PERSPECTIVE FROM MASSACHUSETTS

SHARON HARTMAN STROM

In the fall of 1915 Massachusetts voters defeated an amendment to the state constitution granting women the suffrage by a margin of 132,000 votes. Suffrage workers predicted that defeat because they knew Massachusetts had long been the center of popular and well-organized resistance to votes for women. Yet in 1919, when the Congress of the United States passed the Nineteenth Amendment and sent it to the states for ratification, Massachusetts was the eighth state to ratify, a month after the amendment left Washington. Massachusetts may have been the eastern locus of anti-suffrage sentiment, but it was also the home of a dynamic and politically sophisticated state suffrage movement. Determined women suffragists had gained enough experience by 1919 to crown ten years of innovative and aggressive political agitation with victory.

The history of the woman suffrage movement has traditionally focused on a group of titanic figures: the pioneers, Elizabeth Cady Stanton, Susan B. Anthony, and Lucy Stone; the inspirational leader of the middle years, Anna Howard Shaw; and the great organizer of the final drive for the federal amendment between 1914 and 1920, Carrie Chapman Catt. Accounts by contemporary chroniclers and autobiographies of leaders of the movement are in large part responsible for this focus on a few personalities,[1] and most recent historians have largely

---

From the *Journal of American History* 62 (September 1975). Reprinted by permission.

taken these uncritical assessments on faith. While historians of other social movements have begun to move away from reliance on such egocentric sources and conclusions, historians of the suffrage movement give the impression that the success of the cause resulted from the drive and determination of these gifted women, especially in the last campaigns for a federal amendment.[2]

Even the most recent histories convey the feeling that the mass of the American movement was curiously isolated from any contact with its foreign counterparts. Although women in both England and America were fighting for the suffrage at the same time and shared a common ideological heritage, surprisingly few women in the American movement seem to be responsible for the adoption of English militant suffragist tactics.[3] Again, a few unusual individuals account for whatever English influence was felt in America: Harriot Stanton Blatch, daughter of the invincible Stanton, and Alice Paul, militant leader of the Woman's party, both of whom spent time working in the English movement and tried to adapt English tactics to the American scene.[4]

The history of the woman suffrage movement in Massachusetts between 1901 and 1919, however, indicates that these assumptions may be incorrect. Although studies of other states' suffrage movements will be required to substantiate these new hypotheses completely, the evidence from Massachusetts shows that extensive changes both within the rank and file of the movement and in the wider arena of social reform, not the aggressive leadership of a few personalities, were responsible for a highly mobilized and efficient organization in the years before World War I. Massachusetts sources also indicate that large numbers of ordinary American women suffragists enthusiastically supported their militant English sisters and consciously adapted militant suffragist tactics to the work in America several years before Paul arrived in Washington.

Massachusetts women have long been downgraded in analyses of the national movement. As the nineteenth-century headquarters of the American Woman Suffrage Association, the more conservative of the national organizations, Boston is usually characterized as the capital of stuffy feminism.[5] New York, the home of the founders of the more radical National Woman Suffrage Association, is usually credited with having produced most of the innovative tactics and aggressive leaders. Stanton and Susan B. Anthony were far more catholic in their reform interests and consistently feminist than Stone and Henry Blackwell. By 1890, however, when the two groups merged to become the National American Woman Suffrage Association (NAWSA), most women in the suffrage movement neither knew nor cared about the original quarrel between the two organizations. In fact, there is every reason to believe that, while the New York movement produced the precinct organization method and such personalities as Blatch and Catt, the woman's movement in Massachusetts was an equally rich source of tactics and workers for the final battle.

The fight in Massachusetts for an amendment to the state constitution granting women the vote in the late-nineteenth century was largely an exercise in futility. The road to final adoption was difficult; passage required a two thirds vote in both houses of two sucessive legislatures, as well as approval by referendum. Before 1880, the suffragists followed a well-established routine. Every year they presented petitions to the state legislature, and then eloquent proponents of woman suffrage testified at the subsequent public hearing in the State House, hoping both to convince legislators and obtain publicity. They also sought endorsement of the suffrage by reformers, editors, politicians, and educators, and, whenever they were invited, spoke in churches and lecture halls. They also organized suffrage societies. But after fifteen years of such work, there was still no evidence that the state legislature would enact a suffrage amendment—the yearly hearings had become a barely noticed ritual.[6]

In 1879 suffragists thought they had made a breakthrough. With the temporary support of the Republicans, who controlled the state, they secured the right for women to vote for and serve on their local school committees. Republicans supported school suffrage partly in recognition of the stake women had in the education of their children, but mostly in the hope that middle-class females would help to combat the growing voting power of Catholic immigrant and working-class men in local communities. The School Suffrage Law was possible because bills regarding local elections required only a simple majority in the state legislature. The state constitution, in effect, specified male voters for state offices.

Members of the Massachusetts Woman Suffrage Association (MWSA) immediately moved to take advantage of their 1879 victory and this constitutional exception. They began to work for an additional form of partial suffrage, the municipal vote, and played down their demands for an amendment to the state constitution, which would give women the same voting rights as men.[7] This change of emphasis from their traditional argument to a more "expedient" one led suffragists to imply that voting women in the cities could clean up urban politics, combat boss rule, and restore the municipal order upset by industrialization and immigration.[8] However, the new strategy of the state suffrage organization proved to be a disaster. MWSA found itself not only again allied with the Woman's Christian Temperance Union but also with the virulently anti-Catholic Loyal Women of America.[9] Even this approach failed to reclaim Republican support. The municipal bill passed in the Massachusetts lower house in 1894 but was defeated in the state senate. Abandoned by the Republicans, suffragists also found their campaign had elicited the strongest statewide anti-suffrage movement in the country, whose leaders now maneuvered to get rid of the municipal voting issue once and for all by proposing a mock referendum in the election of 1895. Women eligible to vote for their school committees were asked to participate. Ignoring the fact that women who voted in the referendum overwhelmingly voted "yes," the antis gloated over the poor turnout; only 4 percent of the eligible female voters went to the polls. For years Massachusetts suffragists had to combat the anti-suffrage position that women should not be given the vote because they did not want it anyway.

With Stone's death in 1893 seeming to foreshadow a general dampening of enthusiasm, the suffrage movement in Massachusetts entered a period of steady decline.[10] Ninety local leagues had been organized in 1889; only twenty-six remained in 1895.[11] Yet by 1908, though there had been no apparent significant change in leadership, the Massachusetts Woman Suffrage Association was among the largest in the country.[12]

Many factors account for the resurgence of the suffrage movement in Massachusetts. The lessons learned in the municipal suffrage referendum of 1895 about the specific nature of Massachusetts politics, general social changes which occurred during the Progressive era, and changes among women, especially those in the upper class, were the most important. One of the effects of urbanization and industrialization in America in the late-nineteenth century was a frantic growth in organizations which for many people took the place of the extended family, the church, and the rural village.[13] The concomitant move of middle- and upper-class women into a limited participation in public life and the professions, especially teaching and social work, gave them new skills and self-confidence. In reform circles, these new talents allowed women to move away from their reliance on male reformers, who had always been somewhat dubious allies, and to create their own organizations.[14]

In Massachusetts these trends were well on their way by the time of the municipal suffrage debacle in 1895. That referendum convinced women suffrage workers that they should concentrate entirely on reaching women, who, they decided, must never again be accused of indifference to their own rights and needs. They also learned that their arguments should be as universal as possible, or combined with specific ones for every special interest group in the state, since arraying themselves against so many power blocs had led to defeat. But the crucial point is that, once having made these decisions, Massachusetts suffragists could act on them because of the proliferation of organizations for women at the turn of the century.

There were three important organizations in Massachusetts that worked in concert with dozens of others to promote the suffrage after 1900: MWSA; the College Equal Suffrage League (CESL); and the Boston Equal Suffrage Association for Good Government (BESAGG). This group of organizations provided the impetus for the resurgence of the woman's vote question. The smallest and most specialized of them, BESAGG, was probably the most important. Founded in 1901, BESAGG was initially a civic organization with committees on the schools, sanitation, temperance, vice reform, peace, and the suffrage. By 1904, however, suffrage work dominated its activities.[15] Three of the founders of BESAGG—Pauline Agassiz Shaw, Mary Hutcheson Page, and Maud Wood Park—are typical of the kind of women who reinvigorated the Massachusetts movement and then worked in the national campaign during its final years.[16] They were well-educated, confident, independent, and determined to become first-class citizens. In 1900 they needed a small organization in which to discuss new ideas, unencumbered by the stodgy membership of MWSA and its older, more conservative leaders—Julia Ward Howe and Mary A. Livermore—who were still using all the old tactics.

The first president of BESAGG, Pauline Agassiz Shaw, was the daughter of world-renowned Harvard professor Louis Agassiz and wife of Quincy A. Shaw, owner of the fabulous Calumet and Hecla mines. The most powerful supporter of suffrage in Massachusetts, Pauline Agassiz Shaw moved in the state's most élite circles of education and wealth. She preferred to work behind the scenes and left decision-making and public speaking to friends like Mary Hutcheson Page and Maud Wood Park. Her money kept BESAGG financially sound, and more than once saved the *Woman's Journal* from ceasing publication. It was rumored upon her death in 1917 that she had donated millions to Boston schools and reform groups.[17]

Perhaps it is because she was so adept at manipulating people and at backstage politics that Mary Hutcheson Page's contributions have been overlooked. Born in 1860 to a family of bankers, she was orphaned at the age of sixteen, left "comfortably off" and almost entirely on her own. Unhappy with her traditional finishing school education, she sought tutoring in mathematics and then enrolled in Massachusetts Institute of Technology as a special student. In 1890 she married George Hyde Page, son of James Page, the headmaster of Dwight School. Despite her four young children, but with the hearty endorsement of her husband, she worked in the suffrage movement all through the 1890s. At first she helped to organize a special "Committee of Work" in Massachusetts to raise money for Catt's Colorado campaign. But she soon turned her hand to work closer to home. BESAGG was born in her Committee of Work in 1901, and it was she who convinced Pauline Agassiz Shaw to become its first president. Her fund-raising abilities and powers of persuasion were legendary within the movement. She raised thousands of dollars through her social contacts and had a special genius for finding the right person to do the right job. Convinced, for instance, that Alice Stone Blackwell was an ineffective chairman of the Executive Board of MWSA, she quietly convinced Alice Stone Blackwell in 1901 to step down and be replaced by her personal choice, Maud Wood Park.[18]

In 1895, the year of the municipal suffrage referendum in Massachusetts, Maud Wood had enrolled in Radcliffe, where the faculty was solidly opposed to suffrage for women, and where there were almost no suffragists among her fellow students. In her senior year she was invited to speak at the annual MWSA dinner because she was one of the few college women interested in suffrage. After her marriage in 1898 to Charles Park, an architect in sympathy with the suffrage cause, she became a devoted worker. In 1900, searching for inspiration, she visited NAWSA's convention in Washington. She came away appalled. The meeting was held in the basement of a church and attended by an audience of about 100 middle-aged and elderly women. The first speaker presented a state report from Missouri in rhyme. Convinced something must be done to attract younger, especially educated, women, Maud Wood Park and a college friend, Inez Haynes, decided that spring to form a new organization, a College Equal Suffrage League. Based at first in Boston, CESL was ingeniously designed to interest two groups of women in suffrage. College alumnae were to form chapters in CESL and then were charged with organizing women currently attending their alma maters. In 1901, Maud Wood Park strengthened her suffrage ties by becoming chairwoman of the Executive Board of MWSA, and by founding BESAGG with Mary Hutcheson Page.[19]

CESL mushroomed in Massachusetts among the numerous new college women graduates, and in 1904 Maud Wood Park was invited by Blatch and Caroline Lexow to set up college leagues in New York State. In 1906 NAWSA asked her to organize leagues throughout the country. Pauline Agassiz Shaw missed her so much that she volunteered to pay her salary for five years if she would return to New England and work full time. Maud Wood Park promised to return eventually, but in the meantime continued to travel; and in 1908 along with M. Carey Thomas, president of Bryn Mawr, formed a national CESL, complete with an executive council. The older and more prestigious Thomas was made president of the league and perhaps partly out of resentment Maud Wood Park, now widowed, took temporary leave of suffrage work in 1909 to embark on a tour to study women throughout the world, predictably financed by Pauline Agassiz Shaw. Although Maud Wood Park was out of the country during the summers of 1909 and 1910, when new tactics were introduced, she had been instrumental in laying the organizational groundwork and returned to Massachusetts for full-time work in 1911.[20]

While women like Mary Hutcheson Page and Maud Wood Park formed new organizations, they also sought to strengthen old ones. By 1901 they held powerful positions in MWSA and had begun vigorous new recruitment activities. They contacted women in all the religious denominations and teachers' societies, sent speakers to chapters of the Massachusetts Federation of Women's Clubs, and set up booths at agricultural and county fairs.[21] MWSA and CESL also quickly moved to take advantage of the arrival in Boston in 1903 of the Women's Trade Union League (WTUL), hoping to strengthen ties with the American Federation of Labor and convert more working women to suffrage. Unions and suffrage groups exchanged speakers and held joint meetings.[22] By 1909 Mary Hutcheson Page reported that 235 unions had endorsed woman suffrage.[23]

For the first time since the Civil War the wealthy and college-educated women who made up the suffrage movement found themselves allied with large and potentially powerful segments of the population. Organized labor, consumers, ethnic groups, and progressive reformers were all, like the suffragists, on the outside looking in at the entrenched Republican establishment and the interests it represented. In Massachusetts this establishment had conspired to defeat all of the truly "modern" measures such as factory regulations, child labor laws, temperance, and the suffrage.[24] Most WTUL women were suffragists, and most suffrage workers were genuinely concerned about the plight of working women.[25] Each group needed the others' support to obtain the legislation they wanted; organized labor could reasonably expect that once women had the vote they would help elect progressive candidates pledged to support regulatory factory legislation. To convince the unions of their potential support, suffragist speakers emphasized what the ballot would do for working women. The alliance between organized labor and suffrage organizations was a long-lived and amicable one. The zeal with which Massachusetts women pursued the friendship indicates they were aware of the important role labor would play in the fight for suffrage.[26]

By 1907 the success of the Massachusetts women in rebuilding the suffrage movement had brought them to the point where they were restless. The movement seemed to have reached a hiatus, in which the convinced reinforced their own convictions. The method of reaching women through the endorsements of prominent citizens, labor leaders, and civic-minded organizations seemed to have reached maximum efficiency. Maud Wood Park, on tour for CESL in 1907, expressed these dissatisfactions to Mary Hutcheson Page from San Francisco:

> You know how we are hampered because we are thought to be merely suffragists, how we can seem to go just so far and no farther. For example, when I want to speak to an audience of college girls it's almost impossible to get them together unless someone of great influence works up the meeting. We rarely get a chance to be heard by uninterested persons. . . .[27]

Maud Wood Park was struggling here to articulate two questions asked more and more frequently by members of the Massachusetts suffrage movement. The first was how the suffragists could gain attention strictly on their own. The second was how they could expand their realm of agitation so as to draw in the uninformed citizen. For ultimately, woman suffrage would have to run the gauntlet of popular opinion before the Massachusetts state constitution could be amended.

The answers to these questions were not always self-evident. For the most part these upper- and middle-class women did not expect suffrage to lead to any fundamental change in woman's special function as wife, mother, and civilizer. To think of themselves as political agitators meant calling into question the whole notion of special spheres of female activity, which was especially prevalent in their age.[28] Once given an inkling of how to overcome these obstacles, however, Massachusetts women did so with remarkably little hesitation.

The hint came not from American leadership or from a more dynamic state suffrage movement but from England. British suffragists had been using more aggressive tactics than their American counterparts for some time, largely as a result of women's involvement with the anti-corn law agitation. Even the more conservative constitutionalist suffrage societies in England considered public speaking and barnstorming campaigns legitimate realms of activity for respectable women.[29] Precisely for this reason, however, these activities failed to stir up much interest or notice. The militant groups, of which Emmeline G. Pankhurst's Women's Social and Political Union (WSPU) was the most famous, sought public attention when they introduced more dramatic tactics: interruptions of political meetings; partisan campaigns in by-elections; and enormous processions through the streets of London, culminating in demonstrations at Westminster. The militants, who were quickly labeled "Suffragettes," got what they bargained for and more;

they were in the headlines for years. Police usually turned the processions into ugly riots, and many women were injured and arrested; a few were killed.[30]

Women in America did not evidently become aware of tactics used for some time by English suffragists until the English militants made them famous on both sides of the Atlantic. Not surprisingly, Mary Hutcheson Page was one of the first Massachusetts women to develop contacts with the militants. In 1908 she initiated a correspondence with Emmeline Pethick-Lawrence, subscribed to the militant paper, *Votes for Women,* and began work on an article concerning the English militant suffragists, which appeared in *Colliers* in 1909.[31] Her attitudes toward the English movement were largely the same as those that were to be expressed by most Massachusetts women over the next few years. She explained that English women had been using constitutional methods for years and had never been taken seriously by any government in power. The women were simply forced to take more aggressive steps, none of them illegal, to make their point. For this they had been beaten, arrested, and imprisoned. She was obviously impressed with the respectable origins of the militants, so much like her own, and found them convincing proof of the sincerity and legitimacy of their motives. She portrayed Pankhurst as a fearless heroine, devoted to the suffrage and the cause of working women. "The suffragettes," she explained, "prefer to go to prison rather than politically recant their dearest convictions; namely, the right to demand the vote in a way that they consider necessary and legal."[32] The cause also received sympathetic treatment in the *Woman's Journal.*[33]

The difficulty for the Massachusetts suffragists lay in deciding what lessons could legitimately be drawn from the English experience. Most important, they had to consider the ways in which the methods used to gain the suffrage in Massachusetts were bound to be different from those employed in England. Pressuring the majority government into supporting the suffrage was only one step in most American states, since constitutional amendments would ultimately have to be approved by the voters.[34] The suffrage movement in America had to gain the spotlight without alienating the voting public. The Massachusetts suffrage organizations, while openly sympathetic with the plight of the English militant suffragists, were more interested in finding out about less defiant tactics that could, nonetheless, bring American women publicity. Some discussion of English tactics, including the open-air meeting, took place at a MWSA meeting in October 1908.[35]

The open-air meeting was perfectly suited to the requirements of the Massachusetts suffragists. It was a dramatic new tactic, for unlike their English sisters American women had typically spoken at only carefully prearranged indoor meetings.[36] It was well-suited to the need the women felt to reach a wider range of people on their own. Moreover, it could be defended as a relatively conservative tactic, since even the constitutional societies in England had long used it. Two English suffrage workers visited Boston during the winter of 1908–1909 and became much-sought-after speakers on the subject of their open-air speaking tours.[37] The result was that in the spring and summer of 1909 a virtual revolution in suffragist tactics took place in Massachusetts. Most of them were consciously adopted from the English movement. One suffragist succinctly summarized the new strategy when she told her colleagues that opposition to suffrage was not the major difficulty in winning the vote:

> We are handicapped by indifference and its resulting ignorance . . . we have got to prove our case, not to a small body of lawmakers, but to a large body of the people, those who elect the lawmakers, and to prove it to them we must make them listen. . . . If they are uninterested it is because you have not made the subject interesting. Make it so. Make it picturesque. This is what the English women have accomplished. Then when you have made it picturesque there is one other step; make it easy . . . you must go to him [the voter].[38]

The first steps taken were naturally a bit tentative and timid, for these suffrage workers were about to do something quite novel for women of their rank and class: they were going to speak, not to prearranged audiences with guaranteed manners, but to whatever assortment of listeners might appear, including the possibly rude or hostile. On May 7 in a meeting of MWSA Mary Hutcheson Page proposed that a storefront in downtown Boston be rented for propaganda work. MWSA, in cooperation with BESAGG, opened a suffrage shop in Tremont Street in late May. Speeches were given there every day at noon.[39] On May 29 the *Woman's Journal* reported that even the New England Woman Suffrage Association was discussing English tactics and concluded that although "it would not be useful in America to smash windows or interrupt public speakers . . . most of the other methods of propaganda work invented in England could be well employed here."[40]

By June more vigorous plans were under way. Again, MWSA and BESAGG cooperated by forming a special joint Votes for Women Committee, headed by Mary Hutcheson Page, which would operate outside both organizations, probably to avoid identifying the more radical tactics with either organization.[41] She promptly sought the best person for the job of directing the first open-air meetings. Her choice, Susan Walker Fitzgerald, the daughter of Admiral John G. Walker, and wife of a wealthy, Harvard-trained lawyer, had majored in political science and history at Bryn Mawr and after her graduation in 1893 had done social work on the West Side of New York. A colleague of Ernest Poole, Robert Hunter, and Lillian Wald, she had served as a truant officer and settlement worker before coming to Boston in 1907.[42]

The women chose the quiet village green of Bedford for their first open-air talk.[43] On June 5 it rained, but on June 12 they held "that first painful meeting" with an audience of about 100. Although they tried to prearrange times and places at first, they soon learned "the only thing to do was to reach a town, take possession of the busiest spot and begin to talk."[44] Under the guidance of Fitzgerald, a small corps of women speakers toured the smaller towns, villages, and vacation spots of Massachusetts during the summers of 1909 and 1910 in automobiles, trolley cars, and trains, outfitted with banners, leaflets, petitions, and "Votes for Women" buttons.[45] One of the travellers delightfully described the routine:

> Picture our party unloading from a street-car in the central square of some little country town. . . . Then we make for the nearest drug store, deposit all our luggage in one corner, and to compensate for its storage all of us are in duty bound to buy sodas. . . . While we drink, the drug clerk is crossexamined as to where the best audience can be collected, time of trolleys, hotel for the night, factories and mills in town, number of employees, men or women, union or non-union, what they manufacture, and a few dozen other similar things. Meanwhile, if the town is large enough for us to require a permit to speak, Mrs. Fitzgerald has interviewed the police. Then our leaflets are unpacked, our flag erected, we borrow a Moxie box from the obliging drug clerk and proceed to the busiest corner of the town square. Our chief mounts the box, the banner over her shoulder, and starts talking to the air, three assorted dogs, six kids, and the two loafers in front of the grocery store just over the way. The rest of us give handbills to all the passers-by and the nearby stores. Within ten minutes our audience has increased from twenty-five to five hundred, according to the time and place. We speak in turn for an hour or more, answer questions, sell buttons, and circulate the petition. Then we leave, generally in undignified haste, to catch our car for the next meeting.[46]

The success of the new tactics was indisputable. The suffragists made converts in their open-air meetings but, more important, gained wide coverage in the newspapers. All summer, reporters and photographers followed them around, delighted with the drama of giving some of Boston's élite families prominent news coverage.[47] As the women steadily became more experienced and accomplished, they tried to invade at least two towns a day and worked six days a week.

Although several dozen women became veteran crowd-handlers, two in particular caught the attention of the press. Florence Luscomb, a 1909 graduate from Massachusetts Institute of Technology in architecture, slim and delicately beautiful, was an aggressive and always self-confident speaker. Her mother, Hannah Knox Luscomb, had long been a suffrage worker and had used her private income to help finance the movement.[48] Margaret Foley may have been the only speaker in the first tours with a working-class background. She grew up in Irish Roxbury, worked in a hat factory, joined the hat-trimmers union, and was eventually put on the local board of WTUL. She was certainly the most colorful of the speakers, for as the Boston *Transcript* rhapsodized, "she stands five feet eight and weighs in at one hundred and forty, but she can easily manage seven feet, turn her brown hair to flame, descend like a mountain of brick and extend her mellifluous accent to megaphonics."[49] Some of the women visited factories and spoke at noon to the workers. Florence Luscomb thought those meetings were especially challenging but claimed the mill audiences were "ready to be entertained," and "often sympathetic in advance."[50] Suffrage workers also distributed thousands of leaflets and gave dozens of speeches at county fairs, sent Margaret Foley up in a balloon, put a float in the Waltham Fourth of July parade, and persuaded the manager of a circus to drape his elephant with a Votes for Women sign.[51]

At home, in the Boston headquarters, the response of most suffrage workers was wholly supportive. The patriarch of the New England movement, Henry Blackwell, heartily endorsed the open-air meetings in the *Woman's Journal*, often combining his kudos with admiration for the English militant suffragists.[52] He died in September 1909, but his daughter, Alice Stone Blackwell, the chief editor of the *Woman's Journal*, was even more enthusiastic about new tactics than her father, and tenaciously defended the Pankhursts through some of their most difficult moments in 1909 and 1910.[53] Noting that English women sold suffrage newspapers on the street, she suggested the same might be done in Boston; and in November 1909, Florence Luscomb and Mabel Ewell entered the ranks of the Boston "newsies," most of whom were working-class boys.[54] This tactic also received much attention in the press and got suffragists, probably for the first time, out onto the streets of Boston.[55]

When Pankhurst visited the city in October, she received a tumultuous greeting from Boston women; and the entire issue of October 16 of the *Woman's Journal* was devoted to the English woman suffrage cause. The first suffrage parade in Boston carried Pankhurst from South Station to Boylston Street suffrage headquarters. More than 2000 people heard the English leader at Tremont Theatre, where she was introduced by Fitzgerald. She stayed in the home of Mary Hutcheson Page. Her visit to the city was capped by a luncheon at the Vendome, where Alice Stone Blackwell compared her to Stone, Henry Blackwell, and the other great reformers.[56]

In December, Foley and Gertrude Cliff invaded the floor of the Boston Stock Exchange and Chamber of Commerce and distributed leaflets advertising the visit of Ethel Snowden, then second in command of WSPU.[57] The total hegemony of the younger generation of more militant Massachusetts women was fittingly symbolized by the appearance of Julia Ward Howe, the most ancient and respectable of all New England feminists, on the same platform with Snowden, who, according to the Boston *Herald,* said that classes or sexes with no redress had eventually to resort to violence.[58]

By 1910, enthusiasm for English tactics was so widespread among Massachusetts suffragists that perhaps the greatest danger to the vitality of their movement lay in losing a feel for what might be appropriate in America and in underestimating their abilities. A more practical atmosphere settled over the Massachusetts movement after the summer of 1911, when two of the most popular open-air speakers in the recent campaigns, Foley and Florence Luscomb, went to the convention of the International Woman Suffrage Alliance in Stockholm. In fact, the main purpose of their trip abroad was to study the English suffrage movement. They spent over a month in London, interviewing leaders of all the suffrage societies, attending meetings, marching in parades, attending demonstrations, visiting Parliament, and selling newspapers.

Florence Luscomb, who kept a detailed diary of what she saw and heard, was obviously in sympathy with the militants and carefully recorded all their tactics and lines of argument that might be useful in America. She was particularly taken with the militant campaigns in by-elections to defeat candidates publically opposed to suffrage. However, she found the English suffrage movement to be more complicated than she had believed. Accustomed to a close alliance between trade union women and suffragists, she was disturbed to learn that many English labor leaders distrusted the Pankhursts and other aristocratic militant suffrage leaders because they were willing to work for a limited franchise for women and ignore the question of universal suffrage for adults. The most militant suffragists were not, evidently, the most radical.[59] In general she came away feeling grateful for American institutions and democratic principles, which, she felt, would make suffrage easier to obtain in America than in England. She was also convinced that American women suffragists were at least as competent as their English counterparts, and she wrote her mother:

> Understand, I am not for a moment disparaging the splendid enthusiasm of the WSPU. . . . But with the exception of Mrs. Pankhurst I did not find

many of their speakers or workers superior . . . their methods, ingenuity, etc., seem no better than our own, when we really set about it. . . . I am coming home more encouraged and pleased with our work than ever.[60]

Foley's new inspiration and self-confidence were also immediately apparent. In the fall of 1911 she set out on a personal campaign to initiate in Massachusetts the English technique of quizzing politicians on their suffrage views at public rallies. She and a group of fellow "hecklers," as they were dubbed in the newspapers, set off by automobile to pursue the Republican campaign through the Berkshires. They were followed by newspaper reporters who gleefully reported the politicos' unsuccessful attempts to escape. She also invaded Tammany Hall, where Congressman James M. Curley and other Democrats recognized her right to speak and gave at least tacit support to woman suffrage.[61] The heckling campaign, although not an official activity of MWSA or BESAGG, was clearly a precursor of future developments.

In 1911 and 1912 the national suffrage movement was at a crossroads over the issue of participation in political campaigns. For years the policy of NAWSA had been one of absolute neutrality. At the national convention in 1912 a major controversy would explode over the party affiliations of several members. After an emotional debate the convention voted to allow its officers to work for the political parties of their choice.[62] For years Henry Blackwell had advocated fierce opposition to anti-suffrage candidates, a form of political partisanship which ultimately would be adopted in the last stages of the federal amendment drive.[63] The successful use of the tactic in England helped to revive interest in it in Massachusetts and in 1909 Alice Stone Blackwell editorialized on its merits in the *Woman's Journal.*[64] Such exhortations could seriously be considered by 1911 because women suffragists in the state were now clearly a significant political force. Morever, the policy was well suited to politics in Massachusetts, where the suffrage issue cut across party lines. Although the entrenched Republicans were the most obvious enemies of the cause, the suffragists skillfully refused to ally with the Progressive, Democratic or Socialist parties except on specific issues, in order to avoid being identified with any potential losers. They concentrated instead on identifying specific enemies, supporting friends, and educating the public on the suffrage issue.

By the summer of 1911 they were ready to overcome the largest center of indifference to suffrage in their state, the city of Boston. The method for reaching city voters and potential women supporters was consciously borrowed from the suffrage workers in New York City who had suggested using the precinct organization method to mobilize city residents for the suffrage cause.[65] In Boston each voter was identified from the registration lists. A suffrage worker visited each voter's residence in the hope of enlisting the women of the house in a new Woman Suffrage party, for which no dues were required. Suffrage literature was also distributed for the voting men. Rallies were held on street corners or party headquarters in every ward of the city, with speeches by women in whichever languages predominated.[66] The door-to-door canvassing was probably the final baptism of fire for the elegant Bostonian suffragists. As the state chairman of ward organization reported after a trial effort in 1910:

> It took some sense of duty, some devotion to our cause, to push us up the dim . . . staircase, to knock at any one of the several non-committal doors on the first shabby landing. Probably the woman who answered knew no English, and stared uncomprehendingly. No matter—you did as well as you could, the children, who have learned English, helped; the Yiddish and Italian flyers helped; and best of all the women, as soon as they knew what it was all about, proved so kindly, so approachable, so open-minded and responsive . . . that whatever the future may hold . . . the pilgrimage through Ward 8 proved of the deepest interest and meaning.[67]

In 1912 suffragists in Massachusetts demonstrated their new political power. They defeated Roger Woolcott, an old enemy, who as chairman of the state senate's Constitutional Amendments Committee, had blocked suffrage bills. In the same year the Progressive party endorsed suffrage, and the Progressive members of the state legislature, supported by pro-suffrage lobbyists, defeated conservative attempts to force another referendum. In coalition with Progressive elements suffragists defeated Levi Greenwood, president of the state senate, in 1913, although his district had been a Republican stronghold for years. By 1914 woman suffrage was supported by the Socialists, the Progressives, the Democrats, the State Federation of Labor, and the new Democratic governor of Massachusetts, David Walsh. In 1914 and 1915 the amendment easily passed both houses of the legislature and was on its way to the voters.[68]

Suffragists in Massachusetts expected to lose the referendum battle and did, but when the federal amendment was passed by Congress in 1919, they quickly remobilized for the ratification drive. Calling on the coalition that had put the state amendment through in 1914 and 1915, they defeated a move by their opponents which would have submitted the amendment to referendum. They collected 135,000 petition signatures in two weeks, and spent an "eleventh hour" session with the chairman of the Federal Relations Committee arguing the legal aspects of ratification. The committee produced a favorable report on the floor of the house, and on June 25 ratification carried by a vote of 185 ayes to 47 noes. There were only five votes against the measure in the senate.[69]

The woman suffrage workers of Massachusetts had, by 1919, transformed a dormant, unimaginative state society of suffragists into a network of aggressive organizations, which mobilized thousands of women, many of them young, in suffrage work and a unique political movement. Their energy and success were stimulated by their own self-confidence, talents, rising aspirations, the example of their English sisters, and the assistance given them by organized labor and other progressive elements in Massachusetts. Their history should remind scholars that while national leaders are important, the rank and file of any movement can be more significant.

NOTES

1. The most widely used original accounts of the suffrage movement are Carrie Chapman Catt and Nettie Rogers Shuler, *Woman Suffrage and Politics: The Inner Story of the Suffrage Movement* (Seattle, 1926); Ida Husted Harper, *The Life and Work of Susan B. Anthony* (3 vols., Indianapolis, 1893–1908); Anna Howard Shaw, *The Story of a Pioneer* (New York, 1915); Elizabeth Cady Stanton, *Eighty Years and More 1815–1897: Reminiscences* (New York, 1898); Elizabeth Cady Stanton, Susan B. Anthony, Matilda Joslyn Gage, and Ida Husted Harper, eds., *The History of Woman Suffrage* (6 vols., Rochester, 1899–1922).

2. Eleanor Flexner, *Century of Struggle: The Woman's Rights Movement in the United States* (New York, 1970), 236; Aileen S. Kraditor, *The Ideas of the Woman Suffrage Movement, 1890–1920* (New York, 1965), 9; William L. O'Neill, *The Woman Movement: Feminism in the United States and England* (London, 1969), 73–78. Alan P. Grimes nearly goes to the other extreme by suggesting that the success of the suffrage movement was due, especially in the West, not so much to the work of suffragists as to generally conservative and irrational social forces which viewed woman suffrage as a means of gaining social control. Alan P. Grimes, *The Puritan Ethic and Woman Suffrage* (New York, 1967).

3. For an analysis of the origins of English and American feminism, see James L. Cooper and Sheila M. Cooper, *The Roots of American Feminist Thought* (Boston, 1973), and O'Neill, *Woman Movement.*

4. Flexner, *Century of Struggle,* 249–53, 263; William L. O'Neill, *Everyone Was Brave: A History of Feminism in America* (Chicago, 1971), 126–27.

5. For example, see Flexner, *Century of Struggle,* 216. The bias in the original sources toward New York may possibly be attributed to several factors: New York women wrote almost all of the published autobiographies; the state of Massachusetts was so notorious among suffragists for its anti-suffrage movement that the hundreds of suffrage activists were often forgotten; New York won a popular

referendum for woman suffrage in 1917 while Massachusetts lost one in 1915, leading to the possible but not necessarily logical conclusion that Massachusetts had a weaker suffrage organization; the official history of the movement was edited by New York women, except Ida Husted Harper, who was a devoted biographer and companion of Susan B. Anthony and enthusiastic champion of Carrie Chapman Catt. Whether in a moment of pique or forgetfulness, Harper managed to avoid including Massachusetts in the index of Volume V of the *History of Woman Suffrage;* sixteen states, including New York, had entries.

6. For a history of the Massachusetts suffrage movement in the nineteenth century, see Lois Bannister Merk's, "Massachusetts and the Woman Suffrage Movement" (doctoral dissertation, Northeastern University, 1961). See also Arthur Mann, *Yankee Reformers in the Urban Age* (Cambridge, Mass., 1954), 205–16.

7. Merk, "Massachusetts and the Woman Suffrage Movement," 58–64.

8. For a discussion of the differences between the "justice" and "expediency" arguments, see Kraditor, *Ideas of the Woman Suffrage Movement,* 43–74.

9. Lois Bannister Merk, "Boston's Historic Public School Crisis," *New England Quarterly,* 31 (June 1958), 172–99.

10. Maud Wood Park, "Massachusetts Woman Suffrage Association: Introductory Notes," June 1943, Woman's Rights Collection (Schlesinger Library, Radcliffe College).

11. *Ibid.;* Merk, "Massachusetts and the Woman Suffrage Movement," 330.

12. NAWSA reported in 1908 that Massachusetts was second only to New York in membership: New York had 27,476; Massachusetts had 19,197; and Illinois had 10,080. *Proceedings of the Annual Convention of the National American Woman Suffrage Association* (Warren, Ohio, 1908), 21–22.

13. See Robert H. Wiebe, *The Search for Order, 1877–1920* (New York, 1967), 111–32, 165.

14. O'Neill, *Everyone Was Brave,* 77–106; Mann, *Yankee Reformers in the Urban Age,* 201–04.

15. *First Report of the Boston Equal Suffrage Association for Good Government, 1901–1903* (Boston, 1903); Maud Wood Park, "Boston Equal Suffrage Association for Good Government. (1901–1907) Introductory Note," Woman's Rights Collection.

16. Mary Hutcheson Page retired from the suffrage movement in 1918 and Pauline Agassiz Shaw died in 1917. Maud Wood Park, as chairwoman of the Congressional Committee of NAWSA from 1917 to 1920, was responsible for directing the work of getting the federal amendment through Congress. For her experiences in Washington, see Maud Wood Park, *Front Door Lobby,* Edna Lamprey Stantial, ed. (Boston, 1960).

17. Edward T. James, Janet Wilson James, and Paul S. Boyer, eds., *Notable American Women, 1607–1950: A Biographical Dictionary* (3 vols., Cambridge, Mass., 1971), III, 278–80; Harper, ed., *History of Woman Suffrage,* V, 337; Boston *Transcript,* Feb. 10, 1917.

18. Katherine Page Hersey, "Mary Hutcheson Page," May 1943, Maud Wood Park, "Mary Hutcheson Page," April 1943, Anthony to Mary H. Page, March 15, 1899, Page Scrapbook, Woman's Rights Collection. See also, National American Woman Suffrage Association, *Victory How Women Won It: A Centennial Symposium, 1840–1940* (New York, 1940), 76. Carrie Chapman Catt knew of Mary Hutcheson

Page's abilities: "*Now,* you are the great persuader . . . I've heard how you go in and camp before your object of entreaty and just smile until she does just what you want." Carrie C. Catt to Mary H. Page, Aug. 12, 1905, Page Scrapbook, Woman's Rights Collection.

19. Lois Bannister Merk, "The Early Career of Maud Wood Park," *Radcliffe Quarterly,* 32 (May 1948), 10–17; Maud Wood Park, "Supplementary Notes," Jan. 1943, and "College Equal Suffrage League Introductory Notes," Dec. 1942, Woman's Rights Collection; "Constitution of the College Equal Suffrage League," May 24, 1905, *ibid.*

20. Park, "College Equal Suffrage League Introductory Notes," Dec. 1942; Park, "College Equal Suffrage League Supplementary Notes," Jan., 1943, Woman's Rights Collection; Pauline A. Shaw to Maud W. Park, April 10, 1907 (copy), *ibid.*

21. Merk, "Massachusetts and Woman Suffrage," 340–56.

22. College Equal Suffrage League, *Minutes,* 1 (Dec. 5, 1906), 64–65, Woman's Rights Collection; Massachusetts Woman Suffrage Association, *Records,* 2 (June 1, 1906 and Oct. 28, 1908), 221, 302, *ibid.*

23. Massachusetts Woman Suffrage Association, *Records,* 2 (Oct. 22, 1909), 348, *ibid.*

24. Whether there was a progressive movement in Massachusetts is debatable. Richard M. Abrams believes the state, with a few exceptions, woman suffrage among them, had enacted most progressive reforms by 1900. He says that Republican leaders, who controlled the government, were "conservative," and when a successful challenge came to their rule, it came from Irish-Americans, not progressives. Since Abrams confines his discussion of woman suffrage to one footnote and excludes women as a political force entirely, his book cannot be considered a comprehensive political study of the period or of the progressive movement in Massachusetts. Richard M. Abrams, *Conservatism in a Progressive Era: Massachusetts Politics 1900–1912* (Cambridge, Mass., 1964). That ethnic leaders in Massachusetts might also be labeled progressives is explored by John D. Buenker, "The Mahatma and Progressive Reform: Martin Lomasney as Lawmaker, 1911–1917," *New England Quarterly,* 44 (Sept. 1971), 397–419.

25. The Women's Trade Union League was organized in Boston, in 1903 at a regular convention of AFL. Although Chicagoans soon dominated the national organization, there was a very strong league in Boston that supported striking women, agitated for labor legislation, organized women workers, and supported feminist causes. Gladys Boone, *The Women's Trade Union Leagues in Great Britain and the United States of America* (New York, 1968).

26. For example, see two accounts of speeches given by Florence Luscomb. Bangor (Maine) *Daily News,* April 22, 1909; Richmond (Virginia) *News Leader,* Oct. 4, 1910. The Woman's Rights Collection has a large number of newspaper clippings and suffrage fliers which attest that women suffragists consistently tried to appeal to labor. See also, Merk, "Massachusetts and Woman Suffrage," 269–74.

27. Maud W. Park to Mary H. Page, Nov. 25, 1907 (copy), Woman's Rights Collection.

28. Aileen S. Kraditor, *Up from the Pedestal: Selected Writings in the History of American Feminism* (Chicago, 1968), 7–13.

29. Constance Rover, *Women's Suffrage and Party Politics in Britain 1866–1914* (London and Toronto, 1967), 61.

30. *Ibid.*, 72–101. See also E. Sylvia Pankhurst, *The Suffragette: The History of the Women's Militant Suffrage Movement 1905–1910* (London, 1911); E. Sylvia Pankhurst, *The Life of Emmeline Pankhurst: The Suffragette Struggle for Women's Citizenship* (New York, 1969).

31. Emmeline Pethick-Lawrence to Mary H. Page, Sept. 16, Nov. 12, 1908, Page Scrapbook, Woman's Rights Collection.

32. Mary Hutcheson Page, "Mr. Asquith's Prisoners," *Colliers*, 43 (May 15, 1909), 17. See also, Mary Hutcheson Page, "Letter to the Editor," Boston *Herald*, March 23, 1909.

33. For example, see "The Struggle in England," *Woman's Journal*, 39 (Oct. 31, 1908), 174; "Events in England," *ibid.*, 39 (Nov. 7, 1908), 178; "An American in England," *ibid.*, 40 (Aug. 14, 1909), 130.

34. Harper succinctly made this point in 1907: "In the United States there are forty-five Parliaments to be reckoned with, and that is only the beginning; for, when a majority of their members have been enlisted, they can only submit the question to the electors. It encounters then such a conglomerate mass of voters as exists nowhere else on the face of the earth, and it is doubtful if under such similar conditions women could get the franchise in any country on the globe." Ida Husted Harper, "Woman Suffrage Throughout the World," *North American Review*, 186 (Sept. 1907), 70.

35. Massachusetts Woman Suffrage Association, *Records*, 2 (Oct. 28, 1908), 303–04, Woman's Rights Collection.

36. There were probably many exceptions to this general rule. The chairwoman of the Meetings Committee of MWSA reported in 1908 that as many as 1000 people a day had been spoken to by suffragists at local fairs that summer and fall. *Ibid.*, 304. The first open-air meetings in Boston took place by accident outside the state house because everyone present could not fit into the building. Boston *Herald*, Feb. 24, 1909.

37. *Woman's Journal*, 40 (Jan. 2, 1909), 3; *ibid.*, 40 (Feb. 20, 1909), 29; *ibid.*, 40 (March 6, 1909) 35.

38. Florence H. Luscomb, "Our Open-Air Campaign," circa 1909, p. 1, Woman's Rights Collection.

39. Massachusetts Woman Suffrage Association, *Records*, 2 (May 7, 1909), 327, *ibid.; Woman's Journal*, 40 (May 29, 1909), 86.

40. *Woman's Journal*, 40 (May 29, 1909), 85.

41. Massachusetts Woman Suffrage Association, *Records*, 2 (June 4, 1909), 335, Woman's Rights Collection; *Fifth Report of the Boston Equal Suffrage Association for Good Government, 1908–1910* (Boston, 1910), 9.

42. "Mrs. Susan W. Fitzgerald," *Woman's Journal*, 41 (Feb. 5, 1910), 21. Susan Walker Fitzgerald served as recording secretary for NAWSA from 1912 to 1915. Another original participant in the Massachusetts open-air meetings, Katherine Dexter McCormick, was treasurer of NAWSA in 1913 and 1914, and first vice-president from 1915 to 1920.

43. The question of which group or individual gave the first open-air meeting in the United States remains in doubt. Scholars have generally accepted the contention of Harriot Stanton Blatch that she pioneered the technique in America, but she admits that her first attempt, a trolley car campaign along the Erie Canal in May 1908, was a dismal failure. See Harriot Stanton Blatch and Alma Lutz, *Challenging*

Years: the Memoirs of Harriot Stanton Blatch (New York, 1940), 107. Winifred Cooley, who reported on the use of such tactics in New York City, claimed a group called the Suffragettes, led by Lydia K. Commander, gave the first open-air meetings in New York City during the winter of 1907–1908. Winifred Cooley, "Suffragists and 'Suffragettes' a Record of Actual Achievement," *World To-Day,* 15 (Oct. 1908), 1066–71. Two English suffrage workers instigated a parade followed by an open-air meeting in Boone, Iowa, in 1908. Louise R. Noun, *Strong-Minded Women: The Emergence of the Woman Suffrage Movement in Iowa* (Ames, 1969), 246. Harriot Stanton Blatch's trolley tour was routinely reported in the *Woman's Journal,* 39 (June 13, 1908), 95, with no editorial comment. The crucial point here is that Massachusetts women were convinced that they had adopted the technique from England, not from New York. Certainly the Massachusetts women were the first moderate organization with a statewide membership to use the tactic systematically and consistently. See Florence H. Luscomb, "Brief Biographical Sketch," 1945, pp. 1–3, Woman's Rights Collection; interview with Florence Luscomb, Nov. 6, 1972, Oral History Project of Rhode Island (University of Rhode Island).

44. *Fifth Report of the Boston Equal Suffrage Association for Good Government,* 9.

45. For a description of the tours, see *ibid.*; Luscomb, "Our Open-Air Campaign"; *Woman's Journal,* 40 (Aug. 28, 1909), 138–39; *Proceedings of the Annual Convention of the National American Woman Suffrage Association* (New York, 1910), 118–19.

46. Luscomb, "Our Open-Air Campaign," 4–5.

47. "Annual Report of the Massachusetts Woman Suffrage Association," *Minutes,* 2 (Oct. 22, 1909), 343, Woman's Rights Collection.

48. Interview with Florence Luscomb, July 18, 19, 1972, Oral History Project of Rhode Island; Luscomb, "Brief Biographical Sketch," 1–2.

49. Clipping, circa 1911, Woman's Rights Collection.

50. Luscomb, "Our Open-Air Campaign," 5.

51. Interview with Florence Luscomb, Nov. 6, 1972, Oral History Project of Rhode Island; Luscomb, "Brief Biographical Sketch," 2–4.

52. For example, see "Open-Air Meetings," *Woman's Journal,* 40 (Aug. 14, 1909), 130; "Contrasting Methods," *ibid.,* 40 (Sept. 11, 1909), 146. Meanwhile the open-air technique had captured the interest of women all over the country. At the 1910 NAWSA convention in Washington, D.C., two Massachusetts women were asked to participate in a symposium presided over by Blatch on open-air meetings and help give a "practical demonstration." Mary Hutcheson Page was asked to lead a meeting on "Practical Methods of Work." When the state of California voted in favor of suffrage for women in 1911, workers there enthusiastically reaffirmed that open-air meetings and publicity in the papers were a crucial factor in their success. By 1911 Anna Howard Shaw endorsed open-air campaigns in her presidential address to the convention and in 1912 the tactic was officially introduced on the national level at a huge rally in Independence Square in Philadelphia. See Harper, ed., *History of Woman Suffrage,* V, 286, 317, 333; *Proceedings of the Annual Convention of the National American Woman Suffrage Association* (New York, 1911), 100–07.

53. "Mrs. Pankhurst's Methods," *Woman's Journal,* 40 (Oct. 23, 1909), 170; "Militant Moods," *ibid.,* 40 (Oct. 30, 1909), 174.

54. "Sell the Woman's Journal," *ibid.*, 40 (Sept. 25, 1909), 154.

55. "Selling the Woman's Journal," *ibid.*, 40 (Nov. 13, 1909), 183; "Selling the Woman's Journal," *ibid.*, 40 (Nov. 20, 1909), 186.

56. "Mrs. Pankhurst in Boston," *ibid.*, 40 (Oct. 30, 1909), 174.

57. "The climax of the excitement came when Miss Gertrude Cliff . . . was gently but firmly escorted from the center of the wheat pit." Boston *American,* Dec. 13, 1909.

58. Boston *Herald,* Dec. 15, 1909.

59. This diary is in the possession of Florence Luscomb.

60. Florence H. Luscomb to Hannah K. Luscomb, June 4, 1911, *ibid.*; Boston *Globe,* April 6, 1911.

61. Boston *Globe,* Sept. 9, 1911; Boston *Herald,* Sept. 16, 1911; Boston *Globe,* Sept. 26, Oct. 10, 1911. The Woman's Rights Collection has a large number of clippings about Margaret Foley's "heckling" in the fall of 1911. See also Harper, ed., *History of Woman Suffrage,* VI, 296.

62. *Ibid.*, V, 342.

63. "Militant Woman Suffrage," *Woman's Journal,* 40 (Feb. 20, 1909), 30; Merk, "Massachusetts and Woman Suffrage," 100. After a federal amendment granting woman suffrage was defeated in the United States Senate in 1918 by two votes, NAWSA decided to work for the defeat of one incumbent senator from each party up for election that year. Senators John Weeks of Massachusetts and Willard Saulsbury of Delaware were defeated. See Flexner, *Century of Struggle,* 310–11.

64. "Non-Partisan Influence," *Woman's Journal,* 40 (Sept. 25, 1909), 154.

65. Ronald Schaffer, "The New York City Woman Suffrage Party, 1909–1919," *New York History,* 43 (July 1962), 268–87.

66. *Sixth Report of the Boston Equal Suffrage Association for Good Government, 1910–1912* (Boston, 1912), 14–16.

67. *Quarterly Report of the Massachusetts Woman Suffrage Association,* June 1910 (Boston, 1910), 14. Ward 8 was the political domain of city boss Martin Lomasney. Although he remained opposed to woman suffrage, he gave the suffragists some assistance in their campaign in his district, perhaps one of the best indications of the political power of the suffrage movement in Massachusetts by 1910. For Lomasney's views on suffrage, see Buenker, "The Mahatma and Progressive Reform," 409–10, 412.

68. For a discussion by Alice Stone Blackwell of this sequence of events, see Harper, ed., *History of Woman Suffrage,* VI, 296–99. See also Luscomb, "Brief Biographical Sketch," 5.

69. Harper, ed., *History of Woman Suffrage,* VI, 301–02; interview with Florence Luscomb, Aug. 27, 1973, Oral History Project of Rhode Island.

～18～

WOMEN REFORMERS AND AMERICAN CULTURE, 1870–1930

JILL CONWAY

The history of American feminism has an Alice in Wonderland quality. The story of the achievement of legal and institutional liberties for women in America must be accompanied by an account of their loss of psychological autonomy and social segregation. The historian of American feminism must write a double narrative in which something more than the reversals of Looking-Glass Land must be advanced. The historian must relate the outward story of a successful agitation to some causal analysis of why this agitation first for legal rights, then for access to higher education, then for the franchise and for liberation from a traditional Christian view of marriage had so little influence on actual behavior. For there is no escaping the fact that in the very decade of the twenties when the franchise was secured and when a liberal view of marriage ties had finally gained public acceptance that the vast majority of American women began to find social activism unattractive and to return to an ethic of domesticity as romantic and suffocating as any code of the high Victorian era. In fact the stereotype of femininity which became dominant in the popular culture of the thirties differed little from the stereotype of the Victorian lady except that the twentieth-century American woman had physical appetites which dictated that she could only know fulfillment by experiencing maternity and joyfully adapting to the exclusively feminine world of suburbia.[1]

To some historians and social analysts this paradox has seemed so puzzling that nothing short of a plot theory of history can explain this sudden alteration in what appeared to be the direction of social change. Betty Friedan, for instance, feels that the triumph of domesticity can only be accounted for by the recognition by capitalists that women could best serve the economy of abundance as passive consumers.[2] Yet her diagnosis does not take into account the fact that before the thirties women made the role of consumer an important one for social criticism through the organization of the National Consumers' League, a body which pioneered in legal and political campaigns in favor of state and federal welfare legislation. As the history of the League ably demonstrated between 1899, the year of its foundation, and the beginning of the New Deal welfare programs, consumers need not be passive victims of the capitalist system.

More recently historians of feminism have seen an underlying continuity behind the appearance of change in the social position of American women. Both Aileen Kraditor and William O'Neill have concluded that the remarkable stability of the bourgeois family in the twentieth century was the social fact which led to the frustration of all aspirations for change in the role and status of women.[3] Thus the reformers who made divorce and birth control acceptable in the early decades of the twentieth century put emphasis on the need to strengthen the family in a secular society. Both divorce and limitation of family size finally won popular acceptance when they were advocated as reforms which would allow the bourgeois family the flexibility necessary to survive the pressures of an upwardly mobile urban society rather than as reforms which would permit real changes in sexual behavior.[4] In the light of the evidence of historical demography we see the logic working for this kind of reform to preserve the family. Demographic study indicates that the duration of marriage unions was actually lengthening in the twentieth century as compared with earlier centuries such as the seventeenth, customarily regarded as a period of family stability. In fact, increased life expectancy in the twentieth century meant that fewer marriage partnerships were terminated after a short period by death; consequently, the sanctioning of divorce became a social necessity. There is thus no contradiction between the development of liberal attitudes toward the dissolution of marriage and the renewed stress on the value of maternity and domesticity for women. Divorce and birth control, both reforms which could have been advocated in terms opposed to female domesticity, actually won acceptance as measures to preserve the family and along with it female domesticity.

While historians are correct in emphasizing these underlying continuities in the history of American feminism between the Civil War and the 1930s, it is misleading to do so without drawing attention to the fact that women activists of the period represented a real change in feminine behavior. The failure of feminists to understand the significance of the intense social activism of women reformers during these years indicates that new ways of behaving do not necessarily evoke any new view of the female temperament. Though women of the stature of Jane Addams and Lillian Wald were actually wielding national power and influencing the decisions of the White House, neither they nor any of their contemporaries thought about adjusting the image of the female to this position of command. This failure to see women's activism for what it was, a real departure from women's traditional domesticity, indicates the controlling power of the stereotype of the female temperament which continued unaltered from the 1870s to the 1930s. Acquiescence in this control was indeed the major weakness in the ideology of feminism for the stereotype of the female personality was an essentially conservative one although women reformers coupled it with social innovation and occasionally with trenchant social criticism.

We see the controlling power of the stereotype of the female temperament most clearly in the thought of Jane Addams and Lillian Wald.[5] Both women were aggressive public campaigners who relished a good political fight and who hungered after power. Yet they claimed to be reformers in the name of specialized feminine perceptions of social injustice. These specialized perceptions came from women's innate passivity and from women's ability to empathize with the weak and dependent. Like all reformers with a program for action, Jane Addams and Lillian Wald believed they had found a social group who would bring a new, just social order into being, but theirs was a group defined by sex rather than by class. Lacking a clear class consciousness, they expected a sex group to be agents of social change because of the unique qualities with which they believed the feminine temperament was endowed. Because of these qualities women were capable of direct, intuitive awareness of social injustice exactly in the style of the abolitionists who had been fired for the antislavery crusade through direct intuitive perception of social sin. Just what it was in the psyche of a Jane Addams or a Lillian Wald which would permit empathy with the weak and dependent remains shrouded in mystery for the most assiduous biographer. Both women gave evidence from an early age of the capacity to create and dominate large organizations, and they moved naturally into a position of leadership in any area of reform which they took up, whether it be settlement work, child welfare legislation or the international peace movement.

Even though Jane Addams and Lillian Wald could not recognize their drive to power, their adoption of feminine intuition as a style of reform by which to come to grips with the problems of industrial cities is a puzzling choice. One expects tough-minded economic analysis from critics of industrial society. However, middle-class women reformers of their generation needed to find a basis for criticizing an exploitive economic system in which women of their class played no active part. It was for this reason that they were obliged to make such claims for the intuitive social power of the female temperament. They were encouraged in these claims by the dominant biological view of social evolution which did place great emphasis upon the evolutionary significance of biologically determined male and female temperaments. However, to base one's social criticism upon the idea that feminine intuition could both diagnose and direct social change was to tie one's identity as a social critic to acquiescence in the traditional stereotype of women. Further, to the extent that such women succeeded in gaining popular acceptance as reformers they were lending strength to the stereotype and helping to prepare the ground for the acceptance of another view of sexually specialized intellect, the neo-Freudian, romantic and conservative one, which began to gain acceptance in American culture in the twenties and the thirties.

In my study of American women who were both feminists and social critics in the post-Civil War era, two clearly distinct social types have emerged. The first is a borrowing from European culture, the type of the sage or prophetess who claimed access to hidden wisdom by virtue of feminine insights. The second is the type of the professional expert or the scientist, a social identity highly esteemed in American culture but sexually neutral. Jane Addams represents the best example of the Victorian sage to be found in American culture during her active public career from the 1890s to the 1930s. Florence Kelley, the organizer of the National Consumers' League and a kind of composite Sidney and Beatrice Webb for American industrial society, represents one of the best examples of the professional expert who took on the role of the social engineer. What is interesting about the two types is that the sage had great resonance for American popular culture and was celebrated in endless biographies, memoirs and eulogistic sketches.[6] Women who took on that role became great public figures, culture heroines known in households throughout the nation. But the woman as expert did not captivate the popular imagination and did not become a model of feminine excellence beyond a small circle of highly educated women of a single generation. Julia Lathrop, who was the pioneer strategist of the mental health movement, the innovator responsible for the juvenile court movement and the head of the first Federal Child Welfare Bureau which became the model for many New Deal welfare agencies, simply did not excite the faintest ripple of public attention during a lifetime exactly contemporaneous with Jane

Addams. Indeed this remarkable woman remained so anonymous despite a lifetime devoted to public service that Jane Addams wrote a biography of her so that she could serve as a model for future generations of American women.[7] The biography was little read and could not serve its purpose because Jane Addams lost the substance of this consummate political strategist's life in describing the empathetic and unaggressive woman heroine which the stereotype of female excellence required. Similarly Florence Kelley's biographer, Josephine Goldmark, was unable to preserve for future generations any of the fiery personality of this powerhouse of a woman.[8] The surface account of her lifetime devoted to the welfare of the industrial working class was accurately recorded. But the volcanic personality whose rages were so monumental that she could stamp out of a White House conference slamming the door in the face of Theodore Roosevelt is lost. Since women were supposed to be gentle, none of Mrs. Kelley's passion could come through the uncharacteristic calm imposed by her biographer. Thus the achievements of the experts were lost to subsequent generations and the significance of their actual behavior was completely misunderstood.

What survived for popular consumption was the woman reformer as sage and prophetess, the social type of which Jane Addams is the perfect exemplar. This survival led to an unfortunate association of critical perceptions of society with unquestioning acceptance of traditional views of the female psyche. It is the development of this type which we must understand if we want to comprehend how radical discontent could be expended in every social direction except the one which required questioning the stereotype of women.

The path to Jane Addams' identity as a sage lay through the experience of higher education and the recognition that she had access to learning of a scale and quality not available to preceding generations. The Addams family was involved in the abolition movement and important in local Republican politics and through these concerns became committed to equality with men in women's legal rights and educational opportunities. Daughters of the Addams family thus inherited a family tradition of reform without the corresponding obligation to business success which was imposed by such families on their sons. However, the standard curriculum for women's colleges like Rockford Seminary which Jane Addams attended entirely neglected the question of relevance for future vocational or intellectual purposes. Jane Addams was exposed at Rockford to the standard Victorian literary culture together with a high saturation of Protestant Christianity since the seminary's founder hoped to raise up a race of Christian women who could civilize the West.

The result of rigorous training in moral and aesthetic concerns was considerable disorientation when Jane Addams left college and began to try to define some social role in which her education could be put to use. Not only did her education fail to relate her in any significant way to the occupational structure of society, it had also trained her to be a moral agent in a society which expected middle-class women to be passive spectators and consumers. Two possible responses to this situation seem to have attracted the post-Civil War generation of college-educated women. The first was to withdraw to graduate study and acquire a respectable social role through professional training. Graduate school offered both escape from the family and the opportunity to enter a neutral social territory where the traditional rigidity of the American division of labor between men and women had not had time to establish itself. Those of an intellectual bent for graduate work seem to have found this adaptation a satisfactory one. It was the path to the social type of the woman expert. However, for those to whom graduate school was merely a strategy to escape from family discipline, only the second response was possible. Self-deception about an intellectual or professional career culminated in the standard Victorian ailment of emotional prostration. A minor illness took Jane Addams out of the Women's Medical College in Philadelphia in 1882 and kept her an invalid for over twelve months. Travel was of course the major therapy for such persistent nervous and emotional ailments, and it was while visiting London that Jane Addams began to develop the first signs of a nagging social conscience. In England the stereotypes of nativism could not inhibit perception of the sufferings of the London poor. The faces which stared back at the visitor to London's East End were not the faces of degenerate Irish or Poles, but English faces which could arouse the racially selective democratic feelings of young native Americans as no other sight could.[9]

Travel next suggested the idea of expatriation and the refinement of a literary education through involvement in European aristocratic culture. For a woman who had been trained to see herself as an heir to the abolitionist tradition of moral fervor, however, there could be no more than temporary dabbling in the expatriate life. Once she had recognized her common human ties with the urban poor, it was only a matter of time before she put the two styles of life together by visiting an immigrant ghetto in Chicago and espousing the lot of the common man now seen as the logical object of reforming zeal which an earlier generation had directed toward the Negro.

The consequences of the life style which Jane Addams pioneered and other educated women emulated are well known. In New York and Chicago, women were the first founders of settlement houses. They also were preponderant among settlement residents in Philadelphia, Boston and Cleveland. The initial impulse for this kind of feminine migration to the slums was not identification with the working class, as in the European settlement movement, but the recognition that there was a social cure for the neurotic ills of privileged young women in America because their ailments were socially induced. As Jane Addams and Ellen Starr put it when they were looking for a house in an immigrant ward of Chicago in 1889: moving to the ghetto was ". . . more for the benefit of the people who do it than for the other class. . . . Nervous people do not crave rest but activity of a certain kind."[10] By definition "nervous people" in need of releasing activity in American society were not men but women. Men were also discarded as irrelevant in the planning of Hull-House and other women's settlements because they were thought of as "less Christian" in spirit than women and motivated to action entirely by commercial rewards. It was thus as a consequence of an accurate perception of the problems of educated women in American society that middle-class women were brought into contact with the social problems of urban-industrial America. They were on location, settled and ready to become involved in urban problems just before the great depression of 1893–94 struck. Living in an urban slum that winter was the searing, unforgettable confrontation with social injustice which turned all of them into real critics of American society and obliterated their earlier concern with personal adjustment. But in forgetting the reasons for their presence in the urban slums women began to equate their recognition of social problems with special qualities of feminine insight. In *Democracy and Social Ethics* for instance, the work which was the most popular of Jane Addams' early writings on social problems, the culture of poverty is seen through the eyes of a middle-class woman visitor and the perception of the way American society exploited immigrants is made a feminine one. Exploiters are masculine and those who can see the true vision of a democratic society are women.[11]

Quite apart from the process of social selection which took women reformers to the city, there were good intellectual grounds for ascribing special qualities to the female intellect. These were to be found in the current interpretation of the significance of sex differences in the evolution of society. Jane Addams' papers show that she derived her views on this subject from three supposedly unimpeachable sources. She read Herbert Spencer's *Study of Sociology* of 1873 early in her career and accepted from it Spencer's view that the female psyche and mind were of special significance in the evolutionary process because of the innate feminine capacity to empathize with the weak. Once she had met Lester Ward at Hull-House in the decade of the 1890s, she accepted

Ward's assumption that the female was the prototype of the human being and the most highly evolved of the two sexes. In 1900 she met the Scottish biologist and sociologist Patrick Geddes whose *The Evolution of Sex* of 1889 was the major work in English by a biologist of repute on the evolutionary significance of sex differences. Geddes believed that from the smallest single-celled organism to man sex differences were tied to differences in cell metabolism which made female organisms passive and nurturing and male organisms warlike and aggressive. After she met Geddes, she added a natural bent of pacifism to women's special capacity for social insight and played her role as sage with confidence that it conformed to everything current biology and sociology had to say about the place of women in society.[12]

While she held to this traditional picture of women, however, Jane Addams had by 1900 arrived at some fundamental criticisms of American society. She recognized that political institutions which conformed to the classical theory of democracy were incapable of creating the kind of social equality which was central to the American democratic belief. She was convinced that traditional Puritan individualism was no guide to morality in an urban-industrial society. She saw that every social and political institution in America needed radical change if immigrants and workers were to participate in political decisions and receive the benefits of the American industrial economy to the same degree that native Americans did. She thought the family should be modified so that its members could not settle into a private domesticity which made them blind to social suffering outside the family circle; church and charitable institutions needed to be pried loose from adherence to the old Puritan economic ethic and negative morality; business corporations and trade unions needed to be less concerned with productivity and material rewards and more aware of human values; political parties needed to be reformed so that they could become more responsive to the needs and concerns of the urban immigrant. The tendency to violence in American life which she saw as the heritage of the need to coerce a slave population in the South must be eradicated if the divisions in industrial society were not to lead to class warfare. As a diagnosis of American social ills, this was not unimpressive. It was free from the usual Progressive concern with institutionalizing middle-class values. It was future oriented, ready to accept radical change and optimistic about the potential of the American city to become a genuinely creative, pluralistic community.[13]

One can say that important elements of radical discontent are present in this social criticism—an accurate diagnosis of the present and a creative, dynamizing view of the future. Contemporaries certainly thought so. In 1902 when Jane Addams published *Democracy and*

Social Ethics, the work that contained the major themes of her social criticism up to 1900, her mail ranged from appreciative notes from John Dewey and William James calling it "one of the great books of our time" to emotional letters from college students who said they found reading the book a religious experience which liberated them to be moral beings for the first time.[14]

What *Democracy and Social Ethics* lacked was a realistic perception of the social group who would be agents of desirable social change. To Jane Addams and women reformers of her generation, it seemed perfectly clear that women were the only people in America capable of bringing about a new order in which democracy would find social as well as political expression. As an organized force in politics, they would moralize and socialize a state which Jane Addams recognized was at present organized to protect and promote the interests of businessmen. Of even greater importance, women would be able to solve the problems of city government because the efficient management of urban affairs involved generalizing the skills of housekeeping which were exclusively feminine skills.

This celebration of women as makers of the future democratic society was a position from which there was no retreating as the suffrage agitation mounted. Indeed after 1900 the only modification of this feminist creed which Jane Addams made was to celebrate women's unique capacities for internationalism and the mediation of war. The woman as diplomat could settle the problems of world order as well as those of urban government. Such delusions are comic, but they are also very significant when entertained by minds with the range and scope for social analysis which Jane Addams certainly had.

They point to a predicament which was almost universal for middle-class American women of Jane Addams' generation. Intellectually they had to work within the tradition which saw women as civilizing and moralizing forces in society, a tradition given spurious scientific authority in evolutionary social thought. Yet within American society there was no naturally occurring social milieu in which these assumptions about the exclusive attributes of women could be seen for what they were. Women had to create the very institutions which were their vehicle for departure from middle-class feminine life, and in doing so they naturally duplicated existing assumptions about the sexes and their roles. Beatrice Webb remarked after visiting Hull-House that "the residents consist, in the main, of strong-minded energetic women, bustling about their various enterprises and professions, interspersed with earnest-faced self-subordinating and mild-mannered men who slide from room to room apologetically."[15] Since Beatrice Webb knew this model well in herself and Sidney, it is highly probable that the perception was accurate. In settlement houses women could find endless opportunities for social action but no way out of the prevailing romantic stereotypes of men and women as social beings. As social workers struggling to solve the problems of the poor in American cities, women met mostly businessmen—philanthropists and clergymen with wide social concerns. The businessmen could be disregarded as tainted by acquisitiveness and the profits of commercial exploitation. The clergymen were representatives of a religious tradition which had failed to recognize the superior moral qualities of women. Such men could not be accepted as moral or intellectual equals no matter how readily they wrote checks or served on community charities for they were distrusted as agents of a society which subordinated women for economic or religious purposes. Yet without seeing men and women as moral equals, women reformers could find no way out of the traditional stereotype of the female temperament; and they could not see themselves as they really were, notably aggressive, hard-working, independent, pragmatic and rational in every good cause but that of feminism.

The consequence of this failure to question traditional views of femininity meant that the genuine changes in behavior and the impact of women's social criticism were short-lived. On the other hand, the national eminence of the woman reformer as sage merely strengthened sterile romanticism in popular attitudes to women. In this way a generation of women who lived as rebels against middle-class mores was finally imprisoned by them. We see the limitations imposed by this imprisonment in the absence of thought about or concern for sexual liberty in the lives of two women reformers of national eminence always in search of social issues to explore. For them rejection of Victorian bourgeois and economic values was never accompanied by questioning of Victorian sexual stereotypes.

Nothing is more pathetic than the shocked incomprehension of Jane Addams and Lillian Wald when faced with a popularized version of Freudian thought towards the close of their lives. Each in writing the concluding chapters of her memoirs towards the end of the decade of the twenties tried to grapple with the problem of explaining how their intuitive female sage could be distinguished from Freud's irrational woman whose destiny is shaped by her biological nature.[16] They were powerless to deal with the assertion that their long careers as social reformers were merely evidence of failures in sexual adjustment because they had always accepted the romantic view of women as passive and irrational. This acceptance left them with no recourse when they were told their careers of activism represented deviance; for in terms of the stereotype of femininity which they had always accepted, they had been deviant. They had adopted a feminist ideology and a public identity which gave the widest possible currency to a modernized version of the romantic woman. They had acted very differently but had never understood the significance of the difference, much less reflected upon it until it was too late. Quite unwittingly they had helped to prepare a cultural climate ideally suited to the reception of Freudian ideas. Had they ever reflected on the significance of their behavior it is possible that with their superb talents for publicity and popular writing they could have dramatized some other model of feminine excellence besides the gentle, intuitive woman. Certainly they could have brought in question the negative image of the career woman emerging in the mass media of the thirties. As it was they were silent, and the mass media were left free to begin the commercial exploitation of the romantic female without a murmur of dissent from two women who had used the identity of the romantic sage for far more elevated social purposes.

NOTES

1. On this point see Andrew Sinclair, *The Better Half: The Emancipation of American Women* (New York, 1965).

2. Betty Friedan, *The Feminine Mystique* (New York, 1963).

3. See Aileen S. Kraditor, *Up From the Pedestal* (Chicago, 1968), and William L. O'Neill, *Divorce in the Progressive Era* (New Haven, 1967), and *Everyone was Brave: The Rise and Fall of Feminism in America* (Chicago, 1969).

4. See David M. Kennedy, *Birth Control in America: The Career of Margaret Sanger* (New Haven, 1970).

5. Jane Addams' thought on women's role as reformers is most readily available in her *Democracy and Social Ethics* (New York, 1902), *Newer Ideals of Peace* (New York, 1907), *The Long Road of Woman's Memory* (New York, 1916), and *Peace and Bread in Time of War* (New York, 1922). Her two volumes of autobiography are mostly concerned with the question of women's social role. See *Twenty Years at Hull House* (New York, 1910) and *The Second Twenty Years at Hull House* (New York, 1930). Lillian Wald's ideas on women's place in society are only available in print in her two volumes of autobiography, *The House on Henry Street* (New York, 1915), and *Windows on Henry Street* (Boston, 1934). Her speeches and addresses in the Lillian Wald Papers, New York Public Library are a valuable manuscript source for her thought on this question.

6. Winifred E. Wise, *Jane Addams of Hull House: A Biography* (New York, 1935), and R. L. Duffus, *Lillian Wald* (New York, 1953) are examples of the eulogistic biography.

7. Jane Addams, *My Friend Julia Lathrop* (New York, 1935).

8. Josephine Goldmark, *Impatient Crusader,* (University of Illinois Press, Urbana, 1953). See also Dorothy Blumberg, *Florence Kelley: The Making of a Social Pioneer* (New York, 1966).

9. My attention has been drawn to this by Allen F. Davis in his *Spearheads for Reform: The Social Settlements and the Progressive Movement, 1890–1914* (New York, 1967). See also Jane Addams, *Twenty Years at Hull-House,* 66–70.

10. Ellen G. Starr to Sarah A. Haldeman, Chicago, Feb. 23, 1889, Ellen G. Starr Papers, Sophia Smith Collection, Smith College Library.

11. See Jane Addams, *Democracy and Social Ethics,* 13–70, 137–77.

12. Herbert Spencer, *The Study of Sociology* (New York, 1873); Patrick Geddes and J. Arthur Thompson, *The Evolution of Sex* (London, 1889).

13. *Democracy and Social Ethics* was the first systematic statement of her social criticism. It drew on essays and speeches written entirely in the decade of the 1890s.

14. See William James to Jane Addams, New Hampshire, Sept. 17, 1902; Elizabeth D. Stebbins to Jane Addams, New York, July 18, 1909, both letters in the Jane Addams Correspondence, Swarthmore College Peace Collection.

15. *Beatrice Webb's American Diary* (ed. D.A. Shannon, Madison, 1963), 108.

16. See Jane Addams, *Second Twenty Years at Hull House,* 196–99; also Jane Addams, "A Feminist Physician Speaks," a review of *Modern Woman and Sex* by Rachelle S. Yarros, M.D., *Survey,* LXX, 2, (Feb., 1934), 59. See Lillian D. Wald, *Windows on Henry Street,* 5–11, 322.

Suggested Readings for Part III

Baker, Paula. "The Domestication of Politics: Women and American Political Society, 1780-1920." *American Historical Review* 89 (June 1984): 620-47.

Blair, Karen J. *The Clubwoman as Feminist: True Womanhood Redefined, 1868-1914.* New York: Holmes & Meier, 1980.

Bordin, Ruth. *Women and Temperance: The Quest for Power and Liberty, 1873-1900.* Philadelphia: Temple University Press, 1981.

Brumberg, Joan. "'Ruined Girls': Changing Community Responses to Illegitimacy in Upstate New York, 1890-1920." *Journal of Social History* 18 (Winter 1984): 247-72.

Buhle, Mari Jo. *Women and American Socialism, 1870-1920.* Urbana: University of Illinois Press, 1981.

Bularzik, Mary J. "'The Bonds of Belonging': Leonora O'Reilly and Social Reform." *Labor History* 24 (Winter 1983): 60-83.

Butler, Elizabeth B. *Women and the Trades: Pittsburgh, 1907-1908.* Pittsburgh: University of Pittsburgh Press, 1984.

Campbell, Barbara K. *The Liberated Woman of 1914: Prominent Women in the Progressive Era.* Ann Arbor: University of Michigan Press, 1978.

Carter, Susan B. "Academic Women Revisited: An Empirical Study of Changing Patterns in Women's Employment as College and University Faculty, 1890-1963." *Journal of Social History* 14 (Summer 1981): 675-99.

Chudacoff, Howard P. "The Life Course of Women: Age and Age Consciousness, 1865-1915." *Journal of Family History* 5 (Fall 1980): 274-92.

Connelly, Mark Thomas. *The Response to Prostitution in the Progressive Era.* Chapel Hill: University of North Carolina Press, 1980.

Davis, Allan F. "The WTUL Origins and Organization." *Labor History* 5 (1964): 3-17.

_____. *Spearheads For Reform: The Social Settlements and the Progressive Movement, 1890-1914.* New York: Oxford University Press, 1967.

_____. *American Heroine: The Life and Legend of Jane Addams.* New York: Oxford University Press, 1973.

Degler, Carl. "Charlotte Perkins Gilman on the Theory and Practice of Feminism." *American Quarterly* 8 (1956): 21-39.

_____. "What Ought To Be and What Was: Women's Sexuality in the Nineteenth Century." *American Historical Review* 79 (1974): 1467-90.

Drinnon, Richard. *Rebel in Paradise: A Biography of Emma Goldman.* Chicago: University of Chicago Press, 1961.

Dye, Nancy S. *As Equals and As Sisters: Feminism, the Labor Movement, and the Women's Trade Union League of New York.* Columbia: University of Missouri Press, 1980.

Feldman, Egal. "Prostitution, the Alien Woman and the Progressive Imagination, 1910-1915." *American Quarterly* 19 (1967): 192-206.

Fetherling, Dale. *Mother Jones: The Miners' Angel.* Carbondale: Southern Illinois Press, 1974.

Fishbein, Leslie. "Harlot or Heroine? Changing Views of Prostitution, 1870-1920." *Historian* 43 (1980): 23-35.

_____. "The Failure of Feminism in Greenwich Village before World War I." *Women's Studies* 9 (1982): 275-89.

Forster, Margaret. *Significant Sisters: The Grassroots of Active Feminism, 1839-1939.* New York: Knopf, 1985.

Frankfort, Roberta. *Collegiate Women: Domesticity and Career in Turn of the Century America.* New York: New York University Press, 1977.

Freedman, Estelle. *Their Sisters' Keepers: Women's Prison Reform in America, 1830-1930.* Ann Arbor: University of Michigan Press, 1980.

Garcia, Mario T. "The Chicana in American History: The Mexican Women of El Paso, 1880-1920—A Case Study." *Pacific Historical Review* 49 (May 1980): 315-37.

Garrison, Dee. *Apostles of Culture: Public Librarian and American History.* New York: The Free Press, 1979.

_____. "The Tender Technicians: The Feminization of Public Librarianship, 1876-1905." *Journal of Social History* 6 (1972-73): 131-59.

Gordon, Linda. *Woman's Body, Woman's Right: A Social History of Birth Control in America.* New York: Grossman, 1976.

Graham, Patricia Albjerg. "Expansion and Exclusion: A History of Women in American Higher Education." *Signs* 3 (1978): 759-73.

Graham, Sally H. "Woodrow Wilson, Alice Paul, and the Woman Suffrage Movement," *Political Science Quarterly* 98 (Winter 1983-84): 665-79.

Greenwald, Maurine. *Women, War, and Work: The Impact of World War One on Women Workers in the United States.* Westport, CT: Greenwood Press, 1980.

Hall, Jacquelyn Daud. *Revolt Against Chivalry: Jessie Daniel Ames and the Women's Crusade Against Lynching.* New York: Columbia University Press, 1983.

Hapke, Laura. "The Late Nineteenth Century Street-Walker: Images and Realities." *Mid-America* 65 (October 1983).

Hill, Mary. *Charlotte Perkins Gilman: The Making of a Radical Feminist, 1860-1896.* Philadelphia: Temple University Press, 1980.

Hogelund, Ronald W. "Coeducation of the Sexes at Oberlin: A Study of Social Ideas in Mid-Nineteenth Century America." *Journal of Social History* 6 (1972-73): 160-76.

Jones, Beverly W. "Mary Church Terrell and the National Association of Colored Women, 1896 to 1901." *Journal of Negro History* 67 (Spring 1982): 20-33.

Jones, Kathleen W. "Sentiment and Science: The Late Nineteenth Century Pediatrician as Mother's Advisor." *Journal of Social History* 17 (Fall 1983): 79-96.

Kenneally, James J. *Women and the Trade Unions.* St. Albans, Vt.: Eden Press, 1978.

Kennedy, David. *Birth Control in America: The Career of Margaret Sanger.* New Haven: Yale University Press, 1970.

Kraditor, Aileen S. *The Ideas of the Woman Suffrage Movement, 1890-1920.* New York: Columbia University Press, 1965.

Leach, William R. "Transformations in a Culture of Consumption: Women and Department Stores, 1890-1925." *Journal of American History* 71 (September 1984): 319-42.

_____. *True Love and Perfect Union: The Feminist Reform of Sex and Society.* New York: Basic Books, 1980.

Lubove, Roy. "The Progressives and the Prostitute." *The Historian* 25 (1962): 308-30.

Lunardini, Christine A., and Knock, Thomas J. "Woodrow Wilson and Woman Suffrage: A New Look," *Political Science Quarterly* 95 (Winter 1980-81): 655-71.

Marsh, Marsha. *Anarchist Women, 1870-1920.* Philadelphia: Temple University Press, 1980.

May, Elaine T. *Great Expectations: Marriage and Divorce in Post-Victorian America.* Chicago: University of Chicago Press, 1980.

McGovern, James. "Anna Howard Shaw: New Approaches to Feminism." *Journal of Social History* 3 (1969-70): 135-153.

Newcomer, Mable. *A Century of Higher Education for American Women.* New York: Harper & Row, 1959.

O'Neill, William L. *Divorce in the Progressive Era.* New Haven: Yale University Press, 1967.

_____. *The Woman Movement: Feminism in the United States and England.* London: George Allan and Unwin, 1969.

_____. *Everyone Was Brave: A History of Feminism in America.* Chicago: Quadrangle Books, 1971.

Paulson, Ross Evans. *Women's Suffrage and Prohibition: A Comparative Study of Equality and Control,* Glenview, Ill.: Scott, Foresman & Co., 1973.

Reed, James. *From Private Vice to Public Virtue: The Birth Control Movement and American Society Since 1830.* New York: Basic Books, 1978.

Rosen, Ruth. *The Lost Sisterhood: Prostitution in America, 1900-1918.* Baltimore: Johns Hopkins University Press, 1982.

Rossiter, Margaret W. "Women Scientists in Ameria Before 1920." *American Scientist* 62 (1974); 312-23.

Schofield, Ann. "Rebel Girls and Union Maids: The Woman Question in the Journals of the AFL and IWW, 1905-1920. *Feminist Studies* 9 (Summer 1983): 335-58.

Sochen, June. *The New Woman: Feminism in Greenwich Village, 1910-1920.* New York: Quadrangle Books, 1972.

Sugg, Redding S. *Mother Teacher: The Feminization of American Education.* Charlottesville: University of Virginia Press, 1978.

Tax, Meredith. *The Rising of the Women: Feminist Solidarity and Class Conflict, 1880-1917.* New York: Monthly Review Press, 1980.

Tentler, Leslie W. *Wage Earning Women: Industrial Work and Family Life, 1900-1930.* New York: Oxford University Press, 1978.

Walsh, Mary Roth. *"Doctors Wanted: No Women Need Apply": Sexual Barriers in the Medical Profession, 1835-1875.* New Haven: Yale University Press, 1976.

4

THE ILLUSION OF EQUALITY

The paradox of women's position in American society became profoundly evident in the twentieth century. The suffrage victory in 1920, increased numbers of women in the labor force, and women's new sexual freedom, enhanced their status. Yet the promise of emancipation has remained largely unfulfilled. As Max Lerner wrote in the 1950s, "In theory, in law, and to a great extent in fact, the American woman has the freedom to compete with men on equal terms: but psychically and socially she is caught in a society still dominated by masculine power and standards." Women found that gaining the vote did not ensure an effective bloc of women voters, armed with the power and determination to promote women's interests. In spite of new job opportunities for women, employers maintained differences in men's and women's salaries. By the mid-1960s, radicals commonly referred to the illusion of equality, and a new generation of feminists boldly attacked what they termed the sexist attitudes that have remained the last barrier to women's emancipation.

The many women's organizations that had been active during the Progressive era continued the struggle for reform during the 1920s. The General Federation of Women's Clubs (GFWC), National Consumers League (NCL), and National Women's Trade Union League (NWTUL) joined with the League of Women Voters (LWV), which carried on the work of the National American Woman Suffrage Association, to bring pressure on the Congress and the state legislatures in relation to a wide range of matters of concern to women. In 1920, they established the Women's Joint Congressional Committee (WJCC) "as a clearing house for the federal legislative efforts of the affiliated organizations." The most conspicuous success of the WJCC was the short-lived Sheppard-Towner bill, designed to ensure protection to mothers and children through federal aid to maternal and health care programs. Both the NCL, under the direction of Florence Kelley, and the NWTUL continued their campaigns in the interest of working women throughout the decade. Little tangible success marked their efforts until the economic crisis of the 1930s generated social legislation on behalf of workers in general. However, such activity typified the way in which organized women carried on the Progressive spirit in the 1920s, and it kept alive reform issues that became part of the New Deal agenda.

Toward the end of the 1920s, these efforts began to wane. Women's ranks were divided by the issue of an equal rights amendment, which became the sole focus of the Woman's Party. Although the League of Women Voters carried on a widespread effort against discriminatory legislation, its leaders—like those of the NCL and the NWTUL—believed that the amendment would endanger legislation protecting women workers, which they had struggled so vigorously to see implemented.

Within the NCL, resources were strained by preoccupation with a constitutional amendment prohibiting child labor. Aside from internal division, women's organizations suffered from the conservative mood of the decade. Membership in the LWV never reached that of the NAWSA, and it began to drop sharply after 1924. The GFWC grew increasingly conservative, and the work of the WJCC succumbed to the charge of Communist influence, something that plagued women's efforts throughout the 1920s.

The focus on women in the 1920s shifted greatly in ways that feminists of the time deplored. The changes in social life and behavior that characterized the decade—the oft-noted revolution in manners and morals—shifted emphasis from a concern for social justice to one glorifying individual gratification. This represented a major shift in the history of women in American life. Trends in illegitimacy and premarital intercourse at the turn of the century had signaled a change in behavior, and by the 1920s the alteration of sexual norms was clearly apparent. The decade witnessed not only a new emphasis upon sexuality, which permeated popular culture, but also the emergence of women's demands for equality of sexual pleasure, both inside and outside of marriage. In "The American Woman's Pre-World War I Freedom in Manners and Morals," James R. McGovern discusses the nature of these changes and presents clear evidence that a radical shift in sexual behavior and attitudes appeared among urban Americans well before the end of the Great War.

The "new woman" who emerged in the 1920s was neither the creation of the prewar feminists nor of their successors, who remained active during the decade. She was a product of the new moral climate accentuated by postwar prosperity. The stylish Gibson Girl of the 1890s gave way to the flapper who seemed the very essence of modernity. With her bobbed hair and short skirts, she represented a direct challenge to traditional conceptions of the ideal woman. Relating boyishness to female sexuality, she threatened traditional sex roles. Although lesbianism did assume faddish proportions among bohemians during the 1920s, the androgynous flapper was in fact a monument to heterosexuality.

Most women were neither bohemians nor flappers, but in the 1920s they were enthralled with the technological magic represented by the nation's number-one glamour industry, the motion pictures. The media increasingly created idols for young women, and the movies assumed tremendous importance. The sweet innocents portrayed by Mary Pickford continued to be screened, but increasingly the sexually explicit "vamp" dominated the silver screen. Mary P. Ryan has shown the way in which the young movie industry vividly exploited "the flapper's personality complete with her characteristic gestures, energy, and activism." Such films reflected the times and gave role models to young women. They became the most consistent purveyors of the flapper image and the idea of woman as a sexual predator.

The new freedom in morals and manners occurred simultaneously with economic conditions that made it necessary for many women to work. Industrial accidents, sickness and death rates reached extraordinarily high proportions in the first decade of the twentieth century. In addition, cyclical unemployment and low wages made the income of male wage-earners insufficient to meet family needs. It is not surprising that married women's participation in the nonagricultural work force almost doubled between 1890 and 1920. A large number of the women in the working population were immigrants driven by economic necessity and by aspirations toward the American Dream. Native-born Americans' prejudgment of ethnic characteristics as well as group and family mores shaped immigrant women's attitudes toward work. A woman's ethnic background, as Alice Kessler-Harris noted, "determined her image of herself as a worker and the community's approach to her employment."

Economic necessity and a changing conception of "need" continued to draw women into the labor market during the 1920s. The female labor force grew 26 percent during this time, and consumption patterns changed. These changes profoundly affected the response of middle-income families to the Depression, for, in order to maintain a relatively high standard of living, more members of the family were forced to seek paid employment. According to Winifred D. Wandersee Bolin, "many American families owed their middle-class status not to adequate wages of one person, but to the presence of several wage earners in the family." In the course of the 1930s, the numbers of married homemakers with jobs outside the home increased 50 percent, so that approximately one in every seven married women had entered the labor force. While the increase in the number of working wives had occurred in all social groups, a large majority of white women remained in traditional domestic roles.

In the midst of the Depression, a good deal of pressure was put on women to remain in the home. Most cities refused to hire married women as teachers, and eight states excluded them from civil service jobs; a husband and wife could not both hold federal jobs. Although job segregation was so extreme that few women actually competed against men, those who entered the labor force were blamed for taking jobs from male breadwinners. Such prejudices, combined with the stigma upon a husband's masculinity represented by a working wife, reveal the strength of conventional family values in the midst of economic crisis.

Stripped of its traditional functions, the twentieth-century family became primarily concerned with serving the personalities of its members. Its main function was psychological. According to Rowland Berthoff, "Marriage was in a sense displacing the family itself; a husband and wife now referred colloquially to their 'marriage', implying not so much a fixed social institution as a special arrangement between two people who had 'fallen in love.'" Held together solely by the tenuous bonds of personal relationships, marriages dissolved with increasing rapidity. Divorces, which had reached 100,000 per year in 1914, passed the 200,000 mark by 1929. Many women with a degree of economic independence were unwilling to tolerate unhappy marriages. At the same time, the decline in the birth rate indicated that couples deliberately chose to limit their families in order to maintain their standard of living. Children were no longer an economic asset as they had been in the nineteenth century; they had now become a liability.

The emphasis on personal fulfillment that emerged in the 1920s altered the ideals and aspirations of American women. The hard times of the Great Depression dampened the divorce rate as couples chose security above personal happiness and as a confused society tried to reaffirm traditional sex roles in the face of economic crisis and war. Ruth Schwartz Cowan's study, "Two Washes in the Morning and a Bridge Party at Night," traces the evolution of "the feminine mystique" among middle-class women during the interwar period. The image of the cheerful housewife obsessed with dirt and companionate motherhood was a product of unique economic and demographic conditions. The decline of the servant population and profound technological changes spawned an ideology that Cowan argues was a thinly disguised form of consumerism. The postwar economic developments altered the role of housewives as consumers, but failed to free them from domestic life. The emerging "mystique" idealized the relationship between husbands and wives, encouraged family togetherness and discouraged work outside the home. The home economics movement flourished in the 1920s, and middle-class women were exhorted by advertisers to become more "scientific" homemakers.

In the decade after World War II, prosperity made large families possible, and greater numbers of women accepted the cult of domesticity—"the feminine mystique"—which idealized the affluent suburban housewife devoted to home and family. *The Ideal Marriage*, which appeared in the United States in 1931, charted the course to sexual bliss; the emphasis on home economics and the "scientific" home rationalized domestic drudgery. Yet, personal fulfillment escaped women during these years, just as political power had remained beyond their grasp since the 1920s. The suburban wife was sexually discontented. Her role as housewife expanded in the consumption-oriented society of the 1950s, and the number of hours spent doing housework and related tasks actually increased for married women.

In the late 1950s this picture began to change. Sexual norms became increasingly permissive, and alternative modes of child raising and new forms of marriage gained popularity. In the early 1970s, a best-selling book touted the psychological benefits of "open marriage," which stripped marital relationships of the burdensome responsibilities of the past. The new moral climate of the 1960s not only permitted, but almost demanded, explicit self-analysis and open discussion of sexual matters. This climate led two sociologists to comment: "If there has been a sexual revolution . . . it is in terms of frankness about sex and the freedom to discuss it."

There can be no doubt, however, that behavior was also changing. Due to wide use of oral contraceptives, introduced in 1961, and liberalization of abortion statutes following the Supreme Court decision in the early 1970s, the birth rate plummeted to a point where population growth has stopped. Although marriage has been more popular than ever in American history, there has also been an increasing number of women who remain single. The age of first marriage has risen, and the divorce rate has reached staggering proportions. In the first six months of 1970, more new divorces were granted than in the entire previous decade; in some jurisdictions, such as Marin County, California, they outnumbered legal marriages. At the same time, the sexual activity of women has increased and has become more varied and pleasurable. Studies conducted in the 1970s indicated that teenagers were at least twice as likely to have had intercourse as the same age group born during the 1920s. Marital sex had become more satisfying for women, and the traditional gulf between the premarital and extramarital experiences of men and women had closed dramatically.

The changes in attitudes and behavior in recent years have been of immense importance to American women, since they indicate the downfall of the hypocritical double standard and a more equitable distribution of power in sexual and marital relationships. It is easy to overemphasize the "sexual revolution" and place excessive importance on its more bizarre elements, which were in some ways detrimental to the interests of women. The experiences of men and women have been converging; however, there has probably been little actual increase in promiscuity. Women clearly no longer value virginity as they once did. Premarital sexual relations in the early teens are associated with the experimental tenor of this era and are followed by a latency period in the mid-teens. The most common postadolescent sexual behavior involves relationships that generally take the form of trial marriages, in which sexual activity is associated with affection and the expectation of marriage.

From 1920 to the present, the most important change in the lives of American women has been in the area of employment, and it has produced widespread social and political consequences. Although the percentage of working women has risen continuously throughout the twentieth century, most women have been segregated in low-paying and routine "women's jobs." New Deal legislation provided further protection for women in the areas of hours and wages, but both the National Industrial Recovery Act and the Fair Labor Standards Act tolerated wage differentials and set minimums for women at lower rates than those for men.

After 1939, wartime production drew thirteen million women into the ranks of labor, and, for the first time, married women exceeded single women in the working population. Although industry dropped one out of every four women employed at the end of the war, the number of working women has grown yearly since 1947. In 1970, women constituted 40 percent of the American labor force. As one might have suspected from the war experience, the greatest postwar increase in employment occurred among married women, and the age distribution of women shifted dramatically.

World War II was clearly a watershed in the history of American women, but the myth of Rosie the Riveter, who symbolized the women who worked in industry, must be looked upon with a critical eye. For example, the automobile companies that after 1942 produced almost everything but cars were reluctant to employ women. With VJ (Victory in Japan) Day women were expected to return to their families and relinquish their jobs to men. Nancy Gabin reveals how women were treated in the United Auto Workers union during the decade of demobilization in "Women Workers and the UAW." It is important to note that the UAW was one of the most progressive unions at the time, since it was open to both blacks and women. Yet, Gabin shows that even in this progressive-left environment women faced discrimination. Drawn into the factories by the necessities of war they were thought only to be waiting for "Johnny" to come marching home. Many women desired to work and Gabin details the post-war confusion as more and more women entered the labor force.

Even though they played an increasingly important role in the American economy, women continued to be plagued by unequal pay and job segregation. It was not until the 1960s that they were able to force government action on these problems. Although by the 1940s competition from women as a cheap labor source generated solid support for equal pay from the union movement, legislation on this subject failed in 1945 and again in 1947. Women's continuing concern with the issue of equal pay led to the Women's Bureau Conference on Equal Pay and to the inclusion of a demand for it in the Republican and Democratic platforms of the early 1950s. However, little was done until President John F. Kennedy appointed the Commission on the Status of Women in 1961. In "A 'New Frontier' for Women," Cynthia E. Harrison analyzes the background and organization of the Commission, illustrating the limitations of male liberals and the complex divisions among feminists.

The Commission's report focused attention on the problem of equal pay and recommended reform in the areas of job discrimination, federal social security insurance, tax law, and federal and state labor laws regulating hours, wages, and night work. The Commission also concerned itself with other differences in the treatment of men and women, and with services provided for women in education counseling, job training, and day-care centers. Although this report reflected a general climate of opinion in the early 60s that also produced the Equal Pay Act in 1963 and the addition of Title VII to the Civil Rights Act of 1964 (prohibiting employment discrimination by the federal government), a careful student of the matter, Carl Degler, could still argue in 1962 that "the sexual division of labor is so nearly complete that it is difficult to find comparable jobs of the two sexes to make a definitive study [of wage discrimination]."

The sexual division of labor remains the crucial economic problem facing women today and accounts for the eagerness with which most women activists have embraced the Equal Right Amendment (ERA). However, in "The Paradox of Progress," William H. Chafe emphasizes the social and political consequences of changes that have taken place in the economic role of American women in the past half-century. Focusing upon the dialectic between behavioral and attitudinal shifts that comprises the process of social change, Chafe argues that World War II proved to be a watershed in the history of American women because it precipitated a rapid increase in the number of married women employed in the economy and a radical upward shift in the average age of employed women. Once established, this pattern affected all of the crucial relationships in women's lives and undermined traditional attitudes toward sex roles. Ironically, the decade of the 1950s created the seedbed for the flowering of feminism in the 1960s. "Perhaps," Chafe writes, "the most important precondition for the revival of feminism. . . was the amount of change which had already occurred in women's lives."

The rebirth of feminism in the 1960s remains the most enduring and ultimately most radical by-product of that much-disturbed decade. Explanation of this phenomenon is at once simple and complex. Few would deny that women were discriminated against in most salient aspects of American life; however, the historian must explain why long-term conditions generated a specific set of responses among certain groups at the precise time when they were able to erect the structural apparatus of a social movement. Even Chafe's explanation seems exceedingly abstract and fails to account for the grievances specific to groups of women who actually constructed the women's liberation movement.

Ellen Willis, an editor and writer for *The Village Voice*, looks retrospectively at the infighting among New York feminists in the late 1960s and early 1970s in "Radical Feminism and the Feminist Radicalism." Willis gives a sense of the emotional tension within the movement by emphasizing the debate over the relationship between Marxism, in its various forms, and feminism. In analyzing the slogan "the personal is political," she raises important questions about womanhood and society in America. Her sophisticated argument makes a distinction between "radical" and "cultural" feminism that cuts through such divisive issues as lesbianism, abortion, and pornography.

Although the women's liberation movement has gained support from women in all segments of the society, it originated with professional, upper-middle-class women who, during the mid-1960s, found themselves under a form of intense psychological strain that has been termed relative deprivation. Such women perceived their situations relative to those of men of their class whose career patterns they used to evaluate their own lives. The conditions of the 1960s encouraged professional women with long-term political commitments and aspiring professional women in college, who were disillusioned in very special ways by the student civil rights and peace movements, to generate a revival of feminism. Contemporary feminism differs in many ways from its nineteenth-century predecessor. At times, it seems to lack the necessary coherence to be considered a social movement. But the popularity of traditional women's issues today is immense. Although the majority of American women refuse to accept the direction of any single group or leader, few could be called antifeminist, and a growing majority favor all efforts to enhance women's status in American society.

The suffrage movement split asunder on the rock of racial prejudice in the early part of this century, and the relation of black women to the contemporary movement remains a problem. Although they tend to be more receptive than white women to the leading feminist issues, particularly in the economic realm, black women face role conflicts that whites have been able to transcend. Focusing primarily on the struggle for racial dignity, black women have consciously accepted traditional supportive roles in the interest of reversing the history of pathological destruction that white racism has brought to black men. Black women have thus, for the most part, thrown in their lot with efforts to enhance the status of black men, and they have viewed with suspicion feminist efforts that seemed inimical to this goal. To a large degree, black women have remained outside the movement, a fact which the late Pauli Murray, a black Episcopal priest, civil rights lawyer, successful academician, and one of the founders of the National Organization for Women (NOW), deplored. In presenting what might best be termed a "liberal" feminist view, Murray contended that the issue is one of human rights—women must "transcend the radical barrier" and form an alliance beginning with educated, middle-class women of both races.

In response to International Women's Year and Decade proclaimed by the United Nations, women met in Houston in November of 1977, to define their most urgent issues and concerns. White and minority women of all classes gathered in a demonstration of feminist solidarity. Black, Hispanic, Chinese and Native American women organized and spoke eloquently of their specific economic grievances, such as teenage unemployment. Conservative women led by Phyllis Schlafly and the members of the Eagle Forum claimed to speak for the majority of American women, but their demonstration failed to disrupt or detract attention from the meeting, which hammered out a consensus on women's issues.

What the women's movement does, however, may have only peripheral influence upon the generation of middle-class women born since the fifties who have inherited the benefits won by the movement. Younger women insist that discrimination "doesn't apply to me," despite the facts that the government has failed to enforce laws against sex discrimination in the schools, that only one-fifth of the discrimination complaints are resolved by the United States Commission for Civil Rights, and that child-care centers remain inadequate to aid welfare mothers. The conservative administration of Ronald Reagan has placed a woman on the Supreme Court and has cycled several women through the Cabinet, but has also cut most of the social programs beneficial to women.

In the decade since the meeting at Houston, the country has drifted both politically and culturally to the Right and the position of women has become more paradoxical than ever. The women's liberation movement is in disarray. Although the ERA was supported by all factions of feminists and, according to public opinion polls, by a majority of Americans, it was defeated by economic interest groups, antifeminist women, and the conservative nature of the Constitution. The highly emotional abortion issue has divided women and has served as a focus for the resurgence of a rhetorical commitment to traditional sex roles. Although the census of 1980 showed that only a small minority of households conformed to the image of two parents living with their children, the Administration has proclaimed that we have entered the "Decade of the Family." The equally emotional issue of pornography has driven a sizable number of feminists into an unusual alliance with religious conservatives, who are generally antifeminist, against the usually profeminist ACLU.

While their opponents seem organized for Armageddon, most women's advocates perceive only hollow victories. There can be little doubt that the position of women in America has changed dramatically in recent years. Women have greater access to education than ever before. More women than men graduate from high school and more women than ever continue on to college. The percentage of women in the wage economy has continued to grow and there is a more open entrance into what have been "men's" jobs. At the same time, women with comparable education hold lower positions and earn less than men. Secretaries often have more formal education than their bosses. Women's mean income is two-thirds of that of men and has declined comparatively as more women have entered the labor force. The majority of America's poor are women. The Reagan revolution and the revival of fundamentalist religion, have served to glorify the traditional sex/gender system. Equality remains an illusion.

∽19∽

THE AMERICAN WOMAN'S
PRE-WORLD WAR I FREEDOM
IN MANNERS AND MORALS

JAMES R. MCGOVERN

The Twenties have been alternately praised or blamed for almost everything and its opposite;[1] but most historians hold, whether to praise or to condemn, that this decade launched the revolution in manners and morals through which we are still moving today. This judgment seems to be part of an even more inclusive one in American historiography to exceptionalize the Twenties. No other decade has invited such titles of historical caricature as *The Jazz Age, This Was Normalcy, Fantastic Interim,* or *The Perils of Prosperity.* Richard Hofstadter's classic, *The Age of Reform,* subtly reinforces this view by seeing the Twenties as "Entr'acte," an interim between two periods of reform, the Progressive era and the New Deal, which themselves display discontinuity.[2]

Revisionism, in the form of a developmental interpretation of the relationship between the Progressive era and the Twenties, has been gaining strong support in recent years. De-emphasizing the disruptive impact of World War I, Henry F. May asked whether the 1920s could be understood fully "without giving more attention to the old regime."[3] He declared that "Immediately prewar America must be newly explored," especially "its inarticulate assumptions—assumptions in such areas as morality, politics, class and race relations, popular art

From the *Journal of American History* 55 (September 1968): 315–33. Reprinted by permission.

Dr. McGovern is chairman of the History Department at the University of West Florida in Pensacola.

and literature, and family life."[4] May pursued his inquiry in *The End of American Innocence* and showed that for the purposes of intellectual history, at least, the Twenties were not as significant as the preceding decade.[5] Political historians have been reassessing the relationship of the Progressive era to the Twenties as well. Arthur Link has demonstrated that progressivism survived World War I,[6] and J. Joseph Huthmacher has established continuity between progressivism and the New Deal in the immigrant's steadfast devotion to the ameliorative powers of the government.[7] Together with May's analysis, their writings suggest that the 1920s are much more the result of earlier intrinsic social changes than either the sudden, supposedly traumatic experiences of the war or unique developments in the Twenties. Since this assertion is certain to encounter the formidable claims that the 1920s, at least in manners and morals, amounted to a revolution, its viability can be tested by questioning if the American woman's "emancipation" in manners and morals occurred even earlier than World War I.

Even a casual exploration of the popular literature of the Progressive era reveals that Americans then described and understood themselves to be undergoing significant changes in morals. "Sex o'clock in America" struck in 1913,[8] about the same time as "The Repeal of Reticence."[9] One contemporary writer saw Americans as liberated from the strictures of "Victorianism," now an epithet deserving criticism, and exulted, "Heaven defend us from a return to the prudery of the Victorian regime!"[10] Conditions were such that another commentator asked self-consciously, "Are We Immoral?"[11] And still another feared that the present "vice not often matched since [the time of] the Protestant Reformation" might invite a return to Puritanism.[12] Yet, historians have not carefully investigated the possibility that the true beginnings of America's "New Freedom" in morals occurred prior to 1920.[13] The most extensive, analytical writing on the subject of changing manners and morals is found in Federick L. Allen's *Only Yesterday* (1931), William Leuchtenburg's *The Perils of Prosperity* (1958), May's *The End of American Innocence* (1959), and George Mowry's *The Urban Nation* (1965).

Allen and Leuchtenburg apply almost identical sharp-break interpretations, respectively entitling chapters "The Revolution in Manners and Morals" and "The Revolution in Morals."[14] Both catalogue the same types of criteria for judgment. The flapper, as the "new woman" was called, was a creature of the 1920s. She smoked, drank, worked, and played side by side with men. She became preoccupied with sex—shocking and simultaneously unshockable. She danced close, became freer with her favors, kept her own latchkey, wore scantier attire which emphasized her boyish, athletic form, just as she used makeup and bobbed and dyed her hair. She and her comradely beau tried to abolish time and succeeded, at least to the extent that the elders asked to join the revelry. Although there were occasional "advance signals" of "rebellion" before the war, it was not until the 1920s that the code of woman's innocence and ignorance crumbled.

May, who comes closest to an understanding of the moral permissiveness before the 1920s, describes in general terms such phenomena of the Progressive era as the "Dance Craze," birth control, the impact of the movies, and the "white-slave panic."[15] He focuses on the intellectuals, however, and therefore overlooks the depth of these and similar social movements. This causes him to view them as mere "Cracks in the Surface" of an essentially conservative society. He quotes approvingly of the distinction made by the *Nation* "between the fluttering tastes of the half-baked intellectuals, attracted by all these things, and the surviving soundness of the great majority."[16] His treatment also ignores one of the most significant areas of changing manners and morals as they affected the American woman: the decided shift in her sex role and identification in the direction of more masculine norms. Again, *The End of American Innocence* does not convincingly relate these changes to the growth of the cities. Perhaps these limitations explain Mowry's preference for a "sharp-break" interpretation, although he wrote seven years after May.

Mowry, who acknowledges especial indebtedness to Leuchtenburg,[17] is emphatic about the "startling" changes in manners and morals in the 1920s.[18] He highlights "the new woman of the twenties"[19] whose "modern feminine morality and attitudes toward the institution of marriage date from the twenties."[20] Mowry concedes to the libidos of progressives only the exceptional goings-on in Greenwich Village society.

These hypotheses, excluding May's, hold that the flapper appeared in the postwar period mainly because American women en masse then first enjoyed considerable social and economic freedom. They also emphasize the effect of World War I on morals.[21] By inference, of course, the Progressive era did not provide a suitable matrix. But an investigation of this period establishes that women had become sufficiently active and socially independent to prefigure the "emancipation" of the 1920s.

A significant deterioration of external controls over morality had occurred before 1920. One of the consequences of working and living conditions in the cities, especially as these affected women, was that Americans of the period 1900–1920 had experienced a vast dissolution of moral authority, which formerly had centered in the family and the small community. The traditional "straight and narrow" could not serve the choices and opportunities of city life.[22] As against primary controls and contacts based on face-to-face association where the norms of family, church, and small community, usually reinforcing each other, could be internalized, the city made for a type of "individualization" through its distant, casual, specialized, and transient clusters of secondary associations.[23] The individual came to determine his own behavioral norms.

The "home is in peril" became a fact of sociological literature as early as 1904.[24] One of the most serious signs of its peril was the increasing inability of parents to influence their children in the delicate areas of propriety and morals.[25] The car, already numerous enough to affect dating and premarital patterns,[26] the phone coming to be used for purposes of romantic accommodation,[27] and the variety of partners at the office or the factory,[28] all together assured unparalleled privacy and permissiveness between the sexes.

Individualization of members served to disrupt confidence between generations of the family, if not to threaten parents with the role of anachronistic irrelevance. Dorothy Dix observed in 1913 that there had been "so many changes in the conditions of life and point of view in the last twenty years that the parent of today is absolutely unfitted to decide the problems of life for the young man and woman of today. This is particularly the case with women because the whole economic and social position of women has been revolutionized since mother was a girl."[29] Magazine articles lamented "The Passing of the Home Daughter" who preferred the blessed anonymity of the city to "dying of asphyxiation at home!"[30] The same phenomenon helps to explain the popularity in this period of such standardized mothers as Dorothy Dix, Beatrice Fairfax, and Emily Post, each of whom was besieged with queries on the respective rights of mothers and daughters.

Woman's individualization resulted mainly because, whether single or married, gainfully employed or not, she spent more time outside her home. Evidence demonstrates that the so-called job and kitchen revolutions were already in advanced stages by 1910. The great leap forward in women's participation in economic life came between 1900 and 1910; the percentage of women who were employed changed only slightly from 1910 to 1930. A comparison of the percentages of gainfully employed women aged 16 to 44 between 1890 and 1930 shows that they comprised 21.7 percent of Americans employed in 1890, 23.5 percent in 1900, 28.1 percent in 1910, 28.3 percent in 1920, and 29.7 percent in 1930.[31] While occupational activity for women appears to stagnate from 1910 to 1920, in reality a considerable restructuring occurred with women leaving roles as domestics and assuming positions affording more personal independence as clerks and stenographers.[32]

Married women, especially those in the upper and middle classes, enjoyed commensurate opportunities. Experts in household management advised women to rid themselves of the maid and turn to appliances as the "maid of all service."[33] Statistics on money expended on those industries which reduced home labor for the wife suggest that women in middle-income families gained considerable leisure after 1914.[34] This idea is also corroborated from other sources,[35] especially from the tone and content of advertising in popular magazines when they are compared with advertising at the turn of the century. Generally speaking, women depicted in advertising in or about 1900 are well rounded, have gentle, motherly expressions, soft billowy hair, and delicate hands. They are either sitting down or standing motionless; their facial expressions are immobile as are their corseted figures.[36] After 1910, they are depicted as more active figures with more of their activity taking place outside their homes.[37] One woman tells another over the phone: "Yes[,] drive over right away—I'll be ready. My housework! Oh, that's all done. How do I do it? I just let electricity do my work nowadays."[38] Vacuum cleaners permitted the housewife to "Push the Button—and Enjoy the Springtime!"[39] Van Camp's "Pork and Beans" promised to save her "100 hours yearly,"[40] and Campbell's soups encouraged, "Get some fun out of life," since it was unnecessary to let the "three-meals-a-day problem tie you down to constant drudgery."[41] Wizard Polish, Minute Tapioca, and Minute Gelatine also offered the same promise. The advertising image of women became more natural, even nonchalant. A lady entertaining a friend remarks: "I don't have to hurry nowadays. I have a Florence Automatic Oil Stove in my kitchen."[42] It had become "so *very* easy" to wax the floors that well-dressed women could manage them.[43] And they enjoyed a round of social activities driving the family car.[44]

It was in this setting that the flapper appeared along with her older married sister who sought to imitate her. No one at the office or in the next block cared much about their morals as long as the one was efficient and the other paid her bills on time. And given the fact that both these women had more leisure and wished "to participate in what men call 'the game of life' " rather than accept "the mere humdrum of household duties,"[45] it is little wonder that contemporaries rightly assessed the danger of the situation for traditional morals by 1910.

The ensuing decade was marked by the development of a revolution in manners and morals; its chief embodiment was the flapper who was urban based and came primarily from the middle and upper classes.

Young—whether in fact or fancy—assertive, and independent, she experimented with intimate dancing, permissive favors, and casual courtships or affairs. She joined men as comrades, and the differences in behavior of the sexes were narrowed. She became in fact in some degree desexualized. She might ask herself, "Am I Not a Boy? Yes, I Am—Not."[46] Her speech, her interest in thrills and excitement, her dress and hair, her more aggressive sexuality, even perhaps her elaborate beautification, which was a statement of intentions, all point to this. Women, whether single or married, became at once more attractive and freer in their morals and paradoxically less feminine. Indeed, the term sexual revolution as applied to the Progressive era means reversal in the traditional role of women just as it describes a pronounced familiarity of the sexes.

The unmarried woman after 1910 was living in the "Day of the Girl."[47] Dorothy Dix described "the type of girl that the modern young man falls for" in 1915 as a "husky young woman who can play golf all day and dance all night, and drive a motor car, and give first aid to the injured if anybody gets hurt, and who is in no more danger of swooning than he is."[48] Little wonder she was celebrated in song as "A Dangerous Girl"; the lyrics of one of the popular songs for 1916 read, "You dare me, you scare me, and still I like you more each day. But you're the kind that will charm; and then do harm; you've got a dangerous way."[49] The "most popular art print . . . ever issued" by *Puck* depicts a made-up young lady puckering her lips and saying "Take It From Me!"[50] The American girl of 1900 was not described in similar terms. The lovely and gracious Gibson Girl was too idealized to be real.[51] And when young lovers trysted in advertising, they met at Horlick's Malted Milk Bar; he with his guitar, and she with her parasol.[52] Beatrice Fairfax could still reply archaically about the need for "maidenly reserve" to such queries as those on the proprieties of men staring at women on the streets.[53] And the *Wellesley College News* in 1902 reported that students were not permitted to have a Junior Prom because it would be an occasion for meeting "promiscuous men," although the college sanctioned "girl dances."[54]

The girls, however, dispensed with "maidenly reserve." In 1910, Margaret Deland, the novelist, could announce a "Change in the Feminine Ideal."

> This young person . . . with surprisingly bad manners—has gone to college, and when she graduates she is going to earn her own living . . . she won't go to church; she has views upon marriage and the birth-rate, and she utters them calmly, while her mother blushes with embarrassment; she occupies herself, passionately, with everything except the things that used to occupy the minds of girls.[55]

Many young women carried their own latchkeys.[56] Meanwhile, as Dorothy Dix noted, it had become "literally true that the average father does not know, by name or sight, the young man who visits his daughter and who takes her out to places of amusement."[57] She was distressed over the widespread use by young people of the car which she called the "devil's wagon."[58] Another writer asked: "Where Is Your Daughter This Afternoon?" "Are you sure that she is not being drawn into the whirling vortex of afternoon 'trots' . . . ?"[59] Polly, Cliff Sterrett's remarkable comic-strip, modern girl from *Polly and Her Pals,* washed dishes under the shower and dried them with an electric fan; and while her mother tried hard to domesticate her, Polly wondered, "Gee Whiz! I wish I knew what made my nose shine!"[60]

Since young women were working side by side with men and recreating more freely and intimately with them, it was inevitable that they behave like men. Older people sometimes carped that growing familiarity meant that romance was dead[61] or that "nowadays brides hardly blush, much less faint."[62] And Beatrice Fairfax asked, "Has Sweet Sixteen Vanished?"[63] But some observers were encouraged to note that as girls' ways approximated men's, the sexes were, at least, more comradely.[64] The modern unmarried woman had become a "Diana, Hunting in the Open."[65] Dorothy Dix reported that "nice girls, good girls, girls in good positions in society—frankly take the initiative in furthering an acquaintance with any man who happens to strike their fancy." The new ideal in feminine figure, dress, and hair styles was all semi-masculine. The "1914 Girl" with her "slim hips and boy-carriage" was a "slim, boylike creature."[66] The "new figure is Amazonian, rather than Miloan. It is boyish rather than womanly. It is strong rather than soft."[67] Her dress styles, meanwhile, de-emphasized both hips and bust while they permitted the large waist. The boyish coiffure began in 1912 when young women began to tuck-under their hair with a ribbon;[68] and by 1913–1914, Newport ladies, actresses like Pauline Frederick, then said to be the prettiest girl in America, and the willowy, popular dancer Irene Castle were wearing short hair.[69] By 1915, the *Ladies Home Journal* featured women with short hair on its covers, and even the pure type of woman who advertised Ivory Soap appeared to be shorn.[70]

The unmarried flapper was a determined pleasure-seeker whom novelist Owen Johnson described collectively as "determined to liberate their lives and claim the same rights of judgment as their brothers."[71] The product of a "feminine revolution startling in the shock of its abruptness," she was living in the city independently of her family. Johnson noted: "She is sure of one life only and that one she passionately desires. She wants to live that life to its fullest. . . . She wants adventure. She wants excitement and mystery. She wants to see, to know, to experience...." She expressed both a "passionate revolt against the commonplace" and a "scorn of conventions." Johnson's heroine in *The Salamander,* Doré Baxter, embodied his views. Her carefree motto is reminiscent of Fitzgerald's flappers of the Twenties: " 'How do I know what I'll do to-morrow?' "[72] Her nightly prayer, the modest " 'O Lord! give me everything I want!' "[73] Love was her "supreme law of conduct,"[74] and she, like the literary flappers of the Twenties, feared "thirty as a sort of sepulcher, an end of all things!"[75] Johnson believed that all young women in all sections of the country had "a little touch of the Salamander," each alike being impelled by "an impetuous frenzy... to sample each new excitement," both the "safe and the dangerous."[76] Girls "seemed determined to have their fling like men," the novelist Gertrude Atherton noted in *Current Opinion,* "and some of the stories [about them] made even my sophisticated hair crackle at the roots...."[77] Beatrice Fairfax deplored the trends, especially the fact that "Making love lightly, boldly and promiscuously seems to be part of our social structure."[78] Young men and women kissed though they did not intend to marry.[79] And kissing was shading into spooning (" 'To Spoon' or 'Not to Spoon' Seems to Be the Burning Question with Modern Young America")[80] and even "petting," which was modish among the collegiate set.[81] In fact, excerpts from the diary of a co-ed written before World War I suggest that experimentation was virtually complete within her peer group. She discussed her "adventures" with other college girls. "We were healthy animals and we were demanding our rights to spring's awakening." As for men, she wrote, "I played square with the men. I always told them I was not out to pin them down to marriage, but that this intimacy was pleasant and I wanted it as much as they did. We indulged in sex talk, birth control.... We thought too much about it."[82]

One of the most interesting developments in changing sexual behavior which characterized these years was the blurring of age lines between young and middle-aged women in silhouette, dress, and cosmetics.[83] A fashion commentator warned matrons, "This is the day of the figure.... The face alone, no matter how pretty, counts for nothing unless the body is as straight and yielding as every young girl's."[84] With only slight variations, the optimum style for women's dress between 1908 and 1918 was a modified sheath, straight up and down and clinging.[85] How different from the styles of the high-busted, broad-hipped mother of the race of 1904 for whom Ella Wheeler Wilcox, the journalist and poet, advised the use of veils because "the slightest approach to masculinity in woman's attire is always unlovely and disappointing."[86]

The sloughing off of numerous undergarments and loosening of others underscored women's quickening activity and increasingly self-reliant morals. Clinging dresses and their "accompanying lack of undergarments" eliminated, according to the president of the New York Cotton Exchange, "at least twelve yards of finished goods for each adult female inhabitant."[87] Corset makers were forced to make adjustments too and use more supple materials.[88] Nevertheless, their sales declined.[89]

The American woman of 1910, in contrast with her sister of 1900, avidly cultivated beauty of face and form. In fact, the first American woman whose photographs and advertising image we can clearly recognize as belonging to our times lived between 1910 and 1920. "Nowadays," the speaker for a woman's club declared in 1916, "only the very poor or the extremely careless are old or ugly. You can go to a beauty shop and choose the kind of beauty you will have."[90] Beautification included the use of powder, rouge, lipstick, eyelash and eyebrow stain. Advertising was now manipulating such images for face powder as "Mother tried it and decided to keep it for herself,"[91] or "You can have beautiful Eyebrows and Eyelashes. . . . Society women and actresses get them by using Lash-Brow-Ine."[92] Nearly every one of the numerous advertisements for cosmetics promised some variation of "How to Become Beautiful, Fascinating, Attractive."[93]

In her dress as well as her use of cosmetics, the American woman gave evidence that she had abandoned passivity. An unprecedented public display of the female figure characterized the period.[94] Limbs now became legs and more of them showed after 1910, although they were less revealing than the promising hosiery advertisements. Rolled down hose first appeared in 1917.[95] Dresses for opera and restaurant were deeply cut in front and back, and not even the rumor that Mrs. John Jacob Astor had suffered a chest cold as a result of wearing deep decolleté[96] deterred their wearers. As for gowns, "Fashion says—Evening gowns must be sleeveless. . . . afternoon gowns are made with semi-transparent yokes and sleeves."[97] Undoubtedly, this vogue for transparent blouses and dresses[98] caused the editor of the *Unpopular Review* to declare: "At no time and place under Christianity, except the most corrupt periods in France. . . . certainly never before in America, has woman's form been so freely displayed in society and on the street."[99]

In addition to following the example of young women in dress and beautification, middle-aged women, especially those from the middle and upper classes, were espousing their permissive manners and morals.[100] Smoking and, to a lesser extent, drinking in public were becoming fashionable for married women of the upper class and were making headway at other class levels.[101]   As early as 1910, a prominent clubwoman stated: "It has become a well-established habit for women to drink cocktails. It is thought the smart thing to do."[102]   Even before Gertrude Atherton described in the novel *Black Oxen* the phenomenon of the middle-aged women who sought to be attractive to younger men, supposedly typifying the 1920s,[103]   it was evident in the play "Years of Discretion." Written by Frederic Hatton and Fanny Locke Hatton, and staged by Belasco, the play was "welcomed cordially both in New York and Chicago" in 1912. It featured a widowed mother forty-eight years of age, who announces, "I intend to look under forty—lots under. I have never attracted men, but I know I can."[104]   Again, "I mean to have a wonderful time. To have all sorts and kinds of experience. I intend to love and be loved, to lie and cheat."[105]   Dorothy Dix was dismayed over "the interest that women . . . have in what we are pleased to euphoniously term the 'erotic.' " She continued, "I'll bet there are not ten thousand women in the whole United States who couldn't get one hundred in an examination of the life and habits of Evelyn Nesbitt and Harry Thaw. . . ."[106]   Married women among the fashionable set held the great parties, at times scandalous ones which made the 1920s seem staid by comparison.[107]   They hired the Negro orchestras at Newport and performed and sometimes invented the daring dances.[108]   They conscientiously practiced birth control, as did women of other classes.[109]   And they initiated divorce proceedings, secure in the knowledge that many of their best friends had done the same thing.

Perhaps the best insights on the mores and morals of this group are to be found in the writings of the contemporary, realistic novelist, Robert Herrick.[110]   Herrick derived his heroines from "the higher income groups, the wealthy, upper middle, and professional classes among which he preferred to move."[111]   His heroines resemble literary flappers of the 1920s in their repudiation of childbearing. "It takes a year out of a woman's life, of course, no matter how she is situated," they say, or, "Cows do that."[112]   Since their lives were seldom more than a meaningless round of social experiences, relieved principally by romantic literature, many of them either contemplated or consented to infidelity. Thus Margaret Pole confesses to her friend, Conny Wood-yard, " I'd like to lie out on the beach and forget children and servants and husbands, and stop wondering what life is. Yes, I'd like a vacation— in the Windward Islands, with somebody who understood.' 'To wit, a man!' added Conny. 'Yes, a man! But only for the trip.' "[113]   They came finally to live for love in a manner that is startlingly reminiscent of some of the famous literary women of the Twenties.[114]

Insights regarding the attitudes of married women from the urban lower middle class can be found in the diary of Ruth Vail Randall, who lived in Chicago from 1911 to the date of her suicide, March 6, 1920.[115] A document of urban sociology, the diary transcends mere personal experience and becomes a commentary on group behavior of the times. Mrs. Randall was reared in a family that owned a grocery store, was graduated from high school in Chicago, and was married at twenty to Norman B. Randall, then twenty-one. She worked after marriage in a department store and later for a brief period as a model. She looked to marriage, especially its romance, as the supreme fulfillment of her life and was bitterly disappointed with her husband. She began to turn to other men whom she met at work or places of recreation, and her husband left her. Fearing that her lover would leave her eventually as well, she killed him and herself.

The diary focuses on those conditions which made the revolution in morals a reality. The young couple lived anonymously in a highly mobile neighborhood where their morals were of their own making. Mrs. Randall did not want children; she aborted their only child. [116] She was also averse to the reserved "womanly" role, which her husband insisted that she assume.[117] She complained, "Why cannot a woman do all man does?"[118] She wished that men and women were more alike in their social roles.[119] She repudiated involvement in her home, resolved to exploit equally every privilege which her husband assumed, drank, flirted, and lived promiscuously. Telephones and cars made her extramarital liaisons possible. Even before her divorce, she found another companion; flouting convention, she wrote, "He and I have entered a marriage pact according to our own ideas."[120] Throughout her diary she entertained enormous, almost magical, expectations of love. She complained that her lovers no more than her husband provided what she craved—tenderness and companionship. Disillusionment with one of them caused her to cry out, "I am miserable. I have the utmost contempt for myself. But the lake is near and soon it will be warm. Oh, God to rest in your arms. To rest—and to have peace."[121]

That America was experiencing a major upheaval in morals during the Progressive era is nowhere better ascertained than in the comprehensive efforts by civic officials and censorial citizens to control them. Disapproval extended not only to such well-known staples as alcohol, divorce, and prostitution, but also to dancing, woman's dress, cabarets, theaters and movies, and birth control. "Mrs. Warren's Profession" was withdrawn from the New York stage in 1905 after a one night performance, the manager of the theater later being charged with offending public decency.[122] When a grand jury in New York condemned the "turkey trot and kindred dances" as "indecent," the judge who accepted the presentment noted that "Rome's downfall was due to the degenerate nature of its dancers, and I only hope that we will not suffer the same result."[123] Public dancing was henceforth to be licensed. Mayor John Fitzgerald personally assisted the morals campaign in Boston by ordering the removal from a store of an objectionable picture which portrayed a "show-girl" with her legs crossed.[124] Meanwhile, the "X-Ray Skirt" was outlawed in Portland, Oregon, and Los Angeles;[125] and the police chief of Louisville, Kentucky, ordered the arrest of a number of women appearing on the streets with slit skirts.[126] Witnessing to a general fear that the spreading knowledge of contraception might bring on sexual license, the federal and several state governments enacted sumptuary legislation.[127] And in two celebrated incidents, the offenders, Van K. Allison (1916) in Boston and Margaret Sanger (1917) in New York, were prosecuted and sent to jail.[128]

Public officials were apprehensive about the sweeping influence of the movies on the masses, "at once their book, their drama, their art. To some it has become society, school, and even church."[129] They proceeded to set up boards of censorship with powers to review and condemn movies in four states: Pennsylvania (1911), Ohio (1913), Maryland (1916), and Kansas (1917), and in numerous cities beginning with Chicago in 1907.[130] The Pennsylvania board, for example, prohibited pictures which displayed nudity, prolonged passion, women drinking and smoking, and infidelity. It protected Pennsylvanians from such films produced between 1915 and 1918 as "What Every Girl Should Know," "A Factory Magdalene," and "Damaged Goodness."[131]

Such determination proved unavailing, however, even as the regulatory strictures were being applied. According to one critic the "sex drama" using "plain, blunt language" had become "a commonplace" of the theater after 1910 and gave the "tender passion rather the worst for it in recent years."[132] Vice films packed them in every night, especially after the smashing success of "Traffic in Souls," which reportedly grossed $450,000.[133] In Boston the anti-vice campaign itself languished because there was no means of controlling "the kitchenette-apartment section." "In these apartment houses, there are hundreds of women who live as they please and who entertain as they will." [134] Mayor Fitzgerald's "show-girl," evicted from her saucy perch, gained more notoriety when she appeared in a Boston newspaper the following day.[135] Even Anthony Comstock, that indefatigable guardian of public morals, had probably come to look a bit like a comic character living beyond his times.[136]

When Mrs. Sanger was arrested for propagating birth control information in 1917, she confidently stated, "I have nothing to fear. . . . Regardless of the outcome I shall continue my work, supported by thousands of men and women throughout the country."[137] Her assurance was well founded. Three years earlier her supporters had founded a National Birth Control League; and in 1919, this organization opened its first public clinic.[138] But most encouraging for Mrs. Sanger was the impressive testimony that many Americans were now practicing or interested in birth control.[139] When Paul B. Blanchard, pastor of the Maverick Congregational Church in East Boston, protested the arrest of Van K. Allison, he charged, "If the truth were made public and the laws which prevent the spreading of even oral information about birth control were strictly enforced how very few of the married society leaders, judges, doctors, ministers, and businessmen would be outside the prison dock!"[140]

The foregoing demonstrates that a major shift in American manners and morals occurred in the Progressive era, especially after 1910. Changes at this time, though developing out of still earlier conditions, represented such visible departures from the past and were so commonly practiced as to warrant calling them revolutionary. Too often scholars have emphasized the Twenties as the period of significant transition and World War I as a major cause of the phenomenon. Americans of the 1920s, fresh from the innovative wartime atmosphere, undoubtedly quickened and deepened the revolution. Women from smaller cities and towns contested what was familiar terrain to an already seasoned cadre of urban women and a formidable group of defectors. Both in their rhetoric and their practices, apparent even before the war, the earlier group had provided the shibboleths for the 1920s; they first asked, "What are Patterns for?" The revolution in manners and morals was, of course, but an integral part of numerous, contemporary, political and social movements to free the individual by reordering society. Obviously, the Progressive era, more than the 1920s, represents the substantial beginnings of contemporary American civilization.

The revolution in manners and morals, particularly as it affected women, took the twofold form of more permissive sexuality and diminished femininity. Women from the upper classes participated earlier, as is evidenced by their introductory exhibition of fashions, hair styles, dances, cosmetics, smoking, and drinking. Realistic novels concerned with marriage suggest that they entertained ideas of promiscuity and even infidelity before women of the lower classes. Yet the cardinal condition of change was not sophistication but urban living and the freedom it conferred. As technology and economic progress narrowed the gap between the classes, middle-class women and even those below were free to do many of the same things almost at the same time. Above all, the revolution in manners and morals after 1910 demonstrates that sexual freedom and the twentieth-century American city go together.

NOTES

1. Henry F. May, "Shifting Perspectives on the 1920's," *Mississippi Valley Historical Review,* XLIII (Dec. 1956), 405–27.

2. Richard Hofstadter, *The Age of Reform: From Bryan to F. D. R.* (New York, 1955), 282–301.

3. May, "Shifting Perspectives on the 1920's," 426. See also Henry F. May, "The Rebellion of the Intellectuals, 1912–1917," *American Quarterly,* VIII (Summer 1956), 115, wherein May describes 1912–1917 as a "pre-revolutionary or early revolutionary period."

4. May, "Shifting Perspectives on the 1920's," 427.

5. Henry F. May, *The End of American Innocence: A Study of the First Years of Our Own Time, 1912–1917* (New York, 1959).

6. Arthur S. Link, "What Happened to the Progressive Movement in the 1920's?" *American Historical Review,* LXIV (July 1959), 833–51.

7. J. Joseph Huthmacher, "Urban Liberalism and the Age of Reform," *Mississippi Valley Historical Review,* XLIX (Sept. 1962), 231–41. Other political and economic historians concur on a developmental interpretation. Gerald D. Nash, *State Government and Economic Development: A History of Administrative Policies in California, 1849–1933* (Berkeley, 1964), 250, 291, 326, views the period 1900–1933 as a unit because it was characterized by notable coordination and centralization of authority by agencies of state government in California. Donald C. Swain, *Federal Conservation Policy, 1921–1933* (Berkeley, 1963), 6, sees the national conservation program making continuous advances through the 1920s based upon beginnings in the Progressive period.

8. "Sex O'clock in America," *Current Opinion,* LV (Aug. 1913), 113–14. The anonymous author borrowed the phrase from William M. Reedy, editor of the St. Louis *Mirror.*

9. Agnes Repplier, "The Repeal of Reticence," *Atlantic Monthly,* CXIII (March 1914), 297–304, objected to the "obsession of sex which has set us all a-babbling about matters once excluded from the amenities of conversation" (p. 298). Articles on birth control, prostitution, divorce, and sexual morals between 1910 and 1914 were cumulatively more numerous per thousand among articles indexed in the *Reader's Guide to Periodical Literature* than for either 1919 to 1924 or 1925 to 1928. Hornell Hart, "Changing Social Attitudes and Interests," *Recent Social Trends in the United States: Report of the President's Research Committee on Social Trends* (2 vols., New York, 1933), I, 414.

10. H. W. Boynton, "Ideas, Sex, and the Novel," *Dial,* LX (April 13, 1916), 361. In Robert W. Chambers, *The Restless Sex* (New York, 1918), 143, the heroine remarks, "What was all wrong in our Victorian mothers' days is all right now."

11. Arthur Pollock, "Are We Immoral?" *Forum,* LI (Jan. 1914), 52. Pollock remarks that "in our literature and in our life to-day sex is paramount."

12. "Will Puritanism Return?" *Independent,* 77 (March 23, 1914), 397.

13. Mark Sullivan, *Our Times: The War Begins* (New York, 1932), 165–93, states in colorful and impressionistic terms that significant changes in moral attitudes had taken place in the Progressive era. He attributes much of this to the influence of Freud, Shaw, and Omar Khayyám. Preston William Slosson, *The Great Crusade and After: 1914–1928* (New York, 1930), describes the period 1914–1928 as a unit, but his material dealing with morals centers on the 1920s. For example, there are only five footnotes based on materials written between 1914 and 1919 in his chapter, "The American Woman Wins Equality," 130–61. Samuel Eliot Morison makes brief mention of a "revolution in sexual morals" before 1920 in *The Oxford History of the American People* (New York, 1965), 906–08.

14. Frederick Lewis Allen, *Only Yesterday: An Informal History of the Nineteen-Twenties* (New York, 1931), 88–122; William E. Leuchtenburg, *The Perils of Prosperity: 1914–32* (Chicago, 1958), 158–77.

15. May, *The End of American Innocence,* 334–47, is lightly documented; there are only twelve footnotes to support his discussion of these and similar developments.

16. *Ibid.,* 347. May's view of women's changing attitudes is contradicted by Margaret Deland: "Of course there were women a generation ago, as in all generations, who asserted themselves; but they were practically 'sports.' Now, the simple, honest woman . . . the good wife, the good mother—is evolving ideals which are changing her life, and the lives of those people about her." Margaret Deland, "The Change in the Feminine Ideal," *Atlantic Monthly,* CV (March 1910), 291.

17. George E. Mowry, *The Urban Nation: 1920–1960* (New York, 1965), 250.

18. *Ibid.,* 23.

19. *Ibid.*

20. *Ibid.,* 24.

21. "By 1930 more than ten million women held jobs. Nothing did more to emancipate them." Leuchtenburg, *Perils of Prosperity,* 160. See also Allen, *Only Yesterday,* 95–98. For estimates of the effects of World War I on morals, see Leuchtenburg, *Perils of Prosperity,* 172–73; Allen, *Only Yesterday,* 94; Mowry, *Urban Nation,* 24.

22. Population in urban territory comprised only about 28 percent of the total American population in 1880; but by 1920, approximately 52 percent were living there. Department of Commerce, Bureau of the Census, *Historical Statistics of the United States, Colonial Times to 1957* (Washington, 1960), 14.

23. Scott Nearing and Nellie M. S. Nearing, *Woman and Social Progress* (New York, 1912), 137–41. The Nearings wrote: "The freedom which American Women have gained through recent social changes and the significance of their consequent choice, constitutes one of the profoundest and at the same time one of the most inscrutable problems in American life" (p. 138). William I. Thomas, *The Unadjusted Girl: With Cases and Standpoint for Behavior Analysis* (Boston, 1923), 86. Ernest R. Mowrer, *Family Disorganization* (Chicago, 1927), 6–8. Mowrer attributes "Family Disorganization" to the "conditions of city life" which resulted in a "rebellion against the old ideals of family life. . . ."

24. George Elliott Howard, "Social Control and the Functions of the Family," Howard J. Rogers, ed. *Congress of Arts and Sciences: Universal Exposition, St. Louis, 1904* (8 vols., Boston, 1906), VII, 702.

25. Louise Collier Willcox, "Our Supervised Morals," *North American Review,* CXCVIII (Nov. 1913), 708, observes: "The time is past when parents supervised the morals of their children. . . ."

26. There was a surprisingly large number of cars sold and used in America between 1910 and 1920. Approximately 40 percent as many cars were produced each year between 1915 and 1917 as were manufactured between 1925 and 1927. *Facts and Figures of the Automobile Industry* (New York, 1929), 6, 22. There were approximately 7,500,000 cars registered in 1919. "Existing Surfaced Mileage Total" on a scale of 1,000 miles was 204 in 1910, 332 in 1918, 521 in 1925, and 694 in 1930. *Historical Statistics of the United States,* 458. Newspapers reported the impact of the automobile on dating and elopements. For a moralistic reaction to the phenomenon, see Dorothy Dix, Boston *American,* Sept. 5, 1912. For an enthusiast of "mobile privacy" in this period, see F. Scott Fitzgerald, "Echoes of the Jazz Age," *Scribner's Magazine,* XC (Nov. 1931), 460. Fitzgerald wrote: "As far back as 1915 the unchaperoned young people of the smaller cities had discovered the mobile privacy of that automobile given to young Bill at sixteen to make him 'self-reliant.' "

27. Dorothy Dix, "A Modern Diana," Boston *American,* April 7, 1910.

28. Beatrice Fairfax, *ibid.,* May 28, 1908; Dorothy Dix, *ibid.,* Sept. 9, 1912.

29. *Ibid.,* Aug. 21, 1913.

30. Marion Harland, "The Passing of the Home Daughter," *Independent,* LXXI (July 13, 1911), 90.

31. Sophonisba P. Breckinridge, *Women in the Twentieth Century: A Study of Their Political, Social and Economic Activities* (New York, 1933), 112. Overall percentages of women gainfully employed rose from 19 percent of the total work force in 1890 to 20.6 percent in 1900, 24.3 percent in 1910, 24 percent in 1920, and 25.3 percent in 1930. *Ibid.,* 108.

32. While the number of women who worked as domestics declined after 1910, large numbers of women were employed for the first time as clerks and stenographers. In fact, more women were employed in both these occupations between 1910 and 1920 than between 1920 and 1930. *Ibid.,* 129, 177.

33. Martha Bensley Bruere and Robert W. Bruere, *Increasing Home Efficiency* (New York, 1914), 236–41.

34.

Total Amount Expended in Millions of Dollars

Item	1909	1914	1919	1923	1929
(a) canned fruits and vegetables	162	254	575	625	930
(b) cleaning and polishing preparations	6	9	27	35	46
(c) electricity in household operation	83	132	265	389	615.5
(d) mechanical appliances (refrigerators, sewing machines, washers, cooking)	152	175	419	535	804.1

Item	1909	1914	1919	1923	1929
Percentage of expenditures on household equipment to total expenditures	9.9%	9.2%	10.3%	11.6%	13.2%

(a-b) is found in William H. Lough, *High-Level Consumption: Its Behavior; Its Consequences* (New York, 1935), 236, 241. These figures are tabulated in millions of dollars for 1935. Items (c-d) and the percentage of expenditure on household equipment to total expenditures were taken from James Dewhurst, *America's Needs and Resources: A New Survey* (New York, 1955), 702, 704, 180.

35. Realistic novelists note the leisure of the middle-class women. David Graham Phillips, *The Hungry Heart* (New York, 1909) and *Old Wives for New* (New York, 1908); Robert Herrick, *Together* (New York, 1908), especially 515–17.

36. For example, see *Cosmopolitan*, XXXV (May-Oct. 1903); *Ladies Home Journal*, XXI (Dec. 1903–May 1904). A notable exception showing a woman riding a bicycle may be found in *ibid.* (April 1904), 39.

37. *Ladies Home Journal*, XXXIV (May 1917), for example, shows a woman entertaining stylish women friends (34, 89, 92), driving the car or on an automobile trip (36–37, 74), economizing on time spent in housework (42), the object of "outdoor girl" ads (78), beautifying at a social affair or appearing very chic (102, 106). Perhaps the best illustration for woman's activity in advertisements was employed in *Ladies Home Journal* by Williams Talc Powder. It read, "After the game, the ride, the swim, the brisk walk, or a day at the sea-shore, turn for comfort to Williams Talc Powder." *Ibid.*, XXXIV (July 1917), 74.

38. *Collier's*, 56 (Nov. 27, 1915), 4.

39. *Cosmopolitan*, LIX (June 1915), advertising section, 50.

40. *Collier's*, 56 (Sept. 25, 1915), 22.

41. *Ibid.* (Nov. 27, 1915), 25.

42. *Ladies Home Journal*, XXXV (April 1918), 58.

43. *Ibid.*, 57.

44. *Ibid.*, XXXIII (Jan. 1916), 46–47. Women drove their friends and families about in their cars. *Ibid.*, XXXII (July 1915), 34–35; (Aug. 1915), 38–39; (Oct. 1915), 86; XXXIII (Nov. 1916), 71.

45. Susanne Wilcox, "The Unrest of Modern Women," *Independent*, LXVII (July 8, 1909), 63.

46. Nell Brinkley, a nationally syndicated cartoonist and commentator on women's activities, asked this question of one of her young women. Boston *American*, July 14, 1913.

47. Nell Brinkley coined the phrase. *Ibid.*, Nov. 14, 1916.

48. *Ibid.*, May 4, 1915. See also *Ladies Home Journal*, XXXII (July 1915), which depicts a young woman driving a speedboat while her boyfriend sits next to her.

49. Boston *American*, Oct. 1, 1916.

50. *Collier's*, 56 (March 4, 1916), 38.

51. Emma B. Kaufman, "The Education of a Debutante," *Cosmopolitan*, XXXV (Sept. 1903), 499–508.

52. *Cosmopolitan*, XXXIX (Oct. 1905).

53. "Girls, Don't Allow Men to be Familiar," Boston *American*, June 17, 1904; *ibid.*, July 15, 1905.

54. *Wellesley College News*, Feb. 20, 1902. Wellesley relented on "men dances" in 1913.

55. Deland, "The Change in the Feminine Ideal," 291.

56. *Ibid.*, 289.

57. Boston *American*, May 6, 1910.

58. *Ibid.*, Sept. 5, 1912.

59. Ethel Watts Mumford, "Where Is Your Daughter This Afternoon?" *Harper's Weekly*, LVIII (Jan. 17, 1914), 28.

60. Boston *American*, Sept. 5, 1916; *ibid.*, Jan. 4, 1914.

61. Alice Duer Miller. "The New Dances and the Younger Generation," *Harper's Bazaar*, XLVI (May 1912), 250.

62. Deland, "Change in the Feminine Ideal," 293.

63. Boston *American*, March 24, 1916. In a letter to the editor of the New York *Times*, one critic of the "women of New York" complained that they seemed to be part of a "new race" or even a "super-sex." He waxed poetic: "Sweet seventeen is rouge-pot mad, And hobbles to her tasks blase, . . . Where are the girls of yesterday?" New York *Times*, July 20, 1914.

64. Miller, "New Dances and the Younger Generation," 250. According to Helen Rowland, the woman was "no longer Man's plaything, but his playmate. . . ." Helen Rowland, "The Emancipation of 'the Rib,' *Delineator*, LXXVII (March 1911), 233.

65. Boston *American*, April 7, 1910.

66. *Ibid.*, March 20, 1914.

67. *Ibid.*, June 11, 1916.

68. *Ibid.*, Nov. 27, Dec. 8, 1912.

69. On Newport and Boston society women see *ibid.*, July 6, 27, Aug. 10, 24, 1913. Pauline Frederick's picture may be found in *ibid.*, Aug. 2, 1913. For Irene Castle, see Mr. and Mrs. Vernon Castle, *Modern Dancing* (New York, 1914), 98, 105.

70. *Ladies Home Journal*, XXXII (July and Sept. 1915); *ibid.* (Nov. 1915), 8.

71. Owen Johnson, *The Salamander* (Indianapolis, 1914), Foreword, n.p.

72. *Ibid.*, 9.

73. *Ibid.*, 129.

74. *Ibid.*, 66.

75. *Ibid.*, 61.

76. *Ibid.*, Foreword, n.p. Chamber's young heroine Stephanie Cleland in *The Restless Sex*, 191, practiced trial marriage in order to learn by experience. See also Phillips, *Hungry Heart*, 166–80; Terry Ramsaye, *A Million And One Nights: A History of the Motion Picture* (2 vols., New York, 1926), II, 702–04.

77. "Mrs. Atherton Tells of Her 'Perch of the Devil,' " *Current Opinion*, LVII (Nov. 1914), 349.

78. Boston *American*, Feb. 8, 1917.

79. The "kiss of friendship" criticized by Fairfax had become a major issue of her mail by 1913. See, for example, *ibid.,* July 5, 1913. Girls shocked her with inquiries as to whether it was permissible to "soul kiss" on a first date. *Ibid.,* Feb. 13, 1914. An engaged girl asked whether it would be all right to kiss men other than her fiance. *Ibid.,* May 2, 1916.

80. *Ibid.,* Feb. 8, 1917.

81. Fitzgerald, "Echoes of the Jazz Age," 460.

82. Thomas, *Unadjusted Girl,* 95.

83. "Today in the world of fashion, all women are young, and they grow more so all the time." Doeuilet, "When All The World Looks Young," *Delineator,* LXXXIII (Aug. 1913), 20. Advertisements used flattery or played up the value of youth for women and warned that they might age unless certain products were used. *Cosmopolitan,* LIX (Nov. 1915), 112; *ibid.* (July 1915), 81; *Ladies Home Journal,* XXXII (Nov. 1915), 65; *Cosmopolitan,* LIX (Oct. 1915), 57.

84. Eleanor Chalmers, "Facts and Figures," *Delineator,* LXXXIV (April 1914), 38.

85. Boston *American,* March 20, 1910; *Delineator,* LXXXIX (Oct. 1916), 66.

86. Boston *American,* March 28, 1904.

87. New York *Tribune,* April 4, 1912; Eleanor Chalmers, "You and Your Sewing," *Delineator,* LXXXIII (Aug. 1913), 33.

88. Eleanor Chalmers, *Delineator,* LXXIV (April 1914), 38. The sense of relief these changes brought is amusingly described in Dorothy A. Plum, comp., *The Magnificent Enterprise: A Chronicle of Vassar College* (Poughkeepsie, 1961), 43–44.

89. Percival White, "Figuring Us Out," *North American Review,* CCXXVII (Jan. 1929), 69.

90. Boston *American,* Dec. 10, 1916.

91. *Delineator,* LXXXV (July 1914), 55.

92. Boston *American,* Sept. 3, 1916.

93. *Cosmopolitan,* LIX (July 1915).

94. An editorial declared that women's dresses in 1913 had approached "the danger line of indecency about as closely as they could." New York *Times,* July 6, 1914.

95. *Ladies Home Journal,* XXXIV (Oct. 1917), 98.

96. Boston *American,* June 8, 1907. "The conventions of evening dress have changed radically in the last four or five years. Not so very long ago a high-necked gown was considered *au fait* for all evening functions except formal dinners and the opera. Nowadays, well-dressed women wear decolleté dresses even for home dinners, and semi-decolleté gowns for restaurants and theaters." *Delineator,* LXXV (Jan. 1910), 60.

97. *Cosmopolitan,* LIX (July 1915).

98. *Ladies Home Journal,* XXXII (Oct. 1915), 108; *ibid.,* XXXIII (Oct. 1916), 82; *ibid.,* XXXIII (Nov. 1916), 78–79; *ibid.,* XXXIV (Jan. 1917), 53.

99. "The Cult of St. Vitus," *Unpopular Review,* III (Jan.-March 1915), 94.

100. Boston *American,* July 6, 1912. Dix noted "flirtatious" middle-aged women were "aping the airs and graces of the debutante" and "trying to act kittenish" with men.

101. *Ibid.,* Dec. 6, 10, 1912. Anita Stewart, a movie star who wrote "Talks to Girls," though personally opposed to smoking, admitted that "lots of my friends smoke" and "they are nice girls too." *Ibid.,* Dec. 14, 1915. In 1916, the Boston *American* titled a column on a page devoted to women's interests "To Smoke or Not to Smoke." *Ibid.,* April 12, 1916. The *Harvard Lampoon,* LXXI (June 20, 1916), 376, spoofed women smoking: it carried a heading "Roman Society Women Agree to Give Up Smoking" and a commentary below, "Oh, Nero, how times have changed!"

102. Boston *American,* March 7, 1910.

103. Leuchtenburg, *Perils of Prosperity,* 174–75.

104. " 'Years of Discretion'—A Play of Cupid at Fifty," *Current Opinion,* LIV (Feb. 1913), 116.

105. *Ibid.,* 117.

106. Boston *American,* April 10, 1908. Evelyn Nesbitt, the wife of Harry Thaw, was romantically involved with architect Stanford White, whom Thaw shot to death.

107. *Ibid.,* Aug. 25, Sept. 1, 1912.

108. Most of the dances which became very popular after 1910, such as the Turkey Trot, the Bunny Hug, and the Grizzly Bear, afforded a maximum of motion in a minimum of space. The Chicken Flip was invented by a Boston society woman. *Ibid.,* Nov. 11, 1912. See also "New Reflections on The Dancing Mania," *Current Opinion,* LV (Oct. 1913), 262.

109. Louis I. Dublin, "Birth Control," *Social Hygiene,* VI (Jan. 1920), 6.

110. Alfred Kazin, "Three Pioneer Realists," *Saturday Review of Literature,* XX (July 8, 1939), 15. Herrick's biographer, Blake Nevius, declares, "It can be argued that Herrick is the most comprehensive and reliable social historian in American fiction to appear in the interregnum between Howells and the writers of the Twenties. . . ." Blake Nevius, *Robert Herrick: The Development of a Novelist* (Berkeley, 1962), Preface.

111. Nevius, *Robert Herrick,* 177.

112. Herrick, *Together,* 91, 392.

113. *Ibid.,* 263, 250–51, 320–24.

114. Herrick describes the temperament of the modern woman as one of "mistress rather than the wife. . . . 'I shall be a person with a soul of my own. To have me man must win me not once, but daily.' " *Ibid.,* 516. The last sentence above nearly duplicates Rosalind's statement to her beau in *This Side of Paradise,* "I have to be won all over again every time you see me." F. Scott Fitzgerald, *This Side of Paradise* (New York, 1920), 194.

115. Chicago *Herald and Examiner,* March 10–17, 1920.

116. *Ibid.,* March 10, 1920.

117. *Ibid.,* March 11, 1920.

118. *Ibid.*

119. *Ibid.,* March 11, 12, 1920.

120. *Ibid.,* March 13, 14, 1920.

121. *Ibid.,* March 15, 1920.

122. New York *Tribune,* Nov. 1, 1905.

123. New York *Times,* May 28, 1913.

124. *Ibid.,* Dec. 20, 1912.

125. *Ibid.,* Aug. 20, 23, 1913.

126. *Ibid.,* June 29, 1913.

127. Carol Flora Brooks, "The Early History of the Anti-Contraceptive Laws in Massachusetts and Connecticut," *American Quarterly,* XVIII (Spring 1966), 3–23; George E. Worthington, "Statutory Restrictions on Birth Control," *Journal of Social Hygiene,* IX (Nov. 1923), 458–65.

128. Boston *American,* July 14, 21, 1916; New York *Times,* Feb. 6, 1917.

129. *Report of the Pennsylvania Board of Censors,* June 1, 1915 to Dec. 1, 1915 (Harrisburg, 1916), 6.

130. Ellis Paxson Oberholtzer, *The Morals of the Movie* (Philadelphia, 1922), 115–23.

131. *Report of the Pennsylvania State Board of Censors,* 1915, pp. 14–15; *ibid.,* 1916, pp. 24–25; *ibid.,* 1917, pp. 8–9.

132. Boston *American,* Aug. 10, 1913.

133. Ramsaye, *A Million and One Nights,* II, 617.

134. Boston *American,* July 7, 1917.

135. *Ibid.,* Dec. 20, 1912.

136. Heywood Broun, *Anthony Comstock: Roundsman of the Lord* (New York, 1927); Mary Alden Hopkins, "Birth Control and Public Morals: An Interview with Anthony Comstock," *Harper's Weekly,* LX (May 22, 1915), 489–90.

137. Boston *American,* Jan. 4, 1917.

138. Norman E. Himes, "Birth Control in Historical and Clinical Perspective," *Annals of the American Academy of Political and Social Sciences,* 160 (March 1932), 53.

139. Dublin, "Birth Control," 6.

140. Boston *American,* July 16, 1916. According to International News Service, "Mrs. Rose Pastor Stokes was literally mobbed by an eager crowd in Carnegie Hall when she offered, in defiance of the police, to distribute printed slips bearing a formula for birth control." *Ibid.,* May 6, 1916.

～ 20 ～

Two Washes in the Morning and a Bridge Party at Night: The American Housewife between the Wars

RUTH SCHWARTZ COWAN

The "feminine mystique" has been part of American cultural life for quite a long while, far longer than Betty Friedan and others have believed; its origins go back to the period after the First World War, not the Second.[1] Political tracts very often idealize the past, and *The Feminine Mystique* was no exception; the norms for American women between the wars were not nearly as bold and adventurous as Betty Friedan would like to think.[2] The cult of true womanhood—that marvelous Victorian combination of Christian sentimentalism and sexual repression[3]—had indeed died by the early 20's, but the ideology that replaced it was, to all intents and purposes, the same "feminine mystique" that Friedan attributes to the 40's and 50's. Whatever it was that trapped educated American women in their kitchens, babbling at babies and worrying about color combinations for the bathroom, the trap was laid during the roaring 20's, not the quiet 50's.

Friedan bases her appraisal of the period between the wars on the fiction that appeared in women's magazines. To some extent her appraisal is correct; those stories often dealt with adventurous, athletic and unconventional women—many of them pursuing a career. But Friedan neglects two aspects of those stories that are just as significant: the career girls were always single and the unconventional ladies were always attended by a truly unconventional number of servants. The housewives who were reading those stories could not possibly have seen themselves mirrored therein; in fact, those stories, with their exotic settings and fanciful plots, were frankly escapist literature. When

From *Women's Studies* 2 (1976): 147-171. Reprinted by permission of Gordon and Breach, Science Publishing, Ltd.

they weren't about strong-minded career girls, they were often about baronnesses, debutantes and Hollywood stars. Why tastes changed after World War II, why—as Friedan accurately noted—postwar fiction tended to be about housewives and not baronnesses, is anyone's guess, but the fact remains that the fiction in the women's magazines in the 20's and 30's is not a reliable indicator of the attitudes and problems of the vast majority of American women. This does not mean, however, that the mass circulation women's magazines are not a reliable source for social history, but it does suggest that we should look at the non-fiction to find a more accurate reflection of what was happening to American women—not in fields of glorious endeavor, but in front of their kitchen sinks, which is where they happened to be. In the advertisements, the informative articles and the advice columns of *The Ladies' Home Journal, McCall's, American Home,* and other similar magazines, a careful reader can watch the feminine mystique descending upon the minds and hearts of American women during the two decades between the wars.

That mystique, like any system of cultural norms, was a complex and subtle affair, continuous with previous ideologies, yet clearly different from them. The mystique makers of the 20's and 30's believed that women were purely domestic creatures, that the goal of each normal woman's life was the acquisition of a husband, a family and a home, that women who worked outside their homes did so only under duress or because they were "odd" (for which read "ugly," "frustrated," "compulsive," or "single") and that this state of affairs was sanctioned by the tenets of religion, biology, psychology and patriotism. Hardly a surprising ideology to be found between the covers of women's magazines, past or present. The feminine mystique differed from previous value systems in its prescriptions about the details—who might reside in that household, how many children that happy family might contain, what the relationship between husband and wife, mother and children, housewife and household ideally might be.

The ideal housewife of the 20's and 30's did not have servants, or to put it another way, the servants she had were electrical, not human. In *The Ladies' Home Journal* for January 1, 1918 "The Householder's Dream of a Happy New Year," had been a cartoon: "Mandy Offers to Stay for Life and Takes Less Wages."[4] Throughout the monthly issues that year, in advertisement after advertisement, Mandy was repeatedly depicted: if you wanted to sell flannel baby's clothes to the readers of *The Ladies' Home Journal* you drew a baby held by a nursemaid; if you wanted to sell fabric, you drew a maid pinning up hems; shampoo—a maid washing her mistress's hair; talcum powder—"Nurse powders baby;" washing soap—a laundress hanging up clothes. All this in a year when, according to the editorial columns of the magazine, domestic help was scarce because of the wartime restrictions on immigration and the attractive salaries offered to women in industry.[5] By the time a decade had passed Mandy had retreated from the advertisements; by 1928 she had almost entirely disappeared into the realms of fiction. In that year if you wanted to sell radiators to the readers of *The Ladies' Home Journal* you drew a housewife playing on the floor with her children; if you wanted to promote supermarkets, women were shown doing their own shopping; cleansing powder—a housewife wiping her own sink; floor wax—an elegant lady polishing her own floor; hand cream—"They'll never know you mopped the floor yourself;" washing machines—"Two washes in the morning and a bridge party at night."

Even before the Depression struck, at a time when prosperity was widespread, American advertisers idealized the woman who was going to buy their product as a housewife, well dressed, to be sure, neatly coiffed and elegantly manicured, but a housewife who cheerfully and resolutely did her housework herself. The only servant in a full-page ad depicting every aspect of housework, an ad for Ivory Soap which appeared in *The Ladies' Home Journal* in 1933, was a confinement nurse.[6] Mandy had not disappeared entirely. She was still an important character in women's magazine fiction. *American Home* still published house plans that included a maid's room,[7] and *Parents' Magazine* still worried about the ways in which servants influence children,[8] but the days when a housewife of moderate means fully expected that she would have at least a maid of all work, and probably a laundress and nursemaid, were clearly over.[9]

On the matter of servants the feminine mystique was a reversal of older attitudes. The servantless household had once been regarded as a trial and tribulation; now it was regarded as a condition dearly to be wished. Adequate household help had always been a problem in America and women's magazines had repeatedly offered advice to housewives who were, for one unfortunate reason or another, coping with their homes singlehandedly. The emphasis in those articles was often on the word, "unfortunate;" the housewife was told, for example, that if help is scarce, it is easiest to serve children the same food that adults are eating, and at the same time—although clearly it would be better for their digestion and your temperament if they ate with a nursemaid in the nursery; hopefully the servant shortage would soon pass.[10] Occasionally a lone voice (often male) would remind the housewife of her patriotic obligations (wouldn't it be more democratic to fire the servants and have the family pitch in and do the work?) or would appeal to the higher reaches of her intellect (think how much chemistry you could learn if you would only do the cooking yourself!)[11] but the housewives apparently managed—somehow—to resist such blandishments. Housework was regarded as a chore, albeit a necessary one, and if it could be palmed off on someone else, so much the better. If one can gauge from the content and tone of advertisements, advice columns and letters to the editor, the American housewife clearly preferred to employ servants whenever economic and demographic conditions permitted her to do so.

This attitude began to change in the years after the First World War. Housework was no longer regarded as a chore, but as an expression of the housewife's personality and of her affection for her family. In past times the housewife had been judged by the way she organized her servants; now she would be judged by the way she organized her kitchen. If she were strong and proud of herself her workroom would be filled with labor-saving devices, meticulously cleaned and color coordinated; if she were insecure, frustrated and lonely, woe to her kitchen—it would be disorderly, dim and uninviting.[12] When the kitchen had been dominated by servants it had been a dreary room, often in the basement of the house. Now that the kitchen had become the housewife's domain it had to be prettied up.

> Time was when kitchens were big and dark, for keeping house was a gloomy business. . . . But now! Gay colors are the order of the day. Red pots and pans! Blue gas stoves! . . . It is a rainbow, in which the cook sings at her work and never thinks of household tasks as drudgery.[13]

Laundering had once been just laundering; now it was an expression of love. The new bride could speak her affection by washing tell-tale gray out of her husband's shirts.[14] Feeding the family had once been just feeding the family; now it was a way to communicate deep seated emotions.

> When the careful housekeeper turns from the preparation of company dinner to the routine of family meals, she will know that prime rib roast, like peach ice cream, *is a wonderful stimulant to family loyalty,* but that it is not absolutely necessary for every day.[15] (Italics mine.)

Diapering was no longer just diapering, but a time to build the baby's sense of security; cleaning the bathroom sink was not just cleaning, but an exercise for the maternal instincts, protecting the family from disease.

Clearly, tasks of this emotional magnitude could not be relegated to servants. The servantless household may have been an economic necessity in the 20's, as the supply of servants declined and their wages rose, but for the first time that necessity was widely regarded as a potential virtue. The servantless housewife was no longer portrayed as "unfortunate;" she was happy, revelling in her modern home and in the opportunities for creative expression that it provided.

> The fact is that the American home was never a more satisfying place than it is today. Science and invention have outfitted it with a great range of conveniences and comforts. . . . All this is, in the main, women's work. For the first time in the world's history it is possible for a nation's women in general to have or to be able to look forward to having homes and the means of furnishing them in keeping with their instinctive longings. The women of America are to be congratulated, not only in the opportunity but because of the manner in which they are responding to it. When the record is finally written this may stand as their greatest contribution.[16]

And what opportunities there were! In earlier years American women had been urged to treat housework as a science; now they were being urged to treat it as a craft, a creative endeavor. The ideal kitchen of the prewar period had been white and metallic—imitating the laboratory. The ideal kitchen of the postwar period was color coordinated—imitating the artist's studio. Each meal prepared in that ideal kitchen was a color composition in and of itself: "Make Meals More Appetizing by Serving Foods that Have Pleasing Contrast of Color."[17] Ready made clothes could be disguised by adding individual hand sewn touches; patterned towels could be chosen to match the decorative scheme in the bathroom; old furniture could be repainted and restyled. The new housewife would be an artist, not a drudge.

The new housewife would also be a consumer, not a producer.

> A woman's virtue and excellence as a housewife do not in these days depend upon her skill in spinning and weaving. An entirely different task presents itself, more difficult and more complex, requiring an infinitely wider range of ability, and for these very reasons more interesting and inspiring.[18]

That task was, of course, buying. The words come from an article about shopping for linens, but they could have been taken from any one of the numerous articles on wise buying—clothes, sheets, rugs, blankets, silverware, appliances—that began to appear regularly in women's magazines through the 20's.[19] In earlier days the young housewife had to be taught to make things well; in the 20's she had to be taught to buy things well. Magazines and manufacturers created new devices to teach her how to be a "professional" buyer: product testing services, gadget buying services, home shopping guides, home demonstrators, new packages, new grading systems. Apparently the devices worked;

scores of sociologists and economists have noted that consumption is now the most important social function still performed by families.[20] Unlike so many familial functions, consumption has been expanding, not contracting; the 20's appear to be the decade in which the expansion began.[21]

In her physical appearance the new housewife looked quite different from her older counterparts. In earlier days the ideal American matron had been plump; corset makers were happy to send her garments that would add inches to her *derrière* if she were unfashionably skinny. After World War I the corset makers changed their tune; the emphasis was on reducing, not increasing. By the end of the 20's advertising campaigns were predicated on the American woman's passion for slenderizing; Sunkist oranges are nutritious, and non-fattening; Fleischman's yeast will aid your digestion and prevent constipation if you are dieting; Postum should be substituted for coffee while dieting because it calms the nerves.[22] By the end of the 20's articles about exercising to keep fit had become a regular feature in *The Ladies' Home Journal*; before the war they had been unknown.[23]

She was thin, this ideal lady, and she was also elegant; her hands were long and well manicured, so were her legs. If she worked hard at her housework during hot weather, she remained "personally irreproachable"—thanks to cream deodorants. She wore a fashionable wool suit with a fur collar to visit her local A & P and applied Pompeian Night Cream to keep from looking tired after an exhausting night of bridge. If life was creating problems for her she knew that one or two dabs of Raquel Orange Blossom Fragrance would guarantee eternal bliss. This particular form of hidden persuasion, the notion that cosmetics can guarantee happiness, seems to have been invented in the 20's.[24] The cosmetics industry must have entered a boom phase after World War I—if the number and size of its advertisements are any gauge of its economic well-being.

Child rearing was the single most important task that this new housewife had to perform. Experts agreed that a child raised by nursemaids was a child to be pitied. The young boy tended by servants would never learn the upright, go-getting resourcefulness of the truly American child, would never become a useful member of the egalitarian republic, and would—horror of horrors—probably fail in the business world.[25] His sister, deprived of the example of her mother, would not know how to manage the myriad appliances of the modern kitchen; she would never learn how to decorate a pineapple salad, or how to wash silk underwear in an electric machine, and consequently—horror of horrors—she would never attract and keep a truly American husband.[26] Even more worrisome was the thought that children raised by nursemaids might never reach adulthood because they would not be tended by persons who were familiar with the latest medical and nutritional information. American mothers, anxious about infant mortality, were advised not to leave their offspring in the care of illiterate, untutored servant girls. In 1918, the editor of *The Ladies' Home Journal* rejoiced in the knowledge that, if present trends continued, the postwar generation of American children would be the first generation to be raised by its mothers; they would be healthy in mind and body and, as a result, they would lift the sagging fortunes of the race.[27] There was very little Freudianism in this new child psychology; mothers were to take over the rearing of their children, not because of the psychological traumas of separation, but because mothers were likely to be better informed and better educated than nursemaids.[28]

Spending time with her children seems to have been as much a moral imperative for the housewife of the 20's as spending time on Christian good works was for her mother. There were no more socks to be knitted for missionaries, or elderly sick relatives to be visited, or Bible classes to attend; instead there were basketball games to watch with her children, card games to play with them, and piano lessons to help them with. Togetherness had become a fact for middle-class Americans long before the editors of *McCall's* coined the term in 1954.[29]

> I accommodate my entire life to my little girl. She takes three music lessons a week and I practice with her forty minutes a day. I help her with her school work and go to dancing school with her . . .
>
> There are now never ten days that go by without my either visiting the children's school or getting in touch with their teacher. I have given up church work and club work since the children came. I always like to be here when they come home from school so that I can keep in touch with their games and their friends . . .
>
> I certainly have a harder job than my mother did; everything tends to weaken the parents' influence. But we do it by spending time with our children. I've always been a pal with my daughter, and my husband spends a lot of time with the boy. We all go to basketball games together and to the State Fair in the summer . . .
>
> We used to belong to the Country Club but resigned from that when the children came, and bought a car instead. That is something we can all enjoy together.[30]

The advent of the Depression apparently accelerated this trend. Magazine editors noted that families were being forced to rely upon their own devices for entertainment; the end of prosperity meant the end of meals in restaurants and parties in hotels. *American Home* published essays on turning basements into playrooms; *The Ladies' Home Journal* discovered the barbecue; *Parents' Magazine* began denoting with an asterisk the articles that would be of interest to progressive fathers (i.e. those who wished to take a hand in rearing their own children).[31]

Life was not always a bed of roses in the model American household, but if the lady of the house had any complaints, she refrained, whenever possible, from discussing them with her husband. "She must never bring her troubles to the table;" dinner time was a moment of sweetness and light in her husband's weary day; he came home from the office to be greeted with a cheering cup of Steero bouillon; his children were scrubbed ("Self respect thrives on soap and water") and anxious to tell him about their day in school (they have done well because they did not forget to have hot cereal for breakfast).[32] Woe unto the housewife who would mar this scene by reminding her husband that he had failed to clean his hair out of the sink that morning—or other such domestic trivia. She was almost always cheerful, this modern housewife; in fact, the constellation of emotions that she was allowed to display in magazines was really rather limited. She could be happy, loving, tender or affectionate; occasionally she was worried, but she was never, never angry. What, after all, did she have to be angry about?

Only one anxious emotion ever creased her brow—guilt; she felt guilty a good deal of the time, and when she wasn't feeling guilty she was feeling embarrassed: guilty if her infant didn't gain enough weight, embarrassed if her friends arrived to find that her sink was clogged, guilty if her children went to school in soiled clothes, guilty if she didn't eradicate all the germs behind the bathroom sink, embarrassed if her nieces and nephews accused her of having body odor, guilty if her son was a laggard in school, guilty if her daughter was not popular with the crowd (her mother having failed to keep her dresses properly ironed).[33] In earlier times a woman could have been made to feel guilty if she had abandoned her children or been too free with her affections. In the years between the wars American women apparently began to feel guilty if their children were seen in public in scuffed shoes. Between the two sources of anxiety there seems a world of difference. Advertisers may have stimulated these guilt feelings, but they could not have created them singlehandedly; the guilt must have been there or advertisers would not have found that they could be successful by playing upon it.

In 1937 Emily Post coined a name for the new American housewife: Mrs. Three-in-One, the lady who is cook, waitress and hostess at her own dinner parties.[34] In almost every essential, Mrs. Three-in-One was no different from the housewives that Betty Friedan described in *The Feminine Mystique.* She was fairly well educated and somewhat sophisticated. Her family was smaller than her mother's, but more attention was lavished upon it. Her infants were weighed every day and their nutritional intake carefully planned. The development of her youngsters was carefully watched and the social affairs of her adolescents carefully—but discreetly—supervised. She drove a car, played bridge and took vacations. She had very few servants, or none at all. In the morning she served her family a light breakfast; lunch was a can of soup for herself. She shopped by telephone, or in a small supermarket, bought most of her clothes ready-made, wore silk stockings, and tied her hair in a neat scarf when doing housework. She could nurse a child through the measles, repair a dripping faucet, decorate a kitchen, discourse on vitamins, give a speech before her ladies' club or entertain her husband's business associates—all with equal facility. She was always cheerful, healthy, up-to-date, and gracious, never angry, frustrated, sick, old-fashioned or—perish the thought—gainfully employed. She was content with her life and had no doubts about her femininity; if she wished for anything it was another appliance or a better rug for the living room. She had the vote, but rarely discussed politics; believed in divorce, but was not herself divorced; practiced birth control but did not discuss sex with her daughter.

No doubt there were more Mrs. Three-in-Ones after World War II than there had been before. The feminine mystique probably became more pervasive after 1945; before that it was a social ideology to which only the middle classes—perhaps only the upper middle classes—could possibly pretend. But the ideologies of the upper middle classes eventually percolate down to everyone else in our society and I would venture to guess that that is precisely what happened to the feminine mystique in the late 40's and early 50's. As families moved up the economic and social ladder the signs of their success were the signs that the mystique had arrived on their doorstep: the wife stops working; the house becomes neater; new rooms are added; the children wear ready-made clothes; they stay in school longer, take piano and ballet lessons; slenderizing becomes a passion; nails must be manicured; choices must be made between muslin and percale sheets, double-oven or single-oven stoves, wool or nylon carpeting. The mother who had once complained about back-breaking toil to make ends meet now has a daughter who complains that despite her appliances she still works 16 hours a day, seven days a week—and doesn't quite know why. This pattern must have been repeated in millions of American homes after World War II, but the underlying ideology that produced it was formed in the decades between the wars.

Social ideologies are responsive to changes in economic and demographic conditions. The advent of the feminine mystique was a major ideological change, and there must have been major social and economic changes that produced it. Friedan believed that the mystique arose after the Second World War and consequently her list of causal conditions—higher education for women, widespread prosperity, domestic disruptions attendant upon the Depression and the war, functionalism and Freudianism in the social sciences, the advent of new marketing and advertising techniques—warrants reexamination. One crucial aspect of the new ideology was its emphasis on the servant-less household; changes in the supply of domestic servants are likely, therefore, to have been an important precondition.

Household labor was generally performed by five different types of workers in the early years of the 20th century: the housewife herself, her children (primarily her daughters), other female relatives (a maiden aunt perhaps, or a grandmother), dayworkers, and servants who lived in. Data on changes in the number of any of those types of labor are rather hard to come by, or are likely to be quite unreliable when we have them. Domestic servants are one of the most difficult categories of workers to enumerate as their labor is often transient, or part-time, or unreported. In the early decades of this century social commentators believed that in every category (except the housewife herself) the supply of labor was declining, and the data that are available tend to support this conclusion. Certainly wages for paid household employees were rising. Lynes estimates that in 1890 a live-in cook received about $4.00 a week in wages (this does not count the expense of room and board); in 1920 this would have increased to $25.[35] The Lynds estimate that in 1924 a single day's work for a day laborer cost the Muncie housewife approximately what a week's labor would have cost her mother.[36] Similarly the Lynds found that the business class housewives in Muncie had roughly half the number of household servants that their mothers had had; according to the Federal Census for Indiana, the number of families per servant increased from 13.5 in 1890 to 30.5 in 1920.[37] Using nationwide statistics as a guide, it appears that most of this increase occurred in the decade from 1910 to 1920; the number of families per servant was roughly 10 in 1900, 10 in 1910 and 16 in 1920.[38] These data do not, of course, tell us anything specific about the *supply* of labor, but they are suggestive; if wages were rising and the proportion of workers to households falling, contemporary social critics may have been right in their assumption that the supply of household servants was declining because of the twin pressures generated by fewer immigrants and more attractive industrial wages.[39] Data on the other two categories of household help, children and female relatives, are, to all intents and purposes, nonexistent, but here again the remarks of social critics may be suggestive. Many observers noted tendencies toward less available labor from those sources as well: grandparents were not as frequently moving in with their married children (in part because houses were smaller); grown daughters seemed inclined to have apartments and jobs of their own before marriage; maiden aunts, like their unmarried nieces, were apparently living alone and liking it more.[40]

The odd thing about these social commentaries is that they are recurrent American themes. Household help has always been a sore point in American life; servants were constantly disappearing from the labor market or otherwise behaving recalcitrantly, and the daughters of the middle classes, if they weren't actually out working at Macy's, were often balking at household labor. Yet none of the other periods in which this scarcity of household labor was proclaimed produced an ideology like the feminine mystique, an ideology which put a premium on the servantless household. Consequently we must assume that the declining supply of servants (paid or unpaid) although it must have been part of the preconditions leading to that ideology, was by no means the whole story.

The story become more complete if we look at what was happening to domestic technology during those years. For the first time in the history of the republic there was, after 1918, a viable alternative to the labor of housewives, domestic servants, maiden aunts and adolescent daughters—the machine. It was a classic American solution: when in doubt, try a machine. For several years before the war, home economists had been pressing for the rationalization of household labor. After the war, as electrification and assembly-line production of consumer goods increased, that rationalization seemed to be at hand.

Almost every aspect of household labor was revolutionized during the 20's; in good part this was due to electrification. In 1907 (the first year for which data are available) only 8% of dwellings in the U.S. had electric service; by the time we entered the war this had risen to 24.3% and by 1925 more than half the homes in America (53.2%) had been wired. If we consider the data for urban and rural non-farm dwellings the figures are even more striking: almost half of those homes had been electrified by 1920 (47.4%) and more than two-thirds by 1925 (69.4%).[41] During this period the price of electricity fell from 9.5 cents per kilowatt hour to 7.68 cents (for an average monthly use of 25 kilowatt hours, which is the order of magnitude then used in homes).[42] The amount of money spent on mechanical appliances grew from $145 millions in 1909 to $667 millions in 1927, an increase of almost 500%, while at the same time expenditure on clothing increased only 250% and on furniture, 300%; similarly the dollar value (in current prices) of electric household appliances produced for domestic consumption soared from $11.8 millions in 1909 to $146.3 millions in 1927.[43]

With the spread of electrification came the spread of electrical appliances: a small motor to power the family sewing machine, a fan, an electric iron (the earliest models had no thermostats, but they were still easier to use than the irons heated on cooking stoves), a percolator, perhaps a toaster, a waffle iron or a portable heater. Automatic refrigerators went on the market in 1916 (at roughly $900); in 1921, 5,000 units were sold, but by 1929 that figure had risen to 890,000 units and the price had fallen to roughly $180.[44] A study of 100 Ford employees living in Detroit in 1929 revealed that 98 families had an electric iron, 80 had electric sewing machines, 49 had electric washing machines, and 21 had electric vacuum cleaners.[45] The benefits of technology were clearly not limited to the upper middle classes.

As household habits were being changed by the advent of electricity, so eating habits were being changed by the advent of the metal can, the refrigerated railroad car and new notions about diet. Before World War I an average American family ate three extraordinarily hefty meals a day.

> Steak, roasts, macaroni, Irish potatoes, sweet potatoes, turnips, cole slaw, fried apples, and stewed tomatoes, with Indian pudding, rice, cake or pie for dessert. This was the winter repertoire of the average family that was not wealthy, and we swapped about from one combination to another, using pickles and chow-chow to make the familiar starchy food relishing. . . . Breakfast, pork chops or steak with fried potatoes, buckwheat cakes, and hot bread; lunch, a hot roast and potatoes; supper, same roast cold.[46]

In 1908 an article appeared in *The Ladies' Home Journal* describing an ordinary family lunch; were that meal to be served today it would be regarded as a state banquet.[47] By the middle of the 20's such meals were no longer the rule: breakfast had been reduced to eggs and/or cereal; lunch was essentially one course, or perhaps soup and a sandwich; dinner was usually no more than three. Commercially canned fruits and vegetables made variations in the classic winter menu possible. Some canned goods (primarily peas and corn) had been on the market since the middle of the 19th century, but by 1918 the American housewife with sufficient means could have purchased almost any fruit or vegetable, and quite a surprising array of ready-made meals, in a can: Campbell's soups, Heinz's spaghetti (already cooked and ready to serve), Libby's corned beef and chili con carne (heated directly in its package), Stokeley's peas, corn, string beans, lima beans, tomatoes, succotash, LaChoy's bean sprouts, Beechnut's chili sauce, vinegar, and mustard, Purity Cross's creamed chicken, welsh rarebit, lobster à la newburg, Van Camp's pork and beans, Libby's olives, sauerkraut and

Vienna sausages, Del Monte's peaches, pineapples, apricots and plums. In the morning the American housewife of the 20's could have offered her family some of the new cold cereals (Kellogg's Corn Flakes, or Krumbles, or Post's Grape Nuts Flakes); if her family wanted pancakes she could have prepared them with Aunt Jemima's pancake mix. Recipes in the women's magazines in the 20's utilized canned goods as a matter of course: canned peaches in peach blancmange, canned peas in creamed finnan haddie. Very often the recipes did not even include the familiar rubric, "canned or fresh," but simply assumed that "canned" would be used. By the middle of the 20's home canning was on its way to becoming a lost art; the business-class wives of Muncie reported that they rarely put up anything, except an occasional jelly or batch of tomatoes, whereas their mothers had once spent the better part of the summer and fall canning.[48] Increased utilization of refrigerated railroad cars also meant that fresh fruits and vegetables were appearing in markets at reasonable prices all through the year.[49] Fewer family meals were being taken at home; restaurants and businessmen's clubs downtown, cafeterias in schools and factories, after-school activities for teenagers—all meant that fewer members of the family were home for meals.[50] Cooking was easier, and there was less of it to be done.

Part of the reason that cooking became easier was that the coal or wood-burning stove began to disappear. After World War I the women's magazines only carried advertisements for stoves that used natural gas, kerosene, gasoline or electricity; in Muncie in 1924 two out of three homes cooked with gas.[51] The burdensome chore of keeping a coal stove lit and regulated—and keeping the kitchen free of the resultant soot—had probably been eliminated from most American homes by the 30's. The change in routine that was predicated on the change from coal stoves to oil or gas stoves (electric stoves were inefficient and rarely used in this period) was profound; aside from the elimination of such chores as loading the coal and removing the ashes, the new stoves were simply much easier to regulate. One writer in *The Ladies' Home Journal* estimated that kitchen cleaning was reduced by one-half when coal stoves were eliminated.[52] As the coal stove disappeared from the kitchen, the coal-fired furnace also started disappearing from the basement. By the late 20's coal furnaces were no longer being advertised in home equipment magazines and homeowners were being urged to convert to oil or gas or electricity, "so that no one has to go into the basement anymore." A good number of American homes were centrally heated by the mid-20's; in Zanesville, Ohio 48% of the roughly 11,000 homes had basement furnaces in 1924.[53]

As the routines of meal preparation became less burdensome in the 20's, so did the routines of personal hygiene. The early 20's was the time of the bathroom mania; more and more bathrooms were installed in older homes and new homes were being built with them as a matter of course. Sixty-one per cent of those 11,000 homes in Zanesville had indoor plumbing and bathroom in 1924.[54] In Muncie in 1890 ninety-five out of every hundred families took baths by lugging a zinc tub into the kitchen and filling it with water that had been pumped by hand and heated on the stove; by 1924 three out of four Muncie homes had running water.[55] The rapid increase in the number of bathrooms after World War I was the result of changes in the production of bathroom fixtures. Before the war those fixtures were not standardized and porcelain tubs were routinely made by hand; after the war industrialization swept over the bathroom industry: cast-iron enamelware went into mass production and fittings were standardized. In 1921 the dollar value of the production of enamelled sanitary fixtures was $2.4 million, the same that it had been in 1915. By 1923 just two years later, that figure had doubled to $4.8 million; it rose again, to $5.1 million, in 1925.[56] The first one-piece, recessed, double-shell cast iron enamelled bathtub was put on the market in the early 20's; by the time a decade had passed the standard American bathroom had achieved its standard American form: a small room, with a recessed tub, tiled floors and walls, brass plumbing, a single-unit toilet, and an enclosed sink.[57] This bathroom was relatively easy to clean, and—needless to say—it helped revolutionize habits of personal cleanliness in America; the body-odor fetish of the 30's can be partly attributed to the bathroom fetish of the 20's.

Similarly, the "tell-tale gray" syndrome of the 30's had its roots in the changing technologies of clothes washing. Soap powders and flakes arrived on the market in the early 20's, which meant that bars of soap no longer had to be scraped and boiled to make soap paste. Electric washing machines took a good part of the drudgery out of the washing process, although they required a considerable amount of time and attention to operate, as they did not go through their cycles automatically and did not spin dry.[58] There was more variation in methods of handling household laundry than in any other domestic chore; the Lynds noted that on the same street in Muncie, families of the same economic class were using quite different washing technologies: hand washing, electric machines, commercial laundries, laundresses who worked "in," and laundresses who worked "out."[59] Advertisements in the women's magazines do not give a uniform picture either: sometimes showing old-fashioned tubs, sometimes depicting machines. Commercial household laundries entered a boom period in the 20's; they began to expand their services (wet wash, rough dry, etc.) and began to do more personal laundry (as opposed to flat work) than they had in past years;[60] nationwide, the number of power laundries doing more than $5,000 business a year rose from 4,881 in 1919 to 6,776 in 1929, and their receipts more than doubled.[61]

While the processes of cooking, heating, cleaning, lighting and washing were revolutionized, other processes—just as much a part of the housewife's daily routine—were changing, but not quite as drastically. The corner grocer, the door-to-door merchant and the curbside market were slowly being replaced by the telephone and the supermarket. In 1918 *The Ladies' Home Journal* referred to supermarkets as "The New Stores Without Clerks;"[62] by 1928 there were 2,600 Piggly Wiggly markets across the country.[63] Telephone shopping had become routine in many households by the end of the 20's. Instead of purchasing whole cases of canned goods or bushels of apples and onions to be stored and used over the months, housewives were now telephoning daily orders and having them hand-delivered: 1 head of lettuce, 1 pat of cream cheese, 1 can of string beans, ¼-pound of mushrooms.[64] Hardwood floors were replaced by linoleum; instead of tedious hand polishing, only a mop, soap and water was now required. Heavy cast iron pots and pans were giving way to aluminum and Pyrex. Ready-made clothes were no longer thought "poor-folksy;" by 1928 a good part of each monthly issue of the better women's magazines was devoted to photographs and drawings of clothing that could be bought off the rack. Home sewing, home mending, the once ubiquitous practice of making over dresses—all became vestigial crafts; young women were now being taught how to shop for clothes, not how to make them.[65] Home baking also disappeared; the bakers in Muncie estimated that, depending upon the season, they supplied between 55% and 70% of the city's homes with bread.[66]

Many factors must have contributed to the revolution in household production that occurred during the 20's. On the whole those were prosperous years and prosperity made it possible for many people to buy new equipment for their homes. Vast industrial facilities which were created during the war were converted to the production of consumer goods during peacetime. The apparent shortage of servants and the rise in their wages must have encouraged householders to try the new appliances more readily than they would otherwise have done. The growth of magazines devoted to the interests of modern housewives no doubt encouraged the trend, as did the growth of consumer credit arrangements. Whatever the causes were, the event itself seems indisputable; profound changes in household technology occurred between the end of the First World War and the beginning of the Depression—whether we measure those changes by the number of individual innovations or by the rate of their diffusion. Certain changes did occur after the Second World War: the standard American kitchen achieved its present form, with standardized fixtures and continuous counter space; the automatic washing machine (which could spin and go through its cycles itself) became widespread; the laundromat replaced the commercial laundry; the supermarket replaced the grocery store; frozen foods to some extent replaced canned foods; the dishwasher and the home dryer became more reasonable in price; the ranch home with its open room plan, became more popular. However, all those changes pale to insignificance when compared to the change from oil lamps to electric lamps, coal stoves to gas stoves, coal furnaces to gas and oil furnaces, kitchen heating to central heating, outdoor plumbing to indoor plumbing, not having a bathroom to having one, canning tomatoes to buying canned tomatoes, making dresses to buying them, baking bread to buying it, living with servants and living without them.

Thus, a fundamental productive process was revolutionized by the introduction of new technologies; almost simultaneously an ideology developed which insured that those new technologies would be used in very specific and rather limited ways. In the early days the new technology could have been used to communalize housework. The first vacuum cleaners were large mobile units; they were brought into a home by a team of skilled operators to take over the housewife's cleaning chores.[67] The new washing machines could have been placed in communal laundries where paid employees would take over the housewife's washing chores, and the editors of *The Ladies' Home Journal* advocated that this be done.[68] Those same editors also advocated retention of the wartime communal kitchens, so that the wasteful process of cooking each family's meals separately would be eliminated.[69] Many of the early luxury apartment houses had, along with elevators, communal nurseries on their roofs.[70] Within a very few years, needless to say, those visions of communal housekeeping had died a not very surprising death; this was America, after all, not Soviet Russia. The new domestic technology, communalized or not, could have freed American women to do productive work outside their homes; the growth of the feminine mystique insured that they would not do it.

The advertising industry cooperated in this endeavor, even if it did not invent it. As the size and number of women's magazines increased in the 20's, the amount and the variety of advertising increased also. The American woman was becoming the American consumer *par excellence*; automobile manufacturers, cigarette producers, life insurance companies (not to speak of the advertisers whose wares were of traditional interest to women) all discovered the virtues of the women's magazines. The magazines, of course, found ways to encourage this custom. They used their non-advertising space to advertise in subtler ways: listing new products by their brand names, adopting editorial policies that encouraged women to buy, creating "shop at home" columns for mail-order purchases, sponsoring consumption oriented contests.

> Home building, home decoration and furnishing, *home making,* in fact, is the most outstanding phase of modern civilization. . . . The magazines of today have played an important part in this; they have carried on an intensive sincere campaign for better homes. But an even greater part has been that of the manufacturers. . . . Not only has beauty and convenience and efficiency of home equipment been carefully studied to meet the demand of the modern housewife . . . but back of all this stands the guarantee of the maker of his goods.[71]

Late in the 20's those earnest manufacturers (and their sincere advertising agents) discovered that they could sell more gadgets by appealing to the housewife's fears than by appealing to her strengths; advertisements stopped being informative and started pandering to status-seeking and guilt. An advertisement for soap in 1908 was likely to talk about the clean factory in which the soap was produced and the pure ingredients from which it was made; a similar advertisement in 1928 was likely to talk about the psychological trauma experienced by children who go to school with soiled clothes.[72] It would be difficult to prove that manufacturers and advertising agencies invented the feminine mystique, but it would be equally difficult to deny that they did everything they reasonably could to encourage it.

In a quite different way the proponents of the child health movement also helped to encourage the mystique. The infant mortality rate in the United States in 1915 was 100 for every 1,000 live births, one of the highest in the world. There were very few families who were not touched, in some way, by the spectre of infant death. After the war, with its discouraging reports about the health of young recruits, various public agencies began a concerted effort to improve the health and the physique of America's young people, particularly by disseminating information about proper nutrition and proper care of children during illness. The women's magazines were prime agents in the dissemination of this information; *The Ladies' Home Journal,* for example, started a Babies Registry so that the mothers of registered babies could receive monthly instructional booklets. Professional organizations, such as the Child Study Association (which organized child study groups in cities across the country and began publishing *Parents' Magazine* in 1926), and the federal government were also active in the campaign to improve the health of the young. By the end of the 20's advice to parents on the physical care of their children could be had at every turn: in magazine articles, in thousands of new books, in advertisements, in government pamphlets. The health of children became an overriding, perhaps even a compulsive concern for parents; they were urged to buy GE Mazda Sunlamps to provide Vitamin D for their children, to learn which foods would be most helpful in preventing anemia, to keep Vicks VapoRub on hand in case congestion should develop, to wear masks when they entered a sick child's room, to cleanse their bathrooms with BonAmi because the other (scratchier) cleansers would leave places for germs to breed, to guard against pink toothbrush, to watch for the signs of eczema, to use Castoria for constipation, Listerine for sore throats, and VapoCresoline for whooping cough.[73]

This new concern for the health of children was no doubt necessary, and some of it no doubt worked; the infant mortality rate fell to 65 per 1,000 live births by 1930, before the age of the miracle antibiotics—but the burden that it placed upon the new American housewife was immense. Children had to be kept in bed for weeks at a time; bedpans had to be provided and warmed, "since even the slightest chilling is to be avoided carefully;" in some diseases excrement had to be disinfected before being discarded; food had to be specially prepared; leftovers had to be burned after the sick child's meal; utensils had to be boiled, alcohol baths administered, hands scrupulously washed, mouths carefully masked—and through all this the nursing mother was expected to "get plenty of rest and outdoor recreation," and remain unrelentingly cheerful, "for cheerfulness is needed in a sickroom and the attitude of a mother nursing an ailing child largely influences the speed of recovery."[74] Needless to say, mothers had to remain at home in order for all this nursing to be done; the death of a child whose mother had gone out to work, was a recurrent theme in women's magazine fiction. In this sense, the child health movement was paradoxical; many women made careers out of convincing other women to stay at home and tend their children.

Oddly enough the Depression also served to reinforce the feminine mystique, although many commentators worried about what the economic disaster would do to the family as a social institution. The end of prosperity meant that entertainment outside the home had to be curtailed and it also meant that many families would be unable to pay for domestic servants. The genteel housewife who had formerly kept servants but who had let them go in the early years of the Depression became something of a social stereotype: " . . . a college girl who in recent years has been obliged to live the anxious, circumscribed life of the maid-of-all-work wife of a small-time lawyer with vanishing fees," as Anne O'Hare McCormick described a friend of hers in 1933.[75]

"Doing it yourself these days?" asked the makers of La France Bluing over a stark picture of manicured hands immersed in a laundry tub; indeed, many American housewives were.[76] The need to economize to make ends meet meant that meals had to be planned carefully and cash had to be spent wisely; the editors of American Home advised their readers to stop buying over the telephone and go down to the shops in person to make certain they were getting good value for their money.[77] The editors of The Ladies' Home Journal were pleased to note that the new emphasis on home entertainment was leading families to remodel their homes—themselves.[78] To save money women learned how to fix electric motors, paint used furniture, sew curtains and—once again—remake last year's clothes. Manufacturers had to keep selling their goods, so prices came down and credit buying arrangements became more flexible. The more goods there were on shelves, the heavier advertising pressure on women became. Cash wasn't available, but time was—women's time—and since the prohibition against women entering the work force was particularly heavy during the Depression (they would, after all, be stealing jobs from unemployed men) the best place to spend that time was at home and the best way to spend it was in all those multitudinous little jobs that make up the daily routine of the housewife who was convinced that the feminine mystique made sense.

The feminine mystique, the social ideology which was formed during the 20's and solidified during the 30's, was quite a functional solution to real economic and demographic conditions. Servants were scarcer and their wages higher. Electricity could save burdensome labor and washday was unquestionably easier to face when the washing was done by machine than when it was done by hand. Infants' lives could be saved if care were taken to sterilize their bottles and balance their diets. In fact the feminine mystique worked; it kept women at home to do jobs that, in one way or another, American society needed to have done. Unfortunately calling the solution functional does not mean that it was wise; it seems tragic that as a society we could not utilize all that new technology without constructing an ideology which oppressed half our citizens.

NOTES

1. Betty Friedan, The Feminine Mystique (New York: Norton, 1963). Citations are to be paperback edition (New York: Dell, 1963). For Friedan's argument that the feminine mystique took hold after World War II, see Chapter 8. Other

authors have adopted her chronology. See, for example, Sonya Rudikoff, "Marriage and household," *Commentary*, 55 (June 1973), 61.

2. Friedan, Chapter 2.

3. Barbara Welter, "The cult of true womanhood, 1820–1860," *American Quarterly*, 18 (Summer, 1966), 162.

4. *The Ladies' Home Journal* (January, 1918), 4.

5. "Editorial," *The Ladies' Home Journal* (May, 1918), 4.

6. *The Ladies' Home Journal* (January, 1933), 2.

7. *American Home* regularly published house plans in every issue. About half the plans published between 1928 and 1933 had no maid's room, despite the fact that they were very expensive homes ($9,000 up).

8. Ruth Sapin, "For better or worse, servants influence children," *Parents' Magazine* (January 1929), 20.

9. The prevalence of household servants before World War I, and their disappearance thereafter, is discussed in Russell Lynes, *The Domesticated Americans* (New York: Harper & Row, 1957) Ch. 9. As just one example: an article in *The Ladies' Home Journal* (February, 1908), 44, described a young couple who were struggling along on the husband's meagre salary as a newspaper reporter; they did all the gardening, house painting, and repair work themselves and found various ways to economize on food—but they had a maid-of-all-work.

10. Paraphrased from, *The Ladies' Home Journal* (February, 1918), 49.

11. For an example of the genre see, S. M. Eliot, "The normal American woman," *The Ladies' Home Journal* (January, 1908), 15.

12. "What does your kitchen say about you?" *The Ladies' Home Journal* (March, 1933), 34.

13. "Editorial," *The Ladies' Home Journal* (April, 1928), 36.

14. Advertisement for Fels Naphtha, *American Home* (June, 1937), 64.

15. American Home (April, 1931), 66.

16. "Editorial," *The Ladies' Home Journal* (February, 1928), 32.

17. *Parents' Magazine* (February, 1933), 33.

18. *The Ladies' Home Journal* (March, 1928), 43.

19. For example: "How to buy towels," *The Ladies' Home Journal* (February, 1928), 134, or "When the bride selects bed linens," *The Ladies' Home Journal* (January, 1928), 118.

20. On this point see, for example, John Kenneth Galbraith, *Economics and the Public Purpose* (Boston: Houghton Mifflin, 1973), 29–37.

21. Home economists were very much aware of the change, and of the need to educate women in their responsibilities as consumers. See, for example, Margaret Reid, *The Economics of Household Production* (New York: John Wiley, 1934), Ch. XIII.

22. These advertisements appeared regularly in the monthly editions of *The Ladies' Home Journal* in 1927 and 1928.

23. See, for example, "Keeping in shape," *The Ladies' Home Journal* (April, 1928), 191.

24. See, for example, *The Ladies' Home Journal* (March, 1928), 101.

25. "How we raise our children," *The Ladies' Home Journal* (March, 1928), 193.

26. "Christmas gifts for little girls," *American Home* (December, 1928), 227.

27. "Editorial," *The Ladies' Home Journal* (June, 1918), 4.

28. "Editorial," *Parents' Magazine* (October, 1926), 2.

29. Friedan, 41–42, attributes the concept to the editors of *McCall's*.

30. Remarks made by housewives of the business class in Muncie, Indiana in 1924. Robert S. Lynd and Helen M. Lynd, *Middletown: A Study in Contemporary American Culture* (New York: Harcourt Brace, 1929) 146–147.

31. *American Home* (November, 1931), 81. The idea of converting basements into playrooms was part of the magazine's campaign to encourage home remodelling so that jobs might be created during the Depression. The article on barbecues appeared in *The Ladies' Home Journal* (June, 1937).

32. "She must not bring her troubles to the table," was advice given in an article on Blue Monday, *American Home* (April, 1931), 14. The Steero bouillon ads ran in *The Ladies' Home Journal* in the mid 20's. "Self respect thrives on soap and water," was the motto of the Cleanliness Institute, which placed monthly advertisements in *The Ladies' Home Journal* in 1928.

33. This analysis is paraphrased and abstracted from advertisements in the women's magazines, 1923–1933.

34. Emily Post, *Etiquette,* 5th revised edition (New York, 1937), 823.

35. Lynds, 163 and 171.

36. Lynds, 169.

37. Ibid.

38. *Historic Statistics of the United States, Colonial Times to 1957* (Washington: U.S. Government Printing Office, 1960). These estimates were calculated from Series D 457–463, p. 77, "Private Household Workers Employed," and Series A255, p. 16, "Number of households." As the number of households was overestimated in 1910 and 1920 because of the inclusion of quasi-households in the count (rooming houses, dormitories, etc.) the figures are only a very rough guide.

39. See note 5, Lynes, 156, and Lynds, 170.

40. These phenomena were widely remarked upon. See, Lynds, 25, and 99; Edward Bok, "Editorial," *American Home* (October, 1928), 15 *The Ladies' Home Journal* (March, 1928), 35, an article on buying life insurance: "The old days when the maiden aunt or spinster sister was waiting patiently to take over wiping the noses . . . are rapidly passing. Sister is far too busy paying her own lunch check and insurance policies."

41. *Historical Statistics,* 510.

42. Ibid.

43. *Historical Statistics*, 179.

44. Data from Sigfried Giedion, *Mechanization Takes Command* (New York: Oxford University Press, 1948) 602, *Historical Statistics*, 417 (although the column is headed, "Refrigerators produced," in fact the figures are for refrigerators sold, as is explained on p. 407). The price in 1929 is derived from a Frigidaire advertisement, *The Ladies' Home Journal* (January, 1929), 140.

45. Hazel Kyrk, *Economic Problems of the Family* (New York: Harpers, 1933) 368, reporting a study in *Monthly Labour Review,* 30 (1930), 1209–1252.

46. Lynds, 156–157.

47. *The Ladies' Home Journal* (December, 1908), 46.

48. Lynds, 156. With regard to use of canned goods the Lynds made an interesting observation: "A prejudice lingers among these latter (housewives of the medium and smaller income groups) against feeding one's family out of cans."

49. Lynds, 157.

50. Lynds, 134–135, 153–154.

51. Lynds, 98.

52. *The Ladies' Home Journal* (January, 1908), 44.

53. Lynds, 96, citing a survey in *Zanesville and Thirty-six Other American Cities* (New York: Literary Digest, 1927), 65.

54. Ibid.

55. Lynds, 97.

56. Geidion, 659–703.

57. Helen Sprackling, "The modern bathroom," *Parents' Magazine* (February, 1933), 25.

58. *American Home* (April, 1931), 64, describes, in some detail, how complex a process washing with one of these machines was.

59. Lynds, 174.

60. Ibid.

61. *Historical Statistics,* 526.

62. *The Ladies' Home Journal* (April, 1918), 29.

63. *The Ladies' Home Journal* (February, 1928), 170.

64. See, for example, *American Home* (April, 1931), 48—for a typical shopping list.

65. Lynds, 164–167.

66. Lynds, 155.

67. On the earliest vacuum cleaners see, Geidion, 586.

68. "The after the war woman," *The Ladies' Home Journal* (June, 1918), 13.

69. "Editorial," *The Ladies' Home Journal* (May, 1918), 30; and, "The vanishing servant girl," *The Ladies' Home Journal* (May, 1918), 48.

70. Lynes, 107.

71. Edward Bok, "The American home, the joyous adventure," *American Home* (January, 1929), 287.

72. Compare advertisement for Ivory Soap, *The Ladies' Home Journal* (February, 1908), 5 with Fels Naptha advertisement (January, 1928), 35.

73. These examples were taken from a single issue of *Parents' Magazine* (February, 1933) in which 27 out of 79 advertisements were for drugs or health related items, and two out of the nine featured articles were about diseases.

74. All quotes are from Beulah France, "Home care of contagious diseases," *Parents' Magazine* (March, 1933), 26, 27, 57.

75. *The Ladies' Home Journal* (January, 1933), 13. For a fictionalized version of the same lady, see "Love flies out of the kitchen," *The Ladies' Home Journal* (January, 1933), 42.

76. *The Ladies' Home Journal* (February, 1933), 52.

77. *American Home,* (March, 1933), 50.

78. *The Ladies' Home Journal* (January, 1933), 42.

❦21❧

WOMEN WORKERS AND THE UAW IN THE POST-WORLD WAR II PERIOD: 1945–1954

NANCY GABIN

Josephine DiChiera could not understand "why if the company says we'd have to go after we were married . . . the membership and the union wouldn't fight for us also. To all of us girls, it seems as though they are waiting for us all to get married so they can get rid of us. . . . There are some shady deals being pulled somewhere down the line. . . . We all want [to be] reimbursed on our Union dues we've paid. . . . It appears as though they're taking our money for nothing and fighting against us." DiChiera's angry challenge to the men in her United Automobile Workers (UAW) local union reveals the problems that many women in the union confronted in the post-World War II period. Her statement describes the efforts made by management to remove women from the jobs they held during the war; it indicates that men in the union not only shared management's attitudes toward women but often actively assisted in its efforts to deprive them of employment; and it further illustrates the degree of frustration and bitterness women could feel when the union, which claimed to defend its members regardless of sex, acted against the interests of women members.[1]

The auto industry had not been eager to employ women during the war's first years. When management complained of labor shortages, the UAW and other unions responded that the cause was the employers' refusal to hire qualified women and blacks. By 1943, however, it was apparent to management everywhere that women would have to be employed to meet the nation's wartime needs. The number of women

From *Labor History* 21, Winter 1980, pp. 5-30. Reprinted by permission.

in the total labor force jumped from 12,090,000 in the week before Pearl Harbor to 18,740,000 in March 1944. Most dramatic was the increase in the number of women newly employed in manufacturing industries. In 1939, there was an estimated 3,130 female production workers in the transportation equipment and automobile industries; in November 1943 there were 777,400 women in these industries, an increase of nearly 25,000 per cent. Substantial occupational shifts accompanied the expansion of the female labor force; although 43.2 per cent of the women employed in March 1944 in manufacturing came from outside the labor force, 16.6 per cent came from other industry groups, most often the traditionally female trade and service sectors.[2]

By 1941, the Big Three automobile companies—General Motors, Chrysler and Ford—which were soon to convert to war production and to hire great numbers of women, had all recognized the UAW as the bargaining agent for their plant workers. The UAW like other unions benefitted from its wartime no-strike pledge. In return for pledging not to strike, government granted the unions the maintenance-of-union membership formula, which provided that after a grace period of fifteen days, workers had to retain their union membership for the life of the contract. By 1945, the UAW had one million members, 28 per cent (280,000) of whom were women.[3]

The UAW responded to its new female members in an ambivalent manner. During the war, the public's perception of women workers was at odds with the fact that the majority of women employed between 1941-1945 had worked before Pearl Harbor and presumably would continue to work after the war. The glamorized image of Rosie the Riveter, whose commitment to her job was allegedly due more to her sense of patriotism than to her economic need, confirmed the popular belief that women belonged in the home. Women workers were seen as temporarily employed until brothers, sweethearts, and husbands returned home. There was a conflict within the UAW between those who agreed with this popular sentiment and those who feared that management would take advantage of it after the war to justify the replacement of women workers with men.[4]

The problem of discrimination against women workers by both management and organized labor had long been an issue for the labor movement. The American Federation of Labor (AFL) had a history of hostility to women that was the result not only of its refusal to organize the industrial semi- and unskilled labor force (many of whom were female) but also of its adherence to the popular myths about working women. The AFL rationalized its policies by declaring women both unorganizable and unworthy of organization. Women's low pay, lack of skill, and temporary tenure in the labor force were seen as proof of their disinterest in organization rather than as conditions brought about by a sex-biased and class-biased cultural ideology.[5]

The Congress of Industrial Organization (CIO), formed during the middle and late 1930s as a result of a conflict within the AFL over the principles of industrial and craft organization, could have been the force for challenging and changing attitudes toward, and thus the conditions of, women's work. As opposed to craft unionism, industrial unionism was theoretically committed to the organization of all workers regardless of race, national origin, or sex. If workers were organized by the industry in which they worked, management, it was thought, would be less able to divide them according to their ascribed characteristics and would be forced to treat them equally and fairly. The possible benefits for women, who had generally been restricted to occupations simply because of their sex, loomed as considerable.

The advocates of the UAW's female membership wanted the union to fulfill the promise of industrial unionism and to make an effort to secure gains for working women in anticipation of the post-war period when reconversion would eliminate many of the new wartime jobs. Responding to these demands, the UAW created its Women's Bureau in 1944 as a department of the union's War Policy Division, to meet both the wartime and the post-war needs of women members. R.J. Thomas, president of the UAW, explained in a letter to the local unions that the bureau was designed to deal with the special employment problems of the union's female membership, such as day care, the enforcement of state and federal laws regulating the hours and conditions of women's work, equal pay for equal work, and the hostility of management and male workers toward the idea of women working.[6]

Thomas also noted in this letter that the bureau would "develop techniques for interesting women in general union activities." This aspect of the bureau was intended for those who were more interested in the union's welfare and wanted to avoid a conflict after the war. "If a long-range policy covering female workers cannot be worked out before peace is declared abroad," C.G. Edelin, president of Local Union 51, providently warned, "we may find ourselves in some very warm water." Implicit in Edelin's comment was the assumption that women workers would not willingly leave their jobs after the war.[7]

The placing of the bureau in the War Policy Division, however, indicates the limited and short-range character of the UAW's commitment to its female members. The UAW's position on equal pay for equal work further illustrates how shallow was the union's concern for women. Emphasizing that women's employment was expected to "significantly decline" in the postwar period, Thomas stated in his report to the 1942 International Convention that it was necessary to incorporate the principle of equal pay for equal work in bargaining agreements and legislation in order to protect the wage standards of male workers against management attempts to establish lower wage levels for women in jobs previously held by men. Similarly, when the War Policy Division in 1944 issued its suggested policy for filling job openings, it strongly urged the elimination of job classifications by sex "so management can't claim any job or classification strictly for women and use this, especially after the war."[8]

The UAW defined its post-war membership as male, not as both female and male. When, contrary to expectation, 85.5 per cent of female UAW members said they wanted to keep their jobs in industry because they were better-paying and better-protected than the traditionally female jobs in the retail, clerical, and service occupational sectors, the union reacted unfavorably. Fearing that the reduction of wages and a decrease in the availability of jobs would threaten the solidarity of the workers and their faith in the UAW, the male unionists viewed the women in auto plants as competitors for jobs and as a threat to wage standards. During the reconversion process and continuing well into the post-war period, women complained of discrimination in layoffs and in job grading, but the male leadership and membership of the UAW, in the main, did not respond with sympathy or concern. Women discovered that management was not alone in wanting to exclude them from post-war jobs as a variety of jointly negotiated contract clauses served to deny them the benefits that industrial organization was supposed to offer.[9]

Women were not without supporters within the union during the post-war period. In June 1946 the union leadership made the Women's Bureau part of the newly established Fair Practices and Anti-Discrimination Department. William Oliver, co-director of the Department, explained that, although the unit was principally concerned with the employment problems of black workers, it would give "[s]pecial emphasis . . . [to] women's problems in the automobile industry since it is unquestionably the largest single minority group within the jurisdiction of the UAW-CIO." It is to the credit of the union that it identified racism and sexism as specific problems in the auto industry and established the Fair Practices Department and the Women's Bureau to deal with them. The difficulties that the two offices experienced in working with the union leadership and membership, however, confirmed the fact that it was not only the employers who discriminated against women in the post-war period.[10]

The Women's Bureau and the Fair Practices Department attempted to counteract male antagonism to women workers by means of educational materials, International Convention resolutions, and policy statements issued to the membership and leadership which stressed the danger that discrimination posed for the union. A pamphlet published by the Fair Practices Department in 1946 stressed the need for increased vigilance against management's efforts to exclude women from post-war employment and pointed to the UAW's opposition to such practices. "The catch phrase, a woman's place is in the kitchen," the pamphlet stated, "is a silly slander, a cover slogan for tricky attacks on everyone's standard of living and everyone's political rights."[11]

Resolutions submitted for membership approval at the 1946 and 1949 International Conventions underscored the idea that an attack on one worker was a threat to all workers. The 1946 convention adopted a resolution condemning the layoff of women as well as management's efforts to down-grade and reclassify jobs, and the convention resolved that the UAW "must use [its] full collective bargaining power to defeat these moves of management to undermine the workers' condition." A resolution approved at the 1949 convention observed that, contrary to the popular conception, women worked for the same reasons men did to support themselves and their families. "We are going into a period of job scarcity," the resolution noted, "when management will use every effort to take advantage of working women and create disunity among our members by spreading propaganda against women working. This is an attempt to weaken and finally break down our seniority structure."[12]

In an effort to combat discrimination against women, the Women's Bureau and Fair Practices Department, with the approval of the International Executive Board (IEB), dispatched fair practice, anti-discrimination, and seniority policy statements to the UAW membership. These statements were issued with instructions that they serve as guides in the negotiation of contracts and the filing of grievances. Referring to the Fair Practices Model Contract Clause prepared by the department. William Oliver stated, "The real test of fair practices is understanding by the union and management with respect to equal opportunities at the employment gate and equal opportunities for all jobs within the plant or seniority unit. This phase of fair practice is the most vital and most beneficial to our entire membership."[13]

In a much more strongly worded statement on the Department's seniority policy, Oliver explained that, "[i]n many local seniority agreements, industrial minority groups . . . are traditionally remained [sic] there; and are continuously identified with certain types of work in the shops because of their minority characteristics. . . . [T]hese traditional patterns have often reflected themselves in the form of written agreement which tends to sanction historically prejudicial patterns." The statement concluded with a directive to local unions and regional directors to work to eliminate these patterns so as to be consistent with the basic principle of industrial unionism.[14]

Although the policies and activities of the Women's Bureau and the Fair Practices Department carried International approval, the Department expressed frustration at the inaction of the International. A report prepared by the Fair Practices Department in 1947 on women foundry workers in the UAW stated the problem clearly and explicitly. *"The Fair Practices and Anti-Discrimination Department alone cannot solve all of these problems."* the report stated. "It will take the united support and mobilization of all forces within our union to change the one factor which is most difficult—the question of *changing human nature.*" The report concluded with the comment, "No one but a blind fool would believe that in the UAW-CIO prejudice against women . . . has been eliminated." In a plea to the IEB, the Department urged the Board to "recognize the difficulties incumbent upon this department when, on one hand clearly defined policies are to be observed as they appear in the constitution and official records of the Union; and on the other hand observances of these policies are ignored and even flaunted in the absence of appropriate enforcement machinery." The petition closed with a reminder to the IEB of the fundamental principle of the UAW-CIO: "It behooves the International Executive Board to give serious consideration to this aspect of our internal discipline in order that democracy and fair play will be something more than window dressing."[15]

Conflict within the UAW over the issue of "special privileges" for minority groups undermined the authority of the Women's Bureau and the Fair Practices Department in making and enforcing policy. The conflict can be traced to 1943, when the creation of a Minorities Department within the International was proposed at the International convention. Supporters of the defeated proposal stressed the lack of representation of minority members in leadership positions. Opponents claimed that the proposed department would divide workers into discrete categories, discourage the union's collective consideration of the problems of minorities, and encourage tokenism. Pat Sexton, a UAW member and plant steward at the time, recalls that the establishment of the Women's Bureau in 1944 also met with opposition from unionists. "Some," she noted, "thought it would increase the segregation of women, limit rather than broaden the attention given them, and pacify their demand for general representation. Supporters thought that women needed a staff to perform an advocate's role in the union."[16]

Although opposition to special privileges or affirmative action would appear to be a corollary of the principle of industrial unionism, it seems that, in this instance, opposition was due more to a defensive refusal to confront the problem of discrimination than to any commitment to ideological consistency. This was reflected in the manner in which union officials questioned the influence and power of the Fair Practices Department. When William Oliver offered Richard Leonard, head of the UAW's Ford Department, assistance in dealing with company discrimination against women at the Detroit River Rouge and Highland Park plants in 1946, Leonard politely but firmly refused. In so many words, Leonard scolded Oliver for presuming to interfere and for implying that the local unions would act in a discriminatory manner. In replying to Oliver, Leonard wrote:

I am happy to have had your interest in this matter. However, I think you will agree that seniority is a contractual matter and that policing of the contract is a responsibility of the local unions and the Ford Department, and that it is unfair to your department to be involved unless definite proof is advanced that either local unions or the Ford Department have been remiss in their duties.[17]

Although the International Convention established the Fair Practices Department, the International leadership remained mute regarding the extent of the department's sphere of influence and authority. One explanation for the silence of the executive leadership could be that it was reluctant to dictate an unpopular policy to its constituency for fear of risking the loss of a battle over local union autonomy, a highly valued UAW tradition. If this was the fact, the degree of hostility to women among the rank-and-file is confirmed. It has also been argued, however, that the UAW leadership actually consolidated its powers over the locals in this period. If so, the International's silence on the authority of the Women's Bureau and the Fair Practices Department reflected the ambivalence of the leadership itself in regard to discrimination against minorities. Whatever the explanation, the leadership did not pay sufficient heed to the need for antidiscriminatory action.[18]

The UAW did advocate governmental action on the problem of discrimination against minorities. In 1946, Walter Reuther, newly elected president of the UAW, claimed that "the answer to this postwar problem lies not in special privileges but in the creation of 60,000,000 peacetime jobs in America." To this end, the UAW strongly urged the passage of a Full Employment Act and supported national efforts to secure equal pay for equal work legislation and the institution of government-supported day care centers. Although the Women's

Bureau and the female membership agreed that the government had an obligation to aid women workers, they were suspicious of the International's motives in advocating federal and state action against discrimination. Helen McLean, a delegate to the 1946 convention from the Ford Highland Park plant local union, denounced a resolution invoking government responsibility to women workers as an attempt "to pass the buck on to the United States Government rather than setting a policy with our own union."[19]

Despite the efforts of the Fair Practices Department and the Women's Bureau to challenge prejudice against women on the part of management and the union, there was rampant discrimination against women on the local union level. The discrimination took the form of local union toleration of inequitable hiring practices, layoffs of women workers, discriminatory pay scales, and transfers by management. The hostility of male unionists toward female employees was expressed though the harassment and intimidation of women who pressed grievances against management or complained of local union inequities, the obstruction of grievance procedures, and the negotiation of contracts, supplemental agreements and verbal agreements that sanctioned discriminatory practices. The collusion between management and the union limited women's employment opportunities in plants under UAW contract.

Evidence of discrimination against women on the local union level is available in the reports of cases brought to the attention of the Women's Bureau, in unsolicited letters found in the papers of various International leaders, and in the case files of the IEB Appeals Committees. The dates of these documents range from 1945 to 1954; the majority of the IEB appeal hearing cases took place between 1950 and 1954. Although the early 1950s would seem to lie beyond what can appropriately be called the post-World War II period, the substance of these cases indicates that the effort to exclude women from the jobs they held during the war was based on the terms of contracts written during the war and in the immediate post-war period and extended well beyond the initial period of demobilization and reconversion.

Until a systematic analysis of all grievances submitted to management is undertaken, we cannot know for certain how many women protested their treatment in the post-war period. Evidence of the role the local unions played in suppressing grievances and appeals suggests, however, that the number of documented cases of rank-and-file discrimination is only the tip of the iceberg. It has been argued that the limited number of protests filed by women indicates the extent to which, in the post-war period, they willingly acquiesced in their treatment at the hands of management and membership. The evidence of harassment and intimidation, on the other hand, suggests that such a conclusion is erroneous.[20]

Local union hostility to women was for the most part a function of the male workers' view of women as threats to their jobs. The male view that women belonged in the home helped to justify their approval of a variety of discriminatory plant practices. Although married women were the object of some of the most blatantly discriminatory practices, single women were also victimized by inequitable seniority agreements that gave men the right to "bump" women in the event of transfers or lay offs (but did not accord women the same right) and by unequal wage rates on similar jobs performed by men and women. And both married and single women were subject to verbal harassment and intimidation by fellow workers, stewards, and local union officers. Tactics of this sort were used both to coerce women into leaving their jobs and to prevent them from filing grievances against management for sexual discrimination. To the extent that local unionists succeeded in the latter effort, they helped to conceal both to outside observers and sometimes to international officers the extent of their collusion with management in discriminating against female employees.

In a case heard by the IEB Appeals Committee, the appellant, Nettie Bennett, accused Johnnie Kallos, a steward, of conspiring to remove women from jobs improperly and of using verbal harassment and threats to prevent the women from protesting. One witness for the appellant who had also been laid off reported that, because she had refused to date Kallos, he had told her that she would not be recalled to work at the Hudson Motor Car Company as long as he was chief steward in the department. Another woman testified that after she had submitted a request for a pregnancy leave, Kallos "had the gall to walk up and down the line with his stomach stuck out pretending he was me on the job." Kallos told Mildred Westbrook that there would be no women in his department as long as he was steward and that it would be best for her to find employment elsewhere.[21]

In the Bennett case, the local union ordered the steward to reinstate the women against whom he had discriminated in a transfer action. Other UAW locals were less willing to come to the aid of female members victimized by discrimination. Josephine DiChiera, a member of Local Union 1020 in Homewood, Pennsylvania, discussed with her steward her desire to continue working even though she was about to get married. The steward brought her intention to a vote at a local union membership meeting. "Naturally, when you have about 70 or so girls up against a membership of 1,100, with the rest as man [sic], they wouldn't vote to keep us there," DiChiera reported to regional director Ray Ross. "I feel that this should never have been brought up for the membership to vote on because I feel they were voting Union members against Union members. . . . It appears as though they're taking our money for nothing and fighting against us." Dominic Dornetto, an UAW international representative who supported DiChiera, explained to Ross that the motion at the meeting to keep married women on the payroll "was overwhelmingly defeated with many slurs and other improper behavior of the members." Dornetto later reported to Ross that management refused to answer DiChiera's charge that she had been dismissed without cause, a grievance which she had filed in spite of the steward's lack of support, because the local union did not recognize her complaint as a grievance.[22]

Since the Bureau's major strategy for combatting discrimination on the basis of sex was through the negotiating and grievance machinery on the local level, its efforts required the support of stewards and local union committeemen and officers. When that support was not forthcoming, female employees could easily be victimized. A 1947 report of the Fair Practices Department to the IEB noted that women often waited months or years before filing a complaint against discriminatory practices which, the report emphasized, should have been originally handled through the regular grievance machinery. The report suggested that this was "due to [women's] lack of information and proper understanding of the collective bargaining procedures of their local unions." The authors of the report might, in all fairness, have added that the ignorance of women concerning these procedures might have been due to male efforts to conceal the information from them or to suppress their protests.[23]

If procedural and verbal restraints were not effective in silencing women, discriminatory contract clauses and supplemental and verbal agreements often served this purpose. Three types of discrimination were sanctioned by various union and management agreements. There were, first of all, local agreements prohibiting the employment of married women and providing for the discharge of single women who married. Secondly, agreements providing for unequal hiring-in rates for men and women and unequal wage rates on similar jobs discriminated against single and married women. Thirdly, women, under some agreements, were not permitted to exercise seniority rights equal to those of men in transfers and lay offs. These three practices not only conflicted with post-war UAW policies calling for the protection of the rights of women workers but, by dividing workers according to sex, subverted the theory of industrial unionism. Without a systematic analysis of contracts and supplementary agreements negotiated in this period, it is difficult to determine the extent of this type of discrimination. The fact, however, that the union's records refer to practices of the sort indicated as a widespread problem, suggests that the examples noted were not isolated phenomena.

The codification in UAW contracts and agreements of hostility against married women employees originated in the war period when labor shortages demanded the employment of women to fill essential positions. Management and the UAW agreed that married women, who it was assumed were all adequately supported by their husbands, should not accumulate any seniority and should be the first fired in the event of lay offs. These wartime agreements were continued in post-war contracts. Because John Fernandes, a shop committeeman, supported the seniority rights of all workers regardless of sex, management did not fire married women in his plant after the war, and allowed women who married to continue working. Since recent job cutbacks had resulted in the layoff of a number of men with families, local union members critized Fernandes for protecting the seniority of married women. One union member voiced his unhappiness in a letter to the city newspaper:

My main gripe against Local no. 76 [he wrote] is that they are doing nothing about getting rid of 15 women who persist in hanging on to their jobs . . . while veterans with children are being laid off. It's about time these women realized that the war is over, and they they should stay home and tend to their knitting. All of them are married and I believe that the husband's salary should be enough to tide them through.

Fernandes informed Walter Reuther that the local union was "being torn apart over this question."[24]

A 1953 case involving Local Union 85 that was heard by the International Executive Board illustrates not only union and management collusion in denying married women employment but the extent to which such practices were not even recognized as discriminatory. The Walker Manufacturing Company in Racine, Wisconsin, discharged both Bertha French and Grace Fairless because they had married. In defending the discharges, the management and the leadership of the local cited a verbal agreement, supplemental to the 1948 written contract, that forbade the hiring of married women. The local union's Fair Practices Committee, to whom the women appealed the local executive board's decision to reject their grievance and request for reinstatement with back pay, stated the local union's position on the matter: "There was no intention of discrimination then nor is there now. It is simply a working agreement which until this time has been satisfactory to all parties concerned. . . . [W]e cannot see where

Mrs. Fairless has been treated unfairly, nor has she been discriminated against. Her request to be re-instated on her job was refused because it was merely in keeping with this local's present agreement with management."[25]

The IEB appeal hearing report concluded that the local union was ignorant of the discriminatory nature of its agreement and that the local union, in negotiating the supplemental agreement, had believed "since 1947 that they were conforming to area practice consistent with Local autonomous rights and not in violation of policies of the International Union." Local 85 must have known, however, that the International Fair Practices Department in 1946 compelled Racine Local 642 to delete the section of its 1946 contract that denied married women seniority rights. And in 1948 the IEB ordered Local Union 391 of Racine to delete its discriminatory by-laws providing for unequal hiring-in rates for men and women, but the local union refused to comply and proceeded to operate under a contract that was not approved by the International. Between 1946 and 1949 the Fair Practices Department negotiated with three other Racine area locals in an effort to remove discriminatory contract clauses then being renegotiated with management. The fact that Local 85's agreement with the Walker Manufacturing Co. was a verbal, rather than a written, agreement perhaps indicates some awareness on the part of both management and the local union that the agreement was in violation of UAW policy. In attributing the local's actions to ignorance, the IEB was indicating its own unwillingness to take forceful action to curb sex discrimination.[26]

In 1952, during the course of an IEB appeal hearing dealing with four married women from Local Union 206, the local union officers admitted that, although this was the first time one of the local's married women had appealed a case to the International level, a number of married women had taken grievances to the membership in the early post-war period only to have the membership deny the women the right to work. Other women had been laid off without filing formal complaints, although several women had discussed the problem with the local bargaining committee. In late 1951, the officers testified, women employees "had become aware" of International policy forbidding discrimination on the basis of marital status. When the women notified the UAW regional director of sex discrimination in their local union, he convinced the local's bargaining committee to inform the company that the union would no longer tolerate the discharge of married women.[27]

Fearing that it might have to reinstate the women with back pay in the event of an appeal, the company insisted that the local union assume its share of the responsibility for the discriminatory agreements. The local union leadership therefore raised the issue at a membership meeting. Advised that if it approved the layoff of married women it would be in violation of International policy and the mandate of the International Convention, the membership nevertheless approved a motion not only to continue to support the layoff of married women but to require women to sign a statement when they were hired that they would voluntarily resign if they married. The membership approved this decision a second time at a meeting one month later against the advice of Leonard Woodcock, the regional director, who attended the meeting in order to inform the local union of the implications of its actions. During the appeal hearing one male witness arrogantly explained that the International Union could continue to follow its policy without complaint from the local union as long as the local was allowed to follow its own policy.[28]

In April 1953, William McKenna, chairman of the Fair Practices Committee of Local Union 1020, wrote to Caroline Davis, head of the UAW Women's Bureau, requesting advice regarding a grievance that two women from the local had filed to protest their discharge. The women had been dismissed in accordance with a verbal agreement between the local union and management dating from 1946 which provided for the discharge of married women. McKenna acknowledged that the agreement was in violation of International policy but he was not at all certain that this was of any significance. "Exactly what is *insisted* upon and what is *desired* by the International[?]" he asked. "In a sense such a practice is unfair, but it is *not* contrary to the local constitution or contract.... Violation of 'policy' and violation of contract or constitution, to our way of thinking are two different things." Claiming that the local union executive board and membership did not want to change the terms of the agreement, Tom Nolan, the president of the local, bluntly challenged the International Union to act.[29]

The International submitted the grievance against the company to an arbitrator selected by the American Arbitration Association. But it was Tom Nolan who presented the case for the women and the union. Not only did the appellants note his ineffectiveness, but so, too, did the neutral arbitrator, who said, "What am I doing here if the Company and the Union agree to lay off the married women?" Following this farcical hearing, an IEB Appeal Committee directed the local union officers and membership to end their discrimination against married women: "This type of agreement denies rights to members of the Union who are part of the collective bargaining group and provides hiring opportunities to people who have no rights under the collective bargaining agreement."[30]

The continuation of practices initiated during the war to limit and restrict the rights of newly hired women caused employment problems during the post-war period not only for married women workers but also for single women. When the UAW Research Department conducted a survey of wartime contract clauses, it discovered provisions requiring that, in the event of layoff, women were to be laid off before men regardless of their greater seniority and that women hired after July 7, 1942 on what were considered male jobs would be placed on a special list and granted no seniority. The latter clause limited their employment to the duration of the war or whenever a man was available to replace them. The Local Union 217 contract, the Research Department discovered, stated that when a man was transferred to a woman's job, he would receive the male rate, but when a woman resumed the job, she would receive the lower female rate. This practice also worked in reverse: when a woman was placed on a job classifed as male, she received the lower female rate. These practices continued in the post-war period and were incorporated in new contracts. The practice of differentiating workers on the basis of sex penetrated all the aspects of work that the union was supposed to protect. The classification of jobs as male or female permitted unequal wage rates regardless of equal job content. The practice of separate male and female seniority lists, based on the principle of separate, non-interchangeable occupational groups, compounded this problem. Practices of this sort restricted women to jobs which, because they supposedly required less skill, were not as highly paid.[31]

Disputed cases in which management reclassified a female job as male without any change in the nature of the job reveal the extent to which the labelling of jobs as male or female was entirely arbitrary. In late 1950, women on the 8 a.m. to 4 p.m. and 4 p.m. to midnight shifts of the punch press operation at the Auto-Lite Battery Corporation in Vincennes, Indiana (UAW Local Union 675) filed a grievance with the company demanding equal pay with the men on the midnight to 8 a.m. shift—the women were receiving $1.05 an hour while the men on the same operation, but on a different shift, were receiving $1.25 an hour. The company rejected the complaint and, instead, offered to pay male rates on the punch press job only if the local union agreed to put men on all the shifts. If the local union refused, the job was to remain in the "female" classification and receive the lower rate.[32]

The local union membership accepted the company's proposal

to place men on the early shifts in spite of the advice of an International representative, who informed the membership of the International's equal pay for equal work policy. The result was that the women on the two shifts were laid off. Because of the agreement between the local union and the company providing not only for differential pay rates for "male" and "female" jobs but also for separate male and female seniority lists, the only alternative for the women who had been laid off was to replace other women in lower-paid job classifications. To add insult to injury, the local union refused to follow the mandate of the International Fair Practices Department and the Women's Bureau to negotiate with the company for the reinstatement of the women on the jobs on the early shifts at the higher rate of pay. Ignoring the International's conclusion that the women should have had their grievance processed to a successful conclusion with the full support of the local membership, the local union permitted the company to place men with less seniority on the jobs the women had held. In a letter to Caroline Davis, head of the Women's Bureau, the women expressed their frustration and said in desperation that they would accept the lower rate of pay if only they could get their jobs back.[33]

The non-discriminatory intent of a contract provision for plant-wide seniority without reference to sex was sometimes nullified by other provisions within the same contract. The September 1950 agreement between the Newport Steel Corporation-Universal Cooler Division and Local Union 750 in Marion, Ohio, thus provided for plant wide seniority but also provided for the classification of jobs by sex. When, five months later, the Tecumseh Products Company bought Newport Steel, the new president of the company, which was still under UAW contract, made it clear to the local union that he did not approve of women working, stating that he thought women "should be home in the kitchen." He told the local union that he wanted to eliminate the female employees, a proposal with which the male leadership of the union agreed. A supplemental agreement was therefore drawn up which arbitrarily, and without reference to job content, revised the classifications of some female jobs to male, with corresponding rate increases. The remaining female classified jobs were to "constitute the job classifications to which all female employees shall be limited." The women working on the jobs newly classified as male were laid off.[34]

The women then filed grievances with the company to protest what had occurred. Rachel Shaffstall, a woman working on one of the few remaining female classified jobs, demanded a rate of pay equivalent to that paid men on male classified jobs. The arbitrariness of job classifications had restricted her to the lower "female" pay rate although her job was as heavy and demanding of skill as some of the men's jobs. Betty Delaney claimed that the installation of conveyor belts had actually made one of the reclassified soldering jobs less burdensome than when it had been classified as a female position. Glenna Clements claimed she had been laid off without regard to her seniority and requested reinstatement with back pay. In defense of her demand, she cited the 1950 agreement, which provided for plant wide seniority. The company and the local union rejected Clements' grievance, claiming that "past practice and precedent have always dealt with female classifications independently of male classification"; they referred Clements to the negotiated supplemental agreement of January 1951. Evading the women's complaints of violations of the contract, the local union grievance committee superciliously advised all the female grievants to "thoroughly acquaint yourself with the contract and the supplement in regards to female classifications."[35]

The male membership, which outnumbered the women seven to one, sanctioned the behavior of the local union's grievance committee. At a local union meeting, the membership voted down a motion to classify all jobs which women were able to perform according to state law as either male or female so that women could continue working in line with their seniority. In her report of the investigation she conducted at the plant, Caroline Davis noted that the male workers had submitted a petition in 1946 demanding the elimination of female employees. The local union's claim that the management was responsible for the discrimination against the women in 1951 seems rather dubious given the date of the hostile position. The report of the Fair Practices Department and the Women's Bureau Appeal Committee condemned the illegality of the local union's attitude and actions: "There is . . . little question," the report stated, "that the . . . women . . . were dealt a serious injustice since their inability to return to work is brought about not by a lack of seniority but by the manipulation of jobs which deprive them of employment."[36]

The principle of the contract was at the heart of the theory of labor organization; without a contract, workers were powerless to challenge the whims of management. For women workers in the postwar period, the contract, however, often offered no protection. Because of the complicity of their union representatives, the contract simply codified their separate and unequal status.

Discrimination against women in the UAW occurred not only because of the hostility toward women at the local union level but because of the complicity of regional directors and International representatives. These officials were certainly aware of the UAW's policies on discrimination; much of the out-going correspondence in the files of the Fair Practices Department and the Women's Bureau was addressed to International officials outside the Detroit headquarters in an effort to alert them to the problem of the protection of the rights of the women workers. If an International official approved a discriminatory contract and was sufficiently hostile to a woman's attempt to appeal the practices of either management or her local union, the grievant would have to go over his head to the International Fair Practices Department or the Women's Bureau. The same regional officials, however, often challenged the authority of these units.

The behavior of regional directors regarding the contracts written at the Electric Auto-Lite Company and the Newport Steel Corporation illustrates the role played by these officials in furthering discrimination against women. The Electric Auto-Lite Company and the UAW-CIO agreed in 1950 to a company-wide contract that incorporated fair practice and anti-discrimination principles. The Local Union 675 agreement, however, provided for separate seniority lists, differential job listings, and differential wage rates. The Local 675 agreement and the equitable national agreement were signed by Ray Berndt, the regional director. Protesting to the IEB, a number of women who had been laid off after requesting equal pay for equal work referred to the national agreement as justification for their request that the IEB grant their appeal. The IEB appointed Berndt to oversee the local union's negotiations with the company to reinstate the women. There is no reference in the minutes of the appeal hearing or of the IEB meeting to Berndt's participation in the negotiation of the offensive local union agreement.[37]

Regional director Charles Ballard signed a 1950 agreement between the Newport Steel Corporation and Local Union 750 that provided for separate job classifications. When several women protested the supplemental agreement, which further declassified as male jobs many jobs previously allotted to women and explicitly limited women to the remaining female classifications regardless of the original agreement's provision for plant wide seniority, Ballard expressed his disapproval of their protest. Florence Butcher was unable to meet with Ballard to discuss the grievance and appeal procedures as Caroline Davis had directed her to do. Davis herself encountered difficulty in dealing with Ballard. In a letter to Emil Mazey, the secretary-treasurer of the International, Davis said that she had been "unable to impress him [Ballard] sufficiently" with the seriousness of the women's charges and could not get him to arrange a date for a meeting between the local union and the Women's Bureau to investigate the problem. Davis asked Mazey to use "the good influence" of his position to arrange the meeting. Mazey's "influence" apparently was effective since the

Women's Bureau did conduct an investigation three months later. As in the Local Union 675 case, the IEB Appeal Committee directed Ballard (with Davis' assistance) to negotiate with the company for the elimination of the contract clauses that discriminated against women. Again, however, the IEB failed to chastise the regional director for his previous behavior.[38]

The regional directors, International representatives, local union officials and the UAW membership were, of course, all subject to the authority of the IEB. In failing to exercise its power, as for instance when it did not criticize Berndt and Ballard for their behavior, the IEB, in effect, sanctioned discrimination against women. It must be granted that in the appeal cases that were referred to it, the IEB nearly always ruled in favor of the appellants, and it usually condemned blatantly discriminatory behavior that was brought to its attention. But the IEB did not use its full authority to force recalcitrant locals to adhere either to its recommendations or its policies.

Thus, the initial IEB ruling on an appeal of four women requesting reinstatement with restoration of seniority and pay for time lost was in favor of the appellants. The local union was successful in negotiating their reinstatement with seniority, but management refused to reimburse the women for lost wages. The company claimed that, since the local union was responsible for the appealed practice of firing married women, it should be responsible for the back pay. Leonard Woodcock, chairman of the IEB Appeal Committee for the case, advised the IEB that it should close the case because the local union was liable for the lost wages of the four women and to force it to pay "would be just rubbing salt in the wound." Woodcock did not extend his sensitivity regarding the local union's injured pride to the economic distress of the four women workers.[39]

In the case of a Marion, Ohio local union, the IEB ordered the local union to negotiate the reinstatement of nineteen women who had been laid off despite their seniority. When the union failed in its efforts to secure the restoration of the appellants' seniority, Woodcock, who was also the chairman of this IEB Appeal Committee, explained to the members of the IEB that only a strike could achieve the restoration of seniority, but that a successful strike vote from the predominantly male membership on this question was "not a practical possibility." Woodcock requested the IEB to close the case "because of the practical trade union considerations involved."[40]

"Practical trade union considerations," however, did not interfere with the IEB's decision in 1952 to revoke the charter of the Braniff-UAW local union in Dallas, Texas, for racial discrimination against UAW members. The fact that the IEB used its power in this instance but not in cases of discrimination against women workers indicates the extent to which the UAW leadership simply did not take the issue of discrimination against women workers or its female membership as seriously as did the women or the Women's Bureau. In numerous instances, the IEB surrendered to the demands of the male membership rather than assuming its responsibility to uphold and execute the anti-discrimination policy resolutions approved by the delegates at International Conventions. Clearly, the issue of sexual discrimination caused conflict within the union and among the rank-and-file. The rights of its female membership, however, deserved and required the same protection offered the male rank-and-file.[41]

The experience of women in the UAW during the post-war period suggests that women workers did not necessarily acquiesce in the treatment accorded them by management and that the role played by male unionists in obstructing the protests of women workers and in excluding women from employment in industry needs further exploration. In an effort to exclude women from the industrial labor force after World War II, the UAW—despite its image as an especially progressive union—denied women rights that organized labor considered fundamental, such as the principle of seniority and unrestricted access to the grievance machinery. Certain individuals within the UAW condemned the violation of these rights and the division of workers according to sex. Upholding the principle of industrial unionism, these individuals tried to show how threatening such practices were to the goals of the labor movement. The ambivalence with which the UAW responded to such arguments suggests that industrial organization alone was insufficient to change negative attitudes regarding women employees and to end sexual discrimination. This is not to say that women workers gained nothing from organization; their effective organization among themselves enabled them to impress at least the International leadership with the validity of their demands. The degree of hostility that women workers confronted in demanding their rights from their union demonstrates, however, that the problem of discrimination against women workers was not simply the by-product of management prejudice or a particular method of labor organization but was much more deeply rooted in social ideology.

*I would like to thank Sidney Fine, Robin Jacoby, and Jacqueline Jones for their helpful comments and suggestions on earlier drafts of this paper. Whatever errors remain are, of course, my own.

1. Josephine DiChiera to Ray Ross, May 18, 1953, Emil Mazey Collection, Box 35, Local 1020 Folder, Archives of Labor History and Urban Affairs, Walter P. Reuther Library, Wayne State Univ., Detroit (hereafter cited as WSU Archives).

2. *UAW International Convention Proceedings, 1943,* 97-114; Mary Elizabeth Pidgeon, *Changes in Women's Employment During the War-Special Bulletin No. 20, U.S. Women's Bureau* (Washington: Government Printing Office, 1944), 2-3: Pidgeon, "Women Workers and Recent Economic Change," *Monthly Labor Review,* 65 1947), 667; and Pidgeon, *Changes in Women's Employment,* 12, 26. The remaining 38 per cent were those women who had formerly been employed in manufacturing industries (Pidgeon, *Changes in Women's Employment,* 12).

3. Nelson N. Lichtenstein, "Industrial Unionism Under the No-Strike Pledge: A Study of the CIO during the Second World War" (unpublished Ph.D. diss., Univ. of California, Berkeley, 1974), 225; Gladys Dickason, "Women in Labor Unions," *Annals of the American Academy of Political and Social Science,* 251 (May 1947), 72. Figures for female membership in the UAW before World War II are unavailable. Women, however, represented 6.2 per cent of all automobile and transportation equipment workers in Oct., 1939; this figure can serve for comparison with the 1945 female membership figure (Pidgeon, "Women Workers and Recent Economic Change," 669).

4. For the story of women during World War II and the image of Rosie the Riveter, see William Chafe, *The American Woman* (London: Oxford Univ. Press, 1972), 135-195; Paddy Quick, "Rosie the Riveter: Myths and Realities," *Radical America,* 9 (1975), 115-132; Eleanor Straub, "U.S. Government Policy Toward Civilian Women during World War II," *Prologue,* 5 (1973), 240-254; and Joan Ellen Trey, "Women in the War Economy—World War II," *Review of Radical Political Economics,* 4 (July 1972), 40-57.

5. For the background on women workers and the labor movement prior to the formation of the CIO, see Chafe, 66-89; Nancy S. Dye, "Feminism or Unionism? The New York Women's Trade Union League and the Labor Movement," *Feminist Studies,* 3 (Fall 1975), 111-125; Robin Jacoby, "Feminism and Class Consciousness in the British and American Women's Trade Union Leagues, 1890-1925," in Berenice Carroll, ed., *Liberating Women's History* (Urbana: Univ. of Illinois Press, 1976), 137-160; Alice Kessler-Harris, "Organizing the Unorganizable," in Milton Cantor and Bruce Laurie, eds., *Class, Sex and the Woman Worker* (Westport: Greenwood Press, 1977), 144-165; and Kessler-Harris, "Where are the Organized Women Workers?" *Feminist Studies,* 3 (1975), 92-110.

6. R.J. Thomas to All Regional Directors and Local Union Presidents, April 22, 1944, UAW War Policy Division-Women's Bureau Collection, Box 5, Folder 10, WSU Archives.

7. *Ibid;* C.G. Edelin to International Union Executive Board, Feb. 7, 1944, UAW Local 51 Collection, Box 28, Folder 9, WSU Archives.

8. Thomas, *Automobile Unionism* (Detroit: n.p., 1942), 81-82: UAW War

Policy Division, "Recommended Policy on Transfers and Filling Openings with Female Help," n.d. [1944], UAW Local 51 Collection, Box 28, Folder 8, WSU Archives.

9. "Women's Postwar Plans," *UAW Research Department Research Report*, 4 (March 1944), 3, UAW War Policy Division Collection, Series I, Box 21, WSU Archives. With the exception of Lyn Goldfarb, *Separated and Unequal: Discrimination Against Women Workers After World War II* (The Women's Work Project, A Union for Radical Political Economics Political Education Project, n.d.), there are no studies of women workers in trade unions during the immediate post-World War II period. Goldfarb uses the experience of female UAW members in the Detroit area to illustrate the problems that women workers confronted in the post-war era. Although she is not consistent in her use of Detroit materials, and her analysis is suggestive rather than conclusive, Goldfarb makes several important insights into the dynamics of sexual discrimination in unions.

10. "Second Quarterly Report of the Fair Practices and Anti-Discrimination Department, 1946," UAW Fair Practices and Anti-Discrimination Department-Women's Bureau Collection, Box 2, Folder 17, WSU Archives. The Fair Practices Department and the Women's Bureau acknowledged the special problems of black women, whose status was one of double jeopardy. Convention resolution and Department reports and policy statements referred specifically to black women workers as the group against whom management and the union most often discriminated. The two offices jointly handled cases involving discrimination against black women on the basis of either their sex or race. *UAW International Convention Proceedings, 1946*, 328; "Second Quarterly Report, 1946," 15; and William Oliver to Lillian Hatcher, May 4, 1948. Fair Practices and Anti-Discrimination Department-Women's Bureau Collection, Box 5, Folder 7, WSU Archives.

11. *Equal Pay for Equal Work* (Detroit: Fair Practices and Anti-Discrimination Department, n.d. [1946], Women Employment Vertical File, WSU Archives.

12. *UAW International Convention Proceedings, 1946*, 46; *UAW International Convention Proceedings, 1949*, 8.

13. "Fourth Quarterly Report of the Fair Practices and Anti-Discrimination Department, 1947," 19, Fair Practices and Anti-Discrimination Department-Women's Bureau Collection, Box 2, Folder 18, WSU Archives.

14. *Ibid.*, 3-4.

15. Fair Practices and Anti-Discrimination Department, "Report-Conditions Affecting the Equal Status of Women Foundry Workers in the UAW-CIO," n.d. [April 1947], 3, 15, Walter P. Reuther Collection, Box 21, Fair Practices Department 1946-47 Folder, WSU Archives; "Fourth Quarterly Report, 1947," 1-2.

16. *UAW International Convention Proceedings, 1943*, 369-389; Patricia Sexton, "A Feminist Union Perspective," in B.J. Widick, ed., *Auto Work and Its Discontents* (Baltimore: Johns Hopkins Univ. Press, 1976), 27-28. The conflict over special privileges also reflected the political factionalism within the UAW. The Minority Report on the Minorities Department proposal in 1943, which was supported by the Frankensteen-Addes wing, proposed that the director of the department be black. The Majority Report, which opposed the potential Jim Crowism of the Minority Report demand, was coauthored by Victor Reuther.

17. Richard Leonard to William Oliver, Aug. 19, 1946, Walter P. Reuther Collection, Box 21, Fair Practices Department 1945-47 Folder, WSU Archives.

18. Alan Gale Clive, "The Society and Economy of Wartime Michigan, 1939-1945" (unpublished Ph.D. Diss., Univ. of Michigan, 1976), 612-613.

19. Reuther, quoted in Chester W. Gregory, *Women in Defense Work During World War II* (NY: Exposition Press, 1974), 185: *UAW International Convention Proceedings, 1946,* 52.

20. Clive, 539-547. Clive's statement that, "[i]f female workers were outraged by the treatment accorded them, they made no public show of their displeasure" is clearly at odds with even the minimal coverage of female UAW members' protests in the labor press and statements of women delegates during the International conventions (Clive, 542), *Michigan Chronicle, United Automobile Worker,* and *Ammunition* clippings in the Vertical Files-Women, WSU Archives, and the 1944, 1946, 1949 *UAW International Convention Proceedings.*

21. Grace Curcuri to To Whom it May Concern, Sept. 16, 1952, Nina Fuston Maynard to Richard Gosser, Sept. 16, 1952, Mildred Westbrook to Dear Sirs, Sept. 16, 1952, Mazey Collection, Box 37, Local 154 Folder, WSU Archives.

22. Josephine DiChiera to Ray Ross, May 18, 1953, Dominic Dornetto to Ross, June 4, 1953, and Dornetto to Ross, June 17, 1953, Mazey Collection, Box 35, Local 1020 Folder, WSU Archives. The local union did not recognize DiChiera's grievance because of the existence of a verbal agreement dating back to 1946 that forbade the employment of married women (Ida Seibert and Josephine Jurinko [DiChiera] to Ray Ross, Nov. 10, 1953, *ibid*).

23. "Report of the UAW-CIO Fair Practices and Anti-Discrimination Department to the International Executive Board, September 8, 1947," 7, Fair Practices Department-Women's Bureau Collection, Box 2, Folder 18, WSU Archives. When Leona Frifeldt complained to the International's Fair Practices Department that her local union bargaining committee had no heard her grievance against an improper transfer because of her sex, she was advised to exhaust the local union grievance machinery before appealing to the International. Shortly thereafter, she requested the Department to withdraw her appeal "due to incomplete utilization of grievance machinery." Exactly what happened to Frifeldt is unknown, but it is possible that, because of the lack of support from local officers, either the membership or the company rejected her grievance or she ran afoul of the time limits placed on the filing and processing of grievances ("Third Quarterly Report of the Fair Practices and Anti-Discrimination Department, 1947," 4, *ibid*).

24. John Fernandes to Walter Reuther, April 19, 1949, Mazey Collection, Box 21, Local Union 1031 Folder, WSU Archives; newspaper clipping, *Oakland Tribune* (California), n.d., *ibid.*

25. "Agreement between Local 85 and Walker Manufacturing Company," June 1, 1948, Mazey Collection, Box 32, Local 85 Folder, WSU Archive; Walker Manufacturing Company to Local 85, May 28, 1953, *ibid.*; and "Report Form, Local Union Fair Practices Committee," Oct. 1, 1953, *ibid.*

26. "Appeal Hearing Report," April 28, 1954, *ibid.*; William Oliver to Caroline Davis and Lillian Hatcher, April 12, 1949, Fair Practices Department-Women's Bureau Collection, Box 5, Folder 8; William Oliver to Frank Sahorske, May 19, 1949, Walter P. Reuther Collection, Box 20, Fair Practices Department 1948-49 Folder; and George Addes to Local Union 391, n.d. [1948?], Fair Practices Department-Women's Bureau Collection, Box 5, Folder 1, WSU Archive. Under such agreements, the hiring of married women was left to the discretion of the local

union and the company. If a married woman could show cause for employment—for example, if her husband was incapacitated or in the service—she might be allowed to work, but only under certain onerous constraints. Local Union 72 in Racine allowed married women thus hired to accumulate seniority only in the department in which they worked rather than in accordance with the contract's principle of plant-wide seniority. They were, however, the first to be laid off, regardless of any seniority they might have accumulated. The notorious Local Union 391 had a particularly insulting way of ensuring a married woman's gratitude: she had to pay the local union one dollar per week for permission to work. (W.G. Kult to R.J. Thomas, June 22, 1944, UAW War Policy Division-Women's Bureau Collection, Box 5, Folder 12, WSU Archives: George Addes to Local Union 391, n.d. [1948?], Fair Practices Department-Women's Bureau Collection, *ibid*).

27. "Appeal Hearing Report," May 20, 1952, Mazey Collection, Box 40, Local 206-2 Folder, WSU Archives.

28. Paul Luckett to Emil Mazey, April 21, 1952, *ibid*.; "Appeal Hearing Report," May 20, 1952, *ibid*.

29. William McKenna to Caroline Davis, April 27, 1953. Mazey Collection, Box 35, Local 1021 Folder, *ibid*.; Tom Nolan to Ray Ross, June 15, 1953, *ibid*.

30. Josephine Jurinko to Caroline Davis, Dec. 3, 1953, Mazey Collection, Box 35, Local 1021 Folder, *ibid*.; "Appeal Hearing Report," April 29, 1954, *ibid*.

31. "Clauses Pertaining to Seniority of Women," enclosed with R.J. Thomas to Officers and Regional Directors, Nov. 13, 1944, Mazey Collection, Box 13, Women's Division 1941-47 Folder, *ibid*.

32. "Fair Practices and Anti-Discrimination Department-Women's Bureau Appeal Hearing," Oct. 15, 1951, Mazey Collection, Box 39, Local 675 Folder, *ibid*.

33. *Ibid*.; Dorothy Williams to Caroline Davis, Nov. 1, 1951, *ibid*. To reduce the number of female classified jobs in a plant with separate seniority lists was an effective means of limiting the number of women workers.

34. "Agreement between Universal Cooler Division, Newport Steel Corporation and Local 750," Sept. 20, 1950, Mazey Collection, Box 39, Local 750 Folder; Florence Butcher to Caroline Davis, August 28, 1951, Mazey Collection, Box 31, Local Union 750-6/51-5/52 Folder, *ibid*.; "Supplemental Agreement between Universal Cooler Division, Tecumseh Products Company and Local 750," *ibid*.; and "Schedule A of New Hourly Rates," March 26, 1951, Mazey Collection, Box 39, Local 750 Folder, *ibid*.

35. Rachel Shaffstall Grievance," *ibid*.; "Fair Practices and Anti-Discrimination Department-Women's Bureau Appeal Hearing," n.d. [August, 1952?], Mazey Collection, Box 31, *ibid*.; "Glenna Clements Grievance," Box 39, Local 750 Folder, *ibid*.; and Form Letter from Local Union 750 Grievance Committee, Oct. 30, 1951, *ibid*.

36. Minutes of Local 750 membership meeting, Dec., 1951, *ibid*.; "Appeal Hearing," n.d. [Aug., 1952?], Mazey Collection, Box 31, *ibid*.

37. "National Agreement between the Electric Auto-Lite Company and UAW-CIO (12 Locals in Burt Foundry Unit)," n.d. [1950-1951?], Mazey Collection, Box 39, Local 675 Folder, *ibid*.; "Agreement Between Auto-Lite Battery Corporation, Vincennes, Indiana and UAW-CIO Local 675," March 7, 1951, *ibid*.; "Appeal Hearing Report," Sept. 9, 1952, *ibid*.; and Emil Mazey to Richard Gosser and Ray Berndt, Dept. 24, 1952, *ibid*.

38. "Agreement between Newport Steel and Local 750," *ibid.*; Caroline Davis to Charles Ballard, Sept. 6, 1951, Mazey Collection, Box 31; Davis to Emil Mazey, Oct. 29, 1951, *ibid.*; and "Appeal Hearing Report," Jan. 23, 1953, Mazey Collection, Box 39, Local 750 Folder, WSU Archives.

39. Minutes of IEB meeting, Sept. 15-18, 1952, 323-324, UAW International Executive Board Minutes Collection, Box 6, WSU Archives. It must be noted that although the company was justified in its refusal to accept full moral responsibility for the discriminatory practice, it never objected to the procedure.

40. Minutes of IEB meeting, Jan. 18-21, 1954, 338, *ibid.*

41. "Appeal Hearing," May 20, 1952, Mazey Collection, Box 40, Local 206-2 Folder, WSU Archives.

～22 ～

A "New Frontier" for Women: The Public Policy of the Kennedy Administration

Cynthia E. Harrison

In December 1961, more than four years before the emergence of a vigorous wave of feminism, President John F. Kennedy established the President's Commission on the Status of Women. The creation of the commission, which one newspaper hailed as the launching of a "distaff 'Fair Deal,'" denoted a fundamental shift in federal policy, expressed also in the enactment of equal pay legislation and the prohibition of discrimination against women in the federal civil service.[1] These steps, taken without the impetus of either a widespread feminist movement or a national emergency, marked the federal government's assumption of a new responsibility with regard to equal treatment for women in the labor force. How Kennedy came to appoint such a commission, why the departure in policy took place, and what consequences resulted from the change constitute the subjects of this essay.

Throughout the period 1945 to 1960, government agencies, women's organizations, educators, and journalists expressed concern about proper roles for women. Immediately after the war, those who spoke for working women concentrated on the need to "protect" women in the labor force, including their right to jobs, while providing employment for returning service personnel. Reinstitution of "labor standards" or protective labor laws and the attempt to persuade women to leave their "masculine" jobs for more "feminine" ones in the

From *The Journal of American History* 67 (December, 1980). Copyright Organization of American Historians. Reprinted by permission.

burgeoning clerical and service occupations served both purposes, and both were attempted.[2] A desire to resume "normal" family life and the strong reassertion of traditional sex roles in response to wartime dislocations led many women back to being full-time homemakers.[3]

Later in the 1950s, however, many observers began to voice concern about the educated and talented women who, having taken up careers as full-time homemakers, were denying their talents to their country. Schools and hospitals sorely lacked teachers and nurses. Anxiety over the perceived Soviet threat led many to believe that America needed to harness all its scientific talents, including those of women. These circumstances helped to bring the public's attention to the "under-utilization" of women's abilities.[4]

Although many fields indeed suffered shortages of womanpower, the labor force participation rate of women was actually rising, especially that of married women with children. According to census reports, the proportion of women who worked for wages rose from 31.4 percent in 1950 to 34.8 percent in 1960. Moreover, the proportion of married women, with husbands present, who were employed outside the home increased from 23.8 to 30.5 percent, accelerating a long-term trend. Whereas in 1950, 52.1 percent of women in the labor force were married, by 1960 the percentage had swelled to 59.9. Perhaps most significantly, women who had children under the age of six increased their participation rate by 50 percent (from 12.6 percent in 1950 to almost 19 percent in 1960). The biggest share of this increase occurred early in the decade—by 1955, more than 17 percent of mothers of young children were working.[5]

Despite the mounting numbers of women in paid employment, interest in women's rights and opportunities did not follow a similar pattern of growth. Some, but not all, women's organizations continued to consider women's rights worthy of concern. However, those that did, with the exception of the National Woman's party, viewed it as only one among many worthwhile causes. Attention to equal pay legislation and the Equal Rights Amendment (ERA) declined in the 1950s. No new broad-based women's organization developed to address questions concerning the rights of working women. (In fact, the activist National Women's Trade Union League dissolved in 1950.) Consequently, few of the legal disabilities confronting women were alleviated, employers continued to assign jobs to workers by sex, and pay differentials between male and female workers doing the same work were still a matter of course.[6]

One federal government agency, the Women's Bureau in the Department of Labor, did continue to be concerned with women's status, especially that of women within the labor force. The bureau's active constituency comprised women in labor unions and middle-class women's groups who saw themselves as sympathetic to the needs of working women. Throughout the 1940s and 1950s, the Women's Bureau championed the right of women to work on an equal basis with men and the cause of federal legislation to require equal pay. At the same time, the bureau, which had played a major role in the long struggle to enact protective labor laws for women, was committed to preserving those laws.[7]

This stance of the bureau—advocating equal rights for women without disturbing protective labor legislation—placed it in conflict with women's groups that supported the ERA. The National Federation of Business and Professional Women's Clubs and the National Women's party, both oriented toward middle-class women, provided the nucleus of support for the ERA, while the organizations surrounding the Women's Bureau (for example, the National Women's Trade Union League, the American Association of University Women, the National Consumers League, the National Council of Catholic Women) lobbied in opposition to the amendment. They offered instead the alternative of a national commission on the status of women.

Agitation for a national commission to study the status of women had begun in the 1940s when it appeared that the ERA might be added to the Constitution in gratitude for and in recognition of women's contribution to the war effort. Strong liberal opposition to the ERA developed, however, founded on its apparent threat to hard-won protective labor laws. With the hope of uniting all women's groups behind one proposal, this group of adversaries suggested in 1947 the establishment of a congressional commission on the status of women in lieu of adopting the ERA. They intended to improve women's status without what were perceived to be the damaging consequences of a wide-ranging amendment. Yet they made compromise with ERA advocates virtually impossible by including in the bill to create the commission the statement that "it is the declared policy of the United States that in law and its administration no distinctions on the basis of sex shall be made except such as are reasonably justified by differences in physical structure, biological, or social function." Professional women and those in the better-paying and organized trades viewed protective labor legislation as evidence of a desire to hobble women and handicap their advancement; they supported the ERA and dissented from the philosophy expressed in the new bill. Women who identified with the lowest-paid unorganized women workers deemed protective labor legislation essential and the ERA a meaningless abstraction. They believed that women's wages would decline without minimum wage laws and that women's roles differed from men's in ways that the law should recognize. The fierce dissension among organized women's groups meant that neither the ERA nor a national commission had any reasonable chance of winning the approval of the Congress.[8]

In 1957, however, advocates of a commission received support from a prestigious private source. The National Manpower Council published a report noting the revolution in women's employment and recommending public and private action to enlarge openings for women in the paid labor force and to improve their educational preparation for work. In order to obtain additional necessary information, the council members recommended that the secretary of labor appoint a commission to review federal and state legislation bearing on the employment of women.[9]

The Department of Labor rejected the suggestion. Lack of support from Alice K. Leopold, director of the Women's Bureau, may have been decisive. When the undersecretary of labor asked for her opinion of the National Manpower Council's proposal, she responded that the secretary should "utilize existing facilities, including both Governmental agencies and interested non-governmental organizations" rather than create a commission.[10] Plans to establish a commission on women proceeded no further in the Eisenhower administration, although that administration was not in general unsympathetic toward women's rights. Remarkably, in view of the intense competition to have proposals included in presidential messages, the president endorsed equal pay legislation in the State of the Union Message in 1956 and in annual budget messages and economic reports to the Congress from 1957 through 1961.[11] Still, if the director of the Women's Bureau did not recommend a commission, no internal advisor would plausibly overrule her.

After the election of Kennedy, the new director of the Women's Bureau, Esther Peterson, adopted precisely the opposite position to that of her predecessor. She strongly advocated creation of a commission on women, perhaps because she assumed—correctly—that she would determine the nature and direction of the commission. Kennedy readily assented to her proposal, agreeing even to make it a presidential, rather than a merely departmental, commission. Under Peterson's supervision, the President's Commission on the Status of Women became the centerpiece of the administration's actions on behalf of women, serving to effect specific changes and to heighten public awareness of women's issues.[12]

Kennedy's ready acceptance of Peterson's recommendation to establish a commission on women stemmed at least partially from his political need to "do something for women." Women not only made up more than half the electorate; they were well known to perform most of the less attractive jobs associated with electing Democrats (and Republicans) to office. Moreover, prominent Democratic women from Eleanor Roosevelt on down had assured him that he must recognize this constituency.[13]

Although both Dwight D. Eisenhower and Harry S. Truman were subject to a similar political imperative, they responded mainly by appointing women to highly visible political offices, largely at the entreaty of women party officials. These political women, whose own power derived from their ability to influence patronage, argued that such appointments would inspire appreciation and loyalty from female campaign workers. India Edwards, executive director of the Women's Division of the Democratic National Committee (DNC), who had a close personal relationship with Harry Truman, wielded strong influence, and the President usually acceded to her requests for naming women unless he met opposition from other quarters. Eisenhower was also widely known for his record of choosing women for executive posts, largely at the suggestion of Bertha Adkins, who directed women's activities for the Republican National Committee before she herself accepted a position in the Department of Health, Education, and Welfare.[14]

Because women's issues lacked salience, neither Edwards nor Adkins had any competition for the role of women's spokesperson from any other woman (or man) within the Administration. While it was important to create a "record" with which to impress women voters, it seemingly did not matter if the record were based on appointments or on legislative and executive actions that dealt with discrimination. Neither Truman nor Eisenhower (nor, later, Kennedy) viewed the subject as worthy of his personal attention or the concern of too many advisers. As long as one woman was deemed trustworthy and as long as she did not propose anything that conflicted with the chief executive's policies or philosophy, she enjoyed a relatively free hand. Edwards and Adkins both used their access to foster appointive positions for women.

Margaret Price, chosen by Kennedy to be vice-chairman and director of Women's Activities for the DNC, likewise urged vigorously that Kennedy surpass former administrations in his appointments of women. She prepared a transition document on the records of past administrations in which she included the names and biographies of several potential candidates.[15] Kennedy failed to heed Price's advice, however, and thereby encountered much criticism.

Soon after Kennedy assumed the presidency, Democratic party women began to press him to improve opportunities for women in government. For example, Emma Guffey Miller, a well-known ERA supporter and Democratic national committeewoman from Pennsylvania, protested: "It is a grievous disappointment to the women leaders and ardent workers that so few women have been named to worthwhile positions; that the few who have been named by you are merely replacing other women, while the important posts, formerly filled by women, are now being handed over to men." She concluded with a warning: "As a woman of long political experience, I feel the situation has become serious and I hope whoever is responsible for it may be made to realize that the results may well be disastrous."[16]

In fact, Kennedy's record of appointments did not compare so unfavorably with that of his predecessors. He made only ten Senate-confirmed appointments of women to policy-making executive and judicial posts, but Truman, who won high praise for his record, in a comparable period, had made only fifteen and Eisenhower only fourteen. None of the presidents, Kennedy included, utilized the talents of women significantly. In all three administrations, women held only 2.4 percent of all appointive positions. However, Kennedy's neglect of visible appointments brought reproach. Unlike Eisenhower and Franklin D. Roosevelt, Kennedy failed to appoint a women to a cabinet position. Clayton Fritchey, director of public affairs of the United States Mission to the United Nations and long-time Democratic "pol," pointed out to the president that "*notable* appointments" constituted important symbols to women, and that, as of July 1963, "the present Administration has not done all it could in this respect. . . . Today there are no really famous women serving the Government."[17]

The outcry, therefore, probably resulted from three factors: that expectations were not met, since Kennedy's admirers expected him to exceed the performance of his predecessors; that appointments of women were not so visible as in previous administrations and were not so highlighted by the press; and, most important, that the women party loyalists who expected to control appointments of women lacked access to the chief executive. The Democratic party women, who since the Roosevelt years had been rewarding loyal party supporters with administration posts, suddenly found themselves thwarted and they resented their sudden loss of influence. Edwards remarked that in the Kennedy administration "there was no one at the DNC or in the White House who had any influence with them when it came to women's affairs." Price reportedly never held a private conversation with Kennedy. Emma Guffey Miller voiced the dismay of party women over the exclusion of Price from White House inner circles: "the administration has been lax in recognizing Democratic women. . . . In the Roosevelt and Truman Administrations, the Vice Chairman [and head of women's affairs] was always consulted when women were being named to important posts, but now all Margaret Price knows is what she sees in the newspapers. This is not going to help the Party."[18]

The White House appointments procedure did exclude Price. Kennedy, wrote Theodore Sorensen, "wanted a ministry of talent." To get it, the Kennedy staff broke away from past methods of operation with many of their sensitivities to political "musts" and a well-established role for women, and conducted the search from the White House. Except for minor patronage positions, the President's aides ignored the DNC, figuring that it would not be a source of likely candidates. The Talent Search instituted no compensatory method of including women. Dan Fenn, who ran the recruitment effort, had no sense at all that women represented a pool of ability which should be tapped. Moreover, women were not likely to be found in the places the Kennedy staff did look. The quest centered on elite universities, boards and executive suites of major corporations, and prestigious law firms where women were few in number. The blatant discrimination which kept women out of high-level jobs did not have to come from the Kennedy team; it had already taken place.[19]

Margaret Price could not overcome the consequences of the new Kennedy appointment process. First, Kennedy's association with the DNC differed markedly from that of former presidents. The national committees' power had started to decline in general as primaries and television advertising began to play a greater role in the selection of the ca: ʾdates. Kennedy's political organization had been largely an independent creation, based on developing contacts in local areas, and run by close personal associates. He did not have a history of working with the DNC and had little reason to turn to its officers for counsel of any kind. Second, Margaret Price was herself very deferential, unwilling to fight to build a power base. When Kennedy initially declined to address the biennial Campaign Conference for Democratic Women, a gathering of more than three thousand, Price accepted the dictum. India Edwards, on the other hand, wrote to the President threatening to cancel the meeting, and Kennedy acquiesced. Third, as a member of the reform wing of the Democratic party in Michigan, Price felt less commitment to the patronage aspect of party politics; she viewed herself less an advocate of women than an advocate among women for the Democratic party, and she did not work as hard for distaff appointments as Edwards had. Calvin Mackenzie observed in his book on the politics of appointments that "the surest way for a group to shut itself out of the appointment process is for it to blunder into a strategy of reticence." That was just what Price unwittingly did. Finally, Price could not claim that Kennedy's failure to appoint more women would bring retaliation at the polls because Esther Peterson, the Director of the

Women's Bureau and Assistant Secretary of Labor, was making sure that Kennedy had plenty of evidence to assert that he had a genuine interest in the status of women.[20]

Kennedy's association with Peterson dated from his earliest days in the Congress when she was a lobbyist for the Amalgamated Clothing Workers and he sat on the House Education and Labor Committee. He had therefore known her for more than a decade, during which she had earned a reputation with the Congress for being a well-prepared and effective advocate of labor's position. She joined Kennedy's campaign before the primaries and worked to build labor support for him, while most other labor leaders supported Hubert Humphrey or Stuart Symington. To reward her efforts during the campaign, Kennedy offered Peterson her choice of administration jobs. When she selected the Women's Bureau, Kennedy chided her, saying, "You don't just want to be director of the Women's Bureau, do you?" and within eight months he elevated her to a new position, assistant secretary of labor, a position she held in addition to being Women's Bureau chief. As assistant secretary, Peterson spoke with far more authority than she could have had merely as director of the Women's Bureau. No previous chief executive had ever recognized the Women's Bureau in this way.[21] Her assertiveness in her dual capacities gave her an added edge of effectiveness, and Emma Guffey Miller, excluded from the inner circles of power, lamented the ascendancy of a woman "of the Esther Peterson type [who] goes out of her way to do the contrary thing." Peterson, she felt, was not one of the "women who are for women."[22]

Peterson may not have shared Emma Guffey Miller's view of what made a woman be "for women," but she did pursue her own plan to elevate women's status. Peterson, coming out of the labor movement, was an advocate of protective labor laws for women and therefore an opponent of the ERA that Emma Guffey Miller and many other party women, themselves middle-class professionals, had championed. Nevertheless, while cognizant of the widespread desire to protect the family, including women's special relationship to it, Peterson believed in women's right to contribute to the society in ways other than as wives and mothers. Furthermore, she had long been involved in working to organize women, in cooperating with the Women's Bureau, and in working with women's organizations such as the National Women's Trade Union League to achieve long-desired reforms—a commission on women, equal pay legislation, inclusion of the lowest-paying occupations (which employed large numbers of women) under minimum wage legislation, and amelioration of some of the conditions working women encountered. As director of the Women's Bureau she aimed to accomplish these goals. The important roles women were playing in the paid labor force and the interest of women's organizations and educators gave potency to her efforts to augment the influence of the Women's Bureau.

Although the Republican Women's Bureau head Leopold refused to endorse a commission (and lacked the attributes to achieve much else), the creation of the President's Commission on the Status of Women cannot be attributed merely to the presence of a Democratic administration. During the Truman years, the status of women aroused more discussion than it did later. Agitation for a national commission was at its peak. Truman took no such step because Edwards provided certain evidence of Truman's regard for women and because no woman came forward with sufficient authority to urge Truman to follow a different course of action. Frieda Miller, the director of the Women's Bureau from 1944 through 1952, whose agenda was virtually identical to Peterson's, had no White House entrée at all. But Kennedy's ties to labor were closer than Truman's, and Peterson, an astute politician with a strong labor background, had access to the highest levels of executive power. Thus, she acted as the catalyst that resulted in the Kennedy administration's unprecedented response to women's changing roles. The Women's Bureau's role as the source of effective policy innovation was new in the Kennedy years. The program that Peterson implemented, in lieu of focusing on executive appointments for women to governmental posts, had two main facets, both long sought by herself and her associates—equal pay legislation and a commission on the status of women.[23]

Peterson proposed that Kennedy appoint a commission on the status of women largely because of her concern about the negative impact of the ERA. Kennedy had unwittingly expressed support for the ERA during the presidential campaign, and Peterson feared the consequences of the endorsement. In a memorandum of June 2, 1961, to Secretary of Labor Arthur Goldberg, Peterson asserted that "such a commission would substitute constructive recommendations for the present troublesome and futile agitation about the 'equal rights amendment.'"[24]

Still, Peterson's aversion to the ERA was not her only motive for establishing the commission. The memorandum went on to suggest that "the commission would help the nation set forth before the world the story of women's progress in a free, democratic society, and to move further towards full partnership, creative use of skills, and genuine equality of opportunity." Peterson did in fact use the commission to educate certain facets of the American public and to help advance programs and policies already initiated by administration and government women.

Kennedy created the President's Commission on the Status of Women on December 14, 1961, just six months after Peterson's memo. Its stated purpose was "to review progress and make recommendations as needed for constructive action" in the areas of private and federal employment policies and practices, federal social insurance and tax laws, federal and state protective labor legislation, treatment of women under the law, and provision of necessary family services.[25]

Membership on the commission and its subsidiary bodies represented many constituencies. Fifteen women served with eleven men on the commission itself, with ten members of the commission coming from the federal government, including the attorney general, the chairman of the Civil Service Commission, and the secretaries of Commerce, Agriculture, Labor, and Health, Education, and Welfare. Eleanor Roosevelt bestowed considerable prestige on the commission by accepting appointment as its "chairman." Peterson, with Goldberg, dominated the selection procedures, choosing from women's organizations, labor unions, educational institutions, and governmental agencies, to supply more than 120 participants for the commission and its seven technical committees. No official of the National Woman's party was invited to join the commission, although Peterson did include two women identified with the pro-ERA National Federation of Business and Professional Women's Clubs. A commission without any ERA supporters would lack credibility, and Peterson cleared the way for the participation by omitting a statement of purpose indicating a preconceived position on the amendment.

Significantly, no women with an exclusively political party background received an invitation to join the commission. Edwards related in her memoir that a newspaperwoman had asked her, "How can it be that a commission on the status of women could be appointed and India Edwards, who has done more for women than any other living woman, is not on the commission?" Edwards herself was not surprised, in view of the diminished role of the DNC with respect to women in the administration: "My being overlooked was understandable to me. How different from the days of President Truman's Administration, when the name of every woman proposed by anyone else for appointment by the President was submitted to me for an OK." Political women wielded little influence regarding appointments to the commission, and Peterson later recalled that she never considered placing a political woman on the commission. She did not view the commission's goals as being relevant to the aims of women who had had careers in political parties. Katherine Ellickson, assistant director of the social security department of the American Federation of Labor-Congress of Industrial Organizations, became executive secretary of the commission and headed the small paid staff; Peterson herself, as executive vice-chairman, held a key place. Clearly, labor union women were "in" and politicos were "out."[26]

The Women's Bureau and Peterson maintained a careful watch on the president's commission. Women's Bureau personnel and sympathizers dominated the commission's secretariat, which implemented all commission and committee requests, planned meetings, answered mail, and communicated with other government agencies between commission meetings. Since the commission met only eight times in the two years of its existence and was robbed of its chairman by the death of Eleanor Roosevelt in 1962 (the administration decided not to replace her), the staff exerted a great deal of influence.

The Women's Bureau, the commission staff, and the commission members viewed the controversy over the ERA as a matter of paramount concern. Improperly handled, the dispute could render the commission nugatory. Hyman Bookbinder, representing the secretary of commerce, broached the issue at the first meeting, feeling, he said, like "the proverbial fool who likes to move in where angels fear to tread." Remarking that the amendment had "divided the country" for years, he asserted that "if this Commission does nothing else [but] get an accommodation of views on this difficult and delicate area, we will have made a substantial contribution." Viola Hymes, president of the National Council of Jewish Women, agreed that the ERA had been "the most divisive . . . issue . . . among women's organizations," which had frozen their positions on it and had not reexamined them for twenty-five years. The commission would, she felt, "enable the women's organizations to take a new look in the light of developments and changes which will be very helpful." "Maybe," she suggested, "the women's groups will get together." To this Peterson declared: "It will be worth the Commission if we do it."[27]

Although the commission claimed to be approaching the subject of the ERA with no preconceived position, there was never a chance that it would endorse the amendment. By design, too many commissioners came from labor or conservative religious groups that opposed it. Nevertheless, the Committee on Civil and Political Rights, the subunit of the commission under whose purview the issue fell, worked hard to formulate a position that the commission would accept, short of completely condemning the ERA. At the committee's request, the commission report ultimately stated that, while "equality of rights under the law for all persons, male or female, is so basic to democracy . . . that it must be reflected in the fundamental law of the land," the commissioners believed such equality to be embodied in the Fifth and Fourteenth Amendments. This premise required, however, validation by the Supreme Court, and they urged appropriate test cases. In view of this conviction, the commissioners concluded that "a constitutional amendment need not now be sought in order to establish this principle." The "now" in this last sentence was added at the request of ERA supporter Marguerite Rawalt, a day after the initial wording was adopted.[28]

This carefully constructed position constituted a viable compromise. Partisans of protective laws for women believed that the Supreme Court would continue to uphold such laws as reasonable under the Fourteenth Amendment, even while the justices affirmed women's equality in other areas. For their part, ERA proponents managed to forestall outright rejection of the amendment by the commission—a clear possibility—and, still more, elicited acknowledgement of its potential necessity should the Supreme Court prove reluctant to act. Thus, a breach over the ERA was avoided. Ellickson recalled: "We were all relieved when, under Miss Hickey's skillful chairing, the Commission members, including Rawalt, agreed on this section!"[29]

While the commission discussed the ERA almost gingerly, the members debated the underlying issue of protective labor legislation for women more vehemently than any other. After much discussion, and heavily influenced by Mary Dublin Keyserling (future director of the Women's Bureau), final recommendations endorsed enhancing protective laws for women rather than demanding their application to male workers. Although everyone agreed that extending such labor legislation to men was ultimately desirable, the protectionists obtained a recommendation from the commission for the interim, advocating that laws for women be maintained, strengthened, and expanded.[30] However because the commission did endorse constitutional equality for women, and in a manner acceptable to proponents of protective laws, the subject of the laws themselves lost its power to destroy the cordial working relationship of the members. The commission therefore held together and completed its agenda.

The ERA and protective laws for women aside, most questions elicited general agreement from the start. During its brief life, the commission wholeheartedly lent its prestige to several administration actions on behalf of women. The most significant concerned the Civil Service Commission (CSC).

In preparation for the announcement of the president's commission, Peterson urged administration officials to make the federal government a "showcase" of equal opportunity. A CSC review of requests by agency heads for eligible applicants from the civil service lists showed that only 16 percent of requests to fill places in the lowest grades (one through four) specified men, while an overwhelming 94 percent of those in grades thirteen through fifteen excluded women. The CSC, however, had no power to forbid agency heads from making requests by sex. Except for a brief interlude in the early 1930s, an 1870 law had been interpreted to mean that the president could not prohibit an agency head within the civil service from designating whether he preferred a male or a female for a given position. The president's commission suggested a reexamination of the statute at its first meeting, and on April 9, 1962, it requested a ruling from the attorney general on the long-standing interpretation of the law.[31]

When the attorney general proffered the desired reinterpretation, that the president could indeed stop the discriminatory practice, President Kennedy responded immediately. He directed John Macy, chairman of the CSC, to ensure "that selection for any career position will be made solely on the basis of ability to meet the requirements of the position, and without regard to sex." Macy was to provide "Government-wide leadership" to investigate and eliminate discriminatory practices, even in agencies not subject to civil service jurisdiction.[32] The order itself could hardly guarantee equal opportunities for women in the civil service, but it opened the way for monitoring and enforcement in the future. More important, the policy statement constituted a significant symbol and a standard against which the government's performance could be measured.

Peterson also used the president's commission to advance the cause of the other single most important item on her agenda for women—equal pay legislation. Even before the president's commission was launched, Peterson had concerned herself with the problem of moving an equal pay bill through the Congress. Without detailing a full history of the passage of the Equal Pay Act, it can be stated in sum that the efforts of the Women's Bureau, under Peterson, successfully broke the eighteen-year legislative stalemate by a combination of data-gathering and lobbying. President Kennedy signed the bill on June 10, 1963. An amendment to the Fair Labor Standards Act, the Equal Pay Act stipulated that employers involved in interstate commerce could no longer discriminate among employees on the basis of sex by paying unequal wages for jobs which require "equal skill, effort and responsibility and which are performed under similar working conditions." Compromises resulted in the exclusion from coverage of large numbers of women and the substitution of "equal" work for "comparable" work. Furthermore, "equal pay for equal work" could mean little to the majority of women who were working in sexually segregated occupations. Still, the new law represented the first federal antidiscrimination legislation enacted specifically on behalf of women and directed toward private employers.[33]

Although its focus was narrow, the Equal Pay Act marked the entrance of the federal government into the field of safeguarding the right of women to hold employment on the same basis as men. Traditionally, the business community had justified paying women less by claiming that women worked for "pin money," not to support their families. By making wage discrimination illegal, the federal government undermined this view and implicitly supported the contention that paid employment was consonant with a woman's obligations as wife and mother. The federal government's acceptance of responsibility for ensuring women equitable treatment represented a new commitment.

The combined initiatives of the president's commission and of women in the government, including Peterson, led to innovations in other areas during Kennedy's administration. The Congress enacted legislation in 1962 to assist states in setting up day-care facilities and in May 1963 appropriated $800,000 for that purpose, the first such expenditure since World War II. The president's commission convinced Secretary of Defense Robert McNamara to submit legislation removing statutory restrictions on the number of women officers in the military, a problem the Defense Advisory Council on Women in the Services had hitherto been unable to resolve.[34] Both steps, however small in themselves, indicated a growing recognition on the federal government's part that women's sphere outside the home was expanding.

While advocating enlargement of women's roles, however, the president's commission took care to acknowledge the importance of women's traditional responsibilities. Conflict between the desire and/or need of women to work and the ideal of women at home as wives and mothers resulted in ambivalence, which pervaded the commission's discussions and reports, about a woman's right to define her role. The commission's most frequent justification for promoting opportunities for women in the work force rested on the premise that women needed to work to support their families. All concurred that a woman whose family required her earnings to make ends meet had ample reason to secure employment. Yet, in a burgeoning consumer society, where a college education was soon to be considered the birthright of every child, the concept of "need" broadened to include most working women. By advocating the provision of day-care facilities and rejecting discrimination in favor of male "heads of households," the president's commission certainly appeared to many to be encouraging married women to work. Although the commission attempted to avoid such an implication, it found it difficult to do so.[35]

On October 11, 1963, the commission presented a sixty-page report that concluded its task. After two years of study and occasional meetings, the commission had culled numerous recommendations from its subcommittees. With virtual unanimity, it endorsed improving women's access to education, with benefit of skilled counseling; increasing child care services and aid to working mothers; encouraging equal employment opportunity and availability of part-time employment; securing additional financial benefits for low-income women; supporting equality of rights under the law—preferably under the Fifth and Fourteenth Amendments rather than the ERA; and increasing participation of women in government. It also asked the president to provide for continuing governmental action of behalf of women, and in response, on November 1, 1963, Kennedy established the Interdepartmental Committee on the Status of Women and the Citizens' Advisory Council on the Status of Women. These two groups were to evaluate progress made, provide counsel, and stimulate action.[36] The commission recognized the administration's failure to appoint large numbers of women to high positions, but it did not take an emphatic position on this issue.[37]

While advocating freedom of choice for women, the commission's recommendations proceeded from its view of their special function and characteristics as mothers and homemakers. The report maintained that "widening the choices for women beyond their doorstep does not imply neglect of their education for responsibilities in the home." At another point, the report cautioned that "experience is needed in determining what constitutes unjustified discrimination in the treatment of women workers"—an indication that, because women had special attributes, the commission could envision "justified" discrimination. The commissioners therefore did not endorse adding "sex" to Executive Order 10925, which barred discrimination by federal contractors on the basis of race, creed, color, or national origin. They explained that "discrimination based on sex . . . involves problems sufficiently different from discrimination based on the other factors listed." Their neglect of inequities facing women in the armed services and in the social security system followed from the same belief. Not surprisingly, the commission falied to explore its own assumptions about women, nor did it question the prevailing sex-role structure. It could not, therefore, address root causes of discrimination. In order to effect the moderate change the commissioners had in mind, such an examination was not necessary.[38]

When the commission presented its report to Kennedy, an aide, Myer Feldman, took advantage of the occasion to review the administration's actions in the interest of women. Apart from the commission, Feldman listed the equal pay law; increased coverage under the Fair Labor Standards Act (May 1961) to include retail workers, a large number of whom were women; the Consumer Advisory Council (established July 18, 1962, and headed by Helen G. Conoyer, dean of the School of Home Economics at Cornell University);[39] elimination of the quota system applied to officers in the armed forces; increased provision for day care under welfare statutes; and the new ruling regarding nondiscrimination in the federal civil service.[40] Appointment of women to high governmental and judicial posts was not among the achievements recounted.

The President's Commission on the Status of Women was the brainchild of a labor union woman. Because the labor movement had a history of attempting to achieve goals for women at least partially through federal legislation and executive action, a presidential commission seemed to Peterson and her colleagues to be an appropriate avenue for change. Kennedy, breaking with tradition, heeded the advice of a woman with a labor union background instead of one with political debts to repay by administrative appointment, and in 1961 federal policy toward women veered in a new direction.

The change was significant because the attempt to elevate women's position solely by appointing women to high governmental posts represented perforce a limited strategy. Women appointees in a period in which the status of women was low could not function on behalf of women, even if they wished to maintain their own credibility and to escape being labeled as merely token appointees. To say this is not to denigrate the motives of those interested in appointments for women. They believed that their route did assist women generally by providing female role models, and they also believed that women should have these opportunities in recognition of their own talents. The benefits, however, did not appear to filter down.[41]

The course that Kennedy followed constituted a potentially more fruitful one for advancing the status of women, although the events that ensued were unlikely to have been precisely what the members of the president's commission anticipated. The commission made it clear that it did not regard sexual discrimination to be in the same category as racial bias, and thereby in some respects it retarded effective action toward eradication. Nevertheless, the net effect of the list Feldman described was positive. The Equal Pay Act, civil service reform, and the establishment of the commission constituted early, if minor, successes that helped lead to the quest for more meaningful change.[42] The creation of the president's commission gave a new-found legitimacy to the struggle against discrimination based on sex and initiated a national discussion that continued into the

1980s. As Betty Friedan wrote in 1963, "the very existence of the President's Commission on the Status of Women, under Eleanor Roosevelt's leadership, creates a climate where it is possible to recognize and do something about discrimination against women, in terms not only of pay but of the subtle barriers to opportunity."[43]

Furthermore, as a result of the creation of the national commission, every state instituted similar commissions, which provided vehicles for the participation of many women who had not before been engaged in such issues. The Interdepartmental Committee on the Status of Women and the Citizens' Advisory Council on the Status of Women chose to host annual conventions of the state commissions, creating networks among their women members. The federal bodies sought to contain and direct the agenda, however, and as a consequence in 1966 a group of dissatisfied participants at the Third National Conference of Commissions on the Status of Women were impelled to form the National Organization for Women (NOW).[44]

NOW's founders recognized the intrinsic limitations of governmental bodies "to break through the silken curtain of prejudice and discrimination against women." They acknowledged a debt to the commissions, but indicated that they regarded their recommendations as inadequate and unfulfilled promises. "The excellent reports of the President's Commission on the Status of Women and of the State Commissions have not been fully implemented. . . . They have no power to enforce their recommendations. . . . The reports of these Commissions have, however, created a basis upon which it is now possible to build." The architects of NOW established the organization in order to commence "a civil rights movement for women" that would confront law and custom "to win for women the final right to be fully free and equal human beings." Among the crucial items on the new movement's agenda were "a different concept of marriage, an equitable sharing of the responsibilities of home and children and the economic burdens of their support"—in short, a transformation of sex roles.[45]

Had the women's movement not emerged, enactment of equal pay legislation, prohibition of the most obvious and blatant forms of sex discrimination within the federal government, and creation of federal panels on women's status could all quickly have become dead letters. The president's commission, which endorsed these preliminary reforms, neither predicted nor recommended a feminist indictment of the entire sex-role structure. Nevertheless, the initiators of these early moderate changes, however unwittingly, helped elicit just such a challenge.

NOTES

1. *Christian Science Monitor,* Dec. 15, 1961. The National Organization for Women, the first organized feminist group of the 1960s, was founded in June 1966. The commission also predated the publication of Betty Friedan, *The Feminine Mystique* (New York, 1963), customarily considered one of the earliest harbingers of the women's movement, by more than a year.

2. Protective labor legislation in this context refers to those laws which regulated the conditions under which women worked. Such statutes established the minimum wages women could be paid, the maximum number of hours they could labor, the largest amount of weight they could lift, how late at night they could work, and which occupations they could practice.

3. For a fuller discussion of the experience of the postwar period, see William Henry Chafe, *The American Woman: Her Changing Social, Economic and Political Roles, 1920–1970* (New York, 1972), 192–244; Lois W. Banner, *Women in Modern America: A Brief History* (New York, 1974); National Manpower Council, *Womanpower: A Statement by the National Manpower Council with Chapters by the Council Staff* (New York, 1957); Karen Anderson, "The Impact of World War II in the Puget Sound Area on the Status of Women and the Family" (Ph.D. diss., Duke University, 1976).

4. See the sources cited in 3. For a discussion of women and higher education in this period, see Marian E. Strobel, "Ideology and Women's Higher Education, 1945-1960" (Ph.D. diss., Duke University, 1976).

5. United States, Bureau of the Census, *Statistical Abstract of the United States, 1975* (Washington, 1975), 346–47. For a full examination of this phenomenon, see Valerie Kincade Oppenheimer, *The Female Labor Force in the United States: Demographic and Economic Factors Governing Its Growth and Changing Composition* (Berkeley, 1970).

6. The National Woman's party first proposed an Equal Rights Amendment (ERA) in 1923, which read: "Men and woman shall have equal rights throughout the United States and every place subject to its jurisdiction." The present wording—"Equality of rights under the law shall not be denied or abridged by the United States or by any State on account of sex"—was adopted in 1943. Chafe, *American Woman,* 112; Equal Rights Amendment Project, *The Equal Rights Amendment: A Bibliographic Study* (Westport, 1976), xiii-xiv; *Life and Labor Bulletin,* no. 113 (June 1950), "Miscellany, Congressional Testimony (Special Reports)," box 10, Papers of the Women's Joint Congressional Committee (Library of Congress).

7. See Judith Sealander, "The Women's Bureau, 1920–1950: Federal Reaction to Female Wage Earning" (Ph.D. diss., Duke University, 1977). Upon her retirement as director of the Women's Bureau in 1944, Mary Anderson became chair of the National Committee on Equal Pay, composed of representatives from interested women's groups.

8. Chafe, *American Woman,* 187-88; Minutes, 1947, box 8, Papers of the Women's Joint Congressional Committee; U.S. Congress, House, *A Bill to Establish a Commission on the Legal Status of Women in the United States, to Declare a Policy as to Distinctions Based on Sex, in Law and Administration, and for Other Purposes,* H.R. 2007, 80th Cong., 1st sess., 1947. The House held hearings on the ERA in 1945 and 1948; the Senate, in 1945 and 1956. Although attention to the ERA

waned during the 1950s, the pressure of active party women led both national party platforms to endorse the amendment (with no tangible results) in every presidential election year. See Loretta J. Blahna, "The Rhetoric of the Equal Rights Amendment" (Ph.D. diss., Duke University, 1976).

9. National Manpower Council, *Womanpower*, 6. The National Manpower Council, a group of sixteen, comprising educators, business people, labor union officials, and journalists, was established at Columbia University under a grant from the Ford Foundation in 1951. At the time of the *Womanpower* study, the council included one woman.

10. Alice K. Leopold to the Undersecretary [James T. O'Connell], April 15, 1957, "Women," box 5, Papers of Millard Cass, Records of the Office of the Secretary of Labor, RG 174 (National Archives).

11. "Equal Pay—Administration Support," Jan. 24, 1961, Equal Pay—1961 folder, box 7, Office Files (Women's Bureau, Department of Labor, Washington).

12. Despite common beliefs concerning the lack of effectiveness of presidential commissions in general, a study by Thomas R. Wolanin, *Presidential Advisory Commissions: Truman to Nixon* (Madison, 1975), reaches a different conclusion. Wolanin evaluated all the commissions appointed by the five presidents, and concluded that 58 percent led to substantial government actions. Even this figure is low, however, because of the inclusion of President Richard M. Nixon who departed from tradition by paying much less attention to the commissions he created than had his predecessors. John F. Kennedy's response to his commissions was very supportive. Wolanin's judgment on the President's Commission on the Status of Women, which he claims was less effective than Kennedy's other commissions, fails to take into account actions taken during the life of the commission, looking only at responses to final reports.

13. Joseph P. Lash, *Eleanor: The Years Alone* (New York, 1972), p. 312.

14. India Edwards, *Pulling No Punches: Memoirs of a Woman in Politics* (New York, 1977); Republican National Committee, News Release, July 30, 1953, General Correspondence, 1953–54, box 2, India Edwards Papers (Harry S. Truman Library, Independence, Mo.).

15. Margaret Price to John F. Kennedy, Dec. 8, 1960, "Women—Role in Government," box 1072, Pre-Presidential Papers (John F. Kennedy Library, Waltham, Mass.).

16. Emma Guffey Miller to John F. Kennedy, Feb. 21, 1961, PL9, box 696, White House Central Files, *ibid*. See also Muriel Ferris to Lawrence P. O'Brien et al., May 15, 1961, HU3, box 374, *ibid*.

17. Karen Keesling and Suzanne Cavanagh, "Women Presidential Appointees Serving or Having Served in Full-Time Positions Requiring Senate Confirmation 1912–1977," report no. 78-73G, March 23, 1978, Congressional Research Service (Library of Congress). Oveta Culp Hobby served as secretary of health, education, and welfare from 1953 to 1955, and Frances Perkins held the position of secretary of labor from 1933 to 1945. Clayton Fritchey to John F. Kennedy, July 7, 1963, HU3, box 364, White House Central Files (Kennedy Library); President's Commission on the Status of Women, transcript of the meeting of Oct. 2, 1962, Washington, D.C., 252–53 (Women's Bureau). For 1951–1952, women held 79 of 3,273 appointments; for 1958–1959, 84 of 3,491; and for 1961–1962, 93 of 3,807.

18. Edwards, *Pulling No Punches,* 231–32, 252; Miller to Katie Louchheim, Jan. 26, 1963, Department of State Letters of Congratulations M-Z 1962, box C17, Katie S. Louchheim Papers (Library of Congress).

19. G. Calvin Mackenzie, *The Politics of Presidential Appointments* (New York, 1981), pp. 23–33, 84, 198, 255–59; Telephone interview with Dan Fenn, Jr., May 15, 1981, Boston, Mass.

20. Mackenzie, *The Politics of Presidential Appointments,* pp. 84, 196–97, 209; India Edwards to John F. Kennedy, Apr. 8, 1962, Office of Women's Activities, DNC, box 2, Kenneth O'Donnell to India Edwards, Apr. 10, 1962, 1960 clipping material and correspondence, box 1, India Edwards Papers, (Lyndon Baines Johnson Library, Austin, Tex.); *New York Times,* May 23, 1962; Theodore C. Sorensen, *Kennedy* (New York, 1965), 124–25. Myer Feldman, a Kennedy aide, has asserted that Margaret Price and President Kennedy "enjoyed an excellent relationship," but her influence with respect to women remains obscure. Myer Feldman to Cynthia E. Harrison, Oct. 3, 1979, letter in Harrison's possession. Note also that, by the time Price took over, the Women's Division of the Democratic National Committee had been abolished as a separate entity.

21. Sorensen, *Kennedy,* 123–24; Esther Peterson, telephone interview with Harrison, Oct. 4, 1974; Peterson, interview with Harrison, Washington, D.C., Feb. 27, 1978.

22. Miller to Louchheim, Jan. 20, 1962, Department of State Letters of Congratulations M-Z 1962.

23. Sorenson, *Kennedy,* 439–41. For an argument that the Women's Bureau had been handicapped by the political clumsiness of its directors virtually since its inception, see Sealander, "Women's Bureau."

24. *Washington Post,* Oct. 25, 1960; Peterson to Arthur Goldberg, June 2, 1961, FG 737, box 206, White House Central Files (Kennedy Library). Peterson later became an active supporter of ERA.

25. Executive Order 10980, Dec. 14, 1961, 3 C.F.R. (1959–1963), 500–01.

26. For a complete list of participants, see *American Women: Report of the President's Commission on the Status of Women,* 1963 (Washington, D.C., 1963), 77–85. Edwards, *Pulling No Punches,* 231–32. Mary Hilton, who had served as Chief of the Research Division of the Women's Bureau from 1949 to 1955, was designated Katherine Ellickson's "Special Assistant."

27. President's Commission on the Status of Women, transcript of the meeting of Feb. 12, 1962, Washington, D.C., 51–53 (Women's Bureau).

28. *Ibid.,* 131–32; Minutes of the First Meeting—Feb. 12–13, 1962, President's Commission on the Status of Women (PCSW) Document 18, Papers of the President's Commission on the Status of Women (Women's Bureau); Committee on Civil and Political Rights of the President's Commission on the Status of Women, interim report, April 11, 1963, p. 17, Papers of the President's Commission on the Status of Women, folder 21–22 (Kennedy Library); *American Women,* 44–45; President's Commission on the Status of Women, transcript of the meeting of April 24, 1963, Washington, D.C., 461–62 (Women's Bureau).

29. Katherine Pollack Ellickson, "The President's Commission on the Status of Women: Its Formation, Functioning, and Contribution," Jan. 1976, p. 12 (Walter P. Reuther Library, Wayne State University, Detroit, Mich.).

30. *American Women,* 37.

31. "Employment Policies and Practices of the Federal Government," PCSW Document 17, Papers of the President's Commission on the Status of Women (Women's Bureau). The 1870 law reads: "Women may, in the direction of the head of any department, be appointed to any of the clerkships therein authorized by law, upon the same requisites and conditions, and with the same compensations as are prescribed for men." Executive Departments and Government Officers and Employees, 5 U.S.C. sec. 33 (1958). Interestingly, Herbert Hoover had issued an order prohibiting selection by sex, but his ruling was reversed by Franklin D. Roosevelt at the request of Mary Anderson, director of the Women's Bureau. Anderson feared that, because of the preference given to veterans in the civil service, women would never be hired if agency heads could not specify sex. See Mary Anderson, *Women at Work: The Autobiography of Mary Anderson as Told to Mary N. Winslow* (Minneapolis, 1951), 153. Committee on Federal Employment Policies and Practices of the President's Commission on the Status of Women, "Activities since April 9, 1962," Document 1, Papers of the President's Commission on the Status of Women (Women's Bureau).

32. Robert F. Kennedy to John F. Kennedy, June 14, 1962, John F. Kennedy to Eleanor Roosevelt, June 15, 1962, file 4526, and John W. Macy (form letter), July 24, 1962, file 4644, Eleanor Roosevelt Papers (Franklin D. Roosevelt Library, Hyde Park, N.Y.).

33. Fair Labor Standards Act of 1938, as amended, 29 U.S.C. sec. 206, subsec. d (1964). Judith Hole and Ellen Levine assert that "some activists consider the Equal Pay Act the only law dealing with sex discrimination that is anywhere near properly enforced." Judith Hole and Ellen Levine, *Rebirth of Feminism* (New York, 1971), 29.

34. *New York Times,* May 15, 1963; "Status of Women under Proposed Legislation Regulating from the Bolte Committee Report," May 18, 1962, file 4644, Eleanor Roosevelt Papers; and Robert S. McNamara to Eleanor Roosevelt, July 10, 1962, *ibid.*

35. See, for example, *American Women,* 17, and *Report of the Committee on Home and Community to the President's Commission on the Status of Women* (Washington, 1963), 31.

36. *American Women;* Executive Order 11126, 3 C.F.R. (1959-1963), 791-93.

37. *American Women,* 52.

38. *Ibid.,* 10, 16, 30.

39. *New York Times,* Jan. 19, 1962.

40. Feldman to John F. Kennedy, Oct. 9, 1963, FG 737, box 206, White House Central Files (Kennedy Library).

41. For a discussion of women in appointive positions, see Elsie L. George, "The Women Appointees of the Roosevelt and Truman Administrations: A Study of Their Impact and Effectiveness" (Ph.D. diss., American University, 1972).

42. Thomas J. Morain, "The Emergence of the Women's Movement, 1960-1970" (Ph.D. diss., University of Iowa, 1974), cites Murray Edelman's thesis that "success in achieving a political objective leads to demands for larger amounts of the same benefits" to support his argument that the equal pay law and civil service reform influenced later developments in a positive way. See also Murray Edelman, *The Symbolic Uses of Politics* (Chicago, 1964).

43. Betty Friedan, *The Feminine Mystique* (New York, 1974), 361.

44. The analysis of the impact of the president's commission on the formation of NOW and the rise of the women's movement was developed by Jo Freeman. See Jo Freeman, *The Politics of Women's Liberation* (New York, 1975), 44–70. Freeman focuses on the development of networks, the compilation of data, and the creation of a "climate of expectations." Hole and Levine stated that the "Commission's existence and its report created the political and psychological framework for the growth of the current women's rights movement." Hole and Levine, *Rebirth of Feminism*, 402. NOW, of course, represented only one branch of the women's movement. For a discussion of the genesis of the women's liberation groups arising from the new left, see Freeman, *Politics of Women's Liberation*, 44–70, and Sara Evans, *Personal Politics: The Roots of Women's Liberation in the Civil Rights Movement and the New Left* (New York, 1979).

45. National Organization for Women, "Statement of Purpose (1966)," in *Up From the Pedestal: Selected Writings in the History of American Feminism*, ed. Aileen S. Kraditor (Chicago, 1968), 363–69.

～23～

THE PARADOX OF PROGRESS

WILLIAM H. CHAFE

Although historians have largely neglected the role of women in America's past, few groups in the population merit closer study as a barometer of how American society operates. Not only do women comprise a majority of the population, but gender—together with race and class—serves as one of the principal reference points around which American society is organized. The sociologist Peter Berger has observed that "identity is socially bestowed, socially sanctioned and socially transformed," and gender has been one of the enduring foundations on which social identity has rested. It has provided the basis for dividing up the labor of life ("breadwinning" versus "homemaking"), it has been central to the delineation of roles and authority in the family, and it has served as the source for two powerful cultural stereotypes—"masculine" and "feminine." Any change in the nature of male and female roles thus automatically affects the home, the economy, the school, and perhaps above all, the definition of who we are as human beings.[1]

When the nation entered the Depression decade of the 1930s, few people anticipated any major shift in the status of American women. Although the Nineteenth Amendment had enfranchised women in 1920, the ensuing years witnessed none of the revolutionary changes predicted by either proponents or detractors of the suffrage campaign. Many women who were eligible to vote did not register, and those women who did go to the polls generally cast their ballots for the same candidates as their husbands and fathers. The suffragists had optimist-

From *Paths to the Present,* James T. Patterson, ed. (Minneapolis: Burgess Publishing Co., 1975), pp. 8–24. Reprinted by permission.

ically assumed that women would think, act, and vote together as an independent "bloc," but that assumption underestimated the depth and pervasiveness of traditional ideas on woman's "place." Most Americans had grown up believing that within the family fathers and husbands exercised ultimate authority, particularly regarding issues of a "worldly" nature. Thus it seemed perfectly natural that women should follow the lead of men in political or other nondomestic affairs.[2]

Ratification of the suffrage amendment also failed to produce any significant change in the economic opportunities or activities of women. Although the absolute *number* of women in the labor force increased as the population grew, the *proportion* of women at work shifted very little and in 1940 was approximately the same (25 percent) as it had been in 1910. In addition, women made few inroads into the occupational area of greatest interest to feminists—business and the professions. Three out of four new career women in the 1920s and 1930s went into teaching or nursing (already defined as "women's work"), and the percentage of women in male-dominated professions such as law or medicine either remained constant or declined (as late as the 1940s most medical schools had a 5 percent quota on female admissions).[3]

Here too, the principal reason for the absence of change was the persistence of social norms which prescribed separate and segregated spheres of activities for men and women. Since women were expected to make marriage their career, few businessmen showed any interest in training them for management positions. "The highest profession a woman can engage in," one executive wrote, "is that of a charming wife and wise mother." For most people the idea of combining marriage *and* a career was too radical to consider, first because such a notion flew in the face of prevailing beliefs about a woman's primary responsibility, and second because it required a restructuring of the family, with men assuming some of the tasks of cooking, child-care, and homemaking. In light of such a situation, Margaret Mead observed, a woman with career ambitions had to make a choice between irreconcilable alternatives. She could either be "a woman and therefore less an achieving individual, or an achieving individual and therefore less a woman." If she chose the second alternative, she took the risk of losing any opportunity to be "a loved object, the kind of girl whom men will woo and boast of, toast and marry." It was not surprising, then, that most women traveled the prescribed path and decided not to pursue careers, or continue work after marriage.[4]

If anything, the experience of the Depression decade accentuated the difficulty of altering the status of women. Although the Depression encouraged innovations in politics and social welfare policy, it also seemed to have a chastening effect on cultural values, calling people back to the tried and true verities of family, hearth, and home. Nowhere was this better illustrated than in attitudes toward women. Labor, business, and government undertook a concerted campaign to discourage women from taking jobs, especially married women whose employment might deprive an able-bodied man of a job to support his family. At the same time, women's magazines celebrated the virtues of homemaking and lambasted those women who sought careers or employment. "No matter how successful," one article declared, "the office woman. . . . is a transplanted posey. . . . Just as a rose comes to its fullest beauty in its own appropriate soil, so does a home woman come to her fairest blooming when her roots are stuck deep in the daily and hourly affairs of her own most dearly beloved." Perhaps most important, the American people seemed to agree. When the pollster George Gallup asked whether wives should work if their husbands were employed, 82 percent said no, including more than 75 percent of the women.[5]

The eruption of World War II made the first significant dent in this pattern. The national emergency caused new industries to develop and new jobs to open up, providing an opportunity for women, like other excluded groups, to improve their economic position. Almost overnight, the woman munition worker became an accepted part of the labor force. In one California aircraft plant, 13,000 men and no women had been employed in the fall of 1941. A year later there were 13,000 women and 11,000 men. The same story was repeated throughout the nation. The New York Central Railroad doubled the number of its female employees, assigning them to grease and oil locomotives, load baggage, and work on section gangs. Elsewhere, women riveted gun emplacements, welded hatches, took the place of lumberjacks in downing huge redwoods, became precision toolmakers, and ran giant overhead cranes. Hardly a job existed which women did not perform.

The statistics of female employment suggest the dimensions of the change. Between 1941 and 1945 6.5 million women took jobs, increasing the size of the female labor force by 57 percent. At the end of 1940 approximately 25 percent of all women were gainfully employed; four years later the figure had soared to 36 percent—an increase greater than that of the previous forty years combined. Perhaps most important from a social point of view, the largest number of new workers were married and middle-aged. Prior to 1940 young and single women had made up the vast majority of the female labor force. During the war, in contrast, 75 percent of the new workers were married, and within four years the number of wives in the labor force had doubled. Although some of the new labor recruits were newlyweds who might have been expected to work in any event, the majority listed themselves as former housewives and many, including 60 percent of those hired by the War Department, had children of school and preschool age. By the time victory was achieved, it was just as likely that a wife over forty would be employed as a single woman under twenty-five. The urgency of defeating the Axis powers had swept away, temporarily at least, one of America's entrenched customs.[6]

If women took jobs in unprecedented numbers, however, there was little evidence of a parallel shift in attitudes toward equality between the sexes. Women were consistently excluded from top policy-making committees concerned with running the war, and from higher-level management and executive positions. In addition, the war had only a minimal effect on the traditional disparity between men's and women's wages. Although the War Manpower Commission announced a firm policy of equal pay for equal work, enforcement was spotty, and employers continued to pay women less than men simply by changing the description of the job from "heavy" to "light." As a result, a woman inspector in one plant earned 55 cents an hour while her male counterpart was paid $1.20.[7]

The issue of establishing day care centers provided the most revealing example of enduring attitudes. If women were to be equals with men in the labor market, they required some relief from the burden of sole responsibility for homemaking and child-rearing. Government reports showed a direct correlation between female absenteeism and the need to stay at home and care for youngsters, and newspapers were full of stories of children being exiled to neighborhood movie houses while their parents worked. Yet for many Americans, there was no more sacred obligation than that of a woman to rear her children on a full-time basis. "Now, as in peacetime," the Children's Bureau declared, "a mother's primary duty is to her home and children. This duty is one she cannot lay aside, no matter what the emergency." As a result of the profound value conflict over the issue, a federal day care program was at first postponed, then prevented from becoming fully effective.[8]

The staying power of traditional values received vigorous confirmation in the postwar years. Despite effusive expressions of gratitude for women's contribution to the war effort, many Americans believed that women should return to their rightful place in the home as soon as the war had ended. In one of the most popular treatises of the postwar years, Ferdinand Lundberg and Marynia Farnham argued that female employment was a feminist conspiracy to seduce women into betraying their biological destiny. The independent woman, they claimed, was a "contradiction in terms." Women were born to be soft, nurturant, and dependent on men; motherhood represented the true goal of female life. Sounding the same theme, Agnes Meyer wrote in the *Atlantic* that though women had many careers, "they have only one vocation—motherhood." The task of modern women, she concluded, was to "boldly announce that no job is more exacting, more necessary, or more rewarding than that of housewife and mother." Most Americans seemed to agree. A series of public opinion polls taken in the postwar years showed that a large majority of people continued to subscribe to the idea of a sharp division of labor between the sexes, with husbands making the "big" decisions and wives caring for the home.[9]

In fact, the situation was more complicated than either public opinion polls or magazine rhetoric seemed to indicate. It was one thing to focus renewed attention on traditional values, and quite another to eradicate the impact of four years of experience. As observers noted at the time, women had discovered something new about themselves in the course of the war, and many were unwilling to give up that discovery just because the war had ended. Although most of the women workers viewed their employment as temporary when the war began, a Women's Bureau survey disclosed that by war's end, 75 percent wished to remain in the labor force. "War jobs have uncovered unsuspected abilities in American women," one worker commented. "Why lose all these abilities because of a belief that 'a woman's place is in the home'? For some it is, for others not."[10]

The prospect of a job appealed particularly to those women over thirty-five. According to the 1940 Census, the average woman married at age twenty-one and sent her last child off to school when she was thirty-five. With the children out of the house most of the day, many middle-aged women were free to join, or remain in, the labor force. Economic interest in augmenting family income was matched by personal interest in pursuing new activities. Many women workers relished the recognition and sense of accomplishment associated with a job. Work in a factory or office might not seem that much more exciting or fulfilling than washing dishes or cleaning floors, but it had the advantage of providing social companionship, a tangible reward in the form of a paycheck, and contact with the "outside" world.

To a surprising extent, these women succeeded in their desire to remain in the job market. Although the number of women workers declined temporarily in the period immediately after the war, female employment figures showed a sharp upturn beginning in 1947, and by 1950 had once again reached wartime peaks. By 1960 the number of women workers was growing at a rate four times faster than that of men, and 40 percent of all women over sixteen were in the labor force compared to 25 percent in 1940. More important, the women who spearheaded the change were from the same groups that had first gone to work in the war. By 1970, 45 percent of the nation's wives were employed (compared to 11.5 percent in 1930 and 15 percent in 1940), and the 1970 figure included 51 percent of all mothers with children aged six to seventeen. In addition, the economic background of the women workers had shifted significantly. During the 1930s employment of married women had been limited almost exclusively to families with poverty level incomes. By 1970, in contrast, 60 percent of all families with an income of more than $10,000 had wives who worked. In short, the whole pattern of female employment had been reversed. Through legitimizing employment for the average wife and making it a matter of patriotic necessity, the war had initiated a dramatic alteration in the behavior of women and had permanently changed the day-to-day content of their lives.[11]

But if the "objective" conditions of female employment changed so much, why did attitudes toward equality not follow suit? Why, if so many wives and mothers were holding jobs, was there so little protest about continued low pay and discrimination? Why, above all, did the woman's movement not revive in the forties or fifties instead of developing only in the late sixties? Such questions have no easy answers, but to the extent that an explanation is possible, it has to do with the context of the times. The prospect for value changes in any period depends on the frame of reference of the participants, their awareness of the possibility or need for action, and the dominant influences at work in shaping the society. When the appropriate conditions are present, change can be explosive. When they are not present, change can take on the character of an underground fire—important in the long run but for the moment beneath the surface. The latter description fits the situation of women in the forties and fifties and a consideration of the context in which their employment increased during these years is crucial to an understanding of the relationship between behavior and attitudes.

To begin with, most women in the forties and fifties lacked the frame of reference from which to challenge prevailing attitudes on sex roles. Although many women worked, the assumptions about male and female spheres of responsibility were so deeply engrained that to question them amounted to heresy. If social values are to be changed, there must be a critical mass of protestors who can provide an alternative ideology and mobilize opposition toward traditional points of view. In the postwar period, that protest group did not exist. Feminists at the time simply had no popular support and were generally viewed as a group of cranky women who constituted a "lunatic fringe." The Women's Bureau probably represented the views of the majority of the population in 1945 when it described feminists as "a small but militant group of leisure class women [giving vent] to their resentment at not having been born men."[12]

In such a situation, it was not surprising that most women workers exhibited little feminist consciousness. Most had taken jobs because of the benefits associated with employment, not out of a desire to compete with men or prove their equality. When a pattern of discrimination is so pervasive that it is viewed as part of the rules of the game, few individuals will have the wherewithal to protest. It takes time and an appropriate set of social conditions before a basis for ideological protest can develop. With their experience in World War II, women had gone through the first stage of a monumental change. But it would be unrealistic to think that they could move immediately into a posture of feminist rebellion without a series of intervening stages. New perceptions had to evolve; new ideas had to gain currency. And both depended to some extent on the dominant influences at work in the immediate environment.

The second reason for the persistence of traditional attitudes was that women's employment expanded under conditions which emphasized women's role as "helpmates." The continued entry of women into the labor force was directly related to skyrocketing inflation and the pent-up desire of millions of families to achieve a higher living standard. In many instances, husbands and wives could not build new homes, buy new appliances, or purchase new cars on one income alone, and the impulse not to be left behind in the race for affluence offered a convenient rationale for women to remain in the labor force. Men who might oppose in theory the idea of married women holding jobs were willing to have their own wives go to work to help the family achieve its middle-class aspirations. But under such circumstances, the wife who held a job was playing a supportive role, not striking out on her own as an "independent" woman. The distinction was crucial. If women had been taking jobs because of a desire to prove their equality with men, their employment would probably have encountered bitter resistance. In contrast, the fact that they were thought to be only "helping out" made it possible for their efforts to receive social sanction as a fulfillment of their traditional family role.

To say that attitudes did not change, however, did not mean that behavior was without important long-range effects. Indeed, the growing employment of women offers an excellent example of the way in which changes in behavior can pave the way for subsequent changes in attitudes. As more and more wives joined the labor force after 1940, the sexual segregation of roles and responsibilities within the family gradually gave way to greater sharing. Sociological surveys showed that wherever wives held jobs, husbands performed more household tasks, especially in the areas of child care, cleaning, and shopping. In addition, power relationships between men and women underwent some change. Women who worked exercised considerably more influence on "major" economic decisions than wives who did not work. In no instance did the changes result in total equality, nor were they ideologically inspired; but sociologists unanimously concluded that women's employment played a key role in modifying the traditional distribution of tasks and authority within the family.[13]

Similarly, the presence of an employed mother exercised a substantial impact on the socialization patterns of children. Young boys and girls who were raised in households where both parents worked grew up with the expectation that women—as well as men—would play active roles in the outside world. A number of surveys of children in elementary and junior high school showed that daughters of working mothers planned to work themselves after marriage, and the same studies suggested that young girls were more likely to name their mother as the person they most admired if she worked than if she did not work. At the same time, it appeared that these daughters developed a revised idea of what it meant to be born female. On a series of personality tests, daughters of working mothers scored lower on scales of traditional femininity and agreed that both men and women should enjoy a variety of work, household, and recreational experiences. Thus if behavioral change did not itself produce a challenge to traditional attitudes, it set in motion a process which prepared a foundation for such a challenge.[14]

All that was required to complete the process was the development of an appropriate context, and in the early 1960s that context began to emerge. After eight years of consolidation and consensus in national politics during the Eisenhower administration, a new mood of criticism and reform started to surface in the nation. Sparked by the demands of black Americans for full equality, public leaders focused new attention on a whole variety of problems which had been festering for years. Poverty, racial injustice, and sex discrimination had a lengthy history in America, but awareness of them crystallized in a climate which emphasized the need for activism to eradicate the nation's ills. Once the process of protest had begun, it generated a momentum of its own, spreading to groups which previously had been quiescent.

Again, the experience of women dramatized the process of change. Just as World War II had served as a catalyst to behavioral change among women, the ferment of the sixties served as a catalyst to ideological change. The first major sign of the impending drive for women's liberation appeared with the publication in 1963 of Betty Friedan's best-selling *The Feminine Mystique*. Writing with eloquence and passion, Friedan traced the origins of women's oppression to a social system which persistently denied women the opportunity to develop their talents as individual human beings. "The core of the problem of women today," she wrote, "is not sexual but a problem of identity—a stunting or evasion of growth. . . ." Friedan pointed out that while men had abundant opportunities to test their mettle, women saw their entire lives circumscribed by the condition of their birth and were told repeatedly "that they could desire no greater destiny than to glory in their own femininity." If a woman had aspirations for a career, she was urged instead to find a full measure of satisfaction in the role of housewife and mother. Magazines insisted that there was no other route to happiness; consumer industries glorified her life as homemaker; and psychologists warned her that if she left her position in the home, the whole society would be endangered. The result was that she was imprisoned in a "comfortable concentration camp," prevented from discovering who she really *was* by a society which told her only what she *could be*. Although Friedan's assessment contained little that had not been said before by other feminists, her book spoke to millions of women in a fresh way, driving home the message that what had previously been perceived as only a personal problem was in fact a *woman* problem, shared by others and rooted in a set of social attitudes that required change if a better life was to be achieved.[15]

A second—and equally important—influence feeding the woman's movement came from the burgeoning drive for civil rights. Although it was true that blacks and women had strikingly different problems, they suffered from modes of oppression which in some ways were similar. For women as well as blacks, the denial of equality occurred through the assignment of separate and unequal roles. Both were taught to "keep their place," and were excluded from social and economic opportunities on the grounds that assertive behavior was deviant. The principal theme of the civil rights movement was the immorality of treating any human being as less equal than another on the basis of a physical characteristic, and that theme spoke as much to the condition of women as to that of blacks. In its tactics, its message, and its moral fervor, the civil rights movement provided inspiration and an organizational model for the activities of women.

Just as significant, the civil rights movement exposed many women to the direct experience of sex discrimination. Younger activists in particular found that they frequently were treated as servants whose chief function was to be sex partners for male leaders. ("The place of women in the movement," Stokely Carmichael said, "is prone.") Instead of having an equal voice in policy-making, women were relegated to tasks such as making coffee or sweeping floors. Faced with such discrimination, some female activists concluded that they had to free *themselves* before they could work effectively for the freedom of others. The same women became the principal leaders of the younger, more radical segment of women's liberation, taking the organizing skills and ideological fervor which they had learned in the fight for blacks and applying them to the struggle for women.[16]

Perhaps the most important precondition for the revival of feminism, however, was the amount of change which had already occurred in women's lives. As long as the overwhelming majority of women remained in the home, there was no frame of reference from which to question the status quo. Woman's "place" was a fact as well as an idea. With the changes which began in World War II, on the other hand, reality ceased to conform to attitudes. The march of events had already delivered a fatal blow to conventional ideas on woman's place, thereby creating a condition which made feminist arguments both timely and relevant. The experience of *some* change gave millions of women the perspective which allowed them to hear the feminists call for more change. Thus if the women who took jobs during the forties did not themselves mount an ideological assault on the status quo, they prepared a foundation which enabled the subsequent generation to take up the battle for a change in attitudes and ideas.

With the convergence of these forces, the drive for women's liberation surged to national prominence in the late sixties. Like all social movements, the quest for sex equality assumed a variety of political and ideological forms. The more moderate activists found an organizational shelter in the National Organization of Women (NOW), formed in 1966 by Betty Friedan to spearhead the drive for legal and economic reforms. The younger, more radical segment of the movement took root in female cadres of student organizations like SDS and SNCC. Beginning with "consciousness-raising" sessions in which women discussed the common problems they had encountered on the basis of their sex, these more radical activists quickly developed a loose coalition of small cell groups which advocated a revolutionary transformation of society based upon a change in the status of women. Whatever their particular ideological stance, however, all feminists were united in demanding an end to class treatment, to the idea that women—as women—should automatically be expected to take minutes at meetings, get lower pay than men, wash dishes, get up with the baby at night, or place their aspirations behind those of their husbands. Within months, the movement had become a national sensation, its advocates storming professional meetings to demand equal employment opportunities, boycotting the Miss America contest to protest the treatment of women as sex objects, and demonstrating before state legislatures for the repeal of abortion laws. By 1970 the movement was one of the media's biggest news items, rivaling student demonstrations, inflation, and the war in Vietnam for public attention.[17]

The image projected by the mass media told only part of the story, however. While network television and national news magazines focused on splashy demonstrations or the movement's attitude toward lesbianism, women in countless towns and cities were organizing in small groups to consider the reality of discrimination in their own lives and devise a strategy to combat it. Although they never comprised more than a small minority in any community, such women engaged in a remarkable variety of activities and made up in impact what they lacked in numbers. Some joined local NOW chapters and pressured merchants and employers to stop treating women differently from men. Others organized for political action, published children's books which eliminated invidious sexual stereotypes, started abortion and birth control clinics, or established day care centers. Some observers criticized the movement for its lack of focus and organization, but its alleged weaknesses were actually the source of its greatest strength. By not becoming attached to a single issue or piece of legislation, the movement avoided the danger of rising or falling with one victory or defeat. And by emphasizing decentralization and diversity, it gave maximum leeway to the energies and interests of the local women who constituted its lifeblood.

Almost inevitably, the women's movement provoked hostility and controversy. Particularly in its more radical manifestations, it represented an effort to alter the nature of the family, to change the way in which children were raised, and to overthrow conventional attitudes concerning who should hold which jobs. Furthermore, at its foundation the movement was calling for men and women to fashion a new definition of human identity—one which no longer would rely on cultural preconceptions of masculinity and femininity. In the context of such ideas, it was not surprising that a large number of people reacted to the movement with dismay and anger. Many men felt that their authority, their strength, their whole self-image had come under attack. And many women, who had devoted their lives to fulfilling the culturally sanctioned role of homemaker, believed that the movement was judging and indicting them as failures.

The astonishing thing was that in the face of powerful opposition, a considerable change in attitudes did take place. Although opinion surveys in the early seventies showed that many women continued to harbor antagonism toward the movement *per se* ("it's too extreme," "it goes overboard"), the same women in a majority of cases endorsed positive action on feminist issues such as day care centers, repeal of abortion laws, equal career opportunities for women, and a greater sharing of household tasks. Whatever the acceptability of the movement as a movement, its message and ideas seemed to be filtering through. Younger women in particular gave evidence of standing up for their rights. Many women students declared that they were just as committed to careers as men, and announced that they intended to incorporate marriage into their overall work pattern rather than make it the chief end of their existence.[18]

The ultimate test of the movement's impact, of course, was whether the attitudes it espoused had any effect on the behavior of women. Here, the evidence suggested at least some correlation between the campaign to change values and the way in which women conducted their lives. In a survey of women students at a large urban university, two sociologists found that behavior and attitudes toward premarital sex changed significantly in the years after 1965. Prior to that time, rates of premarital intercourse conformed to the pattern established in the 1920s, with engaged women having the highest frequency of premarital sex. After 1965, in contrast, a major increase occurred in the number of women having intercourse while in a "dating" or "going steady" relationship. The same survey showed a sharp drop in guilt feelings related to sexual experience as compared to a similar study done in 1958. Marriage statistics too showed a substantial shift during the 1960s. By 1971 more than half of all women 20 years of age were single in contrast to only one-third in 1960, and the number of unmarried women in the 20–24 age bracket had climbed from 28 percent in 1960 to 37 percent a decade later.[19] If the number of female applicants for graduate study was any indicator, it would seem that some of these single women were postponing marriage in order to pursue a career. Although such developments did not necessarily reflect the overt influence of women's liberation, there seemed to be a common thread uniting the feminists' call for increased autonomy among women, and the growing tendency of younger women to seek professional training and exhibit greater independence in their approach to sex and marriage.

The change in women's roles had perhaps its greatest potential impact in the field of population growth, or demography. Beginning in the 1920s the birth rate went into a gradual decline, reaching a nadir in the midst of the Depression. Although demographers at the time predicted a continued low birth rate, the end of World War II produced a massive upsurge of births which lasted through the late fifties. There then ensued another downturn which in 1967 resulted in a birth rate of 17.9 live births per 1000 persons compared to 27.2 a decade earlier. Some experts believed that the shifts were strictly a function of the economy, with affluence explaining the "Baby Boom" in the fifties. But prosperity had also been cited as a rationale for the *declining* birth rate of the twenties, thereby calling into question its validity as a primary determinant. Others attributed the "Baby Bust" of the sixties to the development of oral contraceptives. But this explanation too had shortcomings. The "pill" had not been available during the low birth period of the thirties, and the decline in birth rate during the sixties had begun three years before the pill was marketed.

A somewhat more persuasive explanation traced the changes in the birth rate to a combination of previous demographic trends and economic developments. According to this analysis, the "Baby Boom" started when young couples began to have families which they had deferred during the war, and continued as the generation born in the twenties and thirties came of age in the midst of an expanding job market. Due to affluence, it was easy for such people to marry early and contemplate large families. By the 1960s, in contrast, a crowded labor market, unsettled social conditions, and the expense of raising families put a damper on the birth rate. Demographers confidently predicted, however, that the "Baby Boom" of the fifties would have an echo effect in the late sixties and seventies, when the children born twenty years earlier began to reproduce. The only problem with this theory was that it failed to anticipate—or explain—the continued decline of the birth rate after 1970. Rather than rising, the birth rate reached an all-time low in 1972 and 1973, achieving the reproduction level required for Zero Population Growth.[20]

Perhaps the best approach to the trends of the sixties and seventies is to see the birth rate as a product of economic and social forces interacting with cultural values. Clearly, it would be a mistake to discount the impact of economic conditions. Concern about the ability to provide for children frequently enters into the decision to limit the size of a family, especially in a time of recession. Similarly, the accessibility of contraceptives provides the means for implementing a decision after it is made. But a crucial variable which demographers have underestimated is the influence of cultural values. Seen in this light, the declining birth rate of the sixties and seventies can be traced to the "multiplier effect" of changing values and economic conditions. During the sixties, women married later, delayed the birth of their first child, and bore their last child at an earlier age. Whether as cause or effect, this trend coincided with many women finding careers and interests outside of the home. The rewards of having a job and extra money tended to emphasize the advantages of a small family and the freedom to travel, entertain, or pursue individual interests. This pattern, in turn, was reinforced during the late sixties by the ideology of feminism and the ecology movement. Two Gallup polls in 1967 and 1971 sharply revealed this shift in values. The earlier survey showed that 34 percent of women in the prime child-bearing years anticipated having four or more children. By 1971, in contrast, the figure had dropped to 15 percent. In the absence of more persuasive explanations, it would appear that female employment and changing attitudes toward the role of women played major parts in confounding the predictions of population experts and producing the low birth rates of the early seventies.[21] The ramifications of these forces—if they continue—promise to have a profound effect not only on the size of the family but, more important, on the roles of men and women within the home.

In the end, of course, the historian's judgment on change depends on the vantage point which he or she adopts. From one point of view, it can be argued that little progress has been made toward sex equality. Great problems remain, particularly in cultural assumptions about woman's "place." Yet, on balance, the trends in employment, marriage patterns, attitudes toward sex and careers, and the birth rate suggest that the world of women has altered greatly since 1930. As the nation entered the mid-seventies, it seemed that for the first time in thirty years, behavior and attitudes were reinforcing each other; and the direction of events indicated that changes in the family, the economy, and women's definition of themselves would continue to be dominant themes in the social history of modern America.

NOTES

1. Peter Berger, "Social Roles: Society in Man," in Dennis H. Wrong and Harry L. Grace, eds. *Readings in Introductory Sociology* (New York, 1967). For a much more detailed discussion of the material covered in this section, see William H. Chafe, *The American Woman: Her Changing Social, Economic and Political Roles, 1920–1970* (New York, 1972).

2. Emily Newell Blair, "Are Women a Failure in Politics?" *Harpers* CLI (October 1925), pp. 513–22; Stuart H. Rice and Malcolm Willey, "American Women's Ineffective Use of the Vote," *Current History* XX (July 1924), pp. 641–47; Seymour M. Lipset, *Political Man* (New York, 1963), pp. 209–11, 217, 221–23.

3. Janet Hooks, "Women's Occupations Through Seven Decades," *Women's Bureau Bulletin* No. 232 (Washington, D.C., 1951), p. 34; Willystine Goodsell, "The Educational Opportunities of American Women, Theoretical and Actual," *Annals* of the American Academy of Political and Social Science CXLIII (May 1929); Florence Lowther and Helen Downes, "Women in Medicine," *Journal of the American Medical Association*, October 13, 1945.

4. *Independent Woman* VI (October 1922); Mabel Lee, "The Dilemma of the Educated Woman," *Atlantic Monthly* CXLVI (November 1930), pp. 590–95; Margaret Mead, "Sex and Achievement," *Forum* XCIV (November 1935), pp. 301–3.

5. Claire Wallas Callahan, "A Woman With Two Jobs," *Ladies Home Journal* XLVII (October 1930), p. 114; "America Speaks, The National Weekly Poll of Public Opinion," November 15, 1936.

6. Katherine Glover, *Women at Work in Wartime* (Washington, D.C., 1943); "Women in Steel," *Life,* August 9, 1943; Eva Lapin, *Mothers in Overalls* (New York, 1943); "Changes in Women's Employment During the War," *Women's Bureau Bulletin* No. 20 (Washington, 1944); International Labor Organization, *The War and Women's Employment* (Montreal, 1946). See also Chafe, *American Woman,* pp. 135–50.

7. Florence Cadman, "Womanpower 4 F," *Independent Woman* XXII (September 1943); Women's Advisory Committee Archives, National Archives, Boxes 133–135; International Labor Organization, *The War and Women's Employment,* p. 221; Women's Bureau memorandum, October 9, 1945, folder entitled "Equal Pay—General," Women's Bureau Archives, Federal Record Center, Suitland, Maryland.

8. Helen Baker, *Women in War Industries* (Princeton, 1942); "Women Drop Out," *Business Week,* August 21, 1943; "More Child Care," *Business Week,* August 26, 1944; G. T. Allen, "Eight Hour Orphans," *Saturday Evening Post,* October 10, 1942; Katherine Lemoof, "The Children's Bureau Program for the Care of Children of Working Mothers," in Women's Bureau Archives.

9. Ferdinand Lundberg and Marynia Farnham, *Modern Woman, The Lost Sex* (New York, 1947); Agnes Meyer, "Women Aren't Men," *Atlantic* CLXXXVI (August 1950); Hadley Cantril, *Public Opinion, 1935–1946* (Princeton, 1951), p. 1047, The *Fortune* Survey, *Fortune* XXXIV (August and September 1946).

10. "Women Workers in Ten Production Areas and Their Postwar Employment Plans," *Women's Bureau Bulletin* No. 209 (Washington, D.C., 1946), p. 5; "Give Back Their Jobs," *Woman's Home Companion* LXX (October 1943), pp. 5–7.

11. National Manpower Council, *Womanpower* (New York, 1955); Elizabeth Baker, *Technology and Women's Work* (New York, 1964), vii; National Manpower Council, *Work in the Lives of Married Women* (New York, 1957), pp. 17, 72; *New York Times,* October 10, 1970; Elizabeth Waldman, "Changes in the Labor Force Activity of Women," *Monthly Labor Review* XCIII (June 1970).

12. Women's Bureau Memorandum, August 22, 1945, Women's Bureau Archives.

13. Mildred Weil, "An Analysis of the Factors Influencing Married Women's Actual or Planned Work Participation," *American Sociological Review* XVI (January 1951), pp. 91–96; Lois Hoffman, "Parental Power Relations and the Division of Household Tasks," in F. Ivan Nye and Lois Wladis Hoffman, eds. *The Employed Mother in America* (Chicago, 1963), pp. 215–30; Robert Blood, "The Husband-Wife Relationship," in Nye and Hoffman, pp. 282–305; Robert Hamblin and Robert Blood, "The Effect of the Wife's Employment on the Family Power Structure," *Social Forces* XXXVI (May 1958), pp. 347–52; David Heer, "Dominance and the Working Wife," *Social Forces* XXXVI (May 1958), pp. 341–47.

14. Ruth E. Hartley, "Children's Concepts of Male and Female Roles," *Merrill-Palmer Quarterly* VI (January 1959–60), pp. 83–91; Selma M. Matthews, "The Effect of Mothers' Out-of-Home Employment Upon Children's Ideas and Atti-

tudes," *Journal of Applied Psychology* XVIII (February 1954), pp. 116–36; Elizabeth Douvan, "Employment and the Adolescent," in Nye and Hoffman, pp. 142–64; Lois Hoffman, "Effects on Children: Summary and Discussion," in Nye and Hoffman, pp. 196–202.

15. Betty Friedan, *The Feminine Mystique* (New York, 1963), especially pp. 11, 69, 271–98.

16. Susan Brownmiller, "Sisterhood Is Powerful," *New York Times Magazine,* March 15, 1970; Allan Matusow, "From Civil Rights to Black Power: The Case of SNCC, 1960–1966," in Barton Bernstein and Allan Matusow, eds. *Twentieth Century America* (New York, 1969); Richard Gillam, "White Racism in the Civil Rights Movement," *Yale Review* LXII (Summer 1973), pp. 520–43.

17. Susan Brownmiller, "Sisterhood Is Powerful"; "Women's Lib: The War on Sexism," *Newsweek,* March 23, 1970; Robin Morgan, ed. *Sisterhood Is Powerful* (New York, 1970); *Notes From the Second Year* (New York, 1970).

18. *The Gallup Opinion Index,* September 1970, Report No. 63; Louis Harris and Associates, "The 1972 Virginia Slims American Woman's Opinion Poll: A Survey of the Attitudes of Women on Their Roles in Politics and the Economy"; Amy Hogue, "Women at Duke: Their Attitudes and Aspirations," unpublished honors paper, 1973; Adeline Levine and Janice Crumrine, "Women and the Fear of Success: A Problem in Replication," paper presented at the American Sociological Association Meeting, August 1973; *New York Times,* March 24, 1972.

19. Robert K. Bell and Jay B. Clarke, "Pre-marital Sexual Experience Among Coeds, 1958 and 1968," *Journal of Marriage and the Family* XXXII (February 1970), pp. 81–84; New York *Times,* November 5, 1971; "Birth Dearth," *Christian Century,* November 24, 1971.

20. Paul Woodring, "There'll Be Fewer Little Noses," *Saturday Review,* March 18, 1967; "End of Baby Boom," *Science Digest,* September 1967; "Falling Birthrate," *Scientific American,* April 1968; "Z.P.G.," *Scientific American,* April 1971; Lawrence A. Mayer, "Why the U.S. Population Isn't Exploding," *Fortune,* April 1967; "Levelling Off," *Scientific American,* February 1973; "The Surprising Decline in the Birth Rate," *Business Week,* June 3, 1972; Herman Miller, *Rich Man Poor Man,* p. 236; Conrad Taueber, "Population Trends and Characteristics," in Sheldon and Moore, pp. 27–76.

21. *New York Times,* February 21, 1972.

⮑ 24 ⮐

RADICAL FEMINISM AND
FEMINIST RADICALISM

ELLEN WILLIS

I was a radical feminist activist in the late 60s. Today I often have the odd feeling that this period, so vivid to me, occurred fifty years ago, not a mere fifteen. Much of the early history of the women's liberation movement, and especially of radical feminism, has been lost, misunderstood or distorted beyond recognition. The left, the right, and liberal feminists have all for their own reasons contributed to misrepresenting and trivializing radical feminist ideas. To add to the confusion, radical feminism in its original sense barely exists today. The great majority of women who presently call themselves "radical feminists" in fact subscribe to a politics more accurately labeled "cultural feminist." That is, they see the primary goal of feminism as freeing women from the imposition of so-called "male values," and creating an alternative culture based on "female values."

Cultural feminism is essentially a moral, countercultural movement aimed at redeeming its participants, while radical feminism began as a political movement to end male supremacy in all areas of social and economic life, and rejected the whole idea of opposing male and female natures and values as a sexist idea, a basic part of what we were fighting. Though cultural feminism came out of the radical feminist movement, the premises of the two tendencies are antithetical.

It was radical feminism that put women's liberation on the map, that got sexual politics recognized as a public issue, that created the

This is an abridged version of an article originally published in *The '60s Without Apology*, ed. Sohnya Sayres et al., © University of Minnesota Press, 1985. Reprinted by permission of the author.

vocabulary ("consciousness-raising," "the personal is political," "sister-hood is powerful," etc.) with which the second wave of feminism entered popular culture. Radical feminists sparked the drive to legalize abortion and created the atmosphere of urgency in which liberal feminists were finally able to get the Equal Rights Amendment through Congress and most of the states. Radical feminists were also the first to demand total equality in the so-called private sphere—equal sharing of housework and child care, equal attention to our emotional and sexual needs.

Yet this movement collapsed as quickly as it had grown. By 1975 radical feminism had given way to cultural feminism. The women's liberation movement [w.l.m.] had become the women's movement, in which liberals were the dominant, not to say hegemonic force. Socialist and Marxist feminism which had come out of other tendencies of the confused and practically marginal.[1] Feminism had become a reformist politics, a countercultural community, and a network of self-help projects (rape crisis centers, battered women's shelters, women's health clinics, etc.).

I joined New York Radical Women, the first women's liberation group in New York City, in 1968, about a year after it had started meeting. By that time the group was deeply divided over what came to be called (by radical feminists) the "politico-feminist split." The "politicos'" primary commitment was to the new left. They saw capitalism as the source of women's oppression: the ruling class indoc-trinated us with oppressive sex roles to promote consumerism and/or keep women a cheap reserve labor force and/or divide the workers; conventional masculine and feminine attitudes were matters of bourgeois conditioning from which we must all liberate ourselves. I sided with the "feminists," who at some point began calling them-selves "radical feminists." We argued that male supremacy was in itself a systemic form of domination—a set of material, institutionalized relations, not just bad attitudes. Men had power and privilege and like any other ruling class would defend their interests; challenging that power required a revolutionary movement of women.

When I joined women's liberation I had no ongoing, organizational ties with the left and my politics were a somewhat confused blend of cultural radicalism, populism and Marxism, but I certainly thought of myself as a leftist. With few exceptions, those of us who first defined radical feminism took for granted that "radical" implied antiracist, anticapitalist, and anti-imperialist. We saw ourselves as radicalizing the left by expanding the definition of radical to include feminism. In accordance with that definition, we agreed that until the left embraced feminism, our movement should not work with leftist men or male-dominated left groups, except perhaps for ad hoc coalitions.

What we didn't do—at least not in any systematic way—was tackle the question of how to integrate a feminist perspective with an overall radical politics. At that stage of the movement it would have been premature. Our overriding priority was to argue, against pervasive resistance, that male-female relations were indeed a valid political issue, and to begin describing, analyzing and challenging those relations. We were really on uncharted territory, and trying to explore that territory while under very heavy pressure from the left and from the "politicos" in the w.l.m. to subordinate feminist questions to traditional leftist concerns. It's hard to convey to people who didn't go through that experience how radical, how unpopular and difficult and scary it was just to get up and say, "Men oppress women. Men have oppressed *me*. Men must take responsibility for their actions instead of blaming them on capitalism. And yes, that means *you*." We were laughed at, patronized, called frigid, emotionally disturbed man-haters and—worst insult of all on the left!—apolitical.

In retrospect I see that we were faced with an insoluble contradiction. To build a women's liberation movement we had to take male supremacy out of the context of social domination in general. Yet from the very beginning we ran into problems of theory and strategy that could only be resolved within a larger context. Radical feminists professed a radical skepticism toward existing political theories, directed as they were toward the study of "man," and emphasized "consciousness-raising"—the process of sharing and analyzing our own experience in a group—as the primary method of understanding women's condition.

This emphasis on personal experience tended to obscure and mystify the fact that we all interpreted our experience through the filter of prior political and philosophical assumptions. Many debates on feminist issues were really debates about differing overall world views. For example, when a group of radical feminists did consciousness-raising on sex, we discovered that most of the women who testified preferred monogamous relationships, and that pressure for more sexual freedom came mostly from men (at that point, heterosexuality was a more or less unchallenged assumption). And to a large extent the differing positions that emerged depended on whether one viewed sexuality from a psychoanalytical perspective (my own ideas were very much influenced by Wilhelm Reich), a behaviorist perspective, a Simone de Beauvoirist existential humanist perspective, or an orthodox Marxist rejection of psychological categories as unmaterialist. Despite its oppositional stance toward the existing left, radical feminism was deeply influenced by Marxism. While many w.l.m. "politicos" tried to fit women's liberation into pre-existing Marxist categories, radical feminists appropriated certain Marxist ideas and assumptions (specifically, concepts of class interest, class struggle, and materialism) and applied them to male-female relations. Maoism, especially, was instrumental in shaping radical feminist ideas about the nature of power and oppression.

Though radical feminists did not deny being influenced by the ideas of other radical movements (on the contrary, we often pointed to those continuities as evidence of our own revolutionary commitment), we acted as if it were somehow possible for women to separate their ideas about feminism from their ideas about everything else. There was an unarticulated assumption that we could work out our differences solely within a feminist framework and ignore or agree to disagree on other political issues. Again, I think that assumption was necessary, in order to create a feminist framework to begin with, but it made for a very fragile kind of solidarity—and it also excluded large groups of women. The question of why the radical feminist movement was overwhelmingly white and mostly middle class is complex, but one reason is surely that most black and working-class women could not accept the abstraction of feminist issues from race and class issues, since the latter were so central to their lives.

At the same time, the narrowness of the movement's demographic base limited the value of generalizations about women and men based on feminists' personal experience. So another of the problems in interpreting data gleaned from consciousness-raising was, to what extent did it reveal patterns of male-female relations in general, and to what extent did it reflect the situation of women in particular social groups?

I don't want to be misunderstood—I think consciousness-raising did reveal a lot about male-female relations in general. In basic ways women's subordination crosses class, racial and cultural lines and it was a strength of radical feminism to insist on that reality. I'll go further and claim that in accumulating detailed information about the interaction of men and women on a day-to-day level, the consciousness-raising process contributed important insights into the nature of power relations in general—not only sexism.

Still, our lack of attention to social differences among women did limit and distort both our analysis and our practice, and it's hard to see how that could have been avoided without reference to a politics about other forms of social domination. When the minority of radical feminists who were working class or from working-class backgrounds began to challenge class bias without the movement, the same problem arose: the movement had no agreed-on politics of class that we could refer to, beyond the assumption that class hierarchy was oppressive. And again the dilemma was that to turn our attention to building such a politics would conflict with the imperatives of the specifically feminist project that had just barely begun.

Very early in the game radical feminists tried to make an end run around this problem by advancing the thesis that women's oppression was not only the oldest and most universal form of domination, but the primary form. We argued that other kinds of hierarchy grew out of and were modeled on male supremacy—were in effect specialized forms of male supremacy. This idea has a surface logic, given that all the hierarchical systems we know about have been rules and shaped by men. But it's a false logic, I think, because it assumes that men in creating and maintaining these systems are acting purely *as men*, in accordance with peculiarly male characteristics or specifically male supremacist objectives. It implicitly denies that the impulse to dominate, or to use a more materialist formulation, an authoritarian response to certain conditions of life, could be a universal human characteristic that women share, even if they have mostly lacked the opportunity to exercise it. It's a logic that excludes women from history not only practically but ontologically, and it leads to an unrealistic view of women as a more or less undifferentiated underclass with no real stake in the power struggles of class, race, and so on that go on among groups of men.

This notion of women's oppression as the primary oppression was very appealing for several reasons. It was a way of countering the left's insistence that class oppression was primary and women's liberation at best a subsidiary struggle—we could claim that on the contrary, all previous revolutions were mere reformist preludes to the real thing. It allowed white middle-class women to minimize the ways in which women participated in and benefited from race and class privilege. Most important, I think, it seemed to offer a resolution to the contradiction I've been talking about: it held out the possibility that a feminist theory could also be a general theory of social transformation. For all these reasons I fairly uncritically bought this thesis—helped to sell it, in fact.

By 1969, radical feminists were beginning to meet in their own small groups. The first group to publicly espouse a radical feminist line was Redstockings, a spinoff from New York Radical Women, which Shulamith Firestone and I started early in 1969. Shortly after that, the October 17th Movement, a radical split-off from NOW led by

Ti-Grace Atkinson, changed its name to The Feminists and proclaimed itself a radical feminist organization. These groups, which were both very influential in the movement, developed distinctive and opposing political stances.

Redstockings' dominant political tendency was a kind of neo-Maoist materialism. In addition to the belief in personal experience as the bedrock of feminist theory, this perspective was grounded in two basic principles. One was a view of sexual class struggle as the direct exercise of power by men, acting in their economic, social and sexual self-interest, over women. In this view institutions were merely tools of the oppressor and had no political significance in and of themselves. The idea that systems (like the family or capitalism) are in some sense autonomous, that they operate according to a logic that in certain ways constrains the rulers as well as the ruled, was rejected as a mystification and a way of letting men off the hook. To say, for instance, that the family oppressed women was to evade the fact that our husbands and fathers oppressed us; to say that men's sexist behavior was in any way dictated by social or familial norms was to deny that men oppressed women by choice, out of self-interest. The other principle was that women's behavior was always and only a rational, self-interested response to their immediate material conditions, i.e. their oppression by men. When women appeared to consent to their oppression, it was because they saw that individual resistance would not get them what they wanted, but only invite the oppressor's anger and punishment. As we built a movement capable of winning real change, more and more women would feel free to speak up and act collectively in their own behalf. The "pro-woman line," as this position was called, was absolutely antipsychological. It rejected as misogynist, psychological explanations for feminine submissiveness or passivity, since they implied that women collaborated in or were responsible for their oppression. Psychological explanations of men's behavior were regarded as yet another way to avoid blaming men for male supremacy.

The most articulate and systematic exponents of these ideas were Kathie Sarachild and Carol Hanisch, both former SNCC activists and founding members of New York Radical Women, Irene Peslikis, who wrote the classic article "Resistances to Consciousness," and Pat Mainardi, author of "The Politics of Housework." I did not fully share these politics—I believed in the importance of the unconscious and thought the pro-woman line was simplistic—but I was profoundly influenced by them. They were quite effective in challenging my tendencies to over-psychologize everything when social explanations were staring me in the face, and to avoid confronting my painful personal relations with men by making abstract arguments about the system. The genius of the Redstockings brand of radical feminist materialism was its concreteness. It demanded that women examine their everyday lives and face the most immediate and direct sources of their pain and anger. For women who responded to that demand, the confrontations inspired a powerful and urgent desire to change things. Activism became a personal emotional necessity—always a more effective spur to organizing than abstract principle or moral sentiment—with specific and immediate as well as long-range goals. As a result the materialist version of radical feminism had by far the most impact on the larger society, in terms of changing women's view of themselves and the world and inspiring both individual rebellion and collective political action.

But the reductionism of the Redstockings line led to basic miscalculations. For one thing, it underestimated the difficulty of change. If, for instance, resistance to feminism or outright antifeminism among women comes solely from rational fears of the consequences of challenging male authority, then the way to combat it is simply to build a movement and convince women that sisterhood really is powerful— that organized and unified we can win. But suppose in addition to the rational fears and hopes, women suffer from deep unconscious convictions of their own powerlessness and worthlessness and the unlimited power of men? Suppose they unconsciously equate being a "good woman" in men's terms not only with survival but with redemption from utter degradation? If that's true, then the successes of a feminist movement may actually intensify women's fears along with their hopes, and provoke unbearable emotional conflict.

Similarly, the dismissal of institutions as "mere tools" was an obstacle to understanding how change takes place, or fails to. It became an excuse not to really study the institutions that affect women, especially the family. From Redstockings' perspective, the problem with the family was simply male supremacy: women were subordinated within marriage and at the same time forced to marry for economic security and social legitimacy; we were assigned the care of children, but denied control of our fertility. Left criticism of the family per se was dismissed as men's resistance to committing themselves to women and children, emotionally and financially.

This analysis was superficial. To begin with it ignored the way the fundamental premise of the family system—the definition of a man, a woman and their biological children as the basic social unit, with the corresponding assumption that the community as a whole has little if any responsibility for children—automatically puts women in an unequal position. Maternity is obvious; paternity must be acknowledged or proved in some formal way. So women in a familialist system need marriage to establish the father's social obligation to his children, and this in itself gives men power to set the terms of the marriage contract. When women seek to change those terms without challenging the family system itself, they run into a double bind. Women's demands for equality in the home come up against male resistance, and if they press their demands "too far," the probable result is not an equal marriage, but no marriage at all.

In short, feminism inevitably destablizes the family, and so long as the family remains an unquestioned given of social relations, women are trapped into choosing between subordination and abandonment. This is the specter haunting contemporary sexual politics, as antifeminist women desperately try to restore the traditional bargain and feminists as desperately try to have it both ways. There's no way to understand, let alone resolve, this dilemma without an institutional analysis. The problem with our system of child rearing, which is absolutely basic to the oppression of women, is not only sexism but familialism—the equation of biological and social parenthood. Unless it's understood that way, the best we'll ever get is a jerry-built system of day-care centers designed to allow women to keep their shit jobs, and here and there the inspiring example of a "nurturing father" who expects the Medal of Honor for doing what mothers have always done.

But again, if it's impossible to understand women's condition without making a real critique of the family as an institution, the radical feminist strategy of isolating male supremacy from other forms of domination breaks down. The family has more than one political dimension: besides subordinating women, it's also a vehicle for getting children of both sexes to submit to social authority and actively embrace the values of the dominant culture. Among other things, that means enlisting both women and men to uphold the family system and its sexual morality, in which sex for its own sake is bad and dangerous and must be subordinated to the "higher" purposes of heterosexual monogamous marriage and procreation. True, men have always had more license to be "bad" than women and have even been *required* to be "bad" to prove their manhood. But all this means is that men experience a conflict between their sexual desire and identity and their "higher" nature—not, as radical feminists have tended to assume, that men are free of sexual guilt and repression. This conflict and its manifestations—the perception of sex and love as separate or opposed, and sex as connected with violence—are integral to the patriarchal concept of masculinity, while femininity, on the other hand, requires the suppression of "bad" desires and a romanticized, spiritualized eroticism.

The sexual revolution loosened the grip of conservative sexual morality but did not basically change its psychic underpinnings. We all to some degree internalize familialist sexual ideology in its feminine or masculine version. To the extent that any of us rejects it, we are rejecting being a woman or a man as the culture defines it and defining ourselves as social, sexual deviants, with all the consequences that entails. We are all oppressed by having this ideology imposed on us, though some groups are particularly oppressed—women, youth, homosexuals and other sexual minorities. So there is a political fault line in the society dividing people who are in one way or another defending this ideology (and the practices that go with it) from people who are in one way or another rebelling against it. This line cuts across gender, and like class or racial difference creates real divisions among women that can't simply be subsumed in an antisexist politics. It also defies analysis strictly in terms of the "self-interest" of one class of people oppressing another. Ultimately the interest of sexual conservatives in suppressing sexual dissidence is their interest in obliterating possibilities they themselves have painfully relinquished. This interest is so powerful that there are few sexual dissidents—and I would call feminists and unapologetic gays dissidents by definition—who are not also conservative in some ways.

While ignoring all these complications, Redstockings' vision of direct confrontation between sexual classes put an enormous premium on unity among women. The idea was that if all women supported each other in demanding equality—if there were no women willing to "scab"—then men would have no choice but to accept the new order. This was the model of struggle put forward in *Fanshen*, William Hinton's account of revolution in a Chinese village, which circulated widely in the movement. It was inspiring reading, but America is not a Chinese village; Hinton's cast of characters, at least as he presented it, was divided by class, sex and age, but not by multiple ethnic and cultural antagonisms.[2] For all the reasons I've been laying out, I don't see universal sisterhood as a practical possibility. Fortunately men are hardly a monolith—they are deeply divided along various social and political axes, disagree with each other on what "male self-interest" is, and don't necessarily support each other in the face of feminist demands. Feminist struggle will never be a matter of women as a united class confronting men as a united class, but rather of particular groups of women pressing on vulnerable points in the structure of male supremacy and taking advantage of divisions among men. Direct personal pressure on men to change their behavior will be more feasible in some communities than in others. Most early radical feminists operated in a social milieu that was middle-class, educated, culturally liberal and politically leftist. A degree of economic opportunity, access to birth control, and the decline or rigidly familialist mores—along with the fact that most of us were young and as yet uninterested in having children—allowed us a certain amount of independence, therefore power, in dealing with "our" men, and we were also in a position to appeal to their proclaimed belief in democracy and equality.

Even under the best conditions, though, direct confrontation has built-in limits, because it requires a level of day-to-day militance that's impossible to sustain over the long haul. After a while even the most passionate feminists get tired, especially when they see how slow the progress is. As soon as they ease the pressure, men take advantage of it and start a backlash, which then touches off a backlash by *women* who feel they've struggled too hard for not enough result. That's part of the story of the 70s. I'm not saying that personally confronting men is not worth doing, or that our doing it hasn't had lasting effects, because it has. But I think it is basically a minority tactic, and one that flourishes in the exceptional moment, rather than *the* model of revolutionary struggle.

When applied beyond the realm of direct personal combat to feminist demands for changes in public policy, the pure class struggle paradigm becomes much more problematic. These demands operate on two levels. They are aimed at men as a group in that they attack the sexist assumptions embedded in social and economic institutions. But they are also aimed more specifically at men (and the occasional woman) with institutional power—corporate, legal, medical, religious or whatever—who by virtue of their positions represent other interests and ideological commitments besides male privilege. Such interests and commitments may have priority over sexist imperatives or even conflict with them. Thus the alliances and oppositions that form around feminist demands are rarely based strictly on gender or sexual class interest.

For instance, although legal abortion reduces women's subordination and dependence on men, men as a class have not closed ranks against it. Rather, the active political opposition has come from sexually conservative familialists of both sexes (most but not all of whom are opposed to feminism across the board). Many men have supported legal abortion on civil liberties or sexual libertarian grounds. Others have supported it on racist grounds, as an antiwelfare or population control measure. Male politicians have more often than not based their position on abortion on one simple criterion: what would get them reelected. The medical establishment supports freedom for doctors to perform abortions while opposing feminist demands that paramedicals be allowed to perform them. And so on. Most men have at worst been indifferent to or ambivalent about the abortion issue; most women, on the other hand, *have* seen abortion rights as in their female self-interest. Without this asymmetry, it is doubtful that feminists could have won legal abortion or kept it in the face of heavy pressure from the right. As it is, our biggest defeat on this issue, the ban on Medicaid funds for abortion, has clearly involved other factors besides sexism. The new right took advantage of middle-class women's apathy toward the poor, while mobilizing antiwelfare sentiment among people outside the hard-core familialist antiabortion constituency. Often a combination of racist, antipoor and sexist feelings motivated men to opposition in a way sexism alone had not ("Let those irresponsible women have their abortions, but not at my expense").

The Feminists agreed with Redstockings that male domination was the primary oppression and that women and men were political classes. Beyond that the groups diverged. For one thing, The Feminists used the terms "sex role" and "sex class" interchangeably—they identified sexism with particular, complementary patterns of male and female behavior. Redstockings' view of sex roles, like its view of institutions, was that they reflected male power but were not primary political categories. The Feminists' conflation of role and class provided a basis for rejecting the pro-woman line: if the female role, per se, defined women's oppression, then conforming to the role was upholding the oppression. The Feminists' attitude toward institutions was even more reductive than Redstockings', in the opposite direction. While Redstockings assumed that the sexist dimension of an institution could somehow be abstracted from the institution itself, the Feminists assumed that the primary institutions of women's oppression—which they identified as marriage and the family, prostitution, and heterosexuality—were entirely defined by sexism, that their sole purpose was to perpetuate the "sex-role system." Therefore, radical feminists must destory them. (The Feminists had a penchant for words like "destroy" and "annihilate.") The Feminists also rejected consciousness-raising in favor of abstract theorizing, but never clearly laid out the philosophical or epistemological basis of their ideas.

For all the limitations of Redstockings' materialism, we at least knew that we had to base a feminist program on women's actual lives and feelings, and that the important thing was to understand women's behavior, not judge it from some utopian moral standpoint. The Feminists were idealist, voluntarist and moralistic in the extreme. They totally disregarded what other women said they wanted or felt, and their idea of organizing was to exhort women to stop submitting to oppression by being subservient or participating in sexist institutions like marriage. Once at an abortion demonstration in front of a legislative committee I had a huge argument with a member of the group who was yelling at the committee's female secretaries and clerks that they were traitors for not walking out on their jobs and joining us. The

Feminists were the first radical feminist group to suggest that living or sleeping with men was collaborating with the system. They shocked the rest of the movement by making a rule that no more than a third of their membership could be married or living with a man.

The Feminists, and in particular their best-known theorist, Ti-Grace Atkinson, also developed a set of ideas about sex that will be familiar to anyone who has followed current movement debates. The first radical feminist to talk about heterosexual intercourse as an institution was probably Anne Koedt, a member of New York Radical Women who later joined The Feminists, in her essay "The Myth of the Vaginal Orgasm." Koedt was careful to distinguish between intercourse as an option and as an institutionalized practice defined as synonymous with "normal" sex. She also assumed that the point of sex was pleasure, the point of institutionalized intercourse was male pleasure, and the point of challenging that construct was equal pleasure and orgasm for women. Atkinson wrote an article elaborating on this idea of "the institution of sexual intercourse," but took it in a different direction. As she saw it the purpose of the institution was getting women to reproduce and the concept of sexual need or drive was mere ideology. What erotic pleasure was or whether it existed was unclear, especially in the present social context. In fact, heterosexual intercouse was so thoroughly corrupted by the sex-role system that it was hard to imagine a future for it even as an optional practice.

The Feminists' organizing manifesto condemned the institution of heterosexual sex very much in Atkinson's terms, and added that since sex was part of the marriage contract, marriage meant legalized rape. It also included the statement—tucked in inconspicuously, so it seemed a lot less significant than it does in retrospect—that in the context of freedom, physical relations between individuals of whatever sex would not necessarily emphasize genital contact. The implication was that any special interest in or desire for genital sex, heterosexual or otherwise, was a function of sexism. This was a mental leap that seems to me clearly grounded in unconscious acceptance of a traditional patriarchal assumption, namely that lust is male.

The Feminists' perspective on sex was a minority view within radical feminism, considered provocative but out on some weird edge. The predominant attitudes in Redstockings were more typical: we took for granted women's desire for genital sexual pleasure (the importance of fucking to that pleasure was a matter of debate) and focused our critique on the ways men repressed and frustrated women sexually. Though we theoretically defended women's right to be lesbian or celibate, there was a strong heterosexual presumption underlying Redstockings politics. It was tacitly assumed, and sometimes explicitly argued, that men's need for sexual love from women was our biggest weapon in both individual and collective struggle—and that our own need for *satisfying* sexual love from men was our greatest incentive for maintaining the kind of personal confrontation feminism required. We rejected sexual separatism as a political strategy, on materialist grounds—that simply refusing to be with men was impractical and unappealing for most women, and in itself did nothing to challenge male power. But beyond that we didn't really take it seriously as a personal choice, let alone an expression of militance. On the contrary, we thought of living without men as the bitter price we might have to pay for our militance in demanding equal relationships. Tension over these issues, among others, led an alienated minority to quit Redstockings and join The Feminists.

At that point lesbianism per se had not yet emerged as an issue, but there were pitfalls for lesbians in both groups' ideas. If you accepted Redstockings' assumption that the struggle for equality in heterosexual relationships was the nerve center of radical feminism, lesbians were by definition marginal to the movement. The Feminists offered a much more attractive prospect—by their logic lesbians were, simply by virtue of rejecting sexual relationships with men, a liberated vanguard. But there was a catch: the vanguard role was available only to lesbians willing to ignore or play down the element of sexual desire in their lesbian identity. As Alice Echols has pointed out, the convergence of homophobic and antisexual pressures from the movement eventually impelled the majority of lesbian feminists to accept this tradeoff and sanitize lesbianism by defining it as a political choice rather than an erotic one.[3] To complicate matters, many of the feminists who "converted" to lesbianism in the wake of lesbian separatism did so not to express a compelling sexual inclination but to embrace a political and cultural identity; some of these converts denied that lesbianism was in any sense a sexual definition, and equated their rejection of compulsory heterosexuality with "liberation" from sex itself, at least insofar as it was "genitally oriented." In this atmosphere, lesbians who see freedom to express their unconventional sexuality as an integral part of their feminism have had reason to wonder if the label "male identifier" is any improvement over "pervert."

Toward the end of 1969, Shulie Firestone and Anne Koedt started a third group, New York Radical Feminists, which rejected both the pro-woman line and The Feminists' arrogant vanguardism. Two of the group's theoretical principles have been important in the later history of the movement. One has to do with the meaning of male power. Most radical feminists assumed men wanted dominance for the sake of material benefits—by which they meant not only the economic, in the broad sense, benefits of the sexual division of labor, but the psychic benefits of having one's emotional needs catered to without any obligation to reciprocate. NYRF proposed in essence that men wanted to exercise power for its own sake—that it was intrinsically satisfying to the ego to dominate others. According to their formulation men do not defend their power in order to get services from women, but demand services from women in order to affirm their sense of power. The group's other important proposition was its entry in the ongoing debate about why women submit to their oppression. While Redstockings' answer was necessity and The Feminists' implicit answer was cowardice, NYRF insisted that feminine behavior was both enforced and internalized: women were trained from birth both to conform to the feminine role and to accept it as right and natural. This pass at an analysis of male and female behavior was incoherent, implicitly biologistic, and sexist. Besides suggesting that men, by virtue of their maleness, had an inherent predilection for power, NYRF's formulation gave men credit for being active agents while implicitly defining women as passive recipients of social indoctrination. The social-learning model, applied to women, also posed the same problem as all behaviorist psychologies—it could not account for resistance to the system. Inevitably it implied its antinomy, moral voluntarism, since the very existence of a feminist movement meant that some women had in some sense transcended their conditioning.

All the disparate versions of radical feminist analysis shared two basic weaknesses that contributed to the movement's demise. First, commitment to the sex-class paradigm pinned women's hopes for radical change on a millennial unity of women across barriers of class, race, cultural values and sexual orientation. The gap between what radical feminism promised and what it could deliver without a more complex, multivalent theory and strategy was immense. That gap was all too soon filled by attempts at individual liberation through "overcoming female conditioning," fantasies of benevolent matriarchies, the equation of woman-bonding, an alternative women's community and/or a "politically correct lifestyle" with feminism, and moralizing about the iniquity of men and "male values." Underlying these individualist and countercultural revisions of radical feminism was an unadmitted despair of real change. That despair is expressed more overtly in the work of cultural feminist theorists like Andrea Dworkin, who has reified the sex-class paradigm, defining it as a closed system in which the power imbalance between men and women is absolute and all-pervasive. Since the system has no discontinuities or contradictions, there is no possibility of successful struggle against it—at best there can be moral resistance.

The movement's second major weakness was its failure to develop a coherent analysis of either male or female psychology—a failure so total that to me it indicates a willed ignorance rooted in terror. While there was a dissenting minority, radical feminists as a group were dogmatically hostile to Freud and psychoanalysis, and psychoanalytic thought—especially its concept of the unconscious and its emphasis on the role of sexual desire in human motivation—had almost no impact on radical feminist theory. Since I agree with Juliet Mitchell that psychoanalysis is not a defense of patriarchal culture but an analysis of it—though I don't subscribe to her Lacanian interpretation of Freud—I think radical feminists' closed-mindedness on the subject was an intellectual and political disaster.[4]

Redstockings did not succeed in defining psychology as a nonissue. Most radical feminists recognized that there were aspects of male and female feelings and behavior that eluded pragmatic, common-sense explanation. But their attempts to acknowledge the psychological dimension have been fragmented and muddled. In general, the inheritors of the radical feminist movement have followed the path of New York Radical Feminists and endorsed some version of behaviorism, biological determinism, or an ad hoc, contradictory mélange of both. Given the history of biologism as the enemy's weapon, most feminists who draw on it prefer to pretend it's something else, and behaviorist terminology can be useful for this purpose. The present "radical feminist" antipornography movement provides a good example. It claims that pornography conditions men to sexual sadism, which is the foundation and primary expression of their power over women, and conditions women to accept their victimization. But if you examine the argument closely, it doesn't hang together. If men have the power, create the pornography, and define the values it embodies, conditioning might perhaps explain how some men transmit a sadistic mentality to others, but not how or why that mentality arose in the first place. And in fact it is clear from the rest of their rhetoric that antiporn theorists equate male sexuality, per se, with sadism. As for women, the antipornography movement explicitly defines authentic female sexuality as tender, romantic, and nongenitally oriented, despite the suspicious resemblance of this description to the patriarchal stereotype of the good woman. It is only women who disagree with this view of their sexuality who are proclaimed to be victims of male-supremacist conditioning. (How antiporn activists have managed to avoid being conditioned is not explained.) In this case, the language of behaviorism serves not only to deflect charges of biologism, but to inflate the importance of pornography as a target and dismiss political opponents.

The disintegration of radical feminism took several forms. First of all, radical feminist ideas caught the attention of large numbers of women, especially educated, upper-middle-class women, who had no radical perspective on other matters and often were uninterested in, if not actively hostile to, left politics as such. These women experienced sexual inequality in their own lives, and radical feminism raised their consciousness. But their awareness of their oppression as women did not make them radicals in the sense of being committed to overall social transformation, as the early radical feminists had naively assumed it would. Instead they seized on the idea of women's oppression as the primary oppression and took it to mean not that feminism was or should be inclusive of other struggles, but that left politics were "male" and could be safely ignored.

This idea became a prominent theme of cultural feminism. It also led to the development of a new kind of liberal feminism. Many women reacted to radical feminism with an intense desire to change their lives, or the social arrangements that immediately affected them, but had no intention of supporting changes that would threaten their (or their husbands') economic and social class status. Many of the same women were reluctant to explicitly attack male power—not only because of the personal consequences of militance, but because the whole subject of power is uncomfortable for people who are basically committed to the existing socioeconomic order. The result was a brand of politics best exemplified by *Ms.* magazine, which began publishing in 1972. The traditional reformism of organizations like NOW was economistic and hostile to the "personal" sexual and emotional issues radical feminists were raising. *Ms.* and the new liberals embraced those issues, but basically ignored the existence of power relations. Though they supported feminist reforms, their main strategy for changing women's lives was individual and collective self-improvement. They were partial to the argument that men and women are fellow victims of sex-role conditioning. But where the "politicos" in the early movement had blamed this conditioning on capitalism, the liberals blamed it vaguely on "society," or the media, or the schools, ignoring the question of who runs these institutions and on whose behalf. In terms of their political ethos and constituency, the difference between the *Ms.*-ites and NOW was roughly analogous to the difference between the McGovern and Humphrey wings of the Democratic Party, and *Ms.* was to radical feminism what the "new politics" Democrats were to the new left.

Within the radical feminist movement itself, the original momentum almost immediately began giving way to a bitter, immobilizing factionalism. The first issue to create permanent rifts was equality in the movement. Partly out of rebellion against hierarchical structures (especially in the new left) partly because consciousness-raising required informality, radical feminists, like the w.l.m. as a whole, had chosen the putatively structureless small group as their main form of organization. Yet every group had developed an informal leadership, a core of women—I was part of that core in Redstockings—who had the most to do with setting and articulating the direction of the group. Women who felt excluded from equal participation challenged not only the existing leaders but the concept of leadership as a holdover from male-dominated organizations. Debates about group process, the oppressive behavior of some members toward others, and leaders' alleged exploitation of the movement for personal ends began to dominate meetings, to the exclusion of any engagement with sexism in the outside world.

The problems of elitism, class bias, differences in power within the movement, and opportunism were certainly real—they were much the same kinds of problems that had surfaced elsewhere on the left—but by and large the attempts to confront them were ineffective and in the long run disastrous. Obviously, there are inherent difficulties in trying to build a democratic movement. You can't create a perfect society in microcosm while the larger society remains the same, and you can't change the larger society if you spend all your time and energy trying to create a utopian microcosm. The goal should be to strike a balance—work on finding ways to extend skills, experience and confidence to everyone, but at the same time encourage people who already have these assets to use them for the movement's benefit, provided they are accountable for *how* they use them in the movement's name. What makes this so difficult is not only the leaders' desire for personal power or their resistance to being held accountable and sharing their skills, but the rage of those who find themselves at the bottom of yet another hierarchy. They tend to want instant redress, and since there's no way to instantly create a situation where everyone has equal power—because the differences come from years of differential opportunities—some people resort to the pseudo-solution of demanding that those who have the skills or other forms of social power not use them, either for the movement or for themselves. Which is a dead end in terms of creating an effective movement, as well as an unreasonable demand on individuals trying to live their lives within the present social system.

These issues come up in all egalitarian movements, but the premises of radical feminism made them especially intense. The assumption that women's oppression is primary, and that the differences among women can be worked out entirely within an antisexist context, shaped the movement's predominant view of women and class: that a woman's position in the class hierarchy derived solely from the men she was attached to, that women could oppress other women by virtue of their class status but not men, that class conflict among women was a product of false consciousness, and that any form of class striving or power-mongering was therefore "male-identified" behavior. For some women this category extended to any form of individual achievement, intellectual activity, articulateness or self-assertion, the assumption being that these could only derive from some unholy connection with male power. The implicit corollary was that traditionally feminine behavior was the only truly sisterly behavior. These ideas too became staples of cultural feminism. Of course, many radical feminists disagreed and pointed out that charges of pushiness and overachieving were always used by dominant groups to keep oppressed groups in their place. But since the dissenters were operating out of the same basic framework as their adversaries, they tended to adopt some version of the mirror-image position that since women's common interest transcended class differences, this democracy in the movement business must be a sexist plot to cut down feminist leadership and keep the movement weak.

During the same period, working-class women in the movement began talking to each other about their experience with class oppression and confronting middle-class feminists. This new application of the consciousness-raising process educated feminists about the workings of the class system on the level of personal relations, but it did not significantly change class relations in the movement or help to unify women across class lines. As I've noted, there was no way within the parameters of radical feminism to connect the struggle for internal democracy with active opposition to the class system per se. This split between internal and externally oriented politics was exacerbated by a total emphasis on class as a set of oppressive personal relations. It was assumed that the strategy of challenging men's sexist behavior could be applied with equal success to challenging women's class-biased behavior. But this assumption overlooked fundamental differences in the dynamics of class and sexual politics. While the basic institutions of sexist oppression are located in personal life, a realm in which men have a great deal of personal power, the basic institutions of class oppression are located in the public world of the political economy, where middle-class people (women, especially) have little power. That does not mean there is no personal aspect to class oppression, but it does suggest that personal politics are not the cutting edge of class struggle.

For some radical feminists, however, consciousness-raising about class led to a political identity crisis. I was one of those who became convinced that women *were* implicated in the class system and had real class interests, that women could oppress men on the basis of class, and that class differences among women could not be resolved within a feminist context alone. Which meant that a feminist movement purporting to represent all women had to connect in some organic way to a workers' movement, and by extension to a black liberation movement and other movements of oppressed groups—in short, to a left. Some women reacted to this realization by going back to the existing left to promote feminism from within; some moved off in search of a socialist-feminist synthesis. My own experience left me with a lot of new questions and no answers. In the fall of 1969 I had moved to Colorado Springs to work in a G.I. organizing project, intending at the same time to start a radical feminist movement in the area. Obviously, I was already interested in somehow combining feminist and leftist organizing, less out of any abstract commitment to the idea than from the impulse to integrate different sides of my life and politics. Two radical feminists from New York, including Joyce Betries, who was working-class and had raised the class issue in Redstockings, came out to work with me, and we started a women's liberation group. Betries also began confronting the oppressive class relations between middle-class and working-class members of the project and between civilians and G.I.s. After going through this confrontation in a sexually mixed group, in which the women were also raising feminist issues, I had no doubt that the standard radical feminist line on class was wrong.

Unlike Betries, who became active in Youth Against War and Fascism, I continued to regard myself as a radical feminist. I still believed that male supremacy was a structure of domination at least as basic as class or race, and so far as I could tell neither the "male" left nor the socialist-feminists—who struck me as updated versions of 60s politicos—agreed. But I rejected the idea of the primacy of women's oppression and began reluctantly to reject the global sisterhood model of feminist revolution. I saw that the fate of feminism at any given time and place was bound up with the fate of the larger left, though I had no idea how to translate this perception into a political strategy. At this point—1971—our G.I. project had fallen apart along with the rest of the new left, radical feminism was doing the same, and the prospects for any kind of radical politics looked grim. If I felt confused and stymied, I was not alone.

The final blow to the radical feminist movement as a vital political force was the gay-straight split, which took place in the early 70s. Lesbian separatists added a crucial ingredient to existing female separatist ideology—a positive vision of community. While early separatism offered only the moral reward of revolutionary purity, lesbian feminism offered in addition the more concrete social and sexual benefits of a women's counterculture. It then defined that culture not simply as a strategy for achieving women's liberation or as a form of sustenance for its troops, but as the meaning and purpose of feminism.

At a time when the enormous obstacles facing the movement were becoming apparent, this vision had an understandable appeal. And while it had particular advantages for women already committed to lesbianism (and oppressed as lesbians), it could not have been a transforming influence on the movement if it had not exerted a strong pull on the feelings of radical feminists generally. Not only did many women break with heterosexuality to join the lesbian feminist counter-culture, and even more experiment with it; many feminists who remained practicing heterosexuals identified with that culture and its ideology and considered themselves failed or incomplete feminists. Others argued that sexual orientation was irrelevant; what mattered was whether a woman accepted the *values* of female culture. By this route, cultural feminism evolved into a politics that anyone could embrace, that had little to do with sexual separatism or lesbianism as a sexual practice. The "female values" cultural feminists proclaimed— either with openly biologistic arguments, as in Jane Alpert's influential article, "Mother Right," or with behaviorist window dressing—were none other than the traditional feminine virtues. Once again we were alleged to be loving, nurturing, in tune with nature, intuitive and spiritual rather than genital in our eroticism, while men were violent, predatory, alienated from nature, committed to a sterile rationalism and obsessed with genital sex. (There was some disagreement on whether men were hopeless cases or whether women could teach them female values and thereby "humanize" them.) Thus "radical feminism" came full circle, from challenging the polarization of the sexes to affirming it and embracing a reverse sexism.

Insofar as cultural feminists translated their ideas into political activism, their chief focus was male violence against women. Radical feminists had defined rape and other forms of male aggression as weapons for enforcing male dominance—for punishing "uppity" female behavior or simply reminding women who was boss. But their lack of attention to psychology had left a gap in their analysis: in discussing sexual violence as a more or less deliberate, instrumental choice, they ignored it as a sexual and emotional experience. The movement was inconsistent in its view of the relation between rape and sexuality. On the one hand it noted the continuity between rape and "normal" male sexual aggressiveness, and the resulting social tendency to rationalize rape as fun and games. Yet in reaction to this confusion, and to the related myth that men rape out of uncontrollable sexual need, the radical feminist mainstream asserted that "rape is violence, not sex"—a tidy slogan that avoided disturbing "unmaterialist" questions about the nature of male desire, the relationship of pleasure to power. And the iconoclastic Feminists, who implicitly equated heterosexuality with rape, declined to recognize sexual pleasure as a motive in either.

Cultural feminists leaped into this psychological breach, rightly (and therefore effectively) insisting on the reality of sexual violence as an erotic experience, an end in itself. Unfortunately, they proceeded to incorporate this insight into their neo-Victorian caricature of men's sexual nature and to generalize it to all patriarchal relations. New York Radical Feminists had broken with earlier radical feminist thought to argue that men wanted power for its intrinsic satisfactions, not its concomitant rewards; cultural feminists spelled out the implication of this position—that all sexist behavior is an extension of the paradigmatic act of rape. From this standpoint sexual violence was the essence and purpose of male dominance, the paradigmatic "male value," and therefore feminism's central concern.

In the late 70s, cultural feminists' emphasis shifted from actual violence against women to representation of sexual violence in the media and then to pornography. Groups like Women Against Pornography and Women Against Violence in Pornography and Media adopted pornography as the quintessential symbol of a male sexuality assumed to be inherently violent and oppressive, then made that symbol the focus of a moral crusade reminiscent of the 19th-century social purity and temperance movements. Predictably, they have aimed their attack not only at male producers and consumers of porn, but at women who refuse to define lust as male or pornography as rape and insist without apology on their own sexual desires. While continuing to call itself radical feminist—indeed, claiming that it represents the only truly feminist position—the antiporn movement has in effect collaborated with the right in pressuring women to conform to conventionally feminine attitudes.

Though there was surprisingly little resistance to the collapse of radical feminism, some movement activists did fight back. In 1973 Kathie Sarachild, Carol Hanisch, and several other women revived Redstockings, which had disbanded three years before, and in 1975 they published a journal, *Feminist Revolution*. *FR* was an ambitious attempt to analyze the deradicalization of the movement and contained the first major critiques of cultural feminism and *Ms.* liberalism. Its publication was an important political act, especially for those of us who felt alienated from what was passing for the radical feminist movement—or, as it was coming to be called, the "feminist community"—and were trying to make sense of what had gone wrong without the help of any ongoing group. But the journal also revealed the limitations of Redstockings politics when carried to their logical conclusions. *FR*'s critique did not contain any second thoughts about the premises of radical feminist materialism, including its rejection of psychology. On the contrary, the editors blamed the devolution of radical feminism entirely on deviations from these premises. From this unreconstructed viewpoint they could explain the deviations only as deliberate sabotage by "Agents, Opportunists, and Fools" (a section heading).[5]

The antiporn groups, which emerged as an organized political force in 1979, quickly captured the attention of the media and dominated public discussion of feminism and sexuality. Because their ideas resonated with the conservative social climate and appealed to women's fears at a time when real freedom and equality seemed increasingly remote, they exerted a strong influence on the liberal mainstream of the women's movement and on the public perception of feminism. I found these developments alarming, as did many other women who felt that feminists should be fighting the right's assault on women's sexual freedom, not reinforcing it. Our opposition has generated a fierce intramovement debate on the significance of sexuality for feminist politics.

The sex debate has recapitulated the old division between those radical feminists who emphasized women's right to equal sexual pleasure and those who viewed sex primarily in negative terms, as an instrument of sexist exploitation and abuse. But contemporary "prosex" feminists (as the dissidents have been labeled) are also doing something new—placing a specifically feminist commitment to women's sexual autonomy in the context of a more general sexual radicalism. Bound by its theoretical framework, the radical feminist movement analyzed sexuality as a function of sex class; it did not concern itself with sexual repression versus liberation as a problematic distinct from that of male power over women. Accordingly, most radical feminists in all factions equated women's sexual oppression with male domination and rejected the idea of sexual liberation for men as at best redundant, at worst a euphemism for license to exploit women with impunity. Within this framework there was no way to discuss the common elements in women's and men's (particularly gay men's) subjection to sexual repression; or to explore the extent to which men's sexual guilt, fear and frustration contribute to their sexism (and specifically to sexual violence); or to understand the complexities of lesbian sexuality; or to examine other variables besides sexism that influence sexual formation—such as the parent-child relationship, race, class and anxieties shared by both sexes about the body, pleasure, emotional vulnerability and loss of control.

The pro-sex feminists are raising all these questions and others, provoking an explosion of intellectual activity and reintroducing the spirit of critical inquiry to a movement all but ossified by cultural feminist dogma. The emphasis has been on questions rather than answers. There is a good deal of ideological diversity within the pro-sex camp, a loose, informal network that consists mostly of lesbian dissenters from the lesbian feminist consensus, women with political roots in early radical feminism, and feminist academics influenced by Marxism, structuralism, and psychoanalysis. We also maintain friendly relations and an ongoing exchange of ideas with parallel tendencies in the gay movement and the neo-Marxist left.

At the same time, black women and other women of color have begun to create the context for a feminist radicalism based on efforts to analyze the web of race, class and sex/gender relations. Like pro-sex theorizing, these explorations break with prevailing assumptions—in this case the competing orthodoxies of radical and cultural feminism, black nationalism and Marxist socialism. Each of these movements has insisted on hierarchies of oppression and primary causes, forcing women who suffer from racial and class oppression to subordinate some aspects of their identity to others or be political schizophrenics. While socialist feminists have purported to address this dilemma, in practice their economistic bias has tended not only to vitiate their feminist analysis but to reduce racism to its economic component. Many women of color have shared this perspective and its limitations. What is novel and exciting about the current discussions is their concern with the totality of a culture and their recognition that sexism, heterosexism, racism, capitalism and imperialism intersect in complex, often contradictory ways. When this multidimensional analysis is applied to bedrock issues of sexual politics—marriage and motherhood, sexual repression and violence, reproductive freedom, homophobia— it does not simply correct for white middle-class feminists' neglect of other women's experience; it shows that whatever a woman's particular social vantage point, her experience of femaleness is charged with class and racial meanings.

Though the emergence of this tendency and the burgeoning of the predominantly white pro-sex coalition happened independently (a small number of black and Hispanic women have been involved in both) they end up raising many of the same questions from different angles. They also reflect a common impulse toward a decentered radicalism sensitive to difference, ambiguity and contradiction, and critical of all forms of hierarchical thinking. The same impulse informs contemporary cultural radical revisions of Marxist and Marxist-feminist theory. It seems to me that these convergences represent a first fragile step toward the creation of a multiracial left that will include feminism as a basic assumption. At the moment, helping this process along is my own political priority; I think a "new new left" is the prerequisite for a third feminist wave.

Still, the paradox posed by early radical feminism remains unresolved and may be unresolvable in any definitive way. An antisexist politics abstracted from a critique of familialism, a commitment to sexual liberation and race and class struggle, cannot sustain itself as a radical force; a movement that attempts such an abstraction is bound to fragment into bitterly opposed factions and/or turn conservative. Yet so long as sexist power relations exist there will be a need for an autonomous, specifically feminist women's movement. It is the legacy of radical feminism that makes it possible to talk even tentatively of a feminist left. And it would be naive to imagine that a left intellectually committed to feminism would automatically be free of sexism either in theory or in practice. In the foreseeable future, any feminist movement that aims to be radical will somehow have to negotiate this tension between the need to preserve its political boundaries and the need to extend them. It will help to remember that radical feminism named the boundaries in the first place.

NOTES

1. In this essay, as in common usage on the left, the term "socialist feminism" refers primarily to an activist tendency and "Marxist feminism" to a body of theory. There is of course some overlap between the two, but by no means a one-to-one correspondence. As a movement, socialist feminism has generally been more socialist than feminist, assuming that economic relations are fundamental, while sexual political questions are "cultural" or "ideological," i.e., epiphenomenal. Often socialist-feminists have adopted a cultural feminist view of these "ideological" questions and thereby reduced feminism to a matter of lifestyle.

Marxist feminism has displayed a similar weakness for economic reductionism, but it has also used Marxist methodology to expand feminist theory; in recent years, especially, Marxist feminists have both influenced and been influenced by the cultural radical critiques that have generated the "crisis in Marxism" debate. On the other hand, since Marxist-feminist theorizing has been carried on mostly in the academy, it has suffered badly from lack of contact with any organized feminist movement.

2. In any case, postrevolutionary China is hardly a model for those of us whose definition of liberation includes individual freedom. This does not invalidate the process of self-assertion by peasants against landlords, women against men and autocratic matriarchs that Hinton describes. But it does raise the question of whether the Maoist model of struggle can have more than limited success only in a revolution in which individual autonomy and cultural diversity are not important values.

3. Alice Echols, "The New Feminism of Yin and Yang," in *Powers of Desire: The Politics of Sexuality,* ed. Christine Stansell, Ann Snitow and Sharon Thompson (Monthly Review Press, 1983).

4. Ellen Willis, "Toward a Feminist Sexual Revolution," *Social Text,* 6, Fall 1982.

5. Before publishing *Feminist Revolution,* Redstockings held a press conference on the Steinem-CIA connection and distributed copies of the *FR* article. At the time I was working part-time at *Ms.,* editing book reviews, and had just concluded that I ought to quit, having come to the limits of my tolerance for the constant (and usually losing) battles involved in being the token radical on a magazine with mushy corporate liberal politics. The Redstockings flap pushed me over the edge. I had mixed feelings about the article and was upset about the press conference, which by villainizing Steinem and implying a conspiracy could only undercut the credibility of Redstockings' valid critique of *Ms.*'s politics and impact on the movement. But I was incensed by Steinem's response, a disdainful who-are-these-people dismissal of Sarachild, Hanisch et al. as crazies and not real Redstockings. I resigned from *Ms.* and wrote an open letter to the movement press detailing my own criticisms of the magazine and its editor. Redstockings included it in *FR.*

In 1979, Random House published an "abridged edition with additional writings" of *Feminist Revolution.* The chief abridgement was "Gloria Steinem and the CIA," which Random House deleted in response to Steinem's threat to sue, although the facts of her involvement with IRS had long been public information and the article had already survived a libel reading. Though Redstockings organized a protest, this act of censorship provoked little interest outside of radical and cultural feminist circles, and cultural feminists mostly supported Steinem. In the end, the entire episode was a depressing defeat for radical feminism, albeit largely self-inflicted. Not only did Redstockings fail to provoke significant debate about *Ms.*-ism; most people who heard about the controversy at all were left with the impression that Steinem had been attacked by a lunatic fringe.

∼ 25 ∼

THE LIBERATION OF BLACK WOMEN

PAULI MURRAY

Black women, historically, have been doubly victimized by the twin immoralities of Jim Crow and Jane Crow. Jane Crow refers to the entire range of assumptions, attitudes, stereotypes, customs, and arrangements which have robbed women of a positive self-concept and prevented them from participating fully in society as equals with men. Traditionally, racism and sexism in the United States have shared some common origins, displayed similar manifestations, reinforced one another, and are so deeply intertwined in the country's institutions that the successful outcome of the struggle against racism will depend in large part upon the simultaneous elimination of all discrimination based upon sex. Black women, faced with these dual barriers, have often found that sex bias is more formidable than racial bias. If anyone should ask a Negro woman in America what has been her greatest achievement, her honest answer would be, "I survived!"

Negro women have endured their double burden with remarkable strength and fortitude. With dignity they have shared with black men a partnership as members of am embattled group excluded from the normal protections of the society and engaged in a struggle for survival during nearly four centuries of a barbarous slave trade, two centuries of chattel slavery, and a century or more of illusive citizenship. Throughout this struggle, into which has been poured most of the resources and much of the genius of successive generations of American Negroes, these women have often carried a disproportionate share of responsi-

From *Voices of the New Feminism*, Mary Lou Thompson, ed. (Boston: Beacon Press, 1970), pp. 88-102. Reprinted by permission of the Marie Rodell-Frances Collin Literary Agency. Copyright © 1970 by Pauli Murray.

bility for the black family as they strove to keep its integrity intact against a host of indignities to which it has been subjected. Black women have not only stood shoulder to shoulder with black men in every phase of the struggle, but they have often continued to stand firmly when their men were destroyed by it. Few Blacks are unfamiliar with that heroic, if formidable, figure exhorting her children and grandchildren to overcome every obstacle and humiliation and to "Be somebody!"

In the battle for survival, Negro women developed a tradition of independence and self-reliance, characteristics which according to the late Dr. E. Franklin Frazier, Negro sociologist, have "provided generally a pattern of equalitarian relationship between men and women in America." The historical factors which have fostered the black women's feeling of independence have been the economic necessity to earn a living to help support their families—if indeed they were not the sole breadwinners—and the need for the black community to draw heavily upon the resources of all of its members in order to survive.

Yet these survival values have often been distorted, and the qualities of strength and independence observable in many Negro women have been stereotyped as "female dominance" attributed to the "matriarchal" character of the Negro family developed during slavery and its aftermath. The popular conception is that because society has emasculated the black male, he has been unable to assume his economic role as head of the household and the black woman's earning power has placed her in a dominant position. The black militant's cry for the retrieval of black manhood suggests an acceptance of this stereotype, an association of masculinity with male dominance and a tendency to treat the values of self-reliance and independence as purely masculine traits. Thus, while Blacks generally have recognized the fusion of white supremacy and male dominance (note the popular expressions "The Man" and "Mr. Charlie"), male spokesmen for Negro rights have sometimes pandered to sexism in their fight against racism. When nationally known civil rights leader James Farmer ran for Congress against Mrs. Shirley Chisholm in 1968, his campaign literature stressed the need for a "strong male image" and a "man's voice" in Washington.

If idealized values of masculinity and femininity are used as criteria, it would be hard to say whether the experience of slavery subjected the black male to any greater loss of his manhood than the black female of her womanhood. The chasm between the slave woman and her white counterpart (whose own enslavement was masked by her position as a symbol of high virtue and an object of chivalry) was as impassable as the gulf between the male slave and his arrogant white master. If black males suffered from real and psychological castration, black females bore the burden of real or psychological rape. Both situations involved the negation of the individual's personal integrity and attacked the foundations of one's sense of personal worth.

The history of slavery suggests that black men and women shared a rough equality of hardship and degradation. While the black woman's position as sex object and breeder may have given her temporarily greater leverage in dealing with her white master than the black male enjoyed, in the long run it denied her a positive image of herself. On the other hand, the very nature of slavery foreclosed certain conditions experienced by white women. The black woman had few expectations of economic dependence upon the male or of derivative status through marriage. She emerged from slavery without the illusions of a specially protected position as a woman or the possibilities of a parasitic existence as a woman. As Dr. Frazier observed, "Neither economic necessity nor tradition has instilled in her the spirit of subordination to masculine authority. Emancipation only tended to confirm in many cases the spirit of self-sufficiency which slavery had taught."

Throughout the history of Black America, its women have been in the forefront of the struggle for human rights. A century ago Harriet Tubman and Sojourner Truth were titans of the Abolitionist movement. In the 1890's Ida B. Wells-Barnett carried on a one-woman crusade against lynching. Mary McLeod Bethune and Mary Church Terrell symbolize the stalwart woman leaders of the first half of the twentieth century. At the age of ninety, Mrs. Terrell successfully challenged segregation in public places in the nation's capital through a Supreme Court decision in 1953.

In contemporary times we have Rosa Parks setting off the mass struggle for civil rights in the South by refusing to move to the back of the bus in Montgomery in 1955; Daisy Bates guiding the Little Rock Nine through a series of school desegregation crises in 1957–59; Gloria Richardson facing down the National Guard in Cambridge, Maryland, in the early sixties; or Coretta Scott King picking up the fallen standard of her slain husband to continue the fight. Not only these and many other women whose names are well known have given this great human effort its peculiar vitality, but also women in many communities whose names will never be known have revealed the courage and strength of the black woman in America. They are the mothers who stood in schoolyards of the South with their children, many times alone. One cannot help asking: "Would the black struggle have come this far without the indomitable determination of its women?"

Now that some attention is finally given to the place of the Negro in American history, how much do we hear of the role of the Negro woman? Of the many books published on the Negro experience and the

Black Revolution in recent times, to date not one has concerned itself with the struggles of black women and their contributions to history. Of approximately 800 full-length articles published in the *Journal of Negro History* since its inception in 1916, only six have dealt directly with the Negro woman. Only two have considered Negro women as a group: Carter G. Woodson's "The Negro Washerwoman: A Vanishing Figure" (14 *JNH,* 1930) and Jessie W. Pankhurst's "The Role of the Black Mammy in the Plantation Household" (28 *JNH,* 1938).

This historical neglect continues into the present. A significant feature of the civil rights revolution of the 1950's and 1960's was its inclusiveness born of the broad participation of men, women, and children without regard to age and sex. As indicated, school children often led by their mothers in the 1950's won world-wide acclaim for their courage in desegregating the schools. A black child can have no finer heritage to give a sense of "somebodiness" than the knowledge of having personally been part of the great sweep of history. (An older generation, for example, takes pride in the use of the term "Negro," having been part of a seventy-five-year effort to dignify the term by capitalizing it. Now some black militants with a woeful lack of historical perspective have allied themselves symbolically with white racists by downgrading the term to lower case again.) Yet, despite the crucial role which Negro women have played in the struggle, in the great mass of magazine and newspaper print expended on the racial crisis, the aspirations of the black community have been articulated almost exclusively by black males. There has been very little public discussion of the problems, objectives, or concerns of black women.

Reading through much of the current literature on the Black Revolution, one is left with the impression that for all the rhetoric about self-determination, the main thrust of black militancy is a bid of black males to share power with white males in a continuing patriarchal society in which both black and white females are relegated to a secondary status. For example, *Ebony* magazine published a special issue on the Negro woman in 1966. Some of the articles attempted to delineate the contributions of Negro women as heroines in the civil rights battle in Dixie, in the building of the New South, in the arts and professions, and as intellectuals. The editors, however, felt it necessary to include a full-page editorial to counter the possible effect of the articles by women contributors. After paying tribute to the Negro woman's contributions in the past, the editorial reminded *Ebony*'s readers that "the past is behind us," that "the immediate goal of the Negro woman today should be the establishment of a strong family unit in which the father is the dominant person," and that the Negro woman would do well to follow the example of the Jewish mother "who pushed her husband to success, educated her male children first and engineered good marriages for her daughters." The editors also declared that the career woman "should be willing to postpone her aspirations until her children, too, are old enough to be on their own," and, as if the point had not been made clear enough, suggested that if "the woman should, by any chance, make more money than her husband, the marriage could be in real trouble."

While not as blatantly Victorian as *Ebony,* other writers on black militancy have shown only slightly less myopia. In *Black Power and Urban Crisis,* Dr. Nathan Wright, Chairman of the 1967 National Black Power Conference, made only three brief references to women: "the employment of female skills," "the beauty of black women," and housewives. His constant reference to Black Power was in terms of black males and black manhood. He appeared to be wholly unaware of the parallel struggles of women and youth for inclusion in decision-making, for when he dealt with the reallocation of power, he noted that "the churches and housewives of America" are the most readily influential groups which can aid in this process.

In *Black Rage,* psychiatrists Greer and Cobbs devote a chapter to achieving womanhood. While they sympathetically describe the traumatic experience of self-deprecation which a black woman undergoes in a society in which the dominant standard of beauty is "the blond, blue-eyed, white-skinned girl with regular features," and make a telling point about the burden of the stereotype that Negro women are available to white men, they do not get beyond a framework in which the Negro woman is seen as a sex object. Emphasizing her concern with "feminine narcissism" and the need to be "lovable" and "attractive," they conclude: "Under the sign of discouragement and rejection which governs so much of her physical operation, she is inclined to organize her personal ambitions in terms of her achievements serving to compensate for other losses and hurts." Nowhere do the authors suggest that Negro women, like women generally, might be motivated to achieve as *persons.* Implied throughout the discussion is the sexuality of Negro females.

The ultimate expression of this bias is the statement attributed to a black militant male leader: "The position of the black woman should be prone." Thus, there appears to be a distinctly conservative and backward-looking view in much of what black males write today about black women, and many black women have been led to believe that the restoration of the black male to his lost manhood must take precedence over the claims of black women to egalitarian status. Consequently, there has been a tendency to acquiesce without vigorous protest to policies which emphasize the "underemployment" of the black male in relation to the black female and which encourage the upgrading and education of black male youth while all but ignoring the educational and training needs of black female youth, although the highest rates of unemployment today are among black female teenagers. A parallel tendency to concentrate on career and training opportunities primarily for black males is evident in government and industry.

As this article goes to press, further confirmation of a patriarchal view on the part of organizations dominated by black males is found in the BLACK DECLARATION OF INDEPENDENCE published as a full-page advertisement in *The New York Times* on July 3, 1970. Signed by members of the National Committee of Black Churchmen and presuming to speak "By Order and on Behalf of Black People," this document ignores both the personhood and the contributions of black women to the cause of human rights. The drafters show a shocking insensitivity to the revitalized women's rights/women's liberation movement which is beginning to capture the front pages of national newspapers and the mass media. It evidences a parochialism which has hardly moved beyond the eighteenth century in its thinking about women. Not only does it paraphrase the 1776 Declaration about the equality of "all Men" with a noticeable lack of imagination, but it also declares itself "in the Name of our good People and our own Black Heroes." Then follows a list of black males prominent in the historical struggle for liberation. The names of Harriet Tubman, Sojourner Truth, Mary McLeod Bethune, or Daisy Bates, or any other black women are conspicuous by their absence. If black male leaders of the Christian faith—who concededly have suffered much through denigration of their personhood and who are committed to the equality of all in the eyes of God—are callous to the indivisibility of human rights, who is to remember?

In the larger society, of course, black and white women share the common burden of discrimination based upon sex. The parallels between racism and sexism have been distinctive features of American society, and the movements to eliminate these two evils have often been allied and sometimes had interchangeable leadership. The beginnings of a women's rights movement in this country is linked with the Abolitionist movement. In 1840, William Lloyd Garrison and Charles Remond, the latter a Negro, refused to be seated as delegates to the World Anti-Slavery Convention in London when they learned that women members of the American delegation had been excluded because of their sex and could sit only in the balcony and observe the proceedings. The seed of the Seneca Falls Convention of 1848, which marked the formal beginning of the women's rights struggle in the United States, was planted at that London conference. Frederick

Douglass attended the Seneca Falls Convention and rigorously supported Elizabeth Cady Stanton's daring resolution on woman's suffrage. Except for a temporary defection during the controversy over adding "sex" to the Fifteenth Amendment, Douglass remained a staunch advocate of women's rights until his death in 1895. Sojourner Truth and other black women were also active in the movement for women's rights, as indicated earlier.

Despite the common interests of black and white women, however, the dichotomy of a racially segregated society which has become increasingly polarized has prevented them from cementing a natural alliance. Communication and the cooperation have been hesitant, limited, and formal. In the past Negro women have tended to identify discrimination against them as primarily racial and have accorded high priority to the struggle for Negro rights. They have had little time or energy for consideration of women's rights. And, until recent years, their egalitarian position in the struggle seemed to justify such preoccupation.

As the drive for black empowerment continues, however, black women are becoming increasingly aware of a new development which creates for them a dilemma of competing identities and priorities. On the one hand, as Dr. Jeanne Noble has observed, "establishing 'black manhood' became a prime goal of black revolution," and black women began to realize "that black men wanted to determine the policy and progress of black people without female participation in decisionmaking and leadership positions." On the other hand, a rising movement for women's liberation is challenging the concept of male dominance which the Black Revolution appears to have embraced. Confronted with the multiple barriers of poverty, race, and sex, the quandary of black women is how best to distribute their energies among these issues and what strategies to pursue which will minimize conflicting interests and objectives.

Cognizant of the similarities between paternalism and racial arrogance, black women are nevertheless handicapped by the continuing stereotype of the black "matriarchy" and the demand that black women now step back and push black men into positions of leadership. They are made to feel disloyal to racial interests if they insist upon women's rights. Moreover, to the extent that racial polarization often accompanies the thrust for Black Power, black women find it increasingly difficult to make common cause with white women. These developments raise several questions. Are black women gaining or losing in the drive toward human rights? As the movement for women's liberation becomes increasingly a force to be reckoned with, are black women to take a backward step and sacrifice their egalitarian tradition?

What are the alternatives to matriarchal dominance on the one hand or male supremacy on the other?

Much has been written in the past about the matriarchal character of Negro family life, the relatively favored position of Negro women, and the tensions and difficulties growing out of the assumptions that they are better educated and more able to obtain employment than Negro males. These assumptions require closer examination. It is true that according to reports of the Bureau of the Census, in March 1968 an estimated 278,000 nonwhite women had completed four or more years of college—86,000 more than male college graduates in the nonwhite population (Negro women constitute 93 per cent of all nonwhite women), and that in March 1966 the median years of school completed by Negro females (10.1) was slightly higher than that for Negro males (9.4). It should be borne in mind that this is not unique to the black community. In the white population as well, females exceed males in median years of school completed (12.2 to 12.0) and do not begin to lag behind males until the college years. The significant fact is that the percentage of both sexes in the Negro population eighteen years of age and over in 1966 who had completed four years of college was roughly equivalent (males: 2.2 per cent; females: 2.3 per cent). When graduate training is taken into account, the proportion of Negro males with five or more years of college training (3.3 per cent) moved ahead of the Negro females (3.2 per cent). Moreover, 1966 figures show that a larger proportion of Negro males (63 per cent) than Negro females (57 per cent) was enrolled in school and that this superiority continued into college enrollments (males: 5 per cent; females 4 per cent). These 1966 figures reflect a concerted effort to broaden educational opportunities for Negro males manifested in recruitment policies and scholarship programs made available primarily to Negro male students. Though later statistics are not now available, this trend appears to have accelerated each year.

The assumption that Negro women have more education than Negro men also overlooks the possibility that the greater number of college-trained Negro women may correspond to the larger number of Negro women in the population. Of enormous importance to a consideration of Negro family life and the relation between the sexes is the startling fact of the excess of females over males. The Bureau of the Census estimated that in July 1968 there were 688,000 more Negro females than Negro males. Although census officials attribute this disparity to errors in counting a "floating" Negro male population, this excess has appeared in steadily increasing numbers in every census since 1860, but has received little analysis beyond periodic comment. Over the past century the reported ratio of black males to black females has decreased. In 1966, there were less than 94 black males to every 100 females.

The numerical imbalance between the sexes in the black population is more dramatic than in any other group in the United States. Within the white population the excess of women shows up in the middle or later years. In the black population, however, the sex imbalance is present in every age group over fourteen and is greatest during the age when most marriages occur. In the twenty-five to forty-four age group, the percentage of males within the black population drops to 86.9 as compared to 96.9 for white males.

It is now generally known that females tend to be constitutionally stronger than males, that male babies are more fragile than female babies, that boys are harder to rear than girls, that the male death rate is slightly higher and life expectancy for males is shorter than that of females. Add to these general factors the special hardships to which the Negro minority is exposed—poverty, crowded living conditions, poor health, marginal jobs, and minimum protection against hazards of accident and illness—and it becomes apparent that there is much in the American environment that is particularly hostile to the survival of the black male. But even if we discount these factors and accept the theory that the sex ratio is the result of errors in census counting, it is difficult to avoid the conclusion that a large number of black males have so few stable ties that they are not included as functioning units of the society. In either case formidable pressures are created for black women.

The explosive social implications of an excess of more than half a million black girls and women over fourteen years of age are obvious in a society in which the mass media intensify notions of glamour and expectations of romantic love and marriage, while at the same time there are many barriers against interracial marriages. When such marriages do take place they are more likely to involve black males and white females, which tends to aggravate the issue. (No value judgment about interracial marriages is implied here. I am merely trying to describe a social dilemma.) The problem of an excess female population is a familiar one in countries which have experienced heavy male casualties during wars, but an excess female ethnic minority as an enclave within a larger population raises important social issues. To what extent are the tensions and conflicts traditionally associated with the matriarchal framework of Negro family life in reality due to this imbalance and the pressures it generates? Does this excess explain the active competition between Negro professional men and women seeking employment in markets which have limited or excluded Negroes? And does this competition intensify the stereotype of the matriarchal society and female dominance? What relationship is there between the high rate of illegitimacy among black women and the population figures we have described?

These figures suggest that the Negro woman's fate in the United States, while inextricably bound with that of the Negro male in one sense, transcends the issue of Negro rights. Equal opportunity for her must mean equal opportunity to compete for jobs and to find a mate in the total society. For as long as she is confined to an area in which she must compete fiercely for a mate, she will remain the object of sexual exploitation and the victim of all the social evils which such exploitation involves.

When we compare the position of the black woman to that of the white woman, we find that she remains single more often, bears more children, is in the labor market longer and in greater proportion, has less education, earns less, is widowed earlier, and carries a relatively heavier economic responsibility as family head than her white counterpart.

In 1966, black women represented one of every seven women workers, although Negroes generally constitute only 11 per cent of the total population in the United States. Of the 3,105,000 black women eighteen years of age and over who were in the labor force, however, nearly half (48.2 per cent) were either single, widowed, divorced, separated from their husbands, or their husbands were absent for other reasons, as compared with 31.8 per cent of white women in similar circumstances. Moreover, six of every ten black women were in household employment or other service jobs. Conversely, while 58.8 per cent of all women workers held white collar positions, only 23.2 per cent of black women held such jobs.

As working wives, black women contribute a higher proportion to family income than do white women. Among nonwhite wives in 1965, 58 per cent contributed to 20 per cent or more of the total family income, 43 per cent contributed 30 per cent or more and 27 per cent contributed 40 per cent or more. The comparable percentages for white wives were 56 per cent, 40 per cent, and 24 per cent respectively.

Black working mothers are more heavily represented in the labor force than white mothers. In March 1966, nonwhite working mothers with children under eighteen years of age represented 48 per cent of all nonwhite mothers with children this age as compared with 35 per cent of white working mothers. Nonwhite working mothers also represented four of every ten of all nonwhite mothers of children under six years of age. Of the 12,300,000 children under fourteen years of age in February 1965 whose mothers worked, only 2 per cent were provided group care in day-care centers. Adequate child care is an urgent need for working mothers generally, but it has particular significance for the high proportion of black working mothers of young children.

Black women also carry heavy responsibilities as family heads. In 1966, one-fourth of all black families were headed by a woman as compared with less than one-tenth of all white families. The economic disabilities of women generally are aggravated in the case of black women. Moreover, while all families headed by women are more vulnerable to poverty than husband–wife families, the black woman family head is doubly victimized. For example, the median wage or salary income of all women workers who were employed full time the year round in 1967 was only 58 per cent of that of all male workers, and the median earnings of white females was less than that of black males. The median wage of nonwhite women workers, however, was $3,268, or only 71 per cent of the median income of white women workers. In 1965, one-third of all families headed by women lived in poverty, but 62 per cent of the 1,132,000 nonwhite families with a female head were poor.

A significant factor in the low economic and social status of black women is their concentration at the bottom rung of the employment ladder. More than one-third of all nonwhite working women are employed as private household workers. The median wages of women private household workers who were employed full time the year round in 1968 was only $1,701. Furthermore, these workers are not covered by the Federal minimum wage and hours law and are generally excluded from state wage and hours laws, unemployment compensation, and workmen's compensation.

The black woman is triply handicapped. She is heavily represented in nonunion employment and thus has few of the benefits to be derived from labor organization or social legislation. She is further victimized by discrimination because of race and sex. Although she has made great strides in recent decades in closing the educational gap, she still suffers from inadequate education and training. In 1966, only 71.1 per cent of all Negro women had completed eight grades of elementary school compared to 88 per cent of all white women. Only one-third (33.2 per cent) of all Negro women had completed high school as compared with more than one-half of all white women (56.3). More than twice as many white women, proportionally, have completed college (7.2 per cent) as black women (3.2 per cent).

The notion of the favored economic position of the black female in relation to the black male is a myth. The 1966, median earnings of full-time year-round nonwhite female workers was only 65 per cent of that of nonwhite males. The unemployment rate for adult nonwhite women (6.6) was higher than for their male counterparts (4.9). Among nonwhite teenagers, the unemployment rate for girls was 31.1 as compared with 21.2 for boys.

In the face of their multiple disadvantages, it seems clear that black women can neither postpone nor subordinate the fight against sex discrimination to the Black Revolution. Many of them must expect to be self-supporting and perhaps to support others for a considerable period or for life. In these circumstances, while efforts to raise educational and employment levels for black males will ease some of the economic and social burdens now carried by many black women, for a large and apparently growing minority these burdens will continue. As a matter of sheer survival black women have no alternative but to insist upon equal opportunities without regard to sex in training, education, and employment. Given their heavy family responsibilities, the outlook for their children will be bleak indeed unless they are encouraged in every way to develop their potential skills and earning power.

Because black women have an equal stake in women's liberation and black liberation, they are key figures at the juncture of these two movements. White women feminists are their natural allies in both causes. Their own liberation is linked with the issues which are stirring women today: adequate income maintenance and the elimination of poverty, repeal or reform of abortion laws, a national system of child-care centers, extension of labor standards to workers now excluded, cash maternity benefits as part of a system of social insurance, and the removal of all sex barriers to educational and employment opportunities at all levels. Black women have a special stake in the revolt against the treatment of women primarily as sex objects, for their own history has left them with the scars of the most brutal and degrading aspects of sexual exploitation.

The middle-class Negro woman is strategically placed by virtue of her tradition of independence and her long experience in civil rights and can play a creative role in strengthening the alliance between the Black Revolution and Women's Liberation. Her advantages of training and her values make it possible for her to communicate with her white counterparts, interpret the deepest feelings within the black community, and cooperate with white women on the basis of mutual concerns as women. The possibility of productive interchange between black and white women is greatly facilitated by the absence of power relationships which separate black and white males as antagonists. By asserting a leadership role in the growing feminist movement, the black woman can help to keep it allied to the objectives of black liberation while simultaneously advancing the interests of all women.

The lesson of history that all human rights are indivisible and that the failure to adhere to this principle jeopardizes the rights of all is particularly applicable here. A built-in hazard of an aggressive ethnocentric movement which disregards the interests of other disadvantaged groups is that it will become parochial and ultimately self-defeating in the face of hostile reactions, dwindling allies, and mounting frustrations. As Dr. Caroline F. Ware has pointed out, perhaps the most essential instrument for combating the divisive effects of a black-only movement is the voice of black women insisting upon the unity of civil rights of women and Negroes as well as other minorities and excluded groups. Only a broad movement for human rights can prevent the Black Revolution from becoming isolated and can insure its ultimate success.

Beyond all the present conflict lies the important task of reconciliation of the races in America on the basis of genuine equality and human dignity. A powerful force in bringing about this result can be generated through the process of black and white women working together to achieve their common humanity.

Suggested Readings for Part IV

Anderson, Karen. *Wartime Women: Sex Roles, Family Relations, and the Status of Women During World War II.* Westport, CT: Greenwood Press, 1981.

Becker, Susan. *The Origins of the Equal Rights Amendment: American Feminism Between the Wars.* Westport, CT: Greenwood Press, 1981.

Bennett, Sheila K. and Elder, Glen, Jr. "Women's Work in the Family Economy: A Study of Depression Hardship." *Journal of Family History* 4 (1974): 153-72.

Benson, Susan Porter. "Palace of Consumption and Machine of Selling: The American Department Store, 1880-1940," *Radical History Review* 21 (1979): 199-221.

_____. "'The Clerking Sisterhood': Rationalization and the Work Culture of Saleswomen in American Department Stores, 1890-1960." James Green, ed. *Workers Struggles, Past and Present.* Philadelphia: Temple University Press, 1982.

_____. "'The Customers Ain't God': The Work Culture of Department-Store Saleswomen, 1890-1940." Michael H. Frisch and Daniel J. Walkowitz, ed. *Working-Class America: Essays on Labor, Community, and American Society.* Urbana: University of Illinois Press, 1983.

Bernard, Jesse. *Women, Wives and Mothers: Values and Opinions.* Chicago: Aldine Publishing Co., 1975.

Bird, Caroline. *The Invisible Scar.* New York: David McKay Co., 1966.

_____. *Born Female: The High Cost of Keeping Women Down.* New York: David McKay Co., 1968.

Blackwelder, Julia Kirk. "Women in the Work Force: Atlanta, New Orleans, and San Antonio, 1930-1940." *Journal of Urban History* 4 (1978): 331-58.

Bolin, Winifred D. Wandersee. *Women's Work and Family Values, 1920-1940.* Cambridge: Harvard University Press, 1980.

_____. "The Economics of Middle Income Family Life: Working Women During the Great Depression." *Journal of American History* 65 (1978): 60-74.

Bose, Christine E., Bereano, Philip L., and Malloy, Mary. "Household Technology and the Social Construction of Housework." *Technology and Culture* 25 (January 1984): 53-82.

Campbell, D'Ann. *Women at War With America: Private Lives in a Patriotic Era.* Cambridge: Harvard University Press, 1984.

Chafe, William H. *The American Woman: Her Changing Social, Economic and Political Role.* New York: Oxford University Press, 1972.

_____. *Women and Equality: Changing Patterns in American Culture.* New York: Oxford University Press, 1977.

Cookingham, Mary E. "Combining Marriage, Motherhood, and Jobs before World War II: Women College Graduates, Classes of 1905-1935." *Journal of Family History* 9 (Summer 1984): 178-95.

Cott, Nancy F. "Feminist Politics in the 1920s: The National Woman's Party." *Journal of American History* 71 (June 1984): 43-68.

Davies, Margery. *A Woman's Place is at the Typewriter.* Philadelphia: Temple University Press, 1984.

Drachman, Virginia. *Hospital With a Heart: Women Doctors and the Paradox Separatism at the New England Hospital, 1862-1969*. Ithaca: Cornell University Press, 1984.

Degler, Carl. "Revolution Without Ideology: The Changing Place of Women in America." *Daedalus* 93 (1964); 653-670.

Elder, Glen H., and Liker, Jeffrey K. "Hard Times in Women's Lives: Historical Influences across Forty Years." *American Journal of Sociology* 88 (September 1982): 241-69.

Evans, Sara. *Personal Politics: The Roots of Women's Liberation in the Civil Rights Movement and the New Left*. New York: Alfred A. Knopf, 1978.

Fass, Paula. *The Beautiful and the Damned: American Youth in the 1920s*. New York: Oxford University Press, 1977.

Filene, Peter Gabriel. *Him/Her/Self: Sex Roles in Modern America*. New York: Harcourt Brace Jovanovich, 1975.

Firestone, Shulamith. *The Dialectic of Sex*. New York: Bantam Books, 1970.

Freeman, Jo. *The Politics of Women's Liberation*. New York: David McKay Co., 1975.

Friedan, Betty. *The Feminine Mystique*. New York: W.W. Norton, 1963.

Gabin, Nancy. "'They Have Placed a Penalty on Womanhood': The Protest Actions of Women Auto Workers in the Detroit Area UAW Locals, 1945-47." *Feminist Studies* 8 (1982): 373-98.

Geidel, Peter. "The National Woman's Party and the Origins of the Equal Rights Amendment, 1920-1923." *Historian* 42 (August 1980): 557-82.

Hammer, Patricia. *Decade of Elusive Promise: Professional Women in the United States 1920-30*. Ann Arbor: University of Michigan Press, 1978.

Hartmann, Susan M. *The Home Front and Beyond: American Women in the 1940s*. Boston: G.K. Hall, 1982.

Haskell, Molly. *From Reverence to Rape: The Treatment of Women in the Movies*. New York: Holt, Rinehart & Winston, 1973.

Hole, Judith and Levine, Ellen. *The Rebirth of Feminism*. New York: Quadrangle Books, 1971.

Hurt, Morton. *Sexual Behavior in the 1970s*. New York: Playboy Press, 1974.

Klaczynska, Barbara. "Why Women Work: A Comparison of Various Groups—Philadelphia, 1910-1930." *Labor History* 17 (1976): 73-87.

Kornbluh, Joyce L., and Frederickson, Mary, eds. *Sisterhood and Solidarity: Workers' Education for Women, 1914-1984*. Philadelphia: Temple University Press, 1984.

Lasch, Christopher. *The Culture of Narcissism; American Life in an Age of Diminishing Expectations*. New York: W.W. Norton, 1979.

———. *Haven in a Heartless World: The Family Besieged*. New York: Basic Books, 1977.

Lemons, J. Stanley. *The Woman Citizen: Social Feminism in the 1920s*. Urbana: University of Illinois Press, 1973.

Litoff, Judy B. *American Midwives, 1860 to the Present*. Westport, CT: Greenwood Press, 1978.

May, Martha. "The Historical Problem of the Family Wage: The Ford Motor Company and the Five Dollar Day." *Feminist Studies* 8 (1982): 399-424.

Melosh, Barbara. *"The Physician's Hand:" Nurses and Nursing in the Twentieth Century.* Philadelphia: Temple University Press, 1982.

Milkman, Ruth. "Redefining 'Women's Work': The Sexual Division of Labor in the Auto Industry during World War II." *Feminist Studies* 8 (Summer 1982): 337-72.

Reiss, Ira. *The Social Context of Premarital Sexual Permissiveness.* New York: Holt, Rinehart & Winston, 1967.

Robinson, Paul A. *The Modernization of Sex: Havelock Ellis, Alfred Kinsey, William Masters, and Virginia Johnson.* New York: Harper & Row, 1976.

Rosenberg, Rosalind. *Beyond Separate Spheres: The Intellectual Roots of Modern Feminism.* New Haven: Yale University Press, 1982.

Rossiter, Margaret, *Women Scientists in America: Struggles and Strategies to 1940.* Baltimore: John Hopkins Unversity Press, 1982.

Rubin, Lillian Breslow. *Worlds of Pain: Life in the Working-Class Family.* New York: Basic Books, 1976.

Rupp, Leila. "'Imagine My Surprise': Women's Relationships in Historical Perspectives." *Frontiers* 56 (1981).

_____. *Mobilizing Women for War: German and American Propaganda, 1936-1945.* Princeton: Princeton University Press, 1978.

Sahli, Nancy. "Smashing Women's Relationships Before the Fall." *Chrysalis* 8 (1979): 17-29.

Sealander, Judith. *As Minority Becomes Majority: Federal Reaction to the Phenomenon of Women in the Work Force, 1920-1983.* Westport, CT: Greenwood Press, 1983.

_____. "Feminist against Feminist: The First Phase of the Equal Rights Amendment Debate, 1923-1963." *South Atlantic Quarterly* 81 (1982): 147-61.

Scharf, Lois. *To Work and To Wed: Female Employment, Feminism and the Great Depression.* Westport, CT: Greenwood Press, 1980.

Scharf, Lois, and Jensen, Joan M., eds. *Decades of Discontent: The Women's Movement, 1920-1940.* Wesport, CT: Greenwood Press, 1983.

Sherfy, Mary Jane. *The Nature and Evolution of Female Sexuality.* New York: Vintage Books, 1973.

Shorter, Edward. *The Making of the Modern Family.* New York: Basic Books, 1976.

Smuts, Robert W. *Women and Work in America.* New York: Columbia University Press, 1959.

Steere, Geoffrey H. "Freudianism and Childrearing in the Twenties." *American Quarterly* 20 (1968): 759-65.

Stricker, Frank. "Cookbooks and Law Books: The Hidden History of Career Women in Twentieth Century America." *Journal of Social History* 10 (1976): 1-19.

Strom, Sharon H. "Challenging 'Woman's Place': Feminism, the Left and Industrial Unionism in the 1930s." *Feminist Studies* 9 (Summer 1983): 359-86.

Swerdlow, Amy. "Ladies' Day at the Capitol: Women Strike for Peace versus HUAC." *Feminist Studies* 8 (Fall 1982): 493-519.

Vanek, Joann. "Work, Leisure, and Family Roles: Farm Households in the United States, 1920-1955." *Journal of Family History* 5 (Winter 1980): 422-31.

_____. "Time Spent in Housework." *Scientific American* 231 (1974): 116-21.

Vinoskis, Maris A. "An Epidemic of Adolescent Pregnancy? Some Historical Considerations." *Journal of Family History* 6 (1981): 205-30.

Ware, Susan. *Beyond Suffrage: Women in the New Deal.* Cambridge: Harvard University Press, 1970.

Westin, Jeanne. *Making Do: How Women Survived in the '30s.* Chicago: Follett Publishing Co., 1976.

Yellis, Kenneth A. "Prosperity's Child: Some Thoughts on the Flapper." *American Quarterly* 21 (1969): 44-64.

Zaretsky, Eli. *Capitalism, The Family and Personal Life.* New York: Harper & Row, 1976.

1 2 3 4 5 6 7 8 9 0